The Complete Guide to Buddhist America

THE COMPLETE GUIDE TO
Buddhist America

✳

EDITED BY

Don Morreale

Foreword by

H. H. THE DALAI LAMA

Introductions by

Jack Kornfield *and* Joseph Goldstein

SHAMBHALA

Boston & London

1998

SHAMBHALA PUBLICATIONS, INC.
Horticultural Hall
300 Massachusetts Avenue
Boston, Massachusetts 02115
http://www.shambhala.com

9 8 7 6 5 4 3 2 1

FIRST EDITION
Printed in the United States of America
⊗ This edition is printed on acid-free paper that meets the
American National Standards Institute Z39.48 Standard.
Distributed in the United States by Random House, Inc.,
and in Canada by Random House of Canada Ltd

LIBRARY OF CONGRESS CATALOGING-IN-PUBLICATION DATA

Morreale, Don, 1947–
    The complete guide to Buddhist America/by Don Morreale;
introductions by Jack Kornfield and Joseph Goldstein.—1st. ed.
        p.   cm.
    ISBN 1-57052-270-1 (pbk.: alk. paper)
    1. Buddhism—North America.   2.   Spiritual life—Buddhism.
3. Buddhist centers—North America—Directories.   4. Temples,
Buddhist—North America—Directories.   I. Kornfield, Jack, 1945–   .
II. Goldstein, Joseph, 1944–   .   III. Title.
BQ724.M67   1998   97-29992
294.3′0973—dc21   CIP

This book is dedicated to my two
original spiritual teachers,

the Rev. Samuel O. Morreale
and *Eufemia Azzolina Morreale,*

and to the memory of my brother

David Lawrence Morreale

The wise person learns from life itself; the fool waits for the perfect weather.
The wise person learns from all schools of Buddhism; the fool will cling to
one and despise the others—for the wise man knows that any viewpoint
or opinion whatsoever is only a changing condition,
and with its cessation there is peace.
—*Ven. Ajahn Sumedho Bhikkhu*

———————

We Americans can no longer look outside ourselves for peace and
happiness. We have reached the limits of our external expansion. It is now
time to listen to and practice the principles of the Buddhadharma, to turn
our energy inwards, and to discover that the search for paradise that
has always brought people to America ends ultimately in the
discovery and the purification of one's own mind.
—*Bhikshu Heng Chau*

———————

All Dharmas agree at one point.
—*Chekawa Yeshe Dorje*

Contents

✴

Foreword

H.H. TENZIN GYATSO, THE FOURTEENTH DALAI LAMA

⊕

IF WE READ STORIES OF THE GREAT MEDITATIVE adepts of the past, we find that those who attained high realizations always stayed in peaceful isolated places. There are not many accounts of people who attained great realization in the city or town. Therefore, those who wish to meditate are traditionally advised to cast off attachment to worldly pleasures and comforts and to stay in an isolated place in the forest.

What is the benefit of meditating in such an isolated place? You will face no disturbance in relation to either friends or enemies. There will be no one to distract you, either by pleasing you or annoying you. The birds and animals who will be your companions will do you no harm. You will undergo little hardship, but will find peace and happiness, free from distraction. In such circumstances you will be able to do virtuous practices such as calming the mind, recollecting the qualities of the Buddha, meditation on emptiness, or doing the practice of the tantric generation or completion stages.

In the traditional Buddhist countries of Asia, it is still possible in many places to retreat into the forest or mountains to meditate, free from distractions, yet within reach of food and other necessities. But to do so requires time, patience, and much preparation. In Tibet prac-titioners would often retreat to extremely remote and inaccessible places. What is amazing is the relatively high number of meditators who spent many years, if not their entire lives, secluded in such hermitages. The tradition persists even in exile. In the vicinity of Dharamsala, where I live, there are now sixty to seventy dedicated practitioners living in the mountains away from the community, meditating intensely.

In North America, many meditation centers have been founded in suitable locations, which enable people who lead otherwise busy lives to dedicate whatever free time they can spare to meditation. This book contains a list of the names and addresses, and brief descriptions, of such centers. With articles by Buddhist teachers and accounts of Western meditators' experiences of retreat besides, it will be a great boon to people wanting to find out about Buddhist meditation for themselves.

I congratulate all who have contributed to the preparation of this book. Moreover, I pray that everyone desiring to practice meditation may find quiet in solitary places and that, having given up all wandering thoughts, they may meditate with flexible minds.

February 27, 1997

Everything Has Changed in Buddhist America

DON MORREALE

All conditioned things are transitory.

—*the Buddha*

✳

EVERYTHING HAS CHANGED IN BUDDHIST America. The wildness of the early days is over and meditation is no longer the province of a handful of visionaries and poets. Buddhism has gone mainstream. At retreats one is likely to find oneself sitting next to a stockbroker or a therapist or a retired social worker who may or may not claim to be a Buddhist. It is an older crowd as well; fewer and fewer people in their twenties and more and more in their forties, fifties, and sixties.

The teaching situation has changed. Many of the teachers who originally brought the practice to this country, among them the roshis Suzuki, Maezumi, Katagiri, and Jiyu-Kennett, and the rinpoches Trungpa, Kalu, and Kyentse, have all died. Others, notably Robert Aitken Roshi and Philip Kapleau Roshi, have named their successors and retired. The second generation of teachers, many of them trained entirely in the West, have begun to put their own stamp on the practice. The strict, almost martial, discipline that was once the norm in many Zen centers has given way to a freer, lighter approach. Day care is frequently available, as well as flexible schedules to accommodate work and family. Meanwhile, at Gampo Abbey in Cape Breton, Nova Scotia, traditional Tibetan three-year retreats are now being offered in six month

increments. Time at retreat alternates with work in the world, giving participants an opportunity to earn money, to spend time with their families, to integrate what they've learned in seclusion, and so on.

The distinctly Asian flavor that once permeated Western dharma centers has given way to something that feels very familiarly North American. Chanting, done in English at many centers, might these days sound a little less Japanese or Tibetan or Thai, and a little more like plainsong. And what lands in your bowl at mealtime is as likely to be pizza or a bean burrito as it is to be stir-fried veggies, tofu, and brown rice.

More importantly, there has been a shift away from the hierarchical, authoritarian, organizational models imported by teachers steeped in the protocols of Asian monasticism, to one that is more consistent with our own democratic traditions. Instead of decisions emanating from the top down, in many cases the entire *sangha* now meets to discuss pertinent issues until a consensus has been reached. Moreover, we found that while centers were willing to acknowledge a headquarters temple in their listings, they were also very quick to insist that the connection was spiritual as opposed to political. In other words, local *sanghas* have been granted complete autonomy when it comes to running their own affairs, which reflects a growing self-confidence and maturity among Western practitioners.

While the first edition of *Buddhist America* (John Muir Publications, 1988) reflected the bias of its times toward strict practice and intensive retreat, what came across loud and clear as we prepared this edition is that, while retreats might be offered a few times a year at most centers, the real focus has shifted to strong daily practice in the midst of one's ordinary circumstances—dharma in the workplace, dharma at home with one's spouse and children, dharma behind the wheel in a traffic jam, and so on. This is not to say that retreats are no longer valued. They are, and people are flocking to them in record numbers. But the question that remains in most people's minds is: "How can I apply this to my daily life?"

In line with this lay-based approach, there has emerged a strong current of opinion in favor of community service ("engaged Buddhism") as reflected in the teachings of such dharma luminaries as the Ven. Thich Nhat Hanh and the Ven. Bernard Tetsugen Glassman Roshi, and in the activities of organizations like the Buddhist Peace Fellowship, the Asian Classics Input Project, Gaden Relief Projects, the Project on Being with Dying, and the National Buddhist Prison Sangha. In this edition we have widened our perspective to include as many of these new directions and ideas as possible. You will find these in the form of brief vignettes ("Highlights") scattered throughout the listings sections of the book. They make for interesting reading.

How We've Grown

To get some idea of the breadth and scope of the changes going on in North American Buddhism, the centers were asked to answer two questions: (1) "In what year was your center established?" and (2) "Approximately how many people participate in your activities?" Their responses formed the basis for the very unscientific statistical analysis that follows.

Interest in Buddhist meditation has grown dramatically, especially in the last twelve years. (See figure 1.) Of the more than one thousand meditation centers listed in

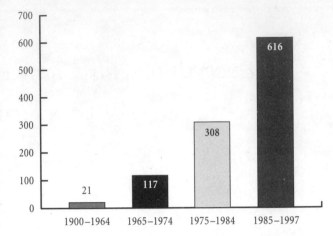

Figure 1. Number of new North American Buddhist meditation centers established, 1900–1997.

this book, only about two percent of them were founded in the years 1900 to 1964. Not surprisingly, the religion made its first great leap forward in the late 1960s and early 1970s, when the number of centers increased more than fivefold. That number more than doubled in the years 1975 to 1984, and then doubled again in the twelve years from 1985 to 1997. Put another way, more Buddhist meditation centers—nearly sixty percent—were established in this last twelve year period than the total number founded in the first eighty-five years of the twentieth century.

During the past decade, both Theravada and Vajrayana Buddhist centers have doubled their numbers. (See figure 2.) The Mahayana centers have nearly tripled. The almost tenfold increase in centers claiming nonsectarian ("Buddhayana") designation signals a growing trend in contemporary Western Buddhism toward ecumenicalism or, more precisely, "polydenominationalism."

Figure 3 shows what the individual meditation groups look like in terms of numbers of participants. Forty-one percent have fewer than twenty-five members. I call these "living room *sanghas*"; small groups who gather in one another's homes for meditation and fellowship. These numbers support the view that the dharma is spreading here on a grassroots level in a very friendly, face-to-face,

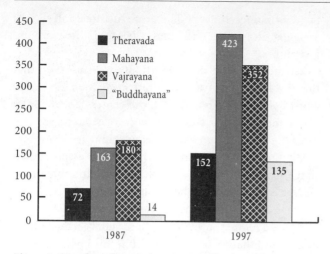

Figure 2. Number of North American meditation centers in the four major Buddhist traditions, 1987–1997.

person-to-person sort of way. The dharma moves from heart to heart and does not aim for mass conversion.

Probably the most frequently asked question about the growing phenomenon of Buddhist meditation in this country is how many people are doing it. As far as I am aware there does not exist at the present time any reliable data to accurately respond. How does one formulate the question? What *is* a Buddhist anyway? Are you a Buddhist if you only attend a retreat now and again? Are you

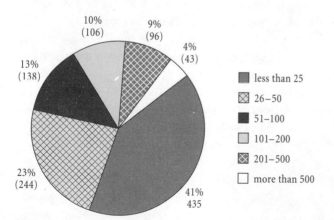

Figure 3. Membership size at North American Buddhist meditation centers.

a Buddhist if you practice at home alone and don't belong to a *sangha*? Are you a Buddhist if you do belong to a *sangha* but don't meditate? An anecdote by Janwillem Van De Wettering, a Dutchman who studied Zen in Japan in the 1950s, illustrates the problem:

> In the garden, I looked for Han-san and found him loading cucumbers into a wheelbarrow.
> "Are you a Buddhist?" I asked.
> Han-san might be a simple country lad, but he was quick on the uptake.
> "I?" he asked innocently. "I study Zen Buddhism . . ."
> "Yes," I said impatiently, "I know. But are you a Buddhist?"
> "You know," Han-san said, "that *I* don't exist. I change all the time. Every moment I am different. I exist in the way a cloud exists. A cloud is a Buddhist too. You call me *Han-san* and pretend that I was yesterday what I shall be today. But that's your business. In reality there is no Han-san. And how can an unreal Han-san be a Buddhist?"
> "Don't be so intricate," I said. "All I ask is whether or not you are a member of the Buddhist brotherhood."
> "Is a cloud a member of the sky?" Han-san asked.

Whatever a "Buddhist" is, there is a surprisingly large number of people on the mailing lists of various dharma centers. Of the more than one hundred centers who shared this information with us, twenty-three reported lists of between one and two thousand, eight said there were between two and four thousand names on theirs, seven claimed lists of between four and ten thousand, and two more said they regularly shipped out program schedules and newsletters to an astounding twenty to thirty thousand interested parties.

Of the different traditions, Mahayana (Zen) has the highest number of centers in the United States (forty-two percent), while Vajrayana Buddhism seems to be more popular in Canada (forty-nine percent). Of additional interest: over one-fifth (twenty-two percent) of United States meditation centers are located in California, while more than a third of Canadian centers (thirty-eight percent) can be found in the Province of Ontario.

How to Use this Book

This book has been divided into four sections, each one devoted to a major *yana,* or denomination. ("Buddha-yana" is technically not a *yana,* but is rather a term employed by many centers where more than one tradition is represented.) Each section is introduced by a recognized Buddhist teacher or scholar in an essay outlining the basic tenets of their respective traditions. These are followed by retreat narratives written by practicing dharma students. The first person accounts have been included to give you a sense of what it's like to attend a zen sesshin, or a Theravada vipassana retreat, or to do thousands of prostrations under the guidance of a Tibetan Vajrayana master. At the end of each section you will find detailed listings of places where these practices are taught.

The listings were supplied by the centers themselves, or else by their parent organizations, and it's worth spending some time reading through them. The centers were asked to provide some basic information (addresses, phone numbers, teachers' names) and to give you some idea of how they are organized and what kinds of programs they offer. In the Appendix, you'll find all of the centers listed alphabetically by name. In the Index, we've listed them under the names of the cities or towns where they are located.

If you see a listing that interests you, it's always a good idea to give the center a call first and find out when would be a good time to visit. Frequently, centers will have an introductory class or a beginners' night that they will invite you to attend. By all means go. Afterward, ask yourself: "Does this place seem open, friendly, and cheerful?" Follow your heart. If you don't feel comfortable with the setup, then it's probably not for you.

This seems like a good place to emphasize that we offer no guarantees here. All the information contained in the listings in this book has come to us in the form of a response to a questionnaire. We have not been to most of these centers, and even if we had there is no way we can tell, much less guarantee, that they offer authen-

tic dharma teachings. "There are no guarantees," as Trungpa Rinpoche once said, "because there are no guarantors."

Let me also take this opportunity to emphasize that this is a book about the Buddhist *meditation* centers of North America. It only lists those centers and temples where meditation is taught, or at least encouraged. Not listed are the vast numbers of temples and centers where meditation is not the focus. These include more than sixty "Culture Centers" of Soka Gakkai International–USA, a significant number of temples in the Nicheren Shoshu sect, and over one hundred Jodo-Shinshu temples throughout the United States and Canada. Please understand that their exclusion from this book does not constitute a judgment as to their truth or efficacy, or an attempt to write them out of existence. With close to eleven hundred meditation centers listed herein, it was simply necessary to limit the scope of the book.

Also not included are many ethnic temples where English is not the principle language. While meditation might be taught there, getting many of them to respond proved way beyond our capabilities. We did try, though. One hundred twenty eight of these centers answered our query; they constitute twelve percent of the centers listed.

Dharma Blessings

Thank you so much for your interest in the Dharma. Hands palm to palm, I wish you all the best of luck in finding a place to learn the Buddha's Way.

> May all sentient beings enjoy happiness and the root of happiness.
> Be free from suffering and the root of suffering.
> May they not be separated from the great happiness devoid of suffering.
> May they dwell in the great equanimity free from passion and aggression and ignorance.*

---

*From the "Bodhisattva Vows for Mahayana Students," translated by the Nalanda Translation Committee and recited at centers affiliated with Shambhala International.

Acknowledgments

✳

This meal is the labor of countless beings: let us remember their toil.

—*Zen Meal Chant*

BUDDHIST AMERICA IS VERY MUCH A GRASSROOTS effort. So to begin with, let me thank everyone who took the time to fill out and return our questionnaires and who has kept us abreast of changes in their groups and centers over the years. A number of people served as contacts in their immediate areas, calling the local centers directly, encouraging them to respond, and in some cases filling out the questionnaires for them over the phone. This book would not have been nearly as complete had it not been for the extremely diligent efforts of Ajahn Amaro Bhikkhu, Randy Baker, Rev. James Ishmael Ford, August Franchimone, Ven. Eshin John Godfrey, Janet Hewins, Patty Smith Puckett, and Marian Smith.

All over the United States and Canada, people have been putting together local dharma center directories, many of which were sent to me with permission to quote from them. Especially helpful were those supplied by Fred Babbin (Buddhist Council of the Midwest), Chris Ng (Buddhist Women's Network of Toronto), John RB Whittlesey (Texas Buddhist Council), Karin Miles (Northwest Dharma Association), Joan Short and Barry Boyce (Shambhala International), Miles Deutch and Michael Doran (Karma Triyana Dharmachakra), Leanne Haglund (Community of Mindful Living), and Barry Kapke (DharmaNet International).

To my utter astonishment, a fax arrived one day from the offices of H. H. the Dalai Lama, informing me that he would be sending a brief foreword. A couple of days later it arrived by registered mail, signed by His Holiness with blessings for all who contributed to the book. How lovely to share our time in the world with this great saint, and how honored and grateful we feel for his kindness in sending us these words of wisdom.

Many thanks to Steve Cary and Ken Luboff of John Muir Publications, who in 1988 first published *Buddhist America*. Steve and Ken, in the true Buddhist spirit of *dana* (generosity), relinquished the rights to this book without asking for remuneration of any kind.

Two people who were quite influential in shaping the manuscript are Leanne Schamp and Bonnie Miller. Leanne spent months entering data and conforming the material. This she did with dedication, precision, and amazing good humor. It was a joy to work with her.

Bonnie Miller, a dharma friend since the very first day I sat down on a meditation cushion, made some extremely helpful suggestions for organizing the material, which resulted in a much more user-friendly publication.

My sweetheart, Nancy Mangus, helped in all kinds of ways, running errands, folding questionnaires, stuffing envelopes, and in general putting up with me during the hectic days and nights when we were pushing to meet our deadline.

Jeff Schmidt and Sister Martha Dharmapali painstakingly compiled the supplementary data on our questionnaires, enabling us to more readily understand the breadth and scope of the changes going on in North America's far-flung dharma community.

As an army travels on its stomach, so a book, in this day and age, travels on the knowledge and skill of its computer wizards. I'm indebted to my friends the Severance family—Tom, Aaron, and Cissy—who patiently showed me how to access the Internet, set up the software on my computers, and copied out the manuscript for me on their whiz-bang ink jet printer.

Peter Turner and Ron Suresha of Shambhala Publications worked diligently to turn a sprawling manuscript into a finished book. Cynthia Baddour did an amazing job of copy editing the manuscript, calling to my attention inconsistencies and contradictions that I never would have spotted.

A host of folks helped in sundry ways both great and small. They're listed here in alphabetical order: Leonard Adamson, Randy Baker, James Baraz, Emma Barrows (Chuan Yuan Shakya), Rev. Kinrei Bassis, Barbara Brodsky, Adrienne Chan, Allen Clevenger, Robina Courtin, Gair Crutcher, Dr. Paul S. Dickman, David Dunley, Dennis and Jo Eberl, Brother Clark Elliot, Doug and Diane Elliot, Clarke Fountain, Wadine Gibbons, Ron Green, Jean Green, Dixie Griffin, Bhante Henepola Gunaratana, Mark and Stephanie Haddad, Kay E. Henry, David Hildebrand, Christy Honigman, Janet Howey, Travis Hunter, Jeanie Johnson (Aurora Public Schools Life Skills Vocational Program), Bruce Sengan Kennedy, Nicole Langley, Toinette Lippe (Bell Tower Books), Albert Low, Sibyl Lundy, Bill Mahoney, Kim McLaughlin, Jane McLaughlin-Dobisz JDPSN, Seamus Miau, Chloe Morreale (Famous Horsewoman), Jesse Morreale (Concertmeister), Lucinda Morreale (Famous Artist), Samantha Morreale (Famous Architect), Sam and Cindy Morreale (Famous Fundraisers), Ven. Mu Soeng Sunim, Sister Nora, Paul Pederson, Linda Petrino, Adele Prager, Dharman Craig Presson, Randall C. Redd, Al Reed, Christopher Reed, Eve Rifkah, Virginia Robinson, Rocky Mountain Internet, Mike Rome, Gail Russel, the late Paul Ruston, Celene Ryan, Ven. Dharman Shakya, Ven. Eido Tai Shimano Roshi, Joye Smith, Nita Sweeney, Greg Tzinberg, Sensei Fred Ulrich, Michael Wick, and Diana Winston.

The retreat narratives and short essays ("Highlights") were supplied gratis by people willing to share their meditation experience with others. Their names appear in the table of contents and in their bylines. Thanks so much to all of them and also to the many writers who submitted articles that space did not permit us to use. We enjoyed reading all of them.

"Entering the Gate of Meditation" was excerpted from *Stumbling toward Enlightenment* by Geri Larkin and is used by permission of Celestial Arts.

"Zen Dance: Meditation in Motion" was adapted from "Yimoko III: Zen Dance Choreography," by Sun Ock Lee, which first appeared in the book *Zen Dance: Meditation in Movement,* by Sun Ock Lee and John Chang McCurdy, published by Seoul International Publishing House.

American Buddhism

JACK KORNFIELD

✳

WHEN I WROTE THE ORIGINAL INTRODUCTION to *Buddhist America* a decade ago, I began with this story:

One day an old woman who lived in New York went to her travel agent and asked him to get her a ticket to Tibet.

"Tibet?!" he exclaimed. "That's a long and difficult journey. You usually go to Miami for the winter. Why not just go there?"

"I must go see the Guru," she replied.

She got a ticket, flew to India, disembarked at the airport in Delhi, and went through all the difficulties of Indian customs. When asked where she was going, she said, "To Tibet, to see the Guru."

After this, her journey continued by train across India to Gangtok, the capitol of Sikkim. Here she secured a visa and traveled by bus up to the Tibetan border, where the guards asked, and again she replied, "I must go see the Guru."

They told her, "You can only say three words to him."

She replied, "I know, I know. I must go anyway."

She then journeyed with her bags across the Tibetan plateau by bus, by jeep, by horse caravan, and finally came to a large mountain with a monastery at the top. There was a long line of pilgrims and she joined the line. After three days of waiting, it was her turn.

The guard at the door reminded her, "Only three words now."

"I know, I know," she said.

She entered the grand chamber and there sat the Guru, a lama with a wispy beard, wearing maroon robes. She sat down opposite him and looked directly at him. After a silent period she simply said, "Sheldon, come home."

Sheldon has now been home for twenty or thirty years. He has been building Buddhist centers and teaching Buddhist meditation in every corner of our continent. He is engaged in the great task of North American Buddhism: bringing the heartfelt practices and awakening of the Buddha to Western soil, and teaching the dharma of liberation in skillful forms for contemporary times. In this chapter I wish to reflect on how Buddhism is changing as it adapts to our North American culture.

It is remarkable that already there is enough history and breadth to the movement of American Buddhism to merit a book as wide-ranging and all-encompassing as this one. A thousand Buddhist centers and practice groups have grown up in one generation. Buddhism in America has already brought great joy and understanding into hundreds of thousands of people's lives. Though predominantly well educated and most often middle class, North American Buddhists are no longer a small, youthful minority. They are young and old, men, women, and children, spread across every state of the union and every province of Canada. And while it is too early to know fully what form North American Buddhism will take, there are many remarkable developments that have begun to give it the flavor of its new home. Let us consider these.

Each time in the past that Buddhism has been integrated into new cultures like those of China, Tibet, and Japan, it has evolved, and new forces, flavors, and qualities have been brought to its practice. Even with this great variety of cultures and lineages, Asian Buddhist practice has been predominantly characterized by a renunciatory and monastic tradition. Whether in Sri Lanka, Tibet, or Japan, most of the best of Buddhist practice has been preserved in monasteries, kept alive by older monks in situations removed from the everyday society around them. For centuries in Asia, Buddhism has had this monastic, masculine, ascetic, and somewhat patriarchal flavor.

While many generations have benefited greatly from the excellent training received in these monasteries (and we certainly hope that a number of well-run and nonsexist monasteries for monks and nuns will grow in this country, providing opportunities for those who wish to experience the life of renunciation), it appears that monasteries with monks and nuns will not be the major focus of Buddhism in America. Instead the focus is shifting to the lay community, which is at the center of practice here.

In this predominantly lay Western Buddhism, which includes Vipassana, Vajrayana, and Zen practitioners, several new forces for the integration and opening of the tradition are at work. There are four key themes that I have noticed developing in the past twenty-five years.

Shared Practice

Buddhism in Asia has been divided for centuries, kept within separate traditions and lineages. American Buddhists have already begun to actively learn from each other's traditions. Many Zen masters and their students have been avidly studying the mindfulness and lovingkindness practices central to Vipassana retreats. Most Vipassana teachers have also practiced with Tibetan lamas and Zen masters. The American Vajrayana tradition has been profoundly influenced by teachings and practice forms from Zen and Vipassana. This is a remarkable development, one that is perhaps unparalleled since the ancient Na-

landa University of early Buddhism. For the first time in thousands of years, Buddhists of each school have direct access to the practices and teachings of every other great tradition. New learnings, cross-fertilization, shared practices, and a more universal ground of Buddhist understanding have already grown. The distant parts of Buddhism are coming together in America.

With this have come unprecedented gatherings of Buddhist teachers from all traditions. In the past ten years I have participated in and sponsored a series of meetings with many of the senior teachers in the West. We have met regularly in Dharamsala with the Dalai Lama, and at places like Spirit Rock Center and San Francisco Zen Center, bringing hundreds of teachers together. We have exchanged teachings and practices, considered what dharma approaches work best in the West, confided in one another our common problems, and gained insight in each other's company. The teachers who gather at these meetings are often struck by the remarkable similarities in their challenges and by the great help that their collective wisdom and practice experience can offer to one another.

Even the greatest remaining divide in North American Buddhism, the gap between the indigenous ethnic temples (such as the Burmese, Chinese, Thai, and Korean) and the quite separate "American" centers, is beginning to respond to this shared practice. Ethnic centers have primarily served the immigrant community with traditional Asian languages and dharma culture, most often offering devotional forms of Buddhism. But in recent years a number of ethnic temples like Lien Hoa Monastery in Irving, Texas, and Wat Buddhawararam in Denver, Colorado, have begun reaching out to the broader American Buddhist world by sponsoring meditation classes and including nonethnic American teachers and programs. Some of the largest American centers have begun to reciprocate. We are learning to support one another.

Democratization

Buddhism is becoming more democratic in our American democracy. Traditionally, most Buddhist communities in Asia were hierarchical and authoritarian. Wisdom, knowledge, and practice were handed down from elders to juniors, and the running of monasteries and the *sangha* (community of monastic practitioners) rested in the hands of the master or a small core of senior monks. What they decided was the way things were, and there was no questioning of their authority; students just followed. In North America, where our culture is at heart much more democratic, this has begun to change. Western Buddhists are trained to think and understand for themselves and are less suited to the hierarchical models of Asia. At present in Western Buddhist communities there are strong forces for democratization and for participation in decision making by the whole community. Rather than hierarchical structures, there are structures of mutual support and appreciation. As students and teachers have matured, our Buddhist communities are no longer totally teacher-centered. Many now are run by elected boards or use the ancient Buddhist practice of council, drawing on the collective wisdom of a group of teachers and committed students. The participation and inclusion of many dedicated voices will be a great vitalizing factor and a major force for change in Buddhism as it evolves in our country.

Feminization

A third and perhaps the most important force affecting Buddhism in America has been the force of feminization. In Asia, through the monasteries and older monks, Buddhism has been primarily a masculine and patriarchal affair: masculine by virtue of the fact that it has been men who have preserved and transmitted it, and more deeply patriarchal in that its language and traditions have been predominantly in the masculine mode. Buddhism has been a practice of the mind, of *Logos*, of understanding, through striving and attainment: of gaining enlightenment through conquering oneself. All of these elements—the mind, logic, striving, the patriarchal structures, which did not allow for a full participation of women and which discounted feminine values—are now being confronted by the powerful force of feminine consciousness that is growing in Western culture. This con-

sciousness is already bringing about a softening and an opening of the Buddhist spirit and practice that allows for strength of mind and the masculine element, and also for the tenderness and earthiness of the feminine element. Not only is there a clear movement to abandon the superficial structures, sexism, and patriarchy, but there is also a more profound movement to develop the dharma as a practice of relationship to the body, the community, and the earth, and to stress interdependence and healing rather than conquering or abandoning. The large number of mature women who are now teaching in all American traditions is a visible reflection of this revitalizing feminization that is taking place.

Integration

The fourth major theme as Buddhism develops in the West is integration. In Asia, Buddhism was primarily characterized by ordained priests, monks, hermits, and forest dwellers who withdrew from worldly life into monasteries, ashrams, caves, and temples, where they created circumstances of simplicity and renunciation for their practice. The rest of the Buddhists, the great majority of laypeople, did not actually practice meditation but remained devoted supporters of the monks. However, here in the West, the laypeople are not content to be only the devotional supporters of other people's practice. Almost all North American students involved want to actually practice the path of liberation. The most frequently asked question in my more than two decades of teaching has been, "How can we *live* the practice in our American lives?" Our practice will emphasize *integration*, not a withdrawal from the world but a discovery of wisdom within the midst of our lives. North American Buddhists have already begun to develop means to integrate and live the practice as householders, as family people, as people with jobs who still wish to partake of the deepest aspects of the dharma—not by running away to caves, but by applying the practice to their daily lives.

In practice, this spirit of integration has already led to new dharma forms such as family retreats, shorter *sesshin*, "sandwich retreats" (two weekends and the weekday evenings in between), urban study groups, "secularized" dharma training like the Shambhala centers, right livelihood groups, and much more. Integration and shared practices are being fostered by a dharma communications revolution, with popular journals like *Tricycle, Shambhala Sun,* and *Inquiring Mind*; on the Internet by groups like CyberSangha and DharmaNet; in a Vietnamese dharma ham radio network in Texas; and in Rev. Kubose's daily Dial-the-Dharma phone teachings in Chicago.

Another powerful new stream in integrated Western dharma has been called Engaged Buddhism by founders like Thich Nhat Hanh, Joanna Macy, Robert Aitken-Roshi, and others. Engagement in compassionate action in our society as a practice has flourished. The Buddhist Peace Fellowship, which is a hub of this activity, catalogues the growing areas of direct service, from prison dharma projects and Buddhist hospices to nonviolent peace crusades, from Buddhist environmental groups to efforts to secure justice for peoples at risk throughout the world. Zen masters like Tetsugen-Roshi have created "street retreats" and projects to deal with homelessness and AIDS. American Buddhist communities are also involved in expressing their gratitude by bringing aid to Buddhist countries in trouble: to Tibet, Burma, Bangladesh, Cambodia, and Vietnam.

Practice has made a significant new entrance into mainstream American culture through the work of teachers like Jon Kabat-Zinn, which brings mindfulness training to hundreds of hospitals, and Dan Goleman, whose *Emotional Intelligence* has offered dharma principles for use in thousands of schools and corporations.

Along with these sweeping changes, Buddhist practitioners across America have been integrating many of the best tools of modern Western psychology into the practice. This powerful change brings a new emphasis on emotional health and wisdom in our personal lives together with the more absolute aspects of traditional dharma practice. The psychological and the spiritual, the personal and the universal have become widely understood as complementary dimensions of the dharma of liberation.

All of these themes are becoming important forces in Buddhist practice as it approaches the twenty-first century in the West. This adaptation is taking place much more quickly here than it did in China and Tibet. For example, when Buddhism went from India to China, it underwent many centuries of integration with an indigenous Chinese culture steeped in Confucian and Taoist values before it became a part of the Chinese way. Here, because of the speed of communication and the rapid pace of our culture, the first developments of a unique North American Buddhism, instead of taking centuries, have become apparent in only decades.

It is not always an easy process, and it has been a struggle for many of us—Buddhist teachers and students alike—to sort out what is valuable and ought to be preserved from what is merely a "container," a structure that could be more suitably reshaped or cast off. Over the years I have struggled with this a great deal. Like a number of other dharma teachers, I had even considered quitting organized Buddhism. Here I'm not speaking of the teachings of the dharma or the discipline for renunciants; nor of the place of silence and celibacy in practice; nor of precepts, forms of bowing, or ceremonies; nor of the hardships and surrender that are, in fact, valuable parts of spiritual practice. What I have struggled with are the limitations of Buddhism as an organized religion; with the sectarianism and attachments of many of the students and teachers involved; and with the territoriality, the patriarchy, and the excessive life-denying tendencies of practice that can leave *it,* and some students, disconnected from their hearts.

For me, this struggle began in Asia. While traveling and practicing there, I discovered that Buddhism was a great religion just like any other—Christianity, Judaism, Hinduism, or Islam. I saw that the majority of Buddhists in Asia do not actually practice. At best, they go to temple devotionally, like Westerners go to church. They go once a week to hear a sermon or a few moral rules, or to leave a little money to make some merit for a better birth in the next life. In fact, even among the monasteries of such countries as Thailand, Burma, Sri Lanka, and Japan, I discovered that only a fraction of the monks and nuns actually practice—perhaps only five or ten percent! The rest are priests (some very kindly) who study and learn the scriptures (preserving the tradition, but rarely prac-

ticing it), or are schoolteachers or village elders who perform ceremonies and live a simple existence. Others are
monks who become part of a whole hierarchy of bishops,
archbishops, and councils of elders who are usually more
involved in the organization of the religion than the practice of liberation taught by the Buddha.

It was inspiring and refreshing to finally discover that
there is a small group of monasteries where the actual
practices of liberation are kept alive and open to sincere
followers of the Buddha's way. Even after discovering
this, it remained necessary to separate the universal
teachings from the cultural container, and to overlook
the problems and difficulties of certain teachers and
practice temples that were "mixed bags," where good
practice was mixed with power trips, blind allegiance, or
other delusions. Perhaps this sorting-out process is always necessary for the maturing of spiritual students.

The struggle has been more than worth it, for the heart
of the Buddha's awakening is an island of sanity in a
world of delusion and suffering. What an extraordinary
vision he had that night under the Bodhi tree. How unut-
terably marvelous that one person could sit down and
see into the truth of life so deeply, with such great clarity,
and with such overwhelming compassion, and that this
one night's vision would have the power to affect one
and a half billion human beings on this earth for twenty-
five hundred years. . . . All of us involved in Buddhist
practice have been touched by the depth and immediacy
of this vision and inspired to continue in the face of both
the external and the internal difficulties that are a part of
any genuine spiritual path.

In order to have access to these teachings, there were
some important lessons I had to learn. One of the first
was how to "take what's good." I had a teacher in one
Burmese monastery, where I undertook a silent retreat
for more than a year, who was renowned as a master of
certain Vipassana meditation practices. I had come there
from the monastery of Ajahn Chah, a teacher of impeccable simplicity, straightforwardness, and wisdom. In this
new Burmese monastery, the cottage I was given was the
most beautiful one, for I was the only Western monk.
Unfortunately, the cottage was also right next to the
teacher's. This teacher was a slob. His robes dragged on
the ground, and he smoked cigars. He used to throw
rocks at the dogs who were getting into his flower garden
and yell at monks who were misbehaving. He spent a
great deal of time gossiping with the nuns and monks.
And I was supposed to practice there! I would close my
eyes and meditate, and because the instructions he gave
me were excellent, after a number of days I began to experience deeper meditations and wonderful results. As
the weeks went by, I would close my eyes and meditate,
have new, important understandings, and then open
them to begin walking meditation. But as soon as I began
to walk, I would see this teacher yelling at a monk, or
throwing rocks at a dog, or sipping his tea and belching
while he smoked his cigar, and think, "I can't learn from
such a person. He's a slob. He's not enlightened. I want
a better and wiser teacher." Then I would go back and
close my eyes and start to sit, and again the fruits of the
practice would show themselves; clarity, understanding,
and insight would arise. Then I would open my eyes and
see him again and wonder what I was doing there. It went
back and forth like this for quite a few weeks. I suffered
tremendously from the tension.

Finally, it dawned on me that it wasn't necessary to
imitate this teacher, that I could simply take from him
what was good. He was an excellent guide for inner meditation. He gave me wonderful interviews every day and
knew quite well how to fine-tune my Vipassana practice.
And as for the rest, I could leave it for him. If he had
some level of realization, which he must have had to
guide my practice, I could take advantage of it, and if his
realization didn't encompass many other parts of his life,
so be it. What a relief to learn that one can take what is
good and leave the rest.

It will take a great deal of courage on the part of North
American Buddhists to face the areas where Buddhism,
in its structures and practices, is not working. To make a
place for the dharma that is open and true, we will need
to look honestly at what brings awakening and where we
are asleep. We will also have to attend to such difficult
issues as abuse of power and authority, alcohol, sexuality,
and money; and attend to our political and social responsibilities. Already upheavals over teacher behavior and
abuse have occurred at dozens (if not the majority) of

the major Buddhist and Hindu centers in America. These are some of the problems that the teacher meetings had to face. Yet, if we respond with courage, these very upheavals can serve to focus our attention on those aspects that need more consciousness. They can help us build wise practice in such areas as sexuality and human relationships, where the expression of Buddhist tradition has been weak or medieval. Similarly, we have to examine ourselves. So many of us come to practice wounded, lonely, or in fear, wanting a loving family as much as enlightenment. That is fine, for we can use the power of practice and the *sangha* to support, heal, and awaken. However, many people also get stuck perpetuating their neuroses in Buddhism itself, abusing practice as a means of escape, using Buddhism to hide from difficult parts of their lives, trying to create an idealistic world, or not dealing with growing and living in the world as mature individuals. The strength of our dharma will depend on the honesty with which we address these issues and our ability to preserve what is good and leave the rest.

Those of us who helped bring Insight meditation to America chose to simplify the practices we learned in an attempt to offer a clear, straightforward form of Buddhist practice in the West. We left much of the Eastern culture, ritual, and ceremony behind in Asia. That is not because we don't value it (I am a great lover of ritual), but we felt that for Americans it was an unnecessary barrier. It seemed to us that for our culture, the simplicity and straightforwardness of mindfulness practice itself would speak best to the heart of those seeking practice. And, in fact, the very simplicity of Insight meditation retreats, without foreign costumes, rituals, and bowing, or the necessity of joining an organized church, has appealed to many thousands of people over the years. Of course, there are those who prefer or benefit from practice that includes more ritual and sacred ceremony. Fortunately, the plurality of Buddhism will provide that, too. We are blessed to have so many ways made available to us.

What matters is that we find a genuine path of practice and do it fully, that we take a practice and go to its very depths, which means going to the very depths of our own being. We must each find a practice that inspires us and follow it over and over again in whatever fashion makes it come alive in our body, in our heart, and in our mind. By doing this, we rediscover the greatness of heart, the truth, and the mystery that were discovered by the Buddha and which he declared should be openhanded and available to all who wish to practice.

Such practice, the practice of liberation, is not exclusive. There is no one tradition, one way, or one particular kind of practice that will awaken people. Although meditation practice seems especially beneficial for our times, there are many ways to realize truth. Even though D. T. Suzuki was a foremost exponent of Zen, he wrote that many more Buddhists were liberated through the heartfelt practices of devotional Buddhism than through all of the insight of Ch'an and Zen put together. In the traditional Pali Buddhist scriptures, most of the people did not become awakened through the systematic process of meditation, but were opened by simply hearing the universal truths proclaimed by the Buddha. When the Buddha spoke the truth of impermanence and invited listeners to the deathless, people became enlightened. As the Buddha described the happiness and freedom that come from letting go, many beings were awakened. Yet these truths are universal and are held by other great traditions as well; enlightenment or liberation is never the possession of any one great teacher or lineage.

What is unique about Buddhism is the clarity and directness of the Buddha's expression of enlightenment and the great number of skillful means that he taught to enable others to realize it. In his forty-five years of teaching and during the twenty-five hundred years of Buddhist history, a vast range of practices for liberation has been taught, encompassing many lands and many cultures. The Buddha himself taught hundreds of techniques of awareness practice, concentration meditation, discipline, and surrender. Since his time, the masters who followed have elaborated even more fully. Now that these techniques are all coming to America, how can we sort through them? How can we understand them as presented in a book such as this?

First we must beware of sectarianism. The history of Buddhism unfortunately contains a great deal of sectarian pain. Zen masters put down other Zen masters. Lamas defend the turf of their own Tibetan sects, waging spiritual—if not actual—warfare with one another. The Sri Lankans or Burmese or Thais denigrate one another's practice. Buddhism has become divided into greater, lesser, and more numerous vehicles. This sectarianism has existed since the time of the Buddha himself. On the day he died sects began springing up based on different aspects of the dharma. Out of ignorance such sects and lineages have fought with one another and continue to do so to this day. Sectarianism grows from the idea that "our way is best," and its divisiveness is actually rooted in misunderstanding and fear. Sectarianism is never true. As the third Zen Patriarch put it, "Distinctions arise from the clinging needs of the ignorant. There is one Dharma, not many." Or as contemporary Buddhist poet Tom Savage wrote, "Greater vehicle, lesser vehicle, all vehicles will be towed at owner's expense."

The many practices of Buddhism are like paths up a mountain—outwardly different approaches that are appropriate for different personalities and character types. Yet, through skillful guidance and practice, these paths can lead one to awakening and freedom at the summit of the mountain.

An early story of the Buddha helps us to understand this. It takes place while the Buddha is standing in a grove at one of his monasteries. A visitor remarks on how tranquil and beautiful the scene is with so many composed monks. The Buddha points to his great disciples and the students gathered around them. He notes that there are many ways that people are practicing. Pointing to Sariputta, the wisest of his disciples, he observes, "Those who have the propensity to practice through wisdom are gathered there with my wisest disciple, Sariputta. And there is my disciple Maha Mogallana, foremost in psychic powers. Those whose propensities draw them to use psychic powers as a part of their path to realization are gathered with Maha Mogallana. There is my great disciple Upali, master of the Vinaya and the discipline, and those whose tendencies would benefit by that way of practice are gathered with him. There again is another great disciple and another group of students. . . ." and so on. It is not helpful to judge one practice against another; in fact, this is a detriment to practice. Our task is simply to find a practice that touches our heart and to undertake it in a committed and disciplined way.

Kindness of Heart, Inner Stillness, and Liberating Wisdom

Our understanding of different practices is also helped by seeing the structure of the entire spiritual path, by understanding its essence and how it brings about human happiness and freedom. The essential path taught by the Buddha has three parts to it. The first is *kindness of heart*, a ground of fundamental compassion expressed through virtue and generosity. The second is *inner stillness* or *concentration*. The third aspect of all Buddhist practice is the awakening of *liberating wisdom*.

All Buddhist practices include ways of expressing compassion through the nonharming of other beings and a generosity of heart. All Buddhist practices offer ways to quiet the mind, nurturing concentration, steadiness, stillness, and clarity or depth of mind. And all Buddhist paths awaken insight and the transcendent wisdom of emptiness, fostering a wise and free understanding of body and mind. These three dimensions and the practices leading to compassion, inner stillness, and wisdom are but means to the final freedom of the heart. As the Buddha himself said, "The purpose of my teaching of the holy life of the Dharma is not for merit, nor good deeds, nor rapture, nor concentration, nor insight, but the sure heart's release. This and this alone is the reason for the teaching of the Buddha." The purpose of all the practices of virtue, kindness, nonharming, generosity, concentration, visualization, devotion, compassion, clarity of mind, and the understanding and wisdom that arises is to bring us to freedom.

As American Buddhism becomes more integrated and inclusive, it follows the historical evolution that marked the dharma's changes in Asia. The earlier forms of Buddhism expressed the path of practice in primarily a renunciatory way. They saw the body and sexuality as impure and the mind and spiritual thoughts as pure, stressing the necessity of withdrawing from the world to embrace a life of solitude as a monk or a nun, emphasizing the need to get out of the rounds of rebirth to the cessation of nirvana, and so forth. As later Buddhist schools developed over the centuries, they shifted from a dualistic approach to a nondualistic one. As the nondualistic expression of Buddhism (which was also taught by the Buddha) grew in predominance, the emphasis shifted to the interdependence of all life and the importance of discovering nirvana in the midst of *samsara*, or a liberation from greed, hatred, and delusion in this very life and on this very earth.

This nondualistic spirit of dharma is particularly important in our times, in a world of turmoil threatened by war and ecological disaster. The mind is able to create weapons of mass destruction and ecological disasters only when it has split off from the heart and the body. If the mind were connected with the heart and the body, with this earth, with children, with cycles of nature, it would not be possible to plan abstractly the mathematics of nuclear arms or the destruction of our environment. A nondualistic understanding, and the wisdom of interdependence, compassion, and nongreed that it teaches, are essential for the very survival of our earth. While this nondualistic flavor is spreading throughout American practice, we must honor both the old and the new perspectives, for they are part of the whole.

Lest we see one as truly separate from another, Lama Govinda gives us the image of a seed and a tree as a way of connecting the variety of Buddhist practices presented in this book. Two thousand five hundred years ago Siddhartha Gautama, through his extraordinary realization, planted a seed of timeless wisdom and compassion. Over the centuries the seed has grown and produced an enormous and wonderful tree, which has a trunk and branches, flowers and fruit. Some people claim that the roots are the true Buddhism. Others claim, "No, it's the fruit or the flowers." Still others say, "No, it's the great trunk of the tree," or "the fruit of Vajrayana," or "the roots of Theravada Buddhism." In fact, all parts of the tree support one another. The leaves give nourishment back to the roots, the roots draw in moisture and minerals, bringing nourishment up to the leaves, and they in turn provide support for the flowers and the fruit. It is all part of the whole, and to understand that is to see the

creative and dynamic forces that were set loose from the seed of the Buddha's awakening.

Preserving and Adapting

Historically, all major religions, including Buddhism, have contained a basic tension—one that persists as Buddhism comes to America. This is the tension between tradition or orthodoxy and adaptation or modernization. Many people involved in Buddhism see it as their purpose and their duty to preserve and sustain the Sutras, the tradition, and the practices just as they were handed down in their lineage from the original teachings and the great masters of old, from the time of the Buddha. Others have found it important to adapt Buddhist practice to new cultures, finding skillful means of allowing access to and understanding of the great wisdom of Buddhism without presenting it in old, ungainly, and inaccessible forms. This tension has been present since the time of the Buddha himself. Since the first council held after the Buddha's death, there have been those great teachers whose main purpose was to preserve, as literally as possible, the practice, style, and teaching of the Buddha without losing any aspect of the original expression of the truth. At the same time, there have been masters and teachers in many cultures who have seen the need to translate and adapt these teachings. Both of these ways, like the great tree of Lama Govinda, are parts of a whole. The ability to adapt Buddhism without losing its essence is dependent on the depth of the tradition that has been preserved. Yet awakening new followers and gaining support for the preservation and depth of practice must come through the translation and creativity of those who have made practice truly alive in new cultures and new times. Each part depends on the other. The very diversity of views, schools, and teachings is Buddhism's health, keeping it vital and true.

In the thirty years of my own study, practice, and teaching of Theravada Buddhism, I have come to recognize very clearly that our tradition contains both— masters who emphasize close adherence to the twenty-five hundred years of Buddhist tradition and masters who insist that practice must also be *practical*, as alive today as it was at the time of the Buddha. After helping to found one center (Insight Meditation Society, Barre, Massachusetts) devoted in a beautiful way to traditional retreat practice, we have now founded a center with a broader purpose in Marin County, California. Spirit Rock Center offers teachings that balance the traditional and integrative aspects of practice. On the one hand, it is a center that preserves a depth of practice through intensive retreats, traditional study, a hermitage, and so forth. On the other hand, the key need to integrate practice into our times is also addressed. We have teachings on right livelihood and service, on right speech and communication, as well as training in the development and expression of compassion in all aspects of life—through Buddhist peace work, through family life, through ecology. This integrative practice has also developed in many other Buddhist centers. We are learning that our practice is not just sitting, not just study, not just belief, but that it encompasses how we actually live, how well we love, and how much we can let go of our small self and care for this earth and all beings.

As Buddhism grows in North America, a wonderful new process is happening. All of us, as laypeople, as householders, want what was mostly the special dispensation of monks in Asia: the real practice of the Buddha. American laypeople are not content to go and hear a sermon once a week or to make merit by leaving gifts at a meditation center. Zen master Suzuki-Roshi observed this when he said,

Here in America we cannot define Zen Buddhists the same way we do in Japan. American students are not priests and yet not completely laymen. I understand it this way: that you are not priests is an easy matter, but that you are not exactly laymen is more difficult. I think you are special people and want some special practice that is not exactly priest's practice and not exactly layman's practice. You are on your way to discovering some appropriate way of life.*

*Shunryu Suzuki, *Zen Mind, Beginner's Mind* (New York: John Weatherhill, 1986), 133.

As lay Buddhists, we too want to *live* the realizations of the Buddha and bring them into our hearts, our lives, and our times. This is why so many Americans have been drawn to the purity of intensive Vipassana retreats, or to the power of Zen *sesshin*, or to the one hundred thousand prostrations and three-year retreats of the Vajrayana tradition. Somehow we have an intuitive sense of the potential of human freedom and the heart of basic goodness—the timeless discovery of the Buddha.

We are drawn not just to study and understand it but to practice it, realize it, and live it in our lives. Practice always involves a great deal of struggle, for it means confronting ourselves, our fears, our territoriality, and our need for security. To do this skillfully, we can use the raft of Buddhism to carry us to the shore of liberation, but we must never mistake the raft for the shore. We are called to go beyond all clinging, beyond the small sense of self to that which is selfless and timeless. When we practice with devotion and a love for truth, we can find the limitless freedom and compassion of the Buddha in our very own heart.

As the many Buddhist traditions are shared by sincere American students, a new freshness, integrity, and questioning have grown. We are open to learning from one another. In my own teaching and practice I have benefited enormously from the privilege of studying with great masters in the Tibetan and Zen traditions. Even though my own heart has found its home in the simplicity of Theravada mindfulness practice, I now discover myself teaching what Suzuki-Roshi called "Hinayana practice with a Mahayana mind." In this spirit, my teaching has shifted from an emphasis on effort and striving to one of opening and healing. So many students come to practice wounded, conditioned to closing off and hating parts of themselves. For them, striving perpetuates their problems. Instead, we now begin by awakening the heart of compassion and inspiring a courage to live the truth as a deep motivation for practice. This heart-centered motivation draws together lovingkindness, healing, courage, and clarity in an interdependent way. It brings alive the compassion of the Buddha from the very first step.

I do not want to be too idealistic. There are many

problems that Buddhist communities must face—unhealthy structures, unwise practices, misguided use of power, and so forth. Still, something new is happening on this continent. Buddhism is being deeply affected by the spirit of democracy, by feminization, by shared practice, and by the integration of lay life. A North American vehicle is being created. Already this vehicle draws on the best of the roots, the trunk, the branches, the leaves, the blossoms, and the fruits—all the parts of Buddhism—and it is beginning to draw them together in a wise and supportive whole.

Let me end with a story that illustrates this. Some years ago we had the privilege of a visit to the Insight Meditation Society by His Holiness, the sixteenth Gyalwa Karmapa, head of the Kagyu sect of Tibetan Buddhism. His Holiness the Karmapa came during one of our three-month retreats. He sat on a gilded throne in our meditation hall, surrounded by 150 yogis and students to whom he gave a dharma talk and ceremonial blessing. As a teacher of the retreat, I sat in the front row next to a sixty-eight-year-old woman from Calcutta named Dipa Ma Barua, who was one of the most highly attained and realized yogis in Theravada Buddhism. She was a visiting master who had developed the highest levels of insight practice and attained all the great *samadhi* practices of compassion and lovingkindness. Because she did not speak English, as the Karmapa's Tibetan was being translated into English by *his* translators, that English was in turn translated into Bengali by *hers*.

After hearing a wonderful talk by the Karmapa on the Buddhist Four Noble Truths and on the great teachings of compassion and emptiness, Dipa Ma turned to me, put her hand on my knee, and exclaimed with delight, "He's a Buddhist!" As an Indian Buddhist she had been going to Bodh Gaya for twenty years, lived right across the street from the Tibetan temple, had seen tens of thousands of Tibetan pilgrims and Tibetan lamas at the Bodhi tree in India during the many years of her practice; yet she had never heard their teachings in translation and had never really understood that they, too, were Buddhists.

The Tibetans, the Burmese, and the Japanese have been hidden from one another for centuries by the heights of mountainous terrain, by the barriers of their cultures, and by the shields of their languages. Their Buddhist traditions, and masters such as Chögyam Trungpa, Rinpoche, and Suzuki-Roshi; or His Holiness the Karmapa and Dipa Ma; or Joshu Sasaki-Roshi and Kalu Rinpoche (who, as the story goes, once met at an airport in Arizona without their translators and could only sit there, hold hands, and smile at each other for an hour), have finally met one another in the great melting pot of our North American culture. And now a whole new generation of North American teachers is continuing the process as leaders of over one thousand Buddhist centers.

In this book and in the West we are seeing the awakening of the Buddha, and the Buddha is smiling very broadly, with the wisdom of Tibet, India, Japan, Thailand, Burma, and America all joined in. We have been given the treasury of Buddhist practices, a cornucopia of compassion and wisdom to nourish and awaken us to our True Nature. It is a remarkable time in the history of Buddhism. For every practitioner it is a privilege to be a part of this process. May we carry the banner of the dharma wisely and offer its blessings to all.

. . .

Jack Kornfield was trained as a monk in the monasteries of Thailand, India, and Burma; for over two decades he has been teaching Vipassana meditation throughout the world. A founding teacher of the Insight Meditation Society and of Spirit Rock Center, he is a psychologist, father, and author whose books include A Path With Heart, Teachings of the Buddha, Seeking the Heart of Wisdom *(with Joseph Goldstein),* Living Dharma, Stories of the Spirit *(with Christina Feldman),* A Still Forest Pool *(with Paul Breider), and* Buddha's Little Instruction Book.

Liberation through Nonclinging Is the Point Where All Buddhist Traditions Agree

JOSEPH GOLDSTEIN

✷

> All Dharmas agree at one point.
>
> —*Chekawa Yeshe Dorje*

ALL OF THE DIFFERENT BUDDHIST TRADITIONS— Theravada, Mahayana, Vajrayana—converge in the understanding of what liberates the mind. The Buddha expressed it many times in the *Suttas*. He said, "The supreme state of sublime peace has been discovered by the Tathagata, namely liberation through nonclinging."

Elsewhere he said, "Nothing whatsoever is to be clung to as I or mine. Whoever has heard this teaching has heard all of the teachings. Whoever puts this into practice has put all of the Dharma into practice."

Down through the centuries, teacher after teacher has emphasized this key point. In a famous exchange between the great Indian sage Tilopa and his disciple Naropa, Tilopa said, "You are not fettered by appearances, Naropa, you are fettered by attachment. So cut your attachment."

One of my students came to me recently with a wonderful image to describe suffering. He called it "rope burn." The rope of experience may be of rough hemp or of the smoothest silk, and yet if we cling or grasp, we get "rope burn," we suffer. Learning to let go of attachment is what meditation is all about.

In hearing the teaching of "liberation through nonclinging," it's important to emphasize right from the start that we don't meditate in order to have a pleasant experience at some later date. Somehow, although we hear this over and over again, we don't want to accept it. Instead we think, "I'll practice real hard and someday it will be nice and easy, it will be wonderful and spacious. . . ." That thought is itself another passing experience. What we are practicing *in this very moment* is the mind of no-attachment. It doesn't matter what experience is coming up; we can practice "liberation through nonclinging" with anything that arises. It's always available and accessible in the moment.

Anicca: Impermanence

How can we accomplish "liberation through nonclinging?" One way is through cultivating an awareness of impermanence. Impermanence can be seen on every level, from macro to micro. Looking at the largest phenomena in the universe—stars, galaxies, clusters of galaxies—we see that they are in continual change. Or we can study the tiniest subatomic particles and recognize that they too are in constant flux. Nothing is static.

We can become aware of impermanence by paying attention to the natural cycles of birth and death of the body, or to the momentary arisings of the mind. Have you found anything in your experience that doesn't change—inside, outside, large, or small? Try to recall—those of you who have already had some experience with Buddhist practice—your most wonderful meditation experience. Maybe you had a moment or two when the mind was clear, open, luminous, radiant; the body didn't hurt and you felt happy and at peace. Where is that experience now? Or think of your worst meditation experience, when your mind was contracted and tight and your body was full of pain and you were restless and you could hardly stand it. Where is that experience now?

Looking back on our experience, it's obvious to us that everything is like a dream. But when we look ahead, somehow we are seduced again and again by the dazzling array of possibilities. Everything in our culture seems to support this fascination with what's coming next. As an example, here's the text of a magazine ad:

> It can take several lifetimes to reach a state of inner peace and tranquillity, or it can take a couple of weeks. Concentrate deeply. Think about a fourteen day ocean journey to Singapore or Bali, Thailand or China. Days when your every whim is anticipated, instantly met. Places where the sights, smells, lights, are a sensual feast imagination can't do justice. Now a flash of insight. Royal Caribbean will soon take you to the Far East. It's a vacation that until now simply did not exist. But you can believe. Call for a free brochure. Or ask your travel agent about the nirvana you have coming. Don't put it off another lifetime.

Those experiences that we so avidly look forward to will be just like all of the other experiences we've had in the past. In the moment they may be wonderful or awful, but when they're gone they lose all sense of substance.

Freedom from clinging does not depend on what the experience is. It's simply a question of letting things be. The Buddha gave very explicit instructions here:

Whatever feeling arises, whether pleasant or unpleasant or neutral, abide contemplating impermanence in those feelings, contemplate fading away, cessation of those feelings. Contemplate relinquishment, letting go. Contemplating thus, we do not cling to anything in the world. When we do not cling, there is no agitation. When not agitated, we personally attain Nibbana.

It's not easy to do because of our strong habituated tendencies, but it is, nonetheless, a very clear, simple, and straightforward teaching. We need to reflect on this and to apply our understanding to the way we relate to the present moment. Because it is through this insight, through the clear seeing and the constant recollection of the momentariness of all arising experience that our grip on the rope is loosened. This is liberation through nonclinging.

Anatta: Selflessness

Awareness of impermanence leads naturally to a deepening insight into selflessness or nonidentification. As we watch the different thoughts, feelings, and sensations coming and going, we notice that they seem to have a life of their own, that the whole process is occurring according to its own laws. Recognizing this, we simply stop identifying with what's coming up. When we don't identify, we stop clinging. In that vast and open mind of not clinging we again see impermanence and selflessness with greater clarity. We enter the great stream of dharma and it carries us along. When nothing is taken to be "I" or "my" or "self," but rather as just this flow of empty phenomena, it's like waking from a dream. When we awaken, the dream disappears.

You don't have to wait for some special "enlightenment" experience to realize selflessness or to practice nonidentification. Any experience will do. This is what gives such power to the practice. It can be done in this very moment with whatever arises in the body, in the mind, in the external world.

In this regard, it's helpful to pay attention to times of suffering. In whatever way suffering arises, try to see it as feedback rather than as a problem. Seeing it as a problem gives rise to discouragement, self-pity, restlessness, aversion. On the other hand, looked upon as feedback, suffering becomes a vehicle for waking up. When we're suffering, it means that in one way or another we are identified with something that has arisen: a thought, an emotion, a reaction, a judgment, a sensation in the body. So suffering is actually a major signal. It invites us to look, right in that moment, see the cause of our suffering, and practice letting go of our identification with it.

Areas Where We Cling

In case there is any confusion about clinging, the Buddha elaborated very specifically on those areas where we tend to hang on most tenaciously. The first of these is attachment to sense pleasures, to pleasant experiences and feelings. When we see for ourselves how strongly the mind holds on to pleasant experience, we learn something about the nature of addiction. Imagine what it would be like to want everything that's advertised on TV. Isn't it obvious that "wanting" is suffering, and that "not wanting" is the release from suffering? To be able to sit back, as most of us do with TV ads, and just let them go by—this is the cooling down of the mind. While it's easy enough to do with the commercials on TV, it's more difficult with our inner advertisements. This, however, is the practice—to investigate how the mind gets enchanted, seduced, pulled in. Can we approach this investigation from a place of interest rather than from one of self-judgment?

At one point in my practice I had the feeling that I was cruising along on this great freeway. Occasionally I'd see a sign by an exit saying "Amusement Park," and I'd watch my mind take the exit, head straight for the park, spend time in whatever fantasy it was, and eventually get back to the highway. After a while I'd see the sign, get off at the exit, realize what was happening, and get right back on again. Finally, with greater clarity and mindfulness, I'd see the sign and just keep on going.

See if you can notice desires as these billboards in the mind. It's one way of beginning to understand the workings of desire and the possibility of not buying in. It's not that all of our desires disappear, but rather that we no longer feel compelled to act on them.

Nonattachment doesn't mean that we close ourselves off to pleasant feelings, or that we push them away or withdraw from them. The mind of no-clinging is not some arid and colorless state. Rather, it's a mind that's open and vast. We're actually opening ourselves to everything, but without attachment or grasping.

The second arena where we get caught is in the attachment to our opinions and viewpoints about things. We cling to our ways of thinking, to being right. How much conflict is there in the world because of this attachment? It's helpful in this regard to notice the difference between what we have an opinion about and what we really know—because we have lots of opinions about things we don't in fact have knowledge of.

It's also helpful to keep an open mind about the things we actually do know; the understandings, insights, and realizations that have come to us through our life experiences, and by way of our practice. We think we really know these things, and very quickly we become attached to what we know. Especially within the context of our dharma practice, such absolute certainty can lead to a kind of dharma pride, which in turn leads to sectarianism; the attitude of mind that asserts "I know this. I'm right. Therefore everybody who has a different point of view must be wrong." Buddhism, like most other traditions, is prey to sectarianism. How much freer it is to rest in the mind of mystery, the "don't know mind."

The third field of clinging is attachment to rites and rituals. I think the Buddha pointed this area out because in his time people believed, mistakenly, that a ritual such as bathing in the Ganges would lead to purification of the heart. While in our time we're less inclined toward this form of attachment, vestiges still remain. Trungpa Rinpoche had an interesting slant on it when he talked of "spiritual materialism." He said that we tend to use our spiritual practice as something to be gained, as one more thing to be acquired in order to bolster the sense of self.

The last great attachment the Buddha mentioned is attachment to "self," attachment to the notion of "I." We create a sense of self in any moment in which we identify with what's happening. Thoughts arise and think themselves, but when we identify with them, when we add that extra piece—"I'm thinking," or "This thought belongs to me,"—in that moment the sense of self is created. This is also true when we identify with emotions, with sensations in the body, with sounds, with sights. It's a subtle form of clinging that is at work in every moment of identification. Even when we're not so caught and can recognize that everything is arising and passing away, we can still be identified with awareness itself, with the sense of being the observer, the witness; "I'm the one who's knowing this."

We also create a sense of self through the stories we make up about ourselves, about who we are, about our life in the world, about our spiritual journey. Creation of that story is the creation of the sense of "I." How many stories have you told yourself about your experience? Here's one: "Maybe if I practice really hard, in twenty years I'll get enlightened." If we believe that story, if we get lost in it, we create someone who needs to practice hard for the next twenty years before something will happen. We solidify the sense of ourselves, when all that has really happened is a passing thought in the moment. When we can rest in the simple awareness of that story as a thought in the moment, there's no problem. The story is there, we see it, and then it's gone.

We also strengthen the sense of self when we get lost in our projections about people and situations. How much do we fabricate in our perceptions of other people? The following story illustrates the point: Back in 1984 my Burmese teacher, U Pandita Sayadaw, came to our center to conduct a retreat. I was doing walking meditation on the sidewalk in front of the building. I happened to glance up and I noticed Sayadaw standing in the window of his room, looking down at me. I straightened up, slowed the pace, and very mindfully and carefully noted each phase of the walking: "Lift, move, place. Lift, move, place." I was really impeccable, or at least pretending to be.

A few minutes later I glanced up again, and there he was, still looking down at me. Fifteen minutes went by, then twenty. I couldn't imagine why he was spending so much time watching me walk. After a half hour of this I looked more carefully and realized it wasn't Sayadaw at all . . . it was a lampshade. My mind had created the whole story, and I was living in that reality, a reality full of self.

As you go through the day, try to notice all those times when you're "selfing." When does the notion of "I" creep in? The late Ven. Buddhadasa of Thailand suggested that in addition to understanding rebirth as happening from lifetime to lifetime, we think of it as a "reincarnation" of the sense of self, of "I" and "mine." When the mind is consumed with hatred, that's a kind of rebirth into the "hell realm." When it gets caught in intense, unfulfilled longing, that's being born into the "hungry ghost realm"; or in conflict, which is the "*Asura* realm"; or in dullness, which is the "animal realm"; or in states of deep concentration, which is the "brahma realm;" or in sense pleasures, which is the "human or *deva* realm." Throughout the day, over and over again, we give birth to the notion of self.

This attachment to self is probably the strongest one we have. But in one of the *suttas*, the Buddha, in a very clear and incisive way, deconstructed this whole notion for us. If we can follow his argument, it opens us immediately to the truth, to the realization, to the experience of nonself. According to the *sutta*, the monk Anuradha was approached by a group of wandering holy men who, in the classical style of Indian philosophical discourse, laid out all the possible alternatives for what happens to the Buddha when he dies: "He exists after death, or he doesn't exist after death, or he both exists and he doesn't exist, or he neither exists nor doesn't exist." But Anuradha replied, "The Buddha is spoken of in ways other than this," at which point the holy men began to make fun of him in no uncertain terms. "You must be a novice," they taunted, "or if you're an elder, you're an ignorant fool."

Troubled, Anuradha went to the Buddha and asked, "How could I have answered these wanderers in a way that's in accord with the dharma?" In reply, the Buddha asked Anuradha a series of questions.

"Is the body permanent or impermanent?"

"Impermanent, oh lord."

"Are feelings, perceptions, all the other mental factors, consciousness, are they permanent or impermanent?"

"Impermanent, Bhante."

"What is impermanent, is that reliable or unreliable?"

"Unreliable, Bhante."

"What is impermanent, unreliable, what is of the nature to change, is it proper to regard those things as 'This is mine, this is myself, this is I?'"

"No, Bhante."

"Now Anuradha, do you regard the Tathagata's body as being the Tathagata?"

"Surely not, oh Lord."

"Do you regard feelings, perceptions, mental activities, consciousness as being the Tathagata?"

"Surely not, Bhante."

"Do you regard the Tathagata as being something apart from these five things?"

"No, Bhante."

"Do you regard the Tathagata as having no body, no feelings, no perceptions, no mental formations, no consciousness?"

"Surely not."

"Then since in just this life the Tathagata is not to be found, is not met with in reality, is it proper to say of him, 'He can be spoken of in some other way?'"

"No, Bhante."

"Well said, Anuradha; both formerly and now also only this do I teach, what suffering is and what is its end."

The body, feelings, perceptions, mental formations, consciousness—are these the self? On the other hand, are we something other than these five things? No. We're not these five things and we're not anything other than these five things either. Do you see? There's nothing there that could even be called self, nothing whatsoever to be clung to as "I" or "mine." We see that the "self" or the "I" is not something we have to get rid of, because it was never there in the first place. As we liberate our minds from the prison of self, as we free ourselves in the moment from the fetter of attachment, the heart-mind of awareness can manifest its true inherent quality of love and compassion.

Lovingkindness and the Realization of Emptiness

The great Hindu saint Maharaji Neem Karoli Baba used to say, "Don't throw anyone out of your heart." In some way I feel that this becomes the bottom-line reference point for our practice. In our lives are we throwing any one, any thing, any situation out of our hearts? Or are we letting it all in? Because when we notice that we're keeping something out, that in itself becomes a reflection for us of the creation of self.

We approach our spiritual practice in two ways: on the one hand from the point of view of love and compassion, on the other from the realization of nonself. As we practice lovingkindness toward ourselves, our friends, benefactors, enemies—all living beings—our hearts expand until they're big enough to let everyone in. And from the realization of selflessness, we see there's no one there to keep anyone out. From both sides, from the expansiveness of lovingkindness and compassion, and from the boundless realization of "no-self," we come to this place that Maharaji was pointing to.

Tulku Urgyen, a great Tibetan master, said that with *relative bodhicitta*—the compassionate wish to alleviate the suffering of all beings—and *absolute bodhicitta*—the wisdom of emptiness, the realization that there is no one there to awaken—"enlightenment is unavoidable." With compassion and emptiness, enlightenment is unavoidable. I like that.

· · ·

Joseph Goldstein is a cofounder and guiding teacher of Insight Meditation Society in Barre, Massachusetts. He has been teaching vipassana *and* metta *retreats worldwide since 1974. In 1989 he helped establish the Barre Center for Buddhist Studies. He is the author of* The Experience of Insight, *and* Insight Meditation: The Practice of Freedom, *and coauthor (with Jack Kornfield) of* Seeking the Heart of Wisdom.

The Complete Guide to Buddhist America

PART ONE

Theravada

The Path of Insight

Theravada: The Path of Insight

GIL FRONSDAL

❋

THERAVADA—LITERALLY, THE TEACHINGS OF the Elders—is an ancient Buddhist tradition that has nurtured practices and teachings of wisdom, love and liberation for over two thousand years. Liberation, the pivotal point around which the tradition revolves, is a deep seeing into and participation in the reality of "things as they are": our ordinary world seen and experienced without the filters of greed, hatred, and delusion.

With the ever present, timeless immediacy of "things as they are" as its central reference point, the Theravada school is a fluid and varied tradition evolving in response to the particular personal, historical, and cultural circumstances of its adherents. Today there are over one hundred million Theravada Buddhists in Sri Lanka and Southeast Asia. The three most influential Theravada countries are Burma, Thailand, and Sri Lanka, and it is from these countries that the tradition has come to the West.

Theravada Buddhism in North America

Since the 1960s, the Theravada tradition has slowly but surely found a home in North America. The two major turning points for its establishment here were the founding—in 1966 by the Sri Lankan Buddhist community in Washington, D.C.—of the first American Buddhist *vihara* (temple) and, ten years later, the establishment of the Insight Meditation Society in Barre, Massachusetts.

Together they represent the two divergent and distinct forms that Theravada Buddhism has taken on this continent, namely, the monastic tradition of Southeast Asian immigrant groups on the one hand, and on the other, the lay-centered *vipassana* movement made up mostly of Americans of European descent. The former tend to be fairly conservative, replicating in America the various forms of Buddhism found in their native countries. The latter take a more liberal and experimental approach in adapting the tradition to its lay-based American setting.

The newest form of American Theravada Buddhism fits into neither of these categories. It is represented by monastic centers run and supported predominantly by Euro-Americans. An example is Abhayagiri Monastery, founded by the English monk Ajahn Amaro in 1996 in Redwood Valley, California. In addition, two other monastic centers—Metta Forest Monastery in San Diego County, California, and the Bhavana Society in High View, West Virginia—are making monastic practice available to Westerners while remaining firmly connected to their traditional Asian communities. It could well be that within these centers we are seeing the beginnings of an authentic American Buddhist monasticism.

Considered an ideal lifestyle for study, practice, service, and the purification of the heart, monasticism has long been a cornerstone of the Theravada tradition. However, in the twentieth century and especially in the modern West, the full range of Theravada practices has been made available to the laity in an unprecedented manner. This being the case, monasticism is no longer seen as the sole carrier of the tradition, although it remains an anchor and a force of preservation.

While it is too early to tell what American Theravada Buddhism will come to look like, it will probably exhibit at least as much diversity as it has in its Southeast Asian homelands and will no doubt stretch the boundaries of what has traditionally defined it.

Basic Teachings

The Buddha encouraged his followers not to believe blindly but to "come and see" for themselves. Consequently his teachings emphasize practice rather than doctrine. In this spirit, Theravada Buddhism promotes awareness "techniques" that are simple in themselves but powerful in their sustained application. It also teaches practices that strengthen such attributes as generosity, lovingkindness, and compassion, thus nurturing the growth of an awakened heart and enabling one to live wisely.

The Buddha's teachings have been preserved in a large body of *suttas* (scriptures) written in Pali, the Theravada equivalent of church Latin. These remarkable texts, known as the *Pali Canon*, contain thorough descriptions of practices, ethics, psychology, and teachings on the spiritual life. Interestingly, they also contain a strong warning not to give up one's own judgment in favor of the tradition or its texts. In the *Kalama Sutta*, the Buddha says that in deciding the truth or falsity of spiritual teachings,

You should decide not by what you have heard, not by following convention, not by assuming it is so, not by relying on texts, not because of reasoning, not because of logic, not by thinking about explanations, not by acquiescing to the views that you prefer, not because it appears likely, and certainly not out of respect for a teacher.

When you would know for *yourselves*, that "these things are unhealthy, these things, when entered upon and undertaken, incline toward harm and suffering"—then you should reject them.

But when you know for yourselves, that "these things are healthy, these things, when entered upon and undertaken, incline toward welfare and happiness"—then having come to them you should stay with them.*

A key reason for such pragmatic criteria is that the Buddha was not particularly interested in establishing correct philosophical views. Rather, he was concerned with pointing out what moves one from suffering to liberation. Thus, the central doctrine of the Theravada tradition is found in the "Four Noble Truths"—the word *truth* here referring to that which is spiritually or therapeutically helpful. First, suffering occurs; second, the cause of suffering is clinging or craving; third, it is possible to put an end to suffering; and fourth, suffering ceases when we follow the "Noble Eightfold Path."

Suffering (*dukkha* in Pali) here does not refer to physical or empathetic pain, but rather to the dissatisfactions and tensions we add to our life through clinging. The first and second Noble Truths are a call to recognize clearly both our suffering and the many variations of grasping and aversion that give rise to it. The third and fourth point to the possibility of ending such clinging-derived suffering and of living with an open, generous, and anxiety-free heart.

The experience of liberation is known as *nibbana* (*nirvana* in Sanskrit, *enlightenment* in English). While the Theravadans sometime describe *nibbana* as a form of great happiness or peace, more often it is defined simply as the complete absence of craving. The primary reason for this negative definition is that *nibbana* is so radically different from what can be described through language that it is best not to try. Furthermore, the tradition discourages attachment to *ideas* of enlightenment as well as to pointless metaphysical speculation. Indeed, the brilliance of the Four Noble Truths is that they offer a guide to the spiritual life without adherence to dogmatic beliefs of any kind.

---

*The Kalama Sutta, translated by Andy Olendzki, in Jack Kornfield and Gil Fronsdal, *The Teachings of the Buddha* (Boston: Shambhala Publications, 1996), 93–95.

The Noble Eightfold Path

Since it is not easy to end all our clinging in "one fell swoop," the Buddha devised a gradual approach, which he called "The Noble Eightfold Path." Here it is:

Panna (Wisdom)
1. Right Understanding
2. Right Intention

Wisdom begins when we see clearly that the Four Noble Truths are not just abstract ideas but refer instead to our own personal situations. It is out of this understanding that a sincere motivation to practice arises.

Sila (Ethics)
3. Right Speech
4. Right Action
5. Right Livelihood

Theravada Buddhism teaches that it is not possible to cultivate an open, trusting, and nonclinging heart if our behavior is motivated by greed, hatred, or delusion. To develop and strengthen an awakened heart we must sincerely align our actions with the values of generosity, kindness, compassion, and honesty.

Samadhi (Awareness Training)
6. Right Effort
7. Right Mindfulness
8. Right Concentration

With an effort that neither strives nor lingers, we cultivate clarity and stability of awareness so that we can see deeply into life. This, in turn, helps facilitate the cessation of clinging.

A Gradual Training

Classically, spiritual training in Theravada Buddhism progresses gradually from the cultivation of generosity, to ethics, to awareness practices, to insight, and finally to liberation. This training model, while ostensibly linear, can also be seen as a description of elements of the spiritual path, which different people develop at different times. Particularly in the West, practitioners tend to skip some of the early stages, preferring instead to jump right into the middle of awareness practice. While there may be good reasons for this in the West, when we start with meditation we often bypass the cultivation of those personal qualities that establish its proper foundation. We can also overlook the fact that, ideally, the awakened heart finds its expression in service to others.

Generosity

Traditional Theravada training begins with the cultivation of generosity (*dana*). In its highest form, *dana* practice is motivated neither by moralistic ideas of right and wrong, nor by the anticipation of future reward. Instead, the aim is to strengthen our ability to be sensitive and appropriately generous in all situations.

As generosity develops, it manifests as an inner openness that supports the more challenging practice of mindfulness. Additionally, the conscious practice of generosity reveals our clinging and attachments and helps us to appreciate how the Four Noble Truths apply in our own lives. Through generosity we connect with others, weakening any tendency toward self-centeredness or self-obsession.

Ethics

From here, our training moves into the realm of ethics, sometimes described as the cultivation of contentment, since ethical transgressions often arise out of discontentment. For a layperson, ethical training means learning to live by the five precepts:

1. To refrain from killing any living being
2. To refrain from stealing or taking what is not given
3. To refrain from sexual misconduct; that is, from hurting others through our sexuality
4. To refrain from speaking what is not true
5. To refrain from using alcohol or drugs that cause us to be careless or heedless

These precepts should not be viewed as moralistic commandments, but rather as guidelines for cultivation. They are taught because they strengthen the qualities of restraint, contentment, honesty, clarity, and respect for life. They also create a healthy relatedness to other people and to other forms of life.

The Theravada tradition advocates the cultivation of four warm-hearted attitudes known as the *Brahmaviharas,* or divine abidings: lovingkindness, compassion, sympathetic joy, and equanimity. Lovingkindness is a selfless friendliness or love that desires the good and happiness of oneself and others. Compassion and sympathetic joy—complementary expressions of lovingkindness—involve sharing in, but in no way clinging to, the suffering and joys of others. Equanimity means to be at ease wherever we find ourselves. Theravada Buddhists use these attitudes as guides for living in relation to others.

Awareness Practice

Once a foundation of generosity and ethics has been established, one begins to cultivate the awareness practices. Theravada Buddhism has a large repertoire of these, including formal sitting and walking meditation and the development of awareness in daily activities. These awareness practices are divided into two categories: concentration and mindfulness.

Concentration emphasizes the development of a stable, one-pointed, fixed focus of mind on such objects as the breath, a mantra, a visual image, or a theme like lovingkindness. Strong concentration engenders helpful, though temporary, states of psychological wholeness and well-being. Lovingkindness (*Metta*) is a particularly useful theme for concentration because it functions as an antidote to all forms of aversion and self-criticism. In addition, it fosters an attitude of friendliness that can support other awareness practices.

Mindfulness or Insight meditation is the cultivation of an undistracted awareness of events unfolding in the present moment. While concentration practices channel the awareness into a controlled focus on a single object to the exclusion of all else, Mindfulness develops an in-clusive, choiceless awareness that notices whatever arises in our experience. It is an accepting awareness that clarifies our feelings, thoughts, motivations, attitudes, and reactions. Such awareness in turn helps us to develop compassion and equanimity, both of which support liberation.

Mindfulness is the most common form of Theravada meditation taught in America today. It is derived from teachings preserved in a scripture called *The Sutta on the Four Foundations of Mindfulness.* The four foundations—the body (physical sensations, the breath, and so on), feelings, mental states, and *dhammas* (the psychological processes and insights that relate to the cultivation of liberated awareness)—are the four areas of experience to which the attention is directed during meditation.

Mindfulness develops the ground of trust and acceptance that enables us to open to whatever our inner and outer life might bring. While this often includes a great deal of self-knowledge, the beauty of this practice is that each clear moment of mindfulness is also a moment of nonclinging and, as such, a taste of liberation.

Insight and Liberation

As Mindfulness becomes stronger, it yields insights into what the Buddha called the Three Characteristics of all experience, namely Impermanence, Unsatisfactoriness, and Selflessness.

All things are impermanent, including the way we experience the world. If our experience of ourselves and of the world is ever changing, then *self* and *world* are inherently unsatisfactory as sources of permanent identity or security. As we see that things in the changeable universe cannot provide us with lasting satisfaction, we also come to realize that our experience does not belong to some fixed, autonomous *self.*

Initially such insights may trigger fear, but as practice matures, we discover that we can function quite happily in the world without needing to cling to anything. Thus the basic insights arising out of Mindfulness help us to cultivate trust and a healthy equanimity in our everyday lives. As this trust grows, it weakens our need to cling. Eventually, the deepest roots of attachment—greed, hatred, and delusion—release themselves and the world of liberation opens up.

The fruit of this liberation is, in a sense, an affirmation of our ordinary world. This is the world of "things as they are," seen clearly, without our projections of hope and fear, desire and aversion, anger and ignorance. If this affirmation is strong enough, we realize directly that our moment-to-moment mindful presence is not a technique or exercise to get us somewhere, but is, in and of itself, the direct experience of the Deathless—the ever present, timeless world of liberation.

Service

While the gradual path of training may end with liberation, this is not the end of the spiritual journey. Liberation is the gate through which compassion, wisdom, and service to others flow without selfish clinging or identification. Before sending his first sixty enlightened disciples out into the world to teach the dharma, the Buddha said to them,

> My friends, I am free from all human and spiritual entanglements. And as you are likewise free of all human and spiritual entanglements, go forth into the world for the good of the many, for the happiness of the many, with compassion for the world, and for the benefit, the blessing, and the happiness of gods and humans. . . . Reveal the spiritual life, complete and pure in spirit and in form.

So the culmination of the spiritual journey is to be of service. Service is a form of generosity. Beginning and ending with generosity, the path has come full circle.

Faith

A key element at every stage of the journey is faith. In Theravada Buddhism, faith does not mean blind belief. Rather, it describes trust or confidence in oneself, in the teachings and practices of liberation, and in the community of teachers and students, both past and present. It is a faith that inspires us to verify for ourselves the experiential possibilities of the spiritual life.

As these possibilities become actualized, we discover increasing levels of trust in our personal capacity for openness and wisdom. This in turn gives rise to a growing appreciation for the people and teachings that support this inner trust. In Buddhism, these are represented by the Three Treasures: the Buddha, the Dharma (teachings), and the Sangha (community of practitioners).

One of the most common rituals for lay practitioners in Theravada Buddhism is Taking Refuge, consciously choosing to be supported and inspired by the Three Treasures. While Taking Refuge is performed as a matter of course at ceremonies and retreats, it represents a pivotal moment when for the first time one does so with the conscious intent of orienting one's life in accordance with one's deepest values and aspirations. Relating our practice to the Buddha, Dharma, and Sangha helps ensure that it is not limited only to intellectual concerns, selfish ambitions, or issues of personal therapy. Taking refuge helps solidify a broad foundation of trust and respect from which true mindfulness and insight can grow.

Theravada Buddhism in Daily Life

Theravada Buddhism distinguishes between the Path of Liberation and the Path of Worldly Well-Being. This corresponds loosely to the Western distinction between spiritual and secular concerns. However, in this tradition no absolute separation exists, and teachers vary in the degree of differentiation (or nondifferentiation) they see between the two. Even when a strong distinction is upheld, the spiritual and the secular are seen as mutually supportive.

The Path of Liberation is concerned with selflessness and *nibbana*, a state that in and of itself does not belong to the conventions, contents, or conditions of the world. The Path of Worldly Well-Being is concerned with how to engage with these conventions and conditions so as to create as much personal, familial, social, economic, and political health as possible.

Traditionally, *vipassana* meditation belongs to the Path of Liberation. This has meant that many Westerners who have devoted themselves to the practice both in Asia and in America have not learned much about the Theravada teachings on worldly well-being. However, to appreciate Theravada Buddhism in its full religious vitality, it is necessary to study both paths. This is particularly true for those who who are trying to integrate the practice with their daily lives.

MONEY

In a number of *suttas* popular in Southeast Asia, the Buddha speaks about how to live well in the world. The *Sigalaka Sutta* addresses the responsibilities of our social and familial roles—parent, child, spouse, teacher, student, friend, employer, employee, monastic, and layperson. One of the *sutta*'s more beautiful and challenging passages deals with earning a living without doing harm in the process:

> The wise who are trained and disciplined
> Shine out like beacon lights.
> They earn money just as a bee gathers honey
> Without harming the flower,
> And they let it grow as an anthill slowly gains in height.
> With wealth wisely gained
> They use it for the benefit of all.

POLITICS

Through the centuries, Theravada Buddhism has had much to say about politics. Many Southeast Asian kings have tried to live up to the ten virtues and duties for political leaders enumerated by the tradition: generosity, ethical conduct, self-sacrifice, honesty, gentleness, lovingkindness, nonanger, nonviolence, patience, and conformity to the *dhamma*. While those who strictly pursue the path of liberation have at times held themselves apart from worldly affairs, Theravada Buddhism as a full religious tradition has been very much engaged with political and social issues: with education, health, public works, and more recently with environmental protection.

To help build a healthy community, the tradition sponsors festivals, ceremonies, and rites of passage that mark major transitions in an individual's life—birth, marriage, death, and even a ceremony of elderhood at a person's sixtieth birthday.

Students and Teachers

Theravada Buddhism teaches that friendship is an invaluable support for the spiritual life, and spiritual friendships among practitioners, and between students and teachers, are encouraged. Indeed, a common title for a teacher is *Kalyana-mitta,* or good spiritual friend. Although teachers may give instruction, reveal delusions and attachments, open new understandings and perspectives, and provide encouragement and inspiration, their role is always limited, since one must walk the spiritual path for oneself. A teacher is pointedly not someone to whom students are to relinquish their own common sense or personal responsibility. Nor is it generally expected in this tradition that students will devote themselves exclusively to one teacher. It is quite common for practitioners to spend time with a variety of teachers, benefiting from their different spiritual strengths.

Retreats

The most popular Theravada practice in North America today is Mindfulness. It was introduced by young Americans who had studied in Southeast Asia and is one of the few Buddhist practices popularized by American as opposed to Asian teachers. Joseph Goldstein, Jack Kornfield, and Sharon Salzberg, to name three, streamlined the practice, freeing it from its traditional Buddhist context in order to make it more easily accessible to their Western students.

"We wanted," says Jack Kornfield "to offer the powerful practices of insight meditation, as many of our teachers did, as simply as possible without the complications of rituals, of robes, chanting, and the whole religious tradition."

Intensive *vipassana* meditation retreats lasting anywhere from one day to three months are conducted in strict silence. A typical day begins around 5:30 AM and ends around 9:30 PM. A simple schedule of sitting and walking meditation, a period of work practice, interviews with teachers, and daily "*dhamma* talks" encourages the cultivation of mindfulness throughout the day.

Alternating periods of intensive retreat with practice in the world has become a hallmark of the American *vipassana* movement. Though Western students are overwhelmingly laypeople, these retreats allow them to practice in a manner traditionally reserved for Theravada forest monks. Such intensive practice not only supports the cultivation of mindfulness, but leads inexorably to "the unshakable deliverance of the heart."

• • •

Gil Fronsdal is a longtime practitioner of Zen and vipassana. He has practiced in monasteries and meditation centers in the United States, Japan, Thailand, and Burma. He is currently a vipassana teacher at both Spirit Rock Center in Marin County, California, and at the Mid-Peninsula Insight Meditation Center in Palo Alto, California.

The Clear-Cut Retreat

G. RICHARD HILL

✸

IT SOUNDED LIKE HEAVEN TO ME. TWELVE DAYS OF silent meditation on a five-acre wooded paradise in southwest Washington. Cloud Mountain Retreat Center—the very name called to mind images of deer grazing in leafy sunlight, birds singing in the trees, and above all, the peace and quiet of the country. So imagine my shock and disappointment when on the morning of the second day I was rudely yanked from sleep by the sound of logging in the surrounding woods. It was loud. Really loud. "How long is *this* gonna last?" I wondered.

Later that morning, Steve Armstrong and Kamala Masters, our teachers, told us the bad news: The entire neighboring property was to be logged during the course of the retreat. The clear-cutting would take place from 6:00 AM to 3:00 PM each day. Three men were hard at work not more than thirty feet from the meditation hall. One was operating a tractor rigged with pincers that gripped the trees in a gargantuan bear hug, snapped them off at the base, lifted them up, and dropped them over with a seismic thud. The second, armed with a chain saw, was hacking off limbs while a third was hooking the stripped trunks to the back of a truck and dragging them down to the main road for loading. The snarl of the chain saw and the roar of the engines were so searingly loud that our skulls literally vibrated.

Here's an entry from my journal on that second day:

The logging disrupts (everything). It's loud. There is grief for the lost trees, the disrupted plants and ani-

mals. I don't think I'll ever feel quite the same way again. We brought our cushions from the meditation hall to the dining hall. It's quieter. I asked Steve how I could feel equanimity about the clear-cutting. He said equanimity is different from detachment. Equanimity is a state where you open up to the pain . . . (but) you remain calm and balanced. It's not passivity. You can still be active. But you act with wisdom, skillfully, without anger or vengeance. Anger is when there's pain and you can't handle it so you lash out so the pain will stop. When you act out of anger, you are hurting yourself. So the point is to open to the pain and learn that you can handle it with calmness and peace and acceptance.

But the next morning the logging started up again and by then I was mad as hell. A lawyer by profession, I spent the entire morning obsessing about how to obtain a court order to stop this desecration, at least until the retreat was over. In my mind I drafted a motion for a temporary restraining order, composed a memorandum of law setting forth the legal basis for the motion (I decided the logging was a legal nuisance), and outlined affidavits. I was all set to break silence, call my office in Seattle, and dictate documents to have the motion heard the next day.

But then I was struck by two very simple realizations: first, it was highly unlikely that in southwest Washington, where logging is the mainstay of the economy, an elected judge would enjoin a clear-cut so that a group of Buddhists could meditate in peace; and second, the logging was happening not because of the law of the state of Washington, but because of the law of cause and effect. The point was not to fix, delay, or change the situation, but rather to learn from my reactions to it, and maybe even to find that space of equanimity that Steve had spoken of the day before.

That afternoon I climbed up to MistHaven, a lovely meditation space at the top of the hill just next to the property line. There I watched the men as they went about their work. They were so efficient as they brought the trees down and dragged them away, leaving only the stubble of stumps. It was beautiful in an odd and eerie way. Strangely enough, a part of me envied them. I wanted to be with them. I wanted to master driving the truck that dragged the logs away. I wanted to learn how to use the chain saw to clear the limbs off the trees. I wanted to know how to operate the tractor that hugged and sliced the trees at their base. In the midst of the noise and the frenzy I felt a kinship with the loggers.

Steve and Kamala encouraged us to see our own role in what was going on next door. The buildings at Cloud Mountain were, after all, constructed of lumber made of logs. We used paper napkins and paper towels each day; we wrote in journals and read books. The loggers were not the "evil" ones, we yogis were not the "good" ones. We were interdependent with one another. If anything, the situation was challenging us to find ways we could ourselves be more responsible in caring for the earth.

As the days progressed, the logging activities began to stretch out, so that sometimes the noise would begin before 6:00 AM and then continue well past three o'clock in the afternoon. Steve and Kamala knew from their interviews with us, from our questions, and from our energy how strained we were. One afternoon when the noise was becoming almost unbearable, Kamala abruptly stood up and—woman with a mission—walked out of the hall.

As she related it to us later, she and the Cloud Mountain Retreat Center manager walked together through the maze of fallen trees to the site of the logging and spoke face to face with the neighboring property owner and the loggers. She explained that, just as they had a job to do, so did she. Weaving metta into the interaction, she told

them that there were thirty retreatants under her care and that the intensely loud sawing noises and the din of falling trees was having a deeply shattering effect on them. He in turn explained why he was logging, and why the job needed to be done right now. While he would not, he said, agree to end the logging, he would abide by a schedule so that we could plan our activities accordingly. For the rest of the retreat he pretty much stuck to his end of the bargain.

In addition to Steve and Kamala's skill in holding the retreat together, the most moving aspect of the twelve days for me was the spirit of my fellow yogis. Despite the far from ideal conditions, no one left before the end of the retreat. Each yogi gave profound support to everyone else, merely by the steadfastness of their practice, and by the small examples of courtesy and generosity that occurred each day—assisting with chores, voluntarily picking up dishes to wash them, being present in the face of each other's pain and sorrow, standing together occasionally in silence during walking periods to watch the logging.

The "Clear-Cut Retreat," as it came to be known, was the most difficult one I ever attended. In many ways it was also the most rewarding. Looking back on those twelve days, what is most striking to me now is not how unusual it all was, but how ordinary. Because of Steve and Kamala's skillful teaching, the intensity, grief, and pain of the experience became a lesson for us in aversion and how to live with it, in powerlessness and how to accept it. Although we were forced to practice in the dining hall instead of the meditation hall, wore ear plugs instead of blissing out on birdsong, and struggled with our anger instead of dealing with the chatter of our monkey minds, we were still doing the very simple vipassana practice of noting what is going on in the present moment, observing the arising and passing away of phenomena. Perhaps for me the greatest lesson was the simplest: that we can be mindful of anything, of everything, and that with mindfulness, no matter what the circumstances, insight will arise.

· · ·

Rich Hill is a land-use attorney in Seattle, Washington. He has practiced vipassana since 1992.

Hi-Tech Dhamma

MICHAEL NAGEL

✳

Were the Buddha alive today, would he spin the Wheel of Dharma on the information superhighway? Would he convene the global *sangha* in virtual reality, or interview distant disciples via satellite, or deliver discourses to us in the comfort of our living rooms over cable TV? We will never know how the Buddha might have harnessed modern technology to extend compassion and alleviate the suffering of sentient beings. Instead it is we who are privileged to serve the dharma's historic migration to the postindustrial West by fostering the integration of modern technology with the ancient path of liberation.

Recently in the backwoods of Washington State, I encountered just such an innovative synthesis at what I thought would be a "typical" six-day *vipassana* meditation retreat with dharma teacher Shinzen Young.

One week before it was to begin I got a call from the retreat registrar. Shinzen had asked that five people volunteer their private rooms for use by fellow retreatants. The rooms would be needed every morning and afternoon.

"What for?" I asked.

"I don't know exactly. It's something unique that Shinzen does. We need to set up the wiring ahead of time?"

"Wiring?"

Later, at the retreat center as I was settling into my room, I noticed the electrical cords that were running out from underneath the doors of the five rooms. They were taped together and fed through the window of a sixth room. What in the world was in there, I wondered. Computers? Biofeedback machines? I'd never seen anything like it at a retreat before.

At 7:00 PM we assembled in the meditation hall to meet each other, the retreat staff, and Shinzen Young. By way of introduction, Shinzen gave us a thumbnail sketch of his life.

He was born, he told us, in Los Angeles and raised in a Japanese-American neighborhood where he'd become not only bilingual but bicultural as well. After graduating from a Japanese-American high school he went on to receive a doctorate in Buddhist Studies from the University of Wisconsin. In 1970 he ordained as a *Shingon* (Japanese Vajrayana) monk and headed for Japan to study and practice for several years before returning to the States to teach. During his brief introduction, Shinzen's humility, wit, intelligence, and clarity of mind were immediately apparent.

The following morning he explained the mystery of the wires. He had, he said, devised a technique of individualized real-time meditation instruction called OnLine Support (OLS), in which the five rooms had been wired to a sixth to create a temporary multichannel telephone switching system. We were to bring our meditation cush-

Shinzen Young. (Photo by Giardini, courtesy of Northwest Vipassana Center.)

ions to one of the rooms where we would find a lightweight telephone headset with a pager button and a microphone positioned over the mouth.

"Just put the headset on and begin meditating," instructed Shinzen. Meanwhile, he would be in the sixth room where he would operate a telephone switchboard. Then, one by one, he would cycle through the five of us, approximately once every ten to fifteen minutes, providing us with individualized, "in-state" meditation instruction.

Shinzen suggested that we use our OLS sessions to get more detailed meditation instruction or to "tune up" our technique. We could also use it to experiment with new techniques, or to work on specific issues in our practice or in our lives in the world.

It is difficult to overemphasize the significance of real-time meditation instruction. Learning relies upon feedback. Buddhism has institutionalized the pedagogical feedback loop in the form of the student/teacher interview. However, the traditional model has some drawbacks. At some three-month courses, students may meet with the teacher only once a week. At shorter retreats, they might interview with the teacher only once every couple of days. Frequently, these long intervals between meetings can result in our forgetting many of the important things we had wanted to say! How often do we forget the details of the teacher's instruction by the time we get back to the cushion? With OLS, the feedback loop tightens significantly, ranging from fifteen minutes to instantaneously. You report your experience, you receive your instruction, and you apply it immediately—*all while in the state of meditation!*

By the middle of the first day, an old "friend" of my meditation practice had reappeared—shortness of breath. The phenomenon had been occurring in my daily meditation fairly regularly for the previous six months. Hoping to learn something at the retreat that would alleviate it, I signed up for an OLS session on the morning of the second day.

"Michael, are you there?" Wow! It's the voice of my meditation teacher—in my mind, while I am meditating!

"Yes, Shinzen," I whisper into the microphone poised over my lips.

"Good. Is everything working and are you comfortable?"

"Yes."

"Before we begin, Michael, would you tell me a little bit about your practice?"

"I've been doing *vipassana* meditation daily for more than ten years. Generally I practice for about forty-five minutes each morning. I go on retreats maybe once a year. I wouldn't describe myself as an advanced meditator."

"Is there anything particular that you want to work on this morning?"

"Yes. Shortness of breath. For the last year or so, I've been practicing *samatha* (concentrative meditation) as often as I practice *vipassana*. It's helped me to learn to balance my practice. But it seems that as my breath approaches the point where it becomes minimal or nonexistent, I often experience severe shortness of breath. It's a real obstacle."

"Are you experiencing it right now?"

"No."

"What I'd like you to do is this. Deepen your state and see if the shortness of breath occurs again. I'll get back to you in about ten minutes or so. Okay?"

"Okay." And off we both go to our respective tasks. Minutes pass. I rediscover my "buddy," shortness of breath.

Shinzen's voice reappears in my meditative stream of awareness. "Michael?"

"Yes, Shinzen."

"Okay, were you able to get in touch with your shortness of breath?"

"Yes."

"Describe for me its location in your body, its 'flavor,' and whether or not you feel it is moving."

"It's in my lower chest. It feels like tight bands of tension radiating out from the center. My breath is quite shallow. And there's a very subtle underlying panicky feeling." Because I am "in-state" and mindful, I'm able to report my experience precisely as it is happening.

"Is the sensation confined to one area or does it spread an influence, perhaps subtly, to other parts of your body?"

"I can feel its effects all over."

"Okay, try this. Focus away from the primary sensation in your sternum and pay attention to the more subtle, global impact. See if you can completely accept those milder sensations even though it may not be possible to completely accept the local, intense sensation."

Five minutes later Shinzen returns. "Were you able to do that?"

"Yes."

"Okay, now focus your attention again on the local, intense sensation. Is it exactly the same or has it changed?"

"It's softer and smoother."

"Okay, now try this. . . ."

In this way, Shinzen took me through a sequence of focusing strategies, each one modified on the basis of the feedback I had given him. By the end of the ninety-minute session the shortness of breath had broken up into a shower of pleasant energy. Since then it has ceased to be a problem in my practice.

Sometimes we worry that Buddhism's embrace of modern technology may distort the "purity" of the ancient dharma. I am reminded of a conversation I had with a friend, a meditation teacher in the Vietnamese tradition. We were speaking about the conditions under which the ancient *Vinaya* (the code of behavior for ordained Buddhists) might be "stretched" to meet the conditions of contemporary life. He reminded me that Buddhism is a living tradition. What matters most, he said, is our motivation and whether the change will help to alleviate the suffering of all sentient beings.

. . .

Michael Nagel has practiced vipassana *since 1982. He lives in Vancouver, Washington, where at midlife he has retired from a data-processing career to pursue a doctorate in the area of his lifelong passion, transpersonal psychology.*

The Natural Vividness of Childhood

MARGARET MANN

✹

EVERY YEAR IN MID-SEPTEMBER, ONE HUNDRED people from all over the world gather at Insight Meditation Society (IMS) in central Massachusetts for the annual three-month *vipassana* retreat. Located on eighty acres of beautiful forestland, the meditation center is housed in an impressive red brick structure with white colonial columns. The word *Metta* (lovingkindness) is inscribed over the entrance. Formerly a home for retired Catholic priests, the building contains a large meditation hall, areas for walking meditation, a dining hall and kitchen, staff areas, teacher interview rooms (popularly known as Guru Alley), sleeping rooms, offices, a yoga room, a library, and a bowling alley where, on a visit to the center, the Dalai Lama is said to have bowled.

Before noble silence begins, a few days are available to ease into the schedule, to get to know your fellow yogis (retreatants), and to make last-minute trips into town for something you're sure you can't do without. Then a bell is rung and the silence descends. We will not speak to each other again for the next three months.

In addition to silence, yogis are expected to keep the traditional five precepts of not killing, not lying, not stealing, refraining from sexual misconduct, and not using intoxicants. These precepts are the basis of our life together in this "intentional community." It is because we adhere to them that a safe and protected space exists in which to let go and open up. (It's worth mentioning here that there are no locks on any doors at IMS). On the opening night of retreat and every night thereafter, the precepts are offered in a brief chanting service. Other than that, there is not much ritual at IMS.

The retreat day begins early with a wake-up bell at 4:45 AM and the first formal sitting forty-five minutes later. The schedule consists of alternating forty-five minute periods of walking and sitting meditation throughout the day, with a few hour-long sittings sprinkled in.

Breakfast is at 6:30 AM, followed by an hour of work. Then the entire community gathers in the meditation hall for the 8:15 sitting. This sitting ends with a freewheeling fifteen-minute question-and-answer period during which the teachers field questions ranging from "What is the balancing factor for concentration?" to "What is the difference between English breakfast tea and Irish breakfast tea?" The rest of the morning is taken up with sitting and walking, and it is at this time that teacher interviews are conducted. Each yogi is assigned to two teachers for a total of three ten-minute interviews a week. During interviews students receive advice and support for their practice. Most yogis keep a notebook next to their sitting cushions to jot down things they want to report to their teachers.

The big event of the day is lunch. Given the lack of other sensory input, the noontime meal receives an inordinate amount of attention. And rightly so, since the food at IMS is delicious. All meals are vegetarian. Evening tea is usually something light; soup, crackers, nut butters,

Entrance to the Insight Meditation Society in Barre, Massachusetts. (Photo courtesy of the Insight Meditation Society.)

fruit, and tea. Evenings are taken up with more sitting and walking. Each night one of the teachers gives a Dhamma talk to inspire, humor, and instruct.

The last formal sitting of the day ends at 10:00 PM, at which time one may either retire or else continue sitting late into the night. After a few weeks of mindfulness practice, I find I can get by with no more than four hours of sleep per day. As my continuity of mindfulness grows, I just go to bed when my head starts to bob, and get up and begin practicing as soon as I awake.

For the most part, yogis are given the latitude to practice at their own pace and intensity, speed and style. At the beginning of retreat, most tend to follow the schedule and then later modify it to fit their own rhythms. (One

year I remember leaving the meditation hall at 1:00 AM and passing another yogi who was just rising to begin her day.) Some opt to sit every sitting in the hall, while others spend the entire retreat in solitude in their rooms.

One is not, however, "confined to barracks" during the course. Yogis are encouraged to go for walks in the surrounding woods. During the autumn months, a walk in the woods is like stepping into a cathedral. The backlit trees blaze with vivid reds, yellows, and oranges. Even the animals feel safe and protected in these forests. Birds will literally eat out of the palm of your hand. On one retreat I was in the woods feeding the chickadees when one landed right on my head! This lightened my heart on a particularly difficult day.

The teachings are what I like to call "old-fashioned Buddhism." *Vipassana* or Insight meditation is taught in the style of the late Burmese meditation master Mahasi Sayadaw and his successor U Pandita Sayadaw. The practice utilizes the technique of mentally noting all arising phenomena (thoughts, sounds, bodily sensations), cultivation of nonattachment, and emphasis on continuity of mindfulness throughout the day. The IMS teachers also stress the *brahma viharas* (the divine abodes or spiritual emotions). These are concentration practices designed to enhance the qualities of lovingkindness, compassion, sympathetic joy, and equanimity.

The extraordinary conditions that prevail at IMS are conducive to sustaining and deepening concentration and mindfulness. The growth of these mental factors causes one's mind and body to open in fascinating and freeing ways. This is what brings me back to IMS again and again.

Typically, what I notice at the beginning of a long retreat is the untying of physical knots. As my awareness grows, I get in touch with the habitually unconscious patterns of tension in my body arising from stress, emotional holding, and reactivity. These manifest for me as heat, tightness, pain, and heaviness. Bringing mindful attention to these knots again and again with acceptance causes them to unravel and clear. What results is an amazing depth of physical relaxation. Mindfulness practice has been for me a very deep form of body work. I have no doubt that this affects my health in positive ways.

As physical knots unravel, so do mental knots. Deeply held memories—many long-forgotten—float to the surface. Sometimes these memories have a theme such as "People-I-Never-Said-Goodbye-To," or "Times-When-Someone-Hurt-Me," or "Times-When-I-Was-Uncaring-Toward-Others." As I relive these painful experiences, I have an opportunity not to react to them by pushing them away, but to just attend to them with as much compassion as possible. Having had their say, the knots untie themselves, sometimes remarkably quickly. As I see it, my job is not to judge my experience in any way, but to accept whatever each moment brings to me with compassion and wisdom. As these mental holdings arise and pass, it is as if I am "lightening" my mind.

As practice deepens, there's a sense of release, of lightening up, of letting go. I'm able to live fully in the moment instead of experiencing things secondhand, lost in thoughts and stories. This direct contact with my experience returns me to the natural vividness of life I remember as a child. Colors, food, sounds, and emotions all take on a richness unique to life as a yogi. It's as if I open a window to seeing more clearly the true nature of experience.

As I react less out of greed or anger, I feel returned to the flow of life, the impersonal flow of thoughts, sensations, emotions, and intentions that make up my world. Life seems less solid and more fluid, and I begin to understand how aversion and grasping cause this flowing quality to contract and solidify.

Seeing these patterns liberates me by giving me the choice not to react unskillfully in ways that bring more suffering. On a recent retreat I had a cancer scare; I'd found a small lump in my breast. I thought it over and decided to stay at the retreat. I scheduled a biopsy for two weeks later. Then I went and saw my teacher. I told him how I was experiencing a lot of fear and agony waiting for the surgery. "But," I told him, "what if I spend these two weeks going crazy with fear and agitation, and then it turns out to be nothing? It would have all been a waste." His response was a revelation to me: "Even if it *is* something, it's a waste. The suffering is extra." I have more choice in my happiness than I realize.

After weeks in silent support of each other's practice, a sense of community emerges. The days pass quickly. By December, the retreat seems to have occurred in the space of a few weeks. I call this the "Post-Retreat Time Warp." I realize that this is how our lives are lived for the most part, gone before we are ready, and all too fast. In my heart, I recommit to living life more fully and with more depth.

No matter how many ups and downs I experience on retreat, I well up with gratitude at its conclusion. A long retreat is a rare and beautiful opportunity in this world. I am thankful for my contact with the Dhamma and the very fortunate circumstances that allow me to spend three months exploring and living life more fully. It is an experience like nothing else in the world. If you are considering it, I encourage you to try it.

· · ·

Margaret Mann works as a freelance technical writer, and she and her two cats make their home in the San Francisco Bay Area. She has been sitting with the Palo Alto Sangha since 1991.

A Lovingkindness Retreat

SHARON SALZBERG

✻

METTA IS A PALI WORD MEANING "loving-kindness" or "friendship." It is part of the living tradition of Buddhist meditation practices that cultivate spaciousness of mind and openness of heart. Classically, *metta* is taught along with three other meditation practices designed to develop compassion, sympathetic joy (the ability to rejoice in the happiness of others), and equanimity. Together these four are known as the *Brahma Viharas*. *Brahma* means "heavenly" or "best," *Vihara*, "dwelling" or "home." So the *Brahma Viharas* represent our heart's most heavenly dwelling, our best home. *Metta* is the foundation practice for the *Brahma Viharas*. Frequently, people will attend an extended *metta* retreat before undertaking the practice on a daily basis.

A *metta* retreat begins with the instruction of the Buddha to "sit comfortably." This direction, implying ease, gentleness, and kindness toward oneself, can be confounding. Many people equate spiritual growth with struggle and suffering. Yet it is not suffering per se that is transformative, but rather our ability to open to it with spaciousness and compassion. That opening itself is lovingkindness. From the continual purification of our motives for doing the practice to the skillful means we employ to persevere in the face of difficulty, to the patience needed to forgive ourselves and begin again after becoming distracted and forgetful, the flavor of lovingkindness permeates the *metta* retreat. Most simply, we

assume a comfortable sitting position so that we can more easily relax and let go of any sense of struggle.

Metta retreats rely on the principle of gladdening the mind . . . that is, practicing gently the reflections and actions that point us back to the radiance and purity of our own hearts. We start, for example, by taking delight in our own goodness—actually calling to mind things we have done out of good-heartedness; perhaps a time when we were generous, or helped someone, or told the truth when it would have been easy to tell a lie. We rejoice in those memories not to develop conceit, but to celebrate the potential for goodness that we all share.

If we can't think of even one good thing we've done, or one thing we like about ourselves, we contemplate the universal wish to be happy. Our innate wish for happiness isn't something to be ashamed or afraid of. In a sense it is one of the best things about us. If we can combine this wish with wisdom instead of ignorance, it will guide us unerringly toward true happiness, toward the realization of our potential as human beings. So we gladden the mind by consciously thinking about these things, and in so doing we engender confidence in our ability to love.

Metta is a concentration practice, which means that we choose an object and continually shepherd the attention back to it whenever the mind wanders. In *metta* the chosen object is a series of phrases, at first directed toward oneself, and subsequently toward other categories of beings. This process of repeatedly returning to the chosen object is what we mean by "concentration."

Just for a moment, consider the amount of energy you expend in daydreaming about the future, in obsessive planning, in ruminating about the past, in comparing yourself to others, in judging yourself, in worrying about what might happen next. That is a huge amount of energy.

Now imagine all of that energy gathered in, restored to you, available. The return of that energy, normally dissipated and lost, is why a concentration practice like *metta* is so healing and empowering. We experience wholeness, the unification of our being, as we gather this energy back in. What is striking is that this is our own energy—we don't have to somehow find it or fabricate it. We already possess it.

When we practice *metta*, we relax, sit comfortably, and allow the phrases to emerge gently from our hearts, rather than pounding them insistently in our heads. So we hold each phrase in our attention, gently, with connection and awareness, as if holding a fragile, precious object; grasp it too tightly and you break it, become lazy or negligent and it falls from your hands and shatters. In just that way we hold, or cherish, the *metta* phrases.

Metta phrases are an expression of the very powerful force of intention in the mind. Every time we silently repeat a *metta* phrase we harness the power of that intention. This is in fact the most important aspect of the practice. The actual emotional tone we experience may vary considerably—sometimes we feel exhilarated and grateful, at other times dubious and uncomfortable. Sometimes we find the practice dry and mechanical, at other times smooth and enjoyable. It's perfectly natural for the feeling tone to change constantly. The important thing is to gently return to the phrases over and over again.

Once I was practicing *metta* and felt extraordinary tension, so much so that at one point I had to stop and investigate the cause. I saw that I was not only trying to do *metta*, but was also continually checking up on myself to see if it was working. "Is this *metta*?" I would ask myself. "Is it genuine? Is it enough? Was there more yester-

day? Is it as much as other people have?" Finally, I realized I had to let go of all that self-doubt, trust in the practice and connect with the phrases.

Developing lovingkindness toward ourselves is our first priority. We repeat phrases that reflect what we wish most deeply for ourselves in an enduring way. The classical formula goes something like this: "May I live in safety. May I have mental happiness (peace, joy). May I have physical happiness (health, freedom from pain). May I live with ease (may the elements of daily life—work, family—go easily, not be a struggle)." One can use these traditional phrases or create others that are more personally meaningful.

People often find it difficult to believe that they deserve to be happy. So we begin with reflections on the good within us and on the rightfulness of the universal wish to be happy. We gently repeat the phrases in our own behalf and in so doing purify our conditioned relationship to ourselves.

The Buddha said, "If you truly loved yourself you would never harm another." Often as we do this practice we find ourselves going through a kind of moral inventory. We remember things we did that were harmful, or times when we spoke in an unkind way, or remained silent when we should have spoken up. When we hurt others we also hurt ourselves, and we inevitably feel the consequences of our misdeeds as we look within. It's important that we learn to see all of this with lovingkindness and forgiveness for ourselves. This is the process of purification.

The next step is to call to mind a benefactor. A benefactor is someone who has inspired us or helped us or been generous toward us in some way. We visualize them or say their name to bring their presence forth, and then send lovingkindness their way by offering them the phrases.

After some time we include a good friend in the field of our *metta* and move on from there to a neutral person, someone for whom we don't feel a strong liking or disliking. Some find that there are few, if any, neutral people in their lives; as soon as they meet someone they form a judgment about them. Others find there are *too many* neutral people in their lives; outside a certain favored circle, people might as well be pieces of furniture for all they care. Regardless of our feelings, when we choose a neutral person and offer them *metta* we are offering it to them simply on the basis that they exist, and therefore that they too must fundamentally wish to be happy.

We then send our good wishes toward someone with whom we have had conflict or difficulty. Students are usually advised to begin with a person who is only mildly difficult, and from there slowly working up to one who might have hurt them more grievously. It is common to feel resentment and anger toward difficult people, and it's important not to judge ourselves for that. Rather, we recognize that our anger burns within our *own* hearts and causes *us* to suffer. So it is out of the greatest respect and compassion for ourselves that we practice letting go of anger.

It's important to recognize that by offering *metta* to a difficult person we are not condoning their actions or pretending that the fact that they have hurt us doesn't matter. Instead we are seeing deeply into our own hearts

and discovering there a capacity for lovingkindness that is not dependent on circumstances or personalities.

We finish the retreat by connecting to the boundlessness of life and offering *metta* to all beings everywhere. We discover that no one stands alone; whether known to us or unknown to us, near or far, female or male, wise or ignorant, cruel or kind, all are part of the infinite fabric of life. We recognize our interconnectedness, our inseparability, and this is the fulfillment of our capacity to care for all living things. Now we see that a loving heart is our natural abode, and that through our practice we can always find our way home.

. . .

Sharon Salzberg is a cofounder of Insight Meditation Society (IMS) and the Barre Center for Buddhist Studies, both located in Barre, Massachusetts. She has studied and practiced Buddhist meditation since 1971 and has been teaching worldwide since 1974. She is a guiding teacher at IMS and the author of A Heart as Wide as the World: Living With Mindfulness, Wisdom, and Compassion *and* Lovingkindness: The Revolutionary Art of Happiness.

War and Catharsis: Letting Go of Vietnam

LLOYD BURTON

❋

I'M OFTEN ASKED WHY I MEDITATE. WHAT GOOD does it do? What purpose does it serve? There are probably as many answers to these questions as there are students of the Dhamma. I can only recount what my experience has been. This, I think, will explain why I practice *vipassana* meditation.

The early days of my first retreat were a veritable symphony of hindrances: aversion to the discomfort of prolonged sitting, attraction to certain other students (complete with lurid Tantric fantasies), sloth, torpor, restlessness, excruciating boredom, and real doubts about the wisdom of enduring what for me seemed like self-imposed spiritual boot camp.

But what gradually began to occur was a deep psychic relaxation—a relaxation that permitted the mind to observe pleasant thoughts, feelings, and sensations without clinging to them; to observe painful, emotionally charged thoughts about my life without reacting against or retreating from them; and to accept the experience of other hindrances as the normal responses of conditioned consciousness.

As the mind relinquished its censorlike control over the flow of experience and the relaxation became deeper, ever more painfully charged visions began to emerge from the recesses of memory—mostly related to my experiences in Vietnam. I had served as a field medical corpsman with Marine Corps ground forces in the early days of the war, in the mountainous provinces on the border between what were then North and South Vietnam. Our casualty rates were high, as were those of the villagers we treated when circumstances permitted.

By the time I attended my first *vipassana* retreat, I'd been back from Vietnam for eight years. At least twice a week during those entire eight years, I had the same recurring nightmare common to many combat veterans: dreaming that I was back there, facing the same dangers, witnessing the same incalculable suffering; waking suddenly, alert, sweating, scared.

At the retreat the nightmares did not occur during sleep. They filled my mind's eye during the day—at sittings, during walking meditation, at meals. Horrific wartime flashbacks were superimposed over a quiet redwood grove at the retreat center; sleeping students in the dormitory became body parts strewn about a makeshift morgue on the DMZ.

What I gradually came to see was that as I relived these memories as a thirty-year-old spiritual seeker, I was also enduring for the first time the full emotional impact of experiences that, as a twenty-year-old medic, I was simply unprepared to withstand. Through private interviews with the teachers at the retreat and through my own continued inner exploration, I began to realize that the mind was gradually yielding up memories so terrifying, so life-denying, and so spiritually eroding that I had ceased to be consciously aware that I was still carrying them around. I was, in short, undergoing a profound catharsis by openly facing what I had most feared and had therefore most strongly suppressed.

At the retreat, I was also plagued by a more current fear: that having released the inner demons of war, I would be unable to control them—that they would now rule my days as they had my nights. But what I experienced instead was just the opposite. The visions of slain friends and dismembered children gradually gave way to other half-remembered scenes from that time and place: the entrancing, intense beauty of a jungle forest that was a thousand different shades of green; a fragrant breeze blowing over beaches so white and dazzling, they seemed carpeted by diamonds.

What also arose at the retreat for the first time was a deep sense of compassion for my past and present selves: compassion for the idealistic young would-be physician forced to witness the most unspeakable obscenities of which humankind is capable, and for the haunted vet-eran who could not let go of memories he was unable to acknowledge carrying.

Since that first retreat, the compassion has stayed with me. Through practice and continued inner relaxation it has grown to sometimes encompass those around me as well—when I'm not too self-conscious to let it do so. And while the memories have also stayed with me, the nightmares have not. The last of the sweating screamers happened in silence, fully awake, high atop a meditation cushion somewhere in northern California.

· · ·

Lloyd Burton has been a student of Jack Kornfield and Joseph Goldstein since 1975. He has a Ph.D. in Law and Public Policy and teaches at the University of Colorado. In 1966 and 1967, he served as a field medical corpsman with the Third Marine Corps Division in the Republic of Vietnam.

Discovering the Source of Suffering

PHIL ALTERMAN

✴

I APPROACHED MY FIRST COURSE IN *VIPASSANA* AS a virtual neophyte, with a strong cynical streak about anything having to do with Eastern religions, mysticism, and gurus. I went because a girlfriend invited me to come along. I figured that once I got there I could talk her out of it and we'd take off for a nice little vacation. Fortunately, things didn't go as planned.

The course description sounded brutal. Ten days? Ten hours of sitting meditation per day? Men and women separated? Complete silence? Were they kidding?! Not really intending to remain for the entire course anyway, I filled out the registration card and sent it in. Besides, it wouldn't cost me anything. The courses were run entirely on the donations of former students who wished to make the *vipassana* experience available to new students.

A few weeks later I arrived at the meditation site clutching my newly purchased *zafu* (meditation pillow). As I signed the registration form, I wondered what I was getting myself into. My friend seemed determined to see it through and, as if to seal my fate, just before the course began one of the staff encouraged each of us to take a vow of determination to remain for the entire ten-day course. In this way we could give it a fair trial. If we weren't willing to do so, it was suggested that we not even begin. Well, I had come this far, so I swore an oath to myself to try.

At about sunset a bell rang, summoning us to the meditation hall. Approximately three hundred students were gathered outside. Students who had taken courses previously were asked to enter first. Entering with the new students a few minutes later, I found a place in the back of the hall and sat down.

The hall was large, about the size of a tennis court. Men and women sat on opposite sides of the room with a long, narrow corridor between the two groups. In the front on a raised platform sat the teacher, Mr. S. N. Goenka, cross-legged on a small cushion and wearing pants and a simple white shirt. He began chanting in a low, melodious voice in a language I did not understand. A few minutes later he addressed the group in English.

We had gathered, he said, to practice the ancient art of *vipassana* meditation as taught by Gautama the Buddha more than twenty-five hundred years ago. He briefly reviewed the rules and asked the students to take refuge in the Buddha, the *Dhamma* (the Path of Enlightenment as taught by the Buddha), and the *Sangha* (the community of meditators). After doing so in both Pali and English, Goenka-ji began giving meditation instruction.

He told us to sit comfortably. No particular posture, such as the lotus position, was required (good thing, since I could barely cross my legs). The most important thing was to keep a straight back and neck as this would be helpful in the long run. In order to avoid distractions, we were to meditate with our eyes closed.

Mr. Goenka instructed us to focus our entire attention on the small area around the nose from the upper lip to the inside of the nostrils. We were to concentrate on the flow of breath as it passed over this small part of the body. The normal, natural breath—without any effort to control it—was to be the focus.

I quickly became aware of its flow as it passed through my nostrils: cold as it entered, warm as it left. While my mind raced with a million thoughts, I tried to remain focused on this "feeling" of the breath. I soon realized that it wasn't going to be easy. My mind constantly wandered off into a quagmire of thought: "What am I doing here? . . . I wish I had eaten more for dinner . . . my aching back . . . did I lock my car? . . . I can't wait for breakfast!" *Anything* except the breath!

In a comforting, reassuring manner, the teacher instructed us to bring our attention gently back to the breath whenever we discovered that the mind had wandered. I wasn't too encouraged on this first evening, although I did notice that the stabbing pain in my back wasn't such a problem if I stayed concentrated on the breath. Maybe I could get through this ordeal after all.

The sound of a bell fluttered through the woods the next morning. With sleep-encrusted eyes, I looked at my watch. "4:00 AM? Whew!" I thought. "These guys are serious." By the time I got to the meditation hall, most of the students were already in their places, immersed in the task of observing the breath as Goenka-ji had instructed. I sat down and did the same.

I struggled with my "monkey mind" for the next four days. Sometimes it would wander away from the breath for hours. Then I would "come to" and realize how little control I actually had over my own mind. I noticed, though, that gradually it was becoming quieter and I was able to focus on the breath for longer and longer periods of time. These stretches of focused attention were peaceful and relaxing, like an oasis in a desert of confusion.

Each evening the teacher delivered a discourse in which he slowly revealed the theory of *vipassana*, unraveling just enough of the puzzle so that we could understand the meditation instructions he had given thus far. He's a very dynamic and sometimes humorous speaker and I found myself looking forward to his discourses. My mind was filled with questions. Though he was speaking to the entire group, it seemed he somehow knew what I was thinking and would address the questions that were foremost in my mind.

Day four, we were told, was to be an important one. For it was on this day that we would be taught the "Art of Vipassana." Having struggled with my "monkey mind" and aching back for three days, I was anxious for day four to arrive. "What could this mysterious *vipassana* be?" I wondered. "What was this field of *panna*, or wisdom, that Goenka-ji kept referring to?"

That afternoon Mr. Goenka began the session by chanting in his low and powerful voice. Then he told us that in order to practice *vipassana* it was necessary to keep the body as still as possible. Any movement would disturb the mind's concentration. He directed us to switch our attention from the breath to a small area at the top of the head and to observe any physical sensations that might be occurring there. We were simply to be aware—in a choiceless fashion—of any sensation that appeared in that part of the body.

I was surprised by the instruction. This was the field of *panna*? What did the top of my head have to do with wisdom? Ignoring my thoughts, I focused on the top of my head as instructed. Sure enough, I felt a slight tingling. Slowly, he guided us through each little part of the body from head to toe, directing us to observe the myriad sensations without clinging to the pleasant ones or avoiding what was painful. The secret lay in learning how *not* to react, in keeping the mind balanced, regardless of the type of sensation. "Let nature take its course," he reminded us. "Be aware of *anicca* (impermanence, or in this case the constant flux of physical sensations in the body)."

By the time we had completed our survey of the entire body (this took well over an hour) I was completely flabbergasted. Though there were many parts of my body in which I was unable to feel any sensations, and though I constantly reacted to the painful ones, it felt as if a light had just gone on inside my mind. My body felt unified in some sort of electric field. I could not believe that I had lived thirty years and had been unaware of what was really going on inside this body. Even more powerful was the realization that my mind was in a constant state of turmoil, reacting to these stimuli. I left the hall stunned by the world that had just opened up to me.

We spent the next six days refining the technique of scanning the body, observing this new continent of sensations. We were taught to vary the method depending upon the quality of the mind and the nature of the sensations springing up at any particular time. Layer upon layer of sensation—some pleasurable, some very painful—rose to the surface, only to disappear after close observation.

Despite the teacher's instructions to the contrary, I often found myself searching for pleasurable sensations and trying to push away the painful ones. I had a particularly nasty burning pain that felt like a knife wound in the center of my back. It lingered for days and the more I tried to fight it, the worse it seemed to get. As I learned to relax and simply observe it, I began to notice that this gross pain was in reality made up of many different types of subtler sensations that, when observed without reaction, would change and sometimes disappear altogether. The more focused and nonreactive my mind became, the less mental suffering there seemed to be. It became clear that my reaction to the pain, and not the pain itself, was the source of suffering.

Each day brought new experiences. There were times when I could barely stay awake. At other times the concentration was so intense that nothing seemed to exist but the sensation and the process of observation. These moments brought feelings of incredible harmony and peace. I also experienced times of extreme doubt, wondering what in the world this was all about, wondering what these sensations had to do with happiness and peace of mind. Under Goenka-ji's sometimes gentle, sometimes stern encouragement, I continued to work, and began to feel lighter, as if the meditation was lifting a burden from my body and mind. I soon came to realize that all of these states of mind were merely *anicca*—constant change. They came and went as quickly as the physical sensations.

By the end of the course I felt as if I had passed through one of the most difficult ordeals of my life, and I was glad that it was over. But I also felt that I had been given an incredible gift, a tool for self-realization that would be with me for the rest of my life.

• • •

Phil Alterman took his first course with S. N. Goenka in California in 1982. In 1984 he traveled to India for further study. He is an immigration lawyer in Denver, Colorado.

Metta Forest Monastery

THANISSARO BHIKKHU

✳

Buddhism's survival in the various cultures to which it has spread over the past twenty-five hundred years has been a story of the interaction of two impulses: the urge to modify the Buddha's teachings to fit with one's way of life, and the inclination to trim down one's way of life to fit with the Buddha's teachings. The first impulse is especially strong in the various forms of Designer Buddhism now being developed in America—so strong that some people have begun to feel the need for places that give expression to the second impulse. Metta Forest Monastery, in its own small way, is an attempt to fill that need.

Located in an avocado orchard on a hill surrounded by the mountains and chaparral of northern San Diego County, Metta follows the traditions of the Thai Forest lineage founded by Phra Ajahn Sao Kantasilo and Phra Ajahn Munn Bhuridatto. This lineage is known for its strict adherence to the *Vinaya* (the monastic discipline), its ascetic lifestyle, and its strong emphasis on full-time meditation practice. Although the lineage has developed a large following in Thailand, its direct, uncompromising ethos sets it apart from many of the typical values of Thai society. This fact makes it an ideal tradition to transplant to America, both because that ethos focuses directly on the major issues of life, death, and the liberation of the mind, with a minimum of cultural trappings, and also because it serves as a reminder that we should not be in too great a hurry to Americanize Buddhism, inasmuch

as the true practice of Buddhism stands apart from the dominant values of lay society no matter where it is found.

Although Metta is primarily a monastery, part of the hill is set aside for lay visitors who want to come on individual retreats and follow our daily schedule. That schedule begins well before dawn, as the monks rise early and meditate individually. A morning chanting service begins at 5:30 AM, followed by a one-hour group meditation session, with instructions or a short reading. After the session, lay visitors help prepare the meal while the monks sweep the monastery grounds and prepare for the alms round at 8:30 AM. Because there is no village of Buddhists in the nearby area, we have developed a small "village" at the monastery itself: the guest house and the area for lay meditators. The monks go to the guest house for their alms and return to the meditation hall at the top of the hill to eat their meal, while the lay visitors do their morning chants. After the monks have had their meal, the lay visitors have theirs, and then there is free time for all to meditate until late afternoon. Sweeping and other chores start in the early evening. Shortly after sundown, the entire community meets for evening chants and a one-hour group meditation session, again with instructions or a reading. After the session there is time for questions, and everyone then returns to his or her private place in the orchard to meditate individually.

We have introduced changes from the parent tradition

only where absolutely necessary. Buildings are a little more substantial than they would be in Thailand in order to meet the county building code and to keep out the chill, damp weather in winter. Mealtime has been moved from early to midmorning, to accommodate donors who may drive from as far away as Los Angeles. The alms round has been shortened in light of the fact that the only potential almsgivers within walking distance live in the lay area of the monastery. Otherwise, the monks adhere strictly to the rules of the *Vinaya*; the lay visitors follow the traditional eight precepts (no killing, no taking what is not offered, no sexual misconduct, no harmful speech, no drugs or alcohol, no solid food after the noon meal, no jewelry or personal adornment, no sleeping on a high bed); and the entire community follows the customary modes of expressing generosity, gratitude, and respect, as inherited from the parent tradition. As in a typical Thai forest monastery, huts and tent platforms—complete with sitting platforms and walking meditation paths—are scattered throughout the orchard, both in the lay and in the monastic sections. For both the monks and the laypeople, most of the day is spent in solitude among the trees.

The support community for Metta is primarily Thai and Laotian, although the number of Euro-American members is slowly growing. The monks are evenly divided between those born in America and those born in Asia. The common interest in meditation and solitude has helped to minimize potential cross-cultural conflicts. In this way, Metta offers an alternative to another common pattern in American Buddhism—the sharp division between Asian and Euro-Buddhist groups—by showing that a return to the basic traditions of the *Dhamma* and *Vinaya* in a natural surrounding provides a common meeting ground where both groups can feel at home.

Theravada monasticism is among the smallest and least appreciated aspects of Buddhism now coming to America, largely because it is so widely misunderstood. Celibate monastic life offers a pattern of freedoms and limitations—quite different from those of lay life—that the Buddha established expressly to help with the training of the mind. There is a common misperception that the rules of the *Vinaya* simply follow the prejudices of

Indians in the Buddha's time and are irrelevant in our own more enlightened times. However, a careful reading of the rules shows that many of them differ markedly from the regulations of other monastic groups in ancient India, and that they find their ultimate justification in the principles of the *Dhamma* itself.

Perhaps the most radical difference between lay and monastic life is that, on entering the monastic *Sangha*, one leaves the lay economy of money and trade and enters an economy of gifts. Monks are not allowed to buy, sell, or even barter goods with laypeople. Lay supporters provide gifts of material requisites for the monks, while the monks provide their supporters with the gift of the teaching. Because these gifts are voluntary, they create a warm and cheerful atmosphere in which to practice. At the same time, this economy teaches many important lessons for the heart. Monastics have no control over the requisites of their life, a fact that forces them to learn many valuable lessons in patience, endurance, and the acceptance of the workings of karma. When they reflect that everything they use is the fruit of other people's generosity, it reminds them that the quality of their practice is not simply their own concern, but that of the entire community of supporters. This spurs them on to even greater efforts in the practice. Having benefited from the generosity of others, they find it natural to share the fruits of their practice with others free of charge when the opportunity or the need arises.

A monastery is designed to benefit not only those who choose to live there as monastics, but also the entire community. The *Vinaya* forces the monks into regular, daily contact with laypeople, and this contact benefits the laity in two major ways. First, simply associating with people who have found happiness by abandoning the material and sensual freedoms of lay life helps a person to keep issues of wealth, status, job, relationships, and so on in a healthy perspective. Second, regular contact with people who have devoted their entire lives to becoming specialists in the practice of the *Dhamma* enables one to learn at any time, free of charge—through words, examples, and a general process of osmosis—lessons that are useful in one's own practice.

In many ways, Metta Forest Monastery is an experiment. In the midst of many movements to create a New Buddhism in America—a country where "new" means "improved"—we are mindful of the fact that the Buddha did not create Buddhism. He found the *Dhamma* and simply taught what he had found. New Buddhism tends to aspire to a harmonious life in a harmonious world, whereas the original teachings claim to come from, and to show the way to, a dimension beyond birth and death in even the best possible world. As a community of lay-people and monastics working together, we at Metta are willing to take those teachings at their word and to give them a serious try.

. . .

Thanissaro Bhikkhu (Geoffrey DeGraff) ordained as a Theravada monk in Thailand in 1976. He trained for ten years under Ajahn Fuang Jotiko of the Thai Forest Tradition and is now abbot of Metta Forest Monastery in Valley Center, California.

A Place for Peace and Happiness

LIBBY REID

✸

I REMEMBER WALKING UP THE PATH TO THE MEDI-tation hall at Bhavana Society on the evening of my first retreat. The forest was incredibly quiet; the only sounds were the crunch of my footsteps on the gravel path and the din from my pounding heart. I didn't know what to expect or how I would possibly react to the rigors of a ten-day retreat.

The Bhavana Society is located on thirty-two acres of secluded forest near High View, West Virginia. It was founded by Bhante Henepola Gunaratana, a native of Sri Lanka who was ordained as a Buddhist monk at the age of twelve, more than fifty years ago. "Bhante G.," as he is affectionately known, is an internationally recognized author and meditation teacher. His book, *Mindfulness in Plain English*, has been published in four languages.

Similar to forest monasteries in Sri Lanka and elsewhere in Southeast Asia, the Bhavana Society provides a home for Buddhist monks and nuns. It is also a place where laypeople can come for retreats and instruction. Just two hours from Washington, D.C., the center is both *in* the world and quite beyond it, an ever changing juxtaposition of East and West, ancient and modern, spiritual and secular—a shaven-headed monk wearing traditional robes and Nike running shoes, the Buddha image on the wall overlooking the computer and the fax machine, the begging bowl on the kitchen counter next to the microwave.

I first turned to the Buddha's teachings in the late 1980s. It seemed, back then, that my life was just one big crisis after another. I had a business that was failing and teenagers with problems beyond my reckoning at home. I was a recovering alcoholic struggling with sobriety, addicted to food, tobacco, work . . . anything that would keep me from facing the emptiness and angst that plagued me.

It was around this time that I began reading the teachings of the Buddha. The more I read, the more appealing I found them, especially the unassailable logic of the Four Noble Truths: "All life is suffering. Suffering comes from desire. There is a way that leads from suffering. The Way is the Eightfold Path." I started practicing meditation on my own but soon realized I needed more guidance. I read about a meditation center a half-day's drive from where I lived, and decided to go there. I knew I had to take this next step.

On the first evening of the retreat, an ancient gong signaled the start of meditation. The deep, low vibrations passed through my heart and drifted out across the forest. Bhante G. began the session with a moving *metta* recitation . . . radiating lovingkindness to all beings. After the sitting he gave a Dhamma talk in which he asked, eyes twinkling, "What is the difference between the man who has everything and the man who wants nothing?"

Often when Bhante G. speaks of the Buddha, his face lights up in a radiant smile. As he tells stories from the Tathagata's life he sometimes lapses into Pali, delighting

Bhante Gunara-tana. (Photo courtesy of the Bhavana Society.)

in the translation and word play. With humor, insight, and great love, he shares the Buddha's teachings.

During the first days of retreat, I struggled with the sheer physical pain of sitting meditation. I had no tolerance whatsoever for discomfort. As an addict of various substances, I was used to running away from even the slightest hint of pain. Here I was on a retreat looking for peace and happiness and all I'd found so far was misery.

I went to see Bhante G. for a private interview and all I could talk about was the pain. He made it clear that if you could stay with the experience, you would discover that "pain" is just a sensation, one of many that arise and fall all the time. What causes us to suffer is our aversive reaction to painful sensations. Once we realize this, the pain disappears. I had not yet had this experience, but I believed Bhante G. and trusted him.

One night during the Dhamma talk he said, "We have a body for one reason and one reason only: to gain insight." I began to see that this limited and very specific physical discomfort provided an opportunity to learn something. If I could understand and deal with physical pain, I might also be able to cope with emotional pain.

I was able to sit comfortably for about forty-five minutes before some excruciating discomfort would set in. Of course I could have easily changed positions and often

did. But as Bhante G. explained, "If you change position, you'll just feel the discomfort again in a different place." How true.

I played all kinds of games with my pain. I watched it carefully, describing every nuance of it to myself. I breathed with it, visualized it, pleaded with it. I prayed for the bell to ring, counting the seconds and then counting those seconds into minutes. Bhante G. kept telling me the same thing over and over again: "Watch your breath. If the pain becomes overwhelming, quit watching the breath and watch the pain. Don't bargain with it. Just feel it." One night in a Dhamma talk, he told us that in all his years of teaching, no one had ever been hurt by meditation. I was comforted by his reassurances.

Eventually I was able to differentiate between pain and fear. The feeling of fear, I discovered, tended to complicate and compound the pain. Without fear, the pain seemed less formidable. I began to see the retreat as a kind of experimental laboratory, a safe haven in which one could explore the maneuverings of one's own mind. Now I found myself looking at the experience of pain with curiosity rather than fear.

One night I was meditating very peacefully. For some time now I had been coping well with the pain. I was working with the breath, fairly concentrated, when all of a sudden I was struck with an excruciating leg cramp. Instead of grabbing my leg in anguish, I decided to let everything go and just watch what happened. For a moment there was intense pain . . . and then almost as suddenly as it came up, it faded away. It was true. I had tested the teachings for myself and in this very specific instance, my faith had been vindicated.

Over the years, I have applied this skill of observation to more than mere physical discomfort. I remember one retreat in particular where I began noticing how often jealousy arose in my mind. It had always been there, of course, but in the retreat setting these mental processes tend to become more obvious.

Jealousy is not a pleasant feeling. For me, it was like a knife wound, a sharp piercing pain. I decided to note how often it came up and was amazed and rather horrified to find how pervasive it was. I coveted the usual things: someone else's body or looks, someone's personality or career, someone's family or good fortune. In the meditation hall, I found myself envying the way someone sat or did walking meditation or asked lucid questions. I could be jealous of another's gentle and loving nature, wishing that I possessed these qualities too. As I became more aware of it, there seemed to be no end to this craving. I could see or experience something about another person and want it somehow, or else feel less adequate because I wasn't that way.

I resolved simply to watch these feelings as they arose . . . just as I had learned to watch physical discomfort when it was present. I didn't try to change it or stop it. I just observed it. Over the years the experience has changed. I no longer feel the pang of jealousy, the sharp emotional pain I used to feel. When I notice jealousy at all, it is more often with amusement than with anguish. Meditation has helped free me from that kind of "psychic irritant." As Bhante G. says, "When you are greedy, are you happy? When you are angry, are you happy? When you are full of craving, are you happy?"

Over the years, the practice of meditation has changed the way I experience the world—something for which I will always be grateful beyond words. I laugh more. I see more joy. Before I got sober, whenever unpleasant feelings arose, I would numb them—at least for the moment—with alcohol. Now, using the observation skills honed in meditation, I can examine those unpleasant feelings and see more clearly how they simply arise and disappear like other sensations. I am less apt to act in some way to escape them unwisely.

My husband has noticed these changes in me. Some-times, when I act unmindfully and start to take things too seriously, when I lose my perspective and my sense of humor, he may ask wryly if it's not time for me to go back to "Buddhist camp." He's right, of course, so back I head to West Virginia for a refresher course in mindfulness.

I have returned to the Bhavana Society each year since that first retreat in 1990. Every time I go back it seems I have to start from the beginning. The first few days my mind is all over the map. I squirm, watch the clock, fight against the slightest discomfort. Then I remember to look at each sensation with curiosity rather than aversion, and it is at this point that the whole experience opens up for me. Sitting becomes a tremendous joy, a fascinating exploration of the processes of the body and mind, not an ordeal to struggle through. My faith is renewed.

For me, the Bhavana Society has provided a refuge, a haven, a safe and beautiful place to explore the Dhamma. At the end of my first retreat, I remember wondering if I would ever be able to describe where I had been. I felt that if I had gone to the most distant corner of the world, I could not have been farther away. Perhaps someday you will have the good fortune to experience this special place and see for yourself.

· · ·

An artist and part-time art teacher, Libby Reid lives with her husband, Ford, in Norfolk, Virginia. Thanks to the first edition of Buddhist America, *she found her way to the Bhavana Society in the spring of 1990 and has been seeking refuge there ever since.*

The Theravada Centers of North America

✳

ALASKA

Wat Dhamma Bhavana

Wat Dhamma Bhavana serves primarily the Thai Buddhist community in Anchorage, though all activities are open to the public. We have Vipassana meditation every evening and services each morning in our *Dhamma* hall. Every Sunday afternoon there is a *Dhamma* talk.

ADDRESS: 738 West 72nd Avenue, Anchorage, AK 99518
PHONE: (907) 344-9994
FAX: (907) 522-2969
LINEAGE: Thai Theravada
SPIRITUAL HEAD: Ven. Amporn Champala, Resident Director
AFFILIATION: Autonomous
ESTABLISHED: 1990
FACILITIES: Thai temple
MEDITATION PROGRAM: *Dhamma* talks on Sunday afternoons; meditation every evening; ceremonies every morning. Call for times.

ARIZONA

Tucson Community Meditation Center

Our group has three meditation periods on Saturday and Sunday mornings. The last sit is a guided *metta* meditation. On Sundays we play a tape by a Vipassana teacher, have a discussion of the practice, and a social hour or a *sangha* meeting. We offer occasional classes oriented to beginners or experienced students. These activities are held in our *zendo*, a converted garage in Mary McWhorter's charming backyard. Our retreats feature various Vipassana teachers, including Shinzen Young and Mary Orr.

ADDRESS: 2033 East Second Street, Tucson, AZ 85719
PHONE: (520) 327-1695
CONTACT: Mary McWhorter
AFFILIATION: Autonomous
ESTABLISHED: 1980
FACILITIES: Meditation hall open to all.
RETREATS OFFERED: About four several-day residential retreats with various teachers offered per year.

Wat Promkunaram (Buddhist Temple of Arizona)

A traditional Thai temple offering devotional services, meditation, and chanting. All are invited to offer food and supplies to the monks, listen to the preaching, and practice meditation.

ADDRESS: 17212 West Maryland, Waddell, AZ 85355
PHONE: (602) 935-2276
FAX: (602) 935-0599
LINEAGE: Thai Theravadan
SPIRITUAL HEAD: Phra Mahawinai Punyayano
CONTACT: Phra Ratana Ratano
AFFILIATION: Autonomous
ESTABLISHED: 1982
FACILITIES: Temple and monastery.
RETREATS OFFERED: Yes

CALIFORNIA

Abhayagiri Buddhist Monastery

Abhayagiri Buddhist Monastery consists of a small house and a *Dhamma* hall in a converted garage on 250 acres of forested hills near the source of the Russian River. Monks and novices live in tents or small huts. As a branch of Amaravati Buddhist Monastery (England) and Wat Pah Nanachat (Thailand), we conform to the traditional standards of Theravada forest monastic life. Simple guest accommodations are available. Those interested in visiting should write well in advance. The monks hold monthly teachings, which are open to the public, in San Francisco.

ADDRESS: 16201 Tomki Road, Redwood Valley, CA 95470
PHONE: (707) 485-1630
FAX: (707) 485-7948

LINEAGE: Thai Forest Tradition

SPIRITUAL HEAD: Ajahn Sumedho (in England)

CONTACT: Ajahn Amaro

AFFILIATION: Amaravati Monastery, United Kingdom

ESTABLISHED: 1996

FACILITIES: Rustic accommodation for monastics and guests.

RETREATS OFFERED: One or two ten-day retreats (off-site) and several five- or six-day retreats are held annually.

PUBLICATIONS: Numerous publications by Ajahn Chah and Ajahn Sumedho (free distribution).

Bell Springs Hermitage

Bell Springs Hermitage is located on a remote 175-acre mountaintop in Mendocino County. It has great views and abundant wildlife. When you're paying hotel rates on retreats, watching your breath can too often lead to watching your wallet, so we offer basic accommodation at very affordable rates for individual and small group retreats. Monks and experienced practitioners of all Buddhist traditions are welcome. Facilities include decks, tents, caravans, yurts, and a cookhouse. Food is not included and retreatants are asked to help with chores. Limited work exchanges are available. Open May to October.

ADDRESS: 4 Cielo Lane, #4D, Novato, CA 94949

PHONE: (415) 883-6111

FAX: (415) 883-6660

LINEAGE: Theravada

CONTACT: Daniel Barnes

AFFILIATION: Autonomous

ESTABLISHED: 1989

RETREATS OFFERED: Available to teachers and small groups.

Berkeley Thursday Night Vipassana Group

The Berkeley Thursday Night Vipassana Group has been meeting since 1980 under the guidance of James Baraz, a co-founder of Spirit Rock Meditation Center. Forty-five-minute sittings are followed by a *Dhamma* talk, discussion, and loving-kindness meditation. James also offers a six-week beginning class in Berkeley two or three times a year. In addition, he leads Spirit Rock-sponsored retreats in the Bay Area and throughout the United States.

ADDRESS: James Baraz, c/o Spirit Rock Meditation Center, PO Box 909, Woodacre, CA 94973

PHONE: (415) 488-0164

LINEAGE: Thai: Ajahn Chah, Burmese: Mahasi Sayadaw

SPIRITUAL HEAD: James Baraz, Resident Teacher

AFFILIATION: Spirit Rock Meditation Center and Insight Meditation Society

ESTABLISHED: 1980

FACILITIES: Meetings at Berkeley Buddhist Monastery, 2304 Mckinley, Berkeley, California.

MEDITATION PROGRAM: Weekly meditation, *Dhamma* talk, discussion.

RETREATS OFFERED: Through Spirit Rock Meditation Center.

California Buddhist Vihara

California Buddhist Vihara is home to the American Buddhist Seminary (ABS), established to provide the academic, religious, and vocational training needed by monastic and secular Buddhist teachers in an English-speaking society. The emphasis is on Theravada monastic training, although programs are being added to accommodate individuals of all Buddhist traditions. Monastics participate in a full-time residential program, receiving religious training at ABS while attending supplemental academic courses at other institutions. Programs: Master and Doctor of Ministry Degrees, Diploma in Buddhist Studies, English Practicum.

ADDRESS: 2717 Haste Street, Berkeley, CA 94704

PHONE: (510) 845-4843

FAX: (510) 644-9739

SPIRITUAL HEAD: Ven. Kokkawita Wipulasara, Resident Teacher

ESTABLISHED: 1985

PUBLICATIONS: Free books on Buddhism are available.

California Vipassana Center/ Dhamma Mahavana

For additional information, please see listing for Vipassana Meditation Center in Shelburne Falls, Massachusetts.

ADDRESS: PO Box 1167, North Fork, CA 93643-1167

PHONE: (209) 877-4386

FAX: (209) 877-4387

E-MAIL: mahavana@aol.com

LINEAGE: Vipassana meditation in the tradition of Burmese teacher Sayagyi U Ba Khin, as taught by S. N. Goenka

SPIRITUAL HEAD: S. N. Goenka of the Vipassana International Academy, near Bombay, India

CONTACT: No resident teachers; numerous assistant teachers conduct courses on a guest basis.

AFFILIATION: Over thirty permanent centers and many associations in thirty-five countries. There is no *parent* group. Timetable, retreat format, and meditation instructions are the same at all courses worldwide.

ESTABLISHED: 1983

FACILITIES: One-hundred-nine-acre retreat facility at 3,000 feet in foothills of Sierra Mountains (capacity: 125).

RETREATS OFFERED: Ten-day courses twice monthly. Periodic introductory

Vassa at Bell Springs Hermitage

ON THE EVENING OF THE FULL MOON IN NOVEMber 1995, four monks and a handful of laypeople celebrated the conclusion of *Vassa*—the traditional three-month rains retreat—at Bell Springs Hermitage in Mendocino County, California. This *Vassa* was unique in that it marked the first time that Western monks from the Thai Forest tradition in the lineage of Ajahn Chah had ever spent a rains retreat in the United States.

Both for advance preparation and for their ongoing material support, monks depended solely on the generosity of the *Sanghapala* (the lay community). In addition to lay attendants who lived with the monks throughout the retreat, some forty additional lay supporters visited the hermitage regularly, bringing needed supplies and offering meals.

Many spoke of the beauty of the setting, the grandeur of the night sky, and the strong effect of being in such close contact with nature. One was startled by the realization that her small pet was potential "bear food."

Several said their understanding was expanded through giving without asking for anything in return; or by having to practice despite not feeling well; or through the experience of moving gradually from "ideas" about the practice to the direct experience of it. Others spoke of how hard the preparations had been. Many who were exhausted from the burden of setting up the retreat discovered renewal of heart while their visit was in progress and were encouraged by its success. For all, a sense of community and "dynamic interdependence" developed out of meeting the challenges posed by this difficult form of practice.

Ajahn Amaro

For more information, contact: Bell Springs Hermitage, 4 Cielo Lane #4D, Novato, CA 94949; (415) 883-6111.

Monks on alms round, high above the clouds at Bell Springs Hermitage in Mendocino in California. (Photo courtesy of Bell Springs Hermitage.)

CALIFORNIA (*cont.*)

three-day and children's courses. Periodic advanced ten- and twenty-day courses and eight-day courses focusing on the *Satipatthana Sutta*.

Davis Unitarian Buddhist Meditation Group

We originally formed as a meditation group for Unitarians with an interest in Buddhism, but our practice has been shaped by a cadre of Sri Lankan friends who continue as active core members of our group. We meet weekly for meditation and dharma discussion. Once a month we plan a half-day "Morning of Mindfulness." Many of our members also have roots in Zen and Tibetan practice, and we welcome both new and long-standing practitioners.

ADDRESS: 27074 Patwin Road, Davis, CA 95616

PHONE: (916) 662-1669

E-MAIL: rjwarg@mother.com

LINEAGE: Sri Lankan Theravada

SPIRITUAL HEAD: Dick Warg, Resident Director

AFFILIATION: Unitarian Universalist Church of Davis

ESTABLISHED: 1994

FACILITIES: Meditation sanctuary.

MEDITATION PROGRAM: Weekly meditation and dharma discussion.

RETREATS OFFERED: Monthly "Morning of Mindfulness."

Dhammachakka Meditation Center

Dhammachakka Meditation Center was established to help Ven. U Silananda share his learning and insight with students in the West. A student of the late Burmese master Mahasi Sayadaw, he teaches Vipassana meditation in that tradition. A well-known scholar of *Abhidhamma* studies, Ven. U Silananda also offers retreats and courses in Buddhist

studies. We have an extensive tape library as well.

ADDRESS: Box 206, 2124 Kittredge Street, Berkeley, CA 94704

PHONE: (408) 567-0616

LINEAGE: Burmese/Vipassana

SPIRITUAL HEAD: Ven. U Silananda

CONTACT: Sarah Marks

AFFILIATION: Autonomous

ESTABLISHED: 1981

RETREATS OFFERED: Weekend and seven- to fourteen-day retreats.

PUBLICATIONS: Some booklets and large cassette library.

Dhamma Dena Desert Vipassana Center

Dhamma Dena is a high-desert sanctuary encircled by mountains and illuminated by constant changes of color. It is a silent, meditative space, permitting insight and

Ruth Denison, Founder and Resident Teacher at Dhamma Dena Desert Vipassana Center in Joshua Tree, California. (Photo by Katherine Tate, courtesy of Dhamma Dena Vipassana Center.)

discovery of communion with all life. Since we live in close relationship with our desert environment, water conservation is practiced. Accommodations are simple. Vegetarian meals are served. Solitary and formal group retreats in Vipassana meditation are available under the guidance of Ruth Denison. During retreats we observe silence and the basic training precepts, refraining from: harming living beings, taking what is not given, unskillful speech, sexual misconduct, and intoxicants and drugs.

ADDRESS: HC-1, Box 250, Joshua Tree, CA 92252

PHONE: (619) 362-4815

LINEAGE: Sayagyi U Ba Khin (Burmese)

SPIRITUAL HEAD: Ruth Denison, Resident Director

AFFILIATION: Autonomous

ESTABLISHED: 1977

FACILITIES: Desert retreat facility.

RETREATS OFFERED: Solitary as well as weekend retreats; nine-day, two- and three-week Vipassana courses.

Dhammakaya International Society of California

Daily meditation practice; weekend retreat every Friday to Sunday; three-day meditation course on the fourth weekend.

ADDRESS: 5950 Heliotrope Circle, Maywood, CA 90270

PHONE: (213) 771-7435

FAX: (213) 771-7437

E-MAIL: vichak@aol.com

LINEAGE: Thai Theravada

SPIRITUAL HEAD: Phra Sudhamayanathera. Phra Vichak Suddhivaro, Resident Teacher

CONTACT: Phra Bhavanaviriyakhun, Resident Director

AFFILIATION: Sister of Dhammakaya Foundation (Thailand)

PUBLICATIONS: *The Light of Peace*, newsletter.

Inquiring Mind

*I*NQUIRING *MIND* IS A JOURNAL DEDICATED TO the creative transmission of Buddha dharma to the West. Published biannually, the journal is distributed worldwide to an estimated readership of fifty thousand.

The journal serves primarily the Theravada Buddhist community of Vipassana (Insight) meditators, but is of interest to Buddhists of all traditions as well as the general public. *Inquiring Mind* has become well known for its excellent interviews and articles featuring Buddhist teachers, philosophers, psychologists, artists, and poets. Regular contributors include Jack Kornfield, Sharon Salzberg, Joseph Goldstein, Thich Nhat Hanh, Joanna Macy, Jon Kabat-Zinn, Gary Snyder, Robert Thurman, Ram Dass, and many others. Each edition includes an extensive international listing of Vipassana retreat schedules and sitting groups. The journal, which is distributed without charge, is funded almost entirely through reader donations.

Barbara Gates and Wes Nisker, editors
Alan Novidor, publisher

For more information, contact: *Inquiring Mind*, PO Box 9999, North Berkeley Station, CA 94709.

CALIFORNIA (*cont.*)

Dharma Vijaya Buddhist Vihara

Urban monastery setting. We offer practice instruction and distribute free books and magazines. Open membership.
ADDRESS: 1847 Crenshaw Boulevard, Los Angeles, CA 90019
PHONE: (213) 737-5084
FAX: (213) 737-7915
LINEAGE: Sri Lankan
SPIRITUAL HEAD: Walpola Piyananda, Resident Teacher
CONTACT: Same
AFFILIATION: Sangha Council of Southern California
ESTABLISHED: 1980
FACILITIES: Two large houses, meditation hall.
MEDITATION PROGRAM: Children's Sunday Dhamma School; instruction in meditation, Pali, and *Tipitaka*.
RETREATS OFFERED: One-day meditation retreats.
PUBLICATIONS: *Old Wisdom in the New World* by Paul Numrich.

Dharmapala Institute for Buddhist Meditation and Research, Incorporated

No description available.
ADDRESS: 110 West Latimer Avenue, Campbell, CA 95008
PHONE: (408) 378-3236
E-MAIL: Dee.Seneviratne@scmh1.nsc.com
LINEAGE: Sri Lankan Theravada
SPIRITUAL HEAD: Ven. Amarabuddhi Thero
ESTABLISHED: 1991

Dolores Street Dharma

Generally about thirty-five people come together each week for sitting meditation, inquiry, discussion, or discourse. We are a "drop-in" group that changes frequently, although over twenty people have been coming weekly for many years. The teacher is Howie Cohn, who has been leading classes and retreats since

Howie Cohn, resident teacher at Dolores Street Dharma in San Francisco, California. (Photo © 1996 by Carol Pratt.)

The Kalyana Mitta Network

THE KALYANA MITTA (SPIRITUAL FRIEND) NET-work was created to serve dharma students interested in having ongoing support for their practice outside of the retreat setting. These "dharma support groups" usually consist of five to twelve members. The small group format provides an intimate setting for the exploration of dharma topics, permitting each member to participate fully and enabling *sangha* bonds to grow strong. Groups vary greatly in how often they meet, but commitment to attend the meetings is a significant factor in the group's success.

We find that when two people who enjoy talking about the dharma are co-coordinators, their enthusiasm becomes contagious to the rest of the group. So a key guideline for Kalyana Mitta groups is that they be run by pairs of facilitators. Group leaders meet under the guidance of James Baraz, Spirit Rock cofounder and teacher.

Each meeting starts with silent meditation followed by a personal "check-in" by each member. Check-in is fol-lowed by group discussion. This might include sharing reflections on an article or book everyone has read or on some issue that the members have been consciously looking at in their daily lives since the previous meeting. Finally, a short sitting, chanting, or Lovingkindness meditation brings a sense of closure to the gathering.

What happens between meetings is as vital as what takes place in them. That is why it's important for members to be working with some dharma issue that has come out of the group discussions. Whatever the group is focusing on comes alive through a commitment to explore patterns in our daily lives. Having some "accountability" to the group helps make the investigation a more conscious part of one's day.

James Baraz

For more information, contact: Kalyana Mitta Network, c/o Spirit Rock Center, PO Box 909, Woodacre, CA 94973.

1985 and has practiced extensively with teachers in many traditions, including Theravada, Zen, Dzogchen, and Advaita Vedanta. The atmosphere is informal and discussion is encouraged.
ADDRESS: 675 Dolores Street, Suite A, San Francisco, CA 94110
PHONE: (415) 821-6378
LINEAGE: Ajahn Chah, Ajahn Buddha-dasa, Mahasi Sayadaw
SPIRITUAL HEAD: Howard Cohn
AFFILIATION: Spirit Rock Center, Woodacre, California
ESTABLISHED: 1985
FACILITIES: Room for forty-five, office for private meetings.
MEDITATION PROGRAM: Ongoing weekly sitting group; revolving five-week introductory series; counseling interviews.
RETREATS OFFERED: Full schedule through Spirit Rock Meditation Center.
PUBLICATIONS: Associated with *Spirit Rock Newsletter* and *Inquiring Mind.*

International Meditation Center

No description available.
ADDRESS: 1331 33rd Avenue, San Francisco, CA 94122
PHONE: (415) 731-1941
LINEAGE: Burmese Theravada
SPIRITUAL HEADS: Sayama and Saya U Chit Tin

Los Angeles Buddhist Vihara

Nonsectarian.
ADDRESS: 1147 North Beechwood Drive, Los Angeles, CA 90038
PHONE: (213) 464-9698
LINEAGE: Sri Lankan Buddhist
SPIRITUAL HEAD: Rev. Ahangama Dham-marama Thero
AFFILIATION: Autonomous
ESTABLISHED: 1978
FACILITIES: Meditation hall, library.
MEDITATION PROGRAM: Insight Meditation; *Dhamma* School; events for youth; lectures; meetings.
PUBLICATIONS: *Sarana*

CALIFORNIA *(cont.)*

Metropolitan Vipassana

Adapting (experimentally) verbal Vipassana to the frenetic Western pace.

ADDRESS: 14713 La Mesa Drive, La Mirada, CA 90638
PHONE: (714) 521-3046
FAX: Same
E-MAIL: robertTHC@aol.com
LINEAGE: Burmese Theravada
SPIRITUAL HEAD: R. H. Hover
CONTACT: Same
AFFILIATION: Autonomous; affiliated with U Ba Khin (deceased).
ESTABLISHED: Mid-1980s
FACILITIES: Sparse
MEDITATION PROGRAM: Verbal Vipassana.
RETREATS OFFERED: None at present.

Metta Forest Monastery

We offer the opportunity for men to ordain and train as *bhikkhus* in a secluded natural setting—an avocado orchard surrounded by the hills and chaparral of northern San Diego County. We also welcome lay visitors for solitary retreats. There is no charge for room or board, as all our activities are funded by donations. However, visitors are asked to observe the precepts and are expected to participate fully in the daily schedule. For the most part, though, the day is open for meditation under the trees in the orchard. Visitors should write in advance.

ADDRESS: PO Box 1409, Valley Center, CA 92082
PHONE: (619) 988-3474
LINEAGE: Thai Forest
SPIRITUAL HEAD: Ajahn Suwat Suvaco
CONTACT: Thanissaro Bhikkhu
AFFILIATION: Autonomous
ESTABLISHED: 1990
FACILITIES: Rural monastery with facilities for lay guests.
RETREATS OFFERED: Opportunity for individual retreats any time of the year.

Metta Meditation Center

Jim Hopper teaches Vipassana meditation as a systematic development of awareness of the mind-body process and as an opening of the heart to *metta* (loving-kindness). Beginning classes and one-day retreats are offered in Pasadena and Riverside. Weekend and longer retreats are offered at Dhamma Dena in Joshua Tree, California. Jim Hopper teaches with the authority and support of Ruth Denison.

ADDRESS: 401 South Fischer Street, #5, Glendale, CA 91205
PHONE: (818) 543-0669
LINEAGE: American Vipassana
SPIRITUAL HEAD: Jim Hopper
CONTACT: Same
AFFILIATION: Autonomous
ESTABLISHED: 1992
FACILITIES: Sitting space until quarters are found.
RETREATS OFFERED: One-day retreats at Pasadena and Riverside Unitarian Universalist Church. Weekend retreats at Dhamma Dena and a ten-day retreat at Thanksgiving.

Mid-Peninsula Insight Meditation Center (MIMC)

MIMC is a community meditation center offering evening sessions of meditation and dharma talks. Introductory classes are periodically given in mindfulness and loving-kindness practice. One- and two-day retreats are offered throughout the year. Participation is informal and teachings are offered on a daily basis.

ADDRESS: 16060 Skyline Boulevard, Woodside, CA 94062
PHONE: (415) 599-3456
SPIRITUAL HEAD: Gil Fronsdal
AFFILIATION: Spirit Rock Center
ESTABLISHED: 1986
FACILITIES: 957 Colorado, Palo Alto, California
RETREATS OFFERED: One-day and weekend silent retreats.

A view of the hills surrounding Metta Forest Monastery in Valley Center, California. (Photo courtesy of Metta Forest Monastery.)

Mountain Stream Meditation Center

Mountain Stream Meditation Center is evolving out of the interest and participation of sitting groups and individuals in the Sierra Nevada foothill communities and surrounds. Our vision is in process and includes Insight Meditation instruction and support for practice, development of practice through intensive retreats, integration of practice into daily living and community, availability of teachings from resident and visiting dharma teachers, and a natural forest setting for inner and outer exploration.

ADDRESS: 13029 Eagle Pine Place, Nevada City, CA 95959

PHONE: (916) 265-0582

LINEAGE: Mahasi Sayadaw, Ajahn Chah, and others

CONTACT: John M. Travis

AFFILIATION: Autonomous. John is also a teacher at the Spirit Rock Center.

ESTABLISHED: 1995

FACILITIES: At present we rent facilities and use a private residence for small retreats. We are looking for property on which to build a small rustic center in a forest setting in the Nevada City area.

MEDITATION PROGRAM: Sitting groups meet in the following areas: Auburn, Grass Valley/Nevada City, Reno/Carson City, and Chico. Six-week introductory classes are taught in the spring and fall of each year in the foothill communities and in Sacramento. These classes are suitable for beginners or as refreshers for experienced sitters.

RETREATS OFFERED: All-day and two- to ten-day retreats. Retreats are typically traditional Vipassana, silent, with alternating sitting and walking meditation, vegetarian meals, meditation instruction, dharma talks, and teacher interviews.

Nama Rupa Foundation

We are a very low-key organization oriented towards facilitating Dhamma teachings and interconnections. We "midwifed" the Sanghapala Foundation until its separate incorporation in 1995 for the support of a Thai forest tradition monastery in the Ajahn Chah/Ajahn Sumedho lineage. We facilitated the historic Jewish-Tibetan Buddhist dialogues described in the book *Jew in the Lotus*, which became the basis for a major film on the subject. We support Dr. Alex Berzin of Dharamsala in his worldwide teachings. Join the fun! There's much to be done!

ADDRESS: 10 Arbor Street, San Francisco, CA 94131

PHONE: (415) 334-4921

FAX: (415) 334-2740

E-MAIL: drmarc@aol.com

LINEAGE: Theravada

SPIRITUAL HEAD: Inspired by Ajahn Chah.

CONTACT: Marc Lieberman, M.D.

AFFILIATION: Autonomous

ESTABLISHED: 1987

FACILITIES: Meditation hall in private home.

MEDITATION PROGRAM: Weekly evening sittings.

RETREATS OFFERED: Associated with Sanghapala Foundation in Amaravati (England), affiliated Theravadan monastic lineage.

Saddhamma Foundation

Saddhamma Foundation was formed by close students of U Pandita Sayadaw to organize meditation retreats under his guidance and to raise funds for *dhamma* projects such as the new eighty-acre forest meditation center outside Rangoon, Burma. We hold a weekly sitting group where detailed *Satipatthana* meditation instructions are given. A *dhamma* talk follows each sitting. The instructor has been a close student of U Pandita Sayadaw for over fifteen years and has done extended retreats with him both in Burma and the United States. *Dhamma* students considering practice in Burma are welcome to call for practical advice and orientation.

ADDRESS: 5459 Shafter Avenue, Oakland, CA 94618

PHONE: (510) 420-1039

E-MAIL: kmorris@pop.slip.net

LINEAGE: Burmese Theravada

SPIRITUAL HEAD: Ven. U Pandita Sayadaw

CONTACTS: Barbara Janus, Kenneth Morris, Stella Valdiviez

AFFILIATION: Panditarama (Burma), Tathagata Meditation Center (San Jose, California)

FACILITIES: No permanent ones in the United States.

MEDITATION PROGRAM: Weekly sittings.

RETREATS OFFERED: Weekend retreats.

San Diego Meditation Community

The San Diego Meditation Community began in 1985 with four members and has grown to its present size of forty members. We meet for meditation followed by a member-initiated dharma talk, a video, an audiotape, or an invited speaker. Breakfast provided by members follows. Meetings are held in private homes and on alternate weeks at a community center in San Diego. All events are free.

ADDRESS: 141 Beechtree Drive, Encinitas, San Diego, CA 92024

PHONE: (619) 436-2368

AFFILIATION: Autonomous

ESTABLISHED: 1985

FACILITIES: Private homes and community center.

MEDITATION PROGRAM: Weekly

CALIFORNIA (*cont.*)

RETREATS OFFERED: Those offered through newsletters. Others organized by members.

San Diego Vipassana Meditation Society

Mark Berger has been practicing Vipassana (Mahasi Sayadaw tradition) since 1974 and has been teaching since 1985. He blends the power of his *shaktipot* with the foundation of awareness to assist students to quickly deepen their meditation. Teaching is given on an individual basis through weekly interviews and guidance. Small classes are held for beginners. Group meditations on weekday evenings. Call for times. Talks focus on the practical application of the Buddha's teachings in our daily lives.

ADDRESS: 1335 Santa Barbara Street, San Diego, CA 92107
PHONE: (619) 225-0817
LINEAGE: Mahasi Sayadaw (Burmese)
SPIRITUAL HEAD: Mark Berger
CONTACT: Same
AFFILIATION: Insight Meditation Society (Barre, Massachusetts) and Spirit Rock Meditation Center
ESTABLISHED: 1985
FACILITIES: Urban meditation house.
RETREATS OFFERED: One-day retreats by announcement.

San Francisco Dhamma

We have a weekly group that meets to meditate, hear *dhamma* talks, and discuss various aspects of traditional teachings and practice.

ADDRESS: c/o Eugene Cash, 1865 Union Street, San Francisco, CA 94123
PHONE: (415) 979-4879
LINEAGE: Theravada, Ajahn Chah, and Mahasi Sayadaw

SPIRITUAL HEAD: Eugene Cash
CONTACT: Same
AFFILIATION: Spirit Rock Meditation Center
ESTABLISHED: 1990
FACILITIES: Small sitting room.
MEDITATION PROGRAM: Weekly sitting group, periodic one-day sits.
RETREATS OFFERED: Irregularly

Sanghapala—East Bay Sitting Group

The Sanghapala East Bay Sitting Group meets weekly for chanting (in Pali and English), sitting meditation, live or recorded dhamma talks by monks in the forest monastery tradition of Ajahn Chah, and tea and conversation. The first week of each month we meet in San Francisco, the other weeks in Berkeley.

ADDRESS: Box 4951, Berkeley, CA 94704-4951
PHONE: (510) 620-0936
FAX: (510) 234-9431
E-MAIL: ebsit@dharmanet.org
LINEAGE: Thai forest tradition.
SPIRITUAL HEAD: Ajahn Chah, Ajahn Sumedho, Ajahn Amaro
CONTACT: Barry Kapke, Director
AFFILIATION: Abhayagiri Forest Monastery
ESTABLISHED: 1996
MEDITATION PROGRAM: Weekly sittings, chanting, dhamma talks.
PUBLICATIONS: Associated with *Fearless Mountain Newsletter*.

Skillful Meditation Project

We publish a free newsletter that contains articles by Southern California Buddhist meditation teachers, which are intended to help meditators cultivate clarity, wisdom, and the skillful means needed to find their own path. Our primary endeavor is to add to the depth and scope of Vipassana meditation practice so that it may always be vital and fresh, and to include the fullest range of human meditative experience. We teach a form of insight meditation that involves the awareness of thoughts and underlying moods as a preparatory process for an individual exploration of the dhamma.

ADDRESS: PO Box 42035, Los Angeles, CA 90042
PHONE: (213) 223-2470
FAX: (213) 222-7990
E-MAIL: skill@deltanet.com
LINEAGE: Theravada
CONTACT: Jason Siff
AFFILIATION: Autonomous
ESTABLISHED: 1995
FACILITIES: Mountain retreat house and urban meeting places.
RETREATS OFFERED: Half-day, weekend, and ten-day retreats.
PUBLICATIONS: *Skillful Means*, free newsletter.

Spirit Rock Meditation Center

Meditation retreat center in the hills of Marin County. Core teachings are Theravada Vipassana meditation with a Mahayana flavor. A collective of teachers presents different styles and emphases within the framework of mindfulness practice. Some focus on traditional teachings of liberation through intensive practice; others, on integrating practice with daily life and involvement in the world. There is a year-round program of classes, daylong sittings, and residential retreats. An active family program provides practice opportunities for parents and children. Spirit Rock teachers also lead weekly sitting groups and daylong retreats throughout the Greater Bay Area, Santa Cruz, and Nevada City.

ADDRESS: PO Box 909, 5000 Sir Francis Drake Boulevard, Woodacre, CA 94973
PHONE: (415) 488-0164

The *"Spirit Rock"* of Spirit Rock Meditation Center in Woodacre, California. (Photo by Lifesigns/Meyer.)

ADDRESS: 3494 21st Street, San Francisco, CA 94110

PHONE: (415) 282-3124

LINEAGE: Burmese Forest Tradition

SPIRITUAL HEAD: The Very Ven. Bhadanda Taungpulu Kaba-Aye Sayadaw Phaya

CONTACT: Rina Sircar, Resident Instructor

AFFILIATION: Autonomous

ESTABLISHED: 1985

FACILITIES: Center with shrine (meditation) room. No residential facilities.

MEDITATION PROGRAM: Daylong sitting once a month. Discussions by monks each week.

RETREATS OFFERED: Retreats are held at the Taungpulu Kaba-Aye Monastery in Boulder Creek, California.

PUBLICATIONS: *Forest Light News*, newsletter.

FAX: (415) 488-0170

E-MAIL: srmc@spiritrock.org

WWW: http://www.spiritrock.org

LINEAGE: Mahasi Sayadaw, Ajahn Chah, Ajahn Buddhadasa, and others

SPIRITUAL HEADS: The Spirit Rock Teacher Collective: Guy Armstrong, James Baraz, Sylvia Boorstein, Eugene Cash, Debra Chamberlin-Taylor, Howard Cohn, Anna Douglas, Gil Fronsdal, Robert Hall, Jack Kornfield, Wes Nisker, Mary Orr, John Travis, and Julie Wester

AFFILIATION: Insight Meditation Society (Massachusetts); Gaia House (England)

ESTABLISHED: 1981, informally; 1985, formally. Previously known as Insight Meditation West (IMW).

FACILITIES: Four-hundred-twelve-acre country retreat facility. Residential buildings will be completed in 1998 and will accommodate over eighty retreatants. Meanwhile a full yearly schedule of residential retreats are held in rented facilities.

RETREATS OFFERED: Approximately twelve one- to three-week intensive Vipassana retreats per year. A year-round schedule of classes and daylong retreats including family practice days.

PUBLICATIONS: *Spirit Rock Newsletter,* biannually. Our program schedule is in our newsletter, *Inquiring Mind,* and on the World Wide Web.

Taungpulu Kaba-Aye Meditation Center

A longtime disciple of the Very Ven. Taungpulu Kaba-Aye Sayadaw Phaya of Upper Burma, Rina Sircar is cofounder of Taungpulu Kaba-Aye (World Peace) Monastery and a professor at the California Institute of Integral Studies in San Francisco. She is also founder of the Taungpulu Kaba-Aye Meditation Center in San Francisco, where she offers ongoing meditation sittings and healing workshops.

Taungpulu Kaba-Aye Monastery

Taungpulu Kaba-Aye Monastery is a monastic training facility in the Theravada tradition. Training under resident monks emphasizes mindfulness and loving-kindness practices for the healing of self and others. Located in the redwood forests of Santa Cruz County, the monastery offers a peaceful environment for practice and study. Per diem donation requested.

ADDRESS: 18335 Big Basin Way, Boulder Creek, CA 95006

PHONE: (408) 338-4050

LINEAGE: Burmese Theravada

SPIRITUAL HEADS: Rina Sircar, Cofounder; U Mandapa, Abbot

CONTACT: Anne Teich, Secretary

AFFILIATION: Taungpulu Kaba-Aye Monastery, Meiktilla District and Yangon, Myanmar

ESTABLISHED: 1981

FACILITIES: World Peace Pagoda, shrine room, guest rooms, tent sites, three cabins.

The pagoda at Taungpulu Kaba-Aye Monastery in Boulder Creek, California. (Photo courtesy of Taungpulu Kaba-Aye Monastery.)

RETREATS OFFERED: Three weekend retreats offered per year; self retreats of up to two weeks duration.

PUBLICATIONS: Free quarterly newsletter: *Forest Light News.* Book: *Blooming in the Desert—Favorite Teachings of Taungpulu Sayadaw.*

Vipassana Meditation with Wes Nisker

Ongoing evenings of sitting, talk, and discussion at St. John's Church. Write for schedule.

ADDRESS: Nisker, Box 9999, North Berkeley Station, Berkeley, CA 94709
LINEAGE: Theravada Vipassana
SPIRITUAL HEAD: Wes Nisker
AFFILIATION: Spirit Rock Meditation Center
FACILITIES: We meet at St. John's Church, 2727 College Avenue, Berkeley, near the University of California campus.
MEDITATION PROGRAM: Weekly Vipassana sitting, talk, discussion.

Vipassana Santa Cruz

Vipassana Santa Cruz is a group of Buddhists and non-Buddhists in the Santa Cruz area who meet regularly for Vipassana meditation. Mary Orr, trained by Jack Kornfield of Spirit Rock, is our guiding teacher. When she is out of town, senior students, other Vipassana teachers, and teachers of other traditions lead the group.

ADDRESS: c/o Mary Orr, 3223 Redwood Drive, Aptos, CA 95003
PHONE: (408) 688-3958
LINEAGE: Theravada via Spirit Rock and Insight Meditation Society
CONTACT: Mary Orr, Resident Teacher
AFFILIATION: Spirit Rock

ESTABLISHED: 1989
FACILITIES: Rented space.
MEDITATION PROGRAM: Two weekly sittings. Beginner's classes several times yearly.
RETREATS OFFERED: Monthly all-day or half-day retreats; "Householder Retreats" (eight days of evening meetings) integrating practice and daily life.
PUBLICATIONS: *Vipassana Santa Cruz Newsletter*

Vipassana Support Institute

Vipassana Support Institute (VSI) trains people in attention and focusing skills using approaches derived from the Buddhist practice of Vipassana Meditation. This training is presented without cultural or religious trappings. VSI also provides innovative support structures to help individuals maintain their ongoing practice, particularly in times of crisis and challenge. Shinzen Young is a Westerner who has trained extensively in Asian monasteries. He is a scholar of languages and science. By drawing parallels between the internal science of mindfulness and the external science of the West, he makes the teachings accessible to the modern mind.

ADDRESS: 4070 Albright Avenue, Los Angeles, CA 90066
PHONE: (310) 915-1943
FAX: (310) 391-7969
E-MAIL: shinlist@together.net
SPIRITUAL HEAD: Shinzen Young, Resident Director
AFFILIATION: Autonomous
ESTABLISHED: 1992
FACILITIES: Retreats are held at various centers.
RETREATS OFFERED: One- to ten-day retreats in Los Angeles; four- to seven-day retreats in Maryland, Colorado, Arizona, and Toronto, making practice approachable to a broad public.

Vipassana Buddy System

THE VIPASSANA SUPPORT INSTITUTE FACILITA-tor Training Program grew out of the combined vision of Shinzen Young and Shirley Fenton. In Shirley's own words, "By 1988, after years of illness, I found myself in chronic pain so intense I truly felt the only option left was suicide. I asked Shinzen if it would be spiritually correct to take my own life. Instead he gave me personalized guided meditation sessions. Through this practice the pain often turns into a kind of purifying energy which deeply and positively affects all aspects of my life. As a successful psychotherapist and trainer for major corporations, I wanted more than anything to help others as I had been helped."

Most people who begin to meditate want to continue but find it difficult to maintain a regular practice. Shinzen noticed that when his students consistently received personalized, step-by-step instruction, they really learned how to meditate and tended to stay with the practice.

In the past, people entered monasteries to find this level of support. But in the modern world, Shinzen rea-soned, different support structures were needed. That's why, in the spring of 1992, Shirley and Shinzen began training facilitators to nurture new meditators in their practice and to support experienced practitioners who found themselves in crises.

Facilitators assist their clients by leading them through "Guided Interactive Meditation." This involves sixty- to ninety-minute sessions in which the facilitator monitors the client's progress by getting direct feedback, usually over the telephone.

In addition, facilitators help by designing a daily practice schedule that meets their client's needs and by informing them of upcoming local and national retreats and other programs that would substantially further their practice. These services are offered free of charge.

Gail Iverson

For more information, contact: Vipassana Support Institute, 4070 Albright Avenue, Los Angeles, CA 90066; (310) 915-1943.

PUBLICATIONS: Tape catalog—over one hundred titles on the theory and practice of meditation; annual teaching schedule.

Wat Buddhanusorn (Thai Temple)

Phranaha Prasert has discussion/meditation groups weekly. The best time to go for a first-time visit is on a Sunday. Call for times.
ADDRESS: 36054 Niles Boulevard, Fremont, CA 94536
PHONES: (510) 790-2294 or (510) 790-2296
FAX: (510) 796-9043
LINEAGE: Thai Theravadan

SPIRITUAL HEADS: Phramaha Somchai, Meditation Master; Phramaha Suchart, Thai Language Teacher
CONTACT: Phramaha Prasert, Abbot
AFFILIATION: Autonomous
MEDITATION PROGRAM: Weekly meditation and discussion.

Wat Thai

No description available.
ADDRESS: 8225 Coldwater Canyon Avenue, North Hollywood, CA 91605-1198
PHONE: (818) 785-9552
FAX: (818) 780-0616
LINEAGE: Thai

SPIRITUAL HEAD: Phrawichin Khunathan
AFFILIATION: Autonomous. Member of Thai Council.
ESTABLISHED: 1971
RETREATS OFFERED: One-week retreat every month.
PUBLICATIONS: *Duangprateep*, in Thai only.

COLORADO

Durango Sangha

Ours is a relatively small but active *sangha* modeled on teachings of the Insight Meditation Society. We meet for evening meditations every week at a member's

COLORADO (cont.)

home and hold retreats here twice a year with visiting teachers from Spirit Rock and Insight Meditation Center.

ADDRESS: c/o Bill Manning, PO Box 2134, Durango, CO 81302

PHONE: (970) 247-8870

E-MAIL: rparker@frontier.net

LINEAGE: Insight Meditation Society

SPIRITUAL HEAD: Board of directors only.

CONTACT: Bill Manning

AFFILIATION: Insight Meditation Society

ESTABLISHED: 1991

FACILITIES: We meet regularly at members' homes and rent facilities for retreats.

MEDITATION PROGRAM: Weekly Vipassana meditation.

RETREATS OFFERED: Twice-yearly silent retreats via teachers from Spirit Rock and Insight Meditation Society.

PUBLICATIONS: *Durango Sangha News & Notes*

Insight Meditation Community

Insight Meditation Community was established to serve the Vipassana community of the Boulder/Denver area. It supports the activities of local teachers and also sponsors three- to ten-day retreats led by visiting teachers from Insight Meditation Society and Spirit Rock Center. The *Insight Meditation Community Newsletter* is sent out three times a year to over a thousand people.

ADDRESS: 780 Union Avenue, Boulder, CO 80304

LINEAGE: Western Theravadan as taught at Insight Meditation Society and Spirit Rock.

SPIRITUAL HEAD: Boulder Vipassana Teachers Collective

CONTACT: Wendy Zerin

AFFILIATION: Informal affiliation with Insight Meditation Society and Spirit Rock.

ESTABLISHED: 1993

FACILITIES: Meetings at The Yoga Workshop, 2020 21st Street, Boulder. Retreats held in rented rural centers.

MEDITATION PROGRAM: Weekly drop-in sitting, dharma discussion.

RETREATS OFFERED: Periodic three- to ten-day retreats with local and visiting teachers.

PUBLICATIONS: *Insight Meditation Community Newsletter*

New Traditions Retreat

A simple, comfortable, solar-warmed mountain cabin, nestled in the piñon pines and wild sage, overlooks the vast San Luis Valley and welcomes the experienced solo meditator. Fireplace, comfy bed, basic kitchen, weekly laundry service, and unobtrusive daily delivery of your "meditation support care basket" assure that you will have nothing to do, nowhere to go. Sunset chanting of coyotes in the arroyos, the song of the high desert breezes, and miles of juniper and pine—no people for miles around. Only for well-practiced, sturdy meditators. By reservation only. References required.

ADDRESS: PO Box 521, Fort Garland, CO 81133

PHONE: (719) 379-2635

FAX: (719) 379-2635

LINEAGE: Theravada Vipassana

CONTACT: Nicole V. Langley

AFFILIATION: Namo Tassa, Inc.

ESTABLISHED: 1990

FACILITIES: Solar-powered remote mountain cabin.

RETREATS OFFERED: Solitary retreats by reservation.

Rocky Mountain Insight

Rocky Mountain Insight offers an opportunity for seekers of the dharma and peace of mind to gather, meditate, study, and share life on the spiritual path in the beauty of the Rockies. Having received transmission from Ruth Denison and

Buddha's birthday celebration at Rocky Mountain Insight in Colorado Springs, Colorado. (Photo by Joe Cadrin.)

Dharma on the Tip of Your Tongue

CHANTING IS COMMON PRACTICE IN THERAVADA Buddhist countries. Not so in America. But now you can have Dharma on the tip of your tongue with "Songs of the Dharma: Buddhist Chants in Pali and English," a booklet and audiocassette created by Lucinda Green, Ph.D., dharma teacher at Rocky Mountain Insight in Colorado Springs, Colorado. "Songs" features the traditional liturgy: *Chant to the Triple Gem, the Metta (Loving Kindness) Chant, Sharing of Merit* and others. All chants in the booklet are duplicated on tape so you, or your sitting group, can learn the tunes.

Dr. Green has also created a series of guided Buddhist meditations on cassette. These are not talks about the topic, but actual guided practice sessions to be done while sitting. One cassette, entitled "In This Very Body," gives instruction in the technique of "Sweeping Meditation," in which the attention is systematically shifted from point to point throughout the body. The practice is designed to increase concentration and bring about deep healing.

In *Developing Loving Kindness,* the listener is introduced to Metta Meditation, a powerful practice that cleanses and purifies the heart by offering unconditional loving kindness to oneself and all beings.

Lucinda Green, Ph.D.

For more information, contact: Treelight Productions, PO Box 6386, Colorado Springs, CO 80934-6386; (719) 685-5528.

---

lived as an *anagarika* in Sri Lanka under the tutelage of Aya Khema, dharma teacher Lucinda Green offers Vipassana courses that cover *anapanasati*, sweeping, and *metta* meditation; the Four Noble Truths; the five precepts for laypeople; and chanting in Pali and English. ". . . a light-hearted heavy-duty Dharma group."
ADDRESS: PO Box 6386, Colorado Springs, CO 80934-6386
PHONE: (719) 685-5528
FAX: (719) 685-5756
LINEAGE: Burma, Sri Lanka
SPIRITUAL HEAD: Lucinda Treelight Green, Ph.D., Resident Teacher
AFFILIATION: Dhamma Dena
ESTABLISHED: 1994
FACILITIES: Urban meditation center with plans for a residential retreat center. Lending library.
MEDITATION PROGRAM: Weekly sitting group; six-week classes; dharma study group.

RETREATS OFFERED: One-day and weekend retreats.
PUBLICATIONS: "Songs of the Dharma: Buddhist Chants in Pali and English" (cassette and booklet); *Metta Meditation in This Very Body: Sweeping Meditation.*

Rocky Mountain Vipassana Association

No description available.
ADDRESS: 760 Northwest Birch Street, Cedaredge, CO 81413
PHONE: (970) 835-8295
LINEAGE: Vipassana meditation in the tradition of Burmese teacher Sayagyi U Ba Khin, as taught by S. N. Goenka
SPIRITUAL HEAD: S. N. Goenka of the Vipassana International Academy near Bombay, India. No resident teachers; numerous assistant teachers conduct courses on a guest basis.

CONTACT: Judi Sammons.
AFFILIATION: Over thirty permanent centers and many associations in thirty-five countries. There is no *parent* group: timetable, retreat format, and meditation instructions are the same at all courses worldwide.
ESTABLISHED: 1989
FACILITIES: Rented sites and rural camp facilities.
RETREATS OFFERED: We organize one or two ten-day courses yearly at rented sites in rural western Colorado; periodic ten-day courses at rural camp facilities in Montana, Utah, Idaho, and in the mountains east of Boulder, Colorado; group sittings and periodic one-day self courses for experienced students.

Tuesday Night Sitting Group

We meet once a week on Tuesday evenings for an hour of Vipassana meditation under the watchful eye of Lotus the Dog. This is usually followed by dinner at a neighborhood restaurant called Cuchina Leone, where we eat pasta and discuss the dharma.

ADDRESS: 140 South Franklin Street, Denver, CO 80209
PHONE: (303) 722-3576
LINEAGE: Burmese Vipassana
CONTACT: Mollie Jankovsky
AFFILIATION: Autonomous
ESTABLISHED: 1995
FACILITIES: Member's home.
MEDITATION PROGRAM: Weekly evening meditation.

Vipassana Dhura Meditation Society

Vipassana meditation is still young in the West, and Ajahn Sobin Namto emphasizes the benefits derived from classical "no-frills" training and from Insight practice as a tool for enlightenment. Originally from Thailand, Ajahn was a monk for thirty-two years and has taught Vipassana meditation for over forty years. His teaching is based on completely setting up your long-term practice and one-on-one interviews. Serious students know that progress of insight depends on the seven Cs: commitment, confidence, correction, continuity, carefulness, and clear comprehension. Ajahn Sobin provides teacher training, and is also available for private consultation.

ADDRESS: 4801 Julian Street, Denver, CO 80221
PHONES: (303) 964-9357 or (303) 778-8012
SPIRITUAL HEAD: Ajahn Sobin S. Namto.
CONTACT: Thomas M. Heron
AFFILIATION: Autonomous
ESTABLISHED: 1986
FACILITIES: Wat Buddhawararam (Den-

ver). Several Thai temples in the United States are used as retreat sites. Extended retreats are held at a rural retreat center near Mexico City.
MEDITATION PROGRAM: Sittings three times a week at Wat Buddhawararam; Sunday morning English-language service.
RETREATS OFFERED: Seven-day to three-month retreats.

Vipassana Towers

Vipassana Towers is a twelve-story, 125-unit apartment building located in the Broadway Terrace area of central Denver. The owners, Dr. David and Woinishet Snyder, provide a meditation hall (capacity: 120) and kitchen/dining area (seats forty) in the building rent-free to area Vipassana groups. All instruction, membership, and retreats are offered free of charge; no donations or fees are accepted. Ajahn Sobin S. Namto lives in an apartment in the building and teaches when he is in town.

ADDRESS: 330 Acoma Street, Denver, CO 80223
PHONE: (303) 778-8883
FAX: Same
LINEAGE: Vipassana/nonsectarian
CONTACTS: Dr. David and Woinishet Snyder, Resident Directors
AFFILIATION: Autonomous
ESTABLISHED: 1996
FACILITIES: Urban meditation center in high-rise apartment building. Large meditation hall and kitchen/dining area.
MEDITATION PROGRAM: Ongoing weekly meditation periods.
RETREATS OFFERED: Retreats, potlucks, other activities as announced. Call or write for current schedule. All activities are open to the general public.

DISTRICT OF COLUMBIA

Washington Buddhist Vihara

The Washington Buddhist Vihara is a Theravadan monastery and Dhamma study center open to all. We have outreach to both the local ethnic Sri Lankan community and the larger American community. A Dhamma bookstore and library are available along with Dhamma classes, weekly meditations, Buddhist celebrations, and retreats offered throughout the year. Resident monks are available for teachings, discussion, and questions. We are building a beautiful seven-acre retreat center in the Maryland suburbs. "To abstain from all evil. To cultivate the good, and to purify one's mind—this is the teaching of the Buddha."

ADDRESS: 5017 16th Street Northwest, Washington, DC 20011
PHONE: (202) 723-0773
LINEAGE: Sri Lankan Theravadan
CONTACT: Ven. Waihene Pannaloka Maha Thera, Director
FACILITIES: Monastery/study center.
RETREATS OFFERED: Various retreats throughout the year.
PUBLICATIONS: *The Washington Buddhist*, newsletter.

FLORIDA

Bodhitree Dhamma Center

Bodhitree Dhamma Center (BTDC) is a suburban meditation center on Florida's central Gulf coast. The one-acre grounds feature a meditation hall and bookstore, areas for outdoor walking meditation, and a specimen of the Bodhi tree. BTDC exists to spread the Buddha's teachings as preserved in the Pali Canon and the Theravadan traditions of Southern Asia. Although Theravadan in orientation,

BTDC also hosts teachers from other Buddhist traditions. Intensive retreats and classes are offered periodically. Regular meetings include periods of Vipassana meditation and a Dhamma talk. The bookstore is open following scheduled events. Mail-order catalog available on request.
ADDRESS: 11355 Dauphin Avenue, Largo, FL 34648-2903
PHONE: (813) 392-7698
LINEAGE: Theravada/Vipassana
CONTACT: Jim Cameron, Resident Director
AFFILIATION: Autonomous. We are slowly developing an affiliation with Abhayagiri Buddhist Monastery in Redwood Valley, California, under the direction of Ajahn Amaro.
ESTABLISHED: 1982
FACILITIES: Meditation hall.
RETREATS OFFERED: Three-day intensives quarterly.
PUBLICATIONS: Flyers, newsletter.

Charlotte County Meditation Society

We gather weekly for meditation, fellowship, and taped instruction. All are invited to join us in celebrating the value that silent spiritual practice gives to our lives. Please contact Rev. Sam Trumbore, the Unitarian Universalist minister of Port Charlotte, for more information and for our meeting location.
ADDRESS: 1532 Forrest Nelson Boulevard, Port Charlotte, FL 33952
PHONE: (941) 627-4303
E-MAIL: trumbore@uua.org
LINEAGE: Mixed. We lean toward American Theravada.
SPIRITUAL HEAD: Lay-led group.
AFFILIATION: Autonomous; sympathetic to Insight Meditation Society in Barre, Massachusetts.
ESTABLISHED: Spring 1995

Circle of Vipassana

We are a small but dedicated *sangha*, meeting sometimes in a local yoga studio, sometimes in private homes. We sit in a circle to emphasize the fact that we are a community of practitioners who come together to reinforce each other's commitment to regular practice. Several times a year we offer a one-day retreat. Every winter we have an intensive weekend retreat in some remote part of Florida, led by Bhante Gunaratana, author of *Mindfulness in Plain English*. The weekly sitting group is designed for experienced students, but instruction is available for beginners.
ADDRESS: 6460 Burning Tree Drive, Largo, FL 33777
PHONE: (813) 392-8103
E-MAIL: malmgren@sptimes.com
SPIRITUAL HEAD: Ven. H. Gunaratana (nonresidential)
CONTACT: Jeanne Malmgren
AFFILIATION: Bhavana Society in West Virginia
ESTABLISHED: 1994
FACILITIES: Member's home or local yoga studio.
MEDITATION PROGRAM: Weekly sitting group.
RETREATS OFFERED: Annual weekend retreat; Day of Vipassana.

Insight Meditation Group

"Come and See!" The Insight Meditation Group strives to avoid exclusivity. We encourage all seekers to practice in order to see clearly the reality of our amazing world. Retreats are held at least once a year, sometimes twice. Outside teachers are brought in.
ADDRESS: 1898 Lodgepole Drive, Milton, FL 32583
PHONE: (904) 673-4290
CONTACT: Gordon O. Meinscher

AFFILIATION: Bhavana Society, High View, West Virginia
ESTABLISHED: 1991
FACILITIES: Meditation hall in Gulf Breeze, Florida.
RETREATS OFFERED: Once or twice yearly.

Wat Buddharangasi of Miami

Suburban meditation center and temple. Space for outdoor walking meditation. Outdoor lecture and tantric hall. Under the care of three Thai monks.
ADDRESS: 15200 Southwest 240 Street, Miami, FL 33032
PHONE: (305) 245-2702
FAX: (305) 247-3092
E-MAIL: mystik@icanect.net
LINEAGE: Thai Theravada
SPIRITUAL HEADS: P. S. Boonnom, Thongchai Yanasangvaro, Thoonthaway Vajaranano, Resident Teachers

HAWAII

Karuna Foundation/Erik Knud-Hansen

The Karuna Foundation has its home on the tropical slopes of Kona, Hawaii. The land is dedicated to awakening awareness and compassion. There is simple accommodation for sincere meditators to live dharma in silence, stillness, and sensitivity.
ADDRESS: PO Box 511, Honaunau, HI 96726
PHONE: (808) 328-9511
SPIRITUAL HEAD: Erik Knud-Hansen
CONTACT: Same
AFFILIATION: Autonomous
ESTABLISHED: 1984
FACILITIES: A place of insight and compassion.
RETREATS OFFERED: Private teachings/occasional groups.

Vipassana Hawaii

Vipassana Hawaii is led by Steven Smith, Michele McDonald Smith (Oahu), and Kamala Masters (Maui), all of whom practice and teach *Insight* and *Metta* meditation with the blessing of the Ven. Sayadaw U Pandita of Burma. On Oahu, the weekly group sittings and monthly daylong retreats are held at a Kahala home. On Maui, the group meets one evening a week in Makawao. Several weeklong retreats and weekend retreats are offered throughout the year at the Palolo Zendo and on Maui. Several members lead weekly meditation classes at the correctional facilities on Oahu.

ADDRESS: 655 Honua Street, Honolulu, HI 96816
PHONES: Oahu, (808) 737-5169. Maui, (808) 878-2994
LINEAGE: Burmese Mahasi Sayadaw
SPIRITUAL HEADS: Steven Smith, Michele McDonald Smith, Kamala Masters
CONTACTS: Thanh and Xuan Huynh
AFFILIATION: Insight Meditation Society, Barre, Massachusetts
ESTABLISHED: 1984
FACILITIES: Private home. Most retreats held at Palolo Zendo/Diamond Sangha.
MEDITATION PROGRAM: Weekly group sittings. Monthly daylong sitting in Oahu.
RETREATS OFFERED: One or more nine-day retreats and several weekend retreats per year.
PUBLICATIONS: *Vipassana News*

Vipassana Metta Foundation

The Vipassana Metta Foundation has evolved out of the Vipassana retreat community on Maui. Awareness is cultivated through the traditional practices of generosity, moral conduct, concentration, loving-kindness, and insight, with the understanding that liberation of the heart brings "the greatest happiness, which is peace." Periodically other senior teachers are invited to offer teachings on Maui. Our vision includes establishing a small, practice-oriented residential community for laypeople.

ADDRESS: PO Box 2523, Wailuku, Maui, HI 96793
PHONE: (808) 878-3760
E-MAIL: metta@maui.net
WWW: http://www.maui.net/~metta/
LINEAGE: Burmese Mahasi/Insight Meditation Society
CONTACTS: Steve Armstrong/Kamala Masters, Resident Teachers
AFFILIATION: Autonomous
ESTABLISHED: 1995
FACILITIES: Rented rooms and retreat facilities.
MEDITATION PROGRAM: Regular weekly sittings with instruction and Dhamma dialogue.
RETREATS OFFERED: "Days of Mindfulness"; weekend and weeklong retreats; New Year's retreat; annual monthlong silent Vipassana-Metta retreats (August).

ILLINOIS

Buddhadharma Meditation Center

Founded by Thai and American Buddhists, Buddhadharma Meditation Center (BMC) is one of the fastest-growing Buddhist organizations in the country. Though rooted in the Theravada tradition, its vision is ecumenical and its emphasis is on meditation. BMC runs a popular Dharma-gift program, a fine library, and an excellent Sunday School. Dharma literature is published and distributed free of charge. Intensive retreats and religious instruction are arranged by appointment. BMC welcomes study groups from colleges and universities and sends representatives to speak at academic institutions. You are invited to visit.

ADDRESS: 8910 Kingery Highway, Hinsdale, IL 60521
PHONE: (630) 789-8866
FAX: (630) 789-8879
LINEAGE: Thai Theravada
SPIRITUAL HEAD: Ajahn Banyat Dammasaro, Resident Teacher
AFFILIATION: Council of Thai Bhikkhus in the USA
ESTABLISHED: 1986
FACILITIES: Urban temple and meditation center.
MEDITATION PROGRAM: Sunday morning meditation, talk, food offering to monks; English-language services; Children's Dharma School; weekly evening meditation. Call for times.
RETREATS OFFERED: Vipassana retreats (May/June); Children's Summer Camp; one-day retreats for Thais; New Year's Retreat.
PUBLICATIONS: *Buddhadharma*, bimonthly newsletter.

Burmese Buddhist Association

The temple of the Burmese Buddhist Association was founded in October 1987. Its present chief monk is U Kay Thawa.

ADDRESS: 15 West 110 Forest Lane, Elmhurst, IL 60657
PHONE: (708) 941-7608
LINEAGE: Burmese Theravada
SPIRITUAL HEAD: U Kay Thawa, Chief Monk
CONTACT: Nay Aung, (708) 424-0072
AFFILIATION: International Organization of Burmese Buddhist Sanghas
ESTABLISHED: 1987
FACILITIES: Urban temple.
MEDITATION PROGRAM: Meditation is part of regular Sunday services, held on the first and third Sunday of the month. Services are in Burmese. Call for times.

Cambodian Buddhist Association/ Wat Khemararan

This is the first Cambodian temple in Chicago. We follow the Khmer (Cambodian) Theravada tradition. All services are conducted in Khmer. Regular Sunday services are held and religious holidays observed according to the lunar calendar. *Attha Sila* (Eight Precepts) are taken every month and Visakha (birth, enlightenment, and death of the Buddha) is celebrated on the fifteenth day (full moon) of the fourth lunar month.

ADDRESS: 1258 West Argyle, Chicago, IL 60640
PHONE: (312) 878-8226
LINEAGE: Khmer Theravada
CONTACT: Savat Khem, (312) 793-7121 (w); (312) 583-0133 (h)
AFFILIATION: Autonomous
FACILITIES: Urban temple.
MEDITATION PROGRAM: Sunday services in Khmer. Call for times.

Dhammaka Meditation Center of Chicago

Activities include meditation, religious services, weekend retreats, and dharma talks.

ADDRESS: 2329 Birch Street, Des Plaines, IL 60018-3109
PHONE: (847) 768-9866
FAX: (847) 768-9862
E-MAIL: dhammakayail@sprintmail.com
LINEAGE: Theravada
SPIRITUAL HEAD: Ven. Phra Bhavanavisut (Dharmachaiya Bhikkhu)
CONTACT: Ven. Suddhivaro Bhikkhu
AFFILIATION: Dhammakaya Foundation, Thailand
ESTABLISHED: 1997
RETREATS OFFERED: Weekend retreats.

Kampuchean Buddhist Society, Inc./Wat Khmer Metta Temple

Though this temple serves the Cambodian, Thai, Laotian, and Vietnamese people of the Chicago area, everyone is welcome. Ven. Sangwoei Khemchom speaks English and will explain activities. We cooperate with other religious and refugee organizations to develop affordable housing, elderly day care, education, job training, and counseling for Cambodians in the Chicago area. Wat Khmer Metta Temple also performs weddings and funeral services.

ADDRESS: 4716 North Winthrop Avenue, Chicago, IL 60640
PHONE: (312) 275-0096
LINEAGE: Cambodian, Thai, Laotian, Vietnamese Theravada
SPIRITUAL HEAD: Chanyann Ven. Sangwoei Khemchom, Resident Teacher
ESTABLISHED: 1986
FACILITIES: Urban ethnic Buddhist temple.

Oak Park Meditation Group

"Beginner's Mind" Buddhist meditation is held on Sunday mornings at the Unity Temple Unitarian Church. We are a lay Buddhist group whose members were trained by Dr. Phangcham of Wat Dhammaram Thai Buddhist Temple, and we emphasize basic Buddhist meditation. All are welcome to sit with us.

ADDRESS: 875 Lake Street, Oak Park, IL 60301
PHONES: (708) 524-1658, (708) 848-4668
LINEAGE: Thai Theravada
CONTACTS: Larry Barr/Alvin Lee Wilcox
AFFILIATION: Autonomous
ESTABLISHED: 1990
FACILITIES: Unity Temple Unitarian Church
MEDITATION PROGRAM: Sunday morning

"Beginner's Mind" meditation. Call for times.

Rock River Meditation Community

"I live in a rural area about forty-five miles southwest of Rockford. The nearest meditation groups are fifty to a hundred miles away—too far away to attend on a regular basis. So, I told all the local folks I knew that I was interested in starting a group in the Rock River Valley and within a few months we were meeting. Regular meetings are held one Sunday each month. Once a quarter we meet for a full day. There are plans to hold weekend retreats in the future."—*Jim Ferolo*

ADDRESS: 4094 West Timberlane, Dixon, IL 61021
PHONE: (815) 652-4742
LINEAGE: Mahasi style as taught by Insight Meditation Society teachers.
CONTACT: Jim Ferolo
AFFILIATION: Autonomous
ESTABLISHED: 1995
FACILITIES: Meet in private homes of members.
MEDITATION PROGRAM: Group meditation once a month.
RETREATS OFFERED: Quarterly daylong retreat.

Wat Dhammaram/Vipassana Meditation Center

Wat Dhammaram is a meeting place for the Buddhist Council of the Midwest and regional headquarters of the American Buddhist Congress. The temple is now a main Theravada Buddhist learning center in the Midwest and a center for the Council of Thai Bhikkhus in the USA. The objectives of the temple are to promote and support Buddhist teaching and Thai culture and to organize and unite Buddhist followers for religious worship and charitable activities.

ADDRESS: 7059 West 75th Street, Chicago, IL 60638-5934

PHONE: (708) 594-8100

FAX: (708) 594-8114

E-MAIL: wat@interaccess.com

LINEAGE: Thai Theravada

SPIRITUAL HEAD: Dr. Chuen Phangcham, Resident Director

AFFILIATION: Council of Thai Bhikkhus in the USA

ESTABLISHED: 1976

FACILITIES: Urban temple with a separate room for group meditation. Facilities available for solitary retreat.

MEDITATION PROGRAM: Buddhist Sunday school; daily chanting and group meditation; meditation instruction twice weekly. Call for times.

RETREATS OFFERED: One-day, weekend, and weeklong Insight meditation retreats for the public are given regularly.

PUBLICATIONS: *Dhammopas*, quarterly magazine; instructional pamphlets and booklets.

Wat Phothikaram Lao Buddhist Temple

Wat Phothikaram was established in 1982 by the Laotian communities of Rockford, Elgin, and other cities in Illinois under the leadership of Phra Maha Khamsene Phanthavong and Phra Ajahn Bounmy Kittiphan. This center serves the Laotian community and helps maintain and preserve Laotian culture. Our temple was the subject of a documentary film, *Buddha and Blue Collar*, which was shown on national television.

ADDRESS: 3328 South Mulford Road, Rockford, IL 61109

PHONE: (312) 874-2176

LINEAGE: Laotian Theravada

SPIRITUAL HEAD: Phra Maha Khamsene Phanthavong, President

ESTABLISHED: 1982

FACILITIES: Urban Buddhist temple.

IOWA

Des Moines Sitting Group

Practice at the Des Moines Sitting Group consists of alternating periods of sitting and walking meditation along with listening to taped Dhamma talks, or reading aloud from Buddhist texts. While the basic orientation is Vipassana, anyone who meditates or wants to "just sit" is welcome. Contact Charlie Day for the times and locations of meetings.

ADDRESS: 3205 Grand Avenue, #317, Des Moines, IA 50317-4178

PHONE: (515) 255-8398

LINEAGE: Theravada

CONTACT: Charles W. Day

AFFILIATION: Autonomous. Mid America Dharma Group, Kansas City, Missouri

ESTABLISHED: 1994

FACILITIES: We meet in members' homes.

MEDITATION PROGRAM: Vipassana meditation one evening a week. Call for times and location.

RETREATS OFFERED: Full day of meditation on the last Sunday of the month.

KANSAS

Lenexa Sitting Group

No description available.

ADDRESS: 9429 Gillette, Lenexa, KS 66215

PHONE: (913) 438-4376

LINEAGE: Theravada as taught by Insight Meditation Society

SPIRITUAL HEAD: None

CONTACT: Jane Vogel

AFFILIATION: Mid America Dharma Group, Kansas City, Missouri

MEDITATION PROGRAM: Meets one morning a week for Vipassana meditation. Call for times.

Prairie Village Sitting Group

No description available.

ADDRESS: 7301 Mission Street, Prairie Village, Kansas 66208

PHONE: (913) 333-0851

LINEAGE: Theravada as taught by Insight Meditation Society

SPIRITUAL HEAD: None

CONTACT: George Drasin

AFFILIATION: Mid America Dharma Group, Kansas City, Missouri

MEDITATION PROGRAM: Vipassana meditation one evening a week. Call for times.

MARYLAND

International Meditation Center/ IMC-USA

IMC-USA offers ten-day residential meditation courses in the practice of the Eightfold Noble Path, which comprises three stages of training: morality (*sila*), concentration (*samadhi*), and wisdom or insight (*panna*). Mindfulness of the breath is practiced for the first five days, with the aim of quieting and concentrating the mind. The remaining days are devoted to Insight Meditation (Vipassana), whereby students can experience firsthand the essential elements of Buddha's teaching: the impermanence of all phenomena (*anicca*), unsatisfactoriness (*dukkha*), and the absence of a permanent self (*anatta*).

ADDRESS: 438 Bankard Road, Westminster, MD 21158

PHONE: (410) 346-7889

FAX: (410) 346-7133

LINEAGE: Sayagyi U Ba Khin

SPIRITUAL HEAD: Sayamagyi Daw Mya Thwin

CONTACT: Orin Hargraves

AFFILIATION: International Meditation

The Sandwich Retreat

THE SANDWICH RETREAT AT CAMBRIDGE INsight Meditation Center is not about mindfully chewing on a foot-long hoagie. Rather, it's a unique opportunity to practice mindfulness in daily life with the support of teachers and *sangha*. It spans five weekday evenings "sandwiched" between two weekends of intensive meditation practice, Dhamma talks, and individual interviews with teachers. As the weekend progresses, the mind settles down. This in turn creates a willingness to look at the mind and life itself with more clarity and depth.

As the first weekend draws to a close, teachers assign "homework," which yogis are expected to carry out during the ensuing week at home, at work, and in their relationships. These homework assignments provide an opportunity to extend mindfulness into the activities of everyday life.

A typical homework assignment might be to work with the *paramita* (perfection) of "right speech" (speaking only what is true, not using divisive or harsh language, and speaking only what is useful by avoiding idle chatter and gossip). Students are encouraged to observe their verbal communication throughout their days, and to really listen while conversing with others. Participants reconvene at the center each weekday evening for more intensive meditation practice and, in rich and lively discussions, to share their homework assignment experiences.

The continuity of practice, the support of teachers and *sangha*, the intention to be mindful, the homework assignments, group discussions, Dhamma talks, personal interviews, and intensive periods of sitting and walking meditation work together to support the development of mindfulness in our busy lives.

Maddy Klyne

For more information, contact: Cambridge Insight Meditation Center, 331 Broadway, Cambridge, MA 02139; (617) 492-0472.

Centers in Burma, United Kingdom, Austria, Australia
ESTABLISHED: 1984
FACILITIES: Pagoda, Dhamma hall, dorms, kitchen, dining room.
RETREATS OFFERED: Six to eight ten-day retreats per year; weekend retreats for established students.
PUBLICATIONS: Many books, all for sale here.

Wat Thai

Thai temple. Free meditation workshops twice a month for all levels. Please call for times.
ADDRESS: 13440 Layhill Road, Silver Spring, MD 20906
PHONE: (301) 251-6101
LINEAGE: Thai Theravada
CONTACT: Deb Hammond

MASSACHUSETTS

Boston West Sitting Group

We are a small group that meets three mornings per week in members' homes for forty-five minutes of sitting meditation. On Sunday mornings the sitting is preceded by a reading.
ADDRESS: 7 Hardy Road, Wellesley, MA 02181
PHONE: (617) 235-3703
E-MAIL: afr@cris.com
LINEAGE: Vipassana
CONTACT: Alex Rose, Director
AFFILIATION: Insight Meditation Society. Cambridge Insight Meditation Center.
ESTABLISHED: 1993
FACILITIES: Members' homes.
MEDITATION PROGRAM: Group meditation three mornings weekly. Please call for times.

Cambridge Insight Meditation Center

Cambridge Insight Meditation Center (CIMC) was established in 1985 as a nonprofit, nonresidential urban center for the practice of Insight meditation. Located in the heart of Cambridge, CIMC provides an environment where the contemplative life can be developed and protected amid the complexities of city living. We offer a place where people come together to learn, support, and deepen practice.

ADDRESS: 331 Broadway, Cambridge, MA 02139

PHONE: (617) 492-0472

LINEAGE: Thai Forest Tradition

SPIRITUAL HEAD: Larry Rosenberg, Resident Teacher

AFFILIATION: Insight Meditation Society, Barre, Massachusetts

ESTABLISHED: 1985

FACILITIES: Meditation hall, Dharma hall, library, interview room, office. Four living arrangements.

RETREATS OFFERED: Many weekend, one-day, and weeklong programs. Sandwich retreats.

PUBLICATIONS: *Insight* (with Insight Meditation Society).

Dharma Seed Tape Library

Dharma Seed Tape Library's mission is to share the dharma by preserving the oral tradition. We support daily practice through preserving and distributing contemporary Theravadan Vipassana teachings. Our goal is to make the teachings available through high-quality audio- and videotapes at the lowest possible prices. Dharma Seed is a nonprofit religious organization guided by a volunteer board of directors.

ADDRESS: PO Box 66, Wendell Depot, MA 01380

PHONE: (800) 969-SEED (7333)

FAX: (413) 772-5599

WWW: http://world.std.com/~metta~

AFFILIATION: Vipassana meditation teachers

ESTABLISHED: 1983

PUBLICATIONS: Three yearly catalogues.

The Insight Meditation Society in Barre, Massachusetts. (Photo courtesy of the Insight Meditation Society.)

Insight Meditation Society (IMS)

Insight Meditation Society operates a center for intensive Insight meditation practice in rural central Massachusetts. Teacher-led retreats for beginning and experienced meditators include sitting and walking meditation, dharma talks and individual or group meetings with teachers. We also offer short- and long-term individual retreats, work retreats, and a yearlong volunteer staff program. Insight meditation is the direct, moment-to-moment observation of the mind/body process through calm and focused awareness from a place of stillness. Learning to observe in this way enables us to relate to life with less fear and clinging and to have peace in our daily lives.

ADDRESS: 1230 Pleasant Street, Barre, MA 01005

PHONE: (508) 355-4378

FAX: (508) 355-6398

LINEAGE: Nonsectarian Theravada

SPIRITUAL HEADS: Joseph Goldstein, Sharon Salzberg, Christina Feldman, Larry Rosenberg, Steven Smith (Guiding Teachers)

CONTACT: The office.

AFFILIATION: Connections with Spirit Rock; Barre Center for Buddhist Studies; Cambridge Insight Meditation Center.

ESTABLISHED: 1975

FACILITIES: Country retreat facility.

RETREATS OFFERED: Weekend to ten-day Vipassana and *metta* retreats; three-month Vipassana course; young adult, family, and supervised individual retreats. Closed during January.

PUBLICATIONS: *Insight* (semiannual).

Newbury Insight Meditation Center

No description available.

ADDRESS: 1 Rolfe's Lane, Newbury, MA 01951-1221

PHONE: (508) 463-0131

FAX: (508) 462-3959
WWW: http://world.std.com/~metta/
centers/nimc.html
LINEAGE: Theravada (Vipassana)
SPIRITUAL HEAD: Daeja Napier
CONTACT: Deborah Breen

Vipassana Meditation Center/ Dhamma Dhara

S. N. Goenka has been teaching Vipassana meditation courses since 1969. VMC was the first of his centers to open outside of India. Intensive silent retreats are held here regularly and are open to the general public. Courses are conducted by authorized assistant teachers using taped instructions by S. N. Goenka. There is no charge for these retreats, even for food and accommodation. All expenses are met by donations from those who, having completed a course and experienced the benefits of the practice, wish to give others the same opportunity. Teachers and staff volunteer their time and receive no remuneration.

ADDRESS: PO Box 24, Shelburne Falls, MA 01370-0024
PHONE: (413) 625-2160
FAX: (413) 625-2170
E-MAIL: VmcDhara@aol.com
WWW: http://www.dhamma.org
LINEAGE: Vipassana meditation in the tradition of Burmese teacher Sayagyi U Ba Khin, as taught by S. N. Goenka
SPIRITUAL HEAD: S. N. Goenka, Vipassana International Academy, near Bombay, India
CONTACT: No resident teachers; numerous assistant teachers conduct courses on a guest basis.
AFFILIATION: Over thirty permanent centers and many associations in thirty-five countries. No "parent" group. Timetable, retreat format, and meditation instructions are the same at all courses worldwide.
ESTABLISHED: 1982
FACILITIES: One-hundred-eight-acre rural retreat complex in the hills of western Massachusetts; winter capacity: sixty-four; summer capacity: 250. Individual meditation cells. Pagoda.

RETREATS OFFERED: Ten-day courses twice monthly; introductory three-day and short children's courses; advanced twenty- to thirty-day courses; eight-day *Satipatthana Sutta* courses.
PUBLICATIONS: Books and cassettes are not sold at North American centers or course sites, in order to keep the meditation environments free from any commercialism.

MICHIGAN

Traipitra's Vipassana Sitting Group

No description available.
ADDRESS: 2427 Hunt Club Drive, Bloomfield, MI 48304
PHONE: (810) 644-7403
SPIRITUAL HEAD: Traipitra (Wisityuthasart) Sarnsethsiri
CONTACT: Traipitra
ESTABLISHED: 1982
RETREATS OFFERED: Occasionally

Upland Hills Ecological Awareness Center

No description available.
ADDRESS: 2575 Indian Lake Road, Oxford, MI 48370
PHONE: (810) 693-2878
FAX: (810) 693-4317
LINEAGE: Vipassana
CONTACT: Marcia Rose, Teacher
AFFILIATION: Insight Meditation Society
ESTABLISHED: 1980

MINNESOTA

Resources for Ecumenical Spirituality

We started with the idea of trying to spread interfaith understanding through shared spiritual practice and dialogue.

The Vipassana Meditation Center, situated on 108 acres in Shelburne Falls, Massachusetts. (Photo by Dhamma Dhara.)

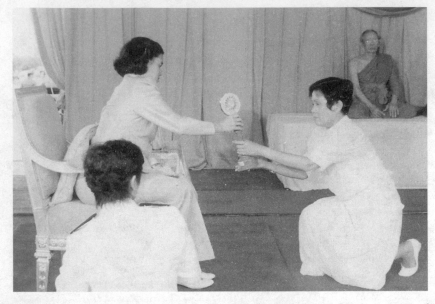

Traipitra Sarnsethsiri, the spiritual leader of Traipitra's Vipassana Sitting Group, received an award from the Princess of Thailand for teaching meditation in the United States, Europe, and Thailand. (Photo courtesy of Traipitra Sarnsethsiri.)

We rather quickly settled into offering regular Theravadan Vipassana retreats—both bringing in teachers and being taught by the resident teacher. We branched out in a few years into presenting Vipassana to Christians in ways that made it apparent how this method could add greatly to their spiritual experience. When several practitioners of Twelve-step spirituality joined us, we started adding retreats emphasizing Vipassana as an excellent method for Twelve-step programs. These three have become the major thrust of this nonprofit corporation.

ADDRESS: PO Box 6, Mankato, MN 56002

PHONE: (507) 387-4276

SPIRITUAL HEAD: Mary Jo Meadow, Resident Teacher

AFFILIATION: Autonomous

ESTABLISHED: 1987

FACILITIES: Forest Monastery in Missouri. We rent facilities for most retreats.

MEDITATION PROGRAM: A sitting group meets twice weekly in southern Minnesota. Classes offering meditation instruction occur annually in both the Mankato, Minnesota, and the Minneapolis areas and we have an affiliated sitting group in Chicago.

RETREATS OFFERED: Daylong Saturday sittings about eight times a year; straight *Buddha-Dhamma* retreats; Vipassana/*metta* retreats for Christians; Vipassana retreats for Twelve-step programs. Weekends to two weeks long.

PUBLICATIONS: Annual offerings brochure, spring update, three annual newsletters for members (donation requested).

Twin Cities Vipassana Cooperative

The Twin Cities Vipassana Cooperative (TCVC) is a network of people interested in practicing Insight meditation. Its mission is to provide opportunities to practice with other like-minded individuals and to obtain instruction from experienced teachers. TCVC is not a formal organization and has neither official membership nor a central location. Activities are administered by volunteers and take place at the facilities of local organizations such as Minnesota Zen Meditation Center and Common Ground Meditation Center (Minneapolis), and the Tau Center in Winona, Minnesota.

ADDRESS: PO Box 14683, Minneapolis, MN 55414

PHONE: (612) 229-3139

LINEAGE: Burmese

CONTACT: Hal Barron

AFFILIATION: Autonomous

ESTABLISHED: 1986

FACILITIES: Use facilities of other groups in the area.

MEDITATION PROGRAM: Group meditation twice a month.

RETREATS OFFERED: Residential retreat, four times a year.

PUBLICATIONS: *Grassroots Dhamma* (three times yearly).

MISSOURI

Heartland Insight Meditation

This is an informal organization supporting the growth of Vipassana practice in the central Midwest. Beginning classes are provided through the Continuing Education Department of Missouri Southern State College (MSSC), Joplin, Missouri, or off campus as demand requires. Contacts with other centers are maintained to make upcoming retreats known to area members. Gregg (Khemacara) Galbraith, a student of Vipassana in the Burmese tradition since 1973, provides teaching and counseling services.

ADDRESS: 427 South Main Street, Carthage, MO 64836

PHONE: (417) 358-5176

CONTACT: Gregg (Khemacara) Galbraith, Resident Director

AFFILIATION: Autonomous

ESTABLISHED: 1982

FACILITIES: At MSSC. An off-campus center is being built.

MEDITATION PROGRAM: Weekly Dhamma support group; sittings.

RETREATS OFFERED: Weekend retreats.

Mid America Dharma Group

Mid America Dharma Group (MADG) is an umbrella organization for sitting groups in Missouri, Kansas, Iowa, and Nebraska. In addition to fostering the dharma teachings in the area, MADG sponsors four three- to ten-day residential retreats and at least two nonresidential retreats annually. Our teachers are primarily from Spirit Rock Center in Woodacre, California, and from the Insight Meditation Society in Barre, Massachusetts. MADG has three affiliated sitting groups in Missouri, four in Kansas, and one in Iowa. MADG sponsors two *Kalyana-Mitta* book study groups—one in Kansas City, Missouri, and one in Columbia, Missouri.

ADDRESSES: Mailing: PO Box 414411, Kansas City, MO 64141-4411. Street: 13741 Pembroke Circle, Leawood, KS 66224

PHONE: (913) 685-3430

WWW: http://www.geocities.com/Athens/3712/index.html

LINEAGE: Theravada as taught by Insight Meditation Society

CONTACT: John van Keppel

AFFILIATION: Autonomous

ESTABLISHED: 1982

FACILITIES: Use other organizations' facilities for retreats and sitting groups.

RETREATS OFFERED: Four residential (three to ten days) and two nonresidential retreats.

PUBLICATIONS: *Mid America Dharma Newsletter* (quarterly); homepage on World Wide Web.

Resources for Ecumenical Spirituality Forest Monastery

When Resources for Ecumenical Spirituality began, we sought a place surrounded by nature where people could come to do their own spiritual work or to sojourn in spiritual company. We have a large house (five bedrooms, five common rooms) surrounded by trees and wildlife. Our seasons are not extreme. Weekend retreat participants share a room; those coming for longer periods have a private room. We serve healthy vegetarian food. Opportunities to house-sit with the entire facility at one's own disposal occur regularly.

ADDRESSES: Mailing: Route 1, Box 1160, Dunnegan, MO 65640-9705. Street: 3704 Highway 13, Dunnegan, MO 65640-9705

PHONE: (417) 754-2562

SPIRITUAL HEAD: Mary Jo Meadow, Resident Teacher

AFFILIATION: Resources for Ecumenical Spirituality, Minnesota

ESTABLISHED: 1992

FACILITIES: Large house on over thirty-five wooded acres. Several smaller structures usable for private retreats.

MEDITATION PROGRAM: Meditation instruction offered in nearby Springfield, Missouri.

RETREATS OFFERED: Straight *Buddha Dhamma* retreats; Vipassana/*Metta* retreats for Christians; Vipassana/Twelve-step program retreats. Six weekend retreats per year. Solitary retreats throughout the year.

PUBLICATIONS: Annual offerings brochure; spring update; three annual members' newsletters (donation requested).

St. Louis Vipassana Meditation Group

This group was brought together by a sincere desire for spiritual peace and equanimity. Members sought a contemplative environment that supported the sacredness of life and a connection with loving-kindness and one's own Buddha nature. We meet once a week and practice a combination of sitting, walking, and *metta* meditation.

ADDRESS: c/o Marty Levinson, 7570 Stanford Avenue, University City, MO 63130

PHONE: (314) 726-3243

LINEAGE: Vipassana

SPIRITUAL HEAD: Cofacilitated

CONTACT: Marty Levinson

AFFILIATION: Autonomous

ESTABLISHED: 1995

FACILITIES: Rented space at Solar Yoga Center.

MEDITATION PROGRAM: Weekly two-hour sittings.

RETREATS OFFERED: Half-day sittings.

Show Me Dharma

Show Me Dharma sponsors two weekly sitting groups in Colombia, Missouri. Following the spirit of Harry Truman, participants are not required to become Buddhists or embrace any particular dogma or philosophy, but are instead encouraged to see for themselves the positive changes that regular mindfulness practice can bring. Show Me Dharma also offers a three-part meditation course, a *Kalyana-Mitta* book study group, and occasionally sponsors local nonresidential retreats.

ADDRESS: 717 Hilltop Drive, Columbia, MO 65201

PHONE: (573) 875-8473

E-MAIL: Morgan@Showme.missouri.edu

LINEAGE: Theravada as taught by Insight Meditation Society

CONTACT: Ginny Morgan

AFFILIATION: Mid America Dharma Group

ESTABLISHED: 1994

MEDITATION PROGRAM: Two sitting groups weekly. *Kalyana-Mitta* book study group. Three-part meditation course.

RETREATS OFFERED: Occasional local nonresidential retreats. We also attend Mid America Dharma retreats. They offer four residential and two nonresidential retreats per year.

PUBLICATIONS: *Mid America Dharma Newsletter*

Wat Phrasriratanaram/Buddhist Temple of St. Louis

No description available.

ADDRESS: 890 Lindsay Lane, Florissant, MO 63031

PHONE: (314) 839-3115

FAX: Same

LINEAGE: Thai Theravada

SPIRITUAL HEAD: Phra Maha Lai Gosako, Abbot

MEDITATION PROGRAM: Weekly Insight Meditation. Program includes dharma discussion, Dynamic Insight Meditation, and a question-and-answer period. Please call for times.

MONTANA

Intermountain Dharma Community

Intermountain Dharma Community (IDC) is an association of Insight medita-

tion (Vipassana) practitioners sponsoring residential and nonresidential meditation retreats throughout the year. IDC draws teachers primarily from Spirit Rock/Insight Meditation Society for these retreats. Residential retreats are conducted at Blacktail Ranch near Wolf Creek, Montana, with plans to expand to the Jackson, Wyoming, area. Nonresidential retreats are currently offered twice yearly in Missoula, Montana, and once yearly in Bozeman, Montana, and Jackson, Wyoming.

ADDRESS: PO Box 1603, Thompson Falls, MT 59873

PHONE: (406) 827-3875

E-MAIL: tfl 3875@montana.com

LINEAGE: Theravada Vipassana

AFFILIATION: Insight Meditation Society/ Spirit Rock

ESTABLISHED: 1992

FACILITIES: Various rented spaces in Montana and Wyoming.

RETREATS OFFERED: Four nonresidential retreats per year in Missoula and Bozeman, Montana, and Jackson, Wyoming. Four-day to two-week retreats at Blacktail Ranch, Wolf Creek, Montana.

NEVADA

Dharma Zephyr Sangha

Dharma Zephyr Sangha is named after the local afternoon wind, the Washoe Zephyr, which Mark Twain reported carried "things living and dead, that flittered hither and thither, going and coming, hats, chickens and parasols sailing through the remote heavens; blankets, tin signs and sagebrush a shade lower; doormats and buffalo hides lower still; shovels and coal scuttles on the next grade; glass doors, cats and little children on the next; disrupted lumberyards, light buggies and wheelbarrows on the next, and down only thirty or forty feet above ground . . .

a scurrying storm of emigrating roofs and vacant lots." We first began sitting together in 1990 in living rooms and offices in Carson City and Washoe Valley. We find there is an interest in Buddhist meditation in northern Nevada, as evidenced by the consistent turnout at our retreats. *Sangha* members have taught a class in Buddhist meditation at the Reno YMCA. We strive to be as strong in our practice as the Washoe Zephyr is every afternoon.

ADDRESS: 6205 Franktown Road, Carson City, NV 89704

PHONE: (702) 882-1662

LINEAGE: All American

SPIRITUAL HEAD: None/all

CONTACT: Christy Z. Tews

AFFILIATION: Informally with Mountain Stream Meditation Center (Nevada City) and Spirit Rock (Woodacre, California).

ESTABLISHED: First incarnation, 1987; second, 1988; third, 1990

MEDITATION PROGRAM: Sit together one night a week (phone for time and place).

RETREATS OFFERED: Three or four nonresidential one-day retreats a year, usually led by John Travis.

Wat Buddhapavana Las Vegas

Wat Buddhapavana's Thailand-ordained monks have been serving the Las Vegas community since 1985. Americans and tourists of every nationality are cordially welcome at the new temple facility, which is open to the public Monday through Friday from 6 AM to 10 PM. Services and instruction for children are offered every Saturday and Sunday. Call for times.

ADDRESS: 2959 West Gowan Avenue, North Las Vegas, NV 89030

PHONE: (702) 648-9975

E-MAIL: Makobdee@aol.com

SPIRITUAL HEAD: Ven. Rev. Vara (Bangkok, Thailand)

Wat Buddhapavana in Las Vegas, Nevada. (Photo courtesy of Wat Buddhapavana.)

CONTACT: Rev. Narong, Resident Director
AFFILIATION: Vajiradhammapadip Temple (Mount Vernon, New York) and Wat Thai of Los Angeles (North Hollywood, California)
ESTABLISHED: 1985
FACILITIES: Urban temple.

NEW MEXICO

Albuquerque Vipassana Community (unofficial)

The Albuquerque Vipassana Community has three small sitting groups and publishes a one-page newsletter called *Grassroots*.
ADDRESS: 11577 Laurel Loop NE, Albuquerque, NM 87122
PHONE: (505) 856-5000
SPIRITUAL HEAD: Eric Kolvig, Teacher
CONTACT: Joan Granger
AFFILIATION: Autonomous
ESTABLISHED: 1996
PUBLICATIONS: *Grassroots* newsletter.

Santa Fe Vipassana Sangha

The Santa Fe Vipassana Sangha is a community of meditators who have joined together to create a support system and opportunities for practice. Since 1993 the *sangha* has grown to include several hundred people throughout northern New Mexico who participate in our twice-weekly sitting groups, discussions, and beginner instruction, as well as daylong, weekend, seven-day, and ten-day retreats. Eric Kolvig is our resident teacher.
ADDRESS: 404 Cortez Street, Santa Fe, NM 87501
PHONE: (505) 988-2560
SPIRITUAL HEADS: Eric Kolvig, Resident Dharma Teacher; Joseph Goldstein, Sharon Salzberg, Jack Kornfield
CONTACT: Joan Kaiser
AFFILIATION: Insight Meditation Society
ESTABLISHED: 1993
FACILITIES: Presently sharing Mount Cloud Zen Center.
MEDITATION PROGRAM: Twice-weekly sitting groups, discussion, and beginner instruction.

RETREATS OFFERED: Two weeklong and two weekend retreats per year.

Southwest Sangha

Southwest Sangha is located on remote high desert land near the Gila National Forest, about twenty-five miles east of Silver City, New Mexico. Through interest-free loans from generous supporters, we were able to purchase a historic rock house and chapel on four acres. Our immediate goal is to provide accommodations for intensive silent self retreats in a variety of traditions, and hope, by the year 2000, to have four *kutis* (huts) for this purpose. All accommodations, teachings, and other services are offered free of charge. We rely solely on *dana* (generosity) to support this project.
ADDRESS: Black Range Station, San Lorenzo, NM 88041
PHONE: (505) 536-9847
CONTACTS: Michael Freeman or Amy Schmidt
AFFILIATION: Autonomous
ESTABLISHED: 1995
FACILITIES: House; chapel; tent sites.
MEDITATION PROGRAM: Saturday morning sitting and walking (half-day).
RETREATS OFFERED: Self retreats only.

Taos Vipassana Sangha

We are a growing group of both new and experienced dharma students. We gather for Vipassana meditation and dharma discussion weekly with our Resident Teacher, Marcia Rose. Marcia also teaches classes in the *Brahma Vihara* practices (loving-kindness, compassion, appreciative joy, and equanimity), and in *Ripa Lila* (Movement and Stillness).
ADDRESS: HCR 74, Box 22215, El Prado, NM 87529
PHONE: (505) 751-2132

SPIRITUAL HEAD: Marcia Rose, Resident Teacher
AFFILIATION: Autonomous
ESTABLISHED: 1995
MEDITATION PROGRAM: Weekly sitting group/class, periodic six- to eight-week classes in *Brahma Vihara* and Movement and Stillness.
RETREATS OFFERED: One-day, weekend, and five- to ten-day retreats, all in the Taos area. Occasionally joined by teachers from Insight Meditation Society or Spirit Rock Center.
PUBLICATIONS: *Southwest Vipassana Newsletter* (occasional).

Wat Buddharam/Buddhist Center of New Mexico

No description available.
ADDRESS: 143-145 Madison Street Northeast, Albuquerque, NM 87108
PHONE: (505) 256-7520
FAX: Same
LINEAGE: Thai
SPIRITUAL HEAD: Buddha
CONTACT: Phramaha Sunthorn Janthawong
AFFILIATION: Autonomous
ESTABLISHED: 1994
FACILITIES: Urban Thai temple.

NEW YORK

Albany Vipassana Sangha

Our small *sangha* meets weekly for a brief reading, then an hour of meditation followed by tea and conversation. About half our members first learned Vipassana at the Insight Meditation Society (IMS) in Barre, Massachusetts. We gratefully acknowledge the inspiration of IMS in maintaining our practice energy. Other people have been drawn by our unadorned, "Western" style of practice and lively discussions. Since we have no teacher, we try to make the best use of our collective wisdom.
ADDRESS: 865 Lancaster Street, Albany, NY 12203
PHONE: (518) 453-6445
LINEAGE: Theravada Vipassana
CONTACTS: Amy Souzis or Sterling Post
AFFILIATION: Autonomous
ESTABLISHED: 1987
FACILITIES: We move among members' homes.
MEDITATION PROGRAM: Weekly meditation, reading, tea, conversation.

American Burma Buddhist Association, Inc.

The American Burma Buddhist Association was established in New York on August 21, 1981. It maintains both the Universal Peace Buddha Temple in Brooklyn, New York, and Mahasi Meditation Center in Englishtown, New Jersey. The Master Monk, Ven. Ashin Indaka, is highly proficient in Pali and has devoted years to the study of Buddhism in and outside of Burma. He teaches meditation and Buddhism at colleges, meditation centers, and elsewhere.
ADDRESS: 619 Bergen Street, Brooklyn, NY 11238
LINEAGE: Burmese Mahasi Sayadaw line
SPIRITUAL HEAD: Ven. Ashin Indaka, Master Monk
AFFILIATION: Autonomous; headquarters center.
ESTABLISHED: 1981
FACILITIES: Temple in Brooklyn, New York; meditation center at 63 Gordon's Corner Road in Englishtown, New Jersey.

Ven. Ashin Indaka, head monk at the American Burma Buddhist Association in Brooklyn, New York. (Photo by ABBA, Inc.)

American Sri Lanka Buddhist Association, Inc./New York Buddhist Vihara

The American Sri Lanka Buddhist Association, Inc., was founded by the Ven. Galboda Gnanissara Thero in 1980 in a small New York apartment. In 1986 it moved to its present location. Resident monks offer instruction in Theravada Buddhist philosophy and meditation and are available as speakers for educational and religious institutions. We welcome Buddhists of all traditions, friends of Buddhism and visitors. Instruction and guidance are given as a gift of the *Dhamma* and are offered without charge.
ADDRESS: 84-32 124th Street, Kew Gardens, New York, NY 11415
PHONE: (718) 849-2637
FAX: Same
LINEAGE: Sri Lankan Theravada
SPIRITUAL HEAD: Ven. Kurunegoda Piyatissa (Maha Thero), Resident Teacher
AFFILIATION: Autonomous
ESTABLISHED: January 1981
FACILITIES: We have a small hall for meditation and *vandana*. A temple with retreat facilities is being built.

MEDITATION PROGRAM: Weekly meditation. Call for times.

PUBLICATIONS: *New York Buddhist Newsletter, Bosat, Prince Good Speaker,* and many other publications.

Buddhist Community of Bangladesh

No description available.

ADDRESS: PO Box 831, Syosset, NY 11791

PHONE: (516) 921-5472

LINEAGE: Bengali Buddhist

SPIRITUAL HEAD: Ven. Dr. Karunananda Thero

AFFILIATION: Autonomous

ESTABLISHED: 1989

MEDITATION PROGRAM: Buddhist community services and religious and cultural services.

Rhinebeck Sitting Group

We sit weekly for forty-five minutes and then share for an hour or more. Call for details.

ADDRESS: 141 Lamoree Road, Rhinebeck, NY 12572

PHONE: (914) 876-7963

FAX: (914) 876-6369

LINEAGE: Theravada Vipassana

CONTACT: Jose Reissig

AFFILIATION: Autonomous

ESTABLISHED: 1993

FACILITIES: Artist's studio used for sittings and retreats.

MEDITATION PROGRAM: Weekly sitting.

RETREATS OFFERED: Every few months there is a one-day sit.

NORTH CAROLINA

Asheville Vipassana Group

Informal and eclectic, the Asheville Vipassana Group meets one evening a week. We sit for an hour—sometimes with *Metta* meditation—have tea and cookies, share a reading or tape and work our way into an often lively *Dhamma* discussion. Because we have no formal teacher, we share experience and insight. Members of our group also participate in other local Buddhist groups and work to foster intergroup communication and activities, such as Buddha's Day celebration. We have sponsored two highly successful community-oriented visits by the Drepung Loseling Lamas and have begun prison outreach.

ADDRESS: 34 Lawrence Place, Asheville, NC 28801

PHONE: (704) 255-7635

FAX: Same (when computer is on)

LINEAGE: Burmese/Thai Theravada

SPIRITUAL HEAD: Mahasi Sayadaw

CONTACT: David Hildebrand

AFFILIATION: Autonomous

ESTABLISHED: 1992

FACILITIES: Members' homes

MEDITATION PROGRAM: Meditation, one evening a week.

Durham Meditation Center

The Durham Meditation Center is composed of devoted practitioners who seek to integrate meditation and spiritual inquiry into our daily lives. Vipassana is the foundation for our practice along with nondual awareness practices such as Dzogchen meditation. We balance insight practice with a deepening awareness of our true nature. Meditations on lovingkindness, compassion, and forgiveness are frequently emphasized. Our approach to dharma is one of genuine spiritual inquiry and service. No special religious beliefs are necessary. Please feel free to contact us.

ADDRESS: 1214 Broad Street, #2, Durham, NC 27705

PHONE: (919) 286-4754

LINEAGE: Thai Theravada

SPIRITUAL HEAD: John Orr

AFFILIATION: Autonomous

ESTABLISHED: 1993

FACILITIES: We meet at Shambhala Center in Durham.

MEDITATION PROGRAM: Beginning and advanced meditation classes. Weekly meditation sessions.

RETREATS OFFERED: Weekend and weeklong residential retreats.

PUBLICATIONS: *Leap of Faith*, newsletter.

OHIO

Mindfulness Meditation of Columbus

In 1991 a woman who had recently transferred from San Diego and a man who had just relocated from New Jersey joined a Columbus resident to form Mindfulness Meditation of Columbus (MMOC). Four to eight meditators typically attend MMOC's weekly sittings. We also sponsor semiannual retreats led by experienced teachers such as Jacqueline Mandell, Arinna Weisman, and Bhante Gunaratana. Between retreats, members listen to tapes, read books, and attend quarterly all-day sits. Beginners welcome.

ADDRESS: 2938 Monarch Drive, Columbus, OH 43235-3209

PHONE: (614) 761-7953

FAX: (614) 761-3605

E-MAIL: wksweeny@freenet.columbus.oh.us

LINEAGE: Theravada Vipassana technique; any lineage

SPIRITUAL HEAD: Members study with a variety of teachers

CONTACTS: Ed or Nita Sweeney

AFFILIATION: Autonomous

ESTABLISHED: 1991

FACILITIES: Weekly meditations and one-day sits are held in homes. Extended retreats at a Catholic retreat facility.

MEDITATION PROGRAM: Weekly group meditation. Call for times. Beginners should come early for brief meditation instruction.

RETREATS OFFERED: Four one-day and two four-day retreats annually.

PUBLICATIONS: *Mindful Message* quarterly (upcoming events, book reviews, quotes).

OREGON

Columbia Sangha

Ours is a leaderless group that meets weekly for sittings and discussion. We encourage newcomers to first receive guidance in Vipassana meditation at a retreat led by any teacher from the Insight Meditation Society. Local instruction can be received from Robert Beatty (503-228-5982) or Janni Stark (503-231-8302).

ADDRESS: 1607 Southeast 41st Street, Portland, OR 97214

PHONE: (503) 233-2813

LINEAGE: Theravada Vipassana

CONTACT: Mike Echols

AFFILIATION: Autonomous

ESTABLISHED: 1984

FACILITIES: We meet in members' homes.

MEDITATION PROGRAM: Weekly evening sitting and discussion or taped talk.

RETREATS OFFERED: Monthly daylong sitting and walking.

Eugene Vipassana Group

"Being new to the Eugene Vipassana group, several things soon made it clear that I had found the right place. Not long after sitting, Mary's cat, 'Anicca,' placed herself quite purposefully in my lap. Obviously Anicca had found the right place, too. At the end of the meditation, the silence and clarity that I so treasure were in great abundance. People gradually began to speak as if among old friends. I was in the right place."—*Robert Bolman*

ADDRESS: 1446 Lawrence Street, Eugene, OR 97401

PHONE: (541) 683-3274

CONTACT: Mary Wall

AFFILIATION: Autonomous

ESTABLISHED: 1988

FACILITIES: Mary's house.

RETREATS OFFERED: Usually one or two times a year.

Eugene Women's Vipassana Group

Silent walking and sitting practice group. All women are welcome.

ADDRESS: 2250 Lorane Highway, Eugene, OR 97405

PHONE: (503) 683-6083

LINEAGE: Theravada Vipassana

CONTACT: Uli

AFFILIATION: Autonomous

MEDITATION PROGRAM: Vipassana meditation one evening a week. Silent walking and sitting, followed by audiotaped teachings. Call for location and details.

Heartsong Sangha

Ongoing instruction and dharma discussion focusing on the integration of heart and mind in everyday life.

ADDRESS: 1844 Southwest Castor, Portland, OR 97219

PHONE: (503) 293-6823

SPIRITUAL HEAD: Ruth Denison

CONTACT: Douglas Pullin

AFFILIATION: Autonomous

ESTABLISHED: 1995

FACILITIES: Art of Living Center (meditation hall).

MEDITATION PROGRAM: Weekly evening Vipassana and *metta* (insight and loving-kindness) practice. Call for times.

Metta Foundation

Metta Foundation supports traditional Vipassana instruction and the development and sharing of the newer practice of Insight Dialogue. Insight Dialogue is the methodical application of mindfulness to word-based communication. Weekly sessions provide training in both of these related techniques, with an emphasis on small groups and personalized instruction. Our on-line program includes regular, though unscheduled, e-mail answers to questions.

ADDRESS: 310 NW Brynwood Lane, Portland, OR 97229

PHONE: (503) 292-8550

FAX: (503) 292-4982

E-MAIL: metta@listen.com

SPIRITUAL HEAD: Gregory Kramer

AFFILIATION: Autonomous

ESTABLISHED: 1981

FACILITIES: Portland, Oregon: meditation space, library, on-line program. Santa Rosa, California: office. Ukiah, California: ranch retreat facility.

MEDITATION PROGRAM: Weekly Vipassana and Insight Dialogue practice; ongoing on-line Insight Dialogue practice.

RETREATS OFFERED: Twice yearly. Traditional Vipassana retreats conducted by resident and/or visiting teachers. Insight Dialogue retreats conducted by Gregory Kramer and Terri O'Fallon.

PUBLICATIONS: *The Dhammapada* (Parallax Press), translated by Ven. Ananda Maitreya Maha Nayaka Thera, edited by R. Kramer.

Portland Vipassana Sangha

This *sangha* is grounded in traditional Buddhism with silent sitting and walking meditation and dharma talks. One need not, however, be a capital "B" Buddhist to participate. Awakening takes many forms and there are several archetypal

Insight Dialogue

INSIGHT DIALOGUE IS AN ENGAGED MEDITATION practice that brings mindful awareness directly into communicative interactions. It can be understood as an extension of the reflective process of meditation into the world of interpersonal communication or, conversely, as an extension of ancient and modern dialogic practices— Native American Council, Quaker meeting, or Bohemian dialogue—into the sensitive inner state of meditation.

It involves deeply intentional spoken or written interchange in both face-to-face and on-line communication. Like Vipassana, upon which it is based, Insight Dialogue facilitates the arising of mental calm, heightened attention, compassion, quickness, and other subtle qualities that support the arising of wisdom.

Thoughts arise stimulated by our interchange with others or due to past conditioning. In Insight Dialogue we observe these thoughts with nonattached clarity. If we feel it is important to share them, we do so. However, even in sharing it is *Mindfulness* that predominates. The practice, over time, leads to the habit of awareness even while engaged with other people.

In its more developed stages, Insight Dialogue proceeds very much like traditional Vipassana. Meditators engaged in a dialogue observe their words as they form (just as they would observe the breath rising and falling) and extend this awareness to the body, feelings, mental states, and mind objects. Close investigation of experience is encouraged, including, for example, conditioned responses. In the context of mutual support offered in a practice community, the impermanent, unsatisfactory and nonself nature of all phenomena is examined. It is perhaps most akin to the practice of *Sampajanna* or "Clear Comprehension" as described in the *Satipatthana Sutta*, "clearly conscious in going and coming . . . eating, drinking, chewing and tasting . . . discharging excrement . . . clearly conscious in speaking and keeping silent."

Gregory Kramer and Terri O'Fallon

For more information, contact: Metta Foundation, 310 NW Brynwood Lane, Portland, OR 97229; (503) 292-8550; e-mail: metta@listen.com.

---

figures that can serve as one's chosen ideal. Members adhere to various religions and join with us for the silence, community, and depth of understanding. Teachings include mystical poetry from the world's spiritual traditions, movement, music, drumming, humor, and mindful discussion. They support a life that is mindfully awake, ethical, deeply alive, and compassionately engaged with the world.
ADDRESS: 3434 Southwest Kelly, Portland, OR 97201
PHONE: (503) 223-2214
FAX: Same
E-MAIL: rbeatty@easystreet.com

LINEAGE: Burmese Vipassana as taught by Ruth Denison.
CONTACT: Robert Beatty, Resident Director
AFFILIATION: Autonomous
ESTABLISHED: 1978
FACILITIES: Portland Dharma Center, 2514 SE Madison Street, Portland, Oregon
MEDITATION PROGRAM: Meditation and dharma talk one evening weekly; reading groups; private instruction. Call for times.
RETREATS OFFERED: Four retreats annually at Cloud Mountain Center.

Weeklong retreat in October at Hollyhock (Canada).

Salem Meditation Circle

Vipassana sitting, chanting, and *metta* practice in the Theravada tradition.
ADDRESS: 2649 Commercial Street Southeast, Salem, OR 97302
PHONE: (503) 581-1545
LINEAGE: Theravada Vipassana
CONTACTS: Bob or Martha
AFFILIATION: Autonomous
MEDITATION PROGRAM: Group meditation, one evening a week. Please call for times.

PENNSYLVANIA

Pittsburgh Vipassana Group

We are a group of individuals devoted to the practice of Insight meditation and to understanding the teachings of the Buddha and their relevance to our daily life. Meetings consist of sitting and walking meditation, taped talks, and dharma discussions. There are no chanting or devotional services and one is not required to become a Buddhist in order to meditate. All who wish to discover the path to understanding are welcome. In the tradition of the Buddha, teachings are offered at no charge; it is assumed that techniques learned in these meetings will not be used for financial gain elsewhere.

ADDRESS: PO Box 175, Library, PA 15129
PHONES: (412) 348-9116 or (412) 621-9799
CONTACTS: Mehrdad Massoudi or Janet Dtantirojanarat
AFFILIATION: Autonomous
ESTABLISHED: 1993
FACILITIES: We meet at Earth and Heaven Books, 214 South Craig Street, Pittsburgh, PA 15213.
RETREATS OFFERED: One-day mindfulness retreats. Occasional weekend retreats by various meditation teachers.

TENNESSEE

Nashville Theravada Meditation Group/Lao Buddhpathip

We are a small sitting group with a core of five to six people. We meet one evening a week in the hall of a local Lao temple for an hour of meditation followed by tea and conversation. The hall could accommodate many more people for sitting or dharma talks. Our spiritual head is Bhante U Sacca Vamsa, a Burmese monk and resident of the Lao Temple. We would like to invite other teachers in the Theravada tradition to give dharma talks and lead retreats. New meditators are always welcome.

ADDRESS: c/o Lao Buddhpathip Temple, 104 Glenmont Drive, Nashville, TN 37210
PHONE: (615) 832-8360
E-MAIL: SSitler@gnn.com
LINEAGE: Burmese. Vipassana meditation in the line of U Ba Khin as taught by S. N. Goenkaji.
SPIRITUAL HEAD: Bhante U Sacca Vamsa
CONTACTS: Stan Sitler, (615) 383-7965 or Lee Olsen, (615) 352-5249
FACILITIES: Meditation hall at Lao Buddhpathip Temple.
MEDITATION PROGRAM: Group meditation, one evening weekly. Please call for times.

TEXAS

Buu Mon Buddhist Temple

We hold weekly evening meditation in our temple. Annual ceremonies include Maghapuja, Vesak, Parent's Day, Children's Festival, Kathina, and Vietnamese New Year.

ADDRESS: 2701 Procter Street, Port Arthur, TX 77640
PHONE: (409) 982-9319
FAX: (409) 985-3749
LINEAGE: Vietnamese Theravada
SPIRITUAL HEAD: Rev. Bhante Huyen Viet, Resident Teacher
AFFILIATION: Autonomous
FACILITIES: Temple
MEDITATION PROGRAM: Weekly meditation group, one evening a week. Call for times.

Houston Buddhist Vihara

Sunday Dharma School is held once a month in Austin. We celebrate Vesak in May, Sinhalese New Year in April, Kathina in October, Western New Year (January) and Chinese New Year in February. Our meditation group meets once a week and has about fifteen members.

ADDRESS: 8727 Radio Road, Houston, TX 77075
PHONE: (713) 944-1334
FAX: (713) 943-1417
LINEAGE: Sinhalese, Vietnamese
SPIRITUAL HEADS: Ven. Kamburagalle Nanda, Ven. Basnagoda Rahula, and Ven. Ratnaguna (Buu Duc)
FACILITIES: New building on Radio Road includes library and bookstore.
MEDITATION PROGRAM: Weekly evening service with meditation; daily morning service; Sunday service and Sunday school. Call for times.
PUBLICATIONS: Annual newsletter.

Insight Meditation Dallas

Insight Meditation Dallas offers an ongoing informal program of weekly sittings, monthly dharma discussion groups, occasional days of mindfulness, community dinners, and two silent weekend retreats each year. Our purpose is to foster the practice of Vipassana (Insight) meditation in Dallas and North Texas.

ADDRESS: PO Box 781632, Dallas, TX 75378
PHONE: (214) 351-3789
E-MAIL: lvw@metronet.com
LINEAGE: Vipassana Meditation
AFFILIATION: Autonomous
ESTABLISHED: 1992
FACILITIES: Rented facilities.
MEDITATION PROGRAM: Weekly sittings, monthly dharma discussion groups.
RETREATS OFFERED: "Days of Mindfulness." Two weekend retreats yearly.
PUBLICATIONS: Occasional newsletter.

Insight Meditation Houston

Insight Meditation Houston was founded in 1985 by Rodney Smith, a teacher in-

Members of Insight Meditation Houston during a retreat at Margaret Austin Center. (Photo by Paul Hester and Lisa Carol Hardaway.)

spired by his years as a monk in Asia and as a yogi at the Insight Meditation Society in Barre, Massachusetts. After two years he left Houston, and we have had to be a light unto ourselves ever since; a circumstance not without its advantages. Each month a different moderator conducts the weekly meetings consisting of an hour's sitting and walking meditation and an hour's spoken program. Beginning classes are offered at no charge, and rural retreats are led by various visiting teachers.

ADDRESS: c/o Sieber, 3621 Georgetown, Houston, TX 77005
PHONE: (713) 667-4397
FAX: Same (call first)
LINEAGE: Theravada Vipassana
CONTACT: John Sieber
AFFILIATION: Autonomous
ESTABLISHED: 1985
FACILITIES: Retreats are held at Margaret Austin Center. Meetings at the Hospice at Texas Medical Center, Houston.
MEDITATION PROGRAM: Meditation and dharma talk one evening weekly. Free introductory classes.

RETREATS OFFERED: Three two- to seven-day retreats yearly.
PUBLICATIONS: *Insight Meditation Houston Newsletter*, every two months; *Margaret Austin Center Newsletter*, twice a year.

Lien Hoa Monastery

Now in his late fifties, our master, Ven. Dr. Khantidhammo, became a *samanera* at the age of twelve. Disciplined in both Mahayana and Theravada teachings, he studied under the Ven. Mahasi Sayadaw. Practice at Lien Hoa is Vipassana meditation and *Metta Bhavana* (loving-kindness meditation). Weekly services are conducted in Vietnamese, English, and Pali. Our congregation's ethnic makeup is 90 percent Vietnamese and Vietnamese-Americans; the other 10 percent is a mix of Chinese, Sri Lankans, and Euro-Americans. Our master speaks English well, as do many of the *sangha* at Lien Hoa.

ADDRESS: 2014 Rose Street, Irving, TX 75061

PHONES: (972) 445-1646 (Viet), (214) 832-5961 (English)
FAX: (972) 579-1527
LINEAGE: Vietnamese Theravada
SPIRITUAL HEADS: Ven. Thich Phan Nhan. Ven. Dr. Khantidhammo Mahathero, Abbot
CONTACT: Sucarita Metta Jon Maslow, Chaplain
AFFILIATION: Vietnamese Theravada Buddhist Sangha
FACILITIES: Monastery and temple.
MEDITATION PROGRAM: Vipassana meditation and *metta bhavana* (loving-kindness meditation) on Sundays.
RETREATS OFFERED: On request.

Phap Luan Buddhist Culture Center

Phap Luan Temple serves as the office of the president of the Vietnamese American Unified Buddhist Congress. Annual ceremonies include Magha Puja, Vesak Puja, Kathina, Parent Day, Vietnamese New Year, and Youth Festival.

ADDRESS: 13913 South Post Oak Road, Houston, TX 77045
PHONE: (713) 433-4364
LINEAGE: Vietnamese Theravada
SPIRITUAL HEAD: Rev. Giac Dang Jotika, Resident Director
AFFILIATION: Vietnamese American Unified Buddhist Congress
MEDITATION PROGRAM: Biweekly dharma class; Sunday Service. Call for times.
RETREATS OFFERED: One week every three months.
PUBLICATIONS: *Phap Luan Newsletter*

Southwest Vipassana Meditation Center—Dhamma Siri

For additional information, please see listing for Vipassana Meditation Center, Shelburne Falls, Massachusetts.

The Buddhist Chaplaincy Program

SINCE ONLY A HANDFUL OF PEOPLE ARE WILLING to ordain as monks or nuns nowadays, we must establish new roles to enable them to serve the community and propagate the Dhamma. Recognizing this need, our abbot, the Ven. Dr. Khantidhammo Mahathero, has established the office of chaplain at Lien Hoa Monastery in Irving, Texas.

While subordinate to *bhikkus* and *bhikkunis* (monks and nuns), chaplains in our community are authorized to perform wedding ceremonies, blessings, and funerals, and to offer teachings in the Theravada tradition as well as instruction in Vipassana meditation.

The abbot selects candidates for the chaplaincy based upon their conduct and character, their knowledge and practice of Dhamma, and their activity in the Buddhist community. Aspirants must be able to recite the traditional Pali chanting service and to memorize a number of *Sutta* texts in the original canonical language. In addition, they are expected to keep forty precepts or, more simply, to abstain from unwholesome actions of body, speech, and mind.

At this time there is no organized training program for chaplains. Selection and training are on an individual basis; from time to time, our Venerable Master looks among the congregation for chaplains to assist him.

Jon Maslow

For more information, contact: Lien Hoa Monastery, 2014 Rose Street, Irving, TX 75061; (972) 445-1646 (Viet); (214) 832-5961 (English).

ADDRESS: PO Box 190248, Dallas, TX 75219-0248
PHONES: (214) 932-7868. Course information, (214) 521-5258
FAX: (214) 522-5973
E-MAIL: vip@onramp.net
LINEAGE: Vipassana meditation in the tradition of the Burmese teacher Sayagyi U Ba Khin, as taught by S. N. Goenka
SPIRITUAL HEAD: S. N. Goenka, Vipassana International Academy
CONTACT: No resident teachers; numerous assistant teachers conduct courses on a guest basis.
AFFILIATION: Over thirty permanent centers and many associations in thirty-five countries. There is no *parent* group. Timetable, retreat format, and meditation instructions are the same at all courses worldwide.
ESTABLISHED: 1990
FACILITIES: Meditation center on twenty acres of agricultural land twenty-five miles southeast of Dallas near Kaufman, Texas; capacity: thirty-five students.
RETREATS OFFERED: Ten-day courses twice monthly; periodic introductory three-day and short children's courses; advanced eight- to ten-day courses on *Satipatthana Sutta.*

Wat Buddhavas Thai Temple

Annual ceremonies include Visakarija, Magarija, Songkran, Kathina, Asalha, New Year.
ADDRESS: 6007 Spindle Drive, Houston, TX 77086-3930
PHONES: (713) 521-5941, (713) 820-3255
FAX: (713) 931-9746
LINEAGE: Thai Theravada
SPIRITUAL HEADS: Vens. Prachan Kamchan, Phol Orapin, Ken Kamala
CONTACT: Suchada Kailey
FACILITIES: Urban temple.
MEDITATION PROGRAM: Weekly meditation and chanting. Call for times.
RETREATS OFFERED: Visakapuja and Maghapuja three-day retreats.
PUBLICATIONS: Bimonthly newsletter.

UTAH

The Last Resort

The Last Resort is located in the mountains of southern Utah about forty miles southwest of Bryce Canyon at an elevation of 8,700 feet. The purifying and majestic environment enhances spiritual practice and inner work. Part of what makes the Last Resort so special is that we limit retreat participation to eight to ten people. We celebrate the New Year with a five- or ten-day Vipassana retreat in total silence. We also utilize Iyengar

The Southwest Vipassana Meditation Center, situated on twenty acres in Kaufman, Texas. (Photo courtesy of Dhamma Siri.)

Yoga to ease muscle tension. No pleasures of this world can compare to the inner stillness of deep meditation.
ADDRESS: PO Box 707, Cedar City, UT 84721
PHONE: (801) 682-2289
LINEAGE: Burmese Theravada and Iyengar Yoga
SPIRITUAL HEADS: Pujari and Abhilasha (Ed and Barbara Keays), Resident Directors
AFFILIATION: Autonomous
ESTABLISHED: 1984
FACILITIES: Country facility for group and solitary retreats.
RETREATS OFFERED: Five- and ten-day Vipassana, Iyengar Yoga, and ten-day detoxification and rejuvenation retreats.

VERMONT

DharmaNet

E-mail teaching group and individual guidance.

ADDRESS: PO Box 78, East Middlebury, VT 05740
PHONE: (802) 388-7329
FAX: (802) 388-6406
E-MAIL: asbarker@sover.net
LINEAGE: Burmese Theravada
CONTACT: Ann Barker
ESTABLISHED: 1996

Green Mountain Sangha

Our quarterly daylong retreats are held in a rambling, remote farmhouse in the mountains, surrounded by fields and gardens. Weekly sitting is in Middlebury, in a pleasant, quiet, borrowed space. Meetings are preceded by half-hour private interviews and followed by a dharma talk or question-and-answer session. There is no charge for anything. Our teacher, Ann Barker, has studied Vipassana with Joseph Goldstein and Sharon Salzberg, and Dzogchen with Lama Khenpo Sonam, Rinpoche. Instruction is in the Burmese Theravadan tradition, although, as there are few centers nearby, practitioners of all

traditions and levels of experience are welcome.
ADDRESS: PO Box 78, East Middlebury, VT 05740
PHONE: (802) 388-7329
FAX: (802) 388-6406
E-MAIL: asbarker@sover.net
LINEAGE: Burmese: Mahasi Sayadaw and U Pandita Sayadaw
CONTACT: Ann Barker
AFFILIATION: Autonomous
ESTABLISHED: 1990
FACILITIES: Weekly meetings in borrowed space. Retreats at a mountain farmhouse.
MEDITATION PROGRAM: Weekly group meditation. Call for times.
RETREATS OFFERED: Quarterly daylong retreats.

VIRGINIA

Ekoji Buddhist Sangha Vipassana Sitting Group

This is an informal group that sits weekly for forty-five minutes to one hour. We are not affiliated with any teacher or particular Vipassana method. We sometimes have group discussions or listen to a tape after the sitting.
ADDRESS: 3411 Grove Avenue, Richmond, VA 23221
PHONE: (804) 355-6657
LINEAGE: Buddhist Theravada
CONTACT: Tom Dorfler
AFFILIATION: Autonomous
ESTABLISHED: 1995
FACILITIES: Urban meditation center.
MEDITATION PROGRAM: Weekly group meditation. Call for times.

The Lotus Meditation Group

Bhante Rahula teaches mindfulness meditation here once a month, while Ta Ma Ha Samerung (abbot of Wat Yarnna

E-mail Sangha

Known as DharmaNet, our "e-mail sangha" was established to make both general Theravada Buddhist teachings and individual guidance in reading and practice more widely available. Participants come from every corner of the country and from overseas as well. Some begin with only mild curiosity and no practical experience, while others come with extensive backgrounds in sitting meditation. (There's even an ordained monk from Southeast Asia among our correspondents.) For many who contact us, access to a teacher is not feasible.

Each person begins by reading books by Joseph Goldstein and Sharon Salzberg that introduce the basic teachings and practices of Theravada Buddhism. Even experienced meditators find these books helpful, and although the reading and particularly the practice are strongly recommended, nothing is required.

We urge our members to e-mail us with questions and feedback. Though most queries are directed toward the teacher, who in turn forwards them with responses to the entire group, communication directly among participants is also encouraged. People join regularly, so there's no need to "catch up."

The group's coordinator, Ann Barker, has been meditating since 1972, and practicing under the direction of Joseph Goldstein and Sharon Salzberg since 1986. She became a teacher in 1991. Her local "real-time" dharma group, Green Mountain Sangha, is open to anyone who is interested and able to come to weekly sittings, dharma talks, and occasional daylong and weekend retreats.

Ann S. Barker

For more information, contact: DharmaNet, PO Box 78, East Middlebury, VT 05740; (802) 388-7329; e-mail: asbarker@sover.net.

Rangsee) and Margeuritte McGee maintain the group the rest of the time. Bhante Rahula begins his sessions with a light, relaxing yoga exercise, progressing to sitting and walking meditation. At the end of the session he gives a Dhamma talk and answers questions. Our focus is on beginning and maintaining a meditation practice at home. We meet one evening per week at Wat Yarnna Rangsee in Fairfax, Virginia. Please phone for specific information.
ADDRESS: 10639 Ashby Place, Fairfax, VA 22030-5111
PHONE: (703) 591-8314
LINEAGE: Sri Lankan, Thai, and American Theravada
SPIRITUAL HEADS: Bhante Yogavacara Rahula, Tan Ma Ha Samerung
CONTACT: Margeuritte G. McGee

AFFILIATION: Bhavana Society and Wat Yarnna Rangsee
ESTABLISHED: 1994
FACILITIES: A room at Wat Yarnna Rangsee or larger room at a local community center.
MEDITATION PROGRAM: Group meditation one evening a week.

WASHINGTON

Bellingham Vipassana Meditation Group

Weekly Vipassana meditation practice, group discussion and monthly potlucks. Beginning instruction available. A group of six to twelve people meets weekly to practice and discuss chapters from Buddhist-oriented books.
ADDRESS: 115 Unity Street, Bellingham, WA 98225
PHONE: (360) 671-5993
LINEAGE: Theravada Vipassana
CONTACT: Dove
AFFILIATION: Autonomous
MEDITATION PROGRAM: Weekly Vipassana sitting meditation. Call for times.

Everett Meditation Society

Insight meditation sitting, but all traditions are welcome. Location for the first three meetings of the month is the Public Utilities District (PUD) Building; then location changes for the fourth week. Call for places and times.

ADDRESS: PUD, 2320 California Street, Everett, WA 98201

PHONE: (360) 691-4284

LINEAGE: Theravada Vipassana

CONTACT: Freda

AFFILIATION: Autonomous

FACILITIES: PUD and various other locations.

MEDITATION PROGRAM: Weekly insight (Vipassana) meditation. Please call for time and location.

Northwest Vipassana Center

Northwest Vipassana Center holds ongoing ten-day residential courses in Vipassana meditation in the tradition of Sayagyi U Ba Khin of Burma. The courses are conducted by assistant teachers appointed by S. N. Goenka of the Vipassana International Academy, Igatpuri, India. Tapes of Mr. Goenka's discourses and instructions are used. Northwest Vipassana Center is one of more than thirty centers worldwide dedicated to the practice of Vipassana in this tradition. Courses are financed solely by donations.

ADDRESS: PO Box 345, Ethel, WA 98542-0345

PHONE: (360) 978-5434

FAX: Same

E-MAIL: DhKunja@aol.com

LINEAGE: Sayagyi U Ba Khin

SPIRITUAL HEAD: S. N. Goenka

CONTACT: Scott Corley, (206) 367-9336

AFFILIATION: Vipassana International Academy, Igatpuri, India

ESTABLISHED: 1992

FACILITIES: Retreat facility on forty acres of agricultural land one hundred miles southeast of Seattle in the foothills of the Cascade Mountain Range; capacity: forty-two students.

RETREATS OFFERED: Ten-day courses twice monthly; introductory three-day and short children's courses; ten- and twenty-day advanced courses; eight-day *Satipatthana Sutta* courses.

PUBLICATIONS: Newsletter

Vipassana Group

Weekly fifty-minute group meditation, followed by tea and dharma practice-oriented group discussion. Monthly daylong retreats.

ADDRESS: 5404 Meridian Avenue North, Seattle, WA 98103

PHONE: (206) 367-0992

LINEAGE: Theravada Vipassana

CONTACT: Charlotte

AFFILIATION: Autonomous

MEDITATION PROGRAM: Weekly sittings. Call for times.

RETREATS OFFERED: Monthly daylong retreats.

Washington Buddhavanaram

Teachers Phra Amaramuni and Phra Boon lead Vipassana and Khammathana practice. Please call Monday through Saturday to verify schedule.

ADDRESS: 4401 South 360th Street, Auburn, WA 98001

PHONE: (206) 927-5408

LINEAGE: Thai Theravada

SPIRITUAL HEADS: Phra Amaramuni, Phra Boon, Resident Directors

FACILITIES: Thai ethnic temple and monastic center with facilities for solitary retreats.

MEDITATION PROGRAM: Vipassana and Khammathana practice. Please call for times.

WEST VIRGINIA

Bhavana Society

The Bhavana Society's forest monastery offers newcomers and experienced students the opportunity to study and practice Vipassana meditation under the guidance of Ven. H. Gunaratana and Bhante Yogavacara Rahula. Monthly weekend retreats are offered, along with several ten-day courses each year. The center is located on thirty forested acres about two hours from Washington, D.C. Facilities allow for training of both men and women who wish to enter the Theravada (monastic) *Sangha*, as well as laypeople wishing to practice for extended periods.

ADDRESS: Route 1, Box 218-3, High View, WV 26808

PHONE: (304) 856-3241

FAX: (304) 856-2111

LINEAGE: Sri Lankan Theravada

SPIRITUAL HEAD: Ven. Henepola Gunaratana

CONTACTS: Bhante Gunaratana, Bhante Rahula, Sister Sucinta

AFFILIATION: Autonomous

ESTABLISHED: 1983

FACILITIES: Forest retreat facility: *kutis* (huts) and shared bedrooms, new meditation hall.

RETREATS OFFERED: Weekend and ten-day retreats

PUBLICATIONS: *Mindfulness in Plain English*, Ven. H. Gunaratana. *Bhavana Society Newsletter.*

CANADA

ALBERTA

Bow Valley Sangha

Meditation can help one let go of the suffering that comes from worry, agitation, and rumination. It can also be a spiritual pathway to realizing the interconnectedness of all beings. The group welcomes those who are simply interested in calming their minds and coping with agitation, as well as those who seek to nurture their spirituality. Although rooted in Buddhism, the practice is consistent with

A kuti (meditation hut) in the woods at Bhavana Society in High View, West Virginia. (Photo courtesy of Bhavana Society.)

Bhante Gunaratana and resident monks and nuns in the meditation hall at Bhavana Society. (Photo courtesy of Bhavana Society.)

any spiritual tradition and acceptable to those without one.

ADDRESS: Box 3285, Canmore, AB T0L 0M0

PHONE: (403) 678-2034

LINEAGE: Sri Lankan Theravadan

SPIRITUAL HEAD: Michele Calvery (Her teacher is Ven. Piyadassi Nyaka Thera.)

CONTACT: Mary Dumka

AFFILIATION: Autonomous

ESTABLISHED: 1994

FACILITIES: Private home.

MEDITATION PROGRAM: Meets weekly for sitting meditation, sharing, teaching. Precepts recitation monthly.

RETREATS OFFERED: Occasional one-day and weekend retreats.

Buddhist Vihara Association of Alberta

No description available.

ADDRESS: 4211 110 Street, Edmonton, AB T6J 2S9

PHONE: (403) 435-8890

LINEAGE: Sri Lankan Theravada

SPIRITUAL HEAD: Ven. Seela Vimala

CONTACT: Mr. Lakshman Samarasinghe, President

AFFILIATION: Autonomous

ESTABLISHED: 1982

FACILITIES: Space rented as needed at Vietnamese temple.

MEDITATION PROGRAM: We meet one Sunday afternoon a month for group meditation; children's program; open to the public.

RETREATS OFFERED: Retreats with visiting monks three or four times yearly.

Calgary Theravada Meditation Society

The Calgary Theravada Meditation Society is a Vipassana (Insight) meditation sitting group that meets twice a month. All experienced meditators are welcomed (no instruction is provided). Each session starts with some chanting followed by sitting meditation and a Dhamma talk. Activities include lectures from visiting monks, one-day workshops, and extended three- to ten-day residential Vipassana retreats.

ADDRESS: 3212 6th Street Southwest, Calgary, AB T2S 2M3

PHONE: (403) 243-3433

FAX: Same

LINEAGE: Theravada

CONTACT: Shirley June Johannesen, Resident Teacher

AFFILIATION: Autonomous

ESTABLISHED: 1975

FACILITIES: Central urban rented facility; retreats at various rented locations.

RETREATS OFFERED: One- to ten-day residential retreats.

Light of Dharma

No description available.

ADDRESS: 15111 Rio Terrace Drive, Edmonton, AB T5R 5M6

LINEAGE: Theravada Abhidharma

CONTACT: The president

ESTABLISHED: 1983

FACILITIES: Private home.

MEDITATION PROGRAM: Lectures, when available.
RETREATS OFFERED: Occasional
PUBLICATIONS: Newsletter

Stretch Awareness, Inc.

Shirley June Johannesen teaches Vipassana meditation, emphasizing the "noting" technique adapted from Burmese meditation master Mahasi Sayadaw. She offers twenty-five years of teaching experience in Vipassana meditation and is an internationally known specialist in therapeutic yoga, stretch, relaxation, and stress management. She conducts weekly classes in both disciplines and offers group and private instruction. A partial client list includes amateur and professional athletic associations, health professionals, corporations, and educational institutions. She has produced a video, *Stretch Breathe Relax,* and two audiotapes, *Relaxation Circle* and *Meditation Circle,* which assist and enhance the in-depth instruction she provides in her classes.
ADDRESS: 3212 6th Street, Southwest, Calgary, AB T2S 2M3
PHONE: (403) 243-3433
FAX: Same
LINEAGE: Burmese Vipassana (Mahasi Sayadaw), Hatha Yoga
SPIRITUAL HEAD: Shirley June Johannesen, Resident Director
AFFILIATION: Autonomous
ESTABLISHED: 1974
MEDITATION PROGRAM: Weekly classes.
RETREATS OFFERED: One-, three-, five-, and ten-day silent retreats.
PUBLICATIONS: Video- and audiotapes.

Vipassana Meditation Center

No description available.
ADDRESS: 616 24th Avenue SW, #11, Calgary, AB T2S 0K6

PHONE: (403) 244-0165
LINEAGE: Burmese Theravada as taught by S. N. Goenka
SPIRITUAL HEAD: U Ba Khin Sayadaw
CONTACT: Ms. Sharon Reed
AFFILIATION: Autonomous
RETREATS OFFERED: Yes

BRITISH COLUMBIA

Birken Forest Monastery

Two forest monks living in seclusion. Experienced meditators welcome. Write ahead. Very little accommodation. Practice must be independent.
ADDRESS: PO Box 46, Mt. Currie, BC V02 2K0
LINEAGE: Thai Forest, Ajahn Chah
SPIRITUAL HEAD: Sona Bhikkhu, Resident Director
AFFILIATION: Autonomous
ESTABLISHED: 1994
FACILITIES: Minimal—two trailers.
MEDITATION PROGRAM: Custom-made.

Vipassana Foundation

Vipassana meditation in the tradition of U Ba Khin of Burma is taught at ten-day residential retreats. S. N. Goenka is the teacher, with courses run by his assistants. Retreats are held at camps in British Columbia and Alberta several times a year.
ADDRESS: 806 West 19th Avenue, Vancouver, BC V5Z 1X3
PHONE: (604) 879-9791
WWW: http://rampages.onramp.net/~vip
LINEAGE: Burmese Theravada, U Ba Khin tradition
SPIRITUAL HEAD: S. N. Goenka
CONTACT: Sheldon Klein
AFFILIATION: Vipassana International Academy
ESTABLISHED: 1982

FACILITIES: Associated with center in Washington State.
RETREATS OFFERED: Local ten-day retreats in British Columbia and Alberta.

Vipassana Foundation

For additional information please see listing for Vipassana Meditation Center in Shelburne Falls, Massachusetts.
ADDRESS: 80 High Street, Victoria, BC V8Z 5C7
PHONES: Victoria, (604) 479-6641/Vancouver, (604) 264-7637
LINEAGE: Vipassana meditation in the tradition of Burmese teacher Sayagyi U Ba Khin, as taught by S. N. Goenka
SPIRITUAL HEAD: S. N. Goenka of Vipassana International Academy near Bombay, India
CONTACT: No resident teachers. Numerous assistant teachers conduct courses on a guest basis.
AFFILIATION: Over thirty permanent centers and many associations in thirty-five countries. There is no *parent* group; timetable, retreat format, and meditation instructions are the same at all courses worldwide.
ESTABLISHED: 1982
FACILITIES: Rented sites; seeking permanent facility.
MEDITATION PROGRAM: Introductory evenings for the public; weekly group meditation.
RETREATS OFFERED: Ten-day courses in British Columbia and Alberta several times a year; periodic one-day self courses for experienced students in six cities.

Westcoast Dharma Society

Registered charity. No description available.
ADDRESS: 2224 Larch Street, Vancouver, BC V6K 3P7

PHONE: (604) 731-5469

E-MAIL: marsha.trew@ubc.ca

SPIRITUAL HEAD: Teachers are primarily from Insight Meditation Society and Spirit Rock.

CONTACT: Linda McDonald

FACILITIES: Tape lending library.

RETREATS OFFERED: Six to ten nonresidential retreats yearly.

PUBLICATIONS: Newsletter twice yearly.

ONTARIO

Arrow River Community Center

A Buddhist forest monastery offering a traditional monastic lifestyle and periodic formal retreats. Founded in 1975 as a lay meditation center by Kema Ananda. The resident *bhikkhu*, Punnadhammo, is a former student of Kema's who took ordination in Thailand in 1990.

ADDRESS: Box 2, RR7, Site 7, Thunder Bay, ON P7C 5V5

PHONE: (807) 933-4434

E-MAIL: stumuirhead@msn.com

LINEAGE: Thai Forest (Ajahn Chah)

SPIRITUAL HEAD: Punnadhammo Bhikkhu, Resident Director

AFFILIATION: Autonomous

ESTABLISHED: 1975; 1996 as a monastery.

FACILITIES: Five *kutis*, meditation hall, workshop, sauna.

MEDITATION PROGRAM: *Anapanasati* and Vipassana primarily; also *metta, asubha,* and so on as required.

RETREATS OFFERED: By arrangement—anything from weekend to three months.

PUBLICATIONS: *Northern Aurora*

Buddha Sasana Yeiktha of Ontario

Buddha Sasana Yeiktha is an international meditation center in the lineage of the late Ven. Mahasi Sayadaw and under the spiritual guidance of Ven. Sayadaw U

Pandita. A rural retreat facility, the Center welcomes meditators (both individuals and groups) to practice at their own convenience rather than having to wait for a scheduled formal retreat. However, well-known senior meditation masters (ordained *sangha*) are invited to conduct organized retreats from time to time and, for those unable to come to the country property, daylong Vipassana sittings are held once a month at our Toronto branch. Open to all.

ADDRESS: RR 1, Severn Bridge, ON P0E 1N0

PHONE: (705) 689-5642

FAX: Same

LINEAGE: Mahasi Vipassana Meditation

SPIRITUAL HEAD: Ven. Sayadaw U Panditabhivamsa

CONTACT: Sr. Khema Nandi, Resident Director

AFFILIATION: Autonomous

ESTABLISHED: 1994

FACILITIES: Rural live-in facilities for on-site retreats.

MEDITATION PROGRAM: Daily meditation and chanting.

RETREATS OFFERED: One-day city retreats; weekends; five- and ten-day retreats; open guided individual retreats.

Buddhist Meditation Hermitage

Mostly Indian, Bangladeshi, and Pakistani membership. Plan to build a temple. We walk for world peace. Donations to food banks. Social welfare work. Meditation and some counseling, mostly to the immigrant community, responding to questions about Buddhism.

ADDRESS: 3 Brimley Road, #405, Scarborough, ON M1M 3W2

PHONE: (416) 269-1056

FAX: Same

LINEAGE: Bangladesh. Ancient Theravada.

SPIRITUAL HEAD: Sumano Muni

CONTACT: Soma Kanti Barul

AFFILIATION: Autonomous

ESTABLISHED: 1992

FACILITIES: Meditation room.

RETREATS OFFERED: Weekends

PUBLICATIONS: *Buddhist Thought and Meditation in the Nuclear Age, Buddhism and Science, In Quest of Truth*, a Buddhist novel (all by Soma Kanti Barul); "Life of the Buddha," a video.

Burmese Buddhist Association of Toronto/Maha Dhammika Temple

No description available.

ADDRESS: 435 Hopewell Avenue, Toronto, ON M6E 2S4

PHONE: (416) 785-7497

FAX: Same. Call first.

LINEAGE: Burmese

CONTACTS: Ven. U Nanda Vumsa/Ven. U Nanda, Resident Teachers

AFFILIATION: Overseas Chinese Burmese temple.

ESTABLISHED: 1988–1989

FACILITIES: One building with monk's residence. Two shrine rooms.

MEDITATION PROGRAM: Sunday prayer meeting with meditation and Dhamma talk. Question-and-answer period.

Insight Retreats

Insight Retreats organizes meditation courses in southern Ontario, led by Norman Feldman and other invited, internationally known teachers in the Insight Meditation (Vipassana) tradition. Retreats are held in silence. The daily schedule includes sitting and walking meditation with instructions, a dharma talk, and individual or small group meetings with the teacher(s). The retreats are suitable for beginning and experienced meditators alike. Weekly classes are also held in Lindsay, Ontario.

ADDRESS: 128 Durham Street West, Lindsay, ON K9V 2R5

PHONE: (705) 799-6992
LINEAGE: Insight Meditation. Theravada tradition.
SPIRITUAL HEADS: Norman Feldman and guest teachers
CONTACT: Ellie Stewart
AFFILIATION: Autonomous
MEDITATION PROGRAM: Weekly classes.
RETREATS OFFERED: Silent Vipassana retreats.

Toronto Insight Meditation Center

Open to anyone willing to accept meditative training and rules.
ADDRESS: 54 Millwood Road, Toronto, ON M4S 1J7
PHONE: (416) 932-0327
FAX: Same
SPIRITUAL HEAD: Alan James
CONTACT: Paul McRae, Resident Director
AFFILIATION: The House of Inner Tranquillity (The Aukan Trust) in England
ESTABLISHED: 1988
FACILITIES: Residential facility in large three-story house.
MEDITATION PROGRAM: Weekly sittings, tape or study evenings.
RETREATS OFFERED: Weekend or longer, several times a year.

Vipassana Meditation Group

No description available.
ADDRESS: c/o Karen Soltys, 1329 Leighs Bay Road, Sault Ste. Marie, ON P6A 6K4
PHONE: (705) 949-9629
LINEAGE: Theravada Vipassana
CONTACT: Karen Soltys
AFFILIATION: Autonomous
ESTABLISHED: 1995
FACILITIES: Private home.
MEDITATION PROGRAM: Group meditation, last Friday evening of the month.
RETREATS OFFERED: One-day silent retreat each season.

PUBLICATIONS: *Spirit Messenger Newsletter*, biannually.

Westend Buddhist Center

Westend Buddhist Center was established in 1992. People from all walks of life visit the center, which is open to everyone. It is a place of Theravada tradition. A number of well-trained monks of different countries reside here. Everyone speaks several languages in addition to English. Open to all people regardless of their faith.
ADDRESS: 1569 Cormack Creek, Mississauga, ON L5E 2P8
PHONE: (905) 891-8412
FAX: Same
LINEAGE: Theravada tradition
SPIRITUAL HEAD: Rev. B. Mudita
CONTACT: Rev. K. Dhammawasa
AFFILIATION: Autonomous
ESTABLISHED: 1992
MEDITATION PROGRAM: Once a week for the public.
RETREATS OFFERED: Once a month.
PUBLICATIONS: *The Wheel*, issued bi-monthly.

QUÉBEC

Fondation Vipassana/Eastern Canada Vipassana Foundation

For additional information, please see listing for Vipassana Meditation Center in Shelburne Falls, Massachusetts.
ADDRESS: C.P. 32083 Les Atriums, Montreal, QC H2L 4Y5
PHONE: (514) 481-3504
FAX: (514) 879-8302
LINEAGE: Vipassana meditation in the tradition of Burmese teacher Sayagyi U Ba Khin, as taught by S. N. Goenka
SPIRITUAL HEAD: S. N. Goenka of Vipassana International Academy near Bom-

bay, India. Numerous assistant teachers conduct courses on a guest basis.
AFFILIATION: Over thirty permanent centers and many associations in thirty-five countries. There is no *parent* group.
ESTABLISHED: 1981
FACILITIES: Rented sites. Seeking permanent site.
MEDITATION PROGRAM: Timetable, retreat format, and meditation instructions are the same at all courses worldwide.
PUBLICATIONS: Books and cassettes are not sold at North American centers or course sites, in order to keep the meditation environments free from any commercialism.

International Buddhist Meditation Center of Canada

The International Buddhist Meditation Center of Canada presents a series of sessions aimed at those who are serious about learning how Buddhist teachings may be applied to their daily lives. Probing discussions and guided meditation explore such subjects as how emotions like anger and fear arise and how we can free ourselves from their harmful effects; various ways to eliminate stress, tension, anxiety, worries, desire, addictions, and so forth; and the root causes of these problems, their effects, and how to recognize and eliminate them. Although there is no charge for these teachings, donations are gratefully accepted.
ADDRESS: 6926 St-Vallier, Montreal, QC H2S 2P9
PHONE: (514) 948-3950
FAX: (514) 879-8329
E-MAIL: ibmcc@colba.net
SPIRITUAL HEAD: Dhamma-Rakita, Resident Director
AFFILIATION: Autonomous
ESTABLISHED: 1995
FACILITIES: Three rooms.
RETREATS OFFERED: Short, long, group,

or individual training. Daily, weekly, longer courses.

SASKATCHEWAN

Insight Meditation Group

Our group meets regularly one evening a week throughout the year. We begin with a forty-five-minute sitting and usually follow it with dharma discussion. We have a library of taped dharma talks, which anyone who is interested can borrow. A small discussion group meets for an hour on alternate Sundays.

ADDRESS: 2672 Robinson Street, Regina, SK S4T 2R4

PHONE: (306) 352-5691

SPIRITUAL HEAD: Sharda Rogell, Guiding Teacher

CONTACT: Dana White, Group Facilitator

AFFILIATION: Autonomous

ESTABLISHED: 1993

RETREATS OFFERED: Sharda Rogell teaches a four-day retreat each June. Informal one-day retreats are organized when group members wish to have them.

PART TWO

Mahayana

The Path of Compassion

Mahayana: The Natural Current of Compassion

BONNIE MYOTAI TREACE

A FRIEND OF MINE ONCE SUMMARIZED THE MA-hayana approach to Buddhism by telling a story about his lifeguard training. He said he'd asked his instructor what he should do if there were several people drowning at once. Whom should he save first? The youngest or the oldest? The women or the men? The instructor didn't bat an eye. Solidly and firmly he answered, "Save 'em all!"

"But what if that's impossible? What if it can't be done?"

"Save 'em all!" the instructor repeated with such quiet force that the dilemma was resolved, not rationally perhaps, but in a way that opened my friend's mind to the reality of his new work.

This vital shot of refreshed commitment to the "whole catastrophe" is in a sense implicit in the Buddha's original teachings. Periodically in Buddhism's history, however, that vitality has dulled into abstract ideas about the nature of reality instead of its direct and immediate expression. To be sure, during the lifetime of any religion's founder the spiritual practice evinces a special integrity and wholeheartedness that seem to dissipate after his or her death. As generations pass, power struggles flare up among those who differ about how the original teachings should be interpreted and implemented. The religion loses its power to transform as it becomes locked into

ideology and structure. About five hundred years after the Buddha's death, a wave of freshness began to re-emerge. This fresh blast of energy came to be known as the Mahayana tradition. Offering a paradoxical twist on tradition itself, Mahayana was that eternal rascal impulse to cut to the quick, insisting that each practitioner realize not just the doctrine, but the uncodifiable spirit of the teaching as well.

What is the "quick," the nerve-rich center of Buddhism? There is a moment described in a Zen *koan* when a student who has just had a deep insight into reality is instructed by his teacher to "Go out now. Don't hide yourself in the mountains or the temple. Build a big boat and carry people out of their suffering."

Build a big boat. Over and over again in so many contexts, that is the instruction: open up your heart-mind to the whole thing, take care of it all. That is the basic challenge Mahayana Buddhism emphasizes. "Be big," the teachers intone, "because that is who you really are: the whole catastrophe is nothing other than you."

"Fine idea, but how do I do that?" the student asks. As we explore Mahayana as a path of practice, that question is at the core. As we look briefly at how Mahayana is distinguished historically and philosophically from other forms of Buddhism, the central issue that needs to be held close to the heart is: "How does it live?"

Sensei Bonnie Myotai Treace, Vice-Abbot of Zen Mountain Monastery in Mt. Tremper, New York. (Photo courtesy of Dharma Communications.)

Bodhisattvas: Lives of Mystical Giving

Mahayana means "Great Vehicle," which indicates that this is a lifeboat so big that no one is excluded, smart or dumb, good or bad. Everybody is free, although few of us realize it; everyone has ultimate responsibility, although we deny it. Those who recognize that responsibility to all of life and live their lives in complete, unrestricted responsiveness to the suffering of the world are the truly free. They are called bodhisattvas.

The ideal of bodhisattvahood is daunting for most of us. Offered as inspiration to help us get over our self-preoccupation in all its subtle forms and dedicate ourselves to lives of compassion, the bodhisattva ideal was a reply to the earlier Buddhist ideal of the arhat. The paradigm of the arhat is often critiqued as representing the tendency to seek release from the painful round of cyclic existence (*samsara*) for oneself alone, with little interest in imparting strength to others. Mahayana, in what has been called one of the slickest PR moves in history, is credited historically with framing this individualistic strain of Buddhism as hierarchically inferior to the greater insight and resolve of the bodhisattva, and then dubbing the largely monastic Theravadan tradition *Hinayana* (Lesser Vehicle).

Mahayana's compassionate resolve is known as *bodhicitta*, or "wisdom mind," and reflects not so much a change from the doctrines that preceded it, as a significant shift in emphasis. Early Buddhism recognized the value of providing a place of refuge where its practitioners would be free from social, political, economic, and even religious demands, and emphasized the importance of leaving the attachments of the world. As Mahayana began to emerge, the time for a more altruistic orientation had arrived. This created a very different attitude toward the world in several respects. For the bodhisattva, freedom was not freedom *from* the world, but freedom *within* the world. Therefore, as the teaching of Buddhism increasingly came to be understood not as an escape into an ineffable otherworldliness, but rather a complete "embeddedness" within all things, lay Buddhists practicing in the context of their daily responsibilities were recognized as having an important place in the tradition. Whereas previously the bias had been distinctly monastic, with male monks regarded as the only ones with any chance of realizing enlightenment, suddenly the envelope was stretching—and stretching dramatically.

Mahayana doctrine implied a greater tolerance for a broader range of religious expression, which enabled it to assimilate into diverse cultures, spreading from India to Nepal, Tibet, China, Korea, Japan, and now the Americas and Europe. In each culture, the tradition responded to the conditions in which it found itself, changing its clothes, taking on the traits and habits of the people there. Like water, it took the form of whatever container it was poured into, yet always remained water. When Mahayana reached Tibet it incorporated the core monasticism of the Theravadan tradition that was already there and also, eventually, assimilated aspects of the native (*Bon*) religion involving esoteric rituals and magic formulas. In China, it melded aspects of native Taoist and Confucianist religions into the mix before evolving into the practice-oriented *Ch'an* (or Zen) sect with its unique emphasis on meditation. In several countries, *Ch'an* adopted a particularly devotional aspect from the indigenous religions it encountered, further changing the form of the practice.

Though it has been slow to respond to the reality of

women practitioners, often excluding them from practice opportunities or creating hierarchies based on gender, Mahayana Buddhism has in recent years started to release the male bias it has shared with other major world religions. As it continues to evolve, Mahayana is gradually developing expressions that are more sensitive to disadvantaged peoples living in cultures of domination, who may not relate readily to Buddhism's monastic injunction to leave behind material possessions that they have by definition been excluded from acquiring. In recognizing the validity of these various new forms of lay practice, as well as the importance of centers devoted to a singularly intentioned monastic life, Mahayana continues the seamless process of transforming human society.

The bodhisattva's radical, all-inclusive love is not the selective sentiment of emotional attachment, but arises instead from wisdom, a nonmediated perception of the nature of the self and the universe. To understand how this wisdom becomes inseparably identified with the liberating, completely unhindered compassion of the bodhisattva, we need to explore what Mahayana means by "wisdom," and to see how it differs from any ideas we harbor about truth or matured knowledge. And we need to reflect, again, on what this has to do with how we understand our own lives. In Mahayana that constant collapse back to the one reading this, is key. If we appreciate nothing else about it, we should comprehend its unremitting imperative to close the gap, the distances we create with our minds. "Maybe we should make No-Gap T-shirts," my Zen teacher once said after seeing a Gap ad on TV. How, indeed, does this teaching become the clothes we wear, the breath we breathe? Mahayana teaches that the life of mystical giving cannot be other than *this* life; but then it presses further—what exactly *is* this life?

The Wisdom of Emptiness

The spiritual conquerors have proclaimed *sunyata* to be the exhaustion of all theories and views; those for whom *sunyata* is itself a theory, they declare incurable.

Nagarjuna

Sunyata is probably the most important teaching of the Mahayana tradition. Though earlier philosophical schools in India had debated it for many years before the Buddha ever began to teach, the Mahayanists in a certain sense "popped" the term and pressed it to its fullest. *Sunyata* is not easily translatable. It is derived from the root *su*, which means "to swell" and which has two distinct implications: hollow or empty, and also full, like the womb of a pregnant woman. We can see both of these meanings in the way Mahayana uses the term. In the first sense, the hollowness or "emptiness" (as the term is generally translated) points to the fact that nothing has a fixed, inherent self-nature. In the second sense, there is the connotation of limitless possibilities. The two implications reflect each other: because there are no permanent characteristics, there is an infinite diversity of possible phenomena. As the essence of reality, *sunyata* encompasses all dualities; self and other, nirvana and *samsara*, being and nonbeing, duality and nonduality. When Mahayana's uncompromising logic is brought to bear on *sunyata*, all separation is seen through, and a clarity beyond dualistic thinking is intuited.

The wisdom that constitutes enlightenment is called *prajna*. It has no content and can't be attained or grasped. *Prajna* is often described as "knowing in which there is no distinction between the knower, that which is known, and the act of knowing." *Prajna* as a concept was developed in Mahayana through its vast *prajnaparamita* literature and presented "operationally" as a kind of goal.

The most important thing for us to apprehend about *prajna* is its ungraspability; if you understand it, that's not it. Of course, it follows equally that what is understood is also not *other* than it. There is no separation. A second aspect that should be understood is that *prajna*, in its wholeness, heals the continual yearning, seeking, and discomfort of the mind. When the mind stops objectifying itself in the perpetually exhausting effort to quell its anxiety over its own formlessness, there is what is called an opening. The mind notices its own nonlosing nature—that there is absolutely nothing lacking and never has been. Like the ugly duckling discovering the swan he always was, something changes, yet everything is precisely the same. He's got the same old honk, the same funny way of walking, but having realized his true swan nature, he "gets it" that there is nothing lacking in his capacity to be himself. When Mahayana speaks of wisdom, therefore, there is much more implied than what we ordinarily associate with the word.

Thus nondual perception and action are supported by *sunyata* (emptiness), realized as *prajna* (wisdom), and function as *karuna* (compassion). The ordinary way of thinking about spiritual practice (that it *leads* to spiritual realization, or that one does it in order to arrive at some special state of grace or "enlightenment") takes a radical turn. For the Mahayanist, practice *is* enlightenment, enlightenment *is* practice, *samsara is* nirvana, and nirvana *is samsara*. At the point in its evolution where practice and enlightenment became identified with each other, a vigorous and joyful spiritual training for its own sake began to attract a host of followers.

Practice Paths

How do you teach what fundamentally can't be taught but can only be realized by oneself? How can students reach this place they have never been apart from? The path and the path's fruition are what is called *upaya,* or "skill in means," and during the first several hundred years of its unfolding, Mahayana thinkers treated aspiring bodhisattvas to an unprecedented creative flowering of written teachings on how to realize the Way. As Mahayana Buddhism became more systematic, two main philosophical schools began to hold sway: the *Madhyamaka* and the *Yogacara*. The old debates were renewed under new rubrics: what is the relative importance of meditative experience versus intellectual acuity in realms of nonduality? A fresh wave of the Buddha's teaching rolled in again with the beginnings of *Ch'an* as a distinct tradition. (*Zen* is Japanese for *Ch'an*, which in turn is a transliteration of the Sanskrit word *Dhyana*, meaning "meditation.")

The Rise of Zen

Zen traces its history back to an Indian monk named Bodhidharma, who sailed into the heady scholastic Buddhism of China and quite literally turned his back on it. Upon arriving, Bodhidharma was challenged by Buddhist practitioners and supporters to present his understanding. When he saw that they were unable to grasp the directness of his teaching, he entered a cave and sat facing the wall in deep meditation for nine years, until a student arrived who could realize his meaning. Mind-to-mind, heart-to-heart, Zen teachers transmit to their students what cannot be transmitted or received. Bodhidharma is said to have offered the following definition of Zen:

> Zen is a special transmission
> outside of scriptures
> It doesn't rely on words or letters
> It is a direct pointing to the human heart
> and the realization of Buddhahood.

In Zen we say that to practice means to do. To train means to do. To enter Zen training is to do it: body and mind, breath after breath. It involves the direct study of one's own heart/mind through the development of concentration and awareness. The Sixth Ancestor in the lineage of Chinese masters who realized this "special transmission" once said that Zen was only for realizing the imperturbability of our original nature. *Zazen* (*za*, "sitting"; *zen*, "meditation") is to sit in reality, to sit down in your life itself.

I'll often point out when giving instruction to beginners that it is exactly because it can be done in *any* way that we do it precisely *this* way. Don't change the channel, don't move away at the first sign of discomfort. Just sit down in your life as it is. *This* life! *This* moment! So, during a period of *zazen*, we sit still. Completely still during *zazen*, then completely moving during the walking practice. It has to do with that completeness. It has to do with not being subject to every passing thing, whether it's an itch on the nose or the mood of a coworker or lover. To believe in Buddhism, to understand its principles, doesn't change the way life gets lived. To practice the details does. Suddenly we stop rejecting life, or denying what is real, and begin to settle into the moment. If you miss the moment, you miss your life. So, in Zen training you'll find an emphasis on detail, on commitment, on actually doing the practice rather than talking about it. When a teaching center is alive, the discipline takes place in a context that is palpably human, trustworthy, and generous.

By the time *Ch'an* peaked in China during its Golden Age (618–907 CE), five sects had developed and were going strong. Only two survived, and are popularly known today by their Japanese names, Soto and Rinzai. The distinctions that originally characterized the two schools are much less relevant today, as both have "cross-fertilized" at various points in their history and have adopted many common *upaya*. In general, Soto emphasizes the practice of *shikantaza*, or "just sitting," in which there is no striving whatsoever and the sitter embodies the nonduality of practice and enlightenment. Rinzai training characteristically involves bringing students to a charged state of wakefulness in which dualistic thinking can be blown apart through the use of a *koan*. A koan is a statement or question that contains an apparent paradox. Each koan, however, drives the student to realize the fundamental koan, which is "Who am I?" Instead of approaching it through intellectual thought, which doesn't reach the matter, students are pressed to "Be the koan," to identify with it completely.

The only way to see a koan, or to realize *shikantaza*, is to forget the self. When a student receives instruction in the practice of *zazen*, the specifics of forming a posture that will be most comfortable for long periods of sitting are explained. So is the way of working with the breath and with the thoughts that distract one's concentration. Only when a student's concentration is such that all self-consciousness falls away and there is single-pointedness of mind can a breakthrough occur. As habits and preoccupations are released, one becomes, simply and completely, the moment itself. Life is lived intimately. This is our birthright, this life of no-gap, of intimacy. It is worth paying attention to.

Because of the strength of our habitual ways of using the mind, Zen has developed particularly intensive, even strenuous methods of training in which students sit together and practice in silence for extended periods of time. During weeklong *sesshin* (meditation intensives), students keep their eyes lowered, agree not to read or speak except with the teacher, and rise before dawn for days of fully scheduled practice—*zazen*, liturgy, meals, silent work, more *zazen*—until late into the night. To be sure, there are moments in the training when it is hard to remember what motivated you to do the surprisingly hard work of really being yourself. Then perhaps a leaf falls, resting easily on the air, responding to the currents, landing. No struggle, no complaint, even a bit of a dance. How does Mahayana live? To "save them all" we must be willing to be saved *by* them all.

Front, back
Front, back
Falling autumn leaves

· · ·

Sensei Bonnie Myotai Treace is a successor in the Mountains and Rivers order. Vice-Abbess of Zen Mountain Monastery and primary teacher at the Zen Center of New York City, she began full-time monastic training with Daido Loori Roshi in 1983.

Zen Mountain

JOHN KAIN

✸

A RED-TAILED HAWK IS RIDING THE WARM, strong wind, eyeing the sage for prairie dogs and field mice. My Toyota truck is packed with everything I own, my possessions stripped to a minimum by my divorce and an obsessive urge to travel lightly, as if the weight of a bed, stereo, books, is equal to the weight of recent sorrow. Wind is a Wyoming ritual and seems a natural companion to the rapid dismantling of my life—an affair, divorce, anger, a bit too much bourbon, a desperate spiral down or up or sideways. Confusion.

As things got messy I began sitting *zazen* on my own in Kansas City. My wife and I had moved there from the West Coast because of her job. Our marriage was submerging into a cloudy pool of discomfort, a time of inarticulateness and the start of a marauding hunch that I needed some sort of realignment with the world.

I grew up near San Francisco in the echo of the Beats, latched on to the literary Zen of Kerouac, Snyder, Ginsberg, Whalen. I read R. H. Blythe, D. T. Suzuki, Watts, Shunryu Suzuki. I was drawn to the bare-bones, earthy mysticism of Zen. I'd not been raised in any religious tradition, my parents being "New Agers" before the term was coined: proudly spiritual but anti-institution. With my unraveling I turned to the only thing that felt real to me: Zen. But I needed more than just words. I began to sit. Early in the morning while my wife slept, I'd read a chapter of Suzuki's *Zen Mind, Beginner's Mind* and then sit *zazen* for twenty minutes.

A move to Wyoming to study for my master's degree put the ending touches on my marriage. With my degree completed, divorce papers filed, and no real direction, I decided to make a drastic leap and move to New York City to live the life of a struggling urban writer. But my fledgling Zen practice, along with recent events, had begun to raise deep questions about how I viewed the world, how I viewed myself. In short, I was weary of the stupefying ache and stumble that was passing for my existence. I wanted to strengthen my *zazen*, sit with other people, and get deeper into Zen Buddhism.

I found an ad in a Buddhist magazine for a Zen monastery that was offering monthlong retreats. It was located just two and a half hours from New York, in the Catskill Mountains. The thought of a month of Zen practice before disappearing into the tumult of the city was enticing. I called the monastery, was interviewed and eventually accepted for a month's residency, which included one *sesshin* retreat. This was what I was after— hour after hour of *zazen*.

The hawk screeches and dives, rising with a prairie dog in its talons. I steer east, feeling a little too much like prey, a little too vulnerable, nervous about the monastery and the immensity of New York City. A strong wind is blowing.

The main building at Zen Mountain Monastery rises out of a small bluff that is part of the southern foot of

The zendo *at Zen Mountain Monastery.* (Photo courtesy of Dharma Communications.)

Tremper Mountain, a flat-top peak covered with pine and mixed deciduous forest. The large, four-story, blue-stone and wood-trimmed structure is the first thing you see as you drive though the monastery's front gate. A designated nature sanctuary, its 230 acres encompass forests, meadows, streams, and ponds. Tucked within the property are residential cabins, a workshop, a media production building, and a large garden.

The monastery was originally a Benedictine mountain "getaway" for young men. It was built in the late 1920s by Norwegians who gathered most of the materials from Tremper Mountain: large, rough-hewn, white oak beams and pillars; thick oak windows and doors; bluestone facade, steps, staircases, fireplaces; pine and oak floors. It retains the plain, down-to-earth simplicity of the Lutheran builders that seems a perfect fit with the sparse, no-nonsense attitude of Zen. The place felt homey. Its unpretentiousness lightened my tension. The smell of garlic and the sound of laughter pushed from the kitchen. I had arrived.

Later that night as I lay in my bunk, sleep impossible, I thought about the events of the day. We'd been given a tour that afternoon, and had been instructed in Zen etiquette and zendo procedures. It all seemed so foreign; the monks with shaved heads (both men and women), the bells, the incense, the slap of the *kyosaku* (encourage-

ment stick), the chanting, the bowing—I'd never bowed to anything and I didn't know if it was the bowing itself that felt strange, or the uncomfortable realization of the lack of reverence in my life—none of these thoughts was calming. Also, everything that had happened over the past year was bubbling up: memories of the painful yelling matches between my wife and me, guilt over my affair, the tenacious self-sabotage of my marriage. The warm wind blew through the window, the screen rattled, and in the deep night it struck me that "spiritual practice" was not some abstract, otherworldly concept swimming in shimmering gold light, but was the personal and sometimes stark colors of *my* life. Strangely, this small revelation made me feel better. I'd made it through the first day at least. And, as I was in a worrying mood, I began to think of *sesshin*, coming in two weeks. The sun rising. No sleep.

August heat, pine incense, sweat in the zendo. I fell into the schedule easily, my initial nervousness dissipated by routine and the comradeship I felt with the other residents. My leg was still falling asleep in the zendo, but I was getting used to it. My right knee ached and my lower back was occasionally tightening into a familiar twitch, but it had all been manageable. Now *sesshin* was here.

Over seventy people had come for the retreat and the zendo was full. It started on a Monday evening. Precautions were read: silence was to be maintained for the entire six days except when necessary during "caretaking" (work practice), eyes were to be kept lowered at a forty-five-degree angle, be seated in the zendo by 4:55 AM, no food in the domes or cabins, any problems talk to the monitors, be prompt. I walked slowly up to my cabin. The stars were just beginning to shine; it was still warm, muggy; a weak breeze; dog barking in the distance. I felt light. For no particular reason I began to laugh, which scared a deer into a dash through the trees, made me jump. Crazy human; how easy for a deer to be itself, never any question where to put its next step.

Barry Manilow! "Her name was Lola; she was a show-girl." 4:30 AM. I kept repeating the line in my head as I walked down the hill, flashlight pointed to the gravel road. I hated the song, sensed that it was a blatant warning from my brain—don't count on anything. I'm not a morning person and the first three periods of sitting were a struggle, a strange mix of drowsiness and a speedy tangle of thoughts, but I managed to oust Lola from my mind. When the main bell rang for service I stumbled upright and stood on a *zabuton* (mat). Bows. Chants. *The Heart Sutra*—"So in emptiness there is no form"—it sounded like an echo but came from my throat. Slowly my head began to clear, the chants giving me energy, seventy-plus people chanting. It was powerful; such a help to be with a group.

Oryoki, the ritualized formal meal, is served in the zendo with everyone seated on their zafus and zabutons (cushions and mats) in formal meditation posture. Each *sesshin* participant is given a "mess kit" containing three small bowls, a pair of chopsticks, a spoon, a spatula, and a cloth napkin. The whole lot is tied up in a large cloth that also serves as a place mat. The meal begins with a dramatic drumroll and a food offering to the Buddha. A wooden block is struck, a chant begins and everyone unties their *oryoki* bowls, unfolds their place mats, sets out spoons, chopsticks, and spatulas—all in a particular and precise manner. The chant ends and another begins, signaling the servers to bring out the large bowls of food.

I was starved. With a bow, oatmeal was ladled into my bowl. Another bow, mixed fruit. Yet another bow, and juice, sweet bread, milk, and peanut butter to put in my mush. *Oryoki* and most of the other rituals in Zen are intended to bring the student's awareness back to the task at hand, to focus the attention inward. I found it extremely hard not to look around the zendo and compare notes. The monitors kept urging, "Keep your eyes lowered. Stay within yourself." The taste of oatmeal, peanut butter, banana, my right knee beginning to ache. Was I doing any of this right?

In the afternoon the zendo was hot. Breathe in, out, count up to five. Then: "My brother and I used to catch tarantulas by pouring water down their holes; up they'd come into our jars. Dangerous." Shit! Breathe "one." Breathe "two." And then, "My back is beginning to ache. I can't do this. Why the hell did I give up on my marriage?" And on it went hour after hour, from Technicolor sexual fantasies to stupid TV ad jingles. It was extremely frustrating to keep failing at something that seemed so simple. In *dokusan* (private interview), Daido told me to concentrate, focus on the breath. I kept pushing, beyond frustration. The breath . . . one . . . two.

Anger came with the sunrise. I suddenly hated everything about the monastery, hated the people that had come to this god-awful *sesshin*, hated the monks for orchestrating this dark fiasco. I felt like screaming at them. I thought of a line I'd read in a book: "I piss on you all from a considerable height." The line made me laugh at the absurdity of my anger and criticism. Then, just as suddenly, I was overcome by feelings of gratitude for the place, for Daido, for the monks and the people sitting *sesshin*. I began to weep, continued weeping through *kinhin* (walking meditation).

This roller-coaster ride went on into the third day. The pain that I'd suppressed from the past year rose up. In *dokusan* with the Roshi and in interview with the head monk, I was told to let things come, "just watch them." Tears and snot in my *oryoki* meals. More anger. But always there was the breath, the return to the breath. I began to appreciate the simplicity of returning again and again to the breath. During rest period while walking outside on the large lawn, I passed another person but did not look up. It struck me how much my life was spent reacting to people. I had an eerie, ghostlike feeling. Sadness. I was exhausted.

As the *sesshin* progressed and the pain in my knee and back worsened, I moved from zafu to seiza bench to chair. I was able to manage the pain through my breath; "breathe into it"—as I was told—"don't fight." It worked! My mind was still tenacious in its ability to wander, but for shorter and shorter periods. I began to have brief moments of clarity, a feeling of loose yet sharp awareness. My emotions were still volatile. The dharma talks by the monks and the discourses by Daido went straight to my heart.

At one point I had an overwhelming ache to be loved, deep, infantlike. It scared me because it felt so old and unexplored. I felt like I was dredging the mud of some forgotten river. So this was the spiritual path? Incense, robes, brass bells, chants, bows, and dark muck.

The sixth day came. My back felt like an open wound, my knees like bruised rocks. I made it to the afternoon. I was surprisingly energetic. During rest period I walked up the hill to the pond and came face-to-face with a deer. We looked at each other for a minute or so and then it began to move slowly away. I watched its tan body move, its leg slowly rise and stretch, its taut muscles ripple. I had a strange feeling that its movements were attached to the surrounding forest, somehow attached to my gut, like we were all on one piece of film rolling out from the center of something. It was extraordinarily beautiful. Just a deer. Just my first *sesshin*.

. . .

John Kain is a poet of the mountains and rivers of the West and has completed a year of residency and training at Zen Mountain Monastery.

Noticing Blue Flowers, Seeing Yellow Snails

ANNE RUDLOE

❋

ONE AT A TIME, WE LEAVE THE MEDITATION hall for a private interview with our teacher, Korean Zen Master Seung Sahn Sunim. When it's my turn, I enter the room and sit down on the square mat in front of him. Wanting to make a good impression, to show off in some vague way, I have an opening speech all ready.

"Good morning, how are you?" he says. "Do you have any questions?"

"Yes, I do. Ten thousand times I come into this interview, ten thousand times you ask me a question, ten thousand times I answer wrong, and yet still you sit here!"

There's a pause.

"So what?" the teacher says.

"So what?! So what!! So, how do you do it?"

"The sky is blue, the grass is green."

He leans back, waiting for my response. I don't have one.

He laughs.

"When asked by a visitor to write the essence of practice, Zen Master Ikkyo simply wrote 'Attention!' When pressed for more, he wrote 'Attention! Attention! Attention!' Frustrated, the visitor asked what 'attention' means, and Ikkyo said, 'Attention means attention.' "

He smiles.

"We must learn to pay attention, to be fully present in each moment. It takes a while, but every bit of improvement in this skill is a wonderful gift we give ourselves

each day. And it's done by relaxing, not by forcing. So only stay in the present and give it your full attention. That's Zen. OK?"

"OK," I say hesitantly, thinking that there must be more to it but not quite ready to argue. Back in the meditation room, I try to pay attention but there doesn't seem to be much going on and pretty soon I can't keep my eyes open. Why do we have to get up so damned early anyway? Asking us to do that and then to sit still and be alert all day is like breaking somebody's ankle and then telling them to enjoy the scenery during a hike through the woods.

But as the hours pass, I can't help noticing the bright colors of the mats and the altar, and how the sunlight gleams on the polished oak floors. In its simplicity and openness, the room has a certain aesthetic quality that I have never seen before.

During a break, I go for a walk. A little ways up the path, a blue wildflower blazes in the sun with a clarity and intensity that most flowers don't have. As I squat and stare at it, a single mosquito flies past at eye level and then a spider appears hanging on a thread of silk in mid-air, shining in the afternoon light. As I move slowly and silently, the image of everything is somehow sharper and clearer than usual—like a photographic image suddenly coming into focus. No wonder Zen and the arts have such a close connection in Japanese culture.

By the end of the weekend, I was so sore from the long hours of motionless sitting that I could hardly walk and I still hadn't made much sense of the teacher's comments. But that flower really had seemed different somehow. In my frenetic, rushed lifestyle, maybe I did need to learn how to pay better attention to things. Driving back home to Florida, I wanted more of this elegant, rigorous practice.

When and how to do it wasn't very obvious. There was a lot of work to do at home. I taught marine biology at the local university, and in a few days would be bringing an ecology class to the coast to study the salt marsh ecosystem. I had to scout the trip, figure out the timing and logistics.

A Gulf Coast salt marsh is neither of the land nor of the water—it has its own reality. The pine islands of this one—forested, slightly higher ground surrounded by intertidal grassland—looked like ships at anchor in a sea of grass. Beyond, the marsh opened up into a tan prairie stretching away forever. Smaller pine islands sat on the distant horizon, looking like blue-grey, giant Pleistocene mammoths; mythic, self-aware beasts grazing across an ancient landscape, motionless in eternity. A river of wind and cloud poured overhead, enormous energy sweeping effortlessly past. Carrying butterflies and shining silken grass seeds, it was a wind that had blown for millions of years, long enough for the plants to discover how to ride it.

A storm had pushed the sea up hard against the land, and the salt marsh was flooded. It had rained all night and another storm was coming—not the best weather for scouting, but I needed to know whether or not we could get canoes from the end of the access road out to open water for the field trip.

I waded farther out to the edge of a tidal creek. It looked pretty deep. If we got here near high tide, we wouldn't have to carry the canoes too far. We could probably do a three-hour trip the next day and still be able to get back before the tide drained out again.

Zen Master Ikkyo said, "Pay attention," according to that story at the retreat. Paying such attention to a salt marsh, what might there be to discover? I wondered. I sat down on a wet log to try a little meditation.

The rain moved back in with a vengeance, but instead of fleeing I decided to pay attention to a marsh in the rain. Was it any different then? The tree islands on the horizon seemed to float, embedded in a layer of mist, only their crowns visible, surreal against a sky that moved in and out on fragments of wind. The rain fell harder than ever, soaking through the seams of my poncho and trickling down my back.

White sand, clear water, marsh grass, and streaks of rain—each drop hit with a white flash of light and the water surface shimmered from the vibrations of impact after impact. The interplay of light and water danced and danced. It had something to say but even with all my attention on it, I couldn't quite make out what. Maybe it had something to do with "the sky is blue, the grass is green." Maybe if I paid attention for a longer time, it would come into focus like that flower had. But I only had a little time, couldn't really sit and soak into the slow rhythms of the place in a way that would make it clear. I would have to come back when there was enough time. And somehow I would have to know how much time was enough. A few hours, weeks, a lifetime of seeing?

Several months later I was out in the bay beyond the marsh, where sea whips covered the rocks like a forest. Bright little soft corals about two feet high, they looked a lot like bare-branched trees in winter except that they were bright yellow or purple or orange. The surfaces of their branches were encased in a white fuzz of feeding tentacles, capturing microscopic food out of the current that swept past as the tide rose.

"OK, let's try it here," I thought, putting on a face mask and diving into the water. "Attention!"

And sure enough, the more carefully I looked, the more I saw. Tiny skeleton-shaped, shrimplike creatures hung on to the sea whip branches, bending and flexing as they seized food that was too small for me to see. Little snails, members of a species that occurs only on this particular sea whip, were barely visible, perfectly matched in color with the sea whips. The snails' color came from what they ate, and they ate the sea whips' surface tissue. Yellow sea whips had yellow snails, purple sea whips had purple ones.

I stared at it all for longer than I should have, mumbling to myself. For years I had lectured, drawn diagrams on blackboards, in general taken it for granted and acted like I understood it. But I'd never really looked, never really paid attention, and somehow I'd never truly seen it. At that retreat, we were taught to focus on the phrase, "What is this? Don't know!" and it jumped into my mind now. *What on earth is this??! Don't know!!* The marvel of life on earth, the endless variety of biological form and movement, the absolute mystery of what it ultimately is, how it comes to be, was all there growing on a rock.

Watching the tiny shrimp and snails on the sea whips, I began to grasp a little of what the teacher had tried to explain at the retreat. The world is full of subtleties, and a lot of the time we are so preoccupied with our personal agendas, reviewing the past or anticipating some future moment, that we overlook most of what is before us in the present. If I hadn't looked hard, I never would have noticed the snails at all.

The moments between birth and death are exactly what we have in life. If we just pay full attention to each of them as we live it, the universe will tell us what it's about. And I strongly suspect that it is as much about sea whips, snails, and rain in a marsh as it is about humans.

. . .

Anne Rudloe is a marine biologist, freelance writer, and conservation activist. She teaches at Florida State University and operates Gulf Specimen Marine Laboratory, a nonprofit aquarium and environmental education center in Panacea, Florida. Her research has focused on aquaculture of marine species and the conservation of endangered species, particularly sea turtles. In addition to her professional publications, her writing has appeared in National Geographic, Smithsonian Magazine, *and other national publications. She is currently at work on a book,* Butterflies on a Sea Wind *(from which this essay was excerpted). She has been practicing Zen with Providence Zen Center since 1986.*

To Sit on Ice

NOUK BASSOMB

✳

O N DECEMBER 23, 1993, I RECEIVED AN INVITA- tion to a birthday party. Generally, people's birthdays are celebrated in warm surroundings, with presents and cake. But Bernie Tetsugen Glassman-Roshi's birthday was to be held as a retreat on the steps of the United States Capitol. This four-day "street retreat" would "seek to raise consciousness about homelessness, AIDS, and violence in American society," according to the invitation.

Glassman-Roshi, Zen Buddhist teacher and social activist, is the founder of Greyston Mandala, a network of businesses and nonprofit organizations with a social change agenda. Greyston is located in southwest Yonkers, an impoverished corner of affluent Westchester County, north of New York City.

"This retreat is not a protest," the invitation went on, "but rather a contemplative vigil during which each participant will ponder the questions, 'What is my personal role in homelessness, in the denial of AIDS, and in violence? And what is my own next step toward healing these wounds in society?'" I decided to go. Knowing that there would be no presents and cake, that sleeping would be "in bunk beds at the Center for Creative Nonviolence (a large homeless shelter located close to the Capitol)," and that it might be cold did not stop me. I went, hoping to have fun. It turned out to be quite a trying initiation.

My friends Adalabu, Siddiq, and I arrived at the community center and were directed to a gymnasium that was to be our sleeping quarters for the duration of the retreat. A young, red-bearded man who introduced himself as Jesse approached us. "This is your space right here," he began. "Make yourself comfortable. Mattresses are here." I dropped my bags, pulled out a mat, and lay down. I heard someone ask, "Where is Roshi?"

"He was here earlier in the day and I guess he'll be back," replied Jesse.

It was 9:30 PM and the three of us were the only ones there. Where was everybody else? A thought crossed my mind. Maybe Roshi was sleeping at a hotel and would only show up tomorrow on the steps of the Capitol. Like the pope. When you inquire, they reply, "Security reasons." My response to this has always been, "If the pope cannot give his life for his people, what else can he give them?" I shook my head and closed my eyes. At 10:00 PM, Adalabu touched my foot. I opened my eyes. Roshi was there, smiling as always. We greeted each other and he just pulled out a mat, unfolded the sleeping bag Siddiq had brought him, lay down, and went to sleep almost immediately.

Jesse turned the lights on at eight o'clock the next morning. As we were having breakfast, he told us, "This day is the coldest in a hundred years. So dress accordingly." At nine we sat down in a circle at the steps of the Capitol and officially started the retreat. The snow was everywhere. If I were a phenomenologist, I could talk about the whiteness of the snow and make philosophy out of it. But I am not a phenomenologist and don't want to become one. All I knew at that moment was that it was freezing cold and I was as cold as death.

"We'll go around and everyone will introduce themselves, and maybe say a few words as to their reasons for being here," instructed Bernie. When my turn came, I stated my name and shared that I was born in Africa along the equator where, when the dry season comes, it's 120 degrees in the shade. Everyone chuckled when I said, "I'm a long way from home." Why was I here? Partly out of curiosity, partly to take advantage of a once-in-a-lifetime opportunity to learn about Zen Buddhism. "This is an initiation," I added.

We sat, walked, and sat again. It was cold. More cold than anything I'd ever experienced. I said to myself, "Let the cold penetrate deep inside my body." And the cold did. Quickly. My toes and fingers were frozen. Until then, I felt the cold. After that, I started feeling the bitterness of the cold. I guess the cold reached my bones. A few minutes later I was completely numb. As long as I stayed motionless, I felt nothing. But each time I tried to move, I felt as though my body didn't belong to me anymore. At one point I was so cold that I was warm. Strangely warm. I felt that this wasn't a normal sensation, but I couldn't ask, for everyone was meditating.

"Be careful," I said to myself. "You may get sick. You may even die here." To overcome the cold, or the fear of the cold, one must confront the cold. But was I well protected from it? And from myself? A neophyte needs an initiator. Who was mine? One has to be brought slowly to the truth. What was the truth of the cold? And what, in this instance, was the truth? Was it the cold, the coldness of the cold, or my mind in the state of questioning me about the cold or the coldness of the cold? I looked around and wondered if the others were as cold as I was and what was going through their minds at that very moment.

I also realized that we were, right there, a "House of One People." Both sexes were represented. And we had people from Africa, America, Europe. Muslims, Jews, Christians, agnostics, animists were here. I found myself smiling. Was this not a miracle? We sat until 11:30, when we left for the shelter. There was a huge amount of food, and it was self-service. I ate.

That afternoon we went back to the Capitol and sat down again. "Let's go around," instructed Roshi, "and let everyone say a few words about how they feel about homelessness, AIDS, and violence in America." When Jeannie's turn came, she could not contain herself and burst into tears. That was to me one of the strongest moments of the whole retreat.

"A chief called Hilolombi had a son," I started when my turn came, "who took it upon himself to visit his father five times a day to find out how he was doing and pledge his allegiance. And each time, as he left, Hilolombi's last words were, *Tikkun ha'Olam*."

"The son wondered for years what this expression meant. 'If my father tells me these words each time I visit him,' he thought, 'they must be important.' He asked his father the meaning of the words and never got any response. So one day he set out on a trip around the world to find out for himself. Each time he met somebody, he asked, 'My friend, do you know what these words, *Tikkun ha'Olam*, mean?' 'No!' was the reply he usually got. Then one day he met a wandering tribe. 'My friend,' he asked one of the women, 'Do you know what this expression, *Tikkun ha'Olam*, means?'

" 'Yes,' the woman answered. 'This is the language of my fathers, and the fathers of their fathers before them. We have been speaking this tongue for millennia.'

" 'What do these words say?'

" 'Heal the world!'

"When he got home, the man went back to visit his father. 'Father,' he said, 'why do you always speak to me in a language I can't understand?'

" 'For you to find out, son!'

" 'I did. *Tikkun ha'Olam* means *Heal the world*.'

" 'Who translated these words for you?'

" 'A woman from a wandering tribe. But why is this tribe wandering?'

" 'A plumber cannot fix the plumbing of his customers if he stays at home.'

"Sometimes," I continued, "in our lives, we bump into something extremely wrong, and we want to do something to fix it. Some of us are here, sitting on the ice, for this purpose. And we discover that the forces at play are far stronger than we are. That's when despair overwhelms us. We cry. For no apparent reason. I think that's why Jeannie cried. And I felt deep sympathy, deep connectedness with her . . . for she seemed to be saying to us all, 'What are we going to do?' But we are going to do something about it. We are already doing something about it, sitting here on the ice, with no one around."

Everything I know I learned from the elders. All insisted on *Tikkun ha'Olam* as a principle. While I was speaking I remembered one of them, Rabbi Uriel, who was the first person to call my attention to homeless people and the "divine purpose of homelessness."

"They're the true wandering tribe," he told me. Their purpose is to remind us that there's plenty of healing to do all over the world."

I had met Rabbi Uriel in London and he had invited me to visit him in his flat. There was nothing in there. Nothing at all. No furniture. No silverware, just a bed, a kitchenette, and a few books. "You don't seem to have anything here, Pop," I remarked aloud. (This is what we call the elders in Africa.)

He looked at my hands and said, "You don't seem to have much either."

"But I'm just passing through!"

"So am I, boy, so am I."

We cooked together and ate together, and all the while he kept on teaching me. "Our wandering all over the world is the result of a divine decree. We've got to heal the world wherever it's necessary. Isn't that easy to understand? . . . This task is calling us all now," he added. "Let's make it a big celebration."

I never saw Rabbi Uri again, for I left London and never returned. Instead, I found myself in America, where not a day goes by without Uri's words slapping me in the face like a freezing wind. When the time came for Uri and me to say goodbye, he held my hand and pressed it firmly. It hit me that he was giving me a mission, and the mission was to grasp the torch from his hands and take it further.

The following afternoon as we were getting ready to sit, a homeless guy who called himself Hewitt Hoyt stopped by the circle.

"What's up, men, what's up? What are you doing here? Why are you here?"

Roshi and a few others tried to explain. Hewitt treated us to a fifteen-minute lecture.

"What's the point of sitting here if no one even sees you? What's the point if no one hears you? You're in the wrong place. Where should you be? Pennsylvania Avenue. In front of the White House. They will try to forcibly remove you, then you'll fight. The police will come, TV network crews will follow. The next thing you know, you are on the evening news, and the entire world knows that you are voicing concern about homelessness in America. Listen, men, I was born and raised in this town. I know how it works."

He left, promising that he would go to a shelter and rally the residents and bring them back to sit and meditate with us. We never heard from him again.

We sat. As usual, Roshi asked us to go around the circle and, for ourselves, answer Hewitt's question, "What's the point?" We did. When Roshi's turn came, he told us the story of Indra's net—this mythical king whose people made him a net and wherever the strands crossed there was a jewel that reflected every other jewel in the net.

How to prove it, Indra's net? How to prove that the entire universe was reflected in us being on the steps of the Capitol at that moment, and that we were the reflection of the entire universe, the whole world, the whole of humanity? Does it matter? To me, Indra's net means that if there are any children of violence in our society, they are the reflection of us all, and we all are their reflection. We are the reflection of all these inner-city children who grow up dodging drive-by shootings, bullets, random sniping. We all are dodging bullets, one way or another. Can we all really tell right from wrong? Is it still relevant in our lives? Are we deprived of morality, angry, surrounded by evil and devils who think that the only way out of trouble is through more and more violence?

There was a bell ringing from a nearby church, which Roshi used to mark the end of the sitting period. "Let's sit until the bell rings," he said after everyone had spoken. When the bell rang, we stood up and walked to stretch our legs. We sat again. Roshi was right in front of me. I looked at him. He was enveloped in a white cloud. This man radiates such peace when he meditates that it's impossible not to notice the transformation. I smiled when, going back in time, I remembered the day I first met him.

I had been working on a book about the New York homeless. My editor told me one day that she knew people up in Yonkers who were doing good work for the homeless and that I'd learn something if I were to work with them. She made the connection and asked me to call David Rome, the executive director of Greyston Mandala. I did and he invited me to come and visit them.

"Take the 9:20 Metro North train from Grand Central Station in Manhattan," he advised me. "It will arrive in Yonkers around 9:52. Someone will be there waiting for you."

I was on time that morning. As I walked out of the station door, a man with a green beret touched my hand. "Nouk?" he asked gently. I nodded. "My name is Bernard Glassman. But people usually call me Bernie. I'm here to pick you up and take you to the monastery. The car is right across the street. I'll show you a little bit of Yonkers before we go to the foundation."

"No objection, Bernie," I replied. All this time, I have to admit, to me Bernie was a chauffeur sent by the director to take me to him. But as one who knows the power of the humble, I decided to befriend Bernie the chauffeur. I asked him about himself, about his family. "Fine!" he replied.

"You've got to be strong to keep the family together, Bernie, especially in the New York area. Stay that way."

Bernie turned his head, looked at me, and smiled. Thirty minutes later, I discovered that Bernie, my chauffeur friend, was the president of Greyston Mandala. It was my turn to smile. I remembered my father's teachings. When a father asks his child to be humble, to treat everyone with respect, he is telling him in other words that some day, a chauffeur can become a president, a poor man can become a king, and a homeless person God Himself.

Now at the retreat I looked at Roshi again. He was still surrounded by a white glow. As a matter of fact, I first saw this glow yesterday, but because I was so cold, I didn't pay any attention to it. I also thought that the whiteness of the snow and ice was making me see things that weren't there. But now, better protected against the cold, I was able to focus on other things. The sun's rays were piercing through the clouds. Was that why the glow seemed more pronounced? I looked around. Everyone had this misty cloud around themselves, but the clouds weren't all white. Some were violet, some bluish, some greyish. I looked at myself and couldn't see mine. I looked at Roshi again. I wondered if he ever felt the cold, for he never complained. His eyes were closed. I closed mine too. . . .

Back in New York a few days later, someone asked, "Did the retreat make any difference? Did it achieve anything?"

"It changed something in the people who sat," I answered. "We will never see things the same way again."

One aspect of any initiation is to take a situation to the extreme, so that the student masters the circumstances. The most immediate thing for me was to experience the cold in its extreme. I had never, since I came to the West, spent more than fifteen minutes in the cold. Just the length of time necessary to wait for a bus. And I was always afraid that I might catch pneumonia or something. On this retreat I spent four days sitting on ice, in a temperature that caused Washington, D.C.—the capital of the most powerful nation on earth—to stop functioning, and nothing happened to me. I didn't even get a sore throat.

"Listen, man, I'm no longer afraid to wait for the bus in winter."

· · ·

Nouk Bassomb is a scholar from Cameroon, Africa, who has adopted the homeless lifestyle in New York City. He is a friend-at-large of Zen Center of New York.

Entering the Gate of Meditation

GERI LARKIN

⊛

IT TOOK TEN YEARS OF PASSING THE GATE BEFORE I walked through it. The gate of the Ann Arbor Zen Buddhist Temple. Raised as an agnostic, schooled by Catholics, operating as a card-carrying Unitarian, there was a part of me that was deeply wary of anything foreign. That was the part that gave way—the wary part. The curious part carried me through the gate. The curious part said out loud, "How hard could this be?"

Ann Arbor Zen Buddhist Temple was founded by Venerable Samu Sunim, a Korean Zen monk who now resides mostly in Chicago. He took a large Victorian house located on one of Ann Arbor's busiest streets and, with the help of dharma students and volunteers, transformed it into the thriving center it is today. Each Sunday morning the *Sonbang* (meditation hall) fills with as many as forty people. The formal *sangha* membership is a diverse group, from students to physicians to entrepreneurial types like me who somehow survive the ever shifting world of the self-employed. Together with our sister temples in Chicago and Toronto, we sponsor seven intensive three- to five-day retreats each year. The Korean phrase for extended retreat is revealing. *Yongmaeng Chongjin* means "to leap like a tiger while sitting still."

"How hard could this be?" It took me a year of Sunday services to gain the courage to find out. My first taste was an overnighter in Ann Arbor. I loved it. I loved the quiet. I loved the uninterrupted sittings and the gentle words of encouragement by Reverend Sukha Linda Murray . . .

and the food, and the walking meditation. I even loved the manual work. Since it was such a positive—almost sweet—experience, my obvious next step was a five-day retreat in Toronto.

In the "good old days" stories that will always be a part of our *sangha*, I had heard tales of all-night sittings; of chopping endless wood; of running barefoot in the snow and eating soup made solely from water, salt, and bean sprouts. I packed for the worst. Extra socks and extra layers of clothes. Earplugs. Chocolate bars to hide under my futon. A book in case it all got too scary. Lots of ibuprofen and Tiger Balm. An extra pair of contact lenses in case one dried out from staring at the floor all day. Two kinds of scentless deodorant. An emergency address of a friend of a friend's friend. A living will. I even left instructions with one relative to drive to Toronto to retrieve me if I wasn't back by 10:00 PM on the day the retreat ended. Though I never needed any of the items, it was comforting to know they shared my little sleeping space.

Retreats at our centers always begin in the evening with words of encouragement and several rounds of meditation. A ten-minute break between sittings allows people to get some water, do stretches, visit the bathroom. After every two sittings there is a walking (and occasionally jogging) meditation, which lasts for fifteen to twenty minutes. This overall pattern starts at 5:30 every morning, following wake-up and stretches, and continues until 10:00 PM each evening. Following the last formal sitting of the day, participants are encouraged to continue their practice on their own. Several times now I have found myself at 2:30 AM surrounded by others doing walking or sitting meditation.

The daily schedule also provides time for work practice and a rest period. People who have never napped in their lives become rabid nappers by the second day's rest period. Cleaning and general temple upkeep is always a part of work practice; windows are washed, furniture fixed, food prepared, and always, the sound of wood being chopped. Often, especially in extreme weather, we make meditation mats and cushions.

Over the years I've noticed a pattern to the emotional phases I swim through each time I go on retreat. Excitement is always the overriding feeling at first. I'm excited to be taking time off from work and am eager for uninterrupted, concentrated practice. At the same time a nervousness plays hide and seek with me. Will Sunim yell during my private interviews with him? Will I experience a deeper peace? Will I get enough sleep? Will someone be snoring? Will the bones ache too much?

Day one is always a parade of catnaps. I can begin a retreat fully rested and still manage to sleep through the whole first day. Sitting. Nodding while sitting. Trying not to close my eyes. More nodding. Counting off minutes before the end of the meditation period. Trying to hold on to my concentration. Wondering what the heck ever possessed me to become a Buddhist anyway. More dozing. Then at last, around 11:00 PM, sleep. Real sleep. Dreamless.

Phase two usually starts in the middle of the second day. I call it the "whining mind" phase. About work. About kids—everyone's. About crime. About violence. About my knees hurting. Or the headache that has surfaced because I haven't had any caffeine for two days.

Whining about my teacher and why can't he just pass along a transmission of enlightenment so I don't have to sit on the cushion any more and why didn't anyone warn me that *this is hard work!* Wondering if it is too late to become a Catholic. The whining can last a whole day, sometimes two if I happen to be stuck in a difficult relationship or work environment.

Here is the miracle of retreat for me: the whining always stops. I never know when it will, I just know that it does. And I don't know why it does. I've realized that simply allowing the whining to parade on through somehow gives it the freedom to wind down . . . and stop. Finally, there is just practice. Clear, clear practice. "What is it?" "What is it?" "What is it?" Every move my body makes becomes "What is it?" Every breath is the breath of "What is it?" Interviews get stronger. Breathing softens.

The last few days of retreat are a blur of practice. Everything becomes practice—a practice that stays with me until the next retreat. A practice that sees me through losses, joys, worries, hopes, and the smashed chocolate bar I discover under my sleeping bag as I pack to go home.

Every moment, precious moment.
Every moment, just this.

. . .

Geri Larkin was born in Lafayette, Indiana, and is an ordained dharma teacher and a graduate of the Maitreya Buddhist Seminary. She is president of Strategic Thinking, a management consulting firm located in Ann Arbor, Michigan, and the author of several well-received business books including Woman to Woman: Street Smarts for Woman Entrepreneurs.

Lotus in the Fire: Prison, Practice, and Freedom

ROSHI JOHN DAIDO LOORI

The fire burns
and the lotus
blooms.
It is because the fire
burns
that the lotus
blooms.

Years ago, I received a letter from an inmate of the Green Haven Correctional Facility in Stormville, New York. The inmate had been a Zen Buddhist practitioner for a number of years and was instrumental in starting practice groups in at least three of New York's maximum-security prisons. He was new at Green Haven and requested that I help him start a Zen practice group there. The state maximum-security prison regulations require that religious groups be sponsored by a bona fide member of the clergy affiliated with an outside temple or church.

The letter took me back thirty-five years to my own past karma. While serving in the United States Navy, I received a captain's mast for a minor infraction: refusing to peel potatoes under direct orders from an officer. As a result, the captain awarded me ten days' solitary confinement on bread and water at the Marine prison in the harbor. I was young, and the experience terrified me. The solitary cells were tiny. Three times a day the guard would bring three slices of bread, a bowl of water, and a little bit of salt. Bedding was removed at dawn and returned in the evening. There was nothing to do, nothing to read, no one to communicate with, nothing to watch except for a guard in the distance. It was an incredibly claustrophobic experience that kept the edges of my being raw. By the time the ten days were up I had learned my lesson well. I would avoid that kind of confinement at all costs.

As the years passed, the experience remained in my memory. There was always the fear that somehow I might end up in a prison cell again—maybe for life—and not be able to tolerate it. That fear remained with me for many years until one day in the middle of a *sesshin* I realized I could do it if I had to. I knew I could live a solitary life, that *zazen* (meditation) was the doorway to the strength and the power necessary to do it, and that, clearly, *zazen* is a practice every prisoner should be aware of. I felt the need to do something about bringing Zen practice into prisons, but somehow I didn't quite know where to start. So I kept postponing what I knew would be a very difficult task. I didn't seek it out, but eventually it came to me through this very special prisoner, whom I shall call Brother E. I immediately made an appointment to see him and the senior chaplain of the prison.

Initially, we had some difficulty creating the sitting group simply because the guards didn't know us. They knew the Protestant minister, they knew the Catholic

Roshi John Daido Loori, Abbot of Zen Mountain Monastery. (Photo courtesy of Dharma Communications.)

priest, they knew the Jewish rabbi, and they knew the Islamic imam, but they had no idea who the Zen Buddhists were. All they knew was that we were somehow vaguely connected with kung fu, and they certainly did not want martial arts being taught to prisoners. Consequently, the guards made it difficult to gain entry. There was always some kind of red tape. A two- or three-hour car ride to the prison would result in having to spend most of our time in the waiting room, with hardly a chance to see the inmates.

Now, Brother E was no ordinary prisoner. When we began to encounter difficulties, he immediately went to the prison library and researched the laws on establishing a new religious group in a state prison. Even though he probably had no more than a grade-school education, he wrote a legal brief to a justice of the federal court. Though a federal court justice sees hundreds of complaints of this kind, he chose this one as having enough merit to warrant the attention of the federal judiciary. An attorney was appointed (a fine lawyer from a prestigious New York City firm took the case pro bono), and we went to federal district court for a hearing. That battle continued for about a year and when the dust settled, Zen Buddhism was officially recognized as a legitimate religion to be practiced at the state prisons. This prece-

dent-setting decision was the result of the effort and determination of one bodhisattva prisoner, Brother E.

We then arranged for our first meeting with the inmates. The Protestant chaplain gave us a room to use as a zendo. Of course we had nothing; we had no money, no zendo equipment. I assumed we'd be sitting on the hard wooden floors without *zafus* or *zabutons* (cushions or mats) until we figured out how to get what we needed. As I approached the room escorted by a guard, I was met by prisoners wearing sitting robes. What followed was incredible to see. The students bowed in *gassho* as I walked into a room that had been transformed into a zendo. There were eighty prisoners sitting on *seiza* benches, which they had made. Someone struck the clappers, and they all jumped to their feet. I looked and there was an altar complete with a Buddha and *butsudan* (shrine), a *mokugyo* (a carved, hollow wooden fish used for keeping time during chanting ceremonies), and a *han* (a large block of wood, suspended from the ceiling, struck with a wooden mallet to signal the beginning of a period of meditation), all of which they themselves had made. They had researched it in the prison library, and having examined pictures, they created everything necessary to make a functioning zendo. Brother E had evidently been training them, because when I went to the altar, there was an attendant ready to hand me a stick of incense. When I prepared to do three bows, someone struck a hand bell and they all did the bows with me. At that moment, I knew we had a *sangha*.

As I became familiar with their needs, I was struck by the fact that I was dealing with a kind of monastic environment where poverty, chastity, and obedience were clearly functioning. They even called each other "brother," as Catholic monks do. It was a life of commitment since, whether voluntary or not, most of them were in for life. There seemed to be an incredible level of personal discipline and, most importantly, their questions were real questions; questions regarding the ground of being, the meaning of life and death, what reality is, what truth is, what freedom is.

Our practice is concerned with freedom and, for obvious reasons, this is very important to prison inmates. We talked a great deal in those first days about being stuck in the "bag of skin," the bondage to the illusion of a self that is separate and distinct from everything else. Prison is something we create with our minds because, in fact, the self doesn't exist. The self is an idea, a thought, something we are taught, something we learn, something we believe. In fact, the skin bag doesn't define the boundaries of who we are. Our life is much more than that.

Attachment propagates the illusion of a separate self. Our attachment to things, ideas, and positions constantly reinforces the idea that there is a self. The bonds that restrict us, the cage that confines us, the limits and boundaries that define our lives are all self-created. Each and every one of us is free and unhindered, right from the very beginning. But until we realize this inherent freedom through our own experience, it cannot begin to function in our lives. Once having realized it, there are no boundaries, no limits, no hindrances. It soon became clear to me that there are many prisoners inside Green Haven who are really free, just as there are lots of so-called free people on the outside who are really prisoners. A number of these men had clearly raised the Bodhi mind. I was grateful to have encountered such an extraordinary group of students.

We also focused on the doctrine of karma—cause and effect. What you do and what happens to you are the same thing. What you do with your body, with your words, and with your thoughts. Most of us can understand that we create karma by what we say. But we do not as easily understand that we create karma by what we think. Punching somebody in the nose obviously creates some kind of cause and effect. Saying "I would like to punch you in the nose" creates another kind of cause and effect. Just as certainly, thinking "I would like to punch you in the nose" equally creates some kind of cause and effect. This, in particular, became a topic for much discussion with these students.

For many, their cause for incarceration was violating the precept "Do not kill." The effect of their crime was lifetime imprisonment, a lifetime of being separated from their loved ones, some from their children and families. What does one do about that?

What we do and what happens to us are the same thing. This responsibility—when we truly realize that there is no separation between ourselves and the ten thousand things—is, in itself, freedom. This is an extraordinary thing. It means we are responsible for everything. We are responsible for the past, for the future, and, of course, for this moment that contains the past and the future.

It sounds like a tremendous burden. We are responsible for what is going on in Africa. We are responsible for what is going on in the whole universe. But when we really look at that responsibility, we come to realize that it is actually freedom, because when we are responsible we can no longer blame. Blaming becomes an absurdity. Saying "he made me angry" no longer makes sense. We know that only we can make ourselves angry; we can no longer be a victim. We realize that we are the master of our own life, that what we do and what happens to us are the same thing. This means that there is always something we can do, that we are never helpless victims of circumstance.

Taking responsibility with regards to the Lotus Flower Zendo meant continuous commitment. We therefore established a group of senior students from Zen Mountain Monastery to help share the responsibilities. We trained them to go into the prison to work with the inmates. These students sit with the prisoners, give talks, and help train them in service positions. We call them Lay Buddhist Ministers because they need to have an official title to satisfy the prison authorities.

One thing these lay ministers needed to appreciate before beginning their work was that they weren't bringing anything into the prison. Everything needed was already there; wisdom and compassion were already there. This was particularly important because among prisoners there is always a kind of mystique concerning the outside world. The "cage" is their special world, their special universe. Everything they need and want comes in, somehow, from outside. Suddenly, here was something that did not come from the outside, could not come from the outside because there is no inside or outside, because there is nothing to be given, and nothing to be received—because each one of us right from the beginning is perfect and complete, lacking nothing. Of course, we can lecture about it, but to someone who is being pushed around by guards and locked up in a little room at the end of the day, it takes much sitting and emptying out to begin to realize the truth of it.

Most of the prisoners in the group sit on a regular basis. They sit by themselves in their cells every morning and evening, although they're not really alone because they have begun to understand what the Three Treasures (the Buddha, Dharma, and *Sangha*) are about. So even separated by the courtyards, all of them sit as one in their separate cells, chanting *The Heart Sutra* and renewing their commitment to follow the Precepts.

Racial and ethnic mixing within the prison is rare. The Zen Buddhist group is one of the only racially mixed religious groups. There are whites, blacks, and Hispanics in close to equal proportions. I have no idea why or how any of these inmates came to the dharma, but when you walk into the zendo it becomes obvious that there is an incredible strength to their practice. They are the most determined group of people I have ever encountered. This affiliate group, among several we have along the East Coast, is by far the most powerful and the most rewarding to work with.

The depressing feeling we experienced during those first few days soon ended because the brothers were so appreciative of our presence. I had never felt so appreciated in my entire life. In the early days of our involvement there, we had only ten to fifteen minutes of informal relationship after sitting because the guards would immediately start sending them back to their cells for a head count. The prisoners just wanted to touch, to shake hands with people from the outside. It was obvious that our presence was valued, and this made the whole thing extremely worthwhile. They have repaid us a hundredfold for our smallest efforts. I am convinced that what I and our lay ministers are learning from them is far more than what they are learning from us.

Compassion is the manifestation of the life of Kannon, the Bodhisattva of Compassion. How, indeed, does Kannon Bodhisattva manifest her life within the walls of that prison? Every time an inmate helps another prisoner, the life of Kannon Bodhisattva is manifested right there. Compassion arises from wisdom, and wisdom is the real-

ization of no-separation. Compassion is the activity of that no-separation. It means that when someone falls you pick them up. There is no sense of doer, nor of anything being done. There is no sense of reward, no sense of separation. You do it the way you grow your hair: no-effort. It grows. As the days go by at the prison, the presence of wisdom and compassion seems increasingly evident.

The fire burns, and the lotus blooms. Over the ten years since Lotus Flower Zendo began at Green Haven, the practice has continuously developed. Currently, two meetings are held each week that include *zazen*, liturgy, and a dharma talk when a senior lay minister is in attendance. When I or one of my Dharma Holders visit, we offer face-to-face teaching. The *sangha* holds quarterly one-day *sesshin* and an annual two-day Rohatsu *sesshin*. During the latter, in addition to the usual *sesshin* activities, I also give the Precepts to any students who are at that point in their training.

Another highlight of the year is Buddha's Birthday. This is a rare time when inmates can be with their families and friends in a more natural way without walls or wires between them. In the early years, many of the family members were very tentative about joining our services; what was this strange religion, anyway? But each year, as they've seen the lives of their husbands, brothers, and sons change due to their Zen practice, they have grown to trust it, even if they don't understand it. At our last celebration, every single family member joined us for the service. Thus, as the loved ones of *sangha* members become involved, the practice extends itself even beyond the prison walls.

The fruit of this experience at Green Haven is seeding prison *sangha*s throughout the country. We are now directly involved with *sangha*s in two prisons in New York State and have helped establish a dozen sitting groups at other penal institutions. We carry on a vigorous correspondence program with inmates across the country, offering guidance on practice issues, and sending books and audiotapes. We also serve as advisors to the New York State Department of Corrections concerning Buddhist activities in all New York State prisons. We have even had Lotus Flower *Sangha* members, upon being paroled, spend a year in residential training at the monastery.

Obviously, none of this could have happened without the strong practice of the *sangha* itself. It was, no doubt, that very strength of practice that allowed prison officials and other prison clergy to accept Buddhist meditation there as a serious spiritual endeavor, one that would be of value to the inmates and to the prison. The *sangha* members are now involved in the spread of Zen practice to other prisons throughout the country, and are writing a manual of Zen practice to be made available to inmates in other prisons who wish to develop their own *sangha*s.

It all really points to Ummon's "medicine and sickness curing each other." Ummon, speaking to his assembly, said, "Medicine and sickness heal each other. All the world is medicine; where do you find the self?" The sickness is to violate the precept, 'Do not kill.' What is the medicine? It is atonement, at-one-ment, no separation, taking responsibility for our actions, for our karma. When the cause is *zazen*, what is the effect? Cause and effect is one. When the first thought comes from delusion, all subsequent thoughts are deluded. When the first thought springs from enlightenment, all subsequent thoughts are enlightened. A few of these inmates are looking forward to parole and to continuing their training at the monastery.

There are thousands of prisoners at Green Haven. Sometimes when you walk in there, the air is electric with tension. The atmosphere fills with fear, anger, and hostility as I walk through the halls. It can be felt among the guards and among the prisoners. The fire burns. Then I reach the little *sangha* of Zen Buddhists who are sitting in a room at the Protestant ministry, sitting and emptying themselves. That sitting, that stillness radiates beyond the zendo, beyond the walls of the prison itself. The lotus blooms. Medicine and sickness heal each other. All the world is medicine; where do you find yourself? It is because the fire burns that the lotus blooms.

. . .

The Ven. John Daido Loori-Roshi is abbot of Zen Mountain Monastery in Mt. Tremper, New York. He began his Zen studies under the late Maezumi-Roshi in 1976. This article is derived from a talk given at Zen Center of Los Angeles in July 1986. It has been updated to reflect changes in the Lotus Flower Sangha, and Zen Mountain Monastery's ongoing work with Buddhist inmates nationwide.

Zen Dance: Meditation in Motion

SUN OCK LEE

✴

Korean Zen Dance is an ancient practice rooted in Zen Buddhist philosophy. The purpose of Zen is to find one's "True I," to attain the indescribable *Suchness*—Enlightenment—and to end the suffering of humankind. Words cannot pin down its meaning, nor can rites, rituals, music, or dance. But every human action may be undertaken as an exercise toward Enlightenment and performed in such a way as to suggest the ineffable. Thus Zen Buddhism has given the world Zen archery, Zen karate, Zen swordsmanship, Zen flower arranging, Zen tea drinking, and the art of Zen dance.

For the Zen dancer, dance is not only a medium of artistic expression; it is a path that leads to Enlightenment itself. The basic techniques of Zen meditation have been adapted and applied to dance. Through the use of mantras, *hwa-tous* (*koan* in Japanese), and *tanjun* (lower abdomen) breathing, practitioners learn how to align the mind and body correctly in order to enter the Enlightened state.

In Korea, Zen is known as *Hwalgu-jam Son*, "Utmost Vehicle Meditation." This tradition holds that Enlightenment, or Buddha nature, is the birthright of every human being. Since it already exists within us, it can be neither bestowed by a teacher nor obtained by a disciple—the "Utmost Vehicle" is oneself!

Korean Buddhist Ritual Song and Dance

According to the scriptures, when Gautama Buddha was still a prince in his father's palace, he was entertained by musicians, singers, and dancers. But after his Enlightenment, new forms of music, dancing, and singing were devised to propagate the teachings and encourage the faithful. Unique among Asian Buddhist countries, Korea has maintained the ancient tradition of ritual song and dance.

Known as *Pomp'ae* and *Chakpop*, these artistic performances are very much a part of the religious heritage out of which Zen dance arose. However, where Zen dance is concerned with the attainment of Enlightenment, *Pomp'ae* and *Chakpop* function as a means for propagating the Buddha's teachings and, through invocation and supplication, as expressions of devotion to the Lord Buddha.

The Mantra

Since Enlightenment exists beyond words and concepts, the greatest hindrance to its realization is the human brain, which, in its ordinary state, never ceases to put forth its concepts of reality. The brain not only projects

98

Dr. Sun Ock Lee, performing a Korean Zen dance. (Photo courtesy of the Zen Temple of Cresskill, New York).

a very partial view of reality onto the Universe, but continually works to confirm its interpretations through internal dialogue. Thus a person's awareness of reality is imprisoned by language.

The use of a mantra circumvents this process by employing sound and vibration to transcend the limits of the intellect. Mantras are sacred syllables, like the ancient Vedic OM, which are repeated by the spiritual devotee, either audibly or mentally, with every exhalation of the breath.

The theory is that mantras are a concentrated form of cosmic power. Their recitation may be likened to the repeated stroking of an iron bar with a magnet; eventually, some of the magnetism, or cosmic energy, rubs off on the disciple. For the Zen dancer, the mental repetition of the mantra OM-NAM serves to intensify energy, establish spiritual equilibrium, and hone the power of concentration.

The *Hwa-tou*

While mantras help to eliminate ceaseless mental chatter, something else is needed to rein in the more abstract

workings of the brain. For this the *hwa-tou* is brought into play. A *hwa-tou* is a question for which the rational mind cannot find an answer. The *hwa-tou* most commonly used in Zen dance is *Yimoko*, a Korean word that means "What am I?" or "What is the True Self?" Initially, the question—*Yimoko*?—is repeated one syllable at a time with each breath. Soon this unceasing investigation begins to fill the practitioner's mind and heart with Great Doubt. Great Doubt grows like a filling balloon until it covers the entire Universe. When it bursts, doubt is dispelled and Enlightenment ensues.

For the Zen dancer, the dance itself comes to embody this quest for the "True I," and it is from this vantage point that the dancer and sometimes even the audience may catch a glimpse of "True Self."

Tanjun Breathing

Breathing is the basis for all human activity and death is the final exhalation. In Zen meditation, the *tanjun* area (midway between the navel and the pubic bone) is considered the locus of one's vital energy, or *Ki*. Consciously inhaling and exhaling with the muscles of the lower abdomen—instead of swelling and shrinking the chest—links the breath to the body's center of gravity. This is the source of its vital energy and the place where spirit and body unite.

To maintain the relaxed flow of the breath, one does not inhale or exhale to the maximum in *tanjun* breathing. At the completion of each inhalation and exhalation, the breath is held very briefly. Through this practice, consciousness and concentration are shifted from the head—where they cause top-heaviness and imbalance—to the lower abdomen, a shift that creates the same sense of tranquillity and equilibrium in a dancer in motion as is experienced by a person sitting in meditation.

For the Zen dancer all movement emanates from the *tanjun*. Since the *tanjun* is the source of the body's *Ki* energy and its point of contact with the Universe, movement emanating from it becomes highly energized and as effortless as sailing before the wind. "Effortlessness" is key; as with all Zen-influenced art forms, the practitioner's "not-doing" is more prized than his doing. The highest compliment that can be paid a Zen dancer is to say that she's "at her best when she's doing nothing."

Zen Dance Performance

Zen mind is "everyday mind." Enlightenment does not pertain to some other time or place; it must be here and now or not at all. It must be experienced in every situation, in every moment, whatever one is doing. Zen dancers learn to live with all the elements of the training as part of their continual practice toward Enlightenment. The practice doesn't end just because rehearsal time is over.

It follows, then, that Zen dance performance takes its themes from everyday life. Performers strive to create an atmosphere of tranquillity, reverence, purity, centeredness, balance, and harmony in a meditative state of mind. The dancer shares this meditative state by becoming the medium through which the audience's cloudy thoughts, moods, concepts, and judgments are transformed and distilled into pure, clear essence.

Performances are characterized by slow, spare, essential movement, by economy of space, minimal use of the stage, simplicity, stillness, spontaneity, and immediacy. Total concentration is brought to bear on each and every gesture. Like waves breaking on a shore, or a breeze gusting through leaves, performers move effortlessly, reflecting the rhythms of nature. The performance forms a center in the cosmos where concepts are forgotten and everything is accepted. In that acceptance there is a transformation to a realm beyond words.

. . .

Dr. Sun Ock Lee is one of Korea's foremost dancers and choreographers. Spanning East/West cultural and dance styles, her work has been internationally recognized for its beauty, its power to evoke deep inner feelings, and its innovative approaches to cross-cultural arts. Dr. Lee is Resident Teacher at Zen Temple of Cresskill, New Jersey, and (with photographer John Chang McCurdy) author of Zen Dance: Meditation in Movement.

Sitting in Buddhist Suburbia

JANE MYOJU SHUMAN

✳

RYE, NEW YORK, IS NOT THE KIND OF TOWN where you'd expect to hear sutra chanting three nights a week. Settled in the 1600s, Rye is an established, comfortable "bedroom community" about thirty miles north of New York City on Long Island Sound. Its town center is a four-block stretch of small stores. It prides itself on its many historical buildings, and boasts several golf and yacht clubs. Riding along a tree-lined mile of U.S. Route 1, you'll see a series of old stone churches standing regally one after another: Episcopal, Methodist, Catholic, Presbyterian. Go a mile farther, out toward the harbor, and you'll pass a tiny, grey, antique wooden church with a sign out front that reads "Rye Friends Meeting House." A small sign just below that advertises "Zen Meditation." This is the home of "Empty Hand Zendo," founded in 1986 by Susan Ji-on Postal, Zen priest and student of the late Maurine Stuart-Roshi. Inside, the stodgy ambience of Rye falls away as a mallet strikes the wooden *han*, calling our small group of Zen devotees to a day of practice.

It is a crisp April Saturday morning. The sun is rising over two lines of square brown mats set down on either side of the zendo. On each mat there is a round cushion (zafu) for sitting in cross-legged meditation posture. The altar is set with breathtaking quince blossoms and forsythia; tall white candles in brass holders; pine incense; a statue of Kuan Yin, Bodhisattva of Compassion. A side altar has more candles, incense, and a photograph of

Maurine taken in front of the meeting house when she visited from Cambridge, Massachusetts. Except for the austere and quickening echoes of the *han* (a wooden block struck with a mallet to signal the beginning of a day of meditation), there is silence as twenty-five men and women take their places, bowing first to their seats and then to each other. Susan offers incense, and bows to us all as we bow to her, in gratitude for each other's presence. This bowing is something we do often, putting two palms together in *gassho*, as an expression of "not one, not two," and as a sign of respect for our practice and for those with whom we practice.

Even though it's only a one-day retreat, the traditional rules of Zen *sesshin* are followed. *Sesshin* (a Japanese word that means to gather or collect the mind) comes to us from the Zen monastic tradition. For those of us who have chosen to live in the world as lay practitioners, a day of silent retreat is a taste of a more intense meeting of mind and body than would normally be possible for us. We dress either in lay robes—brown, to blend in with the cushions—or in muted colors. We spend the entire time in silence, not looking around, not wearing perfume or jewelry or in any other way drawing attention to ourselves. The focus is inward: to this end, rather than spending time making decisions about what to do next, we follow a printed schedule, moving, working, and sitting in response to the bells and gongs, as one communal entity.

After everyone is seated, two members of the *sangha* (community) rise and serve tea to the group. As with every other part of the day, drinking tea is done ceremonially, as one, and with mindfulness, paying attention to every sensation: the feel of the cup, the steam rising, the anticipation of the hot liquid about to touch the lips, the taste of the tea, the sound and feel of swallowing, the gratitude to the servers, and so on. After the cups have been collected, the large gong is rung and we begin a series of thirty-minute rounds of *zazen* interspersed with ten-minute periods of *kinhin* (walking meditation). In our zendo, *kinhin* is done slowly, in half steps synchronized with the breath so that we feel we are breathing through our feet. Walking meditation is considered a continuation of seated practice, and it demands the same quality of mindful attention.

In midmorning, Susan gives a talk on the Buddhist Ancestors, whose often colorful and always amazing enlightenment stories serve to invigorate us on our own paths . . . or else to leave us shaking our heads, wondering what was going on back there in India and China and Japan, with the Patriarchs growing robes on their bodies or not speaking a single word until they were fifty!

At noon the bell rings and we eat lunch together in the zendo. Cooked at home by members of the group and reheated, the meals are always vegetarian and usually include soup, bread, and fresh vegetables. We eat in silence and mindfulness, and after lunch work together in the same spirit; cleaning and polishing, vacuuming, wiping windows, pulling weeds, planting flowers, preparing mailings, washing dishes. Work practice, which mirrors the actions of our lives in the world, helps us to refine our awareness of each moment, enabling us to manifest our practice "off the cushion." After work practice, a service is conducted, with sutra chanting in both Japanese and English, preceded and followed by sets of full bows.

Later in the afternoon, there are one-on-one interviews with the teacher. In our tiny zendo, interviews are held behind a folding screen in the kitchen adjoining the main room. This results in much whispering and muffled laughs or cries from both student and teacher. But then, we are an adaptable crew. Having been renters for ten years, we've become experts at producing a complete zendo out of a Quaker meeting house in under half an hour, and doing the reverse in even less time, making sure that everything, each Zen or Quaker object, is well cared for and in its proper place.

Zen Master Dogen said that *zazen* is not just a method to attain awakening, it is awakening itself. So *zazen* is always the prime focus at the Empty Hand Zendo, whether it be in *sesshin* or at a weekday evening sitting. Sitting practice involves many components. In Zen, posture is considered extremely important, and for this reason we have monitors, students who walk around the zendo from time to time checking that spines are straight, hands are in the "cosmic mudra" (one hand resting in the other, thumbs lightly touching, at the level of the *hara*, two inches below the navel), heads are held high with chins tucked in slightly, eyes partly open and directed downward, knees firmly on the mat. In our zendo we do not use the stick (*kyosaku*), but upon request the monitor will hit the large shoulder muscles with a cupped hand as a means of refreshing one's practice. On longer retreats, short back rubs are available and much appreciated.

So, here I am, sitting silently, as I have done for countless hours since the day I first walked past the meeting house and saw the sign. I am facing the bright sun through southeast windows. (We alternate periods, one round facing into the room, the next with faces to the wall). It is rather cool and though the windows are still closed, the meeting house is a porous old building and it is easy to hear the birds singing outside, some nearby in the feeder just outside, others a few hundred feet away in the marsh that leads to the harbor. Soon enough the birdsong and sunshine fade and the thoughts begin. Susan says, "The mind secretes thoughts—that's what the brain does. Our practice is not to get rid of these thoughts, but to notice them without judging, and go back to the breath." Ah. It's the judging part that gives me problems. I hold on to this delusion that after all these years of sitting I should somehow be able to accomplish a half hour of solid, one-pointed, silent, choiceless awareness.

Given all this endless silent time, the mind gets so desperate to be heard that it will talk about almost anything.

If all else fails, it will mutter incoherently or cause deep emotions to arise, until it just gets tired of going on. For me, the first sitting period of the day is the loudest. Twenty minutes into the period my right foot falls asleep, and the mind begins complaining. An inner dialogue ensues:

"My foot is asleep, it hurts."

"You can't hurt, you're a mind. Minds don't hurt. Be quiet."

"I won't be able to stand up when the bell rings."

"You've managed to stand up about ten thousand times before. Why should this time be any different?" Back to the breath. A few minutes of peace, sensing the birds and a few cars passing on Milton Road. Another fleeting thought, some quiet, and the gong. Thirty minutes have passed. The mind tells me that I have wasted a lot of that period. "Who wasted? Wasted what? Just *is*."

Of course, the inner dialogue is how we live our lives; but inside the zendo, we have an opportunity to do it in a different way. The zendo is a laboratory. In it, we sit and let these thoughts happen and we notice them and try not to allow them to take us too far away from our center before we come back to reality. What is reality? Not our thoughts.

Here's a question that Susan often asks us: "If I'm not my thoughts, then who am I? What is there when the thoughts ccasc?" And that is the gift of long sitting. After some time, thoughts do cease, and the "self" that we create with thoughts ceases, and then we can directly experience what might be called our essential nature, our original face. This is why Zen stresses *zazen* over the purely intellectual study of books, or even lectures by teachers, although these can be helpful. Only by actually sitting in silence can one come to know the utter joy and peace of one's true nature. And only through this direct experience can one go back out into the world and have the compassion, understanding, and gratitude necessary to be of service.

Early afternoon; the sun has passed the corner of the church. We have just finished chanting in "voice *zazen*," as Maurine Stuart-Roshi used to call it, and bowed three times, letting go of everything, completely releasing, giving it all away. The mind has long since given up. There is some traffic out on the street, but there is no thought about it, it's just part of the whole. The room feels vast, spacious, and the silence in this space has a wonderful energy, a sweetness and depth that was not there this morning. At *sesshin* there are always many degrees of silence. They say that in Eskimo languages there are ten different words for snow. In zendos there should be ten different words for silence.

The final gong rings and we file into the kitchen for snacks and conversation. The warmth and intimacy are palpable. These are twenty-five souls who might never have met, or had a thing in common in the outside world. Mostly, we don't even know if the people next to us are married, have children, jobs, or even where they live. But the intimacy goes much deeper than all that. It comes from the silent support of *sangha*, one of the Three Treasures of Buddhism, something that is extremely evident to visitors of Empty Hand Zendo.

The sun is getting low, shooting through a lovely stained-glass window above the altar and throwing colors onto the front door. Several people are putting away cushions and setting up pews for tomorrow's Quaker meeting. When we close the door behind us, it looks as if there never was a *sesshin* or even a zendo in that little church today. What we take with us as we leave is exactly what we brought in this morning: a willing heart and an empty hand.

• • •

Jane Myoju Shuman lives in Purchase, New York, with her three girls (one human, two canine). She practices Zen, Tai-Chi, and gardening, and has been a student of Susan Ji-on Postal since 1991.

Sei and Her Soul Are Separated

DONNA THOMSON

❋

IN THE ZEN TRADITION, IT WAS NOT UNCOMMON for monks, after many years in the monastery, to disappear into the world for an extended period of time. There are many stories of this. One lived under a bridge with beggars for twenty years. Another lived with hunters, cooking his vegetables in the pot together with their meat. This time allowed the monks' practice to integrate, gave them experience of the world, scrubbed away the edges of pride that can arise on the spiritual path. Since leaving the Rochester Zen Center I have felt all the koans I worked on working on me, in me. They went deep. Over time, far away from the specialized atmosphere of *sesshin* and the Center, they became real, immediate, present.

A meditation retreat is an intensive, concentrated experience. So much can happen. Vistas open within, insights come, one experiences oneself and the universe in a completely new and different way. Then the time comes to get up from the mat, lift one's eyes, talk to people. How does one integrate the experience of the retreat into one's daily life? How does one live what one experiences in meditation? These are crucial, core issues on the spiritual path. Koans can help with this, but my experience has been that it takes a long, long time. They sink in, are absorbed into one's consciousness, and suddenly arise again years later and one says, "Oh, so that's it."

One koan in particular has stayed with me from the first time I heard it. This is the story of Sei and Her Soul, of separation and reunion. I first worked on it during an early morning *dokusan* (teacher interview) at a spring *sesshin* (retreat). I came downstairs to breakfast in the dawn light. I can still hear the birds. I can still taste the sweet rice cereal in my mouth. That moment, that koan, continued to work in me for years. Here is the story.

Case Number Thirty-five, The Mumonkan: Sei and Her Soul Are Separated

Sei and her soul are separated. When I first began to do *zazen* meditation, I cried every time I heard those words. Roshi used to give *teisho* (discourse) on this koan. He would read the whole story, then he would read the verse. I would feel as though my insides were being drawn up and out of me, as though I too were splitting from the inside out. I remember sitting under an ancient copper beech tree on East Avenue in Rochester, New York. It was summer twilight. The great tree stood tall above me, its long branches brushing the ground. The leaves were purple and green and brown all at once. They whispered. I sat against the tree, knees up, head down, and cried. For hours. Why? Because Sei and her soul were separated. Because, although I did not fully understand it, Donna and her soul were also separated.

I am three years old. My earliest memory is of being split. My grandmother has a bookcase with glass doors. I love to look in the bookcase and see the books. But there, also, in the bookcase is myself. Caught in the glass, unable to move, frozen, my three-year-old self stares back at me now. "Come out, little one, come out and dance, come out and play." She stares back, still caught. I am there with her suddenly, trapped in glass. If it shatters, I shatter. It holds me safe, this glass. It holds that self safe. In the glass I don't feel the hand in my vagina. I don't feel the terror, that I am a hole inside, that there is nothing in me. The hand goes in and in and in, and I am empty. There is nothing inside me, I feel myself falling through endless empty space, black, hole, empty, nothing. Me. You see, Buddha, how well I learned about no-self at such an early age. I don't think this is what you meant. I left a piece of myself there in that empty frozen darkness, in that glass door. That was only the beginning. Over and over I split, left pieces of myself. And years later I cried under a tree because Sei and her soul were separated.

I will tell you the story of Sei as I first heard it. It is not how it was told but it is how I heard it.

Goso asked a monk, "Sei and her soul are separated. Which one is the real Sei?"

That question has echoed in my heart ever since I knew I was supposed to have a self. Long before I ever heard the question, it whispered in my veins. Who is the real Donna? As a child, I also cried for hours, because I did not know what was real.

Sei was a beautiful young girl. She was the only daughter of Chokan. His elder daughter had died. Sei was very much in love with Ochu. I see her now, sitting by the river in her village, playing with the spring flowers, waiting for Ochu. She is small, and her dark hair blows in little wisps around her face. She loves the feel of her own hair. It reminds her of Ochu's lips. She smiles a little at the thought and smells a flower. She watches the ripple of the water. She is in no hurry. He will come. Instead, her father comes.

"I have arranged," he says, "to marry you to Hinryo."

She jumps up. The flowers fall from her hands. Her mind goes blank. She cannot speak.

"He will come at dinner tonight," says Chokan, "but of course you will not see him. He may wish to observe you from a distance after dinner. Be prepared to be called."

He leaves. Ochu arrives. They embrace. Sei is distressed. I see it suddenly like an old silent movie, in black and white, from a great distance. I cannot hear the words. I see Sei throw herself on the ground and sob, Ochu reaches down to her. They sit. He also bursts into tears. It is all so black and white, so silent, so far away. I cannot tell what time it is. Is it still afternoon? Is it night?

Ochu stands, he recedes. Suddenly he is in a boat, he is off down the river. He waves, and I know he is saying to Sei, "I must go away, I must, I cannot bear to see you married to another." Darkness falls, envelops. At midnight Ochu sees a figure beside the boat. Can it be? Not possible. It is! Sei has left her home and followed him; she is running, running beside the boat. He stops and pulls her in.

Now there is color again. Bright daylight. Sei is giving birth. A baby cries. She feels the wetness and blood of it on her breast. The blood is so red, the sun pouring in the window so bright. On the floor by the bed is a vase of pink plum blossoms. Smell the sweetness. Sei gives the baby her breast, feels the small mouth pull and suck. Ah. Ochu enters, smiles, embraces. Oh, he is warm, and big. Laughter. Touch. Warmth. Flesh holds flesh, bodies wrap around each other. I am so happy. Another child. After the second child Sei grows sad. She longs to see her home. She misses her family. Please. I want to go home.

Ochu and Sei return by the river with the two children. They journey on the blue water by day. They sleep deeply at night. Sei is afraid, and happy, and she lets her fingers trail gently in the river. It is cool, good, clear. The sun again is warm on her face; she loosens her robe and feels its warmth upon her breast. Ochu's touch suddenly joins that of the sun. She takes the hand and kisses it. Whose hand? Ochu's, of course. Sei feels a sudden fear, a sudden ripple in her stomach like the ripple of the river. Whose hand? What a foolish question. But she ripples again.

"I do not know," she thinks, "what is real."

Suddenly everything is black and white again as she approaches her home. It is night, it is misty. The water of the river is very still, a glass, a mirror. Sei sees her reflection through the mist. She sees familiar trees by the side of the river. The moon above is full. Everywhere there is frosted light, silver silence. It is all so sharp, like the edge of a gleaming knife blade. Sei is afraid. She can barely see her babies, her husband. She knows they are there in the boat. Aren't they?

"What is it?" asks Ochu. He shakes her a little. "You're dreaming. Look, we are almost there." Almost where? She shakes herself a little, plunges her hands in the cold night water and bathes her flushed face. But the color does not return to the world. The mist rises higher.

"Ochu, Ochu, where is my home?" she cries, "I cannot see it."

"It is here," he says, "it is here."

Sei waits in the boat while Ochu goes to her father. The old man sits on the wooden platform. The moon streams down. His hair is white and very long. There is a little jug of wine at his side. He sips as he watches the moon. The plum blossoms are out. It is the same time of year as when his Sei left. Of course, she did not really leave. Something moves in the mist. It is Ochu, that scoundrel, come back for what purpose? The father sighs. But then, I am an old man with much sorrow in my life. My wife is dead, my daughter. . . . so let me receive him with kindness, and hear his adventures. Ochu bows. The old man gestures that he should sit down and pours him some plum wine. The shadows are deep. Ochu sips the wine, feels its warmth. And stares into the mist.

"Where have you been?" the old man whispers. "And why have you returned? You have caused much suffering."

"Oh, father," cries Ochu. "Forgive me! I am so unworthy! But out of the suffering comes great good. You have two lovely grandchildren. A son and a daughter, born from the greatest love. They await you at the river."

The old man closes his eyes, clutches his beard. "Do not mock me. I have no grandchildren."

"You do, sir, you do. Sei and I have been living. . . ."

The old man leaps to his feet, the wine jug crashes and shatters, the silver silent mirror of the night shatters too. A plum stain spreads on the glistening floor. "How dare you mock me? How dare you!" he cries in a terrible voice. "My daughter lies here, helpless, ill, sleeping, unable to move, in that room, ever since the night you left. No doctor can help her, nothing can rouse her. She lies as though dead, and yet she breathes."

It is in slow motion now, as well as black and white, the old man's rage and grief. He is very white, the night behind him is black, he picks up the shattered jug and hurls it into the dark. It arcs slowly, endlessly, towards the moon. The old man leaps at Ochu, clutches him at the throat.

"No," Ochu cries. "She has been with me. We have plowed fields and planted seeds, we have lain together on long, warm summer evenings. There is no part of me, body or soul, that she has not touched. I have seen her cry, I have felt her tears on my chest. She has given birth, she has nursed her babies, I myself have tasted her mother's milk. You are mad. She cannot be here."

"*You* are mad!" shrieks the old man. "She lies here in her bed—there—go and see for yourself."

They both turn, with infinite slowness, and face the door where the old man points. Faint light streams out from behind the paper screen. The silence settles, swallows them both. Ochu looks at the old man. They stare into each other's eyes.

Suddenly they both know they are both telling the truth. Neither can grasp it, neither can deny it. The silence shifts, something enters it. A ripple. A whisper. They strain to hear.

"Father? Ochu?" They cannot tell the source, the direction. To each, it seems to come from his own heart.

"She is speaking," says the father. He dashes suddenly to the door, and stops.

"We must go gently," says Ochu. Gently, silently, they slide open the door. Gently, silently they step into the room. Each movement, each moment, each thought, echoes.

"Oh," the father is thinking, "my sweet Sei, have you returned to me?"

"Oh," Ochu is thinking, "my sweet Sei, now I know how completely you love." And what is Sei thinking?

At the river, Sei hears a whisper. Father. Ochu. Who said that? She sits up very straight and looks into the darkness. Deep in her body, in its depths, another ripple. It is as though I were with child, she thinks, and awaking in the morning, sick. She holds her belly, she feels the ripples. She waits. She hears a paper screen sliding open. She listens intently.

Ochu and the old man enter Sei's room. She lies very still. "She is so pale," thinks Ochu. She is robed in white, her bed is white, the flowers by her face are white. Even her lips are white, and oh, her hair is so black. A small black Buddha sits serenely looking down on her. Ochu goes to her side, presses his lips to her ear, and begins to whisper. A slight pink flush appears on her cheeks, her chest, her lips.

"Oh, Sei, sweet Sei, I have returned. It is Ochu. And I have brought Sei with me. Come, awake, move, you have two beautiful babies, a husband who loves you, a life to live, love to love, days to be happy, nights to be embraced. Come my Sei, come."

The father watches. He understands. He stays at the door. He knows she is no longer his, but she will again arise, and move and live. He holds himself very still and thinks of her birth, the small baby she was.

Sei opens her eyes. Her hand touches Ochu's. She doesn't speak. She knows exactly what to do, but everything is very blurry. It is hard to see Ochu's face, and her father is lost in the mist. She is alone. They are not important now. What she does see is herself, sharply clear in the silver, knifelike moonlight, on the river, holding the babies. She sees every pore of her silvered skin, gleaming. "Oh," she says, "it is so cold."

In the boat, Sei shivers, and draws her babies closer. She looks to the bank of the river and sees—what? Herself, sharply clear in the knifelike moonlight, standing with arms outstretched. The mist is gone. Sei knows exactly what to do. She puts down her babies and moves, gently, quietly, out of the boat. Her foot feels the cold water, the smooth wet stones of the shore. She holds out her arms. She sees in the achingly silver bright moonlight another pair of arms. There, on the wrist, a small black mole she knows very well. She looks into dark eyes and falls, down, down, into herself. Her fingers brush—what? The edges of herself. Her own hand, there. Slowly, in a great and beautiful dance, in a flash, the two Seis embrace. They match finger for finger, arm for arm, breast for breast, hair for hair, cell for cell. The two Seis become one.

The silence will never end. Moonlight becomes sunlight becomes moonlight. Shadows appear and disappear.

Colors come and go. The moment will never end. Sei stands by the river and looks down at her own hand and knows it, to its depths. The knowledge will never end. She reaches out to Ochu, and all that knowing is in her touch. She smiles. "I am Sei," she says.

Later, much later, when the babies are asleep in the house and the sun is rising, Ochu and Chokan and Sei eat breakfast. The sky is lavender and pink. The grass is wet, golden green. The bowl is blue, the rice is white. The tea is black and very hot. "This is such good rice," Sei thinks. She feels every grain on her tongue. Every grain.

The father says, "Ever since Ochu left, you have not uttered a word or moved from your bed. Now I see that your soul had left your body and followed him." Sei takes a sip of black hot tea and feels it touch her tongue, her throat, her stomach. She feels the warmth of the tea inside, the warmth of the sun outside.

The Zen master asks, "Which one is the real Sei?"

Sei smiles.

As a child I split, dissociated. Years and years later, long after I worked on this koan, long after I had spent many years in *zazen* practice, I began to understand what Sei and Her Soul meant to me. Slowly, painfully at first, then with more and more joy, I finally turned the light of awareness on my childhood. On my self. And found so many selves lost in the dark rooms, sleeping in the cold rooms, hiding in the corners. Welcome, welcome. Come out, come out. All these parts of myself, my dharma practice had never touched. They were hidden. I did so many years of sitting with one little piece of myself. Years later, in a therapist's office, in the moments of my life, in my meditation, finally, week after week, month after month, the pieces appeared. Matched each other. Heads joined bodies, three-year-olds joined five-year-olds. And they began to sit with me. Here we are, Buddha, all of us, all of me. Self. No-self. Countless selves. Hello, Buddha. I am Donna.

Sei dances now by the side of the river. I see her in full color. It is morning. Her children play nearby. She invites me to this dance, always. She invites me to welcome into life a part of myself that has been dead. To give birth deep within. To love myself into being. To come to life, to move, to breathe, to open not only my eyes, my heart, my mind, but my very cells. To awaken myself with the magic touch of my own love, my own awareness. To wake as if from a dream, to break the enchantment of the past, to join with myself in the depths of myself. Sei calls me, always. Into the frozen darkness, out of the frozen darkness. Into the long night, into the morning. Hear her whisper, her song. She calls you. She calls you.

The verse:

Ever the same, the moon among the clouds.
Different from each other, the mountain and the
    valley.
How wonderful, how blessed.
Is this one, is this two?

. . .

Donna Thomson was a member of the Rochester Zen Center from 1970 to 1985. Since that time she has not been formally affiliated with any institution; her path has led her to Ericksonian therapy, Tibetan teachings, Vipassana meditation, and the Divine Mother in her many forms, especially Mother Meera. She has an M.S.W., a background in family and individual therapy, and presently works in the United States and Europe as a channel for a consciousness that calls itself "Awareness." She lives in Santa Fe, New Mexico, with Robert Schrei, her husband of twenty years. She has one grown son, Josh.

The Mahayana Centers of North America

✦

ALABAMA

Green Mountain Zen Center

Green Mountain Zen Center is affiliated with Atlanta Soto Zen Center in Atlanta, Georgia, where Michael Elliston-Roshi lives. Elliston-Roshi conducts single-day *sesshin* at our center from time to time.
ADDRESS: 5014 Sunset Bluff Drive, Huntsville, AL 35803-1941
PHONE: (205) 882-0513
FAX: (205) 880-8928
E-MAIL: jag@hiwaay.net
LINEAGE: Soto Zen
SPIRITUAL HEAD: Michael Zenkai Taiun Elliston-Roshi
CONTACT: Jim Gordon
AFFILIATION: Atlanta Soto Zen Center
ESTABLISHED: 1992
FACILITIES: Floating
RETREATS OFFERED: Irregularly
PUBLICATIONS: *GMZC Newsletter.*

Zen Center of Huntsville

Zen Center of Huntsville, Alabama, is an informal association with a long history. We practice together twice a week. Call or e-mail for directions and times. Besides Dr. Seo, the center is guided by Zen Masters Donald Ta Hui Gilbert and Soeng-ryang Hearn.

ADDRESS: Huntsville, Alabama
PHONE: (205) 776-2290
E-MAIL: fague@hiwaay.net
LINEAGE: Korean Chogye Zen
SPIRITUAL HEAD: Zen Master Kyung-bo Seo
CONTACT: Michael Fague
AFFILIATION: Il-bung Zen Society
ESTABLISHED: 1974

ALASKA

Anchorage Zen Center

For further description please refer to the Community of Mindful Living in Berkeley, California.
ADDRESS: 13852 Caravelle Drive, Anchorage, AK 99502
PHONE: (907) 278-6732
LINEAGE: Mindfulness practice in the tradition of Thich Nhat Hanh.
SPIRITUAL HEAD: Thich Nhat Hanh
CONTACT: Elizabeth McNeil
AFFILIATION: Community of Mindful Living, Berkeley, California
MEDITATION PROGRAM: We sit Sunday mornings and have a short recitation. A dharma discussion on the precepts is held once a week.
RETREATS OFFERED: Days of Mindfulness each month in our forest retreat.

Anchorage Zen Community

Anchorage Zen Community borrows a quotation from Kosho Uchiyama to describe its statement of purpose: "(to) cooperate with one another and aim to create a place where sincere practitioners can practice without trouble."
ADDRESS: 2401 Susitna, Anchorage, AK 99517
PHONE: (907) 248-1049
LINEAGE: Japanese Soto Zen
CONTACT: Judith Haggar
AFFILIATION: Autonomous
ESTABLISHED: 1982
FACILITIES: Use of a yoga studio and a rural retreat house for *sesshin.*
RETREATS OFFERED: Three- to seven-day *sesshin*, three or four times per year.
PUBLICATIONS: Quarterly newsletter.

ARIZONA

Arizona Buddhist Temple

We offer many activities for families and individuals. These include regular Sunday services with dharma school for the children. We also have discussion and study groups, a Desert Dharma Club for adults, a women's association, and a chapter of the Junior Young Buddhists Association. Visitors are always welcome.

ADDRESS: 4142 West Clarendon Avenue, Phoenix, AZ 85019-3617
PHONE: (602) 278-0036
FAX: (602) 278-1939
LINEAGE: Buddhist Churches of America
SPIRITUAL HEAD: Bishop Hakubun Watanabe
CONTACT: Rev. Lee Rosenthal
AFFILIATION: Buddhist Churches of America
ESTABLISHED: 1933
FACILITIES: Temple
RETREATS OFFERED: Yes
PUBLICATIONS: *Prajna*

Desert Cactus Sangha

We gather together on one Sunday each month for a half-Day of Mindfulness, including sitting and walking meditation, readings, discussion, and viewing of videotapes of Thich Nhat Hanh or other spiritual teachers, followed by a silent vegetarian potluck. We also meet one evening a month to meditate. Call for times.
ADDRESS: 5437 East Pinchot Avenue, Phoenix, AZ 85018
PHONE: (602) 952-0915
FAX: (602) 495-2432
E-MAIL: mcolpas@ci.phoenix.az.us
LINEAGE: Mindfulness practice in the tradition of Thich Nhat Hanh.
SPIRITUAL HEAD: Thich Nhat Hanh
CONTACT: Marcie Colpas
AFFILIATION: Autonomous
ESTABLISHED: 1993
FACILITIES: Meet in private home.
RETREATS OFFERED: Annual retreat in early May.

Haku-un-ji Tempe Zen Center

Haku-un-ji was founded by Sokai, a student of Joshu Sasaki-Roshi at Mt. Baldy Zen Center for over five years. The Sunday sitting group, with instruction for beginners, meets at Tempe Bodyworks Studio (1801 South Jentilly, #8). There are also sittings three evenings weekly at the *zendo* on Cedar Street. These include sutra chanting and (sometimes) a discussion group. Please call ahead for directions and times. There are monthly *zazenkai* and periodic retreats. No overnight accommodations are available. The practice is Rinzai, based upon the liturgy of Mt. Baldy Zen Center. Soto practitioners are also welcome.
ADDRESS: 1448 East Cedar Street, Tempe, AZ 85281
PHONE: (602) 894-6353
E-MAIL: TwwX80A@Prodigy.com
LINEAGE: Japanese Rinzai Zen
SPIRITUAL HEAD: Kyozan Joshu Sasaki-Roshi
CONTACT: Sokai Barratt, resident monk
AFFILIATION: Rinzai-ji/Mt. Baldy
ESTABLISHED: 1994
FACILITIES: *Zendo* accommodating approximately twenty practitioners. No overnight accommodations.
RETREATS OFFERED: Monthly one-day and quarterly weekend *zazenkai*.

Jodo Shu Dharma Center

We are a family-oriented Pure Land Buddhist center. We provide Sunday services and a study group. The first Wednesday evening of each month we gather for *nembutsu* practice. Newcomers are welcome.
ADDRESS: 229 East Palo Verde Street, Gilbert, AZ 85296
PHONE: (602) 545-7684
LINEAGE: Jodo Shu
SPIRITUAL HEAD: Bishop Satoru Ryosho Kawai
CONTACT: Terry Lewis
AFFILIATION: Jodo Shu North America Missions
ESTABLISHED: 1992
FACILITIES: Meet in private home.

Peace House

We practice engaged Buddhism, in which we look deeply at our interdependence with all things. We do this through Vipassana meditation as a community, and not just as individuals.
ADDRESS: 4601 East Monte Vista Road, Phoenix, AZ 85008
PHONE: (602) 389-9862
LINEAGE: Tiep Hien Order
SPIRITUAL HEAD: Thich Nhat Hanh
CONTACT: Marvin Brown
AFFILIATION: Tiep Hien order
ESTABLISHED: 1996
FACILITIES: Center
RETREATS OFFERED: Irregularly scheduled.

Satisfied Mind Sangha

For additional information please refer to the Community of Mindful Living in Berkeley, California.
ADDRESS: 113 West Goodwin, Prescott, AZ 86303
PHONE: (602) 776-9766
LINEAGE: Mindfulness practice in the tradition of Thich Nhat Hanh.
SPIRITUAL HEAD: Thich Nhat Hanh
CONTACT: Tom Brodersen
AFFILIATION: Community of Mindful Living, Berkeley, California
MEDITATION PROGRAM: We meet one evening weekly as a nonsectarian Buddhist meditation group.

Valley Unitarian Universalist Zen Group/Desert Lotus Sangha

We are an interfaith Zen meditation group guided by James Ford Osho. Rev. Ford has been ordained both as a Unitarian Universalist minister and a Soto Zen priest. Since 1986 he has been a student of John Tarrant-Roshi, head of the California Diamond Sangha. Our style is informal but follows the Diamond Sangha tradition.

ADDRESS: 1700 West Warner Road, Chandler, AZ 85224

PHONE: (602) 899-4249

E-MAIL: JJFord@Goodnet.com, or UUBF@UUA.org

LINEAGE: Zen

CONTACT: Rev. James Ishmael Ford

AFFILIATION: Autonomous

ESTABLISHED: 1996

FACILITIES: Meetings at Valley Unitarian Universalist Church.

RETREATS OFFERED: Half-day, as announced.

Zen Desert Sangha

Zen Desert Sangha is affiliated with Diamond Sangha, founded by Robert Aitken-Roshi. Our practice combines elements of both the Soto and Rinzai Zen traditions in the spirit of a truly democratic *sangha* that is open to all. While we do not have a resident teacher, we are in close contact with Patrick Hawk-Roshi, a dharma heir of Aitken-Roshi. We have three on-site *sesshin* annually and a variety of other events during the year. We are an active, thriving Zen center. Visitors are always welcome!

ADDRESS: PO Box 44122, Tucson, AZ 85733-4122

PHONE: (520) 327-8460

E-MAIL: rjlane@tmug.com

LINEAGE: Japanese/Sanbo Kyodan/Diamond Sangha

SPIRITUAL HEAD: Robert Aitken-Roshi

AFFILIATION: Diamond Sangha/Three Treasures lineage

ESTABLISHED: 1982

FACILITIES: Large dedicated *zendo*; retreat facilities.

RETREATS OFFERED: Three *sesshin* yearly with Pat Hawk-Roshi.

PUBLICATIONS: *The Buddhist Stew*

ARKANSAS

Eureka Springs Sangha

For additional information please refer to the Community of Mindful Living in Berkeley, California.

ADDRESS: Rt. 1, Box 184A, Eureka Springs, AR 72632

PHONE: (501) 253-6984

LINEAGE: Mindfulness practice in the tradition of Thich Nhat Hanh.

SPIRITUAL HEAD: Thich Nhat Hanh

CONTACT: Tina Moon

AFFILIATION: Community of Mindful Living, Berkeley, California

MEDITATION PROGRAM: We meet monthly for mindfulness practice and precept recitation. As we grow, we will meet more often for sitting meditation.

Zen Center of Hot Springs

Hot Springs National Park is a resort city famous for its pure spring water, lakes, mountains, and southern hospitality. Easy living. Bill Clinton grew up here. Internationally famous artists have established a monthly gallery walk, Documentary Film Festival, Arkansas Arts Festival, and the Hot Springs Music Festival. Howard Lee Kilby, a student of Robert Aitken during the mid-1970s and presently doing *koan* study with Keido Fukushima (Tofukuji Monastery, Kyoto, Japan) has pioneered in this beautiful city, laying the cornerstone for Zen practice to exist. He welcomes those interested in Buddhism.

ADDRESS: Box 1260, Hot Springs National Park, AR 71902-1260

PHONE: (501) 767-6096

LINEAGE: Japanese Rinzai Zen

SPIRITUAL HEAD: Howard Lee Kilby

CONTACT: Same

AFFILIATION: Tofukuji Monastery, Kyoto, Japan

CALIFORNIA

Almond Blossom Sangha

For additional information, please refer to Community of Mindful Living, Berkeley, California.

ADDRESS: 501 Thor Street, Turlock, CA 95380

PHONE: (209) 634-2172

E-MAIL: scunningham@stan-co.k12.ca.us

LINEAGE: Mindfulness practice in the tradition of Thich Nhat Hanh.

SPIRITUAL HEAD: Thich Nhat Hanh

CONTACT: Stan Cunningham

AFFILIATION: Community of Mindful Living, Berkeley, California

MEDITATION PROGRAM: We meet semi-weekly.

Arcata Sangha

For additional information please refer to Community of Mindful Living, Berkeley, California.

ADDRESS: 3471 Jacoby Creek Road, Bayside, CA 95421

PHONE: (707) 443-6558

LINEAGE: Mindfulness practice in the tradition of Thich Nhat Hanh.

SPIRITUAL HEAD: Thich Nhat Hanh

CONTACT: Ginger Kossow

AFFILIATION: Community of Mindful Living, Berkeley, California

MEDITATION PROGRAM: We meet twice monthly for sitting meditation. Call for details.

Bay Zen Center

Bay Zen Center originated in 1985 as a group of students studying with Charlotte Joko Beck. In 1994 Joko's Dharma successor, Diane Eshin Rizzetto, became the Center's teacher and abbot. Practice here is centered in the realization that true liberation rests in the heart of our

Diane Eshin Rizzetto, Dharma successor of Charlotte Joko Beck, is Teacher and Abbot of Bay Zen Center in Oakland, California. (Photo courtesy of Bay Zen Center.)

CALIFORNIA *(cont.)*

worldly activities. In this sense, our work at Bay Zen Center supports an ongoing awareness of life as it is in any moment, in any event, in any place. The center is open to beginners and experienced students and to people of all traditions.

ADDRESS: 5600A Snake Road, Oakland, CA 94611

PHONE: (510) 482-2533

FAX: (510) 482-9531

LINEAGE: Zen

SPIRITUAL HEAD: Diane Eshin Rizzetto

CONTACT: Same

AFFILIATION: Ordinary Mind Zen School/Charlotte Joko Beck

ESTABLISHED: 1985

FACILITIES: Urban Zen center.

MEDITATION PROGRAM: Daily *zazen.* Call for times.

RETREATS OFFERED: *Sesshin*: two- to five-day, five per year. *Zazenkai* (one-day sittings): five per year.

PUBLICATIONS: Newsletter

Berkeley Buddhist Monastery/ Institute of World Religions

Berkeley Buddhist Monastery offers daily and weekly lectures and ceremonies, classes, meditation periods, vegetarian meals, and celebrations of Buddhist holidays. Special ceremonies for taking refuge, receiving precepts and liberating life are held regularly. The Institute of World Religions is an independent institution of higher learning dedicated to research and inquiry into the nature of world religions and spirituality in relation to science. An integral part of Dharma Realm Buddhist University, its focus is on the promotion of mutual understanding among the diverse cultures and citizens of the contemporary world.

ADDRESS: 2304 McKinley Avenue, Berkeley, CA 94703

PHONE: (510) 848-3440

FAX: (510) 548-4551

LINEAGE: We propagate all major Mahayana schools (Ch'an, Pure Land, Vinaya, Scholastic, and Esoteric), and work closely with Theravada.

SPIRITUAL HEAD: Ven. Hsuan Hua

CONTACT: Bhikshu Heng Sure, Resident Director

AFFILIATION: City of Ten Thousand Buddhas/Dharma Realm Buddhist Association

ESTABLISHED: 1994

FACILITIES: Converted church building in Berkeley near University of California campus.

Berkeley Buddhist Priory

Berkeley Buddhist Priory is a church in the Serene Reflection Meditation tradition. It is a branch temple of Shasta Abbey, a Buddhist monastery in Mt. Shasta, California (headquarters of the Order of Buddhist Contemplatives of the Soto Zen Church). Founded in 1973 by the late Rev. Master Jiyu-Kennett,

MOBC, the priory serves the Greater Bay Area as a religious center for the study and practice of Serene Reflection Meditation within the context of a lay community. The prior is Rev. Alden Fulcher, FOBC.

ADDRESS: 1358 Marin Avenue, Albany, CA 94706

PHONE: (510) 528-2139

LINEAGE: Order of Buddhist Contemplatives, Soto Zen Church

SPIRITUAL HEAD: The late Rev. Master Jiyu-Kennett, MOBC

CONTACT: Rev. Alden Fulcher, FOBC

AFFILIATION: Shasta Abbey, Mt. Shasta, California

ESTABLISHED: 1973

FACILITIES: Meditation and ceremony hall, small library, common room.

MEDITATION PROGRAM: Weekly, evening meditation instruction. Meditation and Buddhist services two to three times daily, Tuesday through Sunday. Call for schedule.

RETREATS OFFERED: All-day, Saturday retreats, four times a year. Reservation is required as space is limited.

PUBLICATIONS: *Berkeley Buddhist Priory*, newsletter.

Berkeley Sangha

For additional information please refer to Community of Mindful Living, Berkeley, California.

ADDRESS: 768 Contra Costa Avenue, Berkeley, CA 94707

PHONE: (510) 526-4476

LINEAGE: Mindfulness practice in the tradition of Thich Nhat Hanh.

SPIRITUAL HEAD: Thich Nhat Hanh

CONTACT: Edie Hartshorne

AFFILIATION: Community of Mindful Living, Berkeley, California

MEDITATION PROGRAM: We meet twice a week for sitting and walking meditation. Call for details.

Eye Gazing

PRACTICE AT THE BAY ZEN CENTER IS ROOTED IN an understanding that everything we do in our lives provides an opportunity to become aware. It is centered in the realization that true liberation is at hand whenever we bring attention to the immediate moment.

In learning to bring awareness to the thoughts, emotions and bodily sensations that arise during *sesshin*, we become more intimate with the patterns that dictate our lives and keep us from experiencing things as they are. To help us hone our awareness skills, we've begun incorporating periods of "eye gazing" practice into our retreats at Bay Zen Center.

Here's how it works. Students pair up with the person sitting next to them. Sitting face to face with knees touching, they look deeply into each others' eyes and pay close attention to what comes up: thoughts, emotions, bodily sensations. Each arising phenomenon is labeled: "fear," "anger," "sadness," "joy." Sometimes the emotions express themselves in complete sentences: "Why does he look at me so harshly? I must be doing something wrong." At other times sensations in the body bubble up: tightness, numbness, roller-coaster stomach.

There's a direct correlation between what happens in "eye gazing" and the manner in which we respond to events in our everyday lives. Here's an example: At work a colleague glares at me. The thought arises, "What have I done wrong?" accompanied by a tightening in my stomach and the fear that I am inadequate in some way. Instead of allowing the fear to proliferate unconsciously, I'm able to bring awareness to the situation. I note each sensation in turn, and in the noting there is acceptance and a letting go and I am liberated from my fear.

Venice Wagner

For more information, contact: Bay Zen Center, 5600A Snake Road, Oakland, CA 94611; (510) 482-2533.

Berkeley Zen Center

Berkeley Zen Center is a neighborhood practice center in the Soto Zen tradition. It is led by Abbot Sojun Mel Weitsman, a student of Shunryu Suzuki-Roshi. Practice includes daily *zazen*, service, *sesshin*, classes, practice periods, and social events. Emphasis is on lay practice in the midst of demanding lifestyles; however, opportunities to engage in steady residential training are also offered. We are a friendly place and we eat well!

ADDRESS: 1931 Russell Street, Berkeley, CA 94703
PHONE: (510) 845-2403
LINEAGE: Japanese Soto Zen
SPIRITUAL HEAD: Sojun Mel Weitsman
CONTACT: Alan Senauke
AFFILIATION: Autonomous
ESTABLISHED: 1967
FACILITIES: *Zendo*, five resident apartments, guest room, community room with kitchen.
PUBLICATIONS: Monthly newsletter.

Blessings, Prosperity & Longevity Monastery

For additional information see listing for City of Ten Thousand Buddhas, Talmage, California.
ADDRESS: 4140 Long Beach Boulevard, Long Beach, CA 90807
PHONE: (310) 595-4966
LINEAGE: We propagate all major Mahayana schools (Ch'an, Pure Land, Vinaya, Scholastic, and Esoteric) and work closely with Theravada.
SPIRITUAL HEAD: Ven. Hsuan Hua
AFFILIATION: City of Ten Thousand Buddhas/Dharma Realm Buddhist Association
ESTABLISHED: 1994
FACILITIES: Worship/meditation hall, residential and retreat space for women. Nuns' convent.

California Buddhist University

No description available.
ADDRESS: 1947 Lansdowne Avenue, Los Angeles, CA 90032
PHONE: (213) 628-3449
LINEAGE: Shaolin Zen
SPIRITUAL HEADS: Dr. Jefferson Chan, Ven. Dr. Havanpola Ratanasara
CONTACT: Dr. Jefferson Chan

Sword of Wisdom, Hands of Compassion

EVEN PEOPLE WHO KNOW NOTHING ELSE ABOUT Zen have heard that Zen practitioners are hit with a stick during meditation. The *kyosaku*, a flattened three-foot-long stick used to strike students on the fleshy parts of the shoulders or back, is used, in most American dojos, only on those who request it by placing the palms together as the *sesshin* leader walks past. Ideally, the *kyosaku* is flicked in such a way as to give a momentary sting, without lingering pain, to the muscles beneath.

Those who request the *kyosaku* say it invigorates them, wakes them up, or intensifies their concentration. Others would never dream of asking to be hit and consider the practice a relic of a patriarchal, authoritarian society. The sharp double crack of the stick is deeply meaningful to some in the dojo; to others it is an unnecessary and disturbing distraction.

At our retreats students can ask for either the *kyosaku* or a brief—thirty- to sixty-second—shoulder massage. As one who has given and received both the *kyosaku* and the massage, I can say that the massage is a heart-opening experience for both giver and receiver. And it reflects a growing belief in the West that Zen practice does not have to be austere, daunting, or painful.

Perhaps these two techniques, one steeped in Japanese tradition, the other so characteristically Western, are complementary. If the *kyosaku* could be said to represent the sword of Manjushri, the Bodhisattva of Wisdom who cuts off delusion and inspires us with zeal, the hands of the massager are the thousand all-seeing hands of Avalokiteshvara, the Bodhisattva of Compassion who opens our hearts to the sounds of the many beings.

Bonnie Allen

For more information, contact: California Diamond Sangha, Box 2972, Santa Rosa, CA 95405; (707) 763-9466.

CALIFORNIA *(cont.)*

AFFILIATION: Shaolin Temple/Kewanee Mountain Zen Center
ESTABLISHED: 1988
FACILITIES: One *zendo*, ten rooms.
RETREATS OFFERED: Quarterly residential retreats.
PUBLICATIONS: *Shaolin Monastery*, quarterly.

California Diamond Sangha

California Diamond Sangha is a group of friends who practice the ancient and delightful tradition of Zen meditation together. We have a special interest in the arts, social action, and psychology. The Sanskrit word *sangha* originally referred to the assembly of monks and nuns who heard and preserved the Buddha's teachings. Over the centuries, it has come to mean the community of followers of the way, both monastic and lay. Buddhists of all times and places have understood the value of community and it is our aim to build one that is companionable, democratic, and inclusive of families and children.

ADDRESS: PO Box 2972, Santa Rosa, CA 95405
PHONE: (707) 763-9466
LINEAGE: Rinzai/Soto Zen
SPIRITUAL HEAD: John Tarrant-Roshi
CONTACT: Same
AFFILIATION: Diamond Sangha, but autonomous.
ESTABLISHED: 1987
FACILITIES: Sublet

RETREATS OFFERED: Yes
PUBLICATIONS: Newsletter. *Blind Donkey* (journal).

California Diamond Sangha/ Oakland Dojo

We are the Oakland sitting group of the California Diamond Sangha headquartered in Santa Rosa, California. John Tarrant-Roshi, dharma heir of Robert Aitken-Roshi, is our spiritual head. John and/or one of his senior students is available in Oakland approximately twice monthly for *dokusan* (private interview) or an occasional dharma talk. We meet one evening a week for group practice. *Zazen* instruction is available on request.
PHONE: (510) 531-5779

LINEAGE: Soto/Rinzai Zen, Harada-Yasutani line

SPIRITUAL HEAD: John Tarrant-Roshi

AFFILIATION: California Diamond Sangha, Santa Rosa, California

ESTABLISHED: 1988

MEDITATION PROGRAM: Group practice and *zazen* instruction one evening weekly. Please call for location and times.

Chabolyn Terrace Sangha

For additional information please refer to Community of Mindful Living, Berkeley, California.

ADDRESS: 5995 Chabolyn Terrace, Oakland, CA 94618

PHONE: (510) 654-2456

LINEAGE: Mindfulness practice in the tradition of Thich Nhat Hanh.

SPIRITUAL HEAD: Thich Nhat Hanh

CONTACT: Caleb Cushing

AFFILIATION: Community of Mindful Living, Berkeley, California

MEDITATION PROGRAM: On Sunday mornings we practice sitting and walking meditation, recite the Five Precepts, and discuss the dharma.

Chua Viet Nam (Vietnam Temple)

Chua Viet Nam is the principal cultural center for thousands of Vietnamese Buddhists living in Los Angeles and Orange Counties. The late Dr. Thich Thien An, a Vietnamese Zen Master and scholar of formidable credentials, arrived in the United States in 1966 to teach the dharma to Americans. Eleven years later he founded Chua Viet Nam. Dr. Thich Man Giac, Ph.D., a renowned poet and close friend and classmate of Dr. Thien An, succeeded him and continued his wonderful work at the temple. Here various Mahayana Buddhist traditions (Su-

Lord Buddha's Nativity Festival at Chua Viet-Nam (Vietnam Temple) in Los Angeles, California. (Photo courtesy of Chua Viet-Nam.)

trayana, Vajrayana, Rinzai, Pure Land, etc.) are practiced and preserved.

ADDRESS: 857-871 South Berendo Street, Los Angeles, CA 90005

PHONE: (213) 384-9638

FAX: (213) 384-1547

LINEAGE: Vietnamese *Lam Te* (*Rinzai/Lin-chi*), Vajrayana, Pure Land

SPIRITUAL HEAD: The Abbot Supreme Ven. Dr. Thich Man Giac. Many monks and nuns are Resident Teachers at the temple.

AFFILIATION: Headquarters of Vietnamese Buddhist United Churches in the United States. Also affiliated with the World Buddhist Fellowship organization and the World Buddhist Sangha Council.

ESTABLISHED: 1975

FACILITIES: Urban temple and monastery, a training center for both monastics and the general public.

MEDITATION PROGRAM: Weekend services. Annual ceremonies and Buddhist celebrations. Weddings, funerals, and counseling.

RETREATS OFFERED: Intensive meditation retreats under the guidance of monks and/or nuns.

City of Ten Thousand Buddhas (CTTB)/Dharma Realm Buddhist Association

An ideal environment for spiritual growth and wholesome fellowship, CTTB is set among the groves and meadows of beautiful Ukiah Valley in Mendocino County, California. Everyone shares a common goal: the sincere pursuit of spiritual truth, wisdom, and compassion. Seminars, conferences, and lectures take place under the auspices of Dharma Realm Buddhist University. The City of Ten Thousand Buddhas adheres to the standards of orthodox Pure Land and Ch'an monasteries.

CALIFORNIA (cont.)

CTTB and all branch temples of the Dharma Realm Buddhist Association offer daily meditation, classes, ceremonies, memorial services, and celebrations of Buddhist holidays.
ADDRESS: PO Box 217, Talmage, CA 95481-0217
PHONE: (707) 462-0939
FAX: (707) 462-0949
LINEAGE: We propagate all major Mahayana Schools (Ch'an, Pure Land, Vinaya, Scholastic, and Esoteric), and work closely with Theravada.
SPIRITUAL HEAD: Ven. Hsuan Hua
AFFILIATION: Dharma Realm Buddhist Association
ESTABLISHED: 1976
FACILITIES: Rural, residential monastery and retreat center. The grounds include more than seventy buildings on eighty landscaped acres.
RETREATS OFFERED: Many retreat opportunities throughout the year, following the Buddhist calendar.
PUBLICATIONS: Vajra Bodhi Sea, monthly journal.

City of the Dharma Realm

Nuns' convent. For additional information see listing for City of Ten Thousand Buddhas, Talmage, California.
ADDRESS: 1029 West Capitol Avenue, West Sacramento, CA 95691
PHONE: (916) 374-8268
LINEAGE: We propagate all major Mahayana schools (Ch'an, Pure Land, Vinaya, Scholastic, and Esoteric) and work closely with Theravada.
SPIRITUAL HEAD: Ven. Hsuan Hua
AFFILIATION: City of Ten Thousand Buddhas/Dharma Realm Buddhist Association
ESTABLISHED: 1993
FACILITIES: Worship/meditation hall, residential and retreat space for women.

PUBLICATION: City of the Dharma Realm Newsletter (monthly).

Community of Mindful Living

Since 1983, Thich Nhat Hanh has been leading retreats in North America on the practice of Mindfulness meditation. Community of Mindful Living was formed to help support this practice. We organize and conduct retreats and publish and distribute books, tapes, and a newsletter. We are establishing a rural, residential retreat center and developing programs for war veterans and for those in need in Vietnam and elsewhere. Staff and volunteers try to "practice what we publish"; whenever the telephone rings, for example, we stop and practice mindful breathing for three inhalations and exhalations before continuing the work, refreshed and fully present.
ADDRESS: PO Box 7355, Berkeley, CA 94707
PHONE: (510) 527-3741
FAX: (510) 525-7129
E-MAIL: parapress@aol.com
WWW: http://www.parallax.org
LINEAGE: Vietnamese Rinzai Zen. Mindfulness practice in the tradition of Thich Nhat Hanh.
SPIRITUAL HEAD: Ven. Thich Nhat Hanh
CONTACT: Arnold Kotler, Resident Director
AFFILIATION: Plum Village (France), Maple Village (Quebec), Manzanita Village (Southern California), and sanghas across the United States and Canada.
ESTABLISHED: 1983
FACILITIES: Offices in a former church. The rear house serves as a meditation and meeting hall.
MEDITATION PROGRAM: Weekly meditation and dharma discussion.
RETREATS OFFERED: Nationwide retreats listed in newsletter.

PUBLICATIONS: The Mindfulness Bell, newsletter and Parallax Press catalogue of books.

Desert Zen Center/Monjuji

Desert Zen Center is a monastery and temple dedicated to teaching Buddhism and meditation to all. Formerly used for retreats by members of Long Beach Zen Monastery and the International Buddhist Meditation Center, the property has been occupied since 1982 by the Ven. Thich An Giao, his family, and his senior disciple. Three buildings have been constructed since then, including a new meditation hall. We offer workshops, retreats, Buddhist services, and meditation instruction throughout the year. All are welcome at Desert Zen Center and one's religious affiliation has no bearing on whether one can practice Zen.
ADDRESS: 10989 Buena Vista Road, Lucerne Valley, CA 92356
PHONE: (619) 248-7404
E-MAIL: dbucky@earthlink.net
LINEAGE: Vietnamese Zen, Lam Te order
SPIRITUAL HEAD: Ven. Thich Man Giac
CONTACT: Ven. Thich An Giao, Resident Teacher
AFFILIATION: Autonomous
ESTABLISHED: 1976
FACILITIES: Country retreat facility, residency program for priests and priests-in-training.
MEDITATION PROGRAM: One morning, two evening sessions weekly.
RETREATS OFFERED: Monthly weekend retreats and workshops. Summer Monk's Training ending with seven-day retreat.
PUBLICATIONS: Newsletter

Dharma Eye Zen Center

We are a Zen mushroom that has sprung up in the backyard of our teacher, Myogen Steve Stucky. Dharma Eye Zen Center endeavors to create a place and occasion for the cultivation of the *buddhadharma*. Our work is guided by the teachings of the Soto Zen School as conveyed by Shunryu Suzuki-Roshi and is informed by the wide spectrum of dharma teaching, both historical and contemporary. Based on the Buddha's example of wisdom and compassion, we formally practice the way of *zazen* and extend it through the many activities of our daily life.

ADDRESS: 333 Bayview Street, San Rafael, CA 94901
PHONE: (415) 258-0802
LINEAGE: Soto Zen
SPIRITUAL HEAD: Myogen Steven Stucky
ESTABLISHED: 1996
FACILITIES: *Zendo*
RETREATS OFFERED: Yearly seven-day *sesshin*.

Dharma Gate Sangha

Almost all of us came to Dharma Gate Sangha with no previous experience in Buddhist practice. Many have a dual practice in Buddhism and Christianity or Judaism and some are active in Twelve-step programs. We receive referrals from local physicians and psychotherapists. Several have come through the Mindfulness-based Stress Reduction and Chronic Pain programs taught by Patrick Thornton. Members have expressed interest in developing an organizational structure and acquiring property to expand programs and activities. The *sangha* is grounded in the dharma and welcomes guests and new members with an open heart.

ADDRESS: PO Box 1933, Benicia, CA 94510
PHONE: (707) 747-9550
FAX: (707) 647-1253
E-MAIL: upekkha@well.com

LINEAGE: Mindfulness practice in the tradition of Thich Nhat Hanh.
SPIRITUAL HEAD: Thich Nhat Hanh
CONTACT: Patrick Thornton
AFFILIATION: Community of Mindful Living, Berkeley, California
MEDITATION PROGRAM: One evening weekly for meditation and talk or discussion on practice in daily life. Precept recitations at meeting closest to the new moon.
RETREATS OFFERED: Beginning meditation classes and retreats.

Dharma Kai Zen Center

No description available.
ADDRESS: c/o Aikido Ai Dojo, 6727 South Milton Avenue, Whittier, CA 90601
PHONE: (213) 934-0330
LINEAGE: Korean Zen (Zen Master Seung Sahn)
AFFILIATION: Kwan Um School of Zen

Dharma Zen Center

At Dharma Zen Center we wake early, bow, chant, meditate, and then go off to work or school. In the evenings, more group practice. Residents share in the cooking and cleaning and take part in monthly retreats. Two of our residents are monks, working and teaching full time at the center. Visitors are welcome to join us for practice, for a meal, to stay overnight, or for group or individual retreats. Dharma Zen Center is located two blocks west of La Brea Avenue, just south of Olympic Boulevard in the pleasant Mid-Wilshire area of Los Angeles.

ADDRESS: 1025 South Cloverdale Avenue, Los Angeles, CA 90019
PHONE: (213) 934-0330
FAX: (213) 933-3072
LINEAGE: Korean/Chogye Zen
SPIRITUAL HEAD: Zen Master Seung Sahn (Dae Soen Sa Nim)

CONTACT: Mu Sang Sunim, Abbot
AFFILIATION: Kwan Um School of Zen
ESTABLISHED: 1974
FACILITIES: Urban residential Zen center.
MEDITATION PROGRAM: Bowing, chanting, sitting twice daily.
RETREATS OFFERED: Monthly one- or three-day retreats.

Empty Gate Zen Center

Empty Gate Zen Center is a community-based practice group with members throughout the San Francisco Bay and Monterey, California, areas. We conduct a weekly open house with chanting, meditation instruction, sitting practice, and a short talk and question-and-answer period by Guiding Teacher Jeff Kitzes, JDPSN. Through the Kwan Um School of Zen and its affiliates we provide a full schedule of three-week and three-month meditation retreats called *Kyol Che*. New and longtime students are welcome to join us.

ADDRESS: 3179 College Avenue, Berkeley, CA 94705
PHONE: (510) 653-5991
E-MAIL: egzc@emptygatezen.com
LINEAGE: Korean Zen
SPIRITUAL HEAD: Zen Master Seung Sahn, Founding Teacher. Jeff Kitzes, JDPSN, Guiding Teacher.
AFFILIATION: Kwan Um School of Zen
ESTABLISHED: 1977
FACILITIES: Rented dharma room.
RETREATS OFFERED: One- or three-day retreats eight to ten times per year.
PUBLICATIONS: *Gong Mun*, newsletter.

Fort Bragg Sangha

Our *sangha* is an eclectic group with people who study Theravada, Tibetan, and Zen Buddhism. As Thich Nhat Hanh says, "Sometimes fruit salad is nice." We have formed a subgroup called the Diving

CALIFORNIA (*cont.*)

Deeper Sangha for those who wish to spend more time with Thich Nhat Hanh's teachings. For additional information please refer to Community of Mindful Living, Berkeley, California.

ADDRESS: PO Box 2031, Fort Bragg, CA 95437

PHONE: (707) 964-2931

E-MAIL: ranban@ert.com

LINEAGE: Mindfulness practice in the tradition of Thich Nhat Hanh.

SPIRITUAL HEAD: Thich Nhat Hanh

CONTACTS: Randy and Lisa Bancroft

AFFILIATION: Community of Mindful Living, Berkeley, California

MEDITATION PROGRAM: We meet every Monday night and every other Wednesday night. Call for times and locations.

RETREATS OFFERED: Half-Days of Mindfulness with sitting and walking meditation, silent meal, and taped dharma talk.

Fruitvale Zendo

Street corner wall sitting
Ceaseless traffic sound of cars trucks
busses on San Leandro Street
Union Pacific across from that
BART above that and Amtrak and
Southern Pacific a block away
parallel to I-880
jets flying in and out of Oakland
International
police helicopter circling
dogs barking
sirens blaring
drunken brawlers
hot rodders
boom boxes
car alarms
no bird song
this is my remote mountain temple

ADDRESS: 4001 San Leandro Street #1, Oakland, CA 94601

PHONE: (510) 532-5226

E-MAIL: utapipig@ix.netcom.com

WWW: http://pw2.netcom.com/ ~utapipig/zendo.html

LINEAGE: Japanese Soto Zen

SPIRITUAL HEAD: Sojun Mel Weitsman-Roshi

CONTACT: Greg Fain

AFFILIATION: Berkeley Zen Center

ESTABLISHED: 1996

FACILITIES: Small zendo, maximum occupancy is about five.

MEDITATION PROGRAM: "*Zazen* schedule is kind of wacky—subject to school and work schedules . . . but I am committed to sitting at least once a day. If you're interested, send me an e-mail or do the old-fashioned thing and call or write!"

Gay Zen Group

The purpose of the Gay Buddhist Group is to introduce non-Buddhists to the teachings of Buddhism, especially Zen; to enable people interested in Buddhism to meet and share this interest with others; and to suggest ways a nonhomophobic spiritual practice can enhance all our lives.

ADDRESS: PO Box 29750, Los Angeles, CA 90029

PHONE: (213) 461-5042

LINEAGE: Vietnamese Zen

SPIRITUAL HEAD: Rev. Vajra Karuna

CONTACTS: Rev. Vajra or Norman McClelland

AFFILIATION: International Buddhist Meditation Center (IBMC)

ESTABLISHED: 1986

FACILITIES: Use IBMC (large center).

MEDITATION PROGRAM: Introductory meeting is on second Sunday of each month.

RETREATS OFFERED: Retreats offered through IBMC.

Gold Mountain Monastery

Nuns' convent. For additional information see listing for City of Ten Thousand Buddhas, Talmage, California.

ADDRESS: 800 Sacramento Street, San Francisco, CA 94108

PHONE: (415) 421-6117

LINEAGE: We propagate all major Mahayana schools (Ch'an, Pure Land, Vinaya, Scholastic, and Esoteric) and work closely with Theravada.

SPIRITUAL HEAD: Ven. Hsuan Hua

AFFILIATION: City of Ten Thousand Buddhas/Dharma Realm Buddhist Association

ESTABLISHED: 1970

FACILITIES: Meditation/worship hall.

PUBLICATIONS: *Gold Mountain Monastery Newsletter* (monthly).

Gold Sage Monastery

Nuns' convent. For additional information see listing for City of Ten Thousand Buddhas, Talmage, California.

ADDRESS: 11455 Clayton Road, San Jose, CA 95127

PHONE: (408) 923-7243

LINEAGE: We propagate all major Mahayana schools (Ch'an, Pure Land, Vinaya, Scholastic, and Esoteric) and work closely with Theravada.

SPIRITUAL HEAD: Ven. Hsuan Hua

AFFILIATION: City of Ten Thousand Buddhas/Dharma Realm Buddhist Association

ESTABLISHED: 1995

FACILITIES: Worship/meditation hall, residential and retreat space for women.

PUBLICATIONS: *Pure Sound From Silicon Valley* (monthly newsletter).

Gold Wheel Monastery

Nuns' convent. Chinese school, laity public service programs, recitation, visits to homes for the elderly, bedside support for those on the point of death.

ADDRESS: 235 North Avenue 58, Los Angeles, CA 90042

PHONE: (213) 258-6668

FAX: Same

LINEAGE: We propagate all major Mahayana schools (Ch'an, Pure Land, Vinaya, Scholastic, and Esoteric) and work closely with Theravada.

SPIRITUAL HEAD: Ven. Hsuan Hua

CONTACT: Bhikshuni Heng Chan

AFFILIATION: City of Ten Thousand Buddhas/Dharma Realm Buddhist Association

ESTABLISHED: 1976

FACILITIES: Buddha hall (for meditation and lectures), library, classrooms, dining hall, book display.

MEDITATION PROGRAM: Daily liturgical practice, bowing, chanting, and meditation.

PUBLICATIONS: *Gold Wheel Sagely Monastery Newsletter* (monthly).

Green Gulch Farm/Zen Center

Located in a beautiful valley that opens from the Pacific Ocean, the Green Gulch Farm community includes lay and ordained practitioners, single and married people with children, long-term residents, and short-term guests. We follow a daily schedule of *zazen*, chanting and bowing, and work. A six-month Farm and Garden Apprenticeship Program is offered for people interested in combining the study of organic agriculture and Zen Buddhism. A leader in the organic farming community of Northern California, Green Gulch donates a portion of its fresh produce to shelters and food banks.

ADDRESS: 1601 Shoreline Highway, Sausalito, CA 94965

PHONE: (415) 383-3134

FAX: (415) 383-3128

LINEAGE: Japanese Soto Zen; lineage of Shunryu Suzuki-Roshi

Green Gulch Farm in Sausalito, California. (Photo by Kokai Roberts.)

CONTACTS: Norman Fischer, Abbot; Reb Anderson, Senior Dharma Teacher

AFFILIATION: San Francisco Zen Center

ESTABLISHED: 1972

FACILITIES: *Zendo*, conference room, guest house, organic farm.

MEDITATION PROGRAM: Daily *zazen*, chanting, bowing. Classes in Buddhism. Regular Sunday morning program includes *zazen* instruction and dharma talk.

RETREATS OFFERED: Traditional Soto Zen one- and seven-day *sesshin*; two Practice Periods (*angos*) each year; workshops and retreats such as "The Poetry of Enlightenment," "Women in Buddhism," and "Zen and Bread Baking." Special retreats for HIV-positive patients, hospice workers, and caregivers. Special programs for teachers, business people, and others seeking a spiritual dimension to their work.

PUBLICATIONS: Schedule of events, three times yearly.

The Harbor Sangha

We are a lay Zen Buddhist organization affiliated with the Diamond Sangha, an international Zen society founded by Robert Aitken-Roshi. Our lineage is a mixture of Rinzai and Soto; *koan* study is a part of our practice. Our teacher, Joseph Bobrow, received permission to teach from Aitken-Roshi in 1989. We offer classes in Zen Buddhist philosophy, history, and practice. Various levels of membership are available, based upon

CALIFORNIA (*cont.*)

levels of participation. Beginners are welcome.

ADDRESS: 1032 Irving Street, Box 330, San Francisco, CA 94122

PHONE: (415) 241-8807

LINEAGE: Japanese; mixed lineage of Rinzai and Soto Zen

SPIRITUAL HEAD: Joseph Bobrow

AFFILIATION: The Diamond Sangha

ESTABLISHED: 1989

FACILITIES: No permanent, owned facilities at this time

MEDITATION PROGRAM: *Zazen*, one evening weekly.

RETREATS OFFERED: Monthly one-day sittings; extended *sesshin*, several times yearly; summer wilderness hiking *sesshin*.

PUBLICATIONS: *The Harbor Sangha Newsletter*

Hartford Street Zen Center—Issanji

Hartford Street Zen Center was founded by Issan Dorsey, dharma heir of Zentatsu Baker-Roshi, to provide gay men and lesbians with an opportunity to practice Buddhism in San Francisco's Castro District. Since 1981 the center has offered a full schedule of morning and evening *zazen*, services, lectures, and private interviews with resident Zen teacher Zenshin Philip Whalen. We also hold Buddhist study classes and introductions to Zen practice. All are welcome.

ADDRESS: 57 Hartford Street, San Francisco, CA 94114

PHONE: (415) 863-2507

LINEAGE: Soto Zen (Shunryu Suzuki-Roshi lineage)

SPIRITUAL HEAD: Zenshin Philip Whalen

AFFILIATION: Autonomous

ESTABLISHED: 1980

FACILITIES: Urban meditation center open to all.

RETREATS OFFERED: Occasionally

PUBLICATIONS: Newsletter

Hayward Buddhist Center

Hayward Buddhist Center is dedicated to the study and practice of Buddhist meditation and the education of youth in the Buddha's teachings. We believe that positive attitudes flow from the nourishment of mindfulness. In order to ensure that young people will become good citizens, we have established the Viet-American Buddhist Youth Association to teach them their cultural roots and values. We offer weekly meditation for the Vietnamese community and occasionally for our American friends as well. We also offer training for monks and nuns. Through these goals we hope to contribute to the betterment of our community.

ADDRESS: 27878 Calaroga Avenue, Hayward, CA 94545-4659

PHONE: (510) 732-0728

FAX: (510) 783-3276

E-MAIL: csvvngo@nuc.berkeley.edu

LINEAGE: Vietnamese

SPIRITUAL HEAD: Thich Tu-Luc, Resident Director

AFFILIATION: Autonomous

ESTABLISHED: 1986

FACILITIES: Small property.

MEDITATION PROGRAM: Mindfulness meditation for Vietnamese community, three times a week.

RETREATS OFFERED: Monthly Day of Mindfulness. Annual weeklong retreat.

Hearth Sangha

For additional information please refer to Community of Mindful Living, Berkeley, California.

ADDRESS: 530 Amigo Road, Soquel, CA 95073

PHONE: (408) 462-3703

E-MAIL: hearth@cruzio.com

LINEAGE: Mindfulness practice in the tradition of Thich Nhat Hanh.

SPIRITUAL HEAD: Thich Nhat Hanh

CONTACT: Nanda Currant

AFFILIATION: Community of Mindful Living, Berkeley, California

FACILITIES: We meet at Santa Cruz Zen Center.

MEDITATION PROGRAM: Weekly sitting and walking meditation, followed by a short dharma talk and discussion. Precept recitation ceremony on the Monday closest to the new moon. Call for schedule.

PUBLICATIONS: *Hearth Sangha Newsletter*

Hsi-Lai Temple

The temple has a large and complete faculty of monks, nuns and laypeople—all masters in various aspects of Buddhism. Teachers have undergone extensive training at Oriental Buddhist universities and monasteries. The approach is nonsectarian, with the emphasis on living life as a Bodhisattva. Mindfulness, Rinzai, and Soto Zen meditation, *Nien-fo'* (chanting Buddha's name), mantra/tantra practice, and sutra chanting are among the disciplines taught. Monastic and lay ordination and Bodhisattva precepts are given periodically. Weddings, funerals, and counseling also available. All services open to the public.

ADDRESS: 3456 South Glenmark Drive, Hacienda Heights, CA 91745

PHONE: (818) 961-9697

FAX: (818) 369-1944

LINEAGE: Nonsectarian

SPIRITUAL HEAD: Ven. Master Hsing Yun

AFFILIATION: Buddha's Light International Association

ESTABLISHED: 1978; temple completed 1988.

FACILITIES: Largest Buddhist monastery in the Western Hemisphere, encompassing fifteen acres with a floor area of

102,432 square feet and a capacity for several thousand people. Facilities include many shrine rooms, meditation halls, nunnery, pagoda, offices, gardens, and auditorium.

MEDITATION PROGRAM: Daily open meditation and *puja*.

RETREATS OFFERED: Vipassana and Zen retreats; chanting services; supervised and unsupervised solitary retreats.

The Institute of Buddhist Studies

The Institute of Buddhist Studies offers a master of arts degree in Buddhist Studies. This program is jointly administered with the Graduate Theological Union and is accredited. The institute's Core Program specializes in contemporary Shin Buddhist studies, exploring the application of Shin Buddhist thought to contemporary religious, philosophic, and social issues. This three-year program includes the study of Shinran Shonin's writings and preparation in classical and modern Japanese. Students wishing to specialize in other areas of Buddhism are also encouraged to apply and may take the master of arts in Buddhist Studies as a two-year program.

ADDRESS: 1900 Addison Street, Berkeley, CA 94704

PHONE: (510) 849-2383

FAX: (510) 849-2158

LINEAGE: Shin Buddhist

AFFILIATION: Autonomous

FACILITIES: Seminary and graduate school; includes access to libraries at University of California, Berkeley and Stanford University.

International Buddhist Meditation Center (IBMC)

Nestled in the heart of Los Angeles, IBMC serves as a quiet retreat for those seeking spiritual refuge from the fast-paced hubbub of American city life. Founded in 1971 by the late Dr. Thich Thien-An, it continues to pioneer American Buddhism with its pluralistic, nonsectarian style. It was among the first United States temples established specifically for Westerners and the first to give full *bhikkhu* and *bhikkhuni* ordination to native-born Americans. Since Dr. Thien-An's death in 1980, IBMC has been under the directorship of Ven. Dr. Karuna Dharma, the first American woman to be fully ordained as a *bhikkhuni*.

ADDRESS: 928 South New Hampshire Avenue, Los Angeles, CA 90006

PHONE: (213) 384-0850

FAX: (213) 386-6643

LINEAGE: Vietnamese Zen

SPIRITUAL HEAD: Ven. Dr. Karuna Dharma

AFFILIATION: Autonomous

ESTABLISHED: 1970

FACILITIES: Residence program, college classes, seminars.

RETREATS OFFERED: Bimonthly weekend retreats, semimonthly day retreats.

PUBLICATIONS: *Monthly Guide*

International Translation Institute/Dharma Realm Buddhist Association

The International Translation Institute is the home of the Buddhist Text Translation Society. For additional information see listing for City of Ten Thousand Buddhas, Talmage, California.

ADDRESS: 1777 Murchison Drive, Burlingame, CA 94010-4504

PHONE: (415) 692-5912

FAX: (415) 692-5056

LINEAGE: We propagate all major Mahayana schools (Ch'an, Pure Land, Vinaya, Scholastic, and Esoteric) and work closely with Theravada.

SPIRITUAL HEAD: Ven. Hsuan Hua

AFFILIATION: City of Ten Thousand Buddhas/Dharma Realm Buddhist Association

ESTABLISHED: 1973

FACILITIES: Administrative headquarters and translation offices.

MEDITATION PROGRAM: Weekend lectures and evening meditation.

International Zen Institute of America (IZIA)

The institute's aim is to disseminate Zen Buddhist teaching and practice in Western societies. IZIA offers Zen training, sutra classes, public lectures, and Buddhist ceremonies in the United States and Europe. There is a training program for advanced practitioners that prepares them for the tasks of a Meditation Leader or Zen Teacher. The community of practitioners, Moonheart Sangha, is growing in number and strength. It has developed into an international support network where friendship and compassion for all beings are cultivated.

ADDRESS: PO Box 491218, Los Angeles, CA 90049

PHONE: (310) 472-5707

LINEAGE: Vietnamese Vinitaruci

SPIRITUAL HEAD: Roshi Gesshin Prabhasadharma

AFFILIATION: Headquarters center.

ESTABLISHED: 1983

FACILITIES: Office only.

RETREATS OFFERED: Annual desert spring retreat in Southern California.

PUBLICATIONS: *Zen Life*

Jikoji

Jikoji is a Soto Zen retreat center located in the Santa Cruz mountains amid hundreds of acres of open space preserve. We offer a regular schedule of meditation and *sesshin* and make our space available

Jikoji Soto Zen retreat center, located in the Santa Cruz mountains amid hundreds of acres of open space preserve. (Photo courtesy of Jikoji.)

members, membership is not a prerequisite for participation in its activities.

ADDRESS: 292 College Avenue, Mountain View, CA 94040

PHONE: (415) 903-1935 (to receive brochure)

LINEAGE: Soto Zen, in the tradition of Shunryu Suzuki-Roshi

SPIRITUAL HEAD: Les Kaye (Keido), Abbot

AFFILIATION: Informally affiliated with San Francisco Zen Center and Tassajara Zen Monastery.

ESTABLISHED: 1964

FACILITIES: Moderate-size (fifty people) meditation center.

MEDITATION PROGRAM: Daily morning *zazen*, weekly lecture, longer Saturday schedule includes breakfast and work period.

RETREATS OFFERED: Every other month, varying in length from one or three days to one week.

CALIFORNIA *(cont.)*

to other meditation groups and individuals for rentals. A staff of three to five resident caretakers maintains the facility, supports the practice and guest rentals, and offers hospitality, information, and *zazen* instruction to the public.

ADDRESS: 12100 Skyline Boulevard, Los Gatos, CA 95030

PHONE: (408) 741-9562

LINEAGE: Japanese Soto Zen

SPIRITUAL HEAD: Kobun Chino Otagawa-Roshi

CONTACT: Ryan Brandenburg

AFFILIATION: Autonomous

ESTABLISHED: 1982

FACILITIES: Dorm-style accommodations for twenty-five people.

MEDITATION PROGRAM: Daily morning and evening scheduled practice; Saturday morning practice with talk and potluck lunch. Call for times.

RETREATS OFFERED: Weekend *sesshin*

once a month. Four seven-day *sesshin* per year.

PUBLICATIONS: *Jikoji News*, quarterly.

Kannon Do (Mountain View Zen Meditation Center)

Kannon Do brings the tradition of Soto Zen Buddhism to the Santa Clara Valley and South Peninsula. It provides an opportunity to join with others in meditation, study Buddhist teachings, and explore the meaning of Zen practice in everyday life. Named after Kannon, the Buddhist personification of compassion, the center offers a supportive environment in which centuries-old teachings and traditions complement the creative and caring spirit of contemporary America. Kannon Do is a lay-oriented nonresidential center. Although voluntarily maintained and supported by its

Kanzeonji Non-Sectarian Buddhist Temple

Rev. Ryugen Watanabe, also known as Swami Premananda, Founder of Kanzeonji Non-Sectarian Buddhist Temple, is the sixty-second Patriarch (counting from Bodhidharma) in his line of transmission in the Soto Zen Buddhist tradition. He is a Master of Tantra Yoga, holds the title of Swami, and is also founder of the Siva Ashram Yoga Center, where he provides spiritual instructions and teachings. Rev. Watanabe received inspiration from Kanzeon Bosatsu, the Buddha of Compassion, to bring the teaching and practice of the East to the United States.

ADDRESS: 944 Terrace 49, Los Angeles, CA 90042

PHONE: (213) 255-5345

FAX: (213) 254-5204

LINEAGE: Japanese Soto Zen/Hatha Yoga

SPIRITUAL HEAD: Rev. Ryugen Watanabe,

Abbot and Director

AFFILIATION: Autonomous

ESTABLISHED: 1983

FACILITIES: Guest room for visitors. We sell meditation supplies.

MEDITATION PROGRAM: Yoga classes, *zazen* meditation, Zen healing.

PUBLICATIONS: *The Spiritual*

Kewanee Mountain Zen Center

No description available.

ADDRESS: 4315 Kewanee Street, Los Angeles, CA 90032

PHONE: (213) 342-0744

LINEAGE: Shaolin Zen

SPIRITUAL HEAD: Dr. Ratanasara

CONTACT: Jefferson Chan

AFFILIATION: California Buddhist University

ESTABLISHED: 1992

FACILITIES: *Zendo*, library, six residents' rooms.

RETREATS OFFERED: Quarterly

PUBLICATIONS: *The Shaolin Monastery*, quarterly.

Laguna Beach Sangha

We are an eclectic group. For additional information please refer to Community of Mindful Living, Berkeley, California.

ADDRESS: 639 Pearl Street, Laguna Beach, CA 92651

PHONE: (714) 494-4734

E-MAIL: gmsmith@deltanet.com

LINEAGE: Mindfulness practice in the tradition of Thich Nhat Hanh.

SPIRITUAL HEAD: Thich Nhat Hanh

CONTACT: Greg Smith

AFFILIATION: Community of Mindful Living, Berkeley, California

MEDITATION PROGRAM: We sit together for an hour, one evening a week. Afterward we discuss practice-related topics. Call for times.

RETREATS OFFERED: Day of Mindfulness every Sunday.

Lesbian Buddhist Group

This group meets monthly at the International Buddhist Meditation Center in Los Angeles. There is also an on-line mailing list called Dharma-dykes.

ADDRESS: 920 South New Hampshire Avenue, Los Angeles, CA 90006

PHONE: (213) 739-9952

FAX: (213) 386-6643

LINEAGE: English/all traditions welcome.

SPIRITUAL HEAD: The late Rev. Sarika Dharma

AFFILIATION: International Buddhist Meditation Center

ESTABLISHED: 1993

FACILITIES: *Zendo*, temple, hall, residence.

RETREATS OFFERED: Intermittent

PUBLICATIONS: *IBMC Monthly Guide*

Long Beach Buddhist Temple

We are a nonsectarian, nondenominational Japanese-American Buddhist temple with members representing all of the five major Japanese Buddhist sects found in Southern California. Although nonsectarian, the head minister, Rev. Kokuzo, is a Soto Zen priest. The fundamental teachings of the Buddha are emphasized. Sutras chanted are the *Prajna Paramita Hridaya (Heart) Sutra* and the *Myohorenge Kyo Kanzeon Bosatsu Fumonbonge* (part of *The Lotus Sutra*). Services are held every Sunday morning. Birthday, Enlightenment Day, and Nirvana Day are held on their respective dates. Ullambana and Spring and Autumn Equinoctial services are conducted. All are welcome.

ADDRESS: 2360 Santa Fe Avenue, Long Beach, CA 90810

PHONE: (310) 426-4014

FAX: (310) 426-4014

LINEAGE: Japanese Buddhist

SPIRITUAL HEAD: Buddha Shakyamuni

CONTACT: Rev. Ryosho Kokuzo, Resident Director

AFFILIATION: Los Angeles Buddhist Federation

ESTABLISHED: 1957

FACILITIES: Temple building; meeting rooms and social hall.

MEDITATION PROGRAM: Periodic meditation sessions.

PUBLICATIONS: *The Sangha*, bimonthly newsletter.

Long Beach Monastery

Long Beach Monastery provides training for young novice monks (*shramanera*) within the orthodox Buddhist tradition. The meditation and worship hall is open to all. The public is also invited to take part in the many ceremonies and events that are held here throughout the year. For additional information, please see listing for City of Ten Thousand Buddhas, Talmage, California.

ADDRESS: 3361 East Ocean Boulevard, Long Beach, CA 90803

PHONE: (310) 438-8902

FAX: Same

LINEAGE: We propagate all major Mahayana schools (Ch'an, Pure Land, Vinaya, Scholastic, and Esoteric) and work closely with Theravada.

SPIRITUAL HEAD: Ven. Hsuan Hua

CONTACT: Bhikshu Heng Chang

AFFILIATION: City of Ten Thousand Buddhas/Dharma Realm Buddhist Association

ESTABLISHED: 1990

FACILITIES: Large worship hall, gardens, and residence in former Carmelite convent on the ocean.

RETREATS OFFERED: One-month retreat in summer for young male novices

CALIFORNIA *(cont.)*

(twelve to eighteen years old); winter retreat.

PUBLICATION: *Diligent Cultivation and Study*, quarterly.

Los Gatos Zen Group

Zazen practice at Los Gatos is adapted from Zen Masters Yasutani-Roshi, Soen Nakagawa-Roshi, and Maezumi-Roshi. The practice is formal but not monastic, consisting of thirty-minute meditation periods alternating with chanting, walking meditation, and bowing practice. Some students do koan work. This group has been active for over twenty years, with emphasis on bringing the practice into family life and the workplace. There is no leadership structure.

ADDRESS: 16200 Matilija Drive,
  Los Gatos, CA 95030-3033
PHONE: (408) 354-7506
LINEAGE: Japanese Zen: Soto and Rinzai
SPIRITUAL HEAD: Arvis Joen Justi, Resident Teacher
CONTACT: Same
AFFILIATION: Autonomous
ESTABLISHED: 1963
FACILITIES: *Zendo* in private home.
MEDITATION PROGRAM: Weekly meditation schedule. Introduction and instruction for beginners are by arrangement.
RETREATS OFFERED: Monthly day of Mindfulness or weekend *sesshin.*

Maitri: Residential Care for People Living with AIDS

Maitri provides housing, home-cooked meals, and volunteer support for people living with AIDS. It was founded by Issan Dorsey-Roshi, a disciple of Shunryu Suzuki-Roshi, and dharma heir of Zentatsu Richard Baker-Roshi. We are a nonprofit corporation governed by a board of di-

rectors with a small professional staff supported by volunteers. You are invited and encouraged to attend our volunteer training program.

ADDRESS: 401 Duboce Avenue,
  San Francisco, CA 94117
PHONE: (415) 863-8508
LINEAGE: Soto Zen origins, but nondenominational
SPIRITUAL HEAD: Founded by Issan Dorsey-Roshi
AFFILIATION: Loosely affiliated with Hartford Street Zen Center
ESTABLISHED: 1989
FACILITIES: Fifteen-bed housing for people living with AIDS, small meditation room.
RETREATS OFFERED: Volunteer support program. Visiting Buddhist teachers give talks on issues related to living and dying.
PUBLICATIONS: *Maitri Newsletter*, quarterly.

Middlebar Monastery

Middlebar Monastery was originally named Beikukosan Sanzenji Soto Mission by Rosen Takashima, Primate of the Soto Zen Sect in Japan. Daino Doki MacDonough, an American, was named Chief Priest and later, Abbot. The monastery trains American monastics using traditional Soto methods but without transplanting Japanese culture in the process. Applicants must spend four weeks living at the monastery before requesting ordination. The novitiate year is given over to Buddhist studies, although novices may leave the program without guilt or a sense of failure whenever they choose. Morning *zazen* classes are held for nonresidents. An adjacent convent is planned.

ADDRESS: 2503 Del Rio Drive, Stockton,
  CA 95204
PHONE: (209) 462-9384
LINEAGE: Japanese Soto Zen

SPIRITUAL HEAD: The Ven. MacDonough-Roshi, OSM
CONTACT: Bro. James Percival, OSM
AFFILIATION: Autonomous
ESTABLISHED: 1956
FACILITIES: Suburban center.
MEDITATION PROGRAM: Morning *zazen* classes for nonresidents.

Moon Valley Sangha

For additional information please refer to Community of Mindful Living, Berkeley, California.

ADDRESS: c/o Inner Resources, 255 West Napa Street, Suite E, Sonoma,
  CA 95476
PHONE: (707) 938-8899
LINEAGE: Mindfulness practice in the tradition of Thich Nhat Hanh.
SPIRITUAL HEAD: Thich Nhat Hanh
AFFILIATION: Community of Mindful Living, Berkeley, California

Mt. Baldy Zen Center

Mt. Baldy is a Rinzai Zen Buddhist study and practice community, founded by Joshu Sasaki-Roshi. Through his guidance, monks and nuns conduct the training in a traditional manner: *zazen,* chanting, monastic-style meals, and work-practice. The program serves both ordained and lay residents who, together, strive for the full maturity that is grounded in the awakening of the True Self. The schedule is rigorous and designed to help us abandon our personal interests and enter into the relationships of group practice. The center is open throughout the year and offers different methods of practice each season.

ADDRESS: Box 429, Mt. Baldy, CA 91759
PHONE: (909) 985-6410
LINEAGE: Japanese Rinzai Zen
SPIRITUAL HEAD: Kyozan Joshu Sasaki-Roshi

A Simple Act of Compassion

THE MAITRI AIDS HOSPICE PROGRAM BEGAN AS a simple act of compassion. Issan Dorsey, Zen priest and founder of Hartford Street Zen Center, quietly opened his door to a young Zen student with AIDS. It was this step that brought a group of five friends together to discuss how they could respond to the growing number of people living with AIDS.

In the fall of 1987, Issan opened Maitri Hospice at Hartford Street Zen Center to provide residential care for "homeless" and financially needy people with ARC and AIDS. Two years later, Maitri leased the house next door to provide additional rooms. Issan's magical charm, imagination, and ability to deeply touch people created a warm and nurturing home for those most in need. It is this intimate and friendly atmosphere that Maitri attempts to foster in the midst of the deep tragedy of AIDS.

The hospice provides private rooms for people with the disease regardless of age, gender, ethnicity, religion, sexual orientation, national origin, language, or ability to pay. Working in partnership with Visiting Nurses and Hospice, Maitri staff and volunteers try to meet, in a personal, direct, and heartfelt way, the basic medical requirements as well as the larger psychological, social, and spiritual needs of residents and their friends and families.

In 1997, with favorable news on the AIDS treatment front reducing the immediate need for hospice, Maitri decided to expand its range of services to include skilled nursing, transitional, and respite care for individuals with AIDS, in a new, licensed facility.

Our purpose is twofold: first, to respond to the AIDS crisis by helping those directly in our area who need the supportive care that we can offer; and second, to be a model that establishes the groundwork for other community-based groups. Donations may be sent care of Maitri: Residential Care for People Living with AIDS.

For more information, contact: Maitri: Residential Care for People Living with AIDS, 401 Duboce Avenue, San Francisco, CA 94117; (415) 863-8508.

CONTACTS: Kigen Ekeson, Koshin Cain
AFFILIATION: Autonomous
ESTABLISHED: 1971
FACILITIES: Twenty cabins, *zendo*, dining hall, kitchen, Jacuzzi.

Mountain Spirit Center

Mountain Spirit Center, named after the foremost spirit of the Korean shamanistic pantheon, is the West Coast rural retreat center for the lineage of Zen Master Seung Sahn Dae Soen Sa Nim. We are in a remote area of south central California, a mile from utility power, experimenting with "alternative" renewable energy and reforesting and restoring the land after years of abuse from mining and cattle ranching. Facilities are still primitive; no running water or flush toilets. We're practicing in a mobile home while construction of the residential building is under way.

ADDRESS: 8400 Juniper Way, Tehachapi, CA 93561
PHONE: (805) 333-7204
LINEAGE: Korean Zen Buddhism
SPIRITUAL HEAD: Zen Master Seung Sahn (Dae Soen Sa Nim)
CONTACT: Mu Ryang Sunim
AFFILIATION: Kwan Um School of Zen
ESTABLISHED: 1993
FACILITIES: Primitive mountain retreat center.

MEDITATION PROGRAM: Daily bowing, chanting, sitting, working.
RETREATS OFFERED: Monthly three-day weekend Zen retreats.
PUBLICATIONS: *Mountain Spirit*

Newport Mesa Zen Center

The purpose of the Newport Mesa Zen Center is to encourage and support Zen practice by offering regular opportunities for meditation, education, training, and service. Spiritual Director Deborah Barrett is a Zen monk and Roman Catholic sister. A serious practitioner since the early '70s, her focus is on Christian and Zen awareness methods. Carol Mudd,

CALIFORNIA *(cont.)*

Co-administrator and Program Director, received her training at Zen Center of Los Angeles. She is married and is the mother of a boy and a girl.

ADDRESS: 711 West 17th Street, Suite A-8, Costa Mesa, CA 92663
PHONE: (714) 631-5389
FAX: (714) 631-8891
LINEAGE: Soto Zen
SPIRITUAL HEAD: Deborah Barrett
CONTACT: Carol Mudd, Co-administrator and Program Director
AFFILIATION: Autonomous
ESTABLISHED: 1995
FACILITIES: Urban Zen center.
MEDITATION PROGRAM: Two weekday morning sittings. A Sunday evening program includes sitting and walking meditation, dharma talk, discussion, interview, and work practice.
RETREATS OFFERED: Intensive monthly all-day sittings.

Oakland Sangha

For additional information please refer to Community of Mindful Living, Berkeley, California.

ADDRESS: 574 Forest, Oakland, CA 94618
PHONE: (510) 655-4650
LINEAGE: Mindfulness practice in the tradition of Thich Nhat Hanh.
SPIRITUAL HEAD: Thich Nhat Hanh
CONTACT: Connie Cronin
AFFILIATION: Community of Mindful Living, Berkeley, California
MEDITATION PROGRAM: We meet Sunday afternoons for meditation and discussion. Once a month we recite precepts and have a family potluck.

Ocean Eyes Zen Center (Nae An Soen Won)

Ocean Eyes Zen Center was established by Zen Master Seung Sahn and Robert

Moore, JDPSN, to serve practitioners in the Greater Orange County area. Robert Moore gives monthly Zen interviews and talks, which augment the weekly meditation instruction led by Resident Dharma Teacher and Abbot Paul Lynch. Ongoing one- and three-day retreats are rotated between the six Zen centers that comprise the Southwest Zen Centers of the Kwan Um School of Zen (of which Bob Moore, JDPSN, is the Guiding Teacher and Paul Lynch, the Director).

ADDRESS: 11582 Ale Lane, Stanton, CA 90680-3535
PHONE: (714) 894-0177
FAX: Same
LINEAGE: Korean Chogye Zen
SPIRITUAL HEAD: Zen Master Seung Sahn
CONTACT: Paul Lynch, Resident Teacher and Abbot
AFFILIATION: Kwan Um School of Zen
ESTABLISHED: 1993
FACILITIES: Residential Zen center.
RETREATS OFFERED: Six times per year.
PUBLICATIONS: *Only Go Straight*, newsmagazine.

Palo Alto Friends Mindfulness Sangha

For additional information please refer to Community of Mindful Living, Berkeley, California.

ADDRESS: 2043 El Sereno Avenue, Los Altos, CA 94024
PHONE: (415) 969-3452
E-MAIL: somurphy@email.sjsu.edu
LINEAGE: Mindfulness practice in the tradition of Thich Nhat Hanh.
SPIRITUAL HEAD: Thich Nhat Hanh
CONTACT: Susan Murphy
AFFILIATION: Community of Mindful Living, Berkeley, California
MEDITATION PROGRAM: We meet one morning a week for meditation and discussion based on practices described in Thich Nhat Hanh's book *The Miracle of Mindfulness*.

Ring of Bone Zendo

Nonresidential lay practice center.
ADDRESS: PO Box 510, North San Juan, CA 95960
LINEAGE: Harada/Yasutani line of Zen
AFFILIATION: Diamond Sangha
ESTABLISHED: 1968

Rinzai-Ji Zen Center

Rinzai-Ji Zen Center is the home temple of Rinzai-Ji, the umbrella organization for centers founded by Kyozan Joshu Sasaki of the Myoshinji School of Japanese Rinzai Zen. The center offers a daily schedule of meditation and chanting. Meditation instruction is also available. Our practice consists of two elements—the Diamond Posture and the complete breath (which is soft and quiet and, at the same time, deep).

ADDRESS: 2505 Cimarron Street, Los Angeles, CA 90018
PHONE: (213) 732-2263
LINEAGE: Japanese Rinzai Zen
SPIRITUAL HEAD: Joshu Sasaki-Roshi
AFFILIATION: Headquarters of Rinzai-Ji organization.
ESTABLISHED: 1968
FACILITIES: *Zendo*
MEDITATION PROGRAM: Morning and evening except Sunday night and Monday. Call for times.
RETREATS OFFERED: Monthly one-day retreats. Seven-day *dai sesshin*, spring and fall.

Rinzai Zen Temple of California

We are a small Zen temple offering daily practice which consists of *zazen* (sitting), *kinhin* (walking), and chanting. Our temple is located in the South Bay area of Los Angeles, near the beach cities. If you live or work in the area or are just visiting, please come by and sit with us! All denominations are welcome.

ADDRESS: 1939 West 162nd Street, Unit A, Gardena, CA 90247

PHONE: (310) 327-6823

FAX: Same

LINEAGE: Rinzai Zen

SPIRITUAL HEAD: Roshi Sogen Yamakawa

CONTACT: Rev. Taiu Ogura

AFFILIATION: Shogenji Monastery in Gifu, Japan

ESTABLISHED: 1993

FACILITIES: Temple

MEDITATION PROGRAM: Daily morning and evening sittings.

RETREATS OFFERED: Two three-day *sesshin* per year.

San Francisco Mindfulness Community

We sit as a *sangha* every Monday night. First Monday: precept recitation ceremony; second Monday: tape by Thich Nhat Hanh; third Monday: extended meditation and discussion; fourth Monday: book discussion and reading. All meetings start with sitting and walking meditation. For additional information, please refer to Community of Mindful Living, Berkeley, California.

ADDRESS: 3991 17th Street, San Francisco, CA 94114

PHONE: (415) 252-8452

E-MAIL: SFINSF@aol.com

LINEAGE: Vietnamese

SPIRITUAL HEAD: Thich Nhat Hanh

CONTACT: No resident director. We are a cooperative.

AFFILIATION: Autonomous but affiliated with Community of Mindful Living.

ESTABLISHED: 1994

FACILITIES: We meet at Hartford Street Zen Center (a Japanese-style *zendo*).

MEDITATION PROGRAM: Weekly sitting and walking meditation. Call for schedule and times.

RETREATS OFFERED: Occasional Day of Mindfulness.

San Francisco Zen Center— Beginner's Mind Temple

San Francisco Zen Center was founded by Shunryu Suzuki-Roshi and his early disciples to provide a place in the city for the serious practice of Zen. Since 1969 the center has offered morning and evening *zazen*, chanting services, work/practice, an extensive Buddhist library and

San Francisco Zen Center. (Photo by Don Morreale.)

Interior courtyard at San Francisco Zen Center. (Photo by Barbara Wenger.)

CALIFORNIA (cont.)

bookstore, classes in Buddhist studies, and opportunities for residential practice. Located in a low-income neighborhood, the facility is sometimes used for community meetings and for a wide variety of neighborhood safety and improvement projects. Staff members correspond with prisoners throughout the country, sending them meditation instruction, spiritual books, and encouragement.

ADDRESS: 300 Page Street, San Francisco, CA 94102

PHONE: (415) 863-3136

FAX: (415) 431-9220

LINEAGE: Soto Zen

SPIRITUAL HEADS: Abbot Zoketsu Norman Fischer/Abbess Zenkei Blanche Hartman, Abbot Mel Weitsman, Senior Dharma Teacher Reb Anderson

CONTACT: Abbess Zenkei Blanche Hartman

AFFILIATION: Autonomous

ESTABLISHED: 1962

FACILITIES: Residential and community temple (*zendo* seats eighty), Buddha hall, guest rooms, dining room.

MEDITATION PROGRAM: *Zazen* mornings and evenings.

RETREATS OFFERED: Two *sesshin* a year, residential practice periods, guest program, guest student program.

PUBLICATIONS: *Zen Mind, Beginner's Mind; Book of Serenity, Moon in a Dewdrop; Warm Smiles, Cold Mountains; Jerusalem Moonlight; Windbell* (biannual).

Santa Barbara Buddhist Priory

No description available.

ADDRESS: 1115 Tunnel Road, Santa Barbara, CA 93105

PHONE: (805) 898-0848

FAX: Same

LINEAGE: Soto Zen, Order of Buddhist Contemplatives

SPIRITUAL HEAD: The late Rev. P.T.N.H. Jiyu-Kennett, MOBC

CONTACT: Rev. Jisho Perry, MOBC

AFFILIATION: Shasta Abbey, Mt. Shasta, California

ESTABLISHED: 1979

FACILITIES: One small priory in the foothills.

RETREATS OFFERED: A one-day retreat and one weekend retreat every month.

PUBLICATIONS: *Santa Barbara Buddhist Priory News & Events Calendar*

Santa Cruz Sangha

For additional information please refer to Community of Mindful Living, Berkeley, California.

ADDRESS: 1007 Smith Grade, Santa Cruz, CA 95060

PHONE: (408) 457-2015

LINEAGE: Mindfulness practice in the tradition of Thich Nhat Hanh.

SPIRITUAL HEAD: Thich Nhat Hanh

CONTACTS: Nicola and Thomas Anderson

AFFILIATION: Community of Mindful Living, Berkeley, California

Santa Cruz Zen Center

Santa Cruz Zen Center is a nonresidential lay practice community in the Soto Zen tradition. We offer meditation six days a week, regular daylong sittings, and longer *sesshin*. Practice periods twice a year. Our teacher is Katherine Thanas, a student of Shunryu Suzuki-Roshi, who received dharma transmission in 1988.

ADDRESS: 113 School Street, Santa Cruz, CA 95060

PHONE: (408) 457-0206

LINEAGE: Japanese Soto

SPIRITUAL HEAD: Katherine Thanas

CONTACT: Director duties shared among volunteers.

AFFILIATION: Autonomous, but we are cousins with San Francisco Zen Center. Our teacher Katherine Thanas trained there and at Tassajara Zen Mountain Center.

ESTABLISHED: 1970

FACILITIES: *Zendo*, resident's house, and *dokusan* room.

MEDITATION PROGRAM: Morning and evening Soto Zen meditation, six days a week.

RETREATS OFFERED: Weekend *sesshin*, three times a year; five-day *sesshin*, twice yearly; one-day sitting, six times a year.

PUBLICATIONS: *Sangha* newsletter.

Santa Monica Sangha

For additional information please refer to Community of Mindful Living, Berkeley, California.

ADDRESS: Santa Monica, California

PHONE: (310) 392-1796

LINEAGE: Mindfulness practice in the tradition of Thich Nhat Hanh.

SPIRITUAL HEAD: Thich Nhat Hanh

CONTACTS: Penelope Thompson and Lee Lipp

AFFILIATION: Community of Mindful Living, Berkeley, California

MEDITATION PROGRAM: One evening a week for sitting and dharma discussion. On the Monday evening closest to the new moon, we have a "Beginning Anew Ceremony" to maintain harmony in our *sangha*.

RETREATS OFFERED: On the third weekend of the month, we hold a half-Day of Mindfulness and participate in some form of social action as a *sangha*.

Sebastopol Sangha

For additional information please refer to Community of Mindful Living, Berkeley, California.

ADDRESS: 8915 Barnett Valley Road, Sebastopol, CA 95472

PHONE: (707) 829-6796

FAX: Same

LINEAGE: Mindfulness practice in the tradition of Thich Nhat Hanh.

SPIRITUAL HEAD: Thich Nhat Hanh

CONTACTS: Marg Starbuck and Bill Boykin

AFFILIATION: Community of Mindful Living, Berkeley, California

MEDITATION PROGRAM: We meet one evening a week for meditation and discussion. Please call for times.

RETREATS OFFERED: Veterans' Writing Workshop each season.

Shaolin Buddhist Meditation Center

A division of California Buddhist University, which also includes Kewanee Mountain Zen Center in Los Angeles, and Bodhi Books and Gifts Center at 933¼ Chung King Road, Chinatown, Los Angeles, (213) 628-3449.

ADDRESS: 3165 Minnesota Street, Los Angeles, CA 90031

PHONE: (213) 225-4631

LINEAGE: Shaolin Zen

SPIRITUAL HEAD: Jefferson Chan

CONTACT: Jefferson Chan

AFFILIATION: California Buddhist University

ESTABLISHED: 1988

FACILITIES: *Zendo*, library, sixteen resident rooms.

RETREATS OFFERED: Quarterly

PUBLICATIONS: *The Shaolin Monastery*, quarterly.

Shasta Abbey—The Order of Buddhist Contemplatives

Shasta Abbey is a Buddhist monastery and seminary in the Serene Reflection Meditation (Soto Zen) tradition.

A monk pays homage and prepares to ring the great bell at Shasta Abbey on Mount Shasta, California. (Photo courtesy of Mount Shasta.)

Founded in 1970 by the late Rev. Roshi Jiyu-Kennett, the abbey has a large monastic community of men and women training full time for the Buddhist priesthood. We also offer a year-round schedule of retreats and residential training for laypersons of varying backgrounds and experience. Training at Shasta Abbey encompasses the practice of Serene Reflection meditation, the keeping of the Buddhist Precepts, and the integration of meditation and Buddhist teaching with every activity of one's daily life.

ADDRESS: PO Box 199, 3612 Summit Drive, Mount Shasta, CA 96067-0199.

PHONE: (916) 926-4208

FAX: (916) 926-0428

LINEAGE: Japanese Soto Zen and Chinese Mahayana

SPIRITUAL HEAD: The late Rev. Master Jiyu-Kennett (1924–1996)

CONTACT: Please address inquiries c/o Hospitaller.

The late Rev. Master Jiyu-Kennett (1924–1996). (Photo courtesy of Mount Shasta.)

CALIFORNIA (*cont.*)

AFFILIATION: Shasta Abbey is Headquarters of the Order of Buddhist Contemplatives.

ESTABLISHED: 1970

FACILITIES: Rural monastery.

RETREATS OFFERED: Weekend, weeklong retreats, and short- and long-term stays are offered throughout the year.

PUBLICATIONS: *Journal of the Order of Buddhist Contemplatives*

Signal Hill Zen Center

No description available.

ADDRESS: 2504 E. Willow Street, #107, Signal Hill, CA 90806

PHONE: (310) 424-2929

E-MAIL: becooper@ix.netcom.com

LINEAGE: Korean Zen

SPIRITUAL HEAD: Zen Master Seung Sahn

CONTACT: Bill Cooper

AFFILIATION: Kwan Um School of Zen

ESTABLISHED: 1996

FACILITIES: Urban *zendo*.

RETREATS OFFERED: Periodic one-day retreats. We go to the Dharma Zen Center in Los Angeles for longer retreats.

Sixth Patriarch Zen Center

The main focus at Sixth Patriarch Zen Center is on awakening through traditional Zen practice, with secondary focus on taking care of our health through correct diet, herbs, and a Korean Taoist breath meditation called *Sun-do*. Our teacher, Ven. Hyunoong Sunim, is a Korean Buddhist monk and Oriental herbalist. He gives private nutritional counseling ("Energy Analysis") and treatment with Chinese herbs. We hold regular Zen sittings and ongoing *Sun-do* classes mornings and evenings six days a week. There is a dharma talk every Saturday evening. Zen and *Sun-do* retreats are

offered occasionally.

ADDRESS: 2584 Martin Luther King Jr. Way, Berkeley, CA 94704-2630

PHONE: (510) 486-1762

FAX: (510) 883-0461

LINEAGE: Korean Rinzai Zen

SPIRITUAL HEAD: Ven. Hyunoong Sunim

AFFILIATION: Korean Chogye order

ESTABLISHED: Originally established in 1986 in Vancouver, British Columbia; moved to Berkeley, California, in 1991.

FACILITIES: Zen center near downtown Berkeley in large, old Victorian house. Rooms for resident trainees. Separate meditation hall behind residence.

PUBLICATIONS: *Sun-do: Taoist Breathing Meditation*. Taped dharma talks.

Sonoma Mountain Zen Center

Sonoma Mountain Zen Center was established to continue the Soto Zen lineage of Shunryu Suzuki-Roshi and to make everyday Zen available in Sonoma County. We are situated on eight acres of rolling hills and mountainous land near the town of Santa Rosa. Our *sangha* consists of a small group of residential students and a larger membership from the surrounding towns. We emphasize the practice of sitting meditation every day as a way of deepening our true nature and of actualizing it clearly in our work and activities. We invite you to join us in this wonderful venture.

ADDRESS: 6367 Sonoma Mountain Road, Santa Rosa, CA 95404

PHONE: (707) 545-8105

FAX: (707) 575-7863

LINEAGE: Soto Zen Tradition of Shunryu Suzuki-Roshi

SPIRITUAL HEAD: Jakusho Kwong-Roshi

CONTACT: Sylvia Kincaid, Administrator

AFFILIATION: Autonomous

ESTABLISHED: 1973

FACILITIES: Country retreat property.

RETREATS OFFERED: Extended *sesshin* four times a year.

PUBLICATIONS: *Mountain Wind*, newsletter.

Stone Creek Zendo

Stone Creek Zendo provides a place for investigating the Buddha way. The central practice is *shikantaza*, or "just sitting," being fully present here and now. *Sesshin*, talks, and study classes support meeting the full reality of life in all activities. The *zendo* is open to all who wish to participate and extends a special welcome to women, lesbians, gay men, and people with disabilities. Jisho Warner is a disciple of Rev. Tozen Akiyama of the Milwaukee Zen Center.

ADDRESS: PO Box 1053, Sebastopol, CA 95473

PHONE: (707) 829-9808

FAX: Same

LINEAGE: Soto Zen

SPIRITUAL HEAD: Jisho Warner

CONTACT: Same

AFFILIATION: Autonomous

ESTABLISHED: 1996

FACILITIES: Rural *zendo* with handicapped access.

RETREATS OFFERED: Periodic *sesshin* and one-day sittings.

Taoist Institute

No description available.

ADDRESS: 10630 Burbank Boulevard, North Hollywood, CA 91601

PHONE: (818) 760-4219

LINEAGE: Chinese Taoist/Chan

MEDITATION PROGRAM: Buddhist Chi Kung meditation.

Tassajara Zen Mountain Center

Tassajara was established in 1996 by San Francisco Zen Center to serve as its rural Zen Buddhist training facility. Its hot springs were used by Esselen Indians and it has been a popular hot springs resort since the 1860s. From April through September it is open to guests and offers a variety of work-study programs, workshops, and retreats. For the remainder of the year it is closed to the public so that Zen students can engage in periods of traditional monastic training.

ADDRESSES: September to mid-April: 39171 Tassajara Road, Carmel Valley, CA 93924. Mid-April to August: Tassajara Reservations, 300 Page Street, San Francisco, CA 94102.
PHONE: (415) 431-3771
LINEAGE: Soto Zen (Suzuki-Roshi)
CONTACT: Stuart Kutchens
AFFILIATION: San Francisco Zen Center
FACILITIES: Rural retreat center and Zen monastery.

The Three Treasures Zen Community

Three Treasures Zen Community provides a compassionate and open environment for the study and practice of Zen and offers traditional Buddhist training in a Western context to both lay and monastic students. Nicolee Jikyo Miller-McMahon, Sensei, received Dharma Transmission from the late Taizan Maezumi-Roshi and is also a marriage, family, and child counselor. She uses a variety of traditional approaches including koan study and *shikantaza* (just sitting), as well as art, sacred dance, communication skills, and social concerns to develop and enrich the practice and to help students actualize their understanding in their day-to-day lives.

ADDRESS: 246 Santa Clara Drive, Vista, CA 92083
PHONES: (619) 481-9776 or (619) 724-9541
E-MAILS: Jikyo@aol.com *or* JMGage@aol.com
LINEAGE: Japanese Soto Zen
SPIRITUAL HEAD: Nicolee Jikyo Miller-McMahon, Sensei
AFFILIATION: Autonomous
ESTABLISHED: 1986
FACILITIES: A variety of urban and suburban centers used on various days of the week to accommodate people from a wide geographic area. Call or write for locations and times.
RETREATS OFFERED: Monthly one-day retreats; extended *sesshin* retreats throughout the year; summer *ango* (training period).

Udumbara Sangha—Cuppertino

No description available.
ADDRESS: 10921 Lucky Oak Street, Cuppertino, CA 95014
PHONE: (408) 735-8231
LINEAGE: Japanese Soto (Suzuki-Roshi and Katagiri-Roshi)
SPIRITUAL HEAD: Diane Martin
CONTACT: Val Szymanski
AFFILIATION: Udumbara Zen Center in Evanston, Illinois
PUBLICATIONS: *Central Flower*, quarterly newsletter.

Ukiah Sangha

For additional information please refer to Community of Mindful Living, Berkeley, California.
ADDRESS: 406 West Standley Street, Ukiah, CA 95482
PHONES: (707) 462-7749 or (707) 462-3212
E-MAIL: jrosen@zapcom.net
LINEAGE: Mindfulness practice in the tradition of Thich Nhat Hanh.
SPIRITUAL HEAD: Thich Nhat Hanh
CONTACTS: Jo-ann Rosen and Betty Lacy
AFFILIATION: Community of Mindful Living, Berkeley, California
MEDITATION PROGRAM: We meet on the first Saturday and the third Sunday of the month.

White Heron Sangha

For additional information please refer to Community of Mindful Living, Berkeley, California.
ADDRESS: PO Box 870, Morro Bay, CA 93443
PHONE: (805) 772-4580
LINEAGE: Mindfulness practice in the tradition of Thich Nhat Hanh.
SPIRITUAL HEAD: Thich Nhat Hanh
CONTACT: Rosemary Donnell
AFFILIATION: Community of Mindful Living, Berkeley, California
MEDITATION PROGRAM: We meet every Sunday evening in San Luis Obispo for meditation, followed by dharma discussion or a taped talk. Precepts are recited the first Sunday of the month. There's also a weekday yoga and meditation group, and three study groups: General Buddhism, Women and Buddhism, and Thich Nhat Hanh's Books and Tapes.
RETREATS OFFERED: Days of Mindfulness are scheduled several times a year.
PUBLICATIONS: Quarterly newsletter.

Zen Center of Los Angeles

Zen Center of Los Angeles (ZCLA), established in 1967 by the late Hakuyu Taizan Maezumi-Roshi, is an urban Zen residential community in the heart of Los Angeles. ZCLA offers year-round programs of daily *zazen, sesshin,* classes, talks, access to teachers and liturgy, and an extended weekend program. Its emphasis is on strong *sangha* practice. Sundays are devoted to *The Gate of Sweet Nectar,* a practice which explores our engagement with the community-at-large. ZCLA blends traditional forms of Zen practice with forms growing out of contemporary Western culture.

ADDRESS: 923 South Normandie Avenue, Los Angeles, CA 90006-1301

PHONE: (213) 387-2351

LINEAGE: Japanese Soto Zen

SPIRITUAL HEAD: Roshi Bernard Tetsugen Glassman

CONTACT: Sensei Wendy Egyoku Nakao, Resident Teacher

AFFILIATION: Mother Temple of the White Plum Sangha

ESTABLISHED: 1967

FACILITIES: Urban meditation center with residential community.

RETREATS OFFERED: Monthly *sesshin* and year-round practice programs.

PUBLICATIONS: Bimonthly *Sangha Letter.*

Zen Center of San Diego

As reflected in the name of our lineage, "Ordinary Mind Zen School," the practice at Zen Center of San Diego emphasizes pure awareness and close attention to body experiencing.

ADDRESS: 2047 Felspar Street, San Diego, CA 92109

PHONE: (619) 273-3444

LINEAGE: Ordinary Mind Zen School

SPIRITUAL HEAD: Charlotte Joko Beck

CONTACT: Same

AFFILIATION: Autonomous

ESTABLISHED: 1983

FACILITIES: Urban *zendo.*

RETREATS OFFERED: Nine *sesshin* per year, three to seven days.

PUBLICATIONS: Monthly *sangha* newsletter.

Zen Center of Willits, Inc.

No description available.

ADDRESS: 2085 Primrose Drive, Willits, CA 95490

PHONE: (707) 459-3771

E-MAIL: elihu_smith@RedwoodFN.org

LINEAGE: Ordinary Mind Zen School

SPIRITUAL HEADS: Elihu Genmyo Smith

(Dharma Successor of Charlotte Joko Beck) and Soto priest ordained by the late Hakuyu Taizan Maezumi-Roshi

AFFILIATION: Autonomous. Informal affiliation with Zen Center San Diego.

ESTABLISHED: 1994

MEDITATION PROGRAM: Saturday morning *zazen*; dharma talks and services; teacher interviews by arrangement.

RETREATS OFFERED: *Zazenkai*/one-day sittings in Willits and Garberville periodically. Elihu Genmyo Smith also leads *sesshin* retreats several times a year at Prairie Zen Center in Champaign, Illinois.

Zen Mountain Center

Zen Mountain Center (ZMC) is located in the San Jacinto Mountains of Southern California, 120 miles east of Los Angeles. Nestled in a forested canyon at an altitude of 5,500 feet, the simple and beautiful solar-powered facilities include a *zendo*, which can sit eighty people, a kitchen, bathhouse, and multiple-use buildings. Accommodations are shared or private in trailers, cabins, and dormitories. Camping is permitted. Delicious vegetarian meals are served at all retreats. ZMC offers year-round programs based on the teaching and practice of Zen Buddhism.

ADDRESS: PO Box 43, Mountain Center, CA 92561

PHONE: (909) 659-5272

FAX: Same

E-MAIL: zmc@interserv.com

LINEAGE: Japanese Soto Zen

SPIRITUAL HEAD: Roshi Bernard Tetsugen Glassman

CONTACTS: Sensei Charles Tenshin Fletcher and Sensei Anne Seisen Fletcher, Resident Teachers

AFFILIATION: White Plum Sangha

ESTABLISHED: 1979

FACILITIES: Solitary and group retreat accommodations.

RETREATS OFFERED: Summer and winter ninety-day intensives; extended Zen retreats; yoga, *Tai chi*, and *Qi Gong* retreats; contemplative environmental retreats throughout the year.

PUBLICATIONS: Newsletter

Zenshuji Soto Mission

Zenshuji is a Japanese community temple. It functions also as the Soto Zen headquarters for North America and as *Betsuin*, representing both training monasteries in Japan, Eiheiji and Sojiji.

ADDRESS: 123 South Hewitt Street, Los Angeles, CA 90012

PHONE: (213) 624-8658

FAX: (213) 624-8650

LINEAGE: Japanese Soto Zen

SPIRITUAL HEAD: Bishop Kenko Yamashita

CONTACTS: Rev. Risai Furutani and Shumyo Kojima

FACILITIES: Urban temple.

MEDITATION PROGRAM: *Zazenkai*: meets for *zazen* three times during the weekend and Monday. *Goeika*: women's group that practices formal chanting for services. Other activities: *Zendeko*: young people's *taiko* drumming group. Classes in tea ceremony, flower arrangement, and several other cultural activities throughout the year.

PUBLICATIONS: *Busshin*, bimonthly used by all groups to keep everyone abreast of developments (in Japanese and English). *Zen Quarterly*, topics of current interest for practitioners, (in English). *Zen No Tomo*, current topics (in Japanese).

Zen Wind

Zen Wind has a commitment to a completely lay practice. Accordingly we have no temples, monasteries, centers, professional clergy (or mortgage). We have a three-step approach to practice: intro-

Zenshuji Soto Mission in Los Angeles, the official headquarters for Soto Zen Buddhism in North America. (Photo courtesy of Zenshuji Soto Mission.)

ductory lectures offered on a regular basis, ongoing meditation groups, and individual instruction for those who wish it. We also offer several weekend retreats each year.

ADDRESS: PO Box 4176, Santa Rosa, CA 95402
PHONE: (707) 939-7023
LINEAGE: Korean Chogye Zen
SPIRITUAL HEAD: Tundra Wind
CONTACT: Same
AFFILIATION: Autonomous
ESTABLISHED: 1985
FACILITIES: We meet in practitioners' homes.
RETREATS OFFERED: Two each year.

COLORADO

Boulder Zen Center

No description available.
ADDRESS: PO Box 7283, Boulder, CO 80306

PHONE: (303) 494-3387
LINEAGE: Japanese Zen
CONTACT: Hobart Bell
AFFILIATION: Autonomous
ESTABLISHED: 1978
FACILITIES: Urban meditation hall.
RETREATS OFFERED: Weekend retreats, quarterly.
PUBLICATIONS: Newsletter

Buddhist Association of Colorado (BAC)

Our new temple comprises two floors with three thousand square feet each, on almost four acres of land. BAC consists mostly of Chinese, but Americans are also welcome. Come and visit us when you have time. Sunday morning service is open to the public. Call for times.
ADDRESS: 8965 West Dartmouth Place, Lakewood, CO 80227
PHONE: (303) 985-5506
FAX: Same

LINEAGE: Chinese Pure Land
SPIRITUAL HEAD: Rev. Fat Leong, Resident Director
ESTABLISHED: 1990
FACILITIES: Urban temple.
MEDITATION PROGRAM: Two-hour service every Sunday, which includes chanted recitation of Buddha's name (Namo Amitabha). This is sometimes recited as we walk, following the monk around the temple.

Buffalo Mountain Dharma Center

Located on forty-five Rocky Mountain acres at an altitude of 8,500 feet, Buffalo Mountain Dharma Center was inaugurated in October 1994 with blessings by Prabhasa Dharma-Roshi. The following spring, H. E. Chagdud Tulku Rinpoche consecrated the property as a Nyingma lineage practice place. Led by David Everest, students pooled their efforts to build a thirty-foot yurt, which now houses all Buffalo Mountain practice activities.
ADDRESS: 8901 Hillview Road, Morrison, CO 80465
PHONE: (303) 697-0263
FAX: (303) 837-2595 (attn. Lilliam Valdes-Cruz)
E-MAIL: kanshin@aol.com
LINEAGE: Japanese Rinzai
SPIRITUAL HEAD: Prabhasa Dharma-Roshi
RESIDENT TEACHER: Dharma Prajnabala Kanshin, Sensei
AFFILIATION: Autonomous
ESTABLISHED: 1994
FACILITIES: Yurt for *zendo* and shrine room on mountain property; large house for teacher residence; kitchen; store open during retreats.
RETREATS OFFERED: Weekend *sesshin*, monthly; weeklong *sesshin*, four times per year.

Chan Nhu Buddhist Pagoda in Lakewood, Colorado. (Photo courtesy of Chan-Nhu Buddhist Pagoda.)

COLORADO (*cont.*)

Chan Nhu Buddhist Pagoda

Through her experience as a dharma teacher to both Western and Vietnamese students, Ayya Bhikkuni Chan Nhu came to see that her temple would be of more benefit if she were to open it to Buddhists of all denominations. In recent years Chan Nhu Buddhist Pagoda has been home to a Chinese Pure Land *sangha*, a Tibetan Vajrayana group, and a Vipassana meditation group, as well as to its Vietnamese congregation. The temple is available to all Buddhists who wish to use it for retreats, classes, or weekly meditation.
ADDRESS: 7201 West Bayaud Place, Lakewood, CO 80226
PHONE: (303) 238-5867
LINEAGE: Vietnamese Mahayana
SPIRITUAL HEAD: Thich Nu Chan Nhu
CONTACT: Ayya Chan Nhu
AFFILIATION: Autonomous

ESTABLISHED: 1985
FACILITIES: Suburban house converted into a Vietnamese Buddhist temple. Includes kitchen, overnight accommodations, and meditation room.
RETREATS OFFERED: Any Buddhist group may use the facilities to conduct retreats.
PUBLICATIONS: Newsletter

Colorado Mountain Zen Centers

No description available.
ADDRESS: Box 49, Ouray, CO 81427
PHONE: (970) 325-4440
LINEAGE: Soto Zen
SPIRITUAL HEAD: Matsuoka Soyu-Roshi
CONTACT: Mike Wise
AFFILIATION: Autonomous
ESTABLISHED: 1983
FACILITIES: Private school on loan.
MEDITATION PROGRAM: Weekly *zazen.*
RETREATS OFFERED: Occasional *sesshin.*

Crestone Mountain Zen Center/ Dharmasangha USA

No description available.
ADDRESS: PO Box 130, Crestone, CO 81131
PHONE: (719) 256-4692
FAX: (719) 256-4691
SPIRITUAL HEAD: Richard Baker-Roshi
AFFILIATION: Dharmasangha USA

Great Mountain Zen Center

Our teacher, Gerry Shishin Wick, has trained in both the Soto and Rinzai Zen traditions and is a dharma successor to the late Taizan Maezumi-Roshi. He has a Ph.D. in physics, has worked in both academia and business, and is a family man with five children. Great Mountain Zen Center hosts daily *zazen,* regular *sesshin,* and Zen instruction. Students of all traditions are welcome and family practice is encouraged.
ADDRESS: 1880 Hawthorne Place, Boulder, CO 80304
PHONE: (303) 449-4143
LINEAGE: Japanese Soto Zen
SPIRITUAL HEAD: Gerry Shishin Wick, Sensei, Resident Teacher
AFFILIATION: Autonomous but also affiliated with White Plum Sangha (Maezumi-Roshi lineage).
ESTABLISHED: 1992
FACILITIES: *Zendo*
RETREATS OFFERED: Regular *sesshin.*
PUBLICATIONS: *Hazy Moon,* newsletter.

International Buddhist Progress Society, Denver (IBPS)

This organization propagates the dharma by encouraging lay participation in retreats, lectures, and community works. IBPS-Denver is led by monastic reverends and sponsors dharma functions in the Chinese Mahayana tradition. Activities such as Sunday services, repentance ceremonies, and Pure Land meditation practice sessions are conducted throughout the year.

ADDRESS: 2530 West Alameda Avenue, Denver, CO 80219

PHONE: (303) 935-3889

FAX: (303) 935-1196

LINEAGE: Ch'an

SPIRITUAL HEAD: Ven. Master Hsin-Yun

CONTACT: Rev. Yi-Ray

AFFILIATION: International Buddhist Progress Society, at Hsi-Lai Temple in Los Angeles.

ESTABLISHED: 1988

PUBLICATIONS: Monthly newsletter.

Kwan Um Zen Community of Colorado

Affiliated with Kwan Um Zen School in Providence, Rhode Island, Kwan Um Zen Community of Colorado holds weekly evening Zen meditation sittings and monthly one-day retreats in Denver. We also sponsor periodic weekend retreats with Barbara Rhodes. All activities are open to the public. Call for times.

ADDRESS: 8445 West Elmhurst Avenue, Littleton, CO 80123

PHONE: (303) 979-1655

FAX: Same

E-MAIL: kuzcc@aol.com

LINEAGE: Korean Chogye Zen

SPIRITUAL HEADS: Zen Master Seung Sahn and Zen Master Seong Hyang (Barbara Rhodes)

CONTACT: Richard Baer

AFFILIATION: Kwan Um School of Zen, Providence, Rhode Island

ESTABLISHED: 1992

FACILITIES: Weekly Zen sittings at Unity Church (3021 South University Boulevard, Littleton); small lending library.

RETREATS OFFERED: Weekend sitting retreats three or four times a year in rented facilities; monthly one-day sittings.

Lafayette Sangha

For additional information, please see Community of Mindful Living, Berkeley, California.

ADDRESS: c/o 1345 Elder Avenue, Boulder, CO 80304

PHONE: (303) 413-1543

E-MAIL: Gaia.Mika@Colorado.EDU

LINEAGE: Mindfulness practice in the tradition of Thich Nhat Hanh.

SPIRITUAL HEAD: Thich Nhat Hanh

CONTACTS: Gaia Mika and Hank Brusselback

AFFILIATION: Community of Mindful Living, Berkeley, California

MEDITATION PROGRAM: We meet one evening a month for sitting and dharma discussion.

RETREATS OFFERED: On the first Sunday of each month we gather for a Morning of Mindfulness, which includes sitting, outdoor walking, precept recitation, and tea ceremony. Call for details.

Naropa Zen Group

We meet weekly at Naropa Institute for sitting and walking meditation, service, and dharma discussion under the direction of Cliff Clusin, an ordained priest in the lineage of the late Katagiri-Roshi of Minnesota Zen Center. Retreats are held from time to time with visiting teachers.

ADDRESS: 2130 Arapahoe Avenue, Boulder, CO 80302

PHONE: (303) 442-6297

LINEAGE: Eclectic Zen

CONTACT: Cliff Clusin

AFFILIATION: Autonomous

ESTABLISHED: 1992

FACILITIES: We meet at Naropa Institute.

RETREATS OFFERED: Occasional retreats with guest teachers.

Sugarloaf Mountain Zendo

The Sugarloaf Mountain Zendo arises from Zen practice and Alaya Process, a transpersonal orientation to education and healing. The short distance into the mountains around Boulder offers a unique possibility to enjoy nature's clear inspiration.

ADDRESS: 284 South Peak Road, Boulder, CO 80302

PHONE: (303) 449-4556

LINEAGE: Japanese Rinzai Zen

SPIRITUAL HEAD: Sanchi Reta Lawler, Resident Monk

CONTACT: Same

AFFILIATION: Autonomous

ESTABLISHED: 1986

FACILITIES: Small country zendo.

MEDITATION PROGRAM: Weekly sittings.

RETREATS OFFERED: Monthly weekend sesshin.

University Zen Center

The University Zen Center exists to serve the spiritual needs of the students, faculty, and staff of the University of Colorado, although group meditation and instruction are open to all who care to join us. We meet four nights a week in a classroom on campus to practice zazen as taught by Sasaki-Roshi of Rinzai-ji, Los Angeles. One evening a week we get together at a local restaurant for a postmeditation supper.

ADDRESS: PO Box 1587, Boulder, CO 80306

PHONE: (303) 440-6553

LINEAGE: Japanese Rinzai Zen

SPIRITUAL HEAD: Sasaki-Roshi

CONTACT: Koyo Engennach

AFFILIATION: Rinzai-ji, Los Angeles

ESTABLISHED: 1993

FACILITIES: Meditation room on University of Colorado campus.

RETREATS OFFERED: Daylong retreats from time to time.

Monastery Without Walls

MUCH OF ZEN PRACTICE TODAY IS WEAK AND highly self-directed, resulting in the growth of ego rather than the flowering of selflessness and affection. At the Zen Center of Denver we have been developing a framework for practice within the context of lay life that can provide the same intensive training in all aspects of Zen as is traditionally found only in a monastic setting. While strongly emphasizing practice in everyday life (Householder Zen), the Monastery Without Walls program teaches students to maintain and run every aspect of the temple properly under the guidance of the teachers.

Trainees make a specific commitment to some or all of the temple training forms. These include daily meditation, dharma talks, private interviews with the teacher, daylong sittings, extended *sesshin* retreats, body work (tai chi, hatha yoga), and art practice (calligraphy, photography, drawing, painting, etc.). Participants also serve on the various committees that maintain and run the Center.

In addition, instruction is given in the zendo positions of monitor, timer, lead chanter, altar and flower attendant, retreat cook, ceremony coordinator, and Monastery Without Walls administrator.

Such intensive training is necessarily a long-term endeavor to be balanced reasonably with demands of home, family, and vocation. Commitment to the program is renewed and adjusted yearly, and members may temporarily withdraw when personal circumstances dictate.

Successful participation depends upon aspiration, prioritization, personal circumstances, and fairly close proximity to the temple. But where authentic training takes place, a process of real transformation is begun that can ripen into genuine realization, the dropping away of body and mind for the benefit of all sentient beings.

Danan Henry

For more information, contact: Zen Center of Denver/Lotus in the Flame Temple, 1233 Columbine Street, Denver, CO 80206; (303) 333-4844.

Zazen Group

This is a small group doing *zazen* together. It's just *zazen*. All Zen students are welcome.

ADDRESS: 787 Racquet Lane, Boulder, CO 80303
PHONE: (303) 499-8381
FAX: (303) 494-3023
E-MAIL: burnspc@ucsu.Colorado.edu
SPIRITUAL HEAD: No teacher affiliation or spiritual director.
AFFILIATION: Autonomous
ESTABLISHED: 1994

Zen Center of Denver/Lotus in the Flame Temple

Zen Center of Denver offers serious Zen training in an urban setting under the direction of Danan Henry, Sensei. The center is composed of Lotus in the Flame Temple; The School of Zen Arts & Studies (courses on Buddhism, the arts, and related disciplines); and a Zen-based life counseling service. The Monastery Without Walls program provides intensive Zen training within the context of one's life as a householder. The schedule includes regular morning and evening *zazen*; *dokusan*; all-day sittings; *sesshin*; and work, body, and liturgy practice. The center also hosts community outreach programs and social functions.

ADDRESS: 1233 Columbine Street, Denver, CO 80206
PHONE: (303) 333-4844
FAX: (303) 333-7844
E-MAIL: DZCenter@aol.com
LINEAGE: Harada-Yasutani Lineage, Integral Soto and Rinzai
SPIRITUAL HEAD: Danan Henry-Sensei, Resident Director
AFFILIATION: Diamond Sangha
ESTABLISHED: 1989
FACILITIES: Meditation hall, retrofitted house for center functions.

RETREATS OFFERED: *Sesshin* (four per year), *zazenkai* (eight per year), *naikan* (seven-day retreat first week in January).

PUBLICATIONS: *Mountains Talking, Empty Boat*

CONNECTICUT

The Living Dharma Center

In 1967, psychotherapist Richard Clarke began a fourteen-year period of intensive Zen training in the Harada-Yasutani-Kapleau lineage, at the end of which he received formal transmission as a teacher of Zen. Living Dharma Center promotes the awakening of True Self to be manifested in all aspects of life: "If the mind is free of the obstructive fog of gratuitous thoughts, this place where we are and this present moment are always being accomplished without effort. This is to be con-

Richard Clarke, Resident Teacher at Living Dharma Center in Bolton, Connecticut. (Photo courtesy of Living Dharma Center.)

tent and grateful for our life." —*Richard Clarke*

ADDRESS: PO Box 513, Bolton, CT 06043
PHONE: (860) 742-7049
LINEAGE: The eclectic lineage of Harada-Roshi/Yasutani-Roshi that combines the essence of Soto and Rinzai Zen.
SPIRITUAL HEAD: Richard Clarke, Resident Teacher
AFFILIATION: Autonomous
ESTABLISHED: 1972
FACILITIES: *Zendo* for weekly practice and country monastery for retreats.
MEDITATION PROGRAM: Tuesday in Amherst, Massachusetts; Wednesday in Coventry, Connecticut.
RETREATS OFFERED: Several seven-day *sesshin* offered yearly and periodic *zazenkai* and introductory workshops.
PUBLICATIONS: *Sangha News*, newsletter for members.

Manchester Sangha

For additional information, please see Community of Mindful Living, Berkeley, California.
ADDRESS: 46 Dougherty Street, Manchester, CT 06040
PHONE: (203) 647-0347
LINEAGE: Mindfulness practice in the tradition of Thich Nhat Hanh.
SPIRITUAL HEAD: Thich Nhat Hanh
CONTACT: Deborah Star Conklin
AFFILIATION: Community of Mindful Living, Berkeley, California
FACILITIES: Local Vietnamese temple.
MEDITATION PROGRAM: We meet once a week for meditation, chanting, tea, and discussion.

New Haven Zen Center

No description available.
ADDRESS: 193 Mansfield Street, New Haven, CT 06511

PHONE: (203) 787-0912
E-MAIL: nhzc@aol.com
LINEAGE: Korean Zen, Chogye order, Korea
SPIRITUAL HEAD: Zen Master Seung Sahn, founding teacher
CONTACTS: Paul Bloom, Senior Dharma Teacher; Nancy Brown, Guiding Teacher; Bruce Blair, Abbot
AFFILIATION: Kwan Um School of Zen, Cumberland, Rhode Island
ESTABLISHED: 1977
FACILITIES: Residential center—urban house with grounds.
RETREATS OFFERED: Second weekend of each month.
PUBLICATIONS: *Primary Point*, published by Kwan Um School of Zen, Cumberland, Rhode Island.

DISTRICT OF COLUMBIA

Bright Pearl Zen Group of Washington

We are a small but dedicated group of lay Zen practitioners, some of whom are already formal students of John Daido Loori, Sensei, others of whom have at least spent time in residence or *sesshin* at Zen Mountain Monastery (ZMM). When the time and energy are right, we hope to grow into an affiliate of ZMM. We meet once a week at a member's home for *zazen* and *kinhin* (walking meditation), and to chant *The Heart Sutra* and the Four Bodhisattva Vows. New members are welcome.
ADDRESS: 6813 Fifth Street, Northwest, Washington, DC 20012
PHONE: (202) 722-1511
E-MAIL: danbruner@aol.com
LINEAGE: Soto and Rinzai Zen
CONTACT: Daniel Bruner
AFFILIATION: Autonomous
ESTABLISHED: 1994

FACILITIES: Lay group sitting in members' homes.

MEDITATION PROGRAM: Weekly *zazen, kinhin*, and chanting.

Mintwood Zendo

Created to serve a need in the gay and lesbian community, our *sangha* is not composed entirely of Zen Buddhists, although the form of our sitting together—*zazen*—comes from the Zen tradition. Dealing together with societal oppression and the need for liberation, we also share and support one another's spiritual practice. Some of us have found coming out as a Buddhist more difficult than coming out as a gay or lesbian. So, we meet for support and for the opening of compassion that comes from *zazen*.

ADDRESS: Zen Meditation, PO Box 21022, Kalorama Station, Washington, DC 20009-0522

PHONE: (202) 265-9405

LINEAGE: Gay and Lesbian American

CONTACT: Andrew Hudson, Cofounder

AFFILIATION: Autonomous

ESTABLISHED: 1984

FACILITIES: Centrally located private home.

MEDITATION PROGRAM: *Zazen* and *kinhin*, Wednesday evenings, with readings from a sutra book followed by a potluck dinner. Monthly taped dharma discourse by John Daido Loori, or printed talk by Charlotte Joko Beck. Call for times.

RETREATS OFFERED: Occasional weekend retreats, with a visiting teacher; all-day sit every other month.

PUBLICATIONS: *Mintwood Zendo Newsletter*

Zen Buddhist Center of Washington, DC/Ka Shin Zendo Genzo-ji

Ka Shin Zendo is a *sangha* of area residents with a strong and serious interest in the practice of Zen Buddhist meditation. Basic instruction in *zazen* is offered. The usual schedule during the week and on Sunday mornings consists of three forty-minute sits with *kinhin*. Weekend *sesshin* and all-day sittings are provided during the year.

ADDRESS: 7004 Ninth Street, Northwest, Washington, DC 20012

PHONE: (202) 829-1966

E-MAIL: kashindc@aol.com

LINEAGE: Japanese Rinzai Zen

AFFILIATION: Autonomous

ESTABLISHED: 1970

FACILITIES: Urban meditation center.

RETREATS OFFERED: Weekend *sesshin* and all-day sittings.

FLORIDA

Atlantic Beach Sangha

For additional information please refer to Community of Mindful Living, Berkeley, California.

ADDRESS: 1841 Selva Grande, Atlantic Beach, FL 32233

PHONE: (904) 246-7263

LINEAGE: Mindfulness practice in the tradition of Thich Nhat Hanh.

SPIRITUAL HEAD: Thich Nhat Hanh

CONTACT: Phil Robinson

AFFILIATION: Community of Mindful Living, Berkeley, California

MEDITATION PROGRAM: We sit together three mornings a week. One evening a week we get together for a silent potluck dinner. Please call for times.

RETREATS OFFERED: On the first Saturday of the month we have a half-Day of Mindfulness on a farm near Gainesville.

Cypress Tree Zen Center

We are a small group of Zen students who have met every week since 1986.

This is no small accomplishment since there is very little support for Buddhist practice in the deep South. Lots of interested people come and go, but the core group remains small and steady. Members are affiliated with different teachers; our yearly Buddha's Birthday and Enlightenment Day ceremonies attract practitioners in the Zen and Tibetan traditions who are students of at least seven different teachers.

ADDRESS: PO Box 1856, Tallahassee, FL 32302-1856

LINEAGE: Korean Chogye Zen (Kwan Um)

SPIRITUAL HEADS: Zen Master Seung Sahn and Guiding Teacher Barbara Rhodes

CONTACT: Ellen B. Gwynn, Abbot

AFFILIATION: Kwan Um School of Zen

ESTABLISHED: 1986

FACILITIES: Unitarian Church for weekly meetings; private home for retreats.

MEDITATION PROGRAM: Weekly meditation.

RETREATS OFFERED: Three to four weekend retreats per year.

Gainesville Zen Circle

This is an informal group that meets once a week for two hours of sitting and discussion. Occasionally, we have a Sunday morning "retreat." In this university town, there are few regulars, partly because of the turnover in people and partly because this is a family home and not a full-time temple. So the main function has been to introduce beginners to meditation and to reinforce practical details about "sustaining a deep question" in everyday life.

ADDRESS: 562 Northeast Second Avenue, Gainesville, FL 32601

PHONE: (352) 373-7567

FAX: (352) 335-8521

E-MAIL: jan@zoo.ufl.edu

LINEAGE: Korean Kwan Um School

SPIRITUAL HEAD: Zen Master Barbara Rhodes

CONTACT: Jan Sendzimir, Resident Director

AFFILIATION: Kwan Um Zen School, Providence, Rhode Island

ESTABLISHED: 1986

FACILITIES: Full-time meditation room.

International Zen Institute of Florida

Our group consists of those who wish to seriously pursue meditation while continuing to live and work as members of society. Daily early morning and evening *zazen* is offered during the week.

ADDRESS: 3860 Crawford Avenue, Miami, FL 33133

PHONE: (305) 448-8969

LINEAGE: Rinzai Zen

SPIRITUAL HEAD: Ven. Gesshin Prabhasadharma-Roshi

CONTACT: Rev. Hank Soan Poor, Lay Minister

AFFILIATION: International Zen Institute of America

ESTABLISHED: 1989

FACILITIES: The Dharma House is located in Coconut Grove, a suburb of Miami.

RETREATS OFFERED: Monthly weekend retreats (nonresidential).

Jacksonville Zen Sangha

Daily sittings at a variety of sites around Jacksonville including Arlington, University of North Florida, The Beaches, Westside, Jacksonville University, and Mandarin. A good place to begin, get instruction, and meet other sitters is at 7405 Arlington Expressway on Sunday mornings. Call for times.

ADDRESS: 7405 Arlington Expressway, Jacksonville, FL 32211

PHONE: (904) 721-1050

FAX: (904) 725-8561

E-MAIL: zlewis@osprey.unf.edu

WWW: www.unf.edu/~zlewis

LINEAGE: Japanese Rinzai Zen (Dai Bosatsu Zendo Kongo-ji)

SPIRITUAL HEAD: Zenrin R. Lewis ("More like *Guide* than *Head*.")

CONTACT: Same

AFFILIATION: Autonomous

ESTABLISHED: 1992

FACILITIES: "Floating *zendo*."

MEDITATION PROGRAM: Sunday morning practice. Call for times.

RETREATS OFFERED: Weekend *sesshin* twice yearly.

PUBLICATIONS: *The Book of the Zen Grove*, second edition (both cloth- and paperbound).

Morikami Zen Group

The Oki Pavilion on the beautiful grounds of the Morikami Museum and Japanese Gardens serves as our *zendo*. Early morning *zazen* on Monday and Friday. Wednesday evening's *zazen* is followed by a Zen study group. Our *sangha* serves the area from Ft. Lauderdale to West Palm Beach. Although we are Soto-oriented, a large number of people from other traditions participate actively. The nature of the *sangha* reflects the developing American-Zen tradition supported by our teacher, Peter Muryo Matthiessen, Sensei.

ADDRESS: c/o Cantor, 801 Bridgewood Place, Boca Raton, FL 33434

PHONE: (407) 483-6680

FAX: Same

LINEAGE: Soto Zen

SPIRITUAL HEAD: Peter Muryo Matthiessen, Sensei

CONTACT: Mitchell Doshin Cantor

AFFILIATION: Sagaponack Zendo, Zen Community of New York

ESTABLISHED: 1996

FACILITIES: At Morikami Japanese Museum, Delray Beach, Florida.

RETREATS OFFERED: Yes

Naples Community of Mindfulness

We emphasize mindfulness practice as taught by Thich Nhat Hanh, but influences from all Buddhist traditions are honored and studied. Teachings are offered free of charge. We welcome families with children. Each year in June we rent a summer camp for a five-day retreat during which children and teenagers participate in all activities, such as meditation, dharma talks, swimming, campfires, and sports.

ADDRESS: 99 North Street, Naples, FL 33963

PHONE: (941) 566-1769

LINEAGE: Mindfulness in the tradition of Thich Nhat Hanh with influences from Tibetan Buddhism and Zen.

SPIRITUAL HEAD: Thich Nhat Hanh

CONTACT: Fred Eppsteiner

AFFILIATION: Autonomous

ESTABLISHED: 1994

FACILITIES: Private home.

MEDITATION PROGRAM: Half-Day of Mindfulness and dharma discussion, first Saturday of the month. One evening per month for meditation and dharma study (call for times).

RETREATS OFFERED: Every year in June we do a five-day family retreat at a rented camp in Virginia.

Pure Light Sangha

For additional information, please see Community of Mindful Living, Berkeley, California.

ADDRESS: 1000 East Island Boulevard, #1806, Williams Island, FL 33160

PHONE: (305) 931-4921

LINEAGE: Mindfulness practice in the tradition of Thich Nhat Hanh.

SPIRITUAL HEAD: Thich Nhat Hanh

CONTACT: Wendy Kapner

AFFILIATION: Community of Mindful Living, Berkeley, California

MEDITATION PROGRAM: We meet once a month for meditation, recitation of the precepts, and dharma discussion.

Zen Meditation Center

No description available.

ADDRESS: 4322 Lincoln Street, Hollywood, FL 33021

PHONE: (305) 963-4668

FAX: Same

LINEAGE: Zen

AFFILIATION: Autonomous

Zen Meditation Group of Pinellas

No description available.

ADDRESS: c/o Rosen, 10388 Kumquat Lane, Seminole, FL 33772

PHONE: (813) 391-5735

LINEAGE: Japanese Rinzai and Soto in style of Philip Kapleau

CONTACT: Kenneth Rosen, Resident Director

AFFILIATION: Informally connected with Zen Meditation Center of Hollywood, Florida.

ESTABLISHED: 1992

FACILITIES: Meet at Bodhitree Dhamma Center, Largo, Florida.

MEDITATION PROGRAM: Meet three times a month for *zazen.*

RETREATS OFFERED: Periodic all-day sittings and occasional *yazas* (all-nighters).

GEORGIA

Atlanta Soto Zen Center

Atlanta Soto Zen Center (ASZC) was established under the leadership of Michael Zenkai Taiun Elliston-Roshi, a disciple of Rev. Dr. Soyu Matsuoka-Roshi in Chicago during the 1960s. ASZC supports its members by providing a place to sit, a group to sit with, a full *zazen* schedule, a lending library, and experienced teachers to respond to any questions that might arise. The center operates a prison outreach program and offers meditation instruction to prisoners throughout the state of Georgia.

ADDRESS: 1404 McLendon Avenue Northeast, Atlanta, GA 30307

PHONE: (404) 659-4749

LINEAGE: Japanese Soto Zen

SPIRITUAL HEAD: Resident Director, Michael Zenkai Taiun Elliston-Roshi

AFFILIATION: Autonomous. ASZC has affiliate centers in Charleston, South Carolina, and Huntsville, Alabama.

ESTABLISHED: Early 1970s

FACILITIES: Urban meditation center, *zendo*, library

MEDITATION PROGRAM: Evening meditation seven days per week; morning *zazen*, three days per week; Sunday morning, 8:00–11:00 AM; newcomer's program, Sundays 11:00 AM–12:00 PM. Call for details.

RETREATS OFFERED: Weekend *sesshin* offered on first weekend of even-numbered months; seven-day *sesshin* yearly, May/June.

Atlanta Zen Group

The group started in Atlanta in 1973 with six people in the basement of the home of Charlotte Kramer, a member of the Rochester Zen Center and a student of Roshi Philip Kapleau. People began by sitting on pillows and blankets. Soon, with the establishment of a formal *zendo* (altar, cushions, robes) and with monitored sittings, the group became an affiliate of Rochester Zen Center. At present there are fifteen members, some of whom are students of Roshi Kapleau and some of Abbot Bodhin Kjolhede, who is now head of Rochester Zen Center.

ADDRESS: 5141 Northside Drive Northwest, Atlanta, GA 30327

PHONE: (770) 955-4321

LINEAGE: Japanese Rinzai/Soto Zen

SPIRITUAL HEAD: Roshi Philip Kapleau and Bodhin Sensei

CONTACT: Charlotte Kramer, Group Leader

AFFILIATION: Rochester Zen Center

ESTABLISHED: 1973

FACILITIES: Small formal *zendo* (no overnight).

MEDITATION PROGRAM: Sittings on Sunday mornings.

RETREATS OFFERED: All-day retreats every few months.

HAWAII

Buddhist Study Center

Buddhist Study Center (BSC) is part of the Honpa Hongwanji Mission of Hawaii, a statewide organization affiliated with the worldwide Jodo Shinshu (True Pure Land Buddhism) Hongwanji-ha. Located next to the University of Hawaii at Manoa campus, BSC has a close working relationship with University of Hawaii faculty and departments, in particular with the Religion Department and the Center for Buddhist Studies. It also serves as the Hawaii office of Ryukoku University.

ADDRESS: 1436 University Avenue, Honolulu, Hawaii 96822

PHONE: (808) 973-6555

FAX: (808) 973-6551

LINEAGE: Japanese Jodo Shinshu (True Pure Land)

SPIRITUAL HEAD: Monshu Koshin Ohtani of Nishi Hongwanji

CONTACT: Rev. Toshio Murakami

AFFILIATION: Honpa Hongwanji Mission of Hawaii

ESTABLISHED: 1972

FACILITIES: Office, library, and meeting rooms.

PUBLICATIONS: *Metta*, monthly; Buddhist Study Center Press.

Diamond Sangha/Koko An Zendo

The Diamond Sangha was established in 1959 at the Koko An Zendo as a lay Zen Buddhist society by Anne and Robert Aitken. The *sangha*'s program is designed to help people face matters of life and death, to find their inherent space of peace, and to practice their understanding in daily life. It includes meditation, three- to seven-day *sesshin*, classes, and *dokusan* (interviews) with the Roshi. Other elements of the program include *shingakudo* (movement practice), *samu* (work practice), celebrations, and rituals. Nelson Foster assumed duties as principal teacher following the retirement of Aitken-Roshi in December 1996.

ADDRESS: 2119 Kaloa Way, Honolulu, HI 96822

PHONE: (808) 946-0666

LINEAGE: Zen Buddhist

SPIRITUAL HEADS: Robert Aitken-Roshi, Founder; Nelson Foster, Dharma Heir

AFFILIATION: Autonomous

ESTABLISHED: 1959

FACILITIES: Single-family house in Honolulu—Koko An Zendo.

MEDITATION PROGRAM: Wednesday evening community nights with *zazen* and *dokusan*.

RETREATS OFFERED: None at this site.

PUBLICATIONS: *Blind Donkey*, Diamond Sangha newsletter.

Diamond Sangha/Maui Zendo

This was Robert Aitken-Roshi's original *zendo*. For additional information, see listing under Diamond Sangha/Koko An Zendo.

ADDRESS: 3823 L. Ho'Piilani Road, #110, Lahaina, HI 96761

Robert Aitken-Roshi, Founder of the Diamond Sangha. (Photo © by Tom Haar.)

PHONE: (808) 669-7725

FAX: (808) 669-7735

LINEAGE: Japanese Sanbo Kyodan

SPIRITUAL HEADS: Robert Aitken-Roshi, Founder; Nelson Foster, Dharma Heir

CONTACT: Patti Burke

AFFILIATION: Diamond Sangha/Koko An Zendo

ESTABLISHED: 1975

FACILITIES: Various locations in the community.

MEDITATION PROGRAM: Weekly evening *zazen*. Call for time and location.

RETREATS OFFERED: Monthly *zazenkai* (daylong sitting).

PUBLICATIONS: *Maui Zendo Quarterly Newsletter*

Diamond Sangha/Palolo Zen Center

The Palolo Zen Center is designed for students who seek a residential practice place. It is located in upper Palolo Valley, a rural setting that is, nonetheless, near urban Honolulu.

ADDRESS: 2747 Waiomao Road, Honolulu, HI 96816

PHONE: (808) 735-1347

FAX: (808) 735-4245

LINEAGE: Japanese Zen Buddhist

SPIRITUAL HEADS: Robert Aitken-Roshi, Founder; Nelson Foster, Dharma Heir

CONTACT: Nelson Foster, Resident Teacher

AFFILIATION: Autonomous

ESTABLISHED: 1959

FACILITIES: Rural residential practice center.

MEDITATION PROGRAM: Talk scheduled at *zazen*. Call for times.

RETREATS OFFERED: Periodic retreats.

PUBLICATIONS: *Blind Donkey*, Diamond Sangha newsletter.

Soto Mission

"While we must protect the core of our faith, we desperately need to make whatever changes are necessary to increase its appeal not only to Americans of Japanese descent, but to all people. The essential core of our faith remains forever constant. It is the trappings that will and must change if we want it to survive into the twenty-first century. If we are to succeed, we must work towards making Soto Zen, American Buddhism, so that it will be more easily embraced by all whose minds and hearts are open to the compassionate wisdom of the Buddha."
—*Rev. Shakti Myokan Khan*

ADDRESS: 1708 Nuuanu Avenue, Honolulu, HI 96817

PHONE: (808) 537-9409

FAX: (808) 537-6320

LINEAGE: Japanese Soto Zen

SPIRITUAL HEAD: Bishop Gyokyei Matsuura, Resident Director

AFFILIATION: Hawaii Soto Mission Association

ESTABLISHED: 1913

FACILITIES: *Shoin* or *zazen* room.

MEDITATION PROGRAM: Once a week on Sunday mornings. Call for times. Open to the public.

PUBLICATIONS: *Soto Mission Bulletin*

Zen Center of Hawaii

The Zen Center of Hawaii is located on the island of Hawaii in the town of Waimea (Kamuela). We offer a regular schedule of traditional-style Zen practice, including *sesshin* each month. Our programs are practice-oriented and include broad areas, such as contemplation, right livelihood, and social action. Our Director and Spiritual Teacher is Robert Joshin Althouse. He was a serious student of Taizan Maezumi-Roshi and is presently a Dharmaholder of Bernard Tetsugen Glassman-Roshi.

ADDRESS: PO Box 2066, Kamuela, HI 96743

PHONE: (808) 885-6109

FAX: (808) 885-2009

E-MAIL: zch@aloha.net

LINEAGE: Japanese Soto/Rinzai Zen— White Plum Lineage

SPIRITUAL HEAD: Robert Joshin Althouse, Resident Director

AFFILIATION: Autonomous/White Plum Sangha

ESTABLISHED: 1993

FACILITIES: Three *zendos.*

MEDITATION PROGRAM: Regular weekly meditation schedule at three locations on the Big Island.

RETREATS OFFERED: Regular monthly *sesshin* from three to ten days in length.

PUBLICATIONS: *Muddy Waters,* newsletter.

IDAHO

Beginner's Mind Sangha

For additional information, please see Community of Mindful Living, Berkeley, California.

ADDRESS: 1430 Shenandoah Drive, Boise, ID 83712

PHONE: (208) 336-1525

FAX: (208) 334-2704

LINEAGE: Mindfulness practice in the tradition of Thich Nhat Hanh.

SPIRITUAL HEAD: Thich Nhat Hanh

CONTACTS: Peggy Rowe and Larry Ward

AFFILIATION: Community of Mindful Living, Berkeley, California

MEDITATION PROGRAM: We have meditation and dharma discussion one evening per week. Precept recitation and potluck suppers are scheduled.

RETREATS OFFERED: Occasional Days of Mindfulness and weekend retreats.

Mindfulness Sangha

For additional information, please see Community of Mindful Living, Berkeley, California.

ADDRESS: 106 East Third Street, #3B, Moscow, ID 83843

PHONE: (208) 883-3311

E-MAIL: Pat@uidaho.edu

LINEAGE: Mindfulness practice in the tradition of Thich Nhat Hanh.

SPIRITUAL HEAD: Thich Nhat Hanh

CONTACTS: Pamela Berger and Pat Hine

AFFILIATION: Community of Mindful Living, Berkeley, California

MEDITATION PROGRAM: We practice together two evenings a week and also on Saturday mornings. Our Sunday evening gatherings begin with sitting meditation and are followed by either a precept recitation, a tea ceremony, a sutra recitation, or a dharma discussion.

RETREATS OFFERED: When there is a fifth Sunday in the month, we have special events such as Mindfulness Days, Family Days, or potlucks and planning meetings. Occasional extended retreats.

ILLINOIS

Bloomington-Normal Zen Group

No description available.

ADDRESS: Box 1203, Bloomington, IL 61702-1203

PHONE: (309) 828-4162

E-MAIL: bhodgman@ice.net

LINEAGE: Japanese Soto Zen

CONTACT: Bob Hodgman

AFFILIATION: Autonomous

PUBLICATIONS: *Zen Gazette*

Bong Boolsa Korean Buddhist Temple

Founded in 1982 by Ven. Young Joo Lee according to the tradition of the Chogye Buddhist order of Korea. Activities include a Sunday prayer meeting and Zen meditation. Programs are conducted in Korean.

ADDRESS: 5114 North Elston Avenue, Chicago, IL 60630

PHONE: (312) 286-0307

LINEAGE: Korean Chogye

SPIRITUAL HEAD: Ven. Young Joo Lee

CONTACT: Same

AFFILIATION: Autonomous

ESTABLISHED: 1982

RETREATS OFFERED: Sunday prayer meeting and Zen meditation.

Buddhist Association of Central Illinois

We are a small group of friends who meet weekly for sitting and walking meditation, following primarily the tradition of Soto Zen and the teachings of Thich Nhat Hanh. We occasionally sponsor one-day *sesshin* and visits from Buddhist teachers.

ADDRESS: 1860 East Lakeshore Drive, Springfield, IL 62707

PHONE: (217) 529-6819

E-MAIL: quam.michael@uis.edu

The Fish-Releasing Ceremony

EVERY YEAR IN JUNE, THE *SANGHA* AT BULTASA Korean Buddhist Temple in Chicago holds a traditional ceremony in which fish are released into the Fox River in St. Charles. The temple's two hundred members rent a large "entertainment boat" for half a day and pilot it out to the middle of the river. Then, to the accompaniment of monks chanting, *sangha* members release the fish, one at a time, from small bowls. Fish are purchased at a local pet store, and care is taken to select species appropriate to their new habitat. At the end of the ceremony everyone chants *The Heart Sutra* together and the boat sails back to shore, where a picnic awaits.

The fish-releasing ceremony is a traditional religious rite of spring among Buddhists in Korea and the practice has been imported to Korean temples in the United States. The custom dates back to the Sila dynasty, when fish-releasing ponds were a common fixture in many temple compounds. The ceremony is rooted in the first of the Five Cardinal Precepts: I vow to abstain from the taking of life. Proceeds from this annual event are donated to orphanages or to other temples, a desirable practice of Mahayana Buddhism.

Kay Kim

For more information, contact: Bultasa Korean Buddhist Temple, 4360 W. Montrose Avenue, Chicago, IL 60641; (312) 286-1551.

LINEAGE: Primarily Soto Zen
AFFILIATION: Autonomous
ESTABLISHED: 1992

Buddhist Temple of Chicago

Established in 1944 by the Rev. Gyomay M. Kubose, the Buddhist Temple of Chicago is a nonsectarian temple in the Japanese Mahayana tradition. All ministers are formally trained at Otani University in Kyoto and ordained in the Higashi Honganji School, but hierarchical independence is maintained. Rev. Kubose founded the temple in order to establish a humanistic Buddhism based on the universal teachings of Gautama Buddha, fully accepting that Buddhism in America would take a uniquely American path. The temple is home to the Buddhist Education Center and the American Buddhist Association.
ADDRESS: 1151 West Leland Avenue, Chicago, IL 60640
PHONE: (312) 334-4661

LINEAGE: Jodo Shinshu/Soto Zen
SPIRITUAL HEAD: Rev. Yukei Ashikaga
CONTACT: Richard Brandon, Director, Meditation Program
AFFILIATION: Buddhist Churches of America
ESTABLISHED: 1944
FACILITIES: Urban temple/meditation hall.
MEDITATION PROGRAM: Zen meditation three mornings and two evenings per week. Call for schedule. Buddhist Education Center offers classes in Japanese language, calligraphy, tea ceremony, flower arranging, and martial arts.
RETREATS OFFERED: Combination Rinzai/Soto *sesshin*.
PUBLICATIONS: *BTC Bulletin*

Bultasa Korean Buddhist Temple

Bultasa (the name means "Gathering of Buddhas") is the oldest and largest Korean Buddhist temple in Chicago. Bultasa moved to its present location in 1986, when extensive remodeling transformed the building into a temple complex. A center of the Korean Buddhist community, the complex is staffed by monks of the Chogye order who conduct a variety of services and functions, notably a religious service every Sunday in Korean (English translation available) and commemorative services for the departed.
ADDRESS: 4360 West Montrose Avenue, Chicago, IL 60641
PHONE: (312) 286-1551
LINEAGE: Korean Chogye order
SPIRITUAL HEADS: Ji Hak Sunim (Founder); Hwa Rang Sunim (Abbot)
CONTACTS: Mr. Chung, Kay Kim, Hugh Yoon
AFFILIATION: Autonomous
ESTABLISHED: 1970
FACILITIES: Urban temple complex.
MEDITATION PROGRAM: Sunday services in Korean, services for the departed.
PUBLICATIONS: *Bultasa Weekly News*

Philip Kapleau-Roshi on a visit to Chicago Zen Center. (Photo by Ken Lee.)

ILLINOIS (*cont.*)

Chicago Zen Center

Chicago Zen Center is an affiliate of Rochester Zen Center, Rochester, New York. The Ven. Bodhin Kjolhede, Sensei (Dharma heir of Philip Kapleau-Roshi) is our spiritual head and visits the center frequently. Activities include daily *zazen* and chanting, frequent one-day *sesshin*, occasional two- and four-day *sesshin*, and work days. Regular *zazen* instruction is available from Sensei Kjolhede's senior students. We practice an integrated Rinzai/Soto Zen, as described by Roshi Kapleau in his book, *The Three Pillars of Zen*.

ADDRESS: 2029 Ridge Avenue, Evanston, IL 60201-2713
PHONE: (847) 475-3015
LINEAGE: Integrated Rinzai/Soto Zen
SPIRITUAL HEAD: Ven. Bodhin Kjolhede, Sensei
CONTACT: Ven. Sevan Ross

AFFILIATION: Rochester Zen Center
ESTABLISHED: 1972
FACILITIES: Urban meditation center
RETREATS OFFERED: One-, two-, and four-day *sesshin* scheduled throughout the year.
PUBLICATIONS: Quarterly newsletter.

Han-Ma-Um Zen Center

No description available
ADDRESS: 7852 N. Lincoln Avenue, Skokie, IL 60077
PHONE: (847) 674-0811
FAX: (847) 674-0812
E-MAIL: hanmaum@aol.com
LINEAGE: Korean Seon (Zen), Chogye Order of Korea
SPIRITUAL HEAD: Seon Master Dae Haeng Keun Sunim
CONTACT: Ven. Hye Ji Sunim, Director
AFFILIATION: HanMaUm Seon Won, Chogye Order of Korea

ESTABLISHED: 1992
FACILITIES: Full center
MEDITATION PROGRAM: Regular meeting every Sunday at 10:30 AM
PUBLICATIONS: HanMaUm Hwae Bo

Harmony Zen Center

The Harmony Zen Center operates under the auspices of the Buddhist Temple of Chicago and conducts meditation Monday through Friday. There is also a regular Sunday morning session followed by an optional social breakfast of tea, toast, and fruit. Introduction/instruction available on request (call for appointment). There are no membership fees, although goodwill offerings are accepted. *Zafus*, mats, and *seiza* benches are provided.
ADDRESS: 4645 North Racine Avenue, Second Floor, Chicago, IL 60640
PHONE: (312) 583-5794
LINEAGE: Rinzai/Soto Zen
CONTACT: Richard Brandon
AFFILIATION: Buddhist Temple of Chicago
FACILITIES: Urban *zendo*.
MEDITATION PROGRAM: Meditation three mornings and two evenings per week, plus a regular Sunday morning program. A "special session" is held Tuesday evenings at Second Unitarian Church, 650 West Barry, Chicago. Call for times.

International Zen Dojo Sogenkai

The International Zen Dojo Sogenkai follows the Rinzai Zen tradition and holds introductory six-week Sunday morning sessions. Saturday morning practice consists of a half-hour of *zazen* and two hours of martial arts practice. There are *sesshin* retreats twice a year. Classes are offered on various aspects of Japanese culture.
ADDRESS: 1016 West Belmont, Chicago, IL 60657

Dial-the-Dharma

Dial-the-Dharma offers short, two- to three-minute taped talks, which are changed daily and are accessible twenty-four hours a day. This dharma phone service was started in 1981 by Rev. Sunnan Kubose as a way to promote the teachings and nondualistic approach of his father, the Venerable Gyomay M. Kubose. With roots in Japanese Mahayana Buddhism, Rev. Kubose's teachings can be said to bloom in a universally humanistic manner. His nonsectarian approach focuses on everyday spirituality.

From a library of several hundred tapes, the daily presentations range from vintage talks by Rev. Kubose Senior, to humorous, frequently irreverent commentaries by his son. Religious terminology is minimized in favor of a down-to-earth style that presents the teachings in simple, nonesoteric language. The humorous tone reflects the notion that spirituality does not have to be somber and overly serious. Many of the talks come straight from "Calvin and Hobbes." There's a "Dear Sensei" advice column. "Dharma Dan" and "Sangha Sam" make frequent guest appearances, and callers are sometimes startled by titles such as "BM is fertilizer too!"

Although many of the talks do take a lighthearted tone, there's nothing superficial about them. Rev. Kubose insists that the real importance of laughter lies in its complete and absolute sincerity. Dial-the-Dharma is one way to cultivate an appreciation of everyday spirituality and at the same time to enjoy some dharma laughter. Please write for more information. Better yet, give us a call.

Rev. Sunnan Kubose

For more information, contact: Kubose Dharma Legacy, 8334 Harding Avenue, Skokie, IL 60076; (847) 677-8053.

PHONE: (312) 525-3141
LINEAGE: Japanese Rinzai Zen
CONTACTS: David Miller, Barbara De-Graffe, Resident Teachers
MEDITATION PROGRAM: Regularly scheduled Zen practice twice weekly; Saturday, half-hour *zazen* plus two hours of martial arts.
RETREATS OFFERED: *Sesshin* twice per year. Six-week introductory courses in Zen.

Kubose Dharma Legacy

Kubose Dharma Legacy was established to perpetuate and develop the Buddhist teachings and nondualistic approach of the Ven. Gyomay M. Kubose. With roots in Japanese Mahayana Buddhism, the teachings are expressed in nonsectarian terminology and emphasize the development of a spiritual practice integrated with everyday life. We offer a structured program oriented toward private individual practice at home for people without access to a group. In addition to books and other printed material, short taped talks are accessible on a twenty-four-hour "Dial-the-Dharma" telephone line.
ADDRESS: 8334 Harding Avenue, Skokie, IL 60076
PHONES: (847) 677-8211. "Dial-the-Dharma": (847) 677-8053.
LINEAGE: Japanese Mahayana
SPIRITUAL HEAD: Ven. Gyomay M. Kubose
CONTACT: Rev. Sunnan Koyo Kubose
AFFILIATION: Autonomous
ESTABLISHED: 1996

Lakeside Buddha Sangha

Although Lakeside Buddha Sangha members come from all walks of life, the group's common denominator is an interest in the teachings of Vietnamese Zen Master Thich Nhat Hanh, who encourages a life of awareness, healing, love, and understanding in our communities. Weekly meetings include sitting and walking meditation, and dharma discussions. In June 1992, one of our members was ordained a *dharmacarya* (dharma teacher) by Thich Nhat Hanh in a Transmission of the Lamp ceremony at Plum Village, France. The dharma teacher offers meditation instruction and leads group retreats and Days of Mindfulness.
ADDRESS: PO Box 7067, Evanston, IL 60201

ILLINOIS (cont.)

PHONE: (847) 475-0080
FAX: Same
LINEAGE: Zen Buddhist
SPIRITUAL HEAD: Ven. Thich Nhat Hanh
CONTACT: Jack Lawlor, Dharma Teacher
AFFILIATION: Unified Buddhist Church
of Vietnam
ESTABLISHED: 1991
FACILITIES: Weekly sitting and walking
meditation, dharma discussion.
RETREATS OFFERED: Approximately every
two months.
PUBLICATIONS: Monthly newsletter and a
manual, *Sangha Building: Creating the
Buddhist Practice Community*.

Lotus Sangha (Khom Sen)

We meet once a month for meditation,
chanting, precepts recitation, dharma
talk and discussion, sharing knowledge
and experience, singing, tea meditation, and vegetarian potluck dinners.
Throughout the year we have special
events such as Days of Mindfulness, Tet
(Vietnamese New Year), Buddha's Birthday, Mid-Autumn Festival, and Ullambana Festival. We also do outdoor
gathering and walking meditation in the
local parks.
ADDRESS: 1520 Canyon Run Road,
Naperville, IL 60565
PHONE: (708) 983-6287
LINEAGE: Vietnamese Buddhist
CONTACT: Amelia Nguyen

Midwest Buddhist Temple

Midwest Buddhist Temple teaches the
way of *Nembutsu*, the realization of One-
ness in the Infinite Compassion and Wisdom of Amida Buddha. The temple was
established in 1944 by the late Rev.
Gyodo Kono along with a devoted group
of Japanese-Americans who had just been
discharged from the internment camps of
World War II. The resident minister is

the Rev. Koshin Ogui, Sensei, an eigh-
teenth-generation Buddhist priest from
Japan. Sensei has a sincere desire to open
the Buddha dharma to anyone wishing to
seek the meaning of life in the Buddha's
teachings.
ADDRESS: 435 West Menomonee Street,
Chicago, IL 60614
PHONE: (312) 943-7801
FAX: (312) 943-8069
LINEAGE: Jodo Shin Shu, Kyoto Nishi
Honganji, Japan
SPIRITUAL HEAD: Koshin Ogui, Sensei
CONTACT: Same
AFFILIATION: Buddhist Churches of
America
ESTABLISHED: July 10, 1944
MEDITATION PROGRAM: Sunday morning
zenshin meditation; children's dharma
school; adult *sangha*. Minyo folk dance,
Taiko drumming, and dharma karate.
Call for times.
RETREATS OFFERED: Announced
PUBLICATIONS: *MBT Bulletin*

Northwest Chicago Zen Group

Northwest Chicago Zen Group is led by
Susan Myoyu Andersen, Dharma Holder,
who studied traditional Soto Zen and did
koan practice with the late Taizan Mae-
zumi-Roshi of the Zen Center of Los
Angeles.
ADDRESS: 1433 East Walnut Avenue, Des
Plaines, IL 60016-6621
PHONE: (847) 298-8472
LINEAGE: Soto Zen
SPIRITUAL HEAD: Susan Myoyu Ander-
sen, Dharma Holder
CONTACT: Same
AFFILIATION: Autonomous
FACILITIES: Meets at Countryside Uni-
tarian Church, 1025 North Smith Road,
Palatine, Illinois.
MEDITATION PROGRAM: Regularly sched-
uled weekly *zazen* practice. Children's
classes.
RETREATS OFFERED: *Sesshin* retreats held
throughout the year.

Prairie Buddha Sangha

We sometimes call ourselves the "Traveling Prairie Buddha Sangha" because we
meet at the homes of various *sangha*
members. Our time together includes sitting and walking meditation, readings,
music, and poetry followed by socializing
and refreshments. We offer an open invitation to share knowledge, experience,
presence, and silence. We practice to af-
firm and deepen our understanding of
the dharma, and to recognize that the
truths in all teachings converge into one
whenever people join to share them.
ADDRESS: 136 Ilehamwood, DeKalb, IL
60115
PHONE: (815) 756-2801
LINEAGE: Mindfulness practice in the tradition of Thich Nhat Hanh.
SPIRITUAL HEAD: Thich Nhat Hanh
CONTACTS: Bruce and Estelle von Zellen
AFFILIATION: Community of Mindful
Living, Berkeley, California
FACILITIES: Members' homes.
MEDITATION PROGRAM: We meet twice a
month for mindfulness practice.
RETREATS OFFERED: We join with other
sanghas for a Day of Mindfulness, and
Mindfulness weekends. During the
summer, several of us go to a wonderful
cabin in the woods at Camp Algonquin
to practice mindfulness.

Prairie Zen Center

Prairie Zen Center is comprised of a
group of individuals studying Zen in the
lineage established by Charlotte Joko
Beck at Zen Center of San Diego. We rent
a house for the center's use. Three group
sittings are scheduled each week, and
during at least one of them we listen to
taped dharma talks given by Joko Beck
or her Dharma Successor, Elihu Genmyo
Smith. On the first weekend of each
month we have an overnight intensive.

Three times per year, we offer five-day *sesshin* led by Elihu Genmyo Smith.

ADDRESS: PO Box 1702, Champaign, IL 61824

PHONE: (217) 384-8817

WWW: http://luca.cba.uiuc.edu/PZC/PZCHome.html

LINEAGE: Ordinary Mind Zen School

SPIRITUAL HEADS: Charlotte Joko Beck and Elihu Genmyo Smith

CONTACT: Michael Andrechak

AFFILIATION: Informally with Zen Center of San Diego

FACILITIES: Rented house.

MEDITATION PROGRAM: Three group sittings per week (call for times).

RETREATS OFFERED: Weekend sitting once a month; five-day *sesshin* three times a year.

Quan Am Tu Buddhist Temple

Quan Am Tu Buddhist Temple was founded in 1992 in uptown Chicago. We follow the Pure Land tradition, which had its origins in China in about the fifth century. Pure Land stresses faith in the power and compassion of Amitabha Buddha. We hold daily meditation practice and service on Sunday.

ADDRESS: 5545 North Broadway, Chicago, IL 60640

PHONE: (312) 271-7048

LINEAGE: Chinese Pure Land

CONTACT: Quant Tim

ESTABLISHED: 1992

FACILITIES: Urban temple.

MEDITATION PROGRAM: Daily meditation. Call for times.

Quang Minh Temple

Although Quang Minh Temple serves the Chicago-area Vietnamese community, all are welcome to any of its activities. These include retreats, individual instruction, and Sunday morning service in Vietnamese (Chinese and English services are also provided when required). Monks reside at the facility. Meditation is in the Mahayana tradition.

ADDRESS: 4429 North Damen Avenue, Chicago, IL 60625

PHONE: (312) 275-6859

LINEAGE: Vietnamese Buddhist

SPIRITUAL HEAD: Thich Minh Hanh, Resident Teacher

AFFILIATION: Autonomous

ESTABLISHED: 1982

FACILITIES: Urban temple.

MEDITATION PROGRAM: Daily chanting; Sunday morning service in Vietnamese (call for times).

RETREATS OFFERED: Occasional retreats.

Rissho Kosei-kai of Chicago

Toward the end of his life, Shakyamuni Buddha revealed his supreme wisdom in *The Saddharma-pundarika (Lotus) Sutra*. In it, he taught that all living beings possess an inherent Buddha nature, not yet awakened. Rissho Kosei-Kai was founded to reveal *The Lotus Sutra's* pure doctrine in our contemporary world. Through daily sutra recitation, we manifest the Buddha's wisdom in our daily lives, realize freedom from suffering, and bring about the enlightenment of our ancestors. One of our main practices is *Hoza* (Circle of Compassion), a unique form of group counseling, which takes place after the Sunday prayer service.

ADDRESS: 3754 North Ashland Avenue, Chicago, IL 60613

PHONE: (312) 728-3370

FAX: (312) 728-3390

LINEAGE: Japanese Nichiren

SPIRITUAL HEAD: Rev. Nikkyo Niwano, Founder

CONTACTS: Mrs. Yoshiko Murakami (English: John M. Schuh)

AFFILIATION: Rissho Kosei-kai headquarters, Tokyo, Japan

ESTABLISHED: 1938 in Japan; 1964, Chicago.

FACILITIES: Meeting hall.

PUBLICATIONS: *Dharma World, Everyday Buddhism*

Suma Ching Hai International Association

The Suma Ching Hai International Association follows the Quan Yin method under the leadership of Master Ching Hai. It conducts two-and-a-half-hour meditation sessions for disciples only. These are conducted in English, Chinese, and Vietnamese and include vegetarian meals. Practice retreats last three to six months.

ADDRESS: 8250 South Kedzie Avenue, Chicago, IL 60652

PHONE: (312) 925-1338

LINEAGE: Chinese Quan Yin

SPIRITUAL HEAD: Master Ching Hai

CONTACT: Albert Lai

MEDITATION PROGRAM: Meditation sessions for disciples only.

RETREATS OFFERED: Three- to six-month practice retreats.

PUBLICATIONS: *Suma Ching Hai News*, monthly newsletter.

Udumbara Zen Center

Udumbara Zen Center offers training in Buddhism as a way of life. In addition to meditation, we offer sutra study, a chaplaincy program, and temple officer instruction. Although we are primarily a Zen center in the Soto tradition, we are influenced by both Hinayana and Vajrayana teachings.

ADDRESS: 501 Sherman Avenue, Evanston, IL 60202

PHONE: (847) 475-3264

FAX: (847) 475-8937

LINEAGE: Japanese Soto (Suzuki-Roshi and Katagiri-Roshi)

SPIRITUAL HEAD: Diane Martin

CONTACT: Same

AFFILIATION: Autonomous; informally connected with San Francisco Zen Center, Minnesota Zen Center, and Yvonne Rand of Muir Beach, California.

ESTABLISHED: 1990

FACILITIES: Urban *zendo* with guest accommodations and Wisconsin country retreat house.

MEDITATION PROGRAM: Daily *zazen*. Call for times.

RETREATS OFFERED: Monthly daylong *zazenkai*, five-day summer *sesshin*, three-day winter *sesshin*.

PUBLICATIONS: *Central Flower*, quarterly newsletter.

Won Buddhism of America

Won Buddhism was founded in 1916 through the enlightenment of Ven. Sotaesan Chung Bin Park (1893–1943) in Korea. Il-Won-San (one circle phrase) is used extensively in our practice.

ADDRESS: 6330 North Cicero, Chicago, IL 60630

PHONE: (312) 282-9922

LINEAGE: Korean Won Buddhist

SPIRITUAL HEAD: Ven. Soo Il Yoo

CONTACT: Same

AFFILIATION: Headquarters center.

Zen Buddhist Temple

Located in a renovated Pentecostal church building, Zen Buddhist Temple offers services and meditation courses to the general public, and provides a community for fellowship and support as well as a monastic training center for Buddhist monks and nuns. Among the temple's special events are lecture series, Buddhist art exhibitions, Buddha's Birthday celebrations, and special New Year's Eve and New Year's Day services. The temple serves as a center for study and

Ven. Samu Sunim, founder and president of the Buddhist Society for Contemplative Wisdom and spiritual head of the Zen Buddhist Temple in Chicago. (Photo courtesy of Zen Buddhist Temple.)

practice for students enrolled in the Maitreya Buddhist Seminary. It also runs a year-round solitary retreat center with its own meditation hall, individual rooms, and kitchen.

ADDRESS: 1710 West Cornelia Avenue, Chicago, IL 60657-1219

PHONE: (312) 528-8685

FAX: (312) 528-9909

LINEAGE: Korean/Chogye Zen

SPIRITUAL HEAD: Ven. Samu Sunim (Sam-Woo Kim)

CONTACT: Irjo Mark Gemmill

AFFILIATION: Buddhist Society for Compassionate Wisdom

ESTABLISHED: 1992

FACILITIES: Buddha hall, year-round meditation retreat center, social hall, and garden patio.

MEDITATION PROGRAM: Sunday morning and afternoon services open to the public, as are meditation courses for beginners, retreats, and visitors' programs throughout the year.

RETREATS OFFERED: All-night meditation (January) to commemorate Buddha's Enlightenment; overnight introductory retreat; one- to five-day retreats throughout the year; three-month summer retreat; year-round visitor's program.

PUBLICATIONS: *Spring Wind*, Buddhist Cultural Forum.

The Zen Buddhist Temple of Chicago

The Zen Buddhist Temple of Chicago is the oldest continuously practicing Zen temple in the United States. Its training emphasizes the interplay between Buddhist and Taoist spiritual practices—Tai Chi Chuan and the Chinese Health Methods. In addition to his thirty-five years of experience in Japanese Buddhism, the Rev. Kongo Langlois-Roshi has trained for over three decades in Taoist martial arts and other Chinese traditions. As successor to Professor Huo Chi Kwang, he serves as director of the Chinese Cultural Academy. Our goal is to assist those who would be self-confident, self-responsible, and truly independent.

ADDRESS: 865 Bittersweet, Northbrook, IL 60062

PHONE: (847) 869-0554

E-MAIL: s_ericksen@interramp.com

LINEAGE: Japanese Soto Zen

SPIRITUAL HEAD: Rev. Kongo Langlois-Roshi

CONTACT: Stuart Ericksen

AFFILIATION: Autonomous

ESTABLISHED: 1949

FACILITIES: Meditation center, 608 Dempster Street, Evanston, Illinois.

MEDITATION PROGRAM: Meditation twice a week. Sunday dharma talk.

RETREATS OFFERED: Daylong *sesshin*, first Saturday of the month; three- and four-day retreats, March, June, and November.

PUBLICATIONS: *Diamond Sword Newsletter*

Zen Group of Champaign-Urbana

In addition to weekly *zazen* practice, we celebrate Buddha's Birthday and Bodhi Day and hold an occasional potluck supper.

ADDRESS: Japan House, 902 West California, Urbana, IL 61801

PHONES: (217) 352-1676 or (217) 328-7268

E-MAIL: pgregory@ux1.cso.uiuc.edu

LINEAGE: Japanese Soto Zen (Zen Center of Los Angeles)

CONTACT: Margi Gregory

AFFILIATION: Autonomous

FACILITIES: We meet at Japan House.

MEDITATION PROGRAM: When the University of Illinois is in session, sittings are held one evening a week. Orientation and meditation are held Sundays. Call for times.

RETREATS OFFERED: Occasional weekend *sesshin/zazenkai*.

INDIANA

Indianapolis Zen Group

The Indianapolis Zen group is an affiliate of Furnace Mountain Zen Center, Clay City, Kentucky. There are about two dozen regular participants.

ADDRESS: c/o Walt Johnson, 6009 North Compton, Indianapolis, IN 46220

PHONE: (317) 274-6879

E-MAIL: dubin@chem.iupui.edu

LINEAGE: Korean/Kwan Um Zen

SPIRITUAL HEAD: Dae Gak Sunim, Guiding Teacher

CONTACT: Paul Dubin, Abbot

AFFILIATION: Furnace Mountain Zen Center, Clay City, Kentucky

ESTABLISHED: 1994

MEDITATION PROGRAM: Sitting meditation three evenings a week. Call for times.

RETREATS OFFERED: Biannual weekend retreats.

PUBLICATIONS: *The Ember*, quarterly newsletter.

Kwan Um Zen Community of Chicago (KUZC)

KUZC is an affiliation of several strong practice groups in Chicago, Woodstock, and Wheaton, Illinois, and in Hobart, Indiana. We come together for various "all-sangha" events, which include four annual weekend retreats with Barbara Rhodes, *kidos*, and even joint chanting with a local Sufi group. Like all Kwan Um Zen centers, we practice sitting, bowing, and chanting to connect us more strongly with our original nature. While we do not have a center per se, we practice in a number of wonderful facilities and hold retreats in several locations.

ADDRESS: c/o Bob Kemp, 1101 State Street, Hobart, IN 46342

PHONE: (219) 942-6050

FAX: (312) 867-5197

E-MAIL: ecutler@openport.com

LINEAGE: Korean Zen

SPIRITUAL HEAD: Zen Master Seung Sahn

CONTACT: Bob Kemp, Resident Teacher

AFFILIATION: Kwan Um School of Zen, Providence, Rhode Island

ESTABLISHED: 1981

FACILITIES: We use a number of facilities in the Chicago area.

RETREATS OFFERED: Four times annually with Zen Master Barbara Rhodes (Soeng Hyang Soen Sa).

PUBLICATIONS: *Announcements*, newsletter.

Sensei Richard Sisto, resident teacher at Red Hawk Zendo in Floyd Knobs, Indiana. (Photo by Penny Sisto.)

Red Hawk Zendo

We are a small rural practice center serving Louisville, Kentucky. All are welcome on Sundays (call for time). "My teachers were Soyu Matsuoka-Roshi, Gary Snyder, and Thomas Merton. I teach Zen meditation for continuing education at Bellarmine College in Louisville, and am a full-time jazz musician. I have been sitting since 1965." —*Richard Sisto*

ADDRESS: 6260 Old Vincennes Road, Floyds Knobs, IN 47119

PHONE: (812) 923-7297

LINEAGE: Soto Zen

SPIRITUAL HEAD: "Enlightened Ones"

CONTACT: Richard Sisto, Resident Teacher

AFFILIATION: Autonomous

ESTABLISHED: 1990

FACILITIES: Country zendo (a converted shed).

MEDITATION PROGRAM: Weekly sittings.

RETREATS OFFERED: One- and two-day retreats.

West Lafayette Zazen Group

West Lafayette Zazen Group grew out of a two-year residence at Purdue University by Masao Abe. We're small and informal and draw largely on people from Purdue and the Greater Lafayette area. Membership changes, but there's usually a core of ten to fifteen at any given time. We meet twice a week for a single forty-minute period of group *zazen*. Once a month we do a three-period *zazen-kinhin*. We also receive monthly visits from an ordained member of the Milwaukee Zen Center. Members attend summer *sesshin* at Minnesota Zen Meditation Center/Hokyoji.

ADDRESS: 901 North Chauncey, West Lafayette, IN 47906

PHONE: (317) 743-9806

LINEAGE: Soto Zen

SPIRITUAL HEADS: Sekiun Koretsune, Tozen Akiyama

CONTACT: Neil Myers

AFFILIATION: Autonomous

ESTABLISHED: 1992

FACILITIES: Donated space in a local church.

MEDITATION PROGRAM: Twice weekly group *zazen* practice. Monthly extended group practice.

IOWA

Iowa City Zen Center

Iowa City Zen Center began many years ago as a small sitting group under the guidance of Dainin Katagiri-Roshi. Zen priest Taikin Yokoyama leads a weekly class in *Dogen* study, as well as monthly *sesshin. Sesshin* are conducted in the tradition of Uchiyama-Roshi, with no services, chanting, dharma talk, *dokusan*, or work period—just *zazen*. We also offer four introductory retreats a year led by Shohaku Okumura of the Minnesota Zen Meditation Center. These retreats are more informal and include discussion periods and instruction in *oryoki* and *zazen*.

ADDRESS: 226 South Johnson, #2A, Iowa City, IA 52245

PHONE: (319) 354-1997

LINEAGE: Japanese Soto Zen

SPIRITUAL HEAD: Shohaku Okumura

CONTACT: Taiken Yokoyama, Resident Teacher

AFFILIATION: Autonomous

ESTABLISHED: 1974

FACILITIES: Small apartment with *zendo*.

MEDITATION PROGRAM: Daily morning and evening *zazen*—call for times. Saturday *sangha* meetings or practice and lecture.

RETREATS OFFERED: Monthly two-day *sesshin* and four introductory retreats per year.

PUBLICATIONS: *The Dharma Farmer*, quarterly newsletter.

KANSAS

Kansas Zen Center

Kansas Zen Center is a nonresidential *sangha* in Lawrence, Kansas, affiliated with the Kwan Um School of Zen, which is in turn derived from the Korean Chogye order. We have daily practice, public talks, teacher interviews, intensive meditation retreats, courses, workshops, precept ceremonies, and other life rites of passage (birth, death, marriage). Our *sangha* includes members from the Kansas City area, Topeka, Wichita, and as far away as Arkansas and Oklahoma. Our guiding teacher is Stanley Lombardo. Programs are open to anyone, regardless of previous experience.

ADDRESS: 1423 New York Street, Lawrence, KS 66044

PHONES: (913) 842-7010, (913) 842-4185

E-MAIL: lombardo@kuhub.cc.ukans.edu

LINEAGE: Korean Chogye Zen

SPIRITUAL HEAD: Zen Master Seung Sahn

CONTACT: Stanley Lombardo, JDPSN

AFFILIATION: Kwan Um School of Zen

ESTABLISHED: 1977

FACILITIES: *Dharma* room with detached interview room.

MEDITATION PROGRAM: Daily practice.

RETREATS OFFERED: Two-day retreats three or four times a year.

PUBLICATIONS: *South Wind Newsletter*

Manhattan Zen Group

Our group was established for nonsectarian meditation practice under the guidance of the late Katagiri-Roshi and remains affiliated with Minneapolis Zen Meditation Center. Anyone wishing to practice silent *zazen* is welcome. Participation in Soto Zen service once a week is optional. There are no charges or dues.

ADDRESS: c/o L. Rappoport, Department of Psychology BH416, Kansas State University, Manhattan, KS 66506

PHONE: (913) 532-0616

E-MAIL: rappo@ksu.edu

LINEAGE: Soto Zen

SPIRITUAL HEAD: Shoken Winecoff

AFFILIATION: Minneapolis Zen Meditation Center

ESTABLISHED: 1978

FACILITIES: Donated/rented meditation room.

MEDITATION PROGRAM: Twice-weekly morning *zazen*. Evening *zazen* and reading/discussion once a week. Call for times.

RETREATS OFFERED: Two weekends per year, dates vary.

A traditional Korean meditation temple at Furnace Mountain, Kentucky. (Photo by Dae Gak Soen Sa Nim.)

KENTUCKY

Furnace Mountain

The site of a beautiful traditional temple with a blue tile roof and excellent geomancy, Furnace Mountain is located in the Appalachian foothills, an hour's drive from Lexington, Kentucky, and two and a half hours from Cincinnati, Ohio. Founder and Guiding Teacher Dae Gak Soen Sa Nim is one of six dharma heirs of Korean Zen Master Seung Sahn. He holds a Ph.D. in clinical psychology and has been a practicing psychotherapist for over twenty-five years. He also serves as Guiding Teacher at Zen centers in Cincinnati, Indianapolis, Lexington, and Australia.

ADDRESS: Box 545, Clay City, KY 40312
PHONE: (606) 723-4329
E-MAIL: FMnun@aol.com
LINEAGE: Korean Chogye Zen
SPIRITUAL HEAD: Zen Master Dae Gak
CONTACT: Hyon Do Sunim

AFFILIATION: Kwan Um School of Zen, Providence, Rhode Island
ESTABLISHED: 1986
FACILITIES: Traditional temple, log cabins.
MEDITATION PROGRAM: Daily Zen practice. The center offers a residential program open to students interested in intensive daily Zen practice.
RETREATS OFFERED: Monthly three- or five-day retreats; two-week summer intensive; ninety-day winter *Kyol Che* retreat.
PUBLICATIONS: Newsletter

Lexington Zen Center

Lexington Zen Center was founded in 1981 as an urban retreat center. It offers weekly Zen meditation sessions and sponsors occasional public dharma talks in the Lexington area. Beginning meditation instruction can also be arranged. Zen Master Dae Gak is the guiding teacher.

ADDRESS: 345 Jesselin Drive, Lexington, KY 40503
PHONE: (606) 277-2438
FAX: (606) 277-2438
LINEAGE: Korean Chogye Zen (Kwan Um School)
SPIRITUAL HEAD: Zen Master Dae Gak
CONTACT: Mara Genthner
AFFILIATION: Furnace Mountain
ESTABLISHED: 1981
FACILITIES: Urban practice center.
MEDITATION PROGRAM: Weekly Zen meditation and beginning meditation instruction.
RETREATS OFFERED: At Furnace Mountain.
PUBLICATIONS: Newsletter

LOUISIANA

Blue Iris Sangha

For additional information, please see Community of Mindful Living, Berkeley, California.

ADDRESS: 2419 Chartres, New Orleans, LA 70117
PHONE: (504) 947-6227
E-MAIL: 75716.1124@compuserv.com
LINEAGE: Mindfulness practice in the tradition of Thich Nhat Hanh.
SPIRITUAL HEAD: Thich Nhat Hanh
CONTACT: Dewain Belgard
AFFILIATION: Community of Mindful Living, Berkeley, California
MEDITATION PROGRAM: We meet one evening a week for dharma discussion, precept recitation, and meditation.

New Orleans Zen Temple

Taisen Deshimaru-Roshi was Soto Zen's highest authority in Europe and Africa. During his fifteen years of teaching in the West, he created 120 Zen *dojos* and *zazen* groups in twenty countries. Before his death in 1982, he asked his close disciple

Robert Livingston-Roshi, Abbot and Founder of New Orleans Zen Temple. (Photo by Grevy Photography, New Orleans.)

Robert Livingston to go to the United States and teach the practice of True Zen. At our downtown location we offer year-round residential training and monthly Zen retreats. Morning, noon, and evening *zazen* is open to the public. The temple sponsors affiliate *zazen* groups in Mississippi, Oklahoma, and Louisiana.
ADDRESS: 748 Camp Street, New Orleans, LA 70130
PHONE: (504) 523-1213
FAX: (504) 523-7024
LINEAGE: Japanese Soto Zen
SPIRITUAL HEAD: Robert Livingston-Roshi, Resident Teacher
AFFILIATION: American Zen Association
ESTABLISHED: 1983
FACILITIES: 20,000-sq.-ft., four-story building, downtown New Orleans.
RETREATS OFFERED: Monthly one-day retreat; quarterly one-week retreats.
PUBLICATIONS: Various books, newsletters.

Udumbara Sangha—Breaux Bridge

For additional information, please see Udumbara Zen Center, Evanston, Illinois.
ADDRESS: 1038 Martha Hebert Road, Breaux Bridge, LA 70517
PHONE: (318) 228-7683
LINEAGE: Japanese Soto (Suzuki-Roshi and Katagiri-Roshi)
SPIRITUAL HEAD: Diane Martin
CONTACT: Francine Guillory
AFFILIATION: Udumbara Zen Center, Evanston, Illinois
PUBLICATIONS: *Central Flower*, quarterly newsletter.

Udumbara Sangha—Lafayette

For additional information, please see Udumbara Zen Center, Evanston, Illinois.
ADDRESS: 409 Azalea Street, Lafayette, LA 70506
PHONE: (318) 235-1784
LINEAGE: Japanese Soto (Suzuki-Roshi and Katagiri-Roshi)
SPIRITUAL HEAD: Diane Martin
CONTACT: Virginia de Gravelles
AFFILIATION: Udumbara Zen Center, Evanston, Illinois
PUBLICATIONS: *Central Flower*, quarterly newsletter.

MAINE

Brunswick Sangha

For additional information, please see Community of Mindful Living, Berkeley, California.
ADDRESS: 941 Mere Point Road, Brunswick, ME 04011
PHONE: (207) 721-9005
LINEAGE: Mindfulness practice in the tradition of Thich Nhat Hanh.

SPIRITUAL HEAD: Thich Nhat Hanh
CONTACT: Anne Dellenbaugh
AFFILIATION: Community of Mindful Living, Berkeley, California
MEDITATION PROGRAM: We meet one evening a week for practice and dharma discussion, and recite the precepts on the practice day nearest the new moon.

A Center for the Awareness of Pattern

We train family therapists in a nonrational approach that draws on Zen thought and practice. Zen lends itself particularly well to family therapy because nonrational awareness (as in meditation) enhances our ability to see patterns in families. In addition to family therapy training, we hold semimonthly public Zen meditation sessions in our *zendo* and sponsor public education programs on Zen thought and practice.
ADDRESS: PO Box 407, 10 Cushing Avenue, Freeport, ME 04032
PHONE: (207) 865-3396
FAX: (207) 865-1213
LINEAGE: Soto Zen
SPIRITUAL HEAD: Rev. Nakajima and Rev. Uchiyama
CONTACT: Phoebe Jiko Prosky
AFFILIATION: Autonomous
ESTABLISHED: 1986
FACILITIES: Small *zendo*.
PUBLICATIONS: Papers on Zen and family therapy in book form.

Morgan Bay Zendo

Morgan Bay Zendo offers an opportunity for people to practice Buddhist meditation whatever their background or faith. Meditation is a means of developing the mind so that it may be awakened to its own inherent wisdom and compassion. To facilitate this awakening, we offer daily meditation as well as extended peri-

Zen–New Orleans Style

RESIDENCY AT NEW ORLEANS ZEN TEMPLE provides an opportunity for sincere Zen students to practice and live with the *sangha* while remaining involved in the community at large. Most residents have jobs outside the temple. Others attend school or work full- or part-time for the temple.

Residents attend *zazen* every morning and noontime, and evenings as their work allows. Attendance is required at all monthly "Days of Zen" and quarterly six-day *sesshin*. Residents do at least one hour of work practice for the temple each day, and also help in preparation for retreats.

In addition to the meditation hall, the building—a converted four-story town house/warehouse—contains seven bedrooms, a kitchen, living room, library, sewing room, dining area, workshop, office, storage rooms, and a reception area. The first floor is leased out to a restaurant.

The nominal monthly rental includes daily *genmai* (traditional Zen breakfast), utilities, cleaning supplies, free local phone calls, and use of laundry and kitchen facilities. In addition to rent, residents pay dues to the American Zen Association and cover their own costs for participation in quarterly *sesshin* and monthly "Days of Zen." Charges are minimal and amount to subsidies as our costs are higher. Everyone is encouraged to contribute more if they are financially able.

If you are interested in the residency program, send us a current photo, along with a letter telling us about yourself, your dharma practice experience, any skills or abilities you might have (especially carpentry, sewing, clerical, cooking, foreign language, or computer skills), your financial situation, and when you would like to move in.

For more information, contact: New Orleans Zen Temple, 748 Camp St, New Orleans, LA 70130; (504) 523-1213.

---

ods of retreat from April to December each year. Formerly known as Moonspring Hermitage, it was founded by Walter Nowick in 1971. Subsequent to his resignation in 1985, the Hermitage was renamed and reincorporated as Morgan Bay Zendo.
ADDRESS: PO Box 188, Surry, ME 04684
PHONE: (207) 374-9963
SPIRITUAL HEAD: "A teacher-less *zendo*."
CONTACT: Vicki Pollard
AFFILIATION: Autonomous
ESTABLISHED: 1971. 1985, in its present form.
FACILITIES: *Zendo*, dining hall/kitchen, cabins, tenting area.
RETREATS OFFERED: Varies
PUBLICATIONS: Newsletter twice a year.

True Heart/Mid-Coast Sangha

Our *sangha* shares mindfulness practice in a local state prison. For additional information, please see Community of Mindful Living, Berkeley, California.
ADDRESS: RR2, Box 596, Lincolnville, ME 04849
PHONE: (207) 763-3692
LINEAGE: Mindfulness practice in the tradition of Thich Nhat Hanh.
SPIRITUAL HEAD: Thich Nhat Hanh
CONTACT: Mair Honan
AFFILIATION: Community of Mindful Living, Berkeley, California
FACILITIES: Camden Yoga Studio.
MEDITATION PROGRAM: We meet the first and third Sunday of every month for sitting, walking, precept recitation, and dharma discussion.

Waterville Zazenkai

Our group meets Sunday mornings for two periods of sitting and walking meditation, followed by tea and conversation. We have a small lending library of books and tapes on Zen and Buddhism. We are not affiliated with any particular teacher or Zen center, though a number of us are students or attend *sesshin* at Zen Mountain Monastery. Please phone if you have any questions or would like to attend.
ADDRESS: c/o The Oxbow Center, 32 Western Avenue, Waterville, ME 04901
PHONE: (207) 873-1351

Morgan Bay Zendo, Surry, Maine. (Photo by Chistopher Ayres.)

LINEAGE: Japanese Zen
CONTACTS: Lillian Jakuen McMullin and Dan Mujaku Bloomer
AFFILIATION: Autonomous
FACILITIES: The Oxbow Center. Small library.
MEDITATION PROGRAM: Sunday morning *zazen* (call for times).
RETREATS OFFERED: All-day sittings two or three times yearly.

MARYLAND

American Zen College (AZC)

Zen Master Gosung Shin, Ph.D., and his assistant teachers give instruction in both breath and koan meditation, which is well suited to the needs of American practitioners. AZC is located twenty minutes northwest of Washington, D.C., on a thoroughly converted dairy farm bordering a 350-acre state park in rural Maryland. All activities are open to the general public.

ADDRESS: 16815 Germantown Road, Germantown, MD 20874
PHONE: (301) 428-0665
LINEAGE: Korean Chogye Zen
SPIRITUAL HEAD: Zen Master Gosung Shin, Ph.D.
CONTACT: Steve Kinora
AFFILIATION: South Korean Chogye order
ESTABLISHED: May 30, 1969
MEDITATION PROGRAM: Weekly meditation instruction class and dharma lecture by Zen Master Shin.
RETREATS OFFERED: Weekly half-day of meditation. Monthly three- and six-day *sesshin*.
PUBLICATIONS: *Buddha World*

Avatamsaka Hermitage

Nuns' convent. For additional information see listing for City of Ten Thousand Buddhas, Talmage, California.
ADDRESS: 11721 Beall Mountain Road, Potomac, MD 20854-1128

PHONE: (301) 299-3693
LINEAGE: We propagate all major Mahayana schools (Ch'an, Pure Land, Vinaya, Scholastic, and Esoteric) and work closely with Theravada.
SPIRITUAL HEAD: Ven. Hsuan Hua
AFFILIATION: City of Ten Thousand Buddhas/Dharma Realm Buddhist Association
ESTABLISHED: 1990
FACILITIES: Worship and meditation hall. Nuns' convent.

Baltimore Zendo/Shorin-ji

Most members of Shorin-ji are students of Eido Shimano-Roshi, but students of other teachers are welcome to practice with us. We offer all-day sits and occasional weekend *sesshin*, beginner's classes, weekly sitting, and some social events. See our Home page for more information.
ADDRESS: PO Box 3514, Baltimore, MD 21214-0514
PHONE: (410) 254-5128
E-MAIL: zenisfun@jhunix.hcf.jhu.edu
WWW: http://www.gl.umbc.edu/~jcovey1/zendo.html
LINEAGE: Rinzai Zen
SPIRITUAL HEAD: Eido Shimano-Roshi, Abbot. (Not in residence; he infrequently visits.)
CONTACT: Resident Director Joshin Kado Marci Ziese, Rinzai Zen Buddhist nun/priest
AFFILIATION: Unofficially with Dai Bosatsu Zendo, Kongo-ji, New York.
ESTABLISHED: 1989
PUBLICATIONS: *Facing the Wall*, newsletter three or four times yearly.

Bethesda Sangha

For additional information, please see Community of Mindful Living, Berkeley, California.
ADDRESS: 4340 East-West Highway, Room 709, Bethesda, MD 20814

PHONE: (301) 504-0994 x1388
E-MAIL: wmenza@capaccess.org
LINEAGE: Mindfulness practice in the tradition of Thich Nhat Hanh.
SPIRITUAL HEAD: Thich Nhat Hanh
CONTACT: Bill Menza
AFFILIATION: Community of Mindful Living, Berkeley, California
MEDITATION PROGRAM: We meet three days a week at noon for meditation and dharma discussion.

Bubjusa Buddhist Temple

No description available.
ADDRESS: 17001 Woodale Drive, Silver Spring, MD 20905
PHONE: (301) 924-5050
FAX: (301) 774-1695
SPIRITUAL HEAD: Ven. Poe Hwa
AFFILIATION: The Patriarchal Zen Society in the United States.

MASSACHUSETTS

American Buddhist Shim Gum Do Association

Shim Gwang Sa (Mind Light Temple) is the central teaching center for both the American Buddhist and the World Shim Gum Do Associations. *Shim Gum Do* means "Mind Sword Path" and is composed of hundreds of forms of Sword, *Shin Boep, Ho Shin Sul*, Long Stick, Two Sword, and Short Stick. *Shim Gum Do* is about attaining clear mind, thought, action, and enlightenment. Ongoing classes and residential programs are offered. The center's Founding Teacher, Zen Master Chang Sik Kim, is in residence and oversees all teaching.
ADDRESS: 203 Chestnut Hill Avenue, Brighton, MA 02135
PHONE: (617) 787-1506
FAX: (617) 787-2708
LINEAGE: Korean Zen
SPIRITUAL HEAD: Founding Master Chang Sik Kim
CONTACT: Mary J. Stackhouse
AFFILIATION: World Shim Gum Do Association
ESTABLISHED: 1978
FACILITIES: Urban Zen temple.
PUBLICATIONS: *The Art of Zen Sword*

Cambridge Buddhist Association, Inc.

Cambridge Buddhist Association was founded in 1957. Its first meditation teacher was Shinichi Hisamatsu, who was then a Professor Emeritus of Kyoto University, a Zen teacher, and scholar of Zen art. His *zazenkai* in Cambridge, like its prototype in Japan, was nonsectarian. In 1979, Maurine Stuart-Roshi assumed the position of meditation teacher, a post that she held until her death eleven years later. The present teacher, George Bowman, is in charge of daily sittings and regularly scheduled retreats. Two other groups, one in the Vietnamese tradition, and the other in the Tibetan, use the house on a regular basis.
ADDRESS: 75 Sparks Street, Cambridge, MA 02138
PHONE: (617) 491-8857
LINEAGE: Japanese Zen
SPIRITUAL HEAD: George Bowman
CONTACT: Same
AFFILIATION: Autonomous
ESTABLISHED: 1957 (incorporated in 1959)
FACILITIES: House
MEDITATION PROGRAM: Japanese/Vietnamese/Tibetan programs.
RETREATS OFFERED: Yes
PUBLICATIONS: *The Way of Zazen*, Rindo Fujimoto-Roshi (1961) and *The Chain of Compassion*, Daisetz Suzuki (1966).

Cambridge Sangha

For additional information please see Community of Mindful Living, Berkeley, California.

ADDRESS: 25 Cogswell Avenue, Cambridge, MA 02140
PHONE: (617) 354-7555
FAX: (617) 237-1127
LINEAGE: Mindfulness practice in the tradition of Thich Nhat Hanh.
SPIRITUAL HEAD: Thich Nhat Hanh
CONTACT: Miriam Hawley
AFFILIATION: Community of Mindful Living, Berkeley, California
MEDITATION PROGRAM: We gather one evening of each month for meditation, precept recitation, tea, and discussion.
RETREATS OFFERED: Day of Mindfulness every other month.
PUBLICATIONS: Quarterly newsletter.

Cambridge Zen Center

Cambridge Zen Center is an international Zen Buddhist residential community with an average population of twenty to thirty residents—both lay and monastic—ranging in age from three to sixty-

Abbot Jane McLaughlin gives a dharma talk at Cambridge Zen Center. (Photo courtesy of Cambridge Zen Center.)

Peaceful Heart, Clear Mind: Meditation at the Moment of Death

SINCE THE INCEPTION OF HER WORK WITH THE dying in 1971, Clear Light Society founding director Patricia Shelton has had wide experience in ministering to terminally ill people not only during the weeks and months prior to death, but also at the moment of death itself.

Clear Light Society practitioners, or "guides," each of whom has undergone years of training under Ms. Shelton's direction, provide psychospiritual services tailored to the belief system of each client.

Using special meditative techniques developed by Ms. Shelton, the guides respond to the fundamental need of dying people for a "peaceful heart" and a "clear mind." While these practices offer no miracle cure to save life at the last moment, they do point the way to peace, equanimity, and acceptance.

Through a program of "spiritual befriending," sick people discover that with practice they can create a respite from fear, anxiety, and other painful mental states. Gradually the mind attains the serenity of a still woodland pond. At this point, "peaceful heart, clear mind" are no longer just words, but a harmonious state of being beyond hope and fear.

If you or a loved one are undergoing a life-threatening illness, we warmly invite you to taste for yourself "peaceful heart, clear mind." A telephone call will bring a Clear Light guide to your home for a complimentary visit and a guided meditation session. Family members are welcome to observe. Although the Society does not charge a set fee for services, donations are welcome.

For more information, contact: Clear Light Society, PO Box 306, Brookline, MA 02146; (617) 734-2939.

MASSACHUSETTS (cont.)

three years old! It is a busy, bustling city center with lots of talks, classes, and social activity. The retreat atmosphere, on the other hand, is formal and quiet (though friendly and welcoming). Extra programs include a prison dharma teaching affiliation, college sitting groups, chaplaincies at area hospitals, gay and lesbian Buddhist group meetings, and a strong affiliation with the New England Buddhist Coalition.
ADDRESS: 199 Auburn Street, Cambridge, MA 02139
PHONE: (617) 576-3229
FAX: (617) 864-9025
E-MAIL: cambzen@aol.com
LINEAGE: Korean Zen, Chogye order
SPIRITUAL HEAD: Ven. Seung Sahn Soen Sa Nim, Founder

CONTACT: Jane McLaughlin, JDPSN, Resident Teacher
AFFILIATION: Kwan Um School of Zen, Providence, Rhode Island
ESTABLISHED: 1974
FACILITIES: Forty-room urban residential center; large meditation hall, library, garden, public transportation.
MEDITATION PROGRAM: Daily morning and evening practice.
RETREATS OFFERED: Three-month Kyol Che; weekend retreats.
PUBLICATIONS: Monthly newsletter.

Clear Light Society

Patricia Shelton teaches "Introduction to Zen Practice" at Boston University and leads Zen groups in Massachusetts, Maine, and New Hampshire. Encouraged by the Venerable Rinpoches Trungpa and Kalu and by Zen Master Seung Sahn to engage in a life's work of assisting others at the moment of death, Shelton founded the Clear Light Society in 1971. Here she has pioneered in practices for ministering to people of diverse religious backgrounds and belief systems who are dying, and she has trained hundreds of health care professionals, hospice workers, family members, and Buddhist practitioners in all aspects of her work.
ADDRESS: PO Box 306, Brookline, MA 02146
PHONE: (617) 734-2939
FAX: Same
LINEAGE: Korean Zen (and other sources)
SPIRITUAL HEAD: Patricia Shelton, Resident Teacher
AFFILIATION: Autonomous
ESTABLISHED: 1977

FACILITIES: Centers in Boston, Massachusetts; Nashua, New Hampshire; and Ogunquit, Maine.
RETREATS OFFERED: Monthly, from three days to three weeks.

Community of Interbeing

For additional information, please see Community of Mindful Living, Berkeley, California.
ADDRESS: 20 Elm Street, Maynard, MA 01754
PHONE: (508) 897-0796
E-MAIL: AndreWeiss@aol.com
LINEAGE: Mindfulness practice in the tradition of Thich Nhat Hanh.
SPIRITUAL HEAD: Thich Nhat Hanh
CONTACT: Andrew Weiss
AFFILIATION: Community of Mindful Living, Berkeley, California

Concord Sangha

For additional information, please see Community of Mindful Living, Berkeley, California.
ADDRESS: 321 Bedford Street, Concord, MA 01742
PHONE: (508) 369-6112
FAX: (508) 287-4316
LINEAGE: Mindfulness practice in the tradition of Thich Nhat Hanh.
SPIRITUAL HEAD: Thich Nhat Hanh
CONTACT: Claude An Shin Thomas
AFFILIATION: Community of Mindful Living, Berkeley, California
MEDITATION PROGRAM: Weekly Mindfulness Days for Vietnam War combat veterans.
RETREATS OFFERED: Sundays, Day of Mindfulness for everyone.

Framingham Sitting Group

Framingham Sitting Group meets weekly to do *zazen*. We are loosely affiliated with Zen Mountain Monastery and use their *Eight Gates of Zen* training materials to help us in our practice. Though our group is small, we have met regularly since 1986.
ADDRESS: 24 Vernon Street, Framingham, MA 01701
PHONE: (508) 877-6375, (508) 875-1494
LINEAGE: Soto/Rinzai
SPIRITUAL HEAD: John Daido Loori-Roshi
CONTACTS: Roy Hamilton and Judy Mokyo Perry
AFFILIATION: Zen Mountain Monastery
ESTABLISHED: 1986
FACILITIES: Use of local church.

Golden Wind Temple and White Swan Translation Center

This center is dedicated to the development of Buddhist literary translation and digital media conversion and storage. Eventually the center will provide free tools and access for scholarly and popular presentations through the World Wide Web. We are equipped with advanced computing and scanning systems connected through a 56KB frame relay to outside sources.
ADDRESS: PO Box 323, Concord, MA 01742
E-MAIL: taijuan@aol.com
LINEAGE: Japanese/Rinzai Zen
SPIRITUAL HEAD: Eido Tai Shimano-Roshi
CONTACT: Daien George Burch
AFFILIATION: Daibosatsu Zendo (informally)
ESTABLISHED: 1995
FACILITIES: Ten-seat *zendo*, technical center for translation and multimedia development.

Hopping Tree Sangha

For additional information, please see Community of Mindful Living, Berkeley, California.

ADDRESSES: 80 Silver Lane, Sunderland, MA 01375 or PO Box 443, Northampton, MA 01061
PHONES: (413) 665-3983 or (413) 586-8386
LINEAGE: Mindfulness practice in the tradition of Thich Nhat Hanh.
SPIRITUAL HEAD: Thich Nhat Hanh
CONTACTS: Ann Gibson and Candace Cassin
AFFILIATION: Community of Mindful Living, Berkeley, California
MEDITATION PROGRAM: We meet once a week in Amherst for morning meditation. Depending on the week, we also have precept recitation, reading, and/or dharma discussion.

Interbeing Sangha

For additional information, please see Community of Mindful Living, Berkeley, California.
ADDRESS: 34 Elizabeth Street, Northampton, MA 01060
PHONE: (413) 634-5421
LINEAGE: Mindfulness practice in the tradition of Thich Nhat Hanh.
SPIRITUAL HEAD: Thich Nhat Hanh
CONTACT: Sebern Fisher
AFFILIATION: Community of Mindful Living, Berkeley, California
RETREATS OFFERED: We meet once a month in Haydenville for an Afternoon of Mindfulness including precept recitation.

Keili Meditation Center

For additional information, please see Community of Mindful Living, Berkeley, California.
ADDRESS: 16 Miles Street, Greenfield, MA 01301
PHONE: (413) 773-8259
LINEAGE: Mindfulness practice in the tradition of Thich Nhat Hanh.

SPIRITUAL HEAD: Thich Nhat Hanh

CONTACT: Alice Barrett

AFFILIATION: Community of Mindful Living, Berkeley, California

MEDITATION PROGRAM: The center offers seven sittings a week, as well as classes and discussion groups.

The Living Dharma Center

For additional information, please see Living Dharma Center, Bolton, Connecticut.

ADDRESS: PO Box 304, Amherst, MA 01004

PHONE: (413) 259-1611

LINEAGE: The eclectic lineage of Harada Yasutani-Roshi that combines the essence of Soto and Rinzai Zen.

SPIRITUAL HEAD: Richard Clarke, Resident Teacher

AFFILIATION: Autonomous

ESTABLISHED: 1972

FACILITIES: Urban *zendo*. Country monastery for retreats. No residential accommodations or solitary retreat facilities. Please call for sitting locations.

RETREATS OFFERED: Several seven-day *sesshin* offered yearly and periodic *zazenkai* and introductory workshops.

PUBLICATIONS: *Sangha News* (for members).

Northampton Zendo

No description available.

ADDRESS: 320 Riverside Drive, Northampton, MA 01060

PHONE: (413) 584-6139

FAX: (413) 584-7807

E-MAIL: jbrooks882@aol.com

LINEAGE: Soto Zen

SPIRITUAL HEAD: Issho Fujita

CONTACT: Jeffrey Brooks

AFFILIATION: Valley Zendo

ESTABLISHED: 1995

FACILITIES: Sitting space for thirty.

MEDITATION PROGRAM: Daily *zazen* and karate.

Pond Village Zendo (Old Pond Mind Zen Temple)

In the spring of 1995, before the cushions and folks to sit upon them, there was an automobile. It removed the front wall and settled into the soon-to-be *zendo*. Rising from the wreckage, Pond Village Zendo has evolved into a lovely, still space that invites awareness of the impermanence of things. From the outermost towns of Cape Cod, we gather daily to sit Soto-style *zazen*. A weekly evening event adds tea, talk, and service. Teachers from San Francisco Zen Center visit regularly. We seek to sustain the pure and warm spirit of practice taught by Maurine Stuart-Roshi.

ADDRESS: PO Box 354, 42-44 Shore Road, North Truro (Cape Cod), MA 02652-0354

PHONE: (508) 487-2979

LINEAGE: Japanese Soto Zen

CONTACT: Jishin JC Hotchkiss (Chuck), Director

AFFILIATION: Informally with San Francisco Zen Center

ESTABLISHED: 1995

FACILITIES: Small *zendo* (fourteen to twenty seats).

MEDITATION PROGRAM: Daily morning and evening *zazen*; introductory classes; *zazen* instruction by arrangement.

RETREATS OFFERED: Periodic day-long sittings.

Single Flower Sangha

Single Flower Sangha is a spontaneous gathering of dharma friends touched by the teaching and example of Zen Master Bo Mun (George Bowman). It is free of excess rules and hierarchy, yet characterized by elegant and serious practice—rigorous, not rigid. George has dharma transmission from Seung Sahn Soen-sa Nim of the Korean Chogye order and permission to teach in the lineage of Joshu Sasaki-Roshi of Rinzai-ji. Schedule and other information are periodically updated on the World Wide Web.

ADDRESS: 75 Sparks Street, Cambridge, MA 02138

PHONE: (617) 491-8857

E-MAIL: fcp@traveller.com

WWW: http://www.traveller.com/~fcp/sfs.html

LINEAGE: Rinzai Zen

SPIRITUAL HEAD: Zen Master George Bowman, Resident Teacher

AFFILIATION: Rinzai-ji

ESTABLISHED: 1995

FACILITIES: Shared with Cambridge Buddhist Association.

RETREATS OFFERED: Dates and locations vary.

Stella Blue Sangha

A Zen group for nonsmoking vegetarians. Using the precepts to clean the precepts, we directly actualize the precepts. This is our way. We sit in members' homes, outdoors, and on our island in New Hampshire. Our approach includes (short) dharma talks, Dogen study, chanting, Kundalini yoga, healthy food, new and full moon sittings, together practice, and, mostly, *zazen*.

ADDRESS: 80 Herbert Road, Arlington, MA 02174

PHONE: (617) 648-8462

LINEAGE: Harada-Ban line/Japanese Soto-Rinzai Zen

SPIRITUAL HEAD: DeGuchi Roshi, Ban Roshi

CONTACT: Buddhi Bliss, Director

AFFILIATION: Independent

ESTABLISHED: 1996

FACILITIES: Members' homes. Island retreat center.

MEDITATION PROGRAM: New moon and full moon sittings.
RETREATS OFFERED: Silent sitting weekends.

Stow Sangha

For additional information, please see Community of Mindful Living, Berkeley, California.
ADDRESS: Box 16, Stow, MA 01775
PHONE: (508) 264-9076
E-MAIL: baa@genrad.com
LINEAGE: Mindfulness practice in the tradition of Thich Nhat Hanh.
SPIRITUAL HEAD: Thich Nhat Hanh
CONTACT: Barbara Atenasio
AFFILIATION: Community of Mindful Living, Berkeley, California
FACILITIES: First Parish Church
MEDITATION PROGRAM: We meet one evening a week for sitting, and the last Sunday evening of each month for meditation, precepts recitation, and discussion.

Valley Zendo

Valley Zendo was established in the early 1970s and has strong links with Antai-ji Temple in Japan. From the beginning, Antai-ji has been sending monks to Charlemont to serve as resident teachers. Valley Zendo maintains a rigorous daily sitting practice schedule, frequent extended *zazen* retreats, and occasional visiting dharma lecturers/teachers from Antai-ji and affiliated Zen centers. Monks at Valley Zendo have also offered meditation and tea ceremony classes at Mt. Holyoke College in South Hadley, Massachusetts.
ADDRESS: Warner Hill Road, Charlemont, MA 01330
PHONE: (413) 339-4000
LINEAGE: Soto Zen
SPIRITUAL HEAD: Issho Fujita

AFFILIATION: Antai-ji Temple, Japan (Uchiyama-Roshi)
ESTABLISHED: 1971
FACILITIES: Country retreat facility.
MEDITATION PROGRAM: Daily *zazen*.
RETREATS OFFERED: Frequent Soto Zen *sesshin*.

West County Sangha

For additional information, please see Community of Mindful Living, Berkeley, California.
ADDRESS: Windy Hill-131, Shelburne Falls, MA 01370
PHONE: (413) 625-9495
LINEAGE: Mindfulness practice in the tradition of Thich Nhat Hanh.
SPIRITUAL HEAD: Thich Nhat Hanh
CONTACT: Prudence Grand
AFFILIATION: Community of Mindful Living, Berkeley, California
MEDITATION PROGRAM: We meet three evenings a month for meditation and precept recitation or discussion.

Zenki

Zenki is a newly built meditation center next to farms and wooded conservation land where we explore the many expressions of practice through recycling, composting, gardening, and the arts. We are experimenting with ways to include young people in the practice and are accommodating and increasing the schedule to fit people's lives.
ADDRESS: 70 Littleton County Road, Harvard, MA 01451
PHONE: (508) 456-2740
LINEAGE: Mahayana/nondenominational Rinzai background
SPIRITUAL HEAD: Sheila La Farge, Resident Teacher
AFFILIATION: Autonomous
ESTABLISHED: 1992
FACILITIES: Rural meditation center.

MEDITATION PROGRAM: Evening sittings.
RETREATS OFFERED: Daylong sittings, weekend and longer retreats, workshops.

MICHIGAN

Clear Mind Temple

For additional information, please see Community of Mindful Living, Berkeley, California.
ADDRESS: 2923 Memory Lane, Kalamazoo, MI 49006
PHONE: (616) 344-0836
E-MAIL: holmest@wmich.edu
LINEAGE: Mindfulness practice in the tradition of Thich Nhat Hanh.
SPIRITUAL HEAD: Thich Nhat Hanh. Sister Thich Nu Thanh Luong, Practice Leader.
CONTACT: Tom Holmes
AFFILIATION: Community of Mindful Living, Berkeley, California
MEDITATION PROGRAM: One Saturday of each month we have a half-Day of Mindfulness that includes a meal in mindfulness.

Clear Water Sangha

For additional information, please see Community of Mindful Living, Berkeley, California.
ADDRESS: 6423 Pleasant River Drive, Dimondale, MI 48821
PHONE: (517) 646-9828
LINEAGE: Mindfulness practice in the tradition of Thich Nhat Hanh.
SPIRITUAL HEAD: Thich Nhat Hanh
CONTACTS: Katherine Roth and Greg Holmes
AFFILIATION: Community of Mindful Living, Berkeley, California
MEDITATION PROGRAM: We meet one day a month for meditation, reading, and discussion.

RETREATS OFFERED: During late spring and early summer we meet for retreats at Lake Alward.

Dancing Rabbit Sangha

We welcome visitors. For additional information, please see Community of Mindful Living, Berkeley, California.
ADDRESS: PO Box 422, Elk Rapids, MI 49629
PHONE: (616) 264-8813
LINEAGE: Mindfulness practice in the tradition of Thich Nhat Hanh.
SPIRITUAL HEAD: Thich Nhat Hanh
CONTACT: Trisha Perlman
AFFILIATION: Community of Mindful Living, Berkeley, California
MEDITATION PROGRAM: We gather every other Sunday evening for dharma discussion and meditation using various Plum Village practices.
RETREATS OFFERED: Occasional Day of Mindfulness.

Zen Buddhist Temple/Ann Arbor

Surrounded by a large garden in an idyllic setting, Ann Arbor Temple is located near the University of Michigan. Students are an important component of our *sangha* and there is a strong focus on incorporating Buddhist practice into daily life. Each summer we organize a children's peace camp, which emphasizes cooperation, mindfulness, and fun. The Right Livelihood Fund is a nondenominational four-year pilot program whose goal is funding and assisting the start-up and operation of businesses that embrace the five Buddhist precepts and thus support a strategy of gentle, sustainable development within a context of respect for all people.
ADDRESS: 1214 Packard Road, Ann Arbor, MI 48104-3814

Rev. Sukha Linda Murray, spiritual director of Zen Buddhist Temple in Ann Arbor, Michigan. (Photo courtesy of Ann Arbor Temple.)

PHONE: (313) 761-6520
FAX: (313) 995-0435
LINEAGE: Korean Chogye Zen
SPIRITUAL HEAD: Ven. Samu Sunim (Sam-Woo Kim)
CONTACT: Rev. Sukha Linda Murray
AFFILIATION: Buddhist Society for Compassionate Wisdom
ESTABLISHED: 1981
FACILITIES: Buddha/meditation hall, dorm, workshop, garden.
MEDITATION PROGRAM: Regular meditation schedule; Buddhist services and holiday celebrations; meditation instruction.
RETREATS OFFERED: Overnight introductory retreats; one-, two-, and three-day retreats; visitor's program; summer lecture series.
PUBLICATIONS: *Temple News*

MINNESOTA

Clouds in Water Zen Center

No description available.
ADDRESS: 5701 Garfield Avenue South, Minneapolis, MN 55419-1715
PHONE: (612) 798-5821
LINEAGE: Japanese Soto Zen
SPIRITUAL HEAD: The late Dainin Katagiri-Roshi
CONTACTS: Mike Port and Judith Regir

Minnesota Zen Meditation Center—Ganshoji Temple

The late Dainin Katagiri-Roshi founded Minnesota Zen Meditation Center/Ganshoji Temple in 1972. Like its sister center, Hokyoji Monastery, it is one of the two wings that comprise Minnesota Zen Meditation Center. Ganshoji offers a regular schedule of *zazen*, dharma lectures, *sesshin*, classes, and instruction for beginners. After Katagiri-Roshi's death, Shohaku Okumura-Sensei served as interim spiritual director until a dharma successor could be selected. The new head teacher is Sekijun Karen Sunna.
ADDRESS: 3343 East Calhoun Parkway, Minneapolis, MN 55408
PHONE: (612) 822-5313
E-MAIL: MnZenCtr@aol.com
LINEAGE: Japanese Soto Zen
SPIRITUAL HEAD: The late Dainin Katagiri-Roshi, Founder
CONTACT: Sekijun Karen Sunna, Resident Teacher
AFFILIATION: Autonomous
ESTABLISHED: 1972
FACILITIES: Urban Zen center and temple.
RETREATS OFFERED: Monthly *sesshin* at city or country center.
PUBLICATIONS: Newsletter

Dharma Moon: The American Buddhist Songs Project

The body is a fragile jar
Of brittle dreams that seem so easily
  broken
Floating on a sea of words so easily
  spoken
You never stop them before they start
Like a lotus blooming in a muddy pond
Or a bright moon shining from behind
  the clouds
Find a quiet place among the crowds
Seated in the cave of the heart
from "Seated in the Cave of the Heart"
      © *1995 by Nathaniel Needle*

Dharma Moon songs slip Buddhism out of robes and slap it into jeans. Some of the tunes are contemplative, and some are cute. Some were written for the youngest children. But they all serve a genuine religious purpose: to give a voice to Buddhists who like to sing songs with more than one note!

Core Buddhist teachings receive musical treatment familiar to American ears. There are the Four Noble Truths as a folk lullaby, the Eightfold Path as Bob Wills and the Texas Playboys might have done it, the Three Poisons as an organ-grinder's waltz, and the Three Refuges reminding you of closing time in a quiet piano bar. Calypso, reggae, tango, swing: all are enlisted to serve American dharma. Startling at first, but you may be even more surprised to discover how naturally the music and the message go together.

The tunes encourage meditation, which is sometimes like moonlight "at the bottom of the ocean," and sometimes more like "bailin' out water from a leaky canoe."

Music and lyrics for the twenty-six recorded songs (on two cassettes titled *Dharma Moon* and *Bottom of the Ocean*) were composed by Paramita Nathaniel Needle, a lay Dharma Teacher in the Buddhist Society for Compassionate Wisdom, under the direction of Korean Zen Master Samu Sunim. Both cassettes may be ordered directly from Zen Buddhist Temple, 1214 Packard Road, Ann Arbor, MI 48104. Please include $12 plus $1.50 per tape for shipping.

Paramita Nathaniel Needle

For more information, contact: Zen Buddhist Temple, 1214 Packard Rd., Ann Arbor, MI 48104; (313) 761-6520.

The Buddhist singing group Dharma Moon, under the direction of Paramita Nathaniel Needle. (Photo courtesy of Dharma Moon.)

Minnesota Zen Meditation Center—Hokyoji Monastery

Hokyoji (Catching the Moon Zen Mountain Center) is the country practice facility for Minnesota Zen Meditation Center. It is situated in a remote valley in the scenic Mississippi River basin of southeastern Minnesota, a beautiful three-and-one-half-hour drive south of Minneapolis along the Mississippi River. It's also within driving distance of Milwaukee, Chicago, and the Plains states. Retreat schedules are relaxed and spacious, with time to share silence with birds, trees, and sky. Hokyoji offers regular *zazen* and *sesshin*, a six-week practice period in August/September, and opportunities throughout the year for private retreats. ADDRESS: c/o 3343 East Calhoun Parkway, Minneapolis, MN 55408

PHONE: (612) 822-5313

E-MAIL: MnZenCtr@aol.com

LINEAGE: Japanese Soto Zen

SPIRITUAL HEAD: Sekijun Karen Sunna

CONTACT: Shoken Winecoff, Resident
Priest

AFFILIATION: Minnesota Zen Meditation
Center

ESTABLISHED: 1973

FACILITIES: Rural retreat center; solitary
retreat facilities.

MEDITATION PROGRAM: Regular *zazen*
schedule.

RETREATS OFFERED: Monthly *sesshin*; six-
week residential training program, Au-
gust/September.

MISSISSIPPI

Jackson Zen Group

Our group meets one evening a week for
an hour of sitting and walking meditation, with tea and discussion following.
Every three or four months, we hold a
Day of Zen practice, which is sometimes
led by a visiting monk from the New Orleans Zen Temple. Our group travels to
New Orleans occasionally to participate
in retreats sponsored by New Orleans
Zen Temple.

ADDRESS: 142 Millsaps Avenue, Jackson,
MS 39202

PHONES: (601) 856-7172 or (601) 982-
0402

LINEAGE: Soto Zen

CONTACTS: Linda Townes and Bebe
Wolfe

AFFILIATION: Autonomous. Loose ties to
New Orleans Zen Temple.

ESTABLISHED: 1995

MEDITATION PROGRAM: Weekly group
meditation.

PUBLICATIONS: *MU News*, monthly
newsletter.

Starkville Zen Dojo

Starkville Zen Dojo is a simple sitting
room in a private residence in Starkville,
Mississippi. The group is led by Tony
Bland, a disciple of Robert Livingston-
Roshi of New Orleans Zen Temple. Tony
began studying with Roshi in 1984 and
received monk's ordination in 1992. He
moved to Starkville two years later and
opened the *dojo* with Roshi's permission
and continued guidance. Zen practice
(*zazen, kinhin*, and a brief ceremony) is
held at regularly scheduled times
throughout the week. *Genmai* (traditional Zen breakfast) is served after
morning *zazen*. One-day *sesshin* are held
periodically. Visitors and newcomers are
welcome.

ADDRESS: 231 Santa Anita Drive,
Starkville, MS 39750

PHONE: (601) 324-3622

LINEAGE: Soto Zen

SPIRITUAL HEAD: Robert Livingston-
Roshi

CONTACT: Tony Bland, Resident Teacher

AFFILIATION: New Orleans Zen Temple

ESTABLISHED: 1995

FACILITIES: *Dojo* in private residence.

RETREATS OFFERED: Periodic one-day
sesshin.

MISSOURI

Manchester Sangha

For additional information, please see
Community of Mindful Living, Berkeley,
California.

ADDRESS: 832 King George Court,
Manchester, MO 63021

PHONE: (314) 225-3573

LINEAGE: Mindfulness practice in the tradition of Thich Nhat Hanh.

SPIRITUAL HEAD: Thich Nhat Hanh

CONTACT: Kristen Hunt

AFFILIATION: Community of Mindful
Living, Berkeley, California

MEDITATION PROGRAM: We meet one
evening a week for mindfulness practice.

RETREATS OFFERED: We join the St. Louis
Sangha for occasional Days of Mindfulness.

Missouri Zen Center

No description available.

ADDRESS: 220 Spring Avenue,
Webster Groves (St. Louis), MO 63119

PHONE: (314) 961-6138

E-MAIL: ragrucza@bmb.wustl.edu

LINEAGE: Soto Zen

SPIRITUAL HEAD: Rosan Yoshida

CONTACT: Rick Grucza

MEDITATION PROGRAM: Daily morning
and evening meditation. Sunday service.

RETREATS OFFERED: Monthly extended
zazen. Periodic *sesshin*.

PUBLICATIONS: *Dharma Life*, monthly
newsletter.

St. Louis Sangha

For additional information, please see
Community of Mindful Living, Berkeley,
California.

ADDRESS: 69 Arundel Place, St. Louis,
MO 63105

PHONE: (314) 725-8231

FAX: Same

LINEAGE: Mindfulness practice in the tradition of Thich Nhat Hanh.

SPIRITUAL HEAD: Thich Nhat Hanh

CONTACTS: Louise and Ashley Cadwell

AFFILIATION: Community of Mindful
Living, Berkeley, California

FACILITIES: First Unitarian Church

MEDITATION PROGRAM: We meet one
evening a week for sitting and walking
meditation.

Western Pure Land Buddhist Sangha

We are a small group of Western practitioners of Pure Land Buddhism. We meet and chant *nembutsu* together, study the sutras, and share the dharma with others.

ADDRESS: PO Box 603, Springfield, MO 65801-0603

PHONE: (417) 885-0076

E-MAIL: shaksway@aol.com

LINEAGE: Western Pure Land Buddhism (post-jodo-shin-shu)

CONTACT: Shakudion, Resident Director

ESTABLISHED: 1995

FACILITIES: Meet in each other's homes.

MEDITATION PROGRAM: *Nembutsu* chanting; sutra study.

PUBLICATIONS: *EKO: Newsletter of Western Pure Land Buddhism*

MONTANA

Helena Sangha

For additional information, please see Community of Mindful Living, Berkeley, California.

ADDRESS: 211 East Lawrence, Helena, MT 59601

PHONE: (406) 442-4344

LINEAGE: Mindfulness practice in the tradition of Thich Nhat Hanh.

SPIRITUAL HEAD: Thich Nhat Hanh

CONTACT: David Cooper

AFFILIATION: Community of Mindful Living, Berkeley, California

MEDITATION PROGRAM: We meet one evening a week for sitting and walking meditation and a reading. We recite precepts on the first practice evening of the month.

Open Way Sangha

Open Way is a young and evolving group affiliated with Thich Nhat Hanh and the Tiep Hien order (Order of Interbeing). Everyone who wishes to meditate is welcome, as participation is not limited to members or even to "Buddhists." Open Way is defined as a church and is structured as a nonprofit religious corporation in Montana. Governance is by community meeting and decisions are made by consensus.

ADDRESS: PO Box 7281, Missoula, MT 59807

PHONES: (406) 549-0555, (406) 543-6443, (406) 626-4463, (406) 728-0820

EMAIL: rconrad@selway.umt.edu

LINEAGE: Vietnamese Zen

SPIRITUAL HEAD: Thich Nhat Hanh

CONTACTS: Suzanne Aboulfadl, Michael Colville, Rowan Conrad, Betsy Hart

AFFILIATION: Tiep Hien order

ESTABLISHED: 1989

FACILITIES: Currently meeting in local Quaker church.

MEDITATION PROGRAM: Sunday evening sittings, precept recitations, chanting. Dharma discussion three times per month. Meditation classes and focused dharma study.

RETREATS OFFERED: Spring and fall residential retreats with parallel children's program. Several mindfulness days and/or nonresidential weekend retreats per year.

PUBLICATIONS: *Open Way News & Views*, quarterly.

NEBRASKA

Kearney Zendo

Kearney Zendo is dedicated to the practice of *zazen* in the Soto-shu tradition, as transmitted by the late Dainin Katagiri-Roshi. During fall semesters at University of Nebraska–Kearney, the *zendo* serves as an off-campus classroom where Dr. Mosig, resident monk and practice director, teaches a course on the psychology of Zen. The Zen Shuri-ryu Karate-do and Kobudo Dojo share the facilities and function as a martial arts academy for students who view these disciplines as an extension of their Zen practice. *Karate-do* and *kobudo* are taught to conquer the self rather than to defeat one's enemies.

ADDRESS: 3715 Avenue F (PO Box 370), Kearney, NE 68847

PHONE: (308) 236-5650

FAX: (308) 237-1294

LINEAGE: Japanese Soto Zen

SPIRITUAL HEAD: Dainin Katagiri-Roshi (1928–1990); Shoken Winecoff.

CONTACT: Yozan Mosig, Practice Director

AFFILIATION: Minnesota Zen Meditation Center/Hokyoji

ESTABLISHED: 1984

FACILITIES: *Zendo* with twenty-five *zafu/zabuton*, *butsudan*, library (almost 5,000 books, 600 videotapes), karate *dojo*.

RETREATS OFFERED: Fall *sesshin*; one-day sittings throughout the year.

PUBLICATIONS: Articles in journals; psychology textbooks.

Nebraska Zen Center/Shinkokuji

Nebraska Zen Center (NZC) is a Soto Zen Buddhist practice temple that follows the tradition established in Japan by Zen Master Dogen and transmitted to America by two contemporary masters, the late Shunryu Suzuki-Roshi, founder of San Francisco Zen Center and author of *Zen Mind, Beginner's Mind*; and the late Dainin Katagiri-Roshi. NZC's Head Priest and Teacher is Rev. Nonin Chowaney, an American Zen Master who trained both in Japan and at Tassajara Zen Monastery in California. He was given formal dharma transmission by Rev. Katagiri and certified to teach by the Soto Zen Church in Japan.

Rev. Nonin Chowaney, spiritual director of Nebraska Zen Center. (Photo by Bob Hickman.)

ADDRESS: 3625 Lafayette Avenue, Omaha, NE 68131-1363
PHONE: (402) 551-9035
LINEAGE: Japanese Soto Zen
SPIRITUAL HEAD: Rev. Nonin Chowaney
CONTACTS: Rev. Nonin Chowaney and Kyoki Roberts
AFFILIATION: Autonomous
ESTABLISHED: 1975 by Dainin Katagiri
FACILITIES: Small city temple, *zendo* in four-bedroom house.
MEDITATION PROGRAM: Meditation mornings and evenings, Monday through Saturday; weekly *zazen* instruction; morning service; *ryaku fusatsu* monthly.
RETREATS OFFERED: Monthly one- and two-day *sesshin*; seven-day retreat from Christmas to New Year's; introductory workshops; study seminars.
PUBLICATIONS: *The Nebraska Monkey*

NEVADA

Mojave Desert Zen Center

Practice at Mojave Desert Zen Center is held in the offices of Dr. Ju-Cheon Lee, O.M.D. The center was founded by Thom Pastor, a dharma teacher in the Kwan Um School of Zen. Visitors are welcome to join us for meditation practice, which is free. Instruction is given on chanting and *zazen* as the need arises. If you come regularly you are encouraged to become a member of the Kwan Um Zen School.
ADDRESS: 901 El Camino Way, Boulder City, NV 89005
PHONE: (702) 293-4222
LINEAGE: Korean Chogye order
SPIRITUAL HEAD: Robert Moore Ji Do Poep Sa Nim
CONTACT: Thom "Kwan Jok" Pastor, Resident Director
AFFILIATION: Kwan Um School of Zen, Providence, Rhode Island
ESTABLISHED: 1994
FACILITIES: 919 East Charleston Boulevard, Las Vegas, Nevada
MEDITATION PROGRAM: Sitting, chanting, bowing, work practice, dharma talks, social interaction.
RETREATS OFFERED: One-day, four times yearly; three-day, six times yearly; three-month, yearly; six-week, yearly.
PUBLICATIONS: *Primary Point—Only Go Straight*

Nan Hua Zen Buddhist Society/Zen Center of Las Vegas

The Nan Hua Zen Buddhist Society is led by two priests, Rev. Chuan Yuan Shakya and Rev. Chuan Cheng Shakya, both of whom were ordained in the People's Republic of China at the monastery founded by the Sixth Patriarch, Hui Neng. The society, serving community needs since 1988, produces spiritual liter-

Chuan Cheng Shakya (left) and Chuan Yuan Shakya, codirectors of Nan Hua/Zen Center of Las Vegas. (Photo courtesy of Nan Hua Zen Society.)

ature, maintains a prison ministry, and is active in suicide prevention and Alcoholics Anonymous. Private and group instruction in Zen theology and practice is available. An active Web site is maintained featuring weekly dharma talks and Zen-related topics. Personal contact through the Web site is encouraged.
ADDRESS: 328 Xavier Street, Las Vegas, NV 89107
PHONE: (702) 870-8240
E-MAIL: FaYin@inter-link.com
WWW: http://www.inter-link.com/Dharma
LINEAGE: Order of the Sixth Patriarch, Hui Neng
SPIRITUAL HEAD: Grand Master Jy Din Shakya, Honolulu, Hawaii
CONTACTS: Chuan Yuan Shakya, Chuan Cheng Shakya, Directors
AFFILIATION: Buddhist Association of Colorado

FACILITIES: Private home for individual instruction, rented hall for meditation intensives.

RETREATS OFFERED: Given, but not on regularly scheduled basis.

Quan Am Buddhist Temple

The Quan Am Buddhist Temple is a new branch of the Quan Am Buddhist Fellowship, Inc. Temple meditation and classes are in Vietnamese, but English translators can be found. Please call for meditation schedule.

ADDRESS: 2611 South Buffalo Avenue, Las Vegas, NV 89117
PHONE: (702) 220-3463
E-MAIL: Ryan122@vegas.email.net
LINEAGE: Vietnamese Buddhist
SPIRITUAL HEAD: Thich Gaic Minh, Fellowship President
CONTACT: Rev. Shi Fa-Xian (Conner)
AFFILIATION: Quan Am Buddhist Fellowship, Inc., 3924 Filhurst Avenue, Baldwin Park, CA 91706
FACILITIES: Urban temple.
MEDITATION PROGRAM: Call for meditation schedules.

NEW HAMPSHIRE

Barrington Zen Center

"I was a student of Maezumi-Roshi in the early 1970s. After I left Los Angeles, I only sat sporadically until the summer of 1994 when a friend and I began sitting together three mornings and one evening a week. A few others joined us and we added a one-day retreat on the second Sunday of every month. We have a lovely, simple *zendo* in a quiet place. Perhaps some day we will find a teacher who would like to come at least a few times a year." —*Charter Tosho Weeks*

ADDRESS: 7 Lois Lane, Barrington, NH 03825
PHONE: (603) 664-7654

LINEAGE: Japanese Soto and Rinzai
CONTACT: Charter Tosho Weeks
AFFILIATION: Autonomous
ESTABLISHED: 1994
FACILITIES: Rural *zendo*
MEDITATION PROGRAM: *Zazen* Monday, Wednesday, and Friday mornings; Wednesday evenings.
RETREATS OFFERED: All-day retreat second Sunday of the month.

Bear Tree Zendo

No description available.

ADDRESS: c/o 827 Hatfield Road, Hopkinton, NH 03229
PHONE: (603) 746-5721
LINEAGE: Japanese Rinzai Zen
SPIRITUAL HEAD: Rev. Wade Hancock
AFFILIATION: Autonomous
ESTABLISHED: 1989
FACILITIES: Local *zendo*.
MEDITATION PROGRAM: *Zazen* twice weekly.
RETREATS OFFERED: Monthly all-day sitting.

Peterborough Sangha

For additional information, please see Community of Mindful Living, Berkeley, California.

ADDRESS: 10 Route 101 West, Peterborough, NH 03458
PHONE: (508) 856-3755
E-MAIL: ferris.urbanowski@banyan.ummed.edu
LINEAGE: Mindfulness practice in the tradition of Thich Nhat Hanh.
SPIRITUAL HEAD: Thich Nhat Hanh
CONTACTS: Peggy Cappy and Ferris Urbanowski
AFFILIATION: Community of Mindful Living, Berkeley, California
FACILITIES: Professional health center.
MEDITATION PROGRAM: We meet one evening a week for meditation and discussion or reading from Thây's books.

NEW JERSEY

Central New Jersey Sangha

For additional information, please see Community of Mindful Living, Berkeley, California.

ADDRESS: 37 Maple Street, Princeton, NJ 08542
PHONE: (609) 924-4506
FAX: (609) 924-7477
LINEAGE: Mindfulness practice in the tradition of Thich Nhat Hanh.
SPIRITUAL HEAD: Thich Nhat Hanh

Some of the regulars at Bear Tree Zendo in Hopkinton, New Hampshire. (Photo courtesy of Bear Tree.)

CONTACT: Amy Rhett LaMotte
AFFILIATION: Community of Mindful Living, Berkeley, California
MEDITATION PROGRAM: We meet for an Evening of Mindfulness once a month.
RETREATS OFFERED: Day of Mindfulness every three months. Occasional weekend retreats.

The Engaged Zen Foundation

The Engaged Zen Foundation, Inc., was formed as a not-for-profit corporation to serve the spiritual needs of prisoners and to establish a Zen temple and monastery. All donations, bequests, and gifts of real estate, personal property, securities, and/or equipment are tax-deductible to the full extent of the law.
ADDRESS: PO Box 700, Ramsey, NJ 07446
PHONE: (201) 236-0335
WWW: http://www.teleport.com/~Idotm/Gateway.html
LINEAGE: Rinzai Zen
SPIRITUAL HEAD: Rev. Kobutsu Shindo Kevin Malone
AFFILIATION: Autonomous. Parent temple is Dai Bosatsu Zendo Kongo-ji.
ESTABLISHED: 1991
MEDITATION PROGRAM: Zen training in prisons. Prison and death row chaplaincy.
RETREATS OFFERED: In correctional facilities only.
PUBLICATIONS: Gateway Journal

Juniper Ridge Community

For additional information, please see Community of Mindful Living, Berkeley, California.
ADDRESS: Kitchell Road, Convent Station, NJ 07961
PHONE: (201) 455-7133
E-MAIL: alex322@concentric.net
LINEAGE: Mindfulness practice in the tradition of Thich Nhat Hanh.
SPIRITUAL HEAD: Thich Nhat Hanh

CONTACT: Bill Alexander
AFFILIATION: Community of Mindful Living, Berkeley, California
MEDITATION PROGRAM: We regularly offer meditations and dharma discussions, with an emphasis on the Twelve Steps.

Morristown Sangha

For additional information, please see Community of Mindful Living, Berkeley, California.
ADDRESS: 54 Elm Street, Morristown, NJ 07960
PHONE: (201) 898-9368
LINEAGE: Mindfulness practice in the tradition of Thich Nhat Hanh.
SPIRITUAL HEAD: Thich Nhat Hanh
CONTACTS: Sid Kemp and Kris Lindbeck
AFFILIATION: Community of Mindful Living, Berkeley, California
FACILITIES: Meetings held at the Wholeness Center.
MEDITATION PROGRAM: We meet one evening a week for mindfulness practice. Introductory meditation classes.
RETREATS OFFERED: Monthly Days of Mindfulness.

Princeton Zen Society

Founded in 1985 by Chinzan, one of Sasaki-Roshi's first students in America, the Princeton Zen Society is beautiful and comfortable, overlooking a pond, lawn, and trees. Dai-sesshin occur twice a year with four sanzen per day for seven days by Kyozan Joshu Sasaki-Roshi. Attendance is limited to thirty students.
ADDRESS: 317 Mt. Lucas Road, Princeton, NJ 08540
PHONE: (609) 924-0785
LINEAGE: Rinzai Zen
SPIRITUAL HEAD: Kyozan Joshu Sasaki-Roshi
CONTACT: Chinzan, Resident Director
AFFILIATION: Rinzai-ji of Los Angeles

ESTABLISHED: 1985
FACILITIES: Zendo
MEDITATION PROGRAM: Weekly sitting meditation.
RETREATS OFFERED: Dai-sesshin (weeklong) with sanzen four times per day.

The Zen Society/Jizo-An Monastery

The Zen Society/Jizo-An Monastery is an American Buddhist community and training center dedicated to a single purpose: "to realize tranquillity of mind in communion with one's fellow men and women within our world." Over the years Jizo-An has emerged as a spiritual center for people of all faiths. Nestled in the residential community of Cinnaminson, New Jersey, the monastery offers retreat and refuge from stress, loneliness, confusion, and despair. We conduct comprehensive and authentic nonresidential Zen training programs for laypersons of all ages and religious backgrounds.
ADDRESS: 1603 Highland Avenue, Cinnaminson, NJ 08077
PHONE: (609) 786-4150
FAX: (609) 786-2112
SPIRITUAL HEAD: Seijaku Stephen Reichenbach
AFFILIATION: Autonomous
ESTABLISHED: 1981
FACILITIES: Main building, tea house, garden, outdoor zendo.
MEDITATION PROGRAM: Daily sittings, dharma talks.
RETREATS OFFERED: Sesshin, workshops, tea classes, formal nonresidential training.
PUBLICATIONS: Kokoro, newsletter.

Zen Temple of Cresskill

Zen Temple of Cresskill is a place for Korean Zen practice based on the teaching of Zen Master Songdahm. Our practice is

Zen dance: meditation in motion. (Photo courtesy of Zen Temple of Cresskill, New Jersey.)

Zen dance (meditation in movement) as a ritual and ceremonial multimedia performance. Classes in Zen dance technique and Zen exercise (awakening the body and mind) are offered for dancers and nondancers alike. Cresskill residents are invited to participate.

ADDRESS: 185 Sixth Street, Cresskill, NJ 07626
PHONE: (201) 567-7468
FAX: (201) 567-0831
LINEAGE: Korean Son (Zen)
SPIRITUAL HEAD: Zen Master Songdahm (Inchun, Korea)
CONTACT: Dr. Sun Ock Lee, Resident Teacher
AFFILIATION: Yong Hwa Zen Temple in Korea
ESTABLISHED: 1988
FACILITIES: Dharma room.
RETREATS OFFERED: Two times per year.
PUBLICATIONS: *Zen Quest: Everyday Enlightenment, Zen Dance: Meditation in Movement*

NEW MEXICO

Albuquerque Zen Center

Albuquerque Zen Center creates an oasis of quiet in the noisy world of time constraints, work, family, and political and social involvements. Having a place to practice with others and a reliable practice schedule offers support to those seeking true insight, enabling them to live their lives with understanding, awareness, and compassion. We are a diverse group of people ranging in age from midtwenties to midseventies. Our center is a resource for lay practitioners who value *zazen* as a complement to daily life.

ADDRESS: PO Box 4585, Albuquerque, NM 87196
PHONE: (505) 268-4877
LINEAGE: Japanese Rinzai Zen
SPIRITUAL HEAD: Joshu Sasaki-Roshi
CONTACT: Seiju Mammoser
AFFILIATION: Rinzai-ji, Mt. Baldy Zen Center, Bodhi Manda Zen Center
ESTABLISHED: 1989
FACILITIES: Building new facilities on recently purchased land to replace current rented building.
RETREATS OFFERED: Day/weekend sittings.
PUBLICATIONS: Quarterly newsletter.

Bodhi Manda Zen Center

Bodhi Manda offers a daily schedule of *zazen*, chanting and work practice drawn from the Rinzai Zen tradition. Throughout the year, *zazen* weekends and seven-day *sesshin* are offered for students of all levels. Each summer the Seminar on the Sutras explores Buddhism with various scholars and teachers of the dharma.

ADDRESS: PO Box 8, Jemez Springs, NM 87025
PHONE: (505) 829-3854
FAX: Same
LINEAGE: Japanese Rinzai Zen
SPIRITUAL HEAD: Rev. Joshu Sasaki-Roshi
CONTACT: Hosen
AFFILIATION: Rinzai-ji
ESTABLISHED: 1974
FACILITIES: Country retreat center.
MEDITATION PROGRAM: Daily *zazen*, work, chanting.
RETREATS OFFERED: *Zazen* weekends; two seven-day *sesshin* annually.

Hidden Mountain Zen Center

Alfred Jitsudo Ancheta-Sensei, a dharma heir of the late Maezumi-Roshi, has returned to his native New Mexico to found Hidden Mountain Zen Center. Our new *sangha* occupies a one-hundred-year-old house in downtown Albuquerque, which members have worked hard to convert into a *zendo* and residence. Our future plans call for acquiring a rural retreat center, working with youths at risk, and establishing businesses to provide employment for *sangha* members.

ADDRESS: 216 Ninth Street Northwest, Albuquerque, NM 87102

PHONE: (505) 248-0649

FAX: Same

LINEAGE: Japanese Soto Zen

SPIRITUAL HEAD: Sensei Alfred Jitsudo Ancheta, Resident Teacher

AFFILIATION: White Plum Sangha/Bernard Tetsugen Glassman-Roshi

ESTABLISHED: 1995

FACILITIES: *Zendo* and retreat center.

RETREATS OFFERED: Monthly two- to seven-day retreats.

PUBLICATIONS: *Mountain Path*, newsletter.

The handmade adobe zendo *of Hokoji, near Taos, New Mexico.* (Photo courtesy of Hokoji.)

Hokoji

We, called Ho-ko-ji, are a small *sangha* offering daily *zazen* in the Soto tradition, extended sittings monthly, and four *sesshin* annually in the lineage of Sawaki-Roshi *Di O Sho*, Suzuki-Roshi *Di O Sho*, and Kobun Chino-Roshi. A traditional *Zen Do*. We have some space for indeterminate stays according to circumstances.

ADDRESS: PO Box 238, Arroyo Seco, NM 87514-0238

PHONE: (505) 776-2339

LINEAGE: Japanese Soto Zen

SPIRITUAL HEAD: Kobun Chino-Roshi

CONTACT: Stan Di Shin White, Resident Teacher

ESTABLISHED: 1984

FACILITIES: Country *zendo*.

MEDITATION PROGRAM: Daily *zazen*.

RETREATS OFFERED: Extended sittings monthly; Four *sesshin* annually.

Mountain Cloud Zen Center

Mountain Cloud Zen Center is not a training or residential facility per se, although it does serve as a community center for the Santa Fe Zen (Aitken-Roshi's lineage) and Vipassana *sangha*s. It is used by local Buddhist groups for retreats and shared celebrations of Buddhist holidays. It's also used by non-Buddhist spiritual groups for retreats and self-help workshops. A small but growing Zen *sangha* manages the property.

ADDRESS: PO Box 5768, Santa Fe, NM 87502

PHONE: (505) 988-4396

LINEAGE: Japanese Soto-Rinzai Zen

SPIRITUAL HEADS: Visiting teachers (heirs of Robert Aitken-Roshi).

CONTACT: Head resident

AFFILIATION: Diamond Sangha, Honolulu, Hawaii

ESTABLISHED: 1991

FACILITIES: Meditation hall; dining room; kitchen; three overnight, dorm-style cabins.

RETREATS OFFERED: Weekends and four- to seven-day retreats.

PUBLICATIONS: *Cicada*, quarterly newsletter.

One Zendo

In his book *Living Buddha, Living Christ*, Thich Nhat Hanh says, "On the altar in my hermitage are images of Buddha and Jesus, and I touch both of them as my spiritual ancestors." We do the same in our efforts to transcend concepts and sit with the mystery of the One.

ADDRESS: PO Box 9644, Santa Fe, NM 87504

PHONE: (505) 984-1871

LINEAGE: Japanese Soto Zen
SPIRITUAL HEAD: Buddha
CONTACT: Clark Elliott, Resident Host
AFFILIATION: Plum Village, France
ESTABLISHED: 1994
FACILITIES: Urban meditation center.
MEDITATION PROGRAM: Daily *zazen.*

Open Heart Sangha

We share in socially engaged activities such as working with the Habitat for Humanity house. We have occasional dharma talks by visiting teachers. For additional information, please see Community of Mindful Living, Berkeley, California.
ADDRESS: PO Box 1591, Taos, NM 87571
PHONE: (505) 758-4035
E-MAIL: kate@laplaza.taos.nm.us
LINEAGE: Mindfulness practice in the tradition of Thich Nhat Hanh.
SPIRITUAL HEAD: Thich Nhat Hanh
CONTACT: Susan McCarthy
AFFILIATION: Community of Mindful Living, Berkeley, California
MEDITATION PROGRAM: We meet weekly for sitting and walking meditation, precept recitation, tea ceremonies, and reading from Thich Nhat Hanh's books.
RETREATS OFFERED: Monthly Day of Mindfulness.

Open Way Sangha

For additional information, please see Community of Mindful Living, Berkeley, California.
ADDRESS: Route 4, Box 60B, Santa Fe, NM 87501
PHONE: (505) 982-3846
FAX: (505) 982-9481
LINEAGE: Mindfulness practice in the tradition of Thich Nhat Hanh.
SPIRITUAL HEAD: Thich Nhat Hanh

CONTACTS: Cynthia Jurs and Hugh Wheir
AFFILIATION: Community of Mindful Living, Berkeley, California
MEDITATION PROGRAM: We meet weekly for sitting and walking meditation, and dharma discussion.
RETREATS OFFERED: Days of Mindfulness are held monthly, with precept recitation and writing practice.

NEW YORK

Albany Affiliate/Kinpu-an

Kinpu-an is a lay dharma center whose mission is to provide a space to explore Zen practice. For residents, the center provides a community setting in which to make the practice an integral part of one's daily life. For nonresidents, Kinpu-an offers a schedule of daily sittings, extended retreats, and the use of a library of books and tapes. Retreats are led by senior Mountains and Rivers Order (MRO) students and include talks. Residents also sit with the Lotus Peak Sangha at Great Meadow Prison, Comstock, New York.
ADDRESS: 4 Providence Place, Albany, NY 12202
PHONE: (518) 432-4676
LINEAGE: Soto/Rinzai Zen (Mountains and Rivers Order)
SPIRITUAL HEAD: John Daido Loori
CONTACT: Wally Taiko Edge
AFFILIATION: Zen Mountain Monastery. Mountains and Rivers Order.
ESTABLISHED: 1989
FACILITIES: Urban meditation center, small residential community.
MEDITATION PROGRAM: Daily Zen meditation.
RETREATS OFFERED: Monthly half- or full-day sits.
PUBLICATIONS: Quarterly newsletter.

Bo Kwang Zen Center

No description available.
ADDRESS: 36-25 Union Street, #1C, Flushing, NY 11354
PHONE: (718) 353-2474
LINEAGE: Korean Chogye
SPIRITUAL HEAD: Zen Master Seung Sahn
AFFILIATION: Kwan Um School of Zen

Brooklyn Sangha

For additional information, please refer to Community of Mindful Living, Berkeley, California.
ADDRESS: 412 Ninth Street, #3, Brooklyn, NY 11215
PHONE: (718) 499-5104
LINEAGE: Mindfulness practice in the tradition of Thich Nhat Hanh.
SPIRITUAL HEAD: Thich Nhat Hanh
CONTACT: Patrecia Lenore
AFFILIATION: Community of Mindful Living, Berkeley, California
MEDITATION PROGRAM: Twice a week we have meditation practice followed by a mindful discussion. On Sundays we do outdoor walking meditation in a local park.
RETREATS OFFERED: Monthly Day of Mindfulness.

Brooklyn Zen Urban Temple/Dai Gedatsu An

Located in historic Fort Greene, Brooklyn Zen Urban Temple is a multicultural *sangha* devoted to bringing mindfulness into our daily lives through *samu* (work practice) and public meditation sessions. We specifically urge those not generally represented in the American Zen *sangha* to participate in our projects and programs. Regardless of your race, gender, sexual orientation, or socioeconomic status, we welcome you not just in word, but in practice as well.

NEW YORK (*cont.*)

ADDRESS: 21 South Elliott Place, Brooklyn, NY 11217
PHONE: (718) 243-9040
FAX: (718) 243-9043
E-MAIL: BklynZen@aol.com
LINEAGE: Japanese Soto Zen
SPIRITUAL HEAD: Pat Enkyo O'Hara
CONTACT(S): Angel Kyodo Williams, Director
AFFILIATION: Village Zendo
ESTABLISHED: 1997
RETREATS OFFERED: Monthly *zazenkai. Sesshins.*
PUBLICATIONS: *UPAYA Newsletter*

Budding Flower Sangha

For additional information, please refer to Community of Mindful Living, Berkeley, California.
ADDRESS: 77 Wells Road, RD 7, Newburgh, NY 12550
PHONE: (914) 561-0995
LINEAGE: Mindfulness practice in the tradition of Thich Nhat Hanh.
SPIRITUAL HEAD: Thich Nhat Hanh
CONTACT: Patricia Hunt-Perry
AFFILIATION: Community of Mindful Living, Berkeley, California
MEDITATION PROGRAM: Meditation practice, three times weekly.
RETREATS OFFERED: Occasional weekend mindfulness retreats with guest teachers.

Buffalo Zen Group

Buffalo Zen Group is an informal gathering of people who value the experience of community practice. The style and forms adopted by our *sangha* have been handed down from the Harada/Yasutani/Kapleau-Roshi teaching lineage by way of Rochester Zen Center.
ADDRESS: 4056 North Freeman Road, Orchard Park, NY 14127
PHONE: (716) 662-2904

E-MAIL: dhohman662@aol.com
LINEAGE: Soto/Rinzai Zen
CONTACTS: Dennis Hohman and John Bednarchick
AFFILIATION: Informally with Rochester Zen Center.
ESTABLISHED: circa 1960
FACILITIES: Sittings at East-West Book Store.
MEDITATION PROGRAM: Two-hour sitting every Sunday evening. Sittings consist of three thirty-five-minute rounds of *zazen* interspersed with five-minute periods of walking meditation.
RETREATS OFFERED: All-day *zazen* intensives are conducted three or four times a year.

Ch'an Meditation Center/Dharma Drum Mountain

Ch'an Meditation Center is part of the Institute of Chung-Hwa Buddhist Culture. We began as a small sitting group at the Temple of Great Enlightenment in the Bronx. By 1978, increased membership was making it necessary for us to find a place of our own. In December of the following year, a two-story building located in Elmhurst, New York, was purchased. Eight years later, the center made its third and final move to the three-story building that is its present location.
ADDRESS: 90-56 Corona Avenue, Elmhurst-Queens, NY 11373
PHONE: (718) 592-6593
FAX: (718) 592-0717
SPIRITUAL HEAD: Ch'an Master Sheng-yen
CONTACTS: Master Sheng-yen and disciples Bhikshu Gue-yuan, Guo-Chou, and Guo-gu Shi are Resident Teachers.
AFFILIATION: Foundation of Dharma Drum Mountain, Taipei, Republic of China
ESTABLISHED: 1978
FACILITIES: Urban meditation center. Suburban facilities under construction.

RETREATS OFFERED: One-, two-, three-, and seven-day intensives.
PUBLICATIONS: Over fifty titles by Master Sheng-yen in seven languages.

Chappaqua Sangha

For additional information, please refer to Community of Mindful Living, Berkeley, California.
ADDRESS: 49 Florence Drive, Chappaqua, NY 10514
PHONE: (914) 238-8296
E-MAIL: Judithdav@aol.com
LINEAGE: Mindfulness practice in the tradition of Thich Nhat Hanh.
SPIRITUAL HEAD: Thich Nhat Hanh
CONTACT: Judy Davis
AFFILIATION: Community of Mindful Living, Berkeley, California
MEDITATION PROGRAM: We meet one evening of each month for sitting and walking meditation, with a potluck afterwards.

Zen Master Wu Kwang, Abbot of Chogye International Zen Center of New York. (Photo courtesy of CIZC-NY.)

Compassion for the Dying

THE CH'AN MEDITATION CENTER HAS ESTABlished a unique volunteer program called Compassion for the Dying to help ease the fear, anxiety, and attachment of the dying, the deceased, and their families. When a family calls and requests help, a group of volunteers—from as few as eight to as many as forty—go to the hospital, house, or funeral home to conduct Buddhist services and to provide a peaceful atmosphere.

The service begins with a dharma talk on letting go of attachment to the physical body and life, and is followed by the recitation of the Buddha's name and a chanting of *The Heart Sutra* in low and harmonious tones. The recitation, chanting, and talks help the dying—or those already in the intermediary stage between death and rebirth—to be calm, accepting, and free from confusion and attachment.

Compassion for the Dying has over one hundred volunteers who express their concern by serving the community in this way. The program has helped scores of dying persons to pass away peacefully and has given support to their families in their time of grief. This service is extended to all Ch'an Meditation Center members and their families and friends, but we hope to expand the program as time goes on.

Ven. Guo-gu Bhikshu

For more information, contact: Ch'an Meditation Center, Institute of Chung-Hwa Buddhist Culture, 90-56 Corona Avenue, Elmhurst-Queens, NY 11373; (718) 592-6593.

Chogye International Zen Center of New York

Wu Kwang, Abbot of Chogye International Zen Center of New York, is one of only six individuals to be named Zen Master by the Ven. Seung Sahn Soen Sa Nim. As such, he is authorized to perform all the formal teaching activities of Zen, including the traditional *kong-an* practice of private interchange between teacher and student. He has been practicing meditation since 1966. He is a psychotherapist with an M.S.W., and has a B.A. in music. "Zen," he says, "is everyday life and everyday life is Zen."
ADDRESS: 400 East 14th Street #2D/E, New York, NY 10009
PHONE: (212) 353-0461
FAX: (914) 423-7890
E-MAIL: Ruthin@aol.com
LINEAGE: Korean Zen, Chogye order

SPIRITUAL HEAD: Wu Kwang, Zen Master and Abbot. Founder: Zen Master Seung Sahn.
ESTABLISHED: 1975
FACILITIES: City residential center.
MEDITATION PROGRAM: Daily chanting, bowing, and sitting meditation; Wednesday night, extended sitting practice; Sundays, introduction to Zen practice; monthly Zen talks.
RETREATS OFFERED: Monthly one- and three-day retreats.
PUBLICATIONS: *Woodfish*, newsletter.

Clear Mountain Zen Center

Clear Mountain Zen Center (CMZC) is an interfaith community Zen center blending traditional Rinzai Zen Buddhism with contemporary American life. CMZC offers instruction and training in

zazen, kinhin, chanting, sutra and koan studies, *teisho* (Zen talks), and traditional dharma combat. Abbot Hart integrates Judeo-Christian and Buddhist teachings into a fresh, innovative approach to spirituality in everyday life. We welcome anyone interested in practicing an engaged spirituality and in deepening one's commitment to oneself in a relaxed environment.
ADDRESS: 605 Peninsula Boulevard, Hempstead, NY 11550
PHONE: (516) 564-9808
LINEAGE: Japanese Rinzai
SPIRITUAL HEAD: Kendo Rich Hart, Abbot
CONTACT: Same
AFFILIATION: Autonomous
ESTABLISHED: 1990
FACILITIES: *Zendo*, conference space, living room, library.
MEDITATION PROGRAM: *Zazen* and *teisho*

Kinhin Travels

CLEAR MOUNTAIN ZEN CENTER OFFERS monthly backpacking trips to the Catskill or Adirondack Mountains as a way of Zen training. Inherent in Zen practice is the awareness of stillness while engaged in activity—working, eating, or backcountry traveling. *Kinhin*, or walking meditation, reminds us to pay attention when we're in motion.

Wilderness trips are designed so that people of all levels of fitness may realize *Tathagata Zen*: "just as things are, they are perfect." The sounds present in the outdoors—a valley stream, rambunctious porcupines, or tree frogs beside a pond—reflect their Buddha Nature, and listening to them can lead us back to ourselves.

Wilderness trips are scheduled in advance and are usually held the last weekend of the month. In addition, we sponsor trips of five or more days that are announced well in advance. Participants furnish their own equipment and food. Transportation is arranged by the center.

These excursions are led by Christopher Tenshin Gilhooly. Christopher is an ordained Zen Buddhist monk, psychotherapist, healer, musician, and a licensed guide in the State of New York with over twenty years' experience in wilderness and backcountry travel. Please call for fees and details on upcoming trips.

Christopher Tenshin Gilhooly

For more information, contact: Clear Mountain Zen Center, 605 Peninsula Boulevard, Hempstead, NY 11550; (516) 564-9808.

NEW YORK (*cont.*)

three times weekly. Beginner's introduction on second Sunday of the month.
RETREATS OFFERED: Weekend backpacking trips, all-day sittings.

Empty Hand Zendo

Since 1986 Empty Hand Zendo has been renting an antique chapel (built in 1832) from the Quakers for our weekly meetings. Kwan-Yin sits under an original stained glass window. We are at the edge of a marsh and have twice been severely flooded, gongs filled to the brim. We're on a busy street in a fancy suburb, yet are somehow rustic and simple. Our *zendo* is very *zazen*-centered. We come to sit together, not for social stuff. The result of sitting in silence side by side for all these years is an uncanny bonding and closeness. This is *sangha* being born!
ADDRESS: The Meeting House, 624 Milton Road, Rye, NY 10580
PHONE: (914) 921-3327
LINEAGE: Japanese Rinzai, Maurine Stuart heritage
SPIRITUAL HEAD: The late Maurine Myoon Stuart-Roshi
CONTACT: Rev. Susan Ji-on Postal
AFFILIATION: Autonomous
ESTABLISHED: 1986
FACILITIES: Forty-seat *zendo* in rented Quaker church.
RETREATS OFFERED: One-day retreat each month; weekend *sesshin* at rented conference center twice a year.
PUBLICATIONS: Calendar and newsletter three times a year.

First Zen Institute of America

The institute is a lay organization founded in 1930 by Japanese Zen Master Sokei-an Sasaki. Sokei-an, who immigrated to America in 1906 with his teacher Soyen Shaku, was the first Zen master to settle permanently in America. The institute is governed by its board and is entirely supported by its membership. The institute also publishes *Zen Notes*, a quarterly periodical.
ADDRESS: 113 East 30th Street, New York, NY 10016
PHONE: (212) 686-2520
SPIRITUAL HEAD: Sokei-an Sasaki, Founder
AFFILIATION: Autonomous
ESTABLISHED: 1930
MEDITATION PROGRAM: Meditation two evenings weekly. Open to the public. Call for times.
RETREATS OFFERED: Two-day meditation intensives the second weekend of every month.
PUBLICATIONS: *Zen Notes*, quarterly periodical.

Ithaca Zen Center

No description available.
ADDRESS: 56 Lieb Road, Spencer, NY 14883
PHONE: (607) 272-0694
FAX: Same
E-MAIL: ithacazen@aol.com
LINEAGE: Zen
SPIRITUAL HEAD: Joshu Sasaki-Roshi
CONTACT: David Yoshin Radin, Resident Director
AFFILIATION: Autonomous
ESTABLISHED: 1978
FACILITIES: Retreat facility in upstate New York.
RETREATS OFFERED: Weekend and weeklong *sesshin*; health retreats (body/ mind restoration).

Konzeon Zendo

"When we built our Water Mill house, my husband, Bob, suggested that we add a zendo. The following year, Yasutani-Roshi, Soen-Roshi, and the monk Taisan (now Eido-Roshi) dropped by for a visit. Soen Roshi said, "You need something Japanese." Taisan brought *sumi* ink and a long piece of paper. Roshi knelt on the *tatami* and, using a large brush, did his vital *Mu!* calligraphy. It hangs above the altar, adding his wonderful energies to our *zazen*. Many Roshis, Senseis, Venerables, and students of various traditions have since sat in this *dojo*. All are welcome." —*Jill Jiryu Bart*
ADDRESS: 80 Pauls Lane, Water Mill, NY 11976
PHONE: (516) 537-1163
LINEAGE: Japanese Rinzai Zen
SPIRITUAL HEADS: All attending
CONTACT: Jill Jiryu Bart, Resident Teacher
AFFILIATION: The universe.
ESTABLISHED: Dedicated August 12, 1968, by Yasutani-Roshi, Soen-Roshi,

and the monk Taisan (now Eido-Roshi).
FACILITIES: Small *dojo* seating seven to ten.
MEDITATION PROGRAM: Two half-hour sittings, twice a week.

Long Island Sangha

For additional information, please see Community of Mindful Living, Berkeley, California.
ADDRESS: 10 Gail Court, Huntington, NY 11743
PHONE: (516) 427-9790
LINEAGE: Mindfulness practice in the tradition of Thich Nhat Hanh.
SPIRITUAL HEAD: Thich Nhat Hanh
CONTACT: Tonia Leon-Hysko
AFFILIATION: Community of Mindful Living, Berkeley, California
FACILITIES: The location rotates among members' homes.
MEDITATION PROGRAM: Sitting meditation one evening and one Saturday each month; practice for families and children.
RETREATS OFFERED: Occasional Days of Mindfulness shared with New York City Sangha.

Long Island Zen Center

Since 1976 Genshin Edgar and Rita Kann have dedicated part of their home as a permanent *zendo*. Genshin is an eighty-nine-year-old Zen monk lay-ordained by Joshu Sasaki-Roshi, senior monk of the Myoshinji branch of Rinzai Zen in Japan. Genshin has practiced under him since 1973.
ADDRESS: 6 Brewster Court, Setauket, NY 11733-1424
PHONE: (516) 751-8408
LINEAGE: Rinzai Zen
SPIRITUAL HEAD: Joshu Sasaki-Roshi
CONTACT: Genshin Edgar Kann, Resident Teacher

AFFILIATION: Rinzai-ji, Inc.
ESTABLISHED: 1976
FACILITIES: *Zendo* in private home.
MEDITATION PROGRAM: Formal Zen sittings three days a week. Discussion and study period after one of the sittings.
RETREATS OFFERED: Several formal weekend retreats per year. Call for schedule.

Lotus Flower Zendo

The *sangha* at Lotus Flower Zendo is comprised of prisoners who reside at Greenhaven Correctional Facility, a maximum-security prison in New York State. As an affiliate of Zen Mountain Monastery, we receive regular visits from monastic and lay practitioners who give dharma talks, lead retreats, and provide personal interviews. Our Wednesday meetings are devoted chiefly to sitting and walking meditation, but also include a short service of chanting and bowing. On Fridays, in addition to meditation, we have a training period consisting of body, liturgy, or art practice.
ADDRESS: Greenhaven Correctional Facility, Drawer B, Route 216, Stormville, NY 12582
LINEAGE: Soto Zen
SPIRITUAL HEAD: Abbot John Daido Loori, Sensei
AFFILIATION: Zen Mountain Monastery, Mt. Tremper, New York
ESTABLISHED: 1983
MEDITATION PROGRAM: *Zazen*, Wednesday mornings and Friday evenings for inmates and registered volunteer civilians.
RETREATS OFFERED: Four one-day intensive retreats per year; two-day *rohatsu sesshin* in December.

Lotus Peak Zendo

Since 1994, Lotus Peak Sangha has been meeting at Great Meadow Correctional

Jukai ceremony ("receiving the precepts"), Lotus Peak Zendo at Great Meadow Correctional Facility, near Lake George in New York State. (Photo courtesy of Dharma Communications.)

NEW YORK (*cont.*)

Facility, a maximum-security prison near Lake George, New York. Led by visiting lay students from Zen Mountain Monastery, the *sangha* offers weekly *zazen*, occasional half-day sitting intensives, and an annual Buddha's Birthday celebration. Lotus Peak Zendo is a wellspring of dedicated Zen practice, thriving within a particularly difficult environment.

ADDRESS: c/o Zen Mountain Monastery, PO Box 197, Mt. Tremper, NY 12457

PHONE: (914) 688-2228

FAX: (914) 688-2415

SPIRITUAL HEAD: Abbot John Daido Loori

CONTACT: Geoffrey Shugen Arnold

AFFILIATION: Zen Mountain Monastery

ESTABLISHED: 1994

FACILITIES: Zendo in maximum-security prison.

MEDITATION PROGRAM: Weekly *zazen*.

RETREATS OFFERED: Occasional half-day sitting intensives; annual Buddha's Birthday celebration.

Manhattan Won Buddhism

The Great Master So-Tae-San, the founder of Won Buddhism, stated in 1916, "As material civilization develops, cultivate spiritual civilization accordingly." Our spiritual evolution has not kept pace with our rapidly expanding scientific and economic advancements. Therefore, we must restore our spirituality, allowing it to grow in accordance with scientific and material progress. By cultivating spirituality in our daily lives, we will be led to a state of physical, mental, and emotional equilibrium, a state in which our Buddha Nature can be restored.

ADDRESS: 431 East 57th Street, New York, NY 10022

PHONE: (212) 750-2773

FAX: (212) 750-2774

E-MAIL: Chung_Ok_Lee@together.org

LINEAGE: Korean Won Buddhism

SPIRITUAL HEAD: Prime Master Chawsan

CONTACT: Ven. Dr. Sun Ok Lee, Resident Teacher

AFFILIATION: Zen Temple of Cresskill, New Jersey

ESTABLISHED: 1993

FACILITIES: Urban temple; meditation room; meeting room.

MEDITATION PROGRAM: Daily morning meditation; Sunday Dharma Service; Monday lunch-hour and evening meditations. Call to verify schedule.

RETREATS OFFERED: Four times yearly/seasonal.

New York Buddhist Church

The *sangha* members of New York Buddhist Church (NYBC) welcome you to join us in hearing, learning, and practicing the Buddha-Dharma. NYBC was founded by Rev. Hozen Seki with the assistance of his wife, Satomi, and concerned laypeople. It has been serving the New York community since 1938. May the Wisdom and Compassion of Amida Buddha touch your heart so that you may be awakened to the world of True Dharma with *Nembutsu*.

ADDRESS: 331–332 Riverside Drive, New York, NY 10025

PHONE: (212) 678-0305

FAX: (212) 662-4502

LINEAGE: Japanese Jodo Shin (Pure Land)

SPIRITUAL HEAD: Rev. Hakagaki Kenjitsu, Resident Teacher

AFFILIATION: Nishi-Hongwanji Temple, Kyoto, Japan

ESTABLISHED: 1938

FACILITIES: Temple, library, meditation room, lecture hall.

MEDITATION PROGRAM: The NYBC has

both beginner and regular meditation classes, which include chanting, walking, hearing, and insight. Sunday morning services. Call for times.

RETREATS OFFERED: Late spring and late fall.

PUBLICATIONS: Newsletter

Peaceful Dwelling Project

Peaceful Dwelling Project offers retreats for persons with chronic or life-threatening illnesses and those who care for them. The staff will travel anywhere to facilitate retreats or to train health care professionals in meditation techniques. The director, Madeline Ko-i Bastis, is a Zen priest and certified hospital chaplain who has worked at Memorial Sloan-Kettering Cancer Center and NYU Medical Center. She has led retreats for people with AIDS, psychiatric patients, health care professionals, and the general public. She is a Buddhist delegate to the Long Island Multi-Faith Forum.

ADDRESS: PO Box 3159, East Hampton, NY 11937-3097

PHONE: (516) 324-3736

FAX: Same

E-MAIL: peacefuldwell@hamptons.com

LINEAGE: Japanese Soto Zen

CONTACT: Rev. Madeline Ko-i Bastis, Resident Teacher

AFFILIATION: Zen Community of New York

ESTABLISHED: 1995

FACILITIES: Meditation studio on private property.

MEDITATION PROGRAM: Weekly evening meditation for local community. Weekly meditation meetings for emotionally disadvantaged adults and people who are HIV-positive.

RETREATS OFFERED: Ongoing retreats and workshops.

PUBLICATIONS: Quarterly newsletter.

Plain Water Practice

Plain Water Practice works toward a deep integration of personality and body work with Dogen Zenji's understanding that "when the moon goes down, my shadow becomes me."

ADDRESS: 2997 Route 44-55, Gardiner, NY 12525

PHONE: (914) 255-2918

LINEAGE: Japanese Soto Zen

SPIRITUAL HEADS: The late Taizan Hakuyu Maezumi-Roshi and Bernard Tetsugen Glassman-Roshi

CONTACT: Helen Yuho Harkaspi, Sensei

AFFILIATION: White Plum Sangha Zen Buddhist Association of America

ESTABLISHED: 1992

FACILITIES: Teacher's home, Poughkeepsie Unitarian Church, Grail Retreat House.

RETREATS OFFERED: Three times per year.

Reed Street Sangha

For additional information, please see Community of Mindful Living, Berkeley, California.

ADDRESS: 110 Reed Street, #2, New York, NY 10013

PHONE: (212) 732-4921

LINEAGE: Mindfulness practice in the tradition of Thich Nhat Hanh.

SPIRITUAL HEAD: Thich Nhat Hanh

CONTACT: Phyllis Joyner

AFFILIATION: Community of Mindful Living, Berkeley, California

MEDITATION PROGRAM: We meet weekly for sitting, walking, and chanting.

Rochester Zen Center

Rochester Zen Center celebrated its thirtieth anniversary in June 1996. It was founded by Roshi Philip Kapleau who, along with Robert Aitken-Roshi, is con-

Rock gardens and outdoor meditation path at Rochester Zen Center, Rochester, New York. (Photo by David Sachter.)

NEW YORK (*cont.*)

sidered one of the two elders of American Zen. In 1986, Sensei Bodhin Kjolhede was designated Roshi's Dharma Successor and the center's Resident Director. Under Sensei's guidance, the center offers daily meditation, extended Zen retreats, a full-time staff program, residential training programs, and regular introductory workshops. We're open almost all year-round.

ADDRESS: 7 Arnold Park, Rochester, NY 14607
PHONE: (716) 473-9180
FAX: (716) 473-6846
LINEAGE: Integral Zen (Soto/Rinzai, Harada-Yasutani line)
SPIRITUAL HEAD: Philip Kapleau-Roshi, Founder/Advisor
CONTACT: Sensei Bodhin Kjolhede, Spiritual Director
AFFILIATION: Autonomous
ESTABLISHED: 1966
FACILITIES: Urban meditation center.
MEDITATION PROGRAM: Morning meditation with chanting six days a week. Two-hour evening meditation four days a week.
RETREATS OFFERED: Monthly seven-, four-, or two-day Zen *sesshin*. One-day sittings five or six times a year.
PUBLICATIONS: *Zen Bow*, quarterly journal; *Zen Arrow*, local *sangha* newsletter.

Sagaponack Zendo

No description available.
ADDRESS: PO Box 392, Sagaponack, NY 11962
LINEAGE: Japanese Soto Zen
SPIRITUAL HEAD: Ishin Muryo, Sensei
AFFILIATION: Zen Community of New York
ESTABLISHED: 1984
FACILITIES: *Zendo* only.
MEDITATION PROGRAM: Morning *zazen*, four times weekly. Saturday morning

service and *zazen*. Weekly afternoon discussion group.
RETREATS OFFERED: Monthly *zazenkai*.

Saratoga Center for Meditation and Mindful Living

For additional information, please see Community of Mindful Living, Berkeley, California.
ADDRESS: 11 Marion Place, Saratoga Springs, NY 12866
PHONE: (518) 587-2667
LINEAGE: Mindfulness practice in the tradition of Thich Nhat Hanh.
SPIRITUAL HEAD: Thich Nhat Hanh
CONTACT: Kathryn Tracy
AFFILIATION: Community of Mindful Living, Berkeley, California
MEDITATION PROGRAM: We meet one Sunday morning of each month for sitting and walking meditation, precept recitation, and a children's program.

Soho Zendo

No description available.
ADDRESS: 464 West Broadway, New York, NY 10012
PHONE: (212) 460-9289
LINEAGE: Zen

Village Zendo

Our koan: "How can we facilitate vigorous Zen practice for people living and working in New York City?" We offer flexible *zazen* times (join us during *kinhin*), regular interviews, Friday night study group, Saturday retreats, "sandwich retreats" (two weekends and "drop-in *zazen*" during the week), and quarterly weeklong *sesshin*. In the midst of buzzing doorbells and street sounds, we practice a meticulous form in our *zazen*, services, and *oryoki*. We offer weekly meditation at Gay Men's Health Crisis, scholarships for

people with HIV/AIDS, and ad hoc care for those in need.
ADDRESS: 15 Washington Place, #4E, New York City, NY 10003
PHONE: (212) 674-0832
FAX: (212) 998-1899
E-MAIL: ohara@ls.nyu.edu
LINEAGE: Japanese Soto Zen
SPIRITUAL HEAD: Bernard Glassman-Roshi
CONTACT: Rev. Pat Enkyo O'Hara
AFFILIATION: Zen Community of New York
ESTABLISHED: 1986
FACILITIES: Zendo; longer retreats at rented facilities.
RETREATS OFFERED: Monthly *zazenkai* quarterly; weeklong *sesshin*.
PUBLICATIONS: *Village Zendo*, newsletter.

West 86th Street Sangha

For additional information, please see Community of Mindful Living, Berkeley, California.
ADDRESS: 115 West 86th Street, #9B, New York, NY 10024
PHONE: (212) 873-3142
LINEAGE: Mindfulness practice in the tradition of Thich Nhat Hanh.
SPIRITUAL HEAD: Thich Nhat Hanh
CONTACT: Amy Krantz
AFFILIATION: Community of Mindful Living, Berkeley, California
MEDITATION PROGRAM: We meet for guided meditation one evening a week.

West 97th Street Sangha

For additional information, please see Community of Mindful Living, Berkeley, California.
ADDRESS: 311 West 97th Street, #6E, New York, NY 10025
PHONE: (212) 666-4104
LINEAGE: Mindfulness practice in the tradition of Thich Nhat Hanh.
SPIRITUAL HEAD: Thich Nhat Hanh

CONTACT: David Flint
AFFILIATION: Community of Mindful Living, Berkeley, California
MEDITATION PROGRAM: One evening each week we meet for sitting and a short reading.

Westchester, Rockland, and Fairfield Counties Mindfulness Group

For additional information, please see Community of Mindful Living, Berkeley, California.
ADDRESS: Box 0089, Maryknoll, NY 10545
PHONE: (914) 762-9097
LINEAGE: Mindfulness practice in the tradition of Thich Nhat Hanh.
SPIRITUAL HEAD: Thich Nhat Hanh
CONTACTS: Sally and Eric Taylor
AFFILIATION: Community of Mindful Living, Berkeley, California
FACILITIES: The location alternates between Bailey Farm in Millwood and Hunt Farm in Waccabuc.
RETREATS OFFERED: We meet one Sunday each month for a Day of Mindfulness that includes sitting, indoor and outdoor walking meditation, readings, precept recitation, discussions, and a potluck meal.

Zen Center of New York City

"May we exist in muddy water, with purity like a lotus." At our center, the noise of sirens mixes with the gentle spirals of incense smoke as practitioners come together after work to sit and study the heart of what their lives are about. The tenth-floor *zendo* is both warm and raw; a bank of tall windows brings the hard-edged reality of the cityscape into each *zazen* period, yet the honey-toned hardwood floors, dimmed lights, and serious intention create a sense of private and deep work and support a life that is honest, clear, and kind.
ADDRESS: 119 West 23rd Street, #1009, New York, NY 10011
PHONE: (212) 642-1591
WWW: http://www1.mhv.net/~dharmacom/nycfire.htm
LINEAGE: Soto/Rinzai Zen (Mountains and Rivers Order)
SPIRITUAL HEAD: Roshi John Daido Loori
CONTACT: Sensei Bonnie Myotai Treace
AFFILIATION: The Mountains and Rivers Order
ESTABLISHED: 1984
FACILITIES: Urban retreat center, bookstore.
RETREATS OFFERED: *Zazenkai*; three-month *Ango* training; introduction to Zen retreat; Zen arts, environmental, and academic retreats.
PUBLICATIONS: *Fire Lotus Newsletter*

Zen Center of Syracuse, Inc./Hoen-ji

In 1972 a few graduate students at Syracuse University began doing *zazen* together in a small room on campus. The following year they invited Eido Shimano-Roshi to visit and dedicate the center. Our teacher, the Rev. Roko Sherry Chayat, came to Syracuse in 1976 from Eido's monastery in the Catskills, Dai Bosatsu Zendo, where she had been codirector. Hoen-ji has grown steadily since then, drawing people of all ages from all over upstate New York. In addition to its *zendo*-based programs, the center offers meditation instruction at rehabilitation centers, corporations, health centers, and schools.
ADDRESS: 111 Concord Place, Syracuse, NY 13210
PHONE: (315) 478-1253
FAX: Same
LINEAGE: Japanese Rinzai Zen
SPIRITUAL HEAD: The Rev. Roko Sherry Chayat, Resident Teacher
AFFILIATION: No formal affiliation but close spiritual link with Dai Bosatsu Zendo
ESTABLISHED: 1972
FACILITIES: Urban center: third floor of

Sutra chanting on a Thursday night at Zen Center of Syracuse. (Photo by Christian Sunde.)

NEW YORK (*cont.*)

teacher's house converted to formal *zendo* seating twenty-six.

RETREATS OFFERED: Spring/fall three-day retreats held at Alverna Heights, run by the Sisters of St. Francis; weeklong at Dai Bosatsu Zendo.

PUBLICATIONS: *Hoen-ji News*, quarterly newsletter.

Zen Community of New York

Zen Community of New York (ZCNY) functions as the spiritual core of the Greyston Mandala, which consists of community-building organizations such as Greyston Family Inn, Greyston Bakery, Greyston Health Services, and Pamsula Patchwork and Sewing. ZCNY's ministry consists primarily of social action work. Many retreats are held on the street with the homeless population or in the local community, bearing witness to the social and economic problems that exist in society today. Tetsugen Glassman-Roshi and Sensei Jishu Holmes are currently forming a Zen Peacemaker order, promoting initiatives for social change that are grounded in Buddhist teachings and practice.

ADDRESS: 14 Ashburton Place, Yonkers, NY 10703

PHONE: (914) 376-3900

FAX: (914) 376-1333

E-MAIL: jishusan@aol.com

LINEAGE: White Plum lineage

SPIRITUAL HEADS: Bernard Tetsugen Glassman Roshi and Sandra Jishu Holmes, Sensei

AFFILIATION: Autonomous

ESTABLISHED: 1979

FACILITIES: Meditation space situated in southwest Yonkers.

MEDITATION PROGRAM: Daily *zazen* and private interviews. Weekend program with liturgy service.

RETREATS OFFERED: Street retreats; Bearing Witness retreats.

Zen Dharma Community

Through the practice of loving-kindness, compassion, and mindfulness, the *sangha* realizes that every moment is an opportunity for awakening. We view *zazen* as a way to imbue our lives with spiritual immediacy and as a foundation for engagement with the world. It's a practice for those who consider themselves Buddhists as well as for those who do not.

ADDRESS: 1807 Elmwood Avenue, Buffalo, NY 14207

PHONE: (716) 634-1812

LINEAGE: Soto Zen, founded by Dogen in the thirteenth century.

SPIRITUAL HEAD: Ven. James Kozen Dodson, Resident Director

AFFILIATION: Autonomous

MEDITATION PROGRAM: *Zazen*, classes, counseling, retreats, *sesshin*, weddings, funerals, and an opportunity to become involved in projects that assist others.

Zen Mountain Monastery

From its improbable beginning as a tiny *sangha* huddling through its first winter in an unheated *zendo*, Zen Mountain Monastery has grown to become one of the premier Zen practice centers in the country, providing an authentic, traditional, yet distinctly American Zen training. Located amidst the scenic splendor of Catskill State Park, the monastery's 235 acres unfold gently within the southern bowl of Tremper Mountain. Hundreds of people throughout the world are formal students of the Mountains and Rivers Order, the international umbrella organization for groups, centers, and temples associated with the monastery.

ADDRESS: PO Box 197, South Plank Road, Mt. Tremper, NY 12457

PHONE: (914) 688-2228

Zen Mountain Monastery in Mt. Tremper, New York. (Photo by Dharma Communications.)

Ask Cybermonk

DHARMA COMMUNICATIONS IS THE EDUCA-tional outreach arm of Zen Mountain Monastery. On the verge of the twenty-first century, this organization surfs the wave of today's expanding technological envelope to send nourishing images and words to a global audience. Using its broadcast-quality audio, video, and editing production studios and its state-of-the-art publication facilities, Dharma Communications supports the vitality of spiritual practice by using the powerful tools of communication to heal, inform, and encourage the cultivation of awareness and self-empowerment.

Its quarterly magazine, *Mountain Record: The Practitioner's Journal*, features over one hundred pages of articles on the interface of Zen with art, science, ecology, ethics, psychology, and social action. Each issue presents dharma words from modern American Zen masters, translations of some of the greatest teachings of the Zen tradition, media reviews, and high-quality photography.

Dharma Communications' catalogue offers a wide variety of audio- and videotapes (including an Introduction to Zen Meditation), as well as books, sitting and altar supplies, art practice sets, and Buddha figures.

Dharma Communications is especially sensitive to the needs of practitioners who do not have ongoing access to teachers and centers. To that end it furnishes extensive on-line services. "Cybermonk," for example, provides a senior student to answer e-mailed questions about Zen practice. The World Wide Web site contains information on Zen Mountain Monastery, its calendar of events and retreat schedules, instruction in *zazen*, relevant articles on Zen training, updates on affiliate groups, an electronic journal, a Zen arts gallery, information on ecology programs, and more. For more information, you can contact Dharma Communications at *dharmacom@mhv.net*, or see our Web site at *http://www1.mhv.net/~dharmacom*. You can talk to Cybermonk at *cybermonk@mhv.net*.

For more information, contact: Dharma Communications, P.O. Box 156, Mt. Tremper, NY 12457; (914) 688-7993.

FAX: (914) 688-2415
E-MAIL: dharmacom@mhv.net
WWW: http://www1.mhv.net/
   ~dharmacom
LINEAGE: Japanese Soto/Rinzai (Mountains and Rivers Order)
SPIRITUAL HEAD: John Daido Loori-Roshi, Resident Teacher
AFFILIATION: We are Headquarters, Mountains and Rivers Order.
ESTABLISHED: 1980
FACILITIES: Country retreat facility.
RETREATS OFFERED: Twelve *sesshin*; two ninety-day training intensives per year;

Zen arts, environmental, and academic retreats.
PUBLICATIONS: *Zen Mountain Record*

The Zen Studies Society/Dai Bosatsu Zendo Kongo-ji

The Zen Studies Society was established in 1956 to assist Dr. D. T. Suzuki in his efforts to introduce Zen Buddhism to the West. In 1965 it came under the leadership of Eido Tai Shimano, a Japanese Zen monk who shifted the emphasis towards

zazen practice. Dai Bosatsu Zendo Kongo-ji is located three hours from New York City on Beecher Lake, in the midst of fourteen hundred acres of Catskill Mountain wilderness. It offers an ideal setting for Zen practice for both laypeople and ordained monks and nuns. Guests are welcome to visit the monastery throughout the year.
ADDRESS: HCR 1, Box 171,
   Livingston Manor, NY 12758-9732
PHONE: (914) 439-4566
FAX: (914) 439-3119
LINEAGE: Japanese Rinzai Zen

The National Buddhist Prison Sangha

THERE ARE THOUSANDS OF INMATES ACROSS THE United States who are seeking to engage in Buddhist practice, and yet, because of the constraints due to their incarceration, they have little or no source of support or instruction. There are currently no Buddhist chaplains, so we, the larger *sangha*, provide the only direct means to help these inmates discover and develop their practice.

Zen Mountain Monastery (ZMM) is compiling a National Volunteers List of Buddhist practitioners interested in working with inmates at facilities in their area. We invite you to become a part of this list. The way it will be used is simple: as we receive letters from inmates seeking guidance and support, we will use the list to connect an inmate with a volunteer in their area. Our staff will also be available to offer ongoing instruction and guidance to volunteers.

Due to the tense environment that exists in most prisons, and given the special needs of Buddhist inmates, it is important that volunteers be mature individuals with at least five years of practice experience under the guidance of an authorized Buddhist teacher at a formal training center.

ZMM has been actively involved in prison outreach since the early 1980s. We have a trained staff of senior practitioners who make regular visits to several New York State correctional facilities, helping to lead sessions of meditation, liturgy, classes in basic Buddhist teachings, and religious services for Buddhist holidays. In addition, we respond to hundreds of letters each year from inmates across the country, sending them donated Buddhist books, periodicals, taped talks, and other materials. We also function as an advisor on Buddhist activities to the Commissioner of Ministerial Services for the New York State correctional system.

Geoffrey Shugen Arnold

For more information, contact: The National Buddhist Prison Sangha, Geoffrey Shugen Arnold, Coordinator, Zen Mountain Monastery, Box 197 South Plank Road, Mt. Tremper, NY 12457; (914) 688-2228.

SPIRITUAL HEAD: Ven. Eido T. Shimano-Roshi, Abbot

CONTACT: Jiro-san Andy Afable, General Manager

AFFILIATION: Zen Studies Society

ESTABLISHED: 1976

FACILITIES: Zen monastery and country retreat facility.

MEDITATION PROGRAM: *Kessei/Ango* residents follow a rigorous daily schedule of *zazen*, chanting services, work practice, and formal vegetarian meals.

RETREATS OFFERED: Twice yearly three-month training period; three-, five-, and seven-day *sesshin*; introductory workshops.

PUBLICATIONS: *The Newsletter of the Zen Studies Society*

The Zen Studies Society/New York Zendo Shobo-ji

Shobo-ji celebrated its twenty-fifth anniversary in 1993 as a vital Zen practice center in the heart of New York City. Located on Manhattan's Upper East Side, New York Zendo provides urban people an opportunity for authentic Zen training. For additional information, please see Zen Studies Society/Dai Bosatsu Zendo Kongo-ji.

ADDRESS: 223 East 67th Street, New York, NY 10021-6087

PHONE: (212) 861-3333

FAX: (212) 628-6968

LINEAGE: Japanese Rinzai Zen

SPIRITUAL HEAD: Ven. Eido T. Shimano-Roshi, Abbot

CONTACT: Aiho-san Y. Shimano, Executive Director

AFFILIATION: Zen Studies Society

ESTABLISHED: 1968

FACILITIES: "An elegant ground-floor *zendo* and serene stone garden refresh the eye and epitomize Zen spirit."

MEDITATION PROGRAM: Open five days weekly; evening *zazen*; Tuesday after-

Front view of Dai Bosatsu Zendo Kongo-ji in Livingston Manor, New York. (Photo by Sangen Akihiro Tanaka.)

Eido Shimano Roshi at New York Zendo Shobo-ji, New York City. (Photo by Stephen Ferry.)

noon *zazen*; Saturday morning chanting; Thursday night beginner's program; Buddhist study classes; special events and ceremonies.

RETREATS OFFERED: All-day sittings; weekend *sesshin*.

PUBLICATIONS: *The Newsletter of the Zen Studies Society*

NORTH CAROLINA

Celo Community Sangha

For additional information, please see Community of Mindful Living, Berkeley, California.

ADDRESS: 278 White Oak Creek Road, Burnsville, NC 28714
PHONE: (704) 675-4626
LINEAGE: Mindfulness practice in the tradition of Thich Nhat Hanh.
SPIRITUAL HEAD: Thich Nhat Hanh
CONTACTS: Herb and Marnie Walters
AFFILIATION: Community of Mindful Living, Berkeley, California
MEDITATION PROGRAM: We meet once a week for walking meditation and other mindfulness practices.
RETREATS OFFERED: Order member Herb Walters leads extended Living Earth Meditation Retreats.

Chapel Hill Zen Group

Chapel Hill Zen Group (CHZG) was established by a small group of friends who took turns having meetings in their homes. In the spring of 1991 we asked San Francisco Zen Center (SFZC) to send Taitaku Patricia Phelan to lead the group. (Pat trained at the SFZC and Tassajara from 1971 to 1991.) Members of CHZG have formed a Zen group at the University of North Carolina that meets for *zazen* weekly in the Student Union. Our priest visits Ekoji Buddhist *Sangha* four times a year.

ADDRESS: PO Box 16302, Chapel Hill, NC 27516

PHONE: (919) 967-0861

LINEAGE: Japanese Soto Zen

CONTACT: Taitaku Pat Phelan, Priest and Resident Teacher

AFFILIATION: San Francisco Zen Center

ESTABLISHED: 1981

FACILITIES: Permanent meeting place at 5322 NC Highway 86, Chapel Hill. *Zendo*, kitchen, library, dorm, and priest's office.

RETREATS OFFERED: Monthly all-day meditation intensive; yearly two- and five-day *sesshin*.

PUBLICATIONS: Monthly newsletter.

Charlotte Community of Mindfulness

"As we walk in meditation outside, beneath azure skies and deep green magnolia leaves, even the earth and sky support our practice." For additional information, please see Community of Mindful Living, Berkeley, California.

ADDRESS: 14200 Fountain Lane, Charlotte, NC 28278

PHONE: (704) 588-1413

FAX: (704) 583-1279

E-MAIL: LCRawls@aol.com

LINEAGE: Mindfulness practice in the tradition of Thich Nhat Hanh.

SPIRITUAL HEAD: Thich Nhat Hanh

CONTACT: Leslie Rawls

AFFILIATION: Community of Mindful Living, Berkeley, California

MEDITATION PROGRAM: We meet one evening and one morning a week for sitting, walking, and dharma discussion.

RETREATS OFFERED: Day of Mindfulness and precept recitations on one Saturday of each month.

Charlotte Zen Meditation Society

No description available.

ADDRESS: PO Box 32512, Charlotte, NC 28232

PHONE: (704) 523-7373

LINEAGE: Soto Zen

AFFILIATION: Autonomous

ESTABLISHED: 1990

FACILITIES: Rented sitting space.

MEDITATION PROGRAM: *Shikantaza* sittings three days per week.

RETREATS OFFERED: Usually two long weekend *sesshin* per year.

PUBLICATIONS: *CZMS News*

Cullowhee Zen Group

We meet every Monday evening for *zazen.* Once a month Zen Priest Teijo Munnich facilitates a reading and discussion.

ADDRESS: Route 67, Box 61, Cullowhee, NC 28723

PHONE: (704) 293-5832

E-MAIL: ld10341@wcu.edu

LINEAGE: Soto Zen

SPIRITUAL HEAD: Teijo Munnich

AFFILIATION: Zen Center of Asheville, Asheville, North Carolina

ESTABLISHED: 1996

FACILITIES: Rented church basement.

MEDITATION PROGRAM: Weekly *zazen* and monthly reading and discussion. Call for times.

Durham Unitarian Universalist Buddhist Meditation Group

We meet one evening a week for sitting and walking meditation, reading, discussion, and practice support. There's also tea and cookie meditation, discussions about mindfulness and parenting, and *metta* meditation. The Unitarian Fellowship, where our group meets, holds monthly precept recitation ceremonies led by the senior minister. Participants

include members from our *sangha* and others from the larger fellowship. For additional information, please see Community of Mindful Living, Berkeley, California.

ADDRESS: 4907 Garrett Road, Durham, NC 27704

PHONE: (919) 220-0321

E-MAIL: warre016@mc.duke.edu

LINEAGE: Mindfulness practice in the tradition of Thich Nhat Hanh.

SPIRITUAL HEAD: Thich Nhat Hanh

CONTACT: Kim Warren

AFFILIATION: Community of Mindful Living, Berkeley, California

FACILITIES: Eno River Unitarian Universalist Fellowship

MEDITATION PROGRAM: Weekly meditation.

Mountain Zen Group

No description available.

ADDRESS: 18 Eola Avenue, Asheville, NC 28806-1812

PHONE: (704) 253-4621

FAX: Same

LINEAGE: Soto Zen

SPIRITUAL HEAD: Chere Huber

CONTACT: Chris Larson, Guide

ESTABLISHED: 1992

FACILITIES: Not yet.

Piedmont Zen Group

The Piedmont Zen Group meets regularly three times a week for the group practice of Zen meditation. Basic instruction in Zen practice for beginners is available.

ADDRESS: 3805 Greenleaf Street, Raleigh, NC 27606-2028

PHONE: (919) 833-6200

LINEAGE: Soto and Rinzai Zen

CONTACT: Bob Shuman

AFFILIATION: Autonomous

ESTABLISHED: 1984

FACILITIES: Half of a small house.

MEDITATION PROGRAM: Group *zazen* practice three times a week. Please call for times.

Squirrel Mountain Zendo—North Carolina Zen Center

The crash of hickory nuts bouncing off the *zendo*'s tin roof is one sound that clarifies our Buddha nature at Squirrel Mountain. We're located in a hardwood forest a half-hour's drive from Chapel Hill, where we do walking meditation outside and the meadow serves as a dormitory for weekend gatherings. Sandy Gentei Stewart-Osho, a Zen teacher for twenty-five years, trained with Joshu Sasaki-Roshi, and was on Elisabeth Kubler-Ross's staff.

> Squirreling away
> time after time we gather
> *zendo* full of nuts

ADDRESS: 283 Quartz Hill Road, Pittsboro, NC 27312-8509
PHONE: (919) 542-4234
LINEAGE: Japanese Rinzai Zen
SPIRITUAL HEAD: Sandy Gentei Stewart, Resident Teacher
AFFILIATION: Autonomous
ESTABLISHED: 1974
FACILITIES: Country *zendo* and twelve acres of land for future residential center.
MEDITATION PROGRAM: Daily morning sittings. Evening sittings twice weekly. Sunday morning program.
RETREATS OFFERED: Fall and spring Zen weekends.

Zen Center of Asheville/ Magnanimous Mind Temple

Zen Center of Asheville is a small but growing center with an active *sangha* of approximately twenty people who come regularly to sittings and other events. The center is partially supported by pledges and donations. Much of the care of the facility—mowing grounds and cleaning the *zendo*—is done by *sangha* members.
ADDRESS: PO Box 17274, Asheville, NC 28816-7274
PHONE: (704) 253-2314
LINEAGE: Japanese Soto Zen
SPIRITUAL HEAD: Teijo Munnich, Resident Teacher
AFFILIATION: Autonomous
ESTABLISHED: 1995
FACILITIES: Small house with two-room *zendo*.
MEDITATION PROGRAM: Ongoing schedule of morning and evening sittings; family meditation; a dozen study groups.
RETREATS OFFERED: Monthly daylong sittings; weekend retreat in December; seven-day retreat over New Year's.

OHIO

Cincinnati Sangha

For additional information, please refer to Community of Mindful Living, Berkeley, California.
ADDRESS: 700 Berkshire Lane, Cincinnati, OH 45220
PHONE: (513) 221-1382
LINEAGE: Mindfulness practice in the tradition of Thich Nhat Hanh.
SPIRITUAL HEAD: Thich Nhat Hanh
CONTACTS: Deborah and Keith Andrews
AFFILIATION: Community of Mindful Living, Berkeley, California
MEDITATION PROGRAM: We practice mindful sitting and walking together and discuss the writings of Thich Nhat Hanh.

Cleveland Heights Sangha

For additional information, please refer to Community of Mindful Living, Berkeley, California.
ADDRESS: 2188 Chatfield, Cleveland Heights, OH 44106
PHONE: (216) 932-0579
LINEAGE: Mindfulness practice in the tradition of Thich Nhat Hanh.
SPIRITUAL HEAD: Thich Nhat Hanh
CONTACT: Donna Kwilosz
AFFILIATION: Community of Mindful Living, Berkeley, California
MEDITATION PROGRAM: We meet monthly for meditation, precept recitation, and discussion.

CloudWater Zendo

CloudWater Zendo was established to make Zen and Pure Land teachings available to all. Sunday Dharma Services are held twice a month and meditation practice is conducted four times weekly. Working people's *sesshin*, one-day intensives, monthly lectures on Buddhist teachings and practice, observances of Buddhist holidays, and instruction in Tai Chi and Japanese Tea Ceremony are also offered. The Resident Dharma Instructor is Mike Shu Ho Bonasso, senior student of Rev. Koshin Ogui, Sensei, of Chicago.
ADDRESS: 21562 Lorain Road, Fairview Park, OH 44126
PHONE: (216) 331-8374
E-MAIL: clevezen@aol.com
WWW: http://www.ssp-ii.com/ssp/ Allfaiths/CWZ
LINEAGE: Zen Shin lineage
SPIRITUAL HEAD: Rev. Koshin Ogui, Sensei
CONTACT: Shaku Mike Shu Ho Bonasso, Resident Teacher
AFFILIATION: Autonomous
ESTABLISHED: 1994
FACILITIES: Zendo, dharma hall.
MEDITATION PROGRAM: Zen meditation practice, two evenings and two mornings weekly.

RETREATS OFFERED: Weekend retreats twice yearly; quarterly *sesshin*.

PUBLICATIONS: *Clouds & Water*, quarterly newsletter.

Columbus Zen Corner

Columbus Zen Corner is comprised of individuals who have studied with different teachers and who seek the support of a Zen *sangha* for their established practice. Also among our members are a number of beginners to the path. The group's intention is either to have a teacher in residence, or to be associated with one who would visit periodically to give regular retreats and ongoing training.

ADDRESS: 1954 Indianola Avenue, Columbus, OH 43215

PHONE: (614) 291-2331

LINEAGE: Zen

CONTACT: Wayne Cossin, Director

ESTABLISHED: 1996

MEDITATION PROGRAM: Sittings twice weekly.

RETREATS OFFERED: Occasional half-day sittings.

Toledo Sangha

New and experienced meditators are always welcome. For additional information, please refer to Community of Mindful Living, Berkeley, California.

ADDRESS: 5102 Pickfair Drive, Toledo, OH 43615

PHONE: (419) 534-3063

E-MAIL: jim.lynn@sylvania.sev.org

LINEAGE: Mindfulness practice in the tradition of Thich Nhat Hanh.

SPIRITUAL HEAD: Thich Nhat Hanh

CONTACT: Lynn Lyle

AFFILIATION: Community of Mindful Living, Berkeley, California

FACILITIES: Members' homes.

MEDITATION PROGRAM: We meet for evening meditation twice a month.

RETREATS OFFERED: Day of Mindfulness is held quarterly.

Udumbara Sangha—Cleveland

For additional information, please see Udumbara Zen Center, Evanston, Illinois.

ADDRESS: c/o Department of Religion, Cleveland State University, 1983 East 24th, Cleveland, OH 44115

PHONE: (216) 221-2534

LINEAGE: Japanese Soto (Suzuki-Roshi and Katagiri-Roshi)

SPIRITUAL HEAD: Diane Martin

CONTACT: Ed Brennan

AFFILIATION: Udumbara Zen Center, Evanston, Illinois

PUBLICATIONS: *Central Flower*, quarterly newsletter.

Zen Shin Sangha

Zen Shin Sangha was founded by Sensei Koshin Ogui, an eighteenth-generation Shin minister who worked with Zen masters in Japan and San Francisco before coming to Cleveland. Sensei now resides in Chicago but returns to Cleveland six times a year to conduct services and meditation practice. Each spring, Zen Shin Sangha hosts all the Buddhist groups in the area for a Buddha's Birthday celebration complete with potluck dinner. Dennis, one of our members, defined us this way: "We are an urban guerrilla group with no mountain retreats or extremely long sittings."

ADDRESS: 1573 East 214th Street, Cleveland, OH 44117

PHONE: (216) 692-6509

FAX: (216) 692-2012

LINEAGE: Japanese Zen/Shin

SPIRITUAL HEAD: Koshin Ogui, Sensei

CONTACTS: Mary Gove and Craig Horton

AFFILIATION: Buddhist Churches of America

ESTABLISHED: 1980

FACILITIES: Cleveland Buddhist Temple

MEDITATION PROGRAM: Weekly, introductory classes and evening meditation; Tai Chi; Chi Gong; Yoga; Universal Peace dances.

RETREATS OFFERED: Three- to five-day *sesshin*, sittings mornings and evenings, work/school in between; Naikan workshops and retreats.

PUBLICATIONS: *ZenShin*

OKLAHOMA

Chau Tam Bao Temple

No description available.

ADDRESS: 16933 East 21st Street, Tulsa, OK 74108

PHONE: (918) 438-0714

E-MAIL: bma14432@vax1.utulsa.edu

LINEAGE: Vietnamese

CONTACTS: Ky Nguyen or Mark Brudnak

AFFILIATION: Autonomous

Oklahoma City Zen Group

No description available.

ADDRESS: 5305 North Walker, Oklahoma City, OK 73118

PHONE: (405) 840-4203

LINEAGE: Japanese Soto Zen

SPIRITUAL HEAD: Robert Livingston-Roshi

CONTACT: Carissa Bish

AFFILIATION: American Zen Association/ New Orleans Zen Temple

ESTABLISHED: 1996

FACILITIES: Members' homes.

MEDITATION PROGRAM: Several *zazen* sessions weekly.

RETREATS OFFERED: Occasional

PUBLICATIONS: See New Orleans Zen Temple.

OREGON

Corvallis Zen Circle

Zazen, walking meditation, a reading, and chanting of the Four Great Vows. All are welcome. Orientation is by appointment.

ADDRESS: 111 Northwest Second Street, Corvallis, OR 97330
PHONE: (541) 754-4124
LINEAGE: Zen
CONTACT: Abby
AFFILIATION: Autonomous
MEDITATION PROGRAM: *Zazen*, weekly. Call for time.

Dharma Rain Zen Center

The people of Dharma Rain Zen Center have come together to share meditation practice, study Buddhist principles, and function as a community of support for practice in everyday life. We offer a full array of classes, workshops, meditation periods, and ceremonies. All activities take place in one of two structures: a two-story church building, which houses a large meditation hall, lecture room, and institutional kitchen; and Center House, where a small meditation room, library, office, residences, meeting rooms, and a children's Dharma School are located. The buildings are situated within a block of one another in central Southeast Portland.

ADDRESS: 2539 Southeast Madison Street, Portland, OR 97214
PHONE: (503) 239-4846
E-MAIL: Kyogen@msn.com
LINEAGE: Japanese Soto Zen
SPIRITUAL HEADS: Gyokuko and Kyogen Carlson, Resident Teachers
AFFILIATION: We are a headquarters center.
ESTABLISHED: 1973
FACILITIES: *Zendo* building and residence/office house.

RETREATS OFFERED: Several one- to five-day retreats per year.
PUBLICATIONS: *Still Point Newsletter*

Eugene Buddhist Priory

Eugene Buddhist Priory is an affiliated temple of Shasta Abbey, Headquarters of the Order of Buddhist Contemplatives. Located in Northern California, Shasta Abbey is a Buddhist monastery and seminary in the Serene Reflection Meditation tradition. It was founded in 1970 by Rev. Master Jiyu-Kennett who, until her death in 1996, served as Abbess and Head of the Order of Buddhist Contemplatives. Buddhist training within the order is based upon the practice of Serene Reflection meditation, the keeping of the Buddhist Precepts, and the integration of meditation and Buddhist teaching with daily life.

ADDRESS: PO Box 5369, Eugene, OR 97405
PHONE: (541) 344-7377
LINEAGE: Soto Zen and Chinese Mahayana
SPIRITUAL HEAD: The late Rev. Master Jiyu-Kennett
CONTACT: Reverend Prior
AFFILIATION: Shasta Abbey, Headquarters of the Order of Buddhist Contemplatives
ESTABLISHED: 1973
FACILITIES: Buddhist temple.
RETREATS OFFERED: Yes
PUBLICATIONS: *Journal of the Order of Buddhist Contemplatives* (quarterly).

Eugene Sangha

For additional information, please refer to Community of Mindful Living, Berkeley, California.

ADDRESS: 2430 Cherry Grove Street, Eugene, OR 97403
PHONE: (503) 683-2127

LINEAGE: Mindfulness practice in the tradition of Thich Nhat Hanh.
SPIRITUAL HEAD: Thich Nhat Hanh
CONTACT: Bonnie Whittington
AFFILIATION: Community of Mindful Living, Berkeley, California
RETREATS OFFERED: We have a Day of Mindfulness on one Sunday each month in a beautiful country setting.

Eugene Zendo

"About a dozen people meet in my small house once a week for Evening Service, meditation, reading, discussion, and tea. We close the evening with a brief Vespers service. Kyogen Carlson-Sensei, Abbot of Dharma Rain Zen Center, participates in our activities on a monthly basis. Several of our members are involved in hospice and other types of community work. SAFE (Stop All Female Excision), a project aimed at educating African village girls, has its home in our group. We raise money to send girls from Burkina Faso to school." —*R. Getsushin Brox*

ADDRESS: 3480 Potter Street, Eugene, OR 97405
PHONE: (541) 341-1301
LINEAGE: Japanese Soto Zen
SPIRITUAL HEAD: Kyogen Carlson-Sensei
CONTACT: R. Getsushin Brox
AFFILIATION: Dharma Rain Zen Center, Portland, Oregon
ESTABLISHED: 1989
FACILITIES: Small *zendo* in private home.
RETREATS OFFERED: Retreats at least twice a year.

Independence Sangha

For additional information, please refer to Community of Mindful Living, Berkeley, California.

ADDRESS: 6810 Corvallis Road, Independence, OR 97351
PHONE: (503) 838-0182

OREGON (*cont.*)

LINEAGE: Mindfulness practice in the tradition of Thich Nhat Hanh.

SPIRITUAL HEAD: Thich Nhat Hanh

CONTACT: Jerry Braza

AFFILIATION: Community of Mindful Living, Berkeley, California

MEDITATION PROGRAM: We meet twice a month for meditation, tea, and dharma discussion.

Interfaith Meditation Group

For additional information, please refer to Community of Mindful Living, Berkeley, California.

ADDRESS: 123 West Ninth, Redmond, OR 97756

PHONE: (503) 548-0590

LINEAGE: Mindfulness practice in the tradition of Thich Nhat Hanh.

SPIRITUAL HEAD: Thich Nhat Hanh

CONTACT: Marion Tripp

AFFILIATION: Community of Mindful Living, Berkeley, California

MEDITATION PROGRAM: We meet one night a week in Bend and one night a week in Redmond for meditation.

RETREATS OFFERED: On the second Saturday of each month, we hold a Day of Mindfulness in Bend, Redmond, Sisters, or Tumalo. Occasional weekend retreats.

Portland Buddhist Priory

Portland Buddhist Priory is an affiliated temple of Shasta Abbey, Headquarters of the Order of Buddhist Contemplatives. Located in Northern California, Shasta Abbey is a Buddhist monastery and seminary in the Serene Reflection Meditation tradition. It was founded in 1970 by Rev. Master Jiyu-Kennett who, until her death in 1996, served as Abbess and Head of the Order of Buddhist Contemplatives. Buddhist training within the order is based upon the practice of Serene Reflection meditation, the keeping of the Buddhist Precepts, and the integration of meditation and Buddhist teaching with daily life.

ADDRESS: 3642 Southeast Milwaukee Avenue, Portland, OR 98558

PHONE: (503) 232-0508

LINEAGE: Soto Zen and Chinese Mahayana

SPIRITUAL HEAD: The late Rev. Master Jiyu-Kennett

CONTACT: Reverend Prior

AFFILIATION: Shasta Abbey, Headquarters of the Order of Buddhist Contemplatives

ESTABLISHED: 1973

FACILITIES: Urban temple.

RETREATS OFFERED: Yes

PUBLICATIONS: *Journal of the Order of Buddhist Contemplatives* (quarterly).

Portland Buddhist Temple

No description available.

ADDRESS: 1722 Southeast Madison, Portland, OR 97214

PHONE: (503) 239-5678

FAX: Same

LINEAGE: Taiwan/Chinese

SPIRITUAL HEAD: Hsin Tien

CONTACT: Kwang Ze, Resident Teacher

AFFILIATION: World Buddhism Preaching Association of USA

ESTABLISHED: 1988

Portland Community of Mindful Living

Katie Radditz facilitates a mindfulness group at the Unitarian church in response to interest in Thich Nhat Hanh's books. For additional information, please refer to Community of Mindful Living, Berkeley, California.

ADDRESS: 318 Southwest Taylor, Portland, OR 97204

PHONE: (503) 227-4760

FAX: (503) 227-0829

E-MAIL: lookglas@teleport.com

LINEAGE: Mindfulness practice in the tradition of Thich Nhat Hanh.

SPIRITUAL HEAD: Thich Nhat Hanh

CONTACT: Katie Radditz

AFFILIATION: Community of Mindful Living, Berkeley, California

FACILITIES: Unitarian church.

MEDITATION PROGRAM: We meet one evening a week for meditation and precept recitation.

Salem Zen Sitting Group

Sponsored by the Dharma Rain Zen Center, Salem Zen Sitting Group meets regularly for meditation and study.

ADDRESS: 490 19th Street NE, Salem, OR 97301

PHONE: (503) 623-8600

LINEAGE: Japanese Soto Zen

CONTACT: Jill Bakkai Washburn

AFFILIATION: Dharma Rain Zen Center of Portland

MEDITATION PROGRAM: Soto-style *zazen* one Saturday morning each month. Call for times.

Siskiyou Sansui Sangha

Siskiyou Sansui is a Soto Zen *sangha* for lay practice that meets regularly for meditation and dharma talk, practice discussion, *sesshin,* and special events. Our practice is based on the lineage of Shunryu Suzuki-Roshi. *Zazen* instruction is available and everyone is welcome.

ADDRESS: 777 East Main Street, Ashland, OR 97520

PHONE: (514) 488-0896

LINEAGE: Japanese Soto Zen based on Shunryu Suzuki lineage

CONTACTS: Patty or Harold

AFFILIATION: Autonomous

MEDITATION PROGRAM: *Zazen,* three mornings and one evening weekly; call for times.

Jizo Bodhisattva: Protector of Women and Children

JIZO-IN TEMPLE NEAR PORTLAND, OREGON, TAKES its name from Jizo Bodhisattva. In Japan, Jizo figures are traditionally placed at crossroads to guide those who travel in both the physical and spiritual realms. This bodhisattva has special significance to pregnant women and to those whose children have died. At our temple, his image is used during special ceremonies to honor children who have passed on.

Small sculptures of Jizo Bodhisattva, used to protect a sick child or to remember one who has died. (Photo by Ted Bagley.)

Kids in our *sangha* like to make their own home altars with small statues of Jizo Bodhisattva. However, these images are not worshiped, but are intended to help awaken the energy of compassion and care for women, children, and those who find themselves at a crossroads in life.

Jizo is usually portrayed as a child-monk, often carrying a pilgrim's ringed staff that jingles to warn animals of his approach and prevent mutual harm. He holds the "Wish-fulfilling Jewel of the Dharma" whose light banishes all fear. Jizo is also known as "Kshitagarbha the Earthstore Bodhisattva," guardian of the earth's life-sustaining and protecting energy in the form of water, soil, minerals, and plants. To honor this aspect, our temple planted an organic garden and has developed an educational program.

As a means of supporting the training at Jizo-In Temple, images of this bodhisattva are handmade by our students. These range in size from two-inch altar figures to eighteen-inch garden statues.

Jan Chozen Bays

For more information, contact: Zen Community of Oregon/ Larch Mountain Zen Center/Jizo-In Temple, PO Box 310, Corbett, OR 97109; (503) 695-2103.

Zen Community of Oregon/Larch Mountain Zen Center

The program at Zen Community of Oregon emphasizes practice in daily life and allows students to participate as much or as little as they wish, while holding jobs and taking care of family responsibilities. The local *sangha* is diverse and includes people who work in art, music, sales, medicine, research, education, therapy, ceramics, construction, computers, architecture, law, tree planting, statistics, and bookstores. The teacher and her husband were ordained by the late Maezumi-Roshi and are the only priests.

ADDRESS: PO Box 310, Corbett, OR 97019
PHONE: (503) 695-2103
FAX: (503) 695-2188
E-MAIL: zendust@compuserve.com
LINEAGE: Japanese Soto and Rinzai Zen, Maezumi-Roshi lineage
SPIRITUAL HEAD: Sensei Jan Chozen Bays, Resident Teacher
AFFILIATION: White Plum Sangha and One Drop Zendo
ESTABLISHED: 1980

FACILITIES: Downtown Portland Dharma Center, shared by several Buddhist groups; Larch Mountain Zen Center, country residential and retreat facility. Gift shop/bookstore.
MEDITATION PROGRAM: *Zazen* twice weekly/Portland Dharma Center.
RETREATS OFFERED: Monthly one- to seven-day Zen *sesshin;* Larch Mountain residential training program; Dharma Mind practice two weekends monthly. Talks, interviews, classes.
PUBLICATIONS: *Dharma Dust*

PENNSYLVANIA

Ambler Sangha

For additional information, please refer to Community of Mindful Living, Berkeley, California.
ADDRESS: 29 Cavendish Drive, Ambler, PA 19002
PHONE: (215) 646-1655
E-MAIL: Diep94@aol.com
LINEAGE: Mindfulness practice in the tradition of Thich Nhat Hanh.
SPIRITUAL HEAD: Thich Nhat Hanh
CONTACTS: Eve and David Dimmack
AFFILIATION: Community of Mindful Living, Berkeley, California
MEDITATION PROGRAM: We meet one evening and several mornings a week for sitting meditation. There is weekly recitation of the precepts.

Laughing Rivers Sangha

For additional information, please refer to Community of Mindful Living, Berkeley, California.
ADDRESS: 1006 South Trenton Avenue, Pittsburgh, PA 15221
PHONE: (412) 243-1545
E-MAIL: KHamm11@aol.com
LINEAGE: Mindfulness practice in the tradition of Thich Nhat Hanh.
SPIRITUAL HEAD: Thich Nhat Hanh
CONTACT: Katie Hammond
AFFILIATION: Community of Mindful Living, Berkeley, California
MEDITATION PROGRAM: We meet two Sundays a month in the afternoons to enjoy sitting, walking, and tea meditation followed by dharma discussion and mutual support.
PUBLICATIONS: Local quarterly community newsletter.

Lilac Breeze Sangha

We were thrilled to note that the number of members in our *sangha* more than doubled from 1995 to 1996. For additional information, please refer to Community of Mindful Living, Berkeley, California.
ADDRESS: 267 South Van Pelt Street, Philadelphia, PA 19103
PHONE: (215) 545-3319
LINEAGE: Mindfulness practice in the tradition of Thich Nhat Hanh.
SPIRITUAL HEAD: Thich Nhat Hanh
CONTACT: Joyce Haase
AFFILIATION: Community of Mindful Living, Berkeley, California
MEDITATION PROGRAM: We meet every other week for meditation, precepts recitation, reading, and listening to tapes by Thich Nhat Hanh.
RETREATS OFFERED: Occasional all-day retreats.

Mt. Equity Zendo

"After twelve years of training as a female Soto Zen monk in Japan, I started a *zendo* in the guest room of my mother's apartment. Interestingly, it's located in a Quaker homestead built in 1803 and is called Saints' Rest. Trained by a woman Roshi, I offer *shikan-taza* and the practice of mindfulness. I lead *zazen* at three federal prisons and a university but very much look forward to ending solo work and having residential students to help in reaching a wider spectrum of the vast possibilities for meditation."
ADDRESS: RR4, Box 603, Mt. Equity Road, Muncy, PA 17756-8753
PHONE: (717) 546-2784
FAX: Same
LINEAGE: Japanese Soto Zen
SPIRITUAL HEAD: Patricia Dai-En Bennage, Lineage Holder/*Shike*
CONTACT: Same
AFFILIATION: Autonomous
ESTABLISHED: 1991
FACILITIES: *Zendo* and four apartments. Accommodates up to eighteen. Residency possible.
MEDITATION PROGRAM: Meditation three mornings and one evening weekly; open house; Sunday programs. Call for times.
RETREATS OFFERED: Monthly *zazenkai*, weekend and weeklong *sesshin*.
PUBLICATIONS: Translation of Abbess Aoyama-Roshi's *Zen Seeds*.

Old Path Zendo

For additional information, please refer to Community of Mindful Living, Berkeley, California.
ADDRESS: 2725 Aquetong Road, New Hope, PA 18938
PHONE: (215) 862-2968
LINEAGE: Mindfulness practice in the tradition of Thich Nhat Hanh.
SPIRITUAL HEAD: Thich Nhat Hanh
CONTACTS: Philip and Judith Toy
AFFILIATION: Community of Mindful Living, Berkeley, California
MEDITATION PROGRAM: We sit together every weekday morning at dawn. On Sunday mornings we have sitting and walking meditation, informal tea, and dharma discussions.
RETREATS OFFERED: Days of Mindfulness and weekend retreats.

Plum Tree Zendo

"I am so grateful just to be able to open the doors for those who wish to do *zazen* in this community. . . . I reflect on the special quality of friendship shared by those of us who sit together. Naturally, we all have beloved family and friends, but the deeply shared experience of strong *zazen* practice establishes bonds that somehow transcend the ordinary. As our courage to sit with our own difficulties grows, we more and more appreciate the strength of purpose embodied in our brothers and sisters sitting with us in the *zendo*." —*Rev. Dana Anne Waginger*

ADDRESS: 214 Monroe Street, Philadelphia, PA 19147
PHONE: (215) 625-2601
LINEAGE: Japanese Rinzai Zen
SPIRITUAL HEAD: Rev. Genro Lee Milton
CONTACT: Rev. Dana Anne Waginger
AFFILIATION: Autonomous
ESTABLISHED: 1987
FACILITIES: City *zendo*.
RETREATS OFFERED: Workshops and *sesshin*.
PUBLICATIONS: Schedule of events.

Stillpoint

Our community serves as an organizational catalyst for the dissemination of information about Zen Buddhism to people throughout western Pennsylvania. Stillpoint provides access to leading teachers within the Zen tradition, offers a multimedia library devoted to spiritual practice, and maintains information exchanges with other Zen centers throughout the United States. In past years, Stillpoint has sponsored retreats led by Dai-en Bennage, Chere Huber, and Shohaku Okumura. Our mission is to create a community where individuals come together to sit *zazen* and integrate Zen practice within their daily lives.
ADDRESS: 444 Olympia Road, Pittsburgh, PA 15211
PHONE: (412) 431-8016
FAX: (412) 481-0970
LINEAGE: Japanese Soto Zen
SPIRITUAL HEAD: Dogen
CONTACT: Neal Griebling
AFFILIATION: Autonomous
ESTABLISHED: 1990
FACILITIES: Dedicated *zendo*, lending library of printed and audiovisual material.
MEDITATION PROGRAM: Regular sittings twice weekly. Beginners should arrive thirty minutes early for *zazen* instruction.

RETREATS OFFERED: Monthly one-day, quarterly three-day *sesshin*.
PUBLICATIONS: *Stillpoint Newsletter* and orientation brochure.

Zen Group of Pittsburgh

The Zen Group of Pittsburgh is a local affiliate of the Kwan Um School of Zen, an international network of Zen centers under the direction of Zen Master Seung Sahn-Dae Soen Sa Nim. The group offers meditation instruction and holds weekly sitting and chanting meditation practice. Practice consists of thirty minutes of chanting, thirty minutes of silent meditation, and the reading of teaching letters. Instruction is held before practice or by appointment. Quarterly dues include membership in Kwan Um School of Zen.
ADDRESS: 6331 Walnut Street, Pittsburgh, PA 15206
PHONE: (412) 441-6393
E-MAIL: dickmap@chplink.chp.edu
LINEAGE: Korean Zen
SPIRITUAL HEAD: Zen Master Seung Sahn-Dae Soen Sa Nim
CONTACT: Paul S. Dickman (dharma teacher)
AFFILIATION: Kwan Um School of Zen, Providence, Rhode Island
ESTABLISHED: 1991
FACILITIES: Dharma room for meditation.
MEDITATION PROGRAM: Weekly sitting and chanting meditation. Call for times.

Zen Group of Reading

We are an informal group meeting Sunday evenings for sitting and walking meditation, chanting, and a reading. After *zazen*, there's tea and discussion of issues related to daily practice. Beginners are welcome as are experienced students from all Buddhist traditions looking for a group to sit with. We've held several

formal one- and two-day *sesshin* in conjunction with Zen students from Pennsylvania, Virginia, New Jersey, New York, Maryland, and West Virginia. Participants are urged to bring their own cushions. Chairs are available for those who need them.
ADDRESS: 1808 Perkiomen Avenue, Reading, PA 19606
PHONE: (610) 286-6787
FAX: (610) 373-9858
E-MAIL: nelham@prolog.net
LINEAGE: Japanese Soto with Rinzai influence.
SPIRITUAL HEAD: Bodhin-Sensei
CONTACT: John Sellers
AFFILIATION: Zen Center, Rochester, New York
ESTABLISHED: 1987
FACILITIES: *Zazen* at Aikido Dojo, West Reading, Pennsylvania
MEDITATION PROGRAM: Regular Sunday evening *zazen*.
RETREATS OFFERED: One- and two-day group Zen retreats.

RHODE ISLAND
Providence Zen Center

Providence Zen Center is located twenty minutes from Providence and one hour from Boston. Daily practice of sitting, chanting, and bowing is offered, as well as monthly retreats of one to seven days. There is a three-month retreat in the winter and a three-week retreat in August. Meditation instruction, talks, and teaching interviews are available on a regular schedule. There is space for two dozen residents who work jobs in the outside community and pay training fees. The facilities are available for other groups to rent for retreats and programs.
ADDRESS: 99 Pound Road, Cumberland, RI 02864-2726
PHONE: (401) 658-1464

FAX: (401) 658-1188

E-MAILS: kwanumzen@aol.com *or* 75147.1364@compuserve.com

LINEAGE: Korean Chogye Zen

SPIRITUAL HEAD: Zen Master Seung Sahn

CONTACT: Zen Master Dae Kwang, Resident Director

AFFILIATION: Kwan Um School of Zen

ESTABLISHED: 1972

FACILITIES: Semirural fifty-acre facility for residency and group retreats.

RETREATS OFFERED: Group retreats from one to ninety days.

PUBLICATIONS: *Providence Zen Center Member Newsletter* (monthly).

SOUTH DAKOTA

Laughing Teabowl Zendo

"We met at an open house of a community education program where Francine taught ikebana and I did massage. We got to talking about sitting practice and how nice it would be to have a group to sit with regularly. Two more people joined us and now we sit together two or three times a week. I built a little cabin in the yard that will eventually serve as a sauna and *zendo*. At this time we sit in the room I use for my massage practice." —*Klaus*

ADDRESS: 3326 Harmony Lane, Rapid City, SD 57702

PHONE: (605) 341-6378

E-MAIL: klausan@rapidnet.com

LINEAGE: Japanese Soto Zen

SPIRITUAL HEAD: Gautama Buddha

CONTACTS: Klaus and Francine

ESTABLISHED: 1994

FACILITIES: Space in private home.

MEDITATION PROGRAM: Sittings two or three times weekly

TENNESSEE

Nashville Zen Center

Nashville Zen Center is affiliated with the Kwan Um School of Zen. However, stu-

Nashville Zen Center group. (Photo by Liz Gadbois.)

dents affiliated with other Zen schools and teachers, as well as those new to the practice, are warmly invited to sit with us. Zen meditation enables us to let go of ideas, opinions, and judgments so that we can perceive *this moment* more clearly. As we learn to live our lives simply and mindfully, we not only nourish ourselves, but we begin to touch others with compassion and kindness.

ADDRESS: 1221 Sixth Avenue North, Nashville, TN 37208

PHONES: (615) 255-7715 or (615) 298-3754

LINEAGE: Korean Chogye and Japanese Soto Zen

SPIRITUAL HEAD: Zen Master George Bowman (see Cambridge Buddhist Association)

CONTACTS: Bill Compton or Steve Warren

AFFILIATION: Kwan Um School of Zen/ Zen Master Seung Sahn

ESTABLISHED: 1982

FACILITIES: We use facilities at First Church Unity and Primm Springs Retreat Center.

RETREATS OFFERED: Two three-day retreats with George Bowman, and two one-day retreats each year on our own.

TEXAS

Dallas Community of Mindful Living

For additional information, please refer to Community of Mindful Living, Berkeley, California.

ADDRESS: 8015 Forest Trail, Dallas, TX 75238

PHONE: (214) 342-3309

FAX: (214) 238-6352

E-MAIL: LeePaez@dccd.edu

LINEAGE: Mindfulness practice in the tradition of Thich Nhat Hanh.

SPIRITUAL HEAD: Thich Nhat Hanh

CONTACTS: Luke Barber and Lee Paez

AFFILIATION: Community of Mindful Living, Berkeley, California

MEDITATION PROGRAM: We meet Sunday mornings for meditation practice, readings, and sometimes precepts recitation. On the first Sunday of each month, we have a silent vegetarian potluck meal.

Empty Sky/DeFalco Retreat Center

The practice community at Bishop De-Falco Retreat Center includes people living in the Amarillo area who come for semiweekly sittings, and others who travel to the center for intensive Zen *sesshin*. The local group calls itself Empty Sky. Our contemplative program is modeled after the systematic instructional style established by Father Willigis Jaeger, a Benedictine monk who studied Zen in Japan with Yamada Koun-Roshi. Father Jaeger is a pioneer in adapting Zen techniques to contemplative Christian practice. Empty Sky is affiliated with the Diamond Sangha, an international community of Zen centers founded by Robert Aitken-Roshi.

ADDRESS: 2100 North Spring Street, Amarillo, TX 79107

PHONE: (806) 383-3764

FAX: (806) 383-6919

E-MAIL: bdrcesky@arnet.arn.net

LINEAGE: Diamond Sangha/Zen

SPIRITUAL HEAD: Patrick Hawk Roshi (Resident Teacher)

CONTACT: Glenna Pittock (Assistant to Pat Hawk)

AFFILIATION: Diamond Sangha

ESTABLISHED: 1986

FACILITIES: Private rooms/meals/Zen meditation room

RETREATS OFFERED: Three *sesshin* per year; inquire for dates.

PUBLICATIONS: Newsletter

Houston Zen Community

The Houston Zen Community is a lay Buddhist *sangha* following the teachings of Thich Nhat Hanh, and providing a resource for the study and practice of socially engaged Buddhism. We meet one evening weekly for discussion, dharma talks, precept recitation, and sitting and walking meditation. Each month a different member serves as facilitator. We sponsor at least two retreats per year at the Margaret Austin Center, a contemplative center and farm one hour's drive northwest of Houston.

ADDRESS: P.O. Box 542299, Houston, TX 77254-2299

PHONE: (713) 660-7702

E-MAIL: gduval@hal-pc.org

LINEAGE: Tiep Hien/Vietnamese

SPIRITUAL HEAD: Thich Nhat Hanh

ESTABLISHED: 1989

MEDITATION PROGRAM: We meet one evening weekly for study, talks, precept recitation, and sitting and walking meditation. Open to the public. Call for times and location.

RETREATS OFFERED: Spring and fall weekend retreats. Summer and winter Days of Mindfulness.

PUBLICATIONS: *Houston Zen Community News.*

Linh Son Temple

There are about forty people in our meditation group, which meets daily for sitting practice and once a month for retreat. We also conduct Youth Buddhist activities and Vietnamese martial arts on Sundays. We celebrate Vietnamese New Year (February), Vesak (May), Ullam (August), and Children's Festival (September).

ADDRESS: 13506 Ann Louise, Houston, TX 77086

PHONE: (713) 999-1623

LINEAGE: Vietnamese Zen and Pure Land

SPIRITUAL HEADS: Rev. Thich Tri Hue, Rev. Thich Tri Dung, and Rev. Thich Hue Huong

MEDITATION PROGRAM: Daily morning meditation. Weekly dharma class. Call for times.

RETREATS OFFERED: One day each month.

Maria Kannon Zen Center

Zen Teacher Ruben Habito offers *dokusan* at least once a week at Maria Kannon Zen Center, and conducts *sesshin* for ad hoc groups in New Mexico, Oklahoma, Maine, Mexico, and El Salvador. He is the author of *Healing Breath: Zen Spirituality for a Wounded Earth*, and *Total Liberation: Zen Spirituality for the Social Dimension* (Orbis Press). We practice in the tradition of Yasutani Hakuun-Roshi as transmitted to Yamada Koun-Roshi, bringing together elements of the Soto and Rinzai Schools of Zen. Members are bound together by a common commitment to cultivate wisdom and compassion.

ADDRESS: PO Box 140662, Dallas, TX 75214-0662

PHONE: (214) 361-1066

FAX: (214) 388-5254

E-MAIL: hcortes@msn.com

LINEAGE: Japanese Soto/Rinzai Zen

SPIRITUAL HEAD: Founding teacher Ruben Habito, who received authorization to teach Zen from Yamada Koun-Roshi in 1988.

AFFILIATION: Sanbo Kyodan Foundation, Kamakura, Japan

ESTABLISHED: 1990

MEDITATION PROGRAM: Meditation, four nights weekly in Dallas, one night weekly in Fort Worth. Call for schedule.

RETREATS OFFERED: Six *sesshin* a year. All-day sittings most Saturdays in Dallas.

PUBLICATIONS: *Maria Kannon Zen Center Newsletter* twice yearly.

TEXAS (*cont.*)

Plum Blossom Sangha

For additional information, please refer to Community of Mindful Living, Berkeley, California.

ADDRESS: 1501 Nickerson, Austin, TX 78704

PHONE: (512) 442-8262

LINEAGE: Mindfulness practice in the tradition of Thich Nhat Hanh.

SPIRITUAL HEAD: Thich Nhat Hanh

CONTACT: Nuba Shores

AFFILIATION: Community of Mindful Living, Berkeley, California

MEDITATION PROGRAM: We meet one evening a week for sitting meditation, precept recitation, tea, and discussion. We also have deep relaxation evenings with poetry.

RETREATS OFFERED: Several retreats during the year, usually at Stone Haven Ranch, a beautiful, old, secluded space outside San Marcos.

Sangha del Corazon

The first Sunday of each month we try to meet at Mobi Philips's for precepts and tea; otherwise we celebrate at 121 West Woodlawn Street. For additional information, please refer to Community of Mindful Living, Berkeley, California.

ADDRESS: 11506 Sayanora, San Antonio, TX 78216

PHONE: (210) 344-0681

LINEAGE: Mindfulness practice in the tradition of Thich Nhat Hanh.

SPIRITUAL HEAD: Thich Nhat Hanh

CONTACT: Bonnie Flake

AFFILIATION: Community of Mindful Living, Berkeley, California

ESTABLISHED: 1983

FACILITIES: Meet in members' homes for variety of activities.

MEDITATION PROGRAM: Sunday morning sitting and walking meditation and chanting. Call for times.

RETREATS OFFERED: Occasional retreats.

PUBLICATIONS: Random newsletter.

Sangha of the Rio Grande Valley

Our meditation sessions end with a shared reflection on a topic that someone in the *sangha* suggests. If there is no suggested topic, we read a few pages from books such as Jack Kornfield's *A Path with Heart*. We're most interested in selections on work, family, and social contexts. For additional information, please refer to Community of Mindful Living, Berkeley, California.

ADDRESS: 548 Guava Drive, Harlingen, TX 78552

PHONE: (210) 428-9571

LINEAGE: Mindfulness practice in the tradition of Thich Nhat Hanh.

SPIRITUAL HEAD: Thich Nhat Hanh

CONTACT: Mark Matthews

AFFILIATION: Community of Mindful Living, Berkeley, California

MEDITATION PROGRAM: We meet twice monthly for sitting and walking meditation.

So Lim Korean Buddhist Temple

So Lim means "little forest." This small but comfortable temple serves Korean and other ethnic peoples in the Houston area. The temple, located in southwest Houston, is near Hillcroft Road and West Airport. Two monks minister to the needs of our rapidly growing community; temple abbot Hae Dong Sunim comes from the Pusan area of South Korea and is a member of the Chogye order. Assisting the abbot is an American-born monk.

ADDRESS: 12614 Ashcroft Drive, Houston, TX 77035

PHONE: (713) 729-3928

FAX: (713) 729-4689

LINEAGE: Korean Chogye order

So Lim Temple serves Korean and other ethnic peoples in the Houston area. (Photo courtesy of So Lim.)

SPIRITUAL HEAD: Hae Dong Sunim, Abbot

MEDITATION PROGRAM: Sunday morning services include sitting and walking meditation; Korean language classes; dharma lectures in English; Buddhist holidays and ceremonies throughout the year; funerals and weddings.

Southwestern Son Academy

We have a large facility that is open to all who wish to cultivate their minds in the traditional Zen fashion and to study the words and inner meanings of the Buddha and Patriarchs.

ADDRESS: 1375 Bunker Hill, Houston, TX 77055

PHONES: (713) 467-0998 (English); (713) 467-0997 (Korean)

LINEAGE: Korean Zen

CONTACT: C. E. Lerned, (713) 464-3835 or (713) 366-2472

FACILITIES: Large urban temple.

MEDITATION PROGRAM: Sittings four mornings and two evenings a week. Call for times.

RETREATS OFFERED: Monthly half-day sittings.

Texas Buddhist Association

The Texas Buddhist Association conducts annual ceremonies, including Chinese New Year; Ullambana Festival; Birthdays of Kwan Yin, Sakyamuni, and Amita Buddha. An extensive library is available. There are support programs for homeless people, food drives, a youth group program, and a Chinese school. Dharma talks are given by the monks.

ADDRESS: 6969 West Branch Drive, Houston, TX 77072

PHONE: (713) 498-1616

FAX: (713) 498-8133

LINEAGE: Chinese Pure Land and Zen

FACILITIES: The association maintains a temple at 13210 Land Road, Houston, TX 77047.

SPIRITUAL HEADS: Ven. Jan-Hai, Yuan and Ven. Hung-I, Shih

MEDITATION PROGRAM: Saturday evening meditation and dharma discussion. Sunday services include meditation, chanting, and lecture. Call for times.

RETREATS OFFERED: Three- to five-day retreats quarterly.

PUBLICATIONS: Bimonthly newsletter.

Vietnam Buddhist Center

Our goal is to become a sanctuary for all Buddhist monks and followers, regardless of denomination, locality, or race. A retreat center has been established to nurture the spiritual and intellectual life of the community, and a cultural and education center to preserve and develop Vietnamese culture and ethics in harmony with those of other lands. In order to realize this vision, the center organizes retreat days and Buddhist study classes as well as Vietnamese language classes for Vietnamese children and English classes for newly immigrated Vietnamese.

ADDRESS: 10002 Synott Road, Sugarland, TX 77478

PHONE: (713) 575-0910

LINEAGE: Vietnamese Zen and Pure Land

SPIRITUAL HEAD: Ven. Thich Nguyen Hanh, Resident Teacher

AFFILIATION: Autonomous

ESTABLISHED: 1990

FACILITIES: Ten-acre country retreat; 7,700-square-foot main sanctuary; peace hall, youth activities building; large Avalokiteshvara monument (twenty-eight feet tall).

MEDITATION PROGRAM: Saturday morning sitting and walking meditation in the Zen and Pure Land traditions; Buddhist youth programs; Buddhist amateur radio station; *Vovinam* (Vietnamese martial arts); tai-chi.

RETREATS OFFERED: Twice monthly all-day Saturday retreat.

New main sanctuary building at Vietnam Buddhist Center in Sugarland, Texas. (Photo by Nguyen Xuan Dung.)

Zen Community of Austin

No description available.
ADDRESS: Box 672, Elgin, TX 78621
PHONE: (512) 285-3810
LINEAGE: Rinzai Zen
CONTACT: Chico Wagner
MEDITATION PROGRAM: *Zazen* and
chanting, Saturday mornings in Austin.
Call for times and locations.

UTAH

Kanzeon Zen Center—Utah

Kanzeon Zen Center provides an extensive training program for residents and nonresidents alike. We emphasize the traditional combination of sitting meditation *(zazen)* and frequent individual interviews with the teacher *(daisan)*. The public is welcome to attend any of the scheduled activities, though newcomers usually prefer to receive group instruction first through an introductory course. In the second-floor meditation hall, students are requested to wear black and to follow the traditional forms. The ground-floor meditation room has an informal character consistent with casual clothing.
ADDRESS: 1274 East South Temple,
Salt Lake City, UT 84102
PHONE: (801) 328-8414
FAX: (801) 532-0256
LINEAGE: Japanese Soto Zen
SPIRITUAL HEAD: Dennis Genpo Merzel-Sensei
CONTACT: Anton Tenkei Coppens-Sensei
AFFILIATION: Autonomous
ESTABLISHED: August 13, 1987
FACILITIES: Urban residential center with both formal and informal meditation halls. Overnight nonresident facilities.
MEDITATION PROGRAM: Morning/evening *zazen*: Monday–Thursday; Sunday morning *zazen* and service; introductory courses.
RETREATS OFFERED: *Sesshin* held regu-

larly throughout the year; winter three-month intensive *(ango)* includes a month-long *sesshin*.
PUBLICATIONS: *The Eye Never Sleeps* (Shambhala Publications) and *Beyond Sanity and Madness* (Tuttle) by Genpo Sensei.

Salt Lake Sangha

Our retreats bring old and new students of the dharma together in a situation like that of a one-room schoolhouse, where we learn from each other under the grounded and compassionate guidance of our visiting teachers. For additional information, please refer to Community of Mindful Living, Berkeley, California.
ADDRESS: 1588 Princeton, Salt Lake City, UT 84105
PHONE: (801) 583-9238
LINEAGE: Mindfulness practice in the tradition of Thich Nhat Hanh.
SPIRITUAL HEAD: Thich Nhat Hanh
CONTACTS: Vaughn and Joanne Lovejoy
AFFILIATION: Community of Mindful Living, Berkeley, California
MEDITATION PROGRAM: We meet weekly for sitting and walking meditation, tea, and discussion.
RETREATS OFFERED: Occasional retreats with guest teachers.

Shaolin Chi Mantis

Master Zhen Shen-Lang teaches Ch'an Buddhism, *Shaolin Kung Fu*, and *Luohan Kung Fu* as taught by the Patriarch Bodhidharma and seen in the TV series "Kung Fu." Tai Chi is utilized as a moving meditation by all students to balance the mind and body so that spirituality can become truly attainable. Master Zhen has been teaching in a maximum-security prison, various rehabilitation centers, and public schools since 1984, helping to eliminate violence, stress, and drug addiction.

ADDRESS: PO Box 58547, Salt Lake City, UT 84158
PHONE: (801) 595-1123
LINEAGE: Bodhidharma of Songzhan Shaolin Monastery
SPIRITUAL HEAD: Master Zhen Shen-Lang
CONTACT: Richard O'Connor
AFFILIATION: Shaolin Temple, China
ESTABLISHED: 1984
FACILITIES: Various schools, churches, and sanctuaries.
RETREATS OFFERED: One- and two-day retreats.
PUBLICATIONS: *Shaolin Zen* newsletter. Books available.

VERMONT

Fire on the Mountain

For additional information, please refer to Community of Mindful Living, Berkeley, California.
ADDRESS: RD 1 Box 133S, Woodbury, VT 05650
PHONE: (802) 456-1983
LINEAGE: Mindfulness practice in the tradition of Thich Nhat Hanh.
SPIRITUAL HEAD: Thich Nhat Hanh
CONTACT: Ellie Hayes
AFFILIATION: Community of Mindful Living, Berkeley, California
MEDITATION PROGRAM: During the summer we meet one morning a week for meditation.
RETREATS OFFERED: We are a small but devoted *sangha* of women practitioners.

Pot Lid Sangha

For additional information, please refer to Community of Mindful Living, Berkeley, California.
ADDRESS: PO Box 954, Williston, VT 05495
PHONE: (802) 864-0981

LINEAGE: Mindfulness practice in the tradition of Thich Nhat Hanh.
SPIRITUAL HEAD: Thich Nhat Hanh
CONTACT: Bill Lipke
AFFILIATION: Community of Mindful Living, Berkeley, California
FACILITIES: Vermont Respite House
MEDITATION PROGRAM: We meet Friday afternoons for sitting and dharma discussion. Precepts recitation the first meeting of each month.

Southern Vermont Sangha

For additional information, please refer to Community of Mindful Living, Berkeley, California.
ADDRESS: RR 2 Box 345, Putney, VT 05346
PHONE: (802) 387-4144
LINEAGE: Mindfulness practice in the tradition of Thich Nhat Hanh.
SPIRITUAL HEAD: Thich Nhat Hanh
CONTACT: Eva Mondon
AFFILIATION: Community of Mindful Living, Berkeley, California
MEDITATION PROGRAM: We meet regularly for Days of Mindfulness and recitation of the precepts.

Summer Vine Community Sangha

We try to build neighborhood support for children. Our garden flourishes in Vermont's weather, and we connect with other *sanghas*. For additional information, please refer to Community of Mindful Living, Berkeley, California.
ADDRESS: 19 Vine Street, Montpelier, VT 05602
PHONE: (802) 229-9678
LINEAGE: Mindfulness practice in the tradition of Thich Nhat Hanh.
SPIRITUAL HEAD: Thich Nhat Hanh
CONTACT: Carrie Bagnall
AFFILIATION: Community of Mindful Living, Berkeley, California
MEDITATION PROGRAM: We meet one

evening a week for sitting and walking meditation and read the precepts during the first meeting of the month.

Vermont Zen Center

Sensei Sunyana Graef is a Zen Buddhist priest who trained at Rochester Zen Center with Roshi Philip Kapleau for nineteen years. Kapleau-Roshi's teachings were influenced by Zen Master Harada Daiun-Roshi's blend of the ancient sects of Soto and Rinzai Zen. Hence we meditate facing a wall and practice following the breath (Soto), but also employ koans as in the Rinzai tradition. Most chanting and liturgical recitation is done in English. Zen practice is expressed in our daily lives through the attentiveness and awareness that we bring to every single moment.
ADDRESS: PO Box 880, Shelburne, VT 05482
PHONE: (802) 985-9746
FAX: (802) 985-2668
LINEAGE: Japanese Soto Zen
SPIRITUAL HEAD: Ven. Sunyana Graef, Resident Teacher and Dharma Heir of Roshi Philip Kapleau
AFFILIATION: Autonomous
ESTABLISHED: 1988
FACILITIES: House on over five acres of farmland.
MEDITATION PROGRAM: Regular *zazen*; private instruction; sutra recitation; study groups; ceremonies; dharma talks.
RETREATS OFFERED: Three- to seven-day *sesshin* five times yearly; introductory workshops six times yearly. Calendars with a schedule of these events are available upon request.

Zen Affiliate of Vermont

Zen Affiliate of Vermont consists of three sitting groups located in Burlington, Montpelier, and Springfield. Each group

meets on Monday evenings and all three gather monthly for an all-day retreat that includes *zazen*, chanting, *oryoki* (formal meals), and taped dharma discourse by John Daido Loori. The sitting groups take turns hosting the retreats. Twice yearly we offer a *sesshin* led by a teacher from Zen Mountain Monastery.
ADDRESS: c/o Bob Tokushu Senghas, 54 Rivermount Terrace, Burlington, VT 05401
PHONE: (802) 658-6466
LINEAGE: Japanese Soto/Rinzai Zen
SPIRITUAL HEAD: Abbot John Daido Loori
CONTACTS: Bob Tokushu Senghas, (802) 658-6466; Tom Slayton, (802) 229-0164; Richard Ryoha Dunworth, (802) 228-2476
AFFILIATION: Mountains and Rivers Order, Zen Mountain Monastery, Mt. Tremper, New York
ESTABLISHED: 1984
FACILITIES: Space in churches and in students' homes.
MEDITATION PROGRAM: Weekly evening sittings.
RETREATS OFFERED: Monthly one-day *zazen* retreats.
PUBLICATIONS: Bimonthly newsletter.

VIRGINIA

Blue Ridge Zen Group

Our group started with a few members willing to climb through a second-story window once a week to get to our *zendo* in a condemned building. Presently we have a "walk-in" *zendo* in Charlottesville for daily *zazen* and extended Sunday morning practice. We also have a *zendo* in the Blue Ridge Mountains, where we hold retreats that emphasize *zazen*, work practice, and ample *kinhin* on outdoor trails. Members of our group have studied with various teachers, but our formative connection has been with Rinzai-ji.

VIRGINIA (*cont.*)

ADDRESS: 4460 Advance Mills Road,
Earlysville, VA 22936
PHONE: (804) 973-5435
LINEAGE: Rinzai Zen
SPIRITUAL HEADS: Kyozan Joshu Sasaki-
Roshi and others
CONTACT: Teido Bill Stephens
AFFILIATION: Informally affiliated with
Rinzai-ji.
ESTABLISHED: 1975
FACILITIES: City *zendo* and mountain re-
treat facility.
MEDITATION PROGRAM: *Zazen* daily;
Sunday extended practice.
RETREATS OFFERED: Periodic two- and
three-day retreats.

Charlottesville Sangha

Each year a friendly group of adults and
youngsters from as far away as Missouri,
Florida, and New York joins us for a family retreat at Camp Albemarle where we
enjoy mindful breathing, sitting, swimming, frisbee, and walking meditation
among the huge rocks that overlook the
river. The children make a worthy effort
to sit quietly in the mornings, and at
night there is bonfire meditation. (For
additional information, please refer to
Community of Mindful Living, Berkeley,
California.)
ADDRESS: Box 33, Massie's Mill,
VA 22954
PHONE: (804) 277-8452
LINEAGE: Mindfulness practice in the tra-
dition of Thich Nhat Hanh.
SPIRITUAL HEAD: Thich Nhat Hanh
CONTACT: Kim Cary
AFFILIATION: Community of Mindful
Living, Berkeley, California
FACILITIES: Friends Meeting House
MEDITATION PROGRAM: We meet one
evening a week for meditation, precept
recitation, and discussion.
RETREATS OFFERED: Monthly Days of

Mindfulness; annual family retreat at
Camp Albemarle.

Ekoji Jodo Shin and Chinese Pure Land Group

Services are held weekly. Once a month
Rev. K. T. Tsuji visits from Northern Vir-
ginia and leads the services, which can be
conducted in either Chinese or English,
depending on the makeup of the group.
We chant *The Three Refuges*, the *Juseige*,
Amida's Name, and *Praises of Amida*. Fol-
lowing a short period of meditation, we
have tea, refreshments, and discussion.
Children are welcome.
ADDRESS: 3411 Grove Avenue,
Richmond, VA 23221
PHONE: (804) 355-6657
LINEAGE: Japanese, Chinese
SPIRITUAL HEAD: Rev. Kenryu Tsuji
CONTACTS: C. K. Cheng and Richard
Mercer
AFFILIATION: Buddhist Churches of
America
ESTABLISHED: 1986
FACILITIES: Temple
MEDITATION PROGRAM: Weekly chant-
ing, meditation, discussion.
PUBLICATIONS: *The Dharma Wheel*,
quarterly newsletter.

Ekoji Zen Group

Two groups that had been around for
about ten years merged into what is today
the Ekoji Zen Group. Without a formal
spiritual head or resident teacher, and
unaffiliated with any particular temple or
lineage, we operate by conscientious an-
archy. Members share in the responsibilities and functions of the temple, service,
and orientation of newcomers. Several
times a year we are visited by Pat Phelan,
Zen priest from Chapel Hill Zen Group
(North Carolina). Our *sangha* is growing
slowly but steadily as the dharma takes

root in the granitic bedrock of the former
capital of the Confederacy.
ADDRESS: 3411 Grove Avenue,
Richmond, VA 23221
PHONE: (804) 355-6657
CONTACT: Wyn Jordan
AFFILIATION: Autonomous
ESTABLISHED: 1986
FACILITIES: Urban meditation center.
MEDITATION PROGRAM: *Zazen* twice
weekly. Call for times.
RETREATS OFFERED: Daylong sits four or
five times yearly, when Pat Phelan vis-
its; precepts study group twice monthly.
PUBLICATIONS: *The Dharma Wheel*,
quarterly newsletter.

Loudon County Sangha

For additional information, please refer
to Community of Mindful Living, Berke-
ley, California.
ADDRESS: 20711 Sycolin Road, Leesburg,
VA 22075
PHONE: (703) 777-1618
LINEAGE: Mindfulness practice in the tra-
dition of Thich Nhat Hanh.
SPIRITUAL HEAD: Thich Nhat Hanh
CONTACTS: Alice and Dan Magorian
AFFILIATION: Community of Mindful
Living, Berkeley, California
MEDITATION PROGRAM: We meet once a
month for sitting and walking medita-
tion, a potluck supper, and discussion.

Mindfulness Community of Hampton Roads

For additional information, please refer
to Community of Mindful Living, Berke-
ley, California.
ADDRESS: 612 Westover Avenue, Norfolk,
VA 23507
PHONE: (804) 625-6367
LINEAGE: Mindfulness practice in the tra-
dition of Thich Nhat Hanh.
SPIRITUAL HEAD: Thich Nhat Hanh

CONTACT: Allen Sandler

AFFILIATION: Community of Mindful Living, Berkeley, California

MEDITATION PROGRAM: We meet two Sunday mornings of each month for meditation practice.

New River Zen Community

New River Zen Community meets twice weekly for three periods of *zazen* and a dharma talk. The group includes members from various religious backgrounds who support one another in Zen practice. The third Saturday of each month is reserved for *Morning Zazen*, a half day of sitting.

ADDRESS: 2121 Charlton Lane, Radford, VA 24141

PHONE: (540) 639-4109

E-MAIL: crbirx@runet.edu

LINEAGE: Japanese Soto/Rinzai Zen

SPIRITUAL HEAD: Charles Birx, Dharma Holder, Resident Director

AFFILIATION: White Plum Sangha

ESTABLISHED: 1991

FACILITIES: Meets in local churches.

RETREATS OFFERED: *Morning Zazen* (monthly half-day retreat).

Sai Sho An Zen Group

Sai Sho An Zen Group is a small *sangha* located in a rural/suburban community in Fauquier County, Virginia. One of the oldest Zen *sanghas* in the South, the group is led by Tom Davenport, a Zen layperson and senior student of Joshu Sasaki-Roshi. The *zendo* etiquette is strict, but the atmosphere is warm and encouraging. Sittings are between thirty and forty-five minutes long, and on Saturday mornings after sitting, we talk together about issues raised in koan study. Beginners and newcomers are welcome. Please call Tom Davenport in advance for directions.

ADDRESS: 11324 Pearlstone Lane, Delaplane, VA 22025

PHONE: (540) 592-3701

FAX: (540) 592-3717

E-MAIL: tdavenport@aol.com

LINEAGE: Zen

CONTACT: Tom Davenport, Resident Teacher

AFFILIATION: Blue Ridge Zen Group

ESTABLISHED: 1973

FACILITIES: We meet in an Episcopal church.

MEDITATION PROGRAM: One morning and one evening weekly. Call for times.

RETREATS OFFERED: Occasional weekend and daylong retreats.

PUBLICATIONS: Newsletter

South Anna River Sangha

We are a *sangha* within a land-based, egalitarian, income-sharing, nonreligious community. We are open to new members. (For additional information, please refer to Community of Mindful Living, Berkeley, California.)

ADDRESS: Twin Oaks Community, Louisa, VA 23093

PHONE: (540) 894-5126

LINEAGE: Mindfulness practice in the tradition of Thich Nhat Hanh.

SPIRITUAL HEAD: Thich Nhat Hanh

CONTACT: Craig Green

AFFILIATION: Community of Mindful Living, Berkeley, California

MEDITATION PROGRAM: We share daily morning practice and a weekly sitting and discussion group.

Stone Mountain Zendo

Our teachers have given us an incredible treasure. We established Stone Mountain Zendo to share with others the dharma that has come down to us through twenty-five hundred years of tireless teaching. It is a quiet and peaceful environment where instruction in Zen medi-

tation is offered and one may practice with the support and encouragement of fellow seekers. All are welcome to participate; however, beginners are encouraged to arrange for some preliminary instruction or to attend one of the "Introduction to Zen" workshops that are held twice a year.

ADDRESS: 2702 Avenel Avenue Southwest, Roanoke, VA 24015

PHONE: (540) 345-8209

LINEAGE: Soto Zen

CONTACT: Jacques Kakujo Miller, Resident Teacher

AFFILIATION: Autonomous

ESTABLISHED: 1988

FACILITIES: *Zendo* is a room in the basement of a private home.

MEDITATION PROGRAM: Weekly sitting and walking *zazen*, lecture/discussion period, and a short Buddhist service.

Tuesday Mindfulness Meditation Group

For additional information, please refer to Community of Mindful Living, Berkeley, California.

ADDRESS: 8502 Rehoboth Court, Vienna, VA 22031-5061

PHONE: (703) 356-4912

E-MAIL: wmenza@capaccess.org

LINEAGE: Mindfulness practice in the tradition of Thich Nhat Hanh.

SPIRITUAL HEAD: Thich Nhat Hanh

CONTACT: Bill Menza

AFFILIATION: Community of Mindful Living, Berkeley, California

MEDITATION PROGRAM: We meet one evening weekly for meditation, Five Precepts recitation, and dharma discussion.

RETREATS OFFERED: Every other month we have a morning of mindfulness. Members sometimes join in a Day of Mindfulness with the Washington Mindfulness Community, led by Thich Giac Thanh and Anh Huong Nguyen.

Washington Mindfulness Community

Washington Mindfulness Community was established by a group of women and men inspired by the teachings of Thich Nhat Hanh, a contemporary Vietnamese Zen Master, author, and peace activist. We meet one evening a week for meditation and discussion at the Washington Buddhist Vihara. There is no charge, and beginners are welcome. Meditation instruction and sitting cushions are available.

ADDRESS: 8680 Walutes Circle, Alexandria, VA 22309
PHONE: (703) 799-0441
E-MAIL: childers@erols.com
WWW: http://www.erols.com/sangha/ WMC/
LINEAGE: Vietnamese Zen
SPIRITUAL HEAD: Thich Nhat Hanh
CONTACTS: Richard Brady, Tom Childers, and Mitchell Ratner
AFFILIATION: Plum Village Sangha, France
ESTABLISHED: 1989
FACILITIES: Meetings held at Washington Buddhist Vihara (5017 16th Street Northwest, Washington, D.C.)
MEDITATION PROGRAM: Sunday evening meditation and discussion at Washington Buddhist Vihara. Call for times.
RETREATS OFFERED: Twice a year in May and November.
PUBLICATIONS: Washington Mindfulness Community Newsletter

Zen America

Zen America is an organization for sharing the richness of spiritual and philosophical wisdom that is increasingly commanding the interest of the Western world. Zen is where East meets West, science meets mysticism, and knowledge meets wisdom. This organization is dedicated to spreading the joy and enlightenment of recognized teachers from a wide spectrum of traditions. Zen is for every citizen. All are welcome—both members and the general public. For more information, please contact us.

ADDRESS: c/o Roshan, 1805 Colonial, Virginia Beach, VA 23454
PHONE: (757) 481-4475
CONTACT: Roshan Talreja, Director
ESTABLISHED: 1990
FACILITIES: Private meditation center.
RETREATS OFFERED: Please write to us for program schedules, Zen weekends, and our newsletter.
PUBLICATIONS: Roshni

WASHINGTON

Bellingham Zen Practice Group

Weekly Soto Zen practice group dedicated to helping each other deepen sitting and daily life practice. Zoketsu Norman Fischer, co-Abbot at Green Gulch Farm/ Zen Center in California, leads sesshin twice a year. For information and instruction, please call.

ADDRESS: 115 Unity Street, Bellingham, WA 98225
PHONE: (360) 592-5062
LINEAGE: Japanese Soto Zen
SPIRITUAL HEAD: Zoketsu Norman Fischer (Visiting Teacher)
CONTACT: Florence
AFFILIATION: Autonomous but associated with Green Gulch Farm/Zen Center in California.
MEDITATION PROGRAM: Zazen, one evening a week and first Sunday morning each month. Call for times.
RETREATS OFFERED: Sesshin twice a year.

Dai Bai Zan Cho Bo Zen Temple

In 1978 Genki Takabayashi-Roshi was invited by the Seattle Zen Center to become its resident teacher. By 1983 he had formalized his teaching style around a small group of students and had founded Dai Bai Zan Cho Bo Zen Ji, translated as Great Plum Mountain Listening to the Dharma Zen Temple. Kokan Genjo Marinello Osho, an ordained priest, is our Vice-Abbot.

ADDRESS: 7700 Aurora Avenue North, Seattle, WA 98103
PHONE: (206) 328-3944
FAX: Same
E-MAIL: zenquake@ix.netcom.com
LINEAGE: Japanese Rinzai Zen
SPIRITUAL HEAD: Genki Takabayashi-Roshi, Abbot
CONTACT: Kokan Genjo Marinello Osho, Vice-Abbot
AFFILIATION: Dai Bosatsu Zendo Kongo-Ji, New York (informal)
ESTABLISHED: 1978
FACILITIES: Upstairs Zendo at Seattle Aikikai Dojo.
MEDITATION PROGRAM: Meditation six days a week; introductory class, weekly. Call Genjo for more information.
RETREATS OFFERED: Monthly half-day sittings; quarterly weeklong sesshins.
PUBLICATIONS: Plum Mountain News

Dharma Sound Zen Center

Dharma Sound Zen Center was founded by Zen Master Seung Sahn as a local, nonresidential community of Zen teachers and students. Our Guiding Teacher is Robert Moore-Ji Do Poep Sa Nim. As a member center of the Kwan Um School of Zen, we offer a wide range of activities, including introductory workshops, public talks, and six meditation retreats a year. A solo retreat hut on Vashon Island is available to community members for personal practice, and regular group meditation sessions are held in Seattle, Redmond, and Tacoma.

ADDRESS: PO Box 31003, Seattle, WA 98103
PHONE: (206) 783-8484

LINEAGE: Korean Zen

SPIRITUAL HEAD: Robert Moore, JDPSN

CONTACT: Jeff Tipp, Abbot

AFFILIATION: Kwan Um School of Zen

ESTABLISHED: 1980

FACILITIES: Practice locations in Seattle, Redmond, Tacoma.

MEDITATION PROGRAM: Weekly meditation in three Puget Sound locations.

RETREATS OFFERED: Six retreats per year ranging from three to fourteen days; monthly one-day retreats.

PUBLICATIONS: *Dharma Sound*

Dohn-0 Zen and Sun-do Center

Practice at our center combines traditional Zen Buddhism with a Taoist breath meditation called *Sun-do*. *Sun-do* heals, energizes, and balances so we are better able to approach Zen, a direct path to awakening. We promote the education of the general public concerning Buddhist teachings and doctrines through workshops, dharma talks, and videotapes shown on public access television. Our teacher, Ven. Hyunoong-Sunim, is a Chinese herbalist offering herbs, energy analyses, and diet recommendations to help people regain and/or maintain health.

ADDRESS: 10303 Densmore Avenue North, Seattle, WA 98133-9434

PHONE: (206) 526-1274

LINEAGE: Korean Lin Chi (Rinzai) Zen, and Taoism

SPIRITUAL HEAD: Ven. Hyunoong Sunim (Korean Zen monk)

CONTACT: Ron Hansen, Senior Instructor

AFFILIATION: Sixth Patriarch Zen Center, Berkeley, California

ESTABLISHED: 1988

MEDITATION PROGRAM: Daily classes in *Sun-do* and Zen meditation. Two times yearly, Sunim teaches a Zen and Taoist healing workshop and gives a public dharma talk.

PUBLICATIONS: Sunim's talks on video- and audiocassettes.

Gold Summit Monastery

Gold Summit Monastery is a nuns' convent. For additional information, see listing for City of Ten Thousand Buddhas, Talmage, California.

ADDRESS: 233 First Avenue West, Seattle, WA 98119

PHONE: (206) 217-9320

LINEAGE: We propagate all major Mahayana schools —Ch'an, Pure Land, Vinaya, Scholastic, Esoteric—and work closely with Theravada.

SPIRITUAL HEAD: Ven. Hsuan Hua

AFFILIATION: City of Ten Thousand Buddhas/Dharma Realm Buddhist Association

ESTABLISHED: 1984

FACILITIES: Worship/meditation hall.

HumanKind Sangha

For additional information, please refer to Community of Mindful Living, Berkeley, California.

ADDRESS: 5536 Woodlawn Avenue, North Seattle, WA 98103

PHONE: (206) 632-3551

FAX: (206) 547-7895

LINEAGE: Mindfulness practice in the tradition of Thich Nhat Hanh.

SPIRITUAL HEAD: Thich Nhat Hanh

CONTACTS: Michelle and Joel Levey

AFFILIATION: Community of Mindful Living, Berkeley, California

MEDITATION PROGRAM: We meet one evening a week to share mindfulness and loving-kindness meditation, and to enjoy dharma discussions, *sangha* building, and meditation instruction.

Mountain Lamp Community

Sitting and walking meditation and mindfulness in everyday life. Weekly sitting and "Days of Mindfulness" are led by Eileen Kiera, a dharma teacher appointed by Thich Nhat Hanh. Evening classes are offered throughout the year, along with longer retreats. Call for schedule.

ADDRESS: 115 Unity Street, 3rd Floor, Bellingham, WA 98225

PHONE: (360) 592-5248

LINEAGE: Vietnamese Zen

SPIRITUAL HEAD: Thich Nhat Hanh

CONTACT: Eileen Kiera, Resident Teacher

MEDITATION PROGRAM: Weekly sitting and walking meditation. Call for time.

RETREATS OFFERED: "Days of Mindfulness."

Nipponzan Myohoji

Nichiren Buddhist practitioners meet Sunday mornings to beat the drum, chant, and read *The Lotus Sutra*. Call for more information.

ADDRESS: 6160 Lynwood Center Road, Bainbridge Island, WA 98110

PHONE: Ron, (206) 842-4916; Karen, (206) 780-1215

LINEAGE: Japanese Nichiren

CONTACTS: Ron or Karen

MEDITATION PROGRAM: Chanting on Sunday mornings.

North Cascades Buddhist Priory

North Cascades Buddhist Priory is an affiliated temple of Shasta Abbey, Headquarters of the Order of Buddhist Contemplatives. Located in Northern California, Shasta Abbey is a Buddhist monastery and seminary in the Serene Reflection Meditation tradition. It was founded in 1970 by Rev. Master Jiyu-Kennett who, until her death in 1996, served as Abbess and Head of the Order of Buddhist Contemplatives. Buddhist training within the Order of Buddhist Contemplatives is based upon the practice of Serene Reflection meditation, the keeping of the Buddhist Precepts, and the integration of meditation and Buddhist teaching with daily life.

ADDRESS: PO Box 152, McKenna, WA 98558-0152

PHONE: (360) 458-5075

LINEAGE: Soto Zen and Chinese Mahayana

SPIRITUAL HEAD: The late Rev. Master Jiyu-Kennett

CONTACT: Reverend Prior

AFFILIATION: Shasta Abbey, Headquarters of the Order of Buddhist Contemplatives

ESTABLISHED: 1986

FACILITIES: Rural retreat center and urban (Seattle) temple.

RETREATS OFFERED: Yes

PUBLICATIONS: *Journal of the Order of Buddhist Contemplatives* (quarterly publication).

One Drop Zendo

One Drop Zendo was founded by Shodo Harada-Roshi, Abbot of Sogenji, a three-hundred-year-old Zen monastery in Okayama, Japan. At Sogenji, students from all over the world have received traditional Rinzai training since 1982. Harada-Roshi comes to Seattle every year to teach, give public lectures, and lead weeklong Zen retreats. In the summer of 1996, the group purchased a sixty-acre parcel of land on Whidbey Island, Washington. A Zen monastery is being built. Upon its completion Harada-Roshi will be its full-time Resident Teacher.

ADDRESS: 135 North 75th Street, Seattle, WA 98103

PHONE: (206) 784-1977

FAX: (206) 706-8510

E-MAIL: onedrop@halcyon.com

LINEAGE: Japanese Rinzai Zen

SPIRITUAL HEAD: Shodo Harada-Roshi

CONTACT: Tony Fairbank

AFFILIATION: Sogenji, Okayama, Japan

ESTABLISHED: 1989

FACILITIES: *Zendos* in members' homes. Rural retreat center on Whidbey Island, Washington.

MEDITATION PROGRAM: Weekly *zazenkai* in Seattle.

RETREATS OFFERED: Two seven-day *sesshin* per year (February and September) led by Harada-Roshi.

PUBLICATIONS: Four newsletters.

One Pine Hall Zazen Group

Meditation in the Soto Zen style in a group associated with the San Francisco Zen Center. Robby Pellet (Ryu Zen), ordained priest, leads practice. Tea service is done the last Friday of the month. Bring your own mat and cushion.

ADDRESS: 9515 Linden Avenue North, Seattle, WA 98103

PHONE: (206) 298-3710

LINEAGE: Japanese Soto Zen

SPIRITUAL HEAD: Robby Pellet (Ryu Zen), Resident Director

AFFILIATION: San Francisco Zen Center

MEDITATION PROGRAM: *Zazen* three mornings a week. Please call for times.

Three Treasures Sangha of the Pacific Northwest

Three Treasures Sangha practices in the tradition of Robert Aitken, a teacher in a lay stream of Soto Zen that includes aspects of the Rinzai line, particularly koan work. In addition to offering Zen training and ongoing group practice, Three Treasures encourages its members to apply their practice to environmental and social justice issues. Teacher Jack Duffy was given permission to teach by Robert Aitken in January 1992. He brings to his teaching his experience as spouse, father, psychotherapist, endangered-species activist, and wilderness wanderer.

ADDRESS: PO Box 12542, Seattle, WA 98105

PHONES: (206) 324-5373

LINEAGE: Lay Zen Buddhist

SPIRITUAL HEAD: Jack Duffy, Resident Teacher

CONTACTS: Kay Peters or Kathleen Galvin

AFFILIATION: Diamond Sangha network

ESTABLISHED: 1978

MEDITATION PROGRAM: Morning meditation, Monday through Friday.

RETREATS OFFERED: Two seven-day *sesshin* per year; monthly *zazenkais* of one to three days each.

PUBLICATIONS: *Dharma Currents*, bimonthly newsletter.

Whidbey Island Retreat Center of One Drop Zendo

A sixty-acre wooded site on south Whidbey Island in northern Puget Sound. We are building a full-time residential Zen monastery to which our teacher, Shodo Harada-Roshi, will come to live permanently. The land is beautiful and has a good-size lake on it. Many birds call the place home. For additional information, please refer to One Drop Zendo, Seattle, Washington.

ADDRESS: c/o 135 North 75th Street, Seattle, WA 98103

PHONE: (206) 321-3169

LINEAGE: Japanese Rinzai Zen

SPIRITUAL HEAD: Shodo Harada-Roshi

CONTACT: Tanya

AFFILIATION: Sogenji Temple, Okayama, Japan

FACILITIES: Sixty-acre wooded site on Whidbey Island, where Zen monastery is being built.

MEDITATION PROGRAM: Weekly practice in traditional Rinzai Zen style. Please call for times and location.

WISCONSIN

Crow's Caw/Udumbara Sangha

For additional information, please see Udumbara Zen Center, Evanston, Illinois.

ADDRESS: 4125 North Newhall Street, Milwaukee, WI 53211
PHONE: (414) 964-2652
LINEAGE: Japanese Soto (Suzuki-Roshi and Katagiri-Roshi)
SPIRITUAL HEAD: Diane Martin
CONTACT: Mary Ann Filo, Resident Director
AFFILIATION: Udumbara Zen Center, Evanston, Illinois
ESTABLISHED: 1996
FACILITIES: Meet in Mary Ann's home zendo
MEDITATION PROGRAM: Meet one evening per week for zazen/dharma class.
PUBLICATIONS: Central Flower, quarterly newsletter.

Dragon Flower Ch'an Temple

Regular meditation, dharma instruction, online translations of Chinese Buddhist texts unavailable elsewhere.

ADDRESS: 701 Washington, Rhinelander, WI 54501
PHONE: (715) 362-3371
FAX: (715) 362-5626
E-MAIL: DFCT@bfm.org
WWW: http://www.bfm.org/zen
LINEAGE: Chinese Ch'an (Zen)
SPIRITUAL HEAD: Ven. Ryugen C. Fisher, Resident Director
MEDITATION PROGRAM: Regular meditation and dharma instruction.

East Side Sangha

On the last Sunday of every month, we offer a tea ceremony. Everyone is welcome to bring something personal to share with the Sangha. We also celebrate the solstices and equinoxes. For additional information, please refer to Community of Mindful Living, Berkeley, California.

ADDRESS: 2037 Winnebago Street, Madison, WI 53704
PHONE: (608) 244-2446
LINEAGE: Mindfulness practice in the tradition of Thich Nhat Hanh.
SPIRITUAL HEAD: Thich Nhat Hanh
CONTACTS: Kate Behrens and Cindy Cowden
AFFILIATION: Community of Mindful Living, Berkeley, California
MEDITATION PROGRAM: We meet Sunday evenings for meditation and reading from the books of Thich Nhat Hanh.

Lake Land Zen Center

Lake Land Zen Center has served Lake County, Illinois, and Kenosha County, Wisconsin, since 1986. We follow the Soto-Shu Zen tradition and provide services and instruction on Saturday mornings or by appointment. Resident priest Rev. Suirin Witham is a disciple of Kongo Langlois-Roshi, Abbot of Zen Buddhist Temple of Chicago. We serve as liaison to the Buddhist Council of the Midwest. Rev. Witham organizes the meditation program for the annual International Visakha Festival sponsored by the council.

ADDRESS: 2122 89th Street, #1, Kenosha, WI 53143
PHONE: (414) 942-7052
E-MAIL: Raywith@MSN.com
LINEAGE: Soto Shu Zen
CONTACT: Rev. Ray Witham
ESTABLISHED: 1986
MEDITATION PROGRAM: Zen meditation, Saturday mornings. Meditation instruction available. Call for information.

Madison Zen Center

Madison Zen Center is affiliated with the Rochester (New York) Zen Center. Our spiritual head is Sensei Bodhin Kjolhede, who comes out periodically to teach and conduct sesshin. Although there is no formal teacher in Madison, we do maintain a regular sitting schedule. Many of our members travel regularly to Rochester for sesshin and special ceremonies.

ADDRESS: 1820 Jefferson Street, Madison, WI 53711-2112
PHONE: (608) 255-4488
LINEAGE: Yasutani-Kapleau Soto/Rinzai Zen
SPIRITUAL HEAD: Sensei Bodhin Kjolhede
CONTACT: Lou Kubicka
AFFILIATION: Rochester Zen Center, Rochester, New York
ESTABLISHED: 1974
FACILITIES: House with zendo.
MEDITATION PROGRAM: Regular sitting schedule. Call for times.
RETREATS OFFERED: Two- or four-day sesshin every six months.

Milwaukee Zen Center

Milwaukee Zen Center members "just sit," either at the center or at home, and participate in a weekly study group on Saturdays. "Just sitting" means to "open the hand of thought," letting them go as they arise, and to be complete and present just as we are, here and now. Tosui Ota-Roshi called it "to chop off your head and put it beside you and sit, that's all." The center is open to the public and especially welcomes those who sit for no goal, no merit, no improvement, no accomplishment, and no certification.

ADDRESS: 2825 North Stowell Avenue, Milwaukee, WI 53211-3775
PHONE: (414) 963-0526
FAX: (414) 963-0517
LINEAGE: Japanese Soto Zen
SPIRITUAL HEAD: Tozen Akiyama, Resident Teacher
AFFILIATION: Autonomous
ESTABLISHED: 1979

FACILITIES: Urban sitting center; rooms available for out-of-towners who wish to join in the sitting schedule.

MEDITATION PROGRAM: Regular *zazen* schedule; Saturday study group.

RETREATS OFFERED: Monthly one-day sittings; two-day sittings twice a year.

PUBLICATIONS: Bimonthly newsletter.

Mindfulness Community of Milwaukee

For additional information, please refer to Community of Mindful Living, Berkeley, California.

ADDRESS: 2958 South Mabbett Avenue, Milwaukee, WI 53207

PHONE: (414) 271-9988

LINEAGE: Mindfulness practice in the tradition of Thich Nhat Hanh.

SPIRITUAL HEAD: Thich Nhat Hanh

CONTACTS: Mary Bernau-Eigen and Chuck Eigen

AFFILIATION: Community of Mindful Living, Berkeley, California

FACILITIES: We use facilities at Plymouth Church.

MEDITATION PROGRAM: We meet one evening a week for meditation, discussion, and readings from Thich Nhat Hanh.

RETREATS OFFERED: Occasional half- and full-Days of Mindfulness.

Original Root Zen Center

No description available.

ADDRESS: 600 21st Street, Racine, WI 53403

LINEAGE: Korean Chogye Zen

SPIRITUAL HEAD: Zen Master Dae Kwang, Guiding Teacher

CONTACT: Tony Somlai, Abbot

AFFILIATION: Kwan Um School of Zen

PUBLICATIONS: *Root and Branch Newsletter*

Sacred Lakes Buddha Sangha

For additional information, please refer to Community of Mindful Living, Berkeley, California.

ADDRESS: 2254 Monroe Street, Madison, WI 53711

PHONE: (608) 256-0398

FAX: (608) 223-9767

E-MAIL: Imandt46@execpc.com

LINEAGE: Mindfulness practice in the tradition of Thich Nhat Hanh.

SPIRITUAL HEAD: Thich Nhat Hanh

CONTACTS: Catherine and Larry Mandt

AFFILIATION: Community of Mindful Living, Berkeley, California

MEDITATION PROGRAM: We meet once a month to recite the Fourteen Precepts.

Snowflower Buddhist Sangha

No description available.

ADDRESS: 1836 South Sharpe Corners Road, Mt. Horeb, WI 53572

PHONE: (608) 832-6444

LINEAGE: Vietnamese Zen

SPIRITUAL HEAD: Thich Nhat Hanh

AFFILIATION: Plum Village, Meyrac, France

ESTABLISHED: 1993

FACILITIES: Friends Meeting House, Madison, Wisconsin

MEDITATION PROGRAM: Sitting and walking meditation followed by dharma discussion, one evening weekly. Call for times.

RETREATS OFFERED: Three or four retreats a year with our sister *sanghas* from Illinois and Milwaukee.

Sun Farm Sangha

Lots of people are becoming involved with our *sangha* and we now share Days of Mindfulness in two locations to accommodate everyone. Avocation, labor, work, and fun are blending together and our gatherings are more interesting than ever. For additional information, please refer to Community of Mindful Living, Berkeley, California.

ADDRESS: Route 1 Box 71, Port Wing, WI 54865

PHONE: (715) 774-3374

LINEAGE: Mindfulness practice in the tradition of Thich Nhat Hanh.

SPIRITUAL HEAD: Thich Nhat Hanh

CONTACTS: Chris LaForge and Amy Wilson

AFFILIATION: Community of Mindful Living, Berkeley, California

RETREATS OFFERED: We gather twice a month for a Day of Mindfulness, where we sit for several hours and end the day with a silent meal.

Unitarian Church North Zen Group/Udumbara Sangha

For additional information, please see Udumbara Zen Center, Evanston, Illinois.

ADDRESS: 13800 North Port Washington Road, Mequon, WI 53097

PHONE: (414) 375-3890

LINEAGE: Japanese Soto (Suzuki-Roshi and Katagiri-Roshi)

SPIRITUAL HEAD: Diane Martin

CONTACT: Mary Ann Filo

AFFILIATION: Udumbara Zen Center, Evanston, Illinois

FACILITIES: We sit in the church sanctuary.

MEDITATION PROGRAM: Sitting and dharma class one day a week; Introduction to Meditation. Call for times.

PUBLICATIONS: *Central Flower*, quarterly newsletter.

Wausau Zen Group

The purpose of Wausau Zen Group is to foster the practice of moment-to-moment awareness. This "just now" mind allows us to open to kindness and compassion for others and ourselves. We meet once a week in the evening for formal meditation sitting and dharma talks by members of the group. Meditation instruction is available.

ADDRESS: 5107 River Bend Road, Schofield, WI 54476

PHONE: (715) 355-7050

LINEAGE: Korean Zen

SPIRITUAL HEAD: Master Seung Sahn

CONTACT: Leann Jozefowski-Rudersdorf

AFFILIATION: The Kwan Um School of Zen

ESTABLISHED: 1992

FACILITIES: Meditation room in member's home.

MEDITATION PROGRAM: Chanting, silent meditation, walking meditation, dharma talks, meditation instruction.

RETREATS OFFERED: Half-day retreats monthly; full-day retreats two or three times yearly; a two- to three-day intensive retreat yearly; workshops.

PUBLICATIONS: *Primary Point Journal.* Books by Zen Master Seung Sahn and other teachers.

CANADA
ALBERTA

Avatamsaka Monastery

Freezing, we do not scheme.
Starving, we do not beg.
Dying in poverty, we ask for nothing.
We adapt to conditions, but never waver;
We remain steadfast, yet accord with every situation:
These are our three great principles.
We dedicate our lives to do the Buddha's work.
We forge our lives as our basic duty.
We rectify our lives to fulfill the Sanghan's role.
We express our ideals within our daily affairs,

So that within our daily affairs, our ideals shine forth.
In this way we continue unbroken the legacy of the
Patriarch's mind.

ADDRESS: 1009 Fourth Avenue Southwest, Calgary, AB T2P 0K8

PHONE: (403) 234-0644

FAX: Same

E-MAIL: TSO@freenet.calgary.ab.ca

LINEAGE: Chinese Ch'an/Pure Land

SPIRITUAL HEAD: Ven. Master Hsuan Hua (entered Nirvana 1995)

CONTACT: Heng Tso

AFFILIATION: Dharma Realm Buddhist Association

ESTABLISHED: 1987

FACILITIES: Buddha/meditation halls; dining area; library.

RETREATS OFFERED: Semiannual Pure Land retreats.

PUBLICATIONS: Semiregular newsletter.

Edmonton Shin Buddhist Dojo

We have three meetings a month for both adults and children. The children's *dojo* is run by the parents, who help with teaching and planning. We follow the philosophy of the Pure Land tradition, but do mindfulness meditation as taught by Thich Nhat Hanh. We are attempting to evolve a Canadian form of Buddhism. The group is very active in interfaith affairs with other religions and within Buddhism as well. There is also social action in the form of work with young people, AIDS involvement, prison dharma, hospice work, and community education.

ADDRESS: 6 Keegano, Edmonton, AB T6K 0R3

PHONE: (403) 462-8281

E-MAIL: ulrichs@planet.eon.net

LINEAGE: Japanese Jodo Shinshu

SPIRITUAL HEAD: Gomonshu, Nishihongwan-ji, Kyoto

CONTACT: Ulrich-Sensei, Resident Director

ESTABLISHED: 1970

FACILITIES: Sharing temple with Thai Buddhists.

MEDITATION PROGRAM: Three meetings monthly. Thich Nhat Hanh-style mindfulness practice, and children's *dojo*.

RETREATS OFFERED: Individualized, occasional.

PUBLICATIONS: *Buddha's Smile*

BRITISH COLUMBIA

Gold Buddha Sagely Monastery

Gold Buddha Monastery is a Canadian branch of Dharma Realm Buddhist Association. Our programs follow the format set by our headquarters temple, The City of Ten Thousand Buddhas, in Talmage, California, and are designed to provide an opportunity to practice the Buddhadharma. Also offered are lectures on the sutras to both Chinese and Westerners to help them understand the terminology and grasp the deeper teachings of the Buddhas. Youth Sunday School includes ethics classes, study of the Chinese language, and a basic introduction to Buddhism.

ADDRESS: 301 East Hastings Street, Vancouver, BC V6A 1P3

PHONE: (604) 684-3754

CONTACT: Heng Jen, Resident Director

AFFILIATION: Dharma Realm Buddhist Association

ESTABLISHED: 1984

FACILITIES: Buddha hall; lecture hall; dining hall.

MEDITATION PROGRAM: Saturday morning Introduction to Buddhism class includes twenty minutes of meditation.

RETREATS OFFERED: Seven-day sessions.

PUBLICATIONS: Monthly newsletter.

International Buddhist Society

No description available.
ADDRESS: 9160 Steveston Highway, Richmond, BC V7A 1M5
PHONE: (604) 274-2822
LINEAGE: Chinese Pure Land
AFFILIATION: Autonomous
FACILITIES: Large temple.

Lions Gate Buddhist Priory

Lions Gate Buddhist Priory is an affiliated temple of Shasta Abbey, Headquarters of the Order of Buddhist Contemplatives. Located in Northern California, Shasta Abbey is a Buddhist monastery and seminary in the Serene Reflection Meditation tradition. It was founded in 1970 by Rev. Master Jiyu-Kennett who, until her death in 1996, served as Abbess and Head of the Order of Buddhist Contemplatives. Buddhist training within the order is based upon the practice of Serene Reflection meditation, the keeping of the Buddhist Precepts, and the integration of meditation and Buddhist teaching with daily life.
ADDRESS: 1745 West 16th Avenue, Vancouver, BC V6J 2L9
PHONE: (604) 738-4453
LINEAGE: Soto Zen and Chinese Mahayana
SPIRITUAL HEAD: The late Rev. Master Jiyu-Kennett
CONTACT: Rev. Koten Benson, Prior
AFFILIATION: Shasta Abbey, Headquarters of the Order of Buddhist Contemplatives
ESTABLISHED: 1974
MEDITATION PROGRAM: Weekly schedule of meditation, Buddhist services, ceremonies. Meditation instruction and spiritual counseling available.
RETREATS OFFERED: Monthly daylong retreats.
PUBLICATIONS: *Lions Gate Buddhist Priory Newsletter*, bimonthly.

Mill Hill Mindfulness Society

We would love to have more people join us, and invite anyone who resides on Lower Vancouver Island and the Gulf islands to contact us if they are interested in mindfulness practice. We hope to start a monthly Day of Mindfulness. We are fortunate to be able to gather on occasion with They Tao, resident monk at the local Vietnamese temple, who leads us in sitting and walking meditation. For additional information, please refer to Community of Mindful Living, Berkeley, California.
ADDRESS: 2550 Wentwich Road, Victoria, BC V9B 3N4
PHONE: (604) 478-7098
E-MAIL: pnr@islandnet.com
LINEAGE: Mindfulness practice in the tradition of Thich Nhat Hanh.
SPIRITUAL HEAD: Thich Nhat Hanh
CONTACT: Phil N. Rossner
AFFILIATION: Community of Mindful Living, Berkeley, California
MEDITATION PROGRAM: We meet each week for sitting and walking meditation followed by tea and conversation.

Saltspring Island Meditation Group

Mahayana Buddhism. Meditation. English chants. Dharma talk.
ADDRESS: 1020 Sunset Drive, Saltspring Island, BC V8K 1E6
PHONE: (604) 537-2378
LINEAGE: Mahayana
CONTACT: Matthew Coleman
MEDITATION PROGRAM: Meditation, one evening weekly. Please call for times.

Victoria Zen Centre

Victoria Zen Centre offers an opportunity to practice Zen meditation in the traditional way. Zen emphasizes repeated practice in a formal setting as the way to realize and express our true nature. It does not emphasize the study of Bud-

dhism as an intellectual discipline, so classes in Buddhist philosophy are not offered here. Eshin John Godfrey, the priest at Zen Centre of Vancouver, sits with us twice a month, gives a brief dharma talk, and answers questions on Zen practice. We welcome all who wish to sit with us. Beginner's instruction is available on first visit.
ADDRESS: 4965 Cordova Bay Road, Victoria, BC V8Y 2K1
PHONE: (604) 658-5033
FAX: Same
LINEAGE: Rinzai Zen
SPIRITUAL HEAD: Joshu Sasaki-Roshi
CONTACT: Eshin Godfrey, Priest at Zen Center of Vancouver
ESTABLISHED: 1980
FACILITIES: Interdenominational Chapel at Royal Jubilee Hospital. Retreats at a bed-and-breakfast on Galiano Island.
MEDITATION PROGRAM: Weekly sittings. Call for times.
RETREATS OFFERED: Quarterly five-day *sesshin* with Zen Center of Vancouver.
PUBLICATIONS: Occasional newsletter.

Zen Center of Vancouver

Regular *zazen* meetings are held throughout the week at our city center. Instruction and dharma talks are provided by Eshin John Godfrey, the resident priest. The *sangha* gathers for other functions such as ceremonies, work days, and meetings. Monthly one-day retreats are held on Cypress Mountain. Five-day retreats (*sesshin*) are held quarterly on Galiano Island. The center maintains connections with other Buddhist groups in Vancouver, including the many ethnic ones, and provides speakers for educational institutions when asked.
ADDRESS: 4269 Brant Street, Vancouver, BC V5N 5B5
PHONE: (604) 879-0229
E-MAIL: zcv@vcn.bc.ca
LINEAGE: Japanese Rinzai Zen
SPIRITUAL HEAD: Joshu Sasaki-Roshi

CONTACT: Eshin John Godfrey, Resident Teacher
AFFILIATION: Rinzai-ji Zen Center of Los Angeles, California
ESTABLISHED: 1969
FACILITIES: City *zendo* and residence; mountain retreat cabin.
MEDITATION PROGRAM: *Zazen* scheduled throughout the week.
RETREATS OFFERED: Monthly one-day and quarterly five-day *sesshin.*
PUBLICATIONS: *Waterfall,* newsletter.

Zen Fellowship

We are a lay, nonsectarian Zen group in the backwoods of British Columbia, Canada, at the very end of Highway 101. We trace our links to tradition through Mary Farkas (1911–1992) of the First Zen Institute of America, and her teacher, Sokeian (1882–1945), advancing their efforts to establish a true lay Zen practice in North America. Our *zendo* is located on a homestead, with one hundred members up and down the coast, and a core of around twenty that help to pull the weeds. Robert Heron is our resident scholar.
ADDRESS: PO Box 273, Powell River, BC V8A 4Z6
LINEAGE: Generic Zen
CONTACT: Mr. Gordon Switzer
AFFILIATION: Autonomous
ESTABLISHED: 1993
FACILITIES: *Zendo* in the woods.
MEDITATION PROGRAM: Weekly sittings.
RETREATS OFFERED: Two *sesshin* per year, winter and summer.
PUBLICATIONS: *Zen Views*

NOVA SCOTIA

White Wind Zen Community/ Wolfville Zazenkai

A branch center of White Wind Zen Community (WWZC), Wolfville Zazen-kai is a small group of students studying and practicing Soto Zen under the direction of Zen Master Anzan Hoshin. Sittings are held twice weekly at our Knowlan Mountain Zendo located a few miles outside of Wolfville on the property of one of our members.
ADDRESS: PO Box 96, Wolfville, NS B0P 1X0
PHONE: (902) 542-1728
FAX: (613) 235-0472
E-MAIL: 70670.1514@compuserve.com *or* WhiteWindZenCommunity@ compuserve.com
LINEAGE: Soto Zen
SPIRITUAL HEAD: Zen Master Anzan Hoshin
CONTACTS:Zenki Hope-Simpson, *anagarika*/Jinen Sherman Boates
AFFILIATION: White Wind Zen Community
ESTABLISHED: 1990
FACILITIES: *Zendo*
MEDITATION PROGRAM: Sittings, twice weekly; Introduction to Zen Practice workshops. Call for times.
RETREATS OFFERED: Occasional retreats for WWZC members conducted by Zenki Hope-Simpson, *anagarika,* or by visiting practice advisors. Students travel to Ottawa for *sesshin.*
PUBLICATIONS: *Absolute Zero,* bimonthly newsletter. *Zanmai,* annual journal. Send for catalogue of books and transcripts.

ONTARIO

Ananta Kuan Yin Zen Buddhist Institute

Teachings in Cantonese, Mandarin, and English.
ADDRESS: #326, 200 Silver Star Boulevard, Scarborough, ON M1V 5H4
PHONE: (416) 412-6234
LINEAGE: Chinese Zen

Bul Kwang Sa Temple

No description available.
ADDRESS: 2588 St. Clair, Toronto, ON M6N 1L9
PHONE: (416) 769-1874
FAX: (416) 769-6550
LINEAGE: Korean/Chogye order, Son/Zen
CONTACT: Kwang Ok Sunim
AFFILIATION: We are headquarters center in Canada.
ESTABLISHED: 1976
FACILITIES: *Zendo* in three-story building, library, exhibition room.
MEDITATION PROGRAM: Weekly Sunday service and evening sitting. Celebration of Vesak and Buddha's Enlightenment, Full Moon Days, and other Buddhist holidays.
RETREATS OFFERED: One-day retreats; two ninety-day informal practice periods for individuals.

HanMaUm SeonWon of Toronto

No description available.
ADDRESS: 20 Mobile Drive, Toronto, ON M4A 1H9
PHONE: (416) 750-7943
FAX: (416) 750-7943
E-MAIL: hanmaum@idirect.com
LINEAGE: Korean/Seon (Zen)
SPIRITUAL HEAD: Seon Master Dae Haeng Keun Sunim
CONTACT: Ven. Chong Gak Sunim
AFFILIATION: Chogye order
ESTABLISHED: 1992
FACILITIES: Anyang Head SeonWon

Mountain Moon Sangha

Mountain Moon Sangha consists of students on two continents guided by Sei-un An Roselyn Stone, an authorized Zen master in the Sanbo Kyodan lineage. In 1992 Mountain Moon Sangha *zendos* were established in Brisbane, Australia,

CANADA: ONTARIO (cont.)

and Toronto, Canada. Sei-un An now resides and teaches alternately in Brisbane (June to November) and Toronto (December to May).
ADDRESS: #10, 939 Avenue Road, Toronto, ON M5P 2K7
PHONE: (416) 485-7659
E-MAIL: roselyn.stone@utoronto.ca
WWW: http://student.uq.edu.au/~s311107/mms/
LINEAGE: Sanbo Kyodan
SPIRITUAL HEAD: Sei-un An (Roselyn Stone), Resident Teacher
CONTACT: Same
AFFILIATION: Headquarters center.
ESTABLISHED: 1992
FACILITIES: Apartment *zendo*
MEDITATION PROGRAM: Regularly scheduled meditation program one night a week. Four periods of sitting interspersed with walking meditation (call for times). Dokusan is offered when teacher is in residence. Six orientation lectures and beginning meditation instruction are prerequisites to formal practice with Sei-un An.
RETREATS OFFERED: *Zazenkai* at least once every six weeks. Includes *teisho* and *dokusan* when teacher is in residence.

Nine Mountains Zen Gate Society

Ven. Hwasun Yangil teaches from an extraordinary depth of lucidity and communicates in fluent English. The workshop is ideal for both beginning and advanced meditators.
ADDRESS: 1000 Queen Street, West, Toronto, ON M6J 1H1
PHONE: (416) 588-3251
FAX: (416) 588-7019
LINEAGE: Korean Zen Buddhism
SPIRITUAL HEAD: Ven. Hwasun Yangil, Resident Teacher
AFFILIATION: Headquarters center.

ESTABLISHED: 1987
FACILITIES: Temple, Zen center.
MEDITATION PROGRAM: Weekly Zen meditation class.
RETREATS OFFERED: One-, three-, and seven-day retreats.
PUBLICATIONS: *Energy in Zen*

Ontario Zen Center

No description available.
ADDRESS: c/o John Carducci, 22 Oakmont Street, Toronto, ON M6P 2M7
PHONE: (416) 604-0534
FAX: (416) 314-6202
LINEAGE: Korean Zen (Zen Master Seung Sahn)
SPIRITUAL HEAD: Do An Sunim, Resident Teacher
CONTACT: John Carducci
AFFILIATION: Kwan Um School of Zen

Smiling Flower Sangha

We have been involved with other faith communities in an ongoing vigil and prayer for the poor. We are interested in forming an "Engaged Buddhist" community house that will be interfaith. Those interested in living in community and practicing together are warmly welcome to help us. For additional information please refer to Community of Mindful Living, Berkeley, California.
ADDRESS: 37 Kingsgarden Road, Toronto, ON M8X 1S7
PHONE: (416) 750-2399
FAX: (416) 750-3711
LINEAGE: Mindfulness practice in the tradition of Thich Nhat Hanh.
SPIRITUAL HEAD: Thich Nhat Hanh
AFFILIATION: Community of Mindful Living, Berkeley, California
MEDITATION PROGRAM: We meet for meditation three times a week. Please call for schedule.

The Ha Nguyen

We practice Thich Nhat Hanh's teachings of mindfulness every day. Sangha members take turns inviting the whole group to their home for Days of Mindfulness once a month. For additional information please refer to Community of Mindful Living, Berkeley, California.
ADDRESS: 162 Silver Aspen Crest, Kitchener, ON N2N 1J1
LINEAGE: Mindfulness practice in the tradition of Thich Nhat Hanh.
SPIRITUAL HEAD: Thich Nhat Hanh
FACILITIES: Members' homes.
AFFILIATION: Community of Mindful Living, Berkeley, California
RETREATS OFFERED: Monthly Days of Mindfulness.

Toronto Zen Centre

Toronto Zen Centre was founded in 1968 by Roshi Philip Kapleau, has been in its present location since 1985 and autonomous since 1986. Our teacher, Sensei Sunyana Graef, also teaches at Vermont Zen Center in the United States and Casa Zen in Costa Rica. She visits Toronto frequently. The methods practiced here stem from those taught by Roshi Philip Kapleau at Rochester Zen Center. We sit *zazen* with single-pointed concentration and carry the practice into our daily lives through the attentiveness and awareness that we bring to every single moment.
ADDRESS: 33 High Park Gardens, Toronto, ON M6R 1S8
PHONE: (416) 766-3400
FAX: (416) 769-4880
LINEAGE: Japanese Soto Zen
SPIRITUAL HEAD: Ven. Sunyana Graef, Resident Teacher and Dharma Heir of Philip Kapleau-Roshi
CONTACT: Randy Baker
AFFILIATION: Autonomous
ESTABLISHED: 1968

FACILITIES: Urban *zendo* in large house.

MEDITATION PROGRAM: Daily *zazen*; introductory workshops; study groups; ceremonies; sutra recitation; Zen talks.

RETREATS OFFERED: All-day sittings; three *sesshin* annually, three to seven days.

Tu-An Pagoda

Tu-An Pagoda is a Vietnamese Buddhist temple that also serves as a meeting place in Ottawa for Buddhists of other traditions. There are weekly evening practice sessions that include sitting, walking, and reclining meditation, as well as dharma discussions in both English and Vietnamese. The group's focus is on the practice of Mindful Living as taught by the Vietnamese monk Thich Nhat Hanh. For additional information, please refer to Community of Mindful Living, Berkeley, California.

ADDRESSES: 3591 Albion Road, Gloucester, ON K1T 1A2 *or* 40 Landry #601, Ottawa, ON K1L 8K4 (ATTN: Vinh D. Nguyen)

PHONE: (613) 747-9096

LINEAGE: Vietnamese Zen. Mindfulness practice in the tradition of Thich Nhat Hanh.

SPIRITUAL HEAD: Thich Nhat Hanh

CONTACT: Chan Ngo (Vinh D. Nguyen), Resident Teacher

AFFILIATION: Community of Mindful Living, Berkeley, California

FACILITIES: Urban meditation temple.

MEDITATION PROGRAM: Weekly sitting and walking meditation and dharma discussion.

RETREATS OFFERED: Day of Mindfulness.

Vietnamese Zen Meditation Group

No description available.

ADDRESS: 205 Monarch Park Avenue, Toronto, ON M4J 4R9

PHONE: (416) 463-4241

LINEAGE: Vietnamese Rinzai Zen

SPIRITUAL HEAD: Thich Nhat Hanh

CONTACT: Nguyen Trong Phu

AFFILIATION: Plum Village, France/ Maple Village, Montreal

ESTABLISHED: 1988

MEDITATION PROGRAM: Sitting meditation, precept recitation, Mindful Living, every three weeks. Groups for juniors, seniors, professionals, and English speakers.

RETREATS OFFERED: Spring and summer retreats led by dharma teachers from Plum Village.

PUBLICATIONS: Parallax Publications; *Bell of Mindfulness of Plum Village.*

Warm Snow Sangha

For additional information please refer to Community of Mindful Living, Berkeley, California.

ADDRESS: Ottawa, ON

PHONE: (613) 236-8662

FAX: Same

E-MAIL: ah529@freenet.carleton.ca

LINEAGE: Mindfulness practice in the tradition of Thich Nhat Hanh.

SPIRITUAL HEAD: Thich Nhat Hanh

CONTACT: Gabrielle Yensen

AFFILIATION: Community of Mindful Living, Berkeley, California

MEDITATION PROGRAM: With Chan Ngo's guidance, we meet Saturday mornings for sitting and walking meditation followed by tea, precept recitation, and/or dharma discussion. On the first Saturday of the month, a Buddhist study session is led by Vinh Nguyen or Hoa Nguyen.

White Wind Zen Community

White Wind Zen Community (WWZC) is an international association of students and centers studying and practicing

under the direction of Zen Master Anzan Hoshin. Its several wings reflect aspects of the training offered here. These include Northern Mountain Order, a *sangha* of monks and Soto Zen priests; Buddhavacana Translation Group, translating classical texts from Sanskrit, Pali, Tibetan, Chinese, and Japanese; WWZC Archives, a comprehensive scholastic library for use by monastics and formal students; and Great Matter Publications. Zen Centre of Ottawa (Dainen-ji) is headquarters. Branch centers in Nova Scotia and Great Britain.

ADDRESS: PO Box 203, Stn. A, Ottawa, ON K1N 8V2

PHONE: (613) 562-1568

E-MAIL: 70670.1514@compuserve.com *or* WhiteWindZenCommunity@ compuserve.com

LINEAGE: Soto Zen

SPIRITUAL HEAD: Zen Master Anzan Hoshin

CONTACT: Ven. Joan Shikai Woodward, *godo*

ESTABLISHED: 1985

FACILITIES: Zen monastic training center in Ontario; branch centers in Nova Scotia and Great Britain.

PUBLICATIONS: *Absolute Zero*, bimonthly newsletter; *Zanmai*, annual journal. Send for catalogue of books, tapes, and transcripts.

White Wind Zen Community/Zen Centre of Ottawa

After ten years of renting buildings, we somehow managed to acquire a 9,700-square-foot, thirty-four-room mansion to serve as our new headquarters. We practice Soto Zen under the direction of Zen Master Anzan Hoshin, author of *The Heart of This Moment, Mountains and Rivers, The Straight Path,* and other books. Our teacher provides a strong foundation of *gyoji dokan* (continuous

Maitreya Buddhist Seminary

RECOGNIZING THE NEED IN NORTH AMERICA FOR qualified Buddhist clergy with Western culture in their bones, the Buddhist Society for Compassionate Wisdom, under the direction of the Ven. Samu Sunim, instituted a three-year seminary program in 1987 to train Buddhist priests and dharma teachers. The curriculum has five basic components: meditation, study, ritual practice, the nurturance of spiritual attributes (sincerity, honesty, simplicity, genuine innocence), and the development of "people skills" (attentiveness, listening with compassion, and so on).

In the first year novice students focus on meditation and devotional practice. They also learn various Buddhist rituals and ceremonies. Study revolves around selected texts from the Pali canon and historical readings related to the life of the Buddha and his disciples.

Year Two is more intensive. Chanting is added to the daily practice and students aim for a deeper understanding of nonduality, both as a Buddhist truth and as personal life experience. Ritual and ceremonial training continues. Study texts include *Awakening of Faith*, *The Diamond* and *Platform Sutras,* and various histories of Mahayana Buddhism.

As apprentices to the society's priests, third-year students conduct Sunday services and teach basic meditation. Readings concentrate on *The Avatamsaka Sutra*, Zen texts, history of Buddhism in the West, and contemporary writings on the social teachings of Buddhism.

For three to five years after completing the program, graduates serve as "junior" priests or dharma teachers. Whatever path they choose to follow, these monks, teachers, and priests have been well trained in the West— *for* the West—with all the spunk and tenacity they need to spread the dharma for the benefit of all beings.

For more information, contact: Maitreya Buddhist Seminary, 86 Vaughan Road, Toronto, Ontario M6C 2M1; (416) 658-0137. Maitreya Buddhist Seminary, 1710 West Cornelia Avenue, Chicago, IL 60657-1219; (773) 528-8685. Maitreya Buddhist Seminary, 1214 Packard Road, Ann Arbor, MI 48104-3814; (313) 761-6520.

---

practice) through a strenuous schedule of daily meditation and extended retreats. Classes and workshops in Zen arts, *Naikan*, and *Maitri Bhavana* are presented by senior monastics. Individual retreats are a prominent part of our practice.

ADDRESS: 240 Daly, Ottawa, ON K1N 6G2

PHONE: (613) 562-1568

E-MAIL: 70670.1514@compuserve.com *or* WhiteWindZenCommunity@ compuserve.com

LINEAGE: Soto Zen

SPIRITUAL HEAD: Zen Master Anzan Hoshin

CONTACT: Ven. Jinmyo Fleming, *shuso*

AFFILIATION: White Wind Zen Community (WWZC)

ESTABLISHED: 1985

FACILITIES: Monastic training center in large mansion.

MEDITATION PROGRAM: For WWZC members: forty hours a week of formal meditation practice. For the public: monthly introduction to Zen; Zen arts/ cooking classes; *Naikan* and *Maitri Bhavana* intensives; Zen retreats.

RETREATS OFFERED: Four seven-day *sesshin*, seven two-day *sesshin*, and a *yaza* (all-night sitting) annually.

PUBLICATIONS: *Absolute Zero*, bimonthly newsletter; *Zanmai*, annual journal.

Catalogue of books, tapes, and transcripts.

Zen Buddhist Temple/Toronto

Dedicated to providing peace and quiet to all who visit, Zen Buddhist Temple offers services and meditation instruction, fellowship and support, and a monastery for cultivation and training. The temple is also home to the Buddhist Institute of Canada, an organization dedicated to informing the public about basic Buddhist teachings and to exploring Buddhist solutions to contemporary social problems. The temple organizes an art exhibition each fall to introduce traditional and contemporary Buddhist art to the community. It also serves as a study and practice center for students enrolled at Maitreya Buddhist Seminary.

ADDRESS: 86 Vaughan Road, Toronto, ON M6C 2M1
PHONE: (416) 658-0137
FAX: (416) 658-5855
LINEAGE: Korean/Chogye Zen
SPIRITUAL HEAD: Ven. Samu Sunim (Sam-Woo Kim)
CONTACTS: Sylvia McCormick or Susan Blersh
AFFILIATION: Buddhist Society for Compassionate Wisdom
ESTABLISHED: 1975
FACILITIES: Buddha/meditation hall; social hall; dormitory.
MEDITATION PROGRAM: Daily meditation. Sunday morning/evening meditation open to the public. Year-round visitor's program.
RETREATS OFFERED: Overnight introductory; one- to five-day retreats throughout the year; two-month summer retreat.
PUBLICATIONS: *Spring Wind—Buddhist Cultural Forum*

QUÉBEC

Association Zen de Montreal

No description available.
ADDRESS: 982 Rue Gilford, Montreal, QC H2J 1P4
PHONE: (514) 523-1534
SPIRITUAL HEAD: Taisen Deshimaru
CONTACT: Lise Lambert
AFFILIATION: Association Zen Internationale
ESTABLISHED: 1979
MEDITATION PROGRAM: Sittings, Monday, Wednesday, and Friday evenings and Tuesday, Wednesday, and Thursday mornings. Group practice on Saturday and Sunday mornings. Call for times.

Bo De Pagoda

For additional information please refer to Community of Mindful Living, Berkeley, California.
ADDRESS: Beauport, QC
PHONE: (418) 660-6407
LINEAGE: Mindfulness practice in the tradition of Thich Nhat Hanh.
SPIRITUAL HEAD: Thich Nhat Hanh
CONTACT: M. Bach Vo
AFFILIATION: Community of Mindful Living, Berkeley, California
MEDITATION PROGRAM: Sitting meditation sessions are organized on Friday nights at Bo De Pagoda.

Centre Zen de la Main

Centre Zen de la Main is an urban practice center situated in the heart of Montreal. It was established in 1995 by Myokyo Judith McLean, an ordained Zen monk sent here from Mt. Baldy, California, by her teacher, Rinzai Zen Master Joshu Sasaki-Roshi. Almost from its inception, the center has opened its doors for daily morning and evening *zazen* and chanting. A schedule of intensive *sesshin* retreats is expanding in response to requests from practitioners. The bilingual nature of Montreal and the diverse cultures that are represented here enrich this practice environment.
ADDRESS: 30, Rue Vallieres, Montreal, QC H2W 1C2
PHONE: (514) 842-3648
FAX: (514) 842-7367
E-MAIL: myokyomclean@babylon .montreal.qc.ca
LINEAGE: Japanese Rinzai Zen
SPIRITUAL HEAD: Joshu Sasaki-Roshi
CONTACT: Myokyo Judith McLean

AFFILIATION: Mt. Baldy Zen Center, California
ESTABLISHED: 1995
FACILITIES: Urban meditation center.
MEDITATION PROGRAM: Daily morning and evening *zazen* and chanting. Call for times.
RETREATS OFFERED: Monthly one-day, bimonthly weekend, and annual seven-day retreats.

Maple Village

"In the morning, as sunlight shone through the windows, we recited the precepts of the Order of Interbeing. We felt happy in each of our breaths and knew that the forests around us were also happy. We breathed for them and they breathed for us. The bell master invited the sound of the bell after each precept. On the altar, two candles were lit and the fragrance of sandalwood incense filled the air. The space was filled with peace and calm, bringing us back to our True Home."
ADDRESS: 1730 Crescent Suede Brossard, Village des Erables, QC J4X 1N7
PHONE: (514) 466-8726 or (514) 465-0618
E-MAIL: nguyenn@paprican.ca
LINEAGE: Mindfulness practice in the tradition of Thich Nhat Hanh.
SPIRITUAL HEAD: Thich Nhat Hanh
CONTACT: Chan Huy, Resident Director
AFFILIATION: Plum Village, France; Community of Mindful Living, Berkeley, California
ESTABLISHED: 1985
FACILITIES: Rural retreat house, residential facility.
MEDITATION PROGRAM: Evenings of meditation are held on Mondays, Wednesdays, and Fridays in Montreal.
RETREATS OFFERED: Summer Days of Mindfulness every two weeks at Maple Village. We organize four retreats a year.

Montreal Zen Centre

We have regularly scheduled morning and evening *zazen* throughout the week. Once a month we have a beginner's workshop followed by a one-day sitting. Approximately every month we have *sesshin*: four seven-day, two four-day, three three-day, and one two-day.

ADDRESS: 824 Park Stanley, Montreal, QC H2C 1A2

PHONE: (514) 388-4518

E-MAIL: zenlow@aei.ca

LINEAGE: Japanese Soto and Rinzai

SPIRITUAL HEAD: Albert Low, Resident Teacher

CONTACT: Same

AFFILIATION: Autonomous

ESTABLISHED: 1975

FACILITIES: House and *zendo*.

MEDITATION PROGRAM: *Zazen* five mornings and three evenings weekly.

RETREATS OFFERED: Monthly beginner's workshops; monthly one- to seven-day retreats.

PUBLICATIONS: *Zen Gong*, a bilingual periodical.

Albert Low, resident teacher at Montreal Zen Centre. (Photo courtesy of Montreal Zen Centre.)

YUKON TERRITORY

Yukon Dharma Society

The society has worked since 1976 to provide the Yukon community with an opportunity to meditate and to learn about Buddhism. Classes usually follow a discussion format. We teach breath meditation (Anapanasati) and, when appropriate, Vipassana.

ADDRESS: 2 Redwood, Whitehorse, YT Y1A 4B3

PHONE: (403) 668-7675

FAX: (403) 633-6038

E-MAIL: tigger@polarcom.com

LINEAGE: Mahayana

CONTACT: L. Kwiat, director

AFFILIATION: (loosely) Dharma Centre of Canada

ESTABLISHED: 1976

FACILITIES: House, meditation room, retreat center.

MEDITATION PROGRAM: Three meetings per week. Personal interview is available by appointment. Aikido classes are available on a biweekly basis.

RETREATS OFFERED: As requested. No regular schedule.

PART THREE

Vajrayana

The Path of Devotion

✻

Vajrayana: The Path of Devotion

ROBIN KORNMAN

✳

WHEN TROOPS FROM THE PEOPLE'S REPUBLIC of China entered Tibet in 1956, they caused a massive exodus of Tibetan Buddhist religious practitioners, who traveled across the Himalayas to India and little by little further west. Refugees of the Tibetan diaspora, Tibetan lamas (gurus) and scholars of Buddhist philosophy reached the United States in less than ten years and, with their emphasis on meditation in action and the transmutation of daily life into enlightenment, rapidly spread the teachings of Buddhist Tantra throughout North America. The spiritual and philosophical experimentation fashionable in the early '70s gave particular impetus to this movement and a generation of American Tantric Buddhists was created—thousands of Westerners living or studying closely with their Tibetan masters, who lived much of the year in North America in order to be close to their new disciples.

Since the first edition of *Buddhist America* in 1988, much has changed in this community of allied Western students and Eastern teachers. Some of the Westerners, having studied Tibetan Tantra for twenty-five years, have begun to teach. The death of their gurus has been a consistent theme as well, for many of the founding fathers of American-Tibetan Buddhism have died in the last ten years and have been replaced by their chosen regents and by a new wave of Tibetan teachers brought to us courtesy of the continuing Tibetan diaspora.

In the last ten years our knowledge of this complex and multifaceted religion has improved as well. The practice of American Tantric Buddhists has in general matured, becoming less naive and more nuanced. It has become clear that Tibetan Buddhism is vastly more complex than its Western devotees had originally suspected; this is not a path whose practices can be learned in a mere ten years. In fact, only a fraction of the main teachings of Tibetan Buddhism have so far been communicated in English. The long and arduous process of transferring the lore and wisdom of Tibetan religion from a conquered land to a busy, burgeoning commercial and industrial society will easily take several more generations before it is completed.

Tibetan teachers have established hundreds of meditation centers in Canada and the United States. Most of them are small urban groups meeting weeknights for a few hours and meditating intensively on weekends. A few large-scale meditation centers and monasteries have been built in rural spots. These are the loci of more intensive practice programs and places of individual retreat. These groups and centers are serviced by a handful of lamas who travel on circuits around the country.

Vajrayana

The tantric approach to Buddhist practice is called Vajrayana, the indestructible vehicle. Actually the *vajra* is a kind of brass scepter held by lamas and advanced tantric

Dr. Robin Kornman, assisting traditional Tibetan musicians at the cremation of Chögyam Trungpa Rinpoche in 1987. (Photo by Don Morreale.)

practitioners during ceremonies. Mythologically, the *vajra* was the weapon held by Indra, the king of the gods. It was forged from the bones of a *rishi*, one of the legendary Aryan supermeditators who in ancient times brought the practice of yoga to the Indian subcontinent. Because it is made of this magical material, the *vajra* is adamantine; that is, it is the hardest substance in existence, capable of cutting anything, though itself is uncuttable. Whenever Indra launched the *vajra* at an enemy, it was a law of nature that defense was impossible and that the enemy would be completely destroyed.

In the same way, Vajrayana Buddhism is supposed to be not merely psychologically but also *magically* effective, employing devastating and irresistible techniques to destroy ego. If it is used correctly, it can be "the quick path to Enlightenment." If misused, it can destroy the practitioner.

The principal distinction between Vajrayana and other forms of Mahayana is its emphasis on *transmutation*—as opposed to destruction—of neurosis. Where other approaches seek to destroy passion, aggression, and ignorance so that the practitioner can be free from ego clinging, Vajrayana endeavors to transform the three poisons directly into wisdom, actually transmuting the constituents of ego directly into the principles of Buddhahood.

For this reason Vajrayana is often compared to medieval Western alchemy, which seeks to transmute lead into gold as a symbol for magically turning the unspiritual in human nature into the spiritual. However, unlike Western alchemy, Buddhist Tantra does not believe in a fundamentally unspiritual element in reality. Lead can be transformed into gold because there is, in the end, no such thing as lead, but only gold.

The Buddhist understanding of why transmutation is possible involves this precise peculiarity in the tantric view. According to Buddhist Tantra, neurosis can be transformed into wisdom because, in essence, it is already wisdom in an unrecognized form. So in a sense no real change is necessary. All we have to do is recognize the basic nature of our problems, and the problems become in themselves solutions. Tantric meditation is thus primarily a method of developing confidence—confidence in the self-enlightened self-nature of mind and phenomena.

This philosophy is simple in expression but very complex in application. In expression it simply means that there is no difference between illusory cyclic existence (*samsara*) and nirvana. Enlightenment is not the destruction of *samsara*, but the realization of its inseparability from its supposed opposite, liberation. In application this means that almost any human activity can be turned into a method for gaining enlightenment. Thus, tantric teachers give their students an amazing variety of exercises. Each guru seems to have his own special path and tradition. Consequently, students of different tantric teachers are typically incredulous of each other's paths when they compare notes.

A few things, however, are obvious and common to all lineages of Vajrayana Buddhism: secrecy, personal transmission and guru devotion, visualization practice and symbolic teachings, lengthy group and individual retreats, and a special emphasis upon profound, wordless meditation.

Secrecy

Vajrayana is sometimes called Esoteric Buddhism because the principal teachings are supposed to be secret—

given only to the most sophisticated and devoted disciples. Traditionally, these disciples will have already studied Hinayana (Theravada) and Mahayana Buddhism for many years before they receive real Vajrayana teachings, which are presented as long-withheld secrets, finally revealed during elaborate occasions of ceremonial instruction. Actually, many of the so-called secret teachings can easily be found in popular translations of tantric texts—texts such as *The Life and Teachings of Naropa* and the various biographies of Padmasambhava. Still, even though they are widely available, the tantric teachings are considered "self-secret" because, unless they are given to the disciple in a personal, face-to-face oral transmission by a qualified guru, they will never be intuitively understood. The theory is that in the teacher-disciple relationship there is a special power of direct communication—a power that transcends words and ordinary experience.

In actual fact, even if the mysterious power of oral transmission were not necessary, the teachings would still be more or less secret because they are usually written down in symbolic form, almost as iconographic codes. Without personal instruction from a qualified teacher, most tantric books would be misunderstood because all of the symbolic sections would be misread. For example, an uninstructed student would take the deities to be actual supernatural entities instead of symbols of principles of enlightened human nature.

So the oral instructions are necessary. Typically a student will prepare for years to receive them. The preparation involves a variety of preliminary practices that aim to soften and open the mind. Equally important is the life of serious study and attendance upon a guru—a life of devotion and passionate discipleship that forges an almost telepathic link between the teacher and the student. In the end, if the two succeed in creating this special connection, then the guru should be able to communicate the experience of enlightenment to the disciple through words, esoteric symbols, and gestures in special teaching situations called transmissions. Sometimes the transmissions are quite formal and occur in groups. But many also occur suddenly in the midst of casual communication.

As a result, Vajrayana is preeminently a devotional path. Disciples must love their gurus and worship them as higher beings. Tantric students take special vows of obedience and imitation called *samaya* vows. The word *samaya* is very important. It literally means "commitment" or "promise." Some *samayas* are quite literal and involve promising to complete specific undertakings, such as the daily performance of a set number of mantras or the bimonthly performance of ritual feasts in honor of tantric deities. Other *samayas* are very subtle and involve promises to regard the guru not as an ordinary human being, but as the Buddha himself.

The essence of the *samaya* vow is actually the concept of transmutation through recognition of the indestructible Buddha nature of all things. A person who keeps the *samayas* will see the world as self-existing and sacred, beyond pure and impure. Such an attitude should make it easy to transmute neuroses into enlightenment, because the neurosis is fundamentally respected as a slightly twisted version of Buddha nature.

If the *samaya* that links guru and disciple is unobstructed, the guru can transmit a temporary experience of the Goal or Fruition. This sudden glimpse is terribly important. It is the aim, for example, of most of the special ceremonies students go through as they study Tantra in weekend programs and retreats. It is also the reason that students experiment with numerous teachers until they find one to whom they can be devoted. It may take years to find somebody worthy of this trust, but the search is worth the trouble because an attitude of rapt, devoted attention makes the transmission of glimpses of awakened mind relatively easy.

If the student actually has a momentary glimpse of the nature of awakened mind, then the next step is to adjust one's practice until it is in harmony with this special dispensation. Thus, Vajrayana is sometimes called the Vehicle of Fruition because one is supposed to see the journey in terms of fruition—to be drawn along by a memory of the goal, instead of merely being driven away from illusion.

In other vehicles the meditator practices in order to escape *samsara* (cyclic existence), and "revulsion for the dharmas of *samsara*" is the primary motivation. In Tantra, on the other hand, one develops a kind of passionate yearning for the goal, which is actually nothing more than the state of mind of one's guru. Instead of mere escape from illusion, there is a positive sense of the pursuit of awakening.

A major problem for modern Western tantric practitioners is the difficulty of finding a qualified guru to give them the secret oral instructions. Many of the great masters and lineage hierarchs who brought Buddhism to the West have now died or are quite old. The Gyalwang Karmapa, the head of the Karma Kagyü lineage, died more than a decade ago. The much beloved head of the Nyingma lineage, Dudjom Rinpoche, is also dead. His successor, Dilgo Khyentse Rinpoche, one of the most respected and active teachers in the world, died in 1991. Dezhung-Rinpoche, the famous Shakya teacher; Chögyam Trungpa-Rinpoche, who commanded a worldwide network of meditation centers; the great Shangpa Kagyü ascetic, Kalu-Rinpoche; and, tragically, the young Kagyü-Nyingma prince of the Eclectic tradition, Jamgön Kongtrül of Pepung; have all died, leaving behind masses of Western students who had expected to be able to study with them for many years, but who now must either find a new teacher or fend for themselves.

A whole generation of North American students received their oral instructions from these great gurus and built centers around them. People who come to the centers today receive adequate instruction from the students of these masters, but who will give them the precious oral transmissions that were the special private possession of the old lineage holders? The traditional answer is that a special successor is named to carry and pass on the innermost experiential teachings of the old master. These successors, called regents, replace the gurus until their reincarnations are discovered and fully trained—a matter of some twenty-plus years.

Westerners, however, are not always comfortable with this kind of switch, for they come to the meditation centers not so much because of faith in a particular lineage or sect, but rather because of faith in a single guru they have met. Faced with a replacement teacher, Westerners ask, "Does the regent possess the same insight and powers as his or her teacher?" Will the new students, drawn to the center because of its reputation or the teaching abilities of one of its Western teachers, be able to find in the regent the personal relationship the old students had with the founder?

These questions plague Tibetan Buddhism in its third decade of flowering in North America. In the near future more of the charismatic gurus who grew up in Tibet will die. They will be replaced by their chief disciples, their children, and by younger teachers dispensed from the ancient, newly restored monasteries of Tibet. The moment when the torch is lineally passed to the next guru is all-important. Not only must there be a successor master, but the disciples must successfully transfer their loyalty to that new teacher. For the continuity of tantric lineages has always been maintained in only this way—not by the legal establishment of church institutions, but by the strength of the cord that connects guru to guru down through the ages.

The transferal of authority, respect, loyalty, and care has begun to take place—sometimes peacefully, sometimes not. The old students have begun to deal with their new masters, expressing loyalty to the lineages of their original teachers, or if that is not possible for them, finding new teachers. New students seek in the next generation of teachers the same sort of wonderful relationship the previous generation shared with theirs. They must find their own transmitting gurus and sterling dharma exemplars.

One of the strangest experiences for American Tantric Buddhists has been the repercussions of the Tibetan theory of reincarnation—or to speak more precisely, "emanation." Most of the great masters who taught in America and then died were *tulkus*, reincarnations of previous gurus. Having died, in due course their next "reincarnations" were discovered, identified, and confirmed by the Dalai Lama. Westerners must now come to terms with the idea that their beloved gurus are children again—children who must be educated and taken through two decades of training before they can teach again. Sometimes the reincarnation has occurred in a Western family, sometimes in Tibet or in China. In any case, there is an interesting temporal gap while these *tulkus* go through their minority.

During this time regents must run the communities

their teachers established in America. Meanwhile, the *tulkus* are being trained in another place, usually by other people—Tibetans, not Americans. And it may be that one day a young Tibetan man or woman is presented to an American community as its rightful head, returned in a new body after a twenty-year hiatus.

Symbolism

Another important characteristic of Tantra is the use of complex symbolism in meditation practice. Vajrayana ritual texts use symbolic diagrams called mandalas to represent the phenomenal world from the point of view of fruition—that is, as seen by a Buddha. In such a world, all sounds are regarded as the sacred formulas known as mantra: every human being is one of the five Buddhas who reside in the mandala; and all thoughts are the naked mind of the Buddha—nondiscursive insight beyond distinctions. These are just three among literally thousands of other symbolic figures that are used to describe every aspect of daily reality. Through these myriad symbols, the practitioner sees the phenomenal world as a naturally occurring mandala and moves toward instead of away from it. This leads to a series of special practices called meditation in action—practices that use the symbolic element to transform ordinary activities into an enlightened path.

The aim of this sophisticated system is to enable Buddhist students to live in the world without sacrificing their spiritual principles or slowing their advancement. Vajrayana practitioners should be able to transform every daily activity—livelihood, eating, social relations, even entertainment—into a sort of tantric yoga to speed themselves along the path.

Retreat

In theory, through tantric practice one should be able to abandon ego without abandoning the world. In practice, however, there are times when a tremendous amount of meditation is appropriate and necessary. The tradition of long, ascetic retreats has successfully been transplanted to the West. These retreats may be as short as a weekend or a week, but often are months in length.

Some are even longer. The most famous of these is the strict, rigorous, and altogether difficult retreat of three years, three months, and three days. Disciples who do this are bent upon mastering the most esoteric tantric practices. Three-year retreats are done by a small group of people: ten, perhaps twenty. Ideally, a lama experienced in the practices of tantric yoga, which include strenuous exercises and working with energy channels in the body, shares the retreat with the students.

It took a decade for the fact to sink in that these group retreats were not like the long solitary cave experiences of famous tantric yogins such as Milarepa. Rather, they are more typically schools where a student receives a sort of M.A. in ritual practice and elementary yogic technique. In the end, one leaves retreat knowing an amazing range of practices; ready, perhaps, to focus on one method in order to gain complete enlightenment, or in some cases, ready to enter a second and even third three-year retreat in order to achieve the originally hoped-for depth of experience. Graduates of these retreats are given the title "lama."

Recently, a new sort of program has been developed exclusively to meet the needs of Western disciples—a three-year retreat broken up into six six-month sessions. Although the students live like monks during the retreat, they return to lay life and ordinary jobs during the intervening months between sessions. (For additional information, please see the listing for Gampo Abbey in Nova Scotia, Canada.)

Some Western students have actually entered what is known as "lifetime retreat." They will not enter the world again until their gurus declare them realized or until the fundamental breakthrough is somehow demonstrated. For these people there is no term to their ascetic practice, although in Tibet such yogins surface again as magnificent, aged teachers—guides who suddenly appear after most people had forgotten they existed. On the other hand, many die in retreat, unknown, forgotten, nonentities to the *samsaric* world. This is considered a beautiful death by tantric practitioners.

Although these retreats are lonely and rigorous, they are not, by definition, ascetic. The unworldliness of Tibetan tantra is not the same as that of other world-denying religions. There are basically two sorts of full-time practitioners in Tibet: monastics, who have taken vows of poverty, chastity, and so on; and lay *tantrikas*. Both groups follow the same basic pattern of alternating long solitary retreats with periods of domestic life. This has developed in North America into a system of training that combines thorough engagement in worldly life with a series of carefully supervised meditation retreats of medium length—from a few weeks to a few months. For most practitioners in the West, this is the only way they can manage to put their training into full application. Those who have ordinary nine-to-five jobs save their vacations for intensive practice, attending group and individual retreats at a variety of meditation centers.

Initiation

Ceremonies of empowerment or initiation are an essential component of Esoteric Buddhism. Since the teachings are secret, students must receive, in person from enlightened masters, permission to practice them. In some cases this is not enough, and students must also receive special blessings and dispensations of spiritual energy before they can perform a specific practice. These ceremonies are called *wang* or *abhisheka*. There is actually an art to receiving such empowerments, one that *tantrikas* gradually learn as they journey from one meditation workshop to another.

Empowerment is particularly necessary in the case of the complex mandala visualizations, which are a specialty of Vajrayana. Mandalas are matrices of symbolic entities or deities who stand for different aspects of enlightenment and for the mind of the practitioner as a potentially enlightened being. Tantric students are trained to visualize in a prescribed manner the symbolic beings depicted in the mandalas.

Some of these practices are quite gentle and harmless and are given to beginners as tantric approaches to mindfulness and insight meditation. Others are more complex and in fact are psychologically dangerous for the unschooled. Those who perform them should already have been trained in Hinayana (Theravada) and Mahayana Buddhism. They must also have received *abhisheka* from

an authentic guru who knows them well and has agreed to undertake their education in exchange for obedience and loyalty.

Meditation

Group meditation practice has never, to my knowledge, been done by Tibetans. In Tibet, such "formless" practices as breath meditation or the silent contemplation of arising thought were considered beyond the capabilities of all but the most advanced students, who practiced them mainly in private. However, when Vajrayana Buddhism came West, Tibetan gurus noticed that Japanese, Chinese, and South Asian Buddhists were doing formless practice communally for days at a time. Seeing that it could be taught to relative beginners, they followed suit and began holding superorganized, Zen-style group retreats at their North American centers.

Similar to the insight practice of modern Theravadans, as well as to *shikantaza* (just sitting) in Soto Zen, formless meditation involves sitting in stillness and attending to a simple object such as the breath. Beginners receive it and do almost nothing else for years. Advanced meditators, after years of visualization and mantra practice, complex physical yogic exercises, control of vital energies, and arcane magical contemplations, return to it as the culmination of the spiritual path. When beginners do it, it is called *Vipashyana* (Vipassana). When *tantrikas* do it, it is called *Mahamudra*, the Great Symbol, or *Maha Ati*, The Great Perfection (Tibetan, *Dzogchen*).

Study

There has been a change in the study habits of American Tantric Buddhists over the last ten years. When Tibetan Buddhism was first taught in the West, there were very few translations and only one or two Tibetan teachers who could give talks in English. There were not many interpreters. The few who existed were almost as new to Buddhism as were the people in the audiences. These conditions placed severe limitations on what could be taught. Some of the more subtle, complex, and philosophical elements of Tibetan lore were hardly ever discussed except in universities or among an elite group of disciples in Asia who could speak Tibetan.

The average Tibetan teacher in America would travel from one congregation to another giving, again and again, the same introductory set of talks. Today it is possible for these same teachers or their successors to give learned commentaries to their Western students on complicated practice manuals and sophisticated philosophical texts.

The repetitiveness and dryness of these lectures is actually another important characteristic of Tibetan Buddhism—one we have only come to really appreciate in the last decade. Although this religion places tremendous emphasis on wordless intuition and direct perception, it is also famous for promoting a peculiarly wordy sort of ecclesiastical scholarship. Many of the most famous Tibetan lecturers are products of eleven- and thirteen-year seminaries. The medieval scholasticism that was part and parcel of their upbringing was not immediately apparent because there were no translators who could interpret a highly technical lecture and few translations of the commentaries that accompany such studies.

Now all of that has changed. Advanced study workshops—often several months in length—are taking place across the country. Older students, hungry for higher teachings, are going to extraordinary lengths to receive them. However, not all Tibetan lamas are convinced that Westerners can comprehend or make use of such detailed scholastic instruction. They fear that they will be misunderstood or become the property of American public culture.

Those capable of conducting such extensive study programs are a special breed of Tibetan lecturer. Usually they hold a scholastic degree: *khenpo* (if they are of the Nyingma, Kagyü, or Sakya lineage) and *geshe* (if they are of the Dalai Lama's Gelugpa lineage). *Khenpos* and *geshes* are trained in speaking and in the art of oral discourse. Many have studied Tibetan language arts: the writing of court poetry, grammar, logic, and debate. Some specialize in explanatory teachings and detailed instruction. Others are able to impart powerful intuitive transmissions or to give the all-important initiations without which Tantra may not be engaged.

Common to all Tibetan teachers is one surprising pedagogical characteristic: the use of songs and poetry in teaching. It has been this way since the beginning. The early tantric practitioners in Tibet, following an Indian tradition, composed songs about their meditation experiences called *doha*. These verses were sung to indigenous Tibetan tunes as instructional dharma ballads. Famous yogins like Milarepa and Shapkar put all of their teachings into these ballads, making them easy to memorize, easy to understand, and easy to pass on to later generations. Even today Tibetan teachers make up songs on the spot to summarize their lectures. In this country, they are translated immediately into English by a new breed of interpreter and American audiences begin singing them the very hour they are composed!

The Path

Tantric teachings are being taught on this continent in a tremendous variety of ways. Some Tibetan Buddhist churches have organized them into extensive curricula based on a particular view of Buddhism. Training at centers affiliated with Shambhala International, for example, revolves around the Tibetan notion of the Three Yanas: *Hinayana, Mahayana,* and *Vajrayana.* Hinayana here refers to the introductory teachings, which emphasize discipline and personal salvation. More advanced Mahayana teachings stress the altruistic motivation to save all sentient beings. Vajrayana, the highest vehicle, is a branch of Mahayana that can only be entered by students who have taken vows linking them with a specific enlightened master or guru.

Shambhala centers offer a small selection of practices from each of the three vehicles and march students through these phases across a period of education that can easily go on for twenty years. Along the way there are a variety of intensive retreats, some done in groups, some solitarily. Among these is the famous *dathun* (month of meditation). Organized like a Zen *sesshin*, *dathun* is devoted exclusively to the basic Buddhist meditation practice of *shamatha-vipashyana*, or "tranquil abiding and insight."

Shambhala's program extends into the realm of Tantra

as well. Students who decide to enter the program begin with the famous Vajrayana Preliminary Practices, or *ngondro*. *Ngondro* involves some especially rigorous and radical tantric rituals beginning with the performance of one hundred thousand complete prostrations before a tantric shrine. On each prostration the student places the entire body face down on the floor and utters a prayer. There is also the repetition of a hundred-syllable mantra (one hundred thousand times), the formal offering of one hundred thousand mandalas made out of colored rice, and the repetition of a short guru supplication (one million times). The entire series can be done in two years, of which the average student will spend from two to five months in solitary and group retreats. No matter how you look at it, *ngondro* is a supreme test—a terrible challenge that students must overcome in order to receive the powerful and remarkably effective *vajra* teachings.

Students who successfully complete *ngondro* are ready for the profound and subtle psychology of tantric visualization practice. Here they receive empowerment in a deity practice so complicated that it may take a year to master all of its many intricacies. After that there are successions of visualization practices and special retreats stretching out across the years.

Some Tibetan teachers have no single system by which they transmit Tantra. Using the special richness, flexibility, and variety of Vajrayana disciplines, they tailor their teachings to fit the students at hand. A single group of disciples might receive ten or twenty different *abhishekas* and transmissions. Then the guru will recommend to each student which practices should be his or her specialty. A student for whom passion is the salient neurosis might meditate upon deities related to that principle. One for whom the hindrance of aggression is strongest might concentrate on a whole different set of disciplines. Some students do not work with iconography at all, but simply meditate on the nature of their own minds, without any technique. Since the deities are purely symbolic, either approach will work. It simply depends on the personal psychology of the guru and disciple.

Many Gelugpa and Sakyapa centers in North America offer sophisticated programs of Mahayana Buddhist study that concentrate on the philosophy of emptiness (*Madhyamaka*). While studying the nature of emptiness and the arguments that establish the phenomenal world as illusory, the disciple is also doing simple and extremely safe tantric practices. As philosophical understanding ripens, more complex and challenging Vajrayana meditation is introduced.

Generally speaking, however, the path of a *tantrika* is not so systematic or programmed. Students begin to study with a particular teacher after hearing his or her public lectures. Then if they feel an affinity for the teacher, they may seek more opportunities for study— weekend and weeklong intensives, retreats, and so on. Usually the teacher will have one or two practices that are given to all students in common. For example, several masters of the Nyingma lineage in America give their students a *ngondro* ritual as a daily practice. The student chants this text without counting the repetitions and afterward rests in basic meditation. A given disciple may practice in this way for years, seeing the teacher from time to time in private interviews where the instructions are deepened and tailored to the needs of the individual. Meanwhile, the guru is also giving vast teachings on a number of different subjects, which the student accumulates, gradually forming a clearer view of what the tantric path has to offer.

Some teachers begin with a simple visualization such as the practice of *Chenrezig*. Technically this is a tantric visualization, but actually it has all the characteristics of the basic Hinayana practices. Instead of meditating on the breath, one meditates on a luminous, beautiful, and peaceful deity, gradually developing tranquil concentration and insight through this colorful object of contemplation. Typically, a student who begins with *Chenrezig* will journey over the years through more and more rigorous and complicated visualizations.

Some tantric masters teach in the manner of *khenpos*, doctors of philosophy. They begin by teaching Buddhist analytical philosophy and psychology using systems of definitions and classical lists. Through study, disciples learn the profound meaning of a given set of Buddhist contemplative exercises. Ideally, when the day comes to do them, the student has a mind tamed by study and moral discipline—one that easily performs the practices and accomplishes the goals.

A common feature among Tibetan Buddhist schools and centers are the transmutation practices in which rituals are used to turn ordinary *samsaric* activities into sacred ones. There is a tantric ritual performance for practically every lawful activity in a practitioner's domestic world. Probably the most well-known of these is the Vajra Feast or *ganacakra* (Tibetan, *Tsok*). Two days out of every month, tantric students of a given guru gather for a chanting service of several hours culminating in a formal meal. During the meal a feast of ritual cakes and real food is offered to a mandala of Buddhas and then shared with the disciples in the spirit of communion.

Among *tantrikas*, however, the most common practice of all is Guru Yoga. Here a disciple evokes his own teacher as a form of the Buddha and strives to unify his mind with the enlightened mind of his guru.

Having presented this vast and admittedly bewildering panoply of approaches, let me conclude by saying that ultimately all the teachings of the Vajra Vehicle agree at one point—in their faith and respect for an authentic Vajra guru. There are many charlatans in the world and students always run a terrible risk in entering the Vajrayana. But if a Buddhist meditator can find a genuine tantric master who has realized the essence of mind as Buddha and the essence of the phenomenal world as self-existing sacredness, then success is possible. If such a teacher has a karmic link with the meditator, so that the two can come to love and trust each other, then the mind of teacher and disciple will become one and enlightenment can be realized in one lifetime.

. . .

Dr. Robin Kornman is a senior student of the Vidyadhara, the late Ven. Chögyam Trungpa, Rinpoche, and a founding member of the Nalanda Tibetan Translation Committee. He is presently a Bradley Foundation Professor in the Honors Program at the University of Wisconsin at Milwaukee.

Dathun

CLARKE FOUNTAIN

⚹

DATHUN IS TIBETAN FOR "MONTH-LONG PRAC-tice." More specifically, it's a twenty-eight day retreat designed by the late Chogyam Trungpa-Rinpoche to introduce Western students to the practice of meditation. The primary focus is the eight to ten hours of *shamatha* (breath observation or tranquillity meditation) offered daily.

There are a number of idiosyncrasies that give *dathun*—as presented at Shambhala retreat centers—a flavor all its own. "Functional silence" (as opposed to "strict" or "absolute" silence) is the rule—talking is permitted, conversation is not. There's a random element to the daily sitting schedule; one never knows at the beginning of a period of meditation whether it will last for twenty minutes or four hours. Meals are taken "*oryoki-*style"—a traditional Japanese Zen monastic eating meditation modified by Trungpa-Rinpoche to accommodate both Western taste and Tibetan ritual. There's a "day off" at the midpoint when participants can sleep in, take a hike, go to town, watch a video, or schmooze all they like. At retreat's end there's a celebratory banquet that includes singing, dancing, and plenty of sake.

When I entered the Buddhist Studies Program at Naropa Institute, I received in-depth instruction on the fine points of *shamatha* meditation and was told that as part of my course requirements, I would have to sit at least one *dathun*. To toughen myself up, I sat as much as I could during the weeks leading up to it, and also did a lot of yoga. I even brought all my allergy medications with me. No matter. *Dathun* still hit me like a ton of bricks. I have met people at the various *dathuns* I have attended who have endured arduous Rinzai Zen *sesshin* and painstaking three-month-long Vipassana courses, and none of them were ready for the impact of their first dathun.

Perhaps it's the "functional silence"; all those juicy new people to talk to and get to know. But since, in "functional silence," social conversation is never all right, in order to have a conversation you either have to sneak off somewhere, or else keep looking over your shoulder. In short, it becomes a big deal. As for me, the frustration of not being able to talk nearly drove me wild. Without the crutch of wordplay to make people seem less complicated and confusing, I was constantly being thrown back onto my own reactions. Horrors!

At my first *dathun* the directors insisted that everyone sit on a *gomden*, an upholstered box designed by Trungpa Rinpoche to replace *zafus* (sitting cushions) and meditation cushions. *Gomdens* are supposed to make it possible for a wide assortment of people—most of whom have never sat in anything but a chair—to meditate reasonably well on uniform equipment for extended periods of time. For me, however, it was an instrument of pure torture. I was not comfortable sitting on it for more than two minutes running.

Then there was *oryoki*, a ritual as elegant in concept

as it is maddening in execution. The practice involves a sequence of intricate and extremely time-consuming maneuvers. Bowls and eating utensils are set out just so; food is offered and received in what begins to resemble a courtly ceremonial ballet. Chants are chanted, gongs are gonged, clappers are clapped, bows are bowed, offerings are made to hungry ghosts in every direction. Eventually you get to eat.

Teetering precariously on your *gomden*, you grip your chopsticks and skewer your quesadillas or mashed potatoes or peas or cold cornmeal mush with molasses topping. Half of it dumps in your lap on the perilous voyage from bowl to mouth. Your back hurts, your knees are screaming, and your patience is atoms-thin. Finally the meal is over and your gratitude knows no bounds. Your subsequent ambition to go get some ice cream at the commissary also knows no bounds.

Really hungry people cannot be made to enjoy *oryoki*. Fussy eaters really suffer during the ordeal, and hungry fussy eaters are driven to truly extraordinary lengths. Whoever you are, whatever your attitudes toward food, you will discover whole new geographies of food neuroses while doing *oryoki*. Curiously, though, because of the common suffering, a kind of communal bonding takes place. Even the "rules tyrants," those who humorlessly insist on doing everything correctly—yes, even they will eventually suffer some hilarious mishap during a month of eating *oryoki*-style. We laughed a lot and gradually discovered that eating in this way is in fact a real meditation practice.

Reading for pleasure was strongly discouraged. Before the retreat began, someone went around gathering up all the novels, newspapers, magazines, and comic books and locked them away in a secret hiding place. Without the escape of reading, the intense practice kept throwing me back again and again onto my own inner chaos. At times it felt unbearable. Sometimes it seemed like all I was doing was counting the seconds until "day off." I couldn't wait to go into town, read a newspaper, and eat food I had chosen while sitting in a *Chair*.

You might think from what I've said so far that *dathun* is not something I'd recommend, or would recommend solely on the basis of "I-endured-boot-camp-so-you-should-too." While I have not begun to exhaust my catalogue of *dathun* horrors, I should tell you now that by some curious alchemy these "horrors" served to heighten my attention and deepen my sitting, so that at the end of the whole thing I observed a marked and profound presence of unforced, peaceful awakeness. Even my sleep took on this quality. I wouldn't trade that final week for gold. (On the other hand, I've never been offered gold, so I can't be sure. But you get my drift.)

The "turnaround" began for me, oddly enough, during the much longed-for "day off." I went into town and there found myself nearly overwhelmed with the richness of the everyday world. I had not realized how much stimulation I take for granted. The whole world seemed slowed down somehow, and I felt as though I were moving through molasses. Very clear molasses. Everything was distinct. Nothing seemed to happen quickly, no matter how fast things were "really" transpiring. Before the day ended—long before the day ended—I was ready, even eager, to get back to the *dathun*. The same *dathun* I had longed to flee just hours before.

Which is not to say that it was all a bed of roses after that. Very gradually, however, I began to relish things instead of being uniformly bored or miserable. At first, these small epiphanies occurred when I was away from the shrine room, in my "own" time—afternoon tea, the half hour of personal time after meals, the space at the end of work period. Later I began to enjoy—*really* enjoy—the morning session of walking meditation. There was a bright moment when I found myself utterly thrilled by the dance of sunlight across the shrine room floor. By the final week I was enjoying a little bit of everything, and by the last day I was like a dying man soaking up every moment because he knows it will be his last. There was a clarity and an acceptance in these final moments unlike anything I had experienced in my everyday life on the outside.

There's another odd manifestation that bears mentioning here: As the retreat wore on, I found myself falling in love with first this, then that fellow participant. After a while, my heart fluttered on seeing almost any one of them (though I developed major "crushes" on only a few). In the final days I had warm feelings for even the harshest disciplinarians among the staff and wept over the suffering of flies and mosquitoes. I'm told this is normal, and the effect wore off a couple of days after the retreat, to be sure. But I can't help but wonder what the world would be like if it didn't.

The final dinner party signaled an abrupt return to "everyday" life. There was music, talking, dancing, and cups of sake raised in endless toasts all around. It was nearly overwhelming. An Englishwoman who was there told me she takes a month out of her six-week vacation every year to attend the retreat. "This was my eighth," she said. "*Dathun*'s the best vacation I can imagine." After mine, I understood what she meant.

. . .

Clarke Fountain began practicing Buddhist meditation in 1974 and in 1985 became a student of the Ven. Thrangu-Rinpoche. He has an M.A. in Buddhist Studies from the Naropa Institute and works as a writer for Matrix Software Inc. in Big Rapids, Michigan.

One Hundred and Eight Thousand Prostrations

DAVID LEWIS

✳

PROSTRATION PRACTICE IS AN IMPORTANT FEA-ture of *ngondro* (foundation) practice in the Vajrayana system. The *ngondro* in its simplest form has five main sections of one hundred thousand repetitions each. These are refuge, *bodhicitta*, mandala, *Vajrasattva* (purification), and guru yoga. Prostrations are generally related to taking refuge but they can be used in the other four sections as well. The foundation practices are important because they prepare the student's body, speech, and mind for the more profound subtleties of the higher tantric practices.

Without *ngondro* it is almost impossible to correctly progress along the path. Therefore in the beginning everyone in this tradition is required to do the prostrations. In my case, I did them slowly over many years. When I had completed them, my teacher, His Eminence Shenphen Dawa, asked me to do them over again, but this time within a shorter period of two or three months. This came as quite a shock since I had assumed that this hurdle had been jumped. Not so.

I arranged a period for prostration retreat, scheduling it for the next two months. Khenpo Palden Sherab, our resident abbot, suggested that I try to accomplish three thousand prostrations a day. I was able, in the beginning, to do two hundred a day and, after a week, was eking out around seven hundred. My body was out of shape and my muscles and bones felt utterly bruised. I ached to the core. If I rested in any position for longer than five min-utes it required all of my effort to withstand the pain of even the simplest move.

By the following week, things had begun to smooth out somewhat. By this time I was able to do two thousand a day and the exercise had put me into shape. I established a routine of getting up at four AM, doing a session of seven hundred, then after breakfast another session of the same, and finally completing the balance just before supper.

During the prostration sessions I visualized as well as possible the lineage tree surrounded by the Buddhas and their families looking down upon me and blessing the practice. After the first fifteen minutes the acrid sweat would pour out of me; each time my folded hands were raised above my head in salutation it would drip into my eyes and leave them burning.

I was using a polished hardwood board for the prostrations, along with two cloth pot holders to expedite the sliding of my hands along the wood. In order to perform a proper prostration, one first raises the hands over the head, palm to palm, in salutation, and then lays out completely so that the forehead, chest, hands, and knees are touching the ground. How to go down quickly without sustaining injury is important simply because after doing a hundred thousand, one still wants to enjoy the use of one's body. Quite a few practitioners are unable to complete the practice because of improper technique, and they have been known to sustain serious knee and back injuries. I placed a pad for my knees on the board, and would slide down like a falling tree, not letting the knees touch until my chest had taken the brunt of the impact. Consequently my knees rarely hurt and the stale airs were shocked from my body. After a while the force of falling became the force of rising and the prostrations entered an effortless and blissful space.

After completing the first twenty-five thousand, I worked my way up to three thousand prostrations a day. I could only continue at this pace for three days at a time because some obstacle would always manifest itself: an illness or infection, an unexpected visitor who could not be ignored, or a sudden family emergency. I realized that this was my limit and that the activity of purification was affecting my whole environment. I was beginning to comprehend how the prostrations were working on me, and how subtle and inborn were the obstacles that I was hoping to clear. How great are those practitioners who have accomplished the compassion to work for others on this level of penetration! I had touched the very fiber of *bodhisattva beingness* and though it was not mine to keep at this point, at least through raw effort a kind of self-initiation was pointing out this truth. My respect for teachers in general moved from idealism to recognition, and I felt a deep satisfaction in belonging to the *sangha*.

By the time I had accomplished one hundred thousand prostrations, I had lost twenty pounds, my sweat had become sweet instead of salty, and I felt ready for the next hundred thousand.

. . .

David Lewis began studying Nyingmapa Vajrayana in 1971. He has done retreats in India, Africa, and the Pacific Northwest.

All-Night Vigil to Yumka

WEST ABRASHKIN

✳

V ALENTINE'S DAY. A GIANT SNOWSTORM dumped two feet on our little temple. I had been living next door in a small retreat cabin and when I got up that day I was worried that people couldn't get through—especially since the plow had gotten stuck four times just trying to clear the parking lot. I called Tulku, our Tibetan lama. He didn't seem at all concerned.

When we started this group—the Mahasiddha Nyingma Center in Hawley, Massachusetts—back in 1973, we used to joke about how we were "flounders," floundering and flopping in spiritual naivete. Well, people were really floundering that afternoon, but in snow, not dharma! Bundled up, carrying sleeping bags and provisions, they crawled up the hill with the wind howling and snow blowing horizontally.

Once inside, the habits of many years at such retreats revived. Some scurried to the kitchen downstairs to start dinner while the rest of the twenty or so participants started the main practice in the shrine room. Since it was the twenty-fifth of the lunar month, it was Dakini day and our practice was a *tsok* (feast) to the Queen of the Vajra Dakinis, the consort of Guru Padmasambhava, Yeshe Tsogyel.

For an hour we chanted the *sadhana*, everybody settling into it nicely, and when we came to the root mantra to Yumka (Yeshe Tsogyel)—OM PADMO YOGINI JNANA VARAHI HUNG—we divided into three groups,

each continuing the chant for four hours so that it could go on all night.

I was in the first contingent with Tulku, and we recorded ourselves for a while, playing the tape back and chanting with it, going a bit too fast for my taste, but I figured you needed energy to get through and so screwed myself up to speed.

I usually sit in the back, the better to hide (though I'm the oldest student), but this time I found myself near the front. Being lazy, I never bothered to learn to visualize (our main practice), hoping that sometime the visions would spontaneously appear as our chief teacher said they would. But this time, because I was so impressed by Tulku's description of the visualization, and also because it seemed so simple, I resolved to give it a try.

In this visualization, we first transform into the sparkling light-body of the Goddess, red and transparent, holding drum and skinning knife (to skin the ego), dancing in the advancing posture with a great haughty demeanor, sexually magnetic, disciplining the beings. A big problem for me has been imagining myself as a female. But this time—maybe because the Goddess seemed so powerful—I succeeded! Glancing up with my single eye, I saw the Guru above me and he was Rinpoche. I began to spin the root mantra in my heart.

Things were getting sort of twilight, and in such an atmosphere it was OK to bother this deity above me with my revolving chant. He looked at me with compassion and, just like it is supposed to happen, a rain of nectar began to fall on me. Once before I had had the experience of sheets of blessings falling like brown dust or TV snow, making the air tingle. My back crawled, but I was determined to concentrate. I couldn't believe how easily I kept finishing my rosary. Usually I'm aware of each bead.

Suddenly I was transfixed; I mean really lifted. The profound final mantra of all the Buddhas poured forth like thunder: OM GUHYAJNANA BODHISITTA MAHA SUKHA RULU RULU HUNG JHO HUNG! Joy flooded my heart and I could hardly keep back the tears.

I staggered back to my cabin but couldn't drop off to sleep. Waves of blissful energy, like fast-moving clouds, kept running past my eyelids. I finally knew how other disciples must feel who are more proficient at visualization than me and why their faith is so deep. I just wanted to be back in that light-body with my Lama pouring down the sweet elixir that makes my troubles and stupid ego dissolve.

Next morning, after a call from my mother who has a brain tumor near her ear, we completed the *sadhana* and ate the food offerings. I felt that I had succeeded in the practice a little bit, but I was sad that I couldn't sustain the vision in the postmeditative state.

May you all accomplish your virtuous practices,
you great Beings!

. . .

A sculptor, poet, painter, writer, and devoted practitioner, West Abrashkin was a cofounder of Mahasiddha Nyingmapa Temple in Hawley, Massachusetts. At his death in 1992, he had completed his ngondro *practices and seven of the ten million Vajra Guru Mantras he had vowed to accomplish in this lifetime.*

The Three-Year Retreat

KEN MCLEOD

✳

In the Kagyü tradition of Buddhism in Tibet, the three-year retreat provides systematic training in advanced meditation techniques. Selected monks and reincarnated teachers enter a retreat center and spend approximately three years and three months practicing meditation at least sixteen hours a day. The retreat center is totally isolated from the world, no exits are permitted, and only very high lamas or teachers are allowed to visit to give additional instruction.

During the visit of Kalu-Rinpoche to Vancouver, British Columbia, in 1974, we began hearing rumors about a three-year retreat being planned for Westerners. A three-year retreat for Westerners? Most of us had never dared to dream of such an opportunity—the chance to receive instruction and to practice the legendary methods of such teachers as Naropa, Marpa, Milarepa, and others.

We decided to bring the subject up with Rinpoche. Yes, he said, he was planning a retreat for Westerners. It would be in France. Could we be part of it? Yes, but there were certain requirements. . . .

Foundations

"For fundamental change to take place, motivation must change." Our training from Kalu-Rinpoche up to this point had certainly shown that he was familiar with this maxim. He consistently emphasized the general foundations: Human existence provides a precious, rare, and fragile opportunity to practice Buddhism. Death may come at any moment. A moral and ethical way of life is necessary in view of the workings of karma. *Samsaric* or ego-based existence is inherently unsatisfying.

However, these basic motivating reflections, while necessary for the three-year retreat, were not sufficient. The special foundations of the *mahamudra* tradition must also be completed. These involve five simple acts: prostration, refuge prayer, a long purification mantra, a symbolic offering of the universe, and a prayer for union of one's mind with the teacher's. Each is repeated one hundred thousand times. For most of us, this was not a problem since we had all done this set of practices at least once already.

Tibetan

The next requirement was language. Everything would be in Tibetan—the teaching, the texts, the meditation manuals, the rituals. Everything! Without fluency in Tibetan, it would be like attending a school in a country whose language one didn't know. Rinpoche made it clear that the language was very important. We would be dealing with ideas and concepts that had no formulation in English. We would be studying texts written by great masters and it was important to be able to study them directly. We would be performing rituals composed in Tibetan verse and we should understand the sense of what we were doing and not just repeat words. And our

Ken McLeod.
(Photo courtesy of
Ken McLeod.)

retreat director would only be able to instruct us in Tibetan!

Finances

The third requirement was money—basically, enough for food and minimal personal expenses for the period of the retreat. Rinpoche said that he would send word when it was time to come to France. After Rinpoche's departure, we set out to earn what we would need. Some went to work in copper mines in northern British Columbia. I worked as a teaching assistant at the university and helped as a houseparent for children who were government wards.

Preparation

Eventually, we received word to come to France. We arrived at Kagyu Ling in June. At that time, Kagyu Ling consisted of a mock château, built around the turn of the century, with associated buildings. It was situated on fifteen acres of meadows and woods in rolling hills about halfway between Paris and Lyons. There was a bad drought in the whole region. Water was in short supply, and the weather was generally hot. When we asked where the retreat facilities were, we were told that we were going to build them. We laughed.

Construction

A few days later, Rinpoche arrived and we soon found out that, yes, we were going to build our own retreat structures. And while we were doing that, we were also to learn the regular ceremonies, how to prepare shrines, how to play the various musical instruments, and how to lead chanting. It looked like a full summer.

As it happened, it was really quite a wonderful time. Every morning we would get up, chant the Tara ritual, have breakfast, and work and study all day until Mahakala ritual in the evening. As time went on, we even worked nights. We learned how to mix concrete, lay bricks, put in windows, lay floors, and plaster walls. We were also taught how to play cymbals, beat drums, blow instruments while inhaling without breaking the note (that's a nice trick!), make *tormas* (ceremonial confections), and so on.

Within a few months, our retreat structures began to take shape. There were two separate but identical enclosures, one for men and one for women. Each contained eight rooms, one temple, a kitchen, a communal washroom, and a yoga room. Hundreds of people came to help with construction; drywall experts, architects, and carpenters appeared out of thin air just when they were needed. All the construction work was directed and supervised by a young Englishman whose ability to get the best out of people, to teach and train them to work effectively, and to overcome every problem soon won our respect and appreciation.

At a certain point, Rinpoche began giving the thirty or forty empowerments that form the basis of the practices we would be doing in retreat. Our work schedule became even more intense as the date of entry drew closer. We worked harder and longer, sloshing around in the freezing November rains digging drainage ditches, installing shelves, building individual shrines, often working late into the night. All this time, our anxiety about the next step, complete isolation from the world and the engagement of very intensive practice, began to weigh on us.

Entry

The last of the empowerments was completed. Out of appreciation, all the retreatants offered a long-life ceremony to Rinpoche. In this ceremony, an effigy is offered to all the forces that would generally shorten or threaten the teacher's life. The winds, the clouds, and the rainstorm that developed during the course of the ceremony left a very powerful sense of magic and wonder.

A few days later, we gathered in the main temple and were given tea and offerings. We said good-bye to all the people with whom we had worked so closely over the last six months building the retreat structures. I said good-bye to my wife, who was entering the women's retreat. It was sad but somehow it didn't feel like an actual separation. Then we walked in formal procession behind our retreat director and Rinpoche—magnificently arrayed in his ceremonial brocade—to the gates of the men's retreat house.

The sealing ceremonies were done outside in a cold rain, reading the liturgies by a car's headlights. We entered the retreat house one by one and the door closed. We would not see the outside world or anything of it for three years, three months, and three days.

Leaving the World

The first reaction was one of relief. After the frantic pressure of the last few days, we were suddenly free just to sit and practice. However, there were a few things to adjust to.

Our rooms were approximately ten feet square and contained a shrine, shelves for texts and clothes, and a "meditation box." Constructed of unfinished pine boards, the box was about a yard square, eighteen inches high on the front and sides, three feet high in back. A versatile piece of furniture, it served at various times as couch, meditation platform, writing desk, and eating table. At night it became my bed.

I'd heard much about how strenuously meditators in Tibet had applied themselves, never lying down, putting lighted candles on their heads, fighting off sleep in every conceivable way. Rinpoche told me that he had prevented himself from drifting off to sleep by balancing on a window ledge. Whenever he fell asleep, he fell off! Now it was my turn to follow in the footsteps of these great masters. Or so I thought.

Going to sleep sitting up is not so difficult. After a couple of days of three to four thousand prostrations I could fall asleep in any position. However, remaining upright was another matter. I've always been a restless sleeper, so every morning, and sometimes in the middle of the night, I'd find myself in some strange position, curled up like a dog at the bottom of the box, legs up in the air at some impossible angle—stiff, cramped, sore. Some of my fellow retreatants adjusted with only a little trouble, and found that sleeping sitting up brought about a lighter sleep and clearer dreams. Others had as much difficulty as I. They tied strings from the ceiling to their hair, tried to jam extra blocks into the box to keep the body upright—ingenious, diligent, but ultimately ineffective. Sometimes I was so exhausted I would even dream that I was falling asleep. Then I would have to wake up twice, once during the dream, and once again into "real life." After a couple of these episodes, I began to question seriously the conventional distinctions between reality and dreams.

Despite the difficulties, we were all very happy to be in retreat. Through our teacher, through a lot of hard work, and through the kindness of innumerable people who had helped in so many ways, our dream of entering the retreat had been realized. That feeling of gratitude would stay with us for the whole retreat, a constant encouragement to make full use of the precious opportunity we had been given.

Retreat

The first meditation session began at four o'clock in the morning and continued till six. Half an hour later, we'd meet in the temple to recite prayers to Tara, a female bodhisattva who embodies the principle of awakened compassion and protection. Then at eight we'd go to the kitchen to fetch our breakfast (which was prepared by our cook/attendant) and eat in our rooms. The second session began at nine and was two and a half hours long. Lunch was followed by a period for rest, study, or free time. We'd begin sitting again at two, and at five, we'd meet to do the evening protector rituals. Supper in our rooms was at six. Then we'd sit again from seven to nine.

There were a number of supplementary practices to fit into this schedule: a couple of morning meditations—first thing—followed by prostrations, water offerings, and chanting of mantras between the end of the first session and Tara ritual, our own daily practices whenever we could, and two additional meditations in the evening after the final session, one for protection and one for developing compassion. In addition, we studied the commentaries that explained the various meditation practices, both how to do them and what they meant. We met with our retreat director every few days to go over new material and resolve questions and difficulties, and those who were weak in Tibetan endeavored to improve their comprehension and skills. In short, this was no holiday!

Several times a month, we did major rituals together in the temple instead of our regular individual sessions. Full moon days were marked by special prayers to the lineage of teachers. The tenth day of both the waxing and waning moon was celebrated with *yidam* (deity meditation) ceremonies of self-empowerment. On the twenty-ninth day, we did extensive protector rituals, and a ceremony for the renewal of vows on both full moon and new moon days.

While this was our basic schedule, our actual meditation practice during the four daily sessions was constantly changing. Over the course of the retreat, we practiced most of the central meditation techniques of both the Shangpa Kagyu and Karma Kagyu traditions as well as a number of associated practices.

The First Year

The first year was occupied with the establishment of a proper foundation for spiritual development. At the beginning we spent a full week reflecting on the unique opportunity human existence affords for realization, another week on death and impermanence, and a week each on dharma and the nature of suffering in existence. These reflective meditations were difficult. While we were all familiar with this material, spending more than eight hours a day contemplating these themes had a profound effect on outlook and motivation. One began to see life, the world, and existence itself in a very different light and appreciated at a much deeper level the importance of spiritual understanding as an essential part of life and being.

The next four months were occupied with the special foundations. Although we had all completed them before coming into the retreat, these practices are particularly important for generating a sound basis for further development and removing obstacles and impediments through purification. Practicing them in this kind of intensity was a new experience.

We were still becoming accustomed to the strenuous routine. It was midwinter and for many of us, it was the first time we had lived without heat. Yet our enthusiasm and energy carried us through, exhausted though we might be from doing over three thousand prostrations a day.

With this as our basis, we turned to meditations and practices whose focus was the guru, bringing the mind of the guru and the mind of the student together through the power of faith and devotion. Despite the fact that we had virtually no contact with Rinpoche for much of the retreat, these practices made us very aware of his presence and blessing in the retreat.

Next we turned to techniques to develop love, compassion, and *bodhichitta*, the intention to realize awakening in order to help others. For me, this was one of the most wonderful and powerful periods of retreat. Eight to ten hours of intensive reflection on the needs, pain, and yearnings of others in contrast to one's own made me realize how self-centered we really are. Anger, I realized, is based solely on a sense of personal territory; physical, emotional, or intellectual. Through the technique of *taking and sending*, one gradually discovers that it is not necessary to maintain rigid territorial boundaries. The freedom and joy coming from that realization left me with a deep appreciation of the profundity and power of compassion.

The final practice in the first year of retreat was *shamatha/vipassana*, tranquillity and insight. In the Kagyu tradition, there are two special features of these practices. First, because they lead directly into the sutra tradition of *mahamudra* (meditation on what is ultimately real), the method of meditation remains basically the same through all the stages of experience and understanding. Second, since the Kagyu tradition specializes in faith and devotion towards the guru, each period of meditation starts with prayers to the guru for blessing. In the retreat environment, one clearly appreciates the kindness and love of one's teacher, the role his or her inspiration has played in leading one forward on the spiritual path, and the amazing depth and richness of the teacher's concise instructions on this kind of meditation.

Yidams: The Second Year

Virtually the entire second year was taken up with *yidam* practice, or deity meditation. Here I had to assimilate ideas and approaches to the world that have no counterpart in modern Western culture. Identification with a particular symbolic expression of awakened mind day after day gradually leads one to see the world very differently. No longer does it seem solid and rigid; everything takes on a magical, sacred quality and increasingly appears as a reflection or echo of one's own mind.

Perhaps it is worth mentioning at this juncture that life in retreat is not exactly easy. Seven men, each with strong ideas about "how things should be," make for an interesting environment. As time went on, however, we found that we were not seven separate minds. The state or attitude of one person affected everyone else and we learned, sometimes painfully, that what we experienced was directly related to our outlook. In other words the retreat environment provided a very clear mirror of our own state of mind. We were confronted as individuals with deciding whether to ignore the mirror or face ourselves, however difficult or painful that might be.

As we continued working with *yidam* practice, we came to appreciate the tremendous power and support ritual provides in meditation and spiritual development. The ritual becomes an enactment, virtually a drama, of the unfolding of enlightened mind in oneself. In both the daily and monthly rituals, the expression of one's awakened nature is nourished, refined, and made manifest in actual experience. The dreamlike nature of experience is brought out clearly. Gradually, this view colors and transforms one's experience of ordinary reality.

Year Three: Advanced Practices

The third year was filled with advanced practices such as the Six Teachings of Naropa. These practices dissolve still more subtle kinds of clinging, to enable the mind to rest naturally without contrivance, wandering, or reference. Generally, we only had time to become familiar with the meditations but that was enough to convince us of the real possibility of understanding mind's nature through them.

What It Is

The three-year retreat is primarily a program of training in meditation. It is virtually a college of contemplative techniques. There is a considerable amount of material, both theoretical and practical, to assimilate. And it is an important step into the contemplative life, a life of retreat and practice. In many ways, it is the essence of monasticism—a group of people who are occupied totally with spiritual or mystical practice and who have little contact with or interest in the world at large.

In addition, it is an opportunity to practice, and practice very intensively. All the difficulties—the struggle with physical discomfort, interaction with other retreatants, and so forth—become part of one's path. One finishes the retreat with the feeling that one has done something very significant that, at the same time, is just the smallest beginning on the path.

What It Is Not

When I originally went into the retreat, I had the idea that it would somehow be a solution to all my problems, that at last I would receive the most profound instructions, be able to practice them without distraction, and, if not actually attain awakening, at least make some pretty healthy progress along the path. Needless to say, my expectations, both conscious and unconscious, were not fulfilled; at least, not in the way I expected. Oh yes, the profound instructions were given and it was possible to practice them, but there was one big catch and that was "I."

First, I didn't find the retreat easy, nor the meditation particularly blissful. It was hard work from start to finish. The schedule is demanding even if one is in good health both physically and mentally. However, the intensity of practice and the conditions bring up a lot of "stuff." Physical difficulties—from sore knees to actual illness—

have to be faced directly. There is no escape, though one tends to spend a lot of effort trying to find one. In the end, however, one sees more and more clearly how everything begins and ends with oneself and how one creates one's own experience of the world and finally accepts things for what they are. The truly wonderful consequence of that acceptance is that one finds a totally unsuspected freedom and joy independent of any set of conditions or circumstances.

The three-year retreat is certainly not a guarantee of enlightenment. I gained a much better understanding of how deeply our emotional and ego-based patterns are imbedded in us. While I reluctantly came to the realization that the ignorance and confusion of aeons were not going to be removed in a few months, I also saw clearly that the methods of Buddhist practice will, without doubt, clear them away. The only requisite is to work with constant enthusiasm. In short, my confidence and trust in the dharma were firmly established.

Finally, retreat isn't a vacation from *samsara*, from ordinary egocentric experience. In fact, the retreat was more like super-*samsara*—everything intensified and magnified to such an extent that I couldn't avoid the chaos created by my own confusion and ignorance.

Exit

Time passes in retreat at an extraordinary pace. Sometimes, I felt that the seasons were scenes from a movie; spring changing into summer, then fall, then winter, day by day. The time soon came for us to exit. Since this was the first retreat for Westerners, a large crowd had gathered outside the gates. We stepped out straight into the lens of a movie camera and paraded past literally hundreds of cameras clicking and flashing. But the overriding impression was one of spaciousness. It felt like I was walking in the sky! After forty months of a view confined to half an acre, the meadows, sky, clouds, and woods were infinite vistas, brilliantly clear and vivid. It all seemed like a dream, not really real, yet very much there. This feeling endured, and was easily recalled many months later. People's faces seemed different. One could see peace, anxiety, fear, or love written clearly in the set

of the mouth or the chin, the glance of an eye. And riding in a car, for some reason, sent me immediately to sleep.

As time went on, I became aware of less obvious effects of the retreat. It was much easier for me simply to listen to people than it had been before. For some reason, it was easier to understand what was motivating certain types of behavior. My general outlook on the world had changed, too. The impermanence of situations was accepted with much less resistance. I became clearly aware of the fact that how I felt in a situation determined how I experienced it (rather than the opposite).

The most important effect, however, was a solid confidence and trust in the teachings of Buddha and Rinpoche. There was no doubt left in my mind that these teachings could and would lead one to realization and that the obstacle to that was simply one's own habitual patterns.

Finding a Place In or Out of the World

After the retreat, each of us had to decide what to do next. Some (including myself) elected to return and do a second three-year retreat, another small step on the path. Some took monastic ordination in order to lead a simple life and concentrate on practice. Others found themselves teaching in centers. And still others returned to a more normal life with a family and profession.

At this point, there is still very little support for people who have completed this kind of training, and readjustment to life can be difficult. After the second retreat, a fellow retreatant warned me, "It takes two to three years to adjust." She was right! Or maybe one never "adjusts" completely and the understanding and experience of retreat remains always.

. . .

A dharma student since 1970, Ken McLeod completed his second three-year retreat in 1983 and was subsequently authorized to teach by the Ven. Kalu-Rinpoche. He is executive director of Unfettered Mind, a nonprofit organization in Los Angeles, California, dedicated to the application of Buddhist perspectives and methods to the demands of life in contemporary urban America.

Ego's Last Dance

JOANNA MACY

✵

THERE IT IS IN THE MIDDLE OF THE DANCE ground: you can see it in the form of a small clay doll inside an open, black, triangular box. It is the ego, the self-preoccupation that resides at the center of our lives. And the three sides of the box, each bearing a painted skull, represent what holds it together: the three poisons of greed, hatred, and delusion. Forces also exist that undo the ego, freeing us from the suffering it creates—and, in the fresh spring breeze off the Himalayan foothills, these will be summoned today and danced in full regalia.

It is the third day of the great annual lama dances at Tashi Dzong, a Tibetan refugee community in northwest India. These rituals have been part of my life for nearly thirty years, so I know what's coming: the dance for the dismembering of the ego. I have loved it so much that an adapted form of it has turned up, on occasion, in the workshops and courses I teach in the West. Let me tell you how it is performed in the ancient tantric Buddhist ritual, and then describe the truncated version we have played with in the secularized Western world.

This morning the broad hillside terrace in front of the temple has again been swept with brooms and blessings. Once more the big white canopy that billows gently against the blue sky has been erected to demarcate the dancing ground. It now becomes the sacred mandala of mind, a force field of meditation in movement. Along the valley side and facing toward the wide temple steps where the dancers enter, the musician monks are arrayed with the long horns and cymbals and drums that awakened us at dawn. The other two sides are lined with the lay families of Tashi Dzong, with toddlers, umbrellas, prayer wheels, rosaries, dogs, baskets of pastry, bottles of pop, Indian hill folk from nearby villages, and the occasional camera-hung Westerner.

The resounding horns and cymbals suddenly subside, leaving a silence that dissolves into sounds of mountain morning—birds calling and prayer flags flapping and a truck on the distant valley road. Now a sharp rattling begins, the steady staccato beat of hand drums made from human skulls, rapidly rotated in the hands of four spritely young skeletons. The four apparitions are animated with angular vitality, from their grinning death's-head masks to their tattered rags and bare boys' legs—for once not hidden by monastic robes. With their presence the mandala of the mind becomes a cemetery. Riveting our attention like death itself, the skeletons move around the three-cornered box as if it were an open grave. I am told that they symbolize the purity and fearlessness that remain when the flesh of ignorance and the blood of attachment have been consumed.

When the skeletons withdraw into the temple, the long horns blast and wail, then give way to chanting so deep it seems to come out of the earth. Measured, almost majestic in their movements, and robed in shimmering damask, four *dakinis* enter. These female forms are guardians of the mandala of mind. As symbolized by the tools in their hands, they dance the powers of meditation. The one in white grips the hook of mindfulness, which retrieves the distracted and wandering mind; to hold it steady, the red *dakini* brings the chain of one-pointed concentration. The noose that the yellow one carries is clear knowing, which rescues the mind from fear and delusion. The symbol danced by the *dakini* in green is one I can hear as well as see: it is the bell of release, promising freedom from the death grip of ego. Like the process of meditation itself, the *dakinis'* dance is slow and repetitive. Their steadily recurring steps and gestures remind us gently that to begin again, over and over again, is both tolerable and good.

At their departure the tempo accelerates. The focus widens from the schooling of the mind to its action in the world. Two vigorous masked figures fly down the temple steps and career across the dancing ground, flapping their wings and poking their beaks at ego's box. They are crow and owl. They dance the powers of daytime consciousness and nighttime consciousness: complementary perspectives on reality. Owl, as night, moves with a measure of dignity, as befits the realization of the mysterious emptiness at the ground of being, the void from which all things arise. Amid daily activities, this realization takes on a different character: the perception of the radical interdependence of all phenomena, the mutuality between all things. Crow, with his jagged feathers, swift lunges, and fiercely jutting beak, bristles with the energy such insight releases.

Each foray progressively reveals the pathetic insubstantiality of the little ego. It has staked its claims on its own almighty separateness; now confronted with the realization of its inextricable interexistence with all things, it has no choice but to dissolve, to subside again back into Buddha nature. The final act, after Crow and Owl withdraw, is presided over by two stags. In them, I am told, the trained eye can see Padmasambhava himself, the great tantric master and magician who brought Buddhism to Tibet, and in whose honor these ritual dances are performed. So the stags also symbolize the spontane-

ous play of enlightened mind. They are beautiful, with a kind of wild elegance. Their high, many-pointed antlers flutter with flags as they dance closer to ego's box, sidling on legs like coiled springs. Now quivering to the strong, steady beat of drums and cymbals, and reaching right into the three-sided box, the stags make their meal. Ripping ego apart, they break off pieces of arms, legs, trunk, head, lift them to their mouths, then cast the crumbling remains over their shoulders. Finally, repast completed, ego consumed, the stags leap high in glorious, victorious satisfaction. The long horns blast a mighty proclamation that the mountains echo back.

The danced drama has reached its end. Its resolution has occurred without conquest—no Saint George slaying the dragon, no apocalyptic battle between the forces of light and the legions of darkness—just a gradual, almost teasing dismantling of the illusions that ego lives on. The dance itself unfolds as the realization that our self-centeredness, with all its power to create suffering, does not exist as anything permanently, substantially real. Its pretensions and defenses simply become more and more transparent, until they dissolve again into the natural ground from which they arose. Featureless and liberating, the ground is always Dharmakaya, the ever fresh, ever healing well of all that is.

One day, after returning from a trip to Tashi Dzong, I described the dance to a gathering at a New England Quaker retreat center. "Let's try it!" was the response. I hesitated, assuming that it could only really have meaning for those immersed in Buddhist philosophy or practiced in Buddhist meditation, but the eagerness of the group and my own curiosity carried the day. Silently praying that my Tibetan friends and teachers would forgive me for my brashness in borrowing from their ancient ritual, I joined in digging clay from a stream bank and invented directions for the impromptu ritual.

The notion of making an ego doll was so appealing that each person wanted to make their own. My misgivings were forgotten as my hands worked the hunk of clay before me; a crude figure began to emerge. With bulbous forehead, mouth agape, and huge, pompously raised index finger, it portrayed and lampooned my own self-importance as scholar and teacher. I recognized a per-sona I had half-consciously nurtured and defended over the years, and it was a relief to have it sitting in front of me now, objectified; I gazed at it with a tender mixture of pride and pity. I held it aloft as if bearing the most precious of offerings when the time came to join the ceremonial procession to the bonfire. There each of us in turn, and in different ways, expressed compassion for all that had gone into shaping this manifestation of ego, and gratitude for whatever solace and protection it had provided over the years. And one by one, when we felt ready to let go of it, or even to prepare to let go, amid shouts of support and jubilation we cast the doll into the flames.

What happened for us that summer evening in New England inspired me, in subsequent years, to take the process into classes and workshops—usually in more abbreviated form. One of these occasions was in Los Angeles in May 1991, right after the mammoth uprising that burned and wasted vast sections of the city. An empowerment workshop for social change, it was designed to help us gain wider perspectives and deeper inner resources for effective action in the world. The seventy of us were a racially mixed group, with whites predominating.

After sharing what we had experienced during the weeks of rioting, our fears and hopes, we were about to explore strategies for cooperative action. I sensed the seriousness of commitment on the part of each person, and also the burden that such nobility of purpose represented—a burden compounded by inevitable attachments to one's own views and also by inevitable feelings of inadequacy. In each heart, I knew, were questions about whether or not they were strong enough, or even caring enough, to follow through on their dreams for a just society.

Instead of giving a lecture on our capacities to surmount our weaknesses, I brought out the clay. A half-pound hunk was set before each person. Briefly describing the dance at Tashi Dzong, I said, "Now here's our chance to make our own ego doll, so it won't need to get in the way of what wants to happen through us for the healing of our world."

Again there was rapt silence as each person focused in on the material in their hands, and again my bemuse-ment at what took shape under my own—this time I could make out a huge-breasted Earth Mother, all-wise and ever giving. For our ceremonial offering, a drum was brought out and a drumroll dramatically played as one person after another stepped into the large circle to present their ego doll. This particular occasion remains vivid in my memory because many in the group worked in Hollywood's entertainment industry, and they threw themselves into the exercise with obvious relief and a contagious panache.

"Ta-daa!" they'd cry, leaping forward to parade their precious object in front of our noses, before placing it reverently in the center of the circle.

"Presenting, in its first-ever public appearance, the incomparable, one and only . . . smart-ass ego of mine; many hands and mouths to hide the hollow heart."

"Feast your eyes on this sensitive soul, bent over by the woes of the world and afraid of getting her hands dirty."

"This brilliant know-it-all likes to sit real cool on the sidelines and pass judgments."

"See how sweetly this dear little ego smiles, hoping everyone will love her so she can have her own way."

Each ego was greeted by applause and extravagant expressions of appreciation.

When all the crude little sculptures were amassed in the center, the whole group rose to walk ceremoniously and affectionately around them. Since many in the group were familiar with Buddhist practice, it seemed appropriate to chant a beloved ancient mantra from *The Heart Sutra*: "*Gate, gate, paragate, parasam gate; bodhi swaha!*" ("Gone, gone, gone beyond, completely gone beyond, far out!") It was a way of saying goodbye—or of beginning to prepare to say good-bye—to mental fabrications that had outlived their usefulness. When, after lunch, we turned to strategies for collective action, the task felt light, and alive with vitality.

No *dakinis* had appeared, no skeletons, no stags with flagged antlers to make final dismemberment of our attachments. Instead of ornate Tibetan masks, there was here, on the part of each, an unmasking—a self-disclosure that was no less remarkable for being playful. Perhaps, even without the sonorous horns of Tashi

Dzong and the ancient tantric patterns of the dance, a sacred mandala of mind had happened here, too, if only briefly. For here, as well, the realization had come that the self-centeredness and self-image that imprison us are not to be conquered like an enemy. They are not to be punished so much as seen through. Fabricated by us, without objective reality, they can be released. That letting go occurs more easily without recrimination, even if it has to happen over and over and over again.

. . .

Joanna Macy is a teacher of Buddhism and general systems theory, and is the author of World as Lover, World as Self, *and* Despair and Personal Power in the Nuclear Age.

The Vajrayana Centers of North America

ALASKA

Alaska Buddhist Society

After training in and mastering Tae Kwon Do, Kurt Won turned to Buddhism. Following Grand Master Lu, he set up a Buddhist shrine in Anchorage. He frequently invites various masters to Anchorage and acts as their translator.
ADDRESS: 12810 Mission Circle, Anchorage, AK 99516
PHONE: (907) 345-4401
LINEAGE: Chinese True Buddha School
SPIRITUAL HEAD: Grand Master Sheng-yen Lu
CONTACT: Kurt Won

Juneau Forming Dharma Study Group

For description, please refer to Shambhala International, Halifax, Nova Scotia, Canada.
ADDRESS: Box 22146, Juneau, AK 99802-2146
PHONES: (907) 780-6299 (home); (907) 780-5844 (work)
FAX: (907) 789-4904
E-MAIL: chapman@alaska.net
LINEAGE: Tibetan Kagyu-Nyingma
SPIRITUAL HEAD: Sakyong Mipham Rinpoche

CONTACT: Susan Chapman
AFFILIATION: Shambhala International, Halifax, Nova Scotia

Khawachen Dharma Center

Khawachen Dharma Center was founded in 1979 by the late Ngodup Paljor in Anchorage. From 1979 to 1989 Khawachen brought both Tibetan lamas and Zen teachers to Alaska. Since 1989 it has continued, on a less organized basis, to bring Buddhist teachers to Homer. At present

The logo of Khawachen Dharma Center celebrates Alaska's wildlife. (Illustration courtesy of Khawachen Dharma Center.)

the group meets regularly only when a teacher is visiting (once or twice a year). Denise Lassaw Paljor is the director and serves as a resource connection for teachers, books, films, and other dharma centers. Wandering dharma practitioners are welcome to call.
ADDRESS: HC 67 Box 912, Anchor Point, AK 99556
PHONE: (907) 235-4277
FAX: Same
E-MAIL: dpaljor@igc.apc.org
LINEAGE: Tibetan
SPIRITUAL HEAD: Ngodup Paljor (deceased)
CONTACT: Denise Lassaw Paljor
AFFILIATION: Autonomous
ESTABLISHED: 1979
FACILITIES: Rent space at the yoga studio when needed.
MEDITATION PROGRAM: Group meditation whenever visiting teachers are in town (once or twice yearly).
PUBLICATIONS: Occasional newsletter.

Mahakaruna Tibetan Buddhist Study Center

No description available.
ADDRESS: Box 73359, Fairbanks, AK 99707
PHONE: (907) 479-7455

LINEAGE: Tibetan Vajrayana
CONTACT: David Whitmore
FACILITIES: Shrine room
MEDITATION PROGRAM: Meditation once a week. Meditation every night when lama is here.
PUBLICATIONS: Newsletter from time to time.

ARIZONA

Bodhisattva Institute

Bodhisattva Institute is a center devoted to the study and practice of the Karma and Shangpa Kagyu lineages. Our plan is to build a large temple and monastic center in the Southwest for monastics and laypeople alike. Facilities will include lodging and space for long retreats and ongoing studies as well as a complete program of monastic practice.
ADDRESS: 714 North Desert Avenue, Tucson, AZ 85711
PHONE: (520) 325-2272
FAX: Same
E-MAIL: tenpa@azstarnet.com
LINEAGE: Tibetan Kagyu
SPIRITUAL HEAD: His Eminence Kalu Rinpoche
CONTACT: Lama Karma Tenpa Gyeltsen
AFFILIATION: Autonomous
ESTABLISHED: 1994
FACILITIES: Meditation room, library, peace garden.
MEDITATION PROGRAM: Four meditation sessions daily, additional service on Sunday. Visiting teachers are invited throughout the year to give teachings and empowerments. Ongoing classes include Buddhist basics, meditation, tai-chi, yoga, volunteer training and various subjects such as death and dying. Call for times.
RETREATS OFFERED: One-day retreat monthly.
PUBLICATIONS: Quarterly newsletter.

Lhundrub Ling

For description see Rigdzin Ling/Chagdud Gonpa Foundation, Junction City, California.
ADDRESS: PO Box 23558, Flagstaff, AZ 86002
PHONE: (520) 774-6896
LINEAGE: Tibetan
SPIRITUAL HEAD: H. E. Chagdud Tulku Rinpoche
CONTACT: Blake Spalding
AFFILIATION: Chagdud Gonpa Foundation, Junction City, California

Padma Bodhi Ling

We're a Tibetan Buddhist practice center under the guidance of Chagdud Tulku Rinpoche. We encourage and provide regular study in order to build a solid foundation for understanding all levels of Buddhist philosophy and practice. We consider spiritual practice to be an expression of service, and seek to provide an atmosphere that brings sanity, compassion, and kindness into people's lives.
ADDRESS: 13194 North 94th Way, Scottsdale, AZ 85260
PHONE: (602) 860-5636
LINEAGE: Nyingma, Karma Kagyu
SPIRITUAL HEAD: Chagdud Tulku Rinpoche
CONTACT: Christopher May
AFFILIATION: Chagdud Gonpa Foundation, Junction City, California
ESTABLISHED: 1995
FACILITIES: Meditation hall in private residence.
RETREATS OFFERED: Weekly practice group; weekend retreats.

Phoenix Karma Thegsum Choling (KTC)

Phoenix KTC and affiliate centers are involved in a wide range of community activities in addition to our study and practice programs. Our Dharma Basket program provides food and other assistance to families and lamas in need. Under the kind direction of Erma Pounds, this center has been meeting continuously since the late 1970s.
ADDRESS: 605 East Broadway, Tempe, AZ 85282
PHONE: (602) 829-1479
E-MAIL: seed@netzone.com
LINEAGE: Tibetan Karma Kagyu
SPIRITUAL HEAD: Ven. Khenpo Karthar Rinpoche
CONTACTS: Erma Pounds, Director; Bill Glover, Contact
AFFILIATION: Karma Triyana Dharmachakra, Woodstock, New York
ESTABLISHED: Late 1970s
FACILITIES: Urban center.
MEDITATION PROGRAM: Daily meditation practice and study groups. First Friday and third Wednesday monthly: Prescott Affiliate (contact Karen McDowell, (520) 772-0801). Second Friday monthly: Sedona Affiliate (contact Ruth McFarland, (602) 839-4152).
RETREATS OFFERED: Weekend seminar once monthly.
PUBLICATIONS: Lion's Roar Dharma News

Vici Arizona

Informally affiliated with the Foundation for the Preservation of the Mahayana Tradition (FPMT) founded by Lama Thubten Yeshe with Jon Landaw, the Ven. George Churinoff, and other teachers of the FPMT.
ADDRESS: 4540 North 44th Street #15, Phoenix, AZ 85018
PHONE: (602) 912-0096
FAX: (602) 912-0134
E-MAIL: v-west@getnet.com
LINEAGE: Tibetan
CONTACT: Dorothea Watkins
AFFILIATION: Autonomous
ESTABLISHED: 1990
FACILITIES: Meet in private homes.

CALIFORNIA

Aro Ter

No description available.
ADDRESS: 2508 Eagle Avenue, Alameda, CA 94501
PHONE: (520) 865-1394
WWW: http://www.aroter.org
LINEAGE: Tibetan/Nyingma
SPIRITUAL HEADS: Ngak'chang Chogyam Rinpoche; Khandro Dechen
AFFILIATION: Sang-ngak-cho-dzong (United Kingdom)
FACILITIES: Meeting in a private home.
MEDITATION PROGRAM: Group practice one evening a week. Please call for times.
RETREATS OFFERED: Two public retreats yearly, spring and fall.
PUBLICATIONS: Vision (quarterly); Hidden Word (annual).

Ati Ling/Chagdud Gonpa Foundation

For description see Rigdzin Ling/Chagdud Gonpa Foundation, Junction City, California.
ADDRESS: PO Box 90, Oakville, CA 94562
PHONE: (707) 944-1907
LINEAGE: Tibetan
SPIRITUAL HEAD: H. E. Chagdud Tulku Rinpoche
CONTACT: Tulku Jigme Tromge Rinpoche
AFFILIATION: Chagdud Gonpa Foundation

Berkeley Shambhala Center

For description, please refer to Shambhala International, Halifax, Nova Scotia, Canada.
ADDRESS: 2288 Fulton Street, Berkeley, CA 94704
PHONES: (510) 841-3242 or (510) 841-6475
E-MAIL: jgrun@sirius.com
LINEAGE: Tibetan Kagyu-Nyingma
SPIRITUAL HEAD: Sakyong Mipham Rinpoche
CONTACT: Colin Waters, Coordinator
AFFILIATION: Shambhala International, Halifax, Nova Scotia
FACILITIES: Urban meditation center.
MEDITATION PROGRAM: Weekly scheduled meditation, meditation instruction, dharma talk. Open to the public.
RETREATS OFFERED: Free "Shambhala Training, Level I." Call for schedule.
PUBLICATIONS: Books by Trungpa Rinpoche and others.

Buddha Dendo

No description available.
ADDRESS: 167 Vernon Street, San Francisco, CA 94132
LINEAGE: Tendai Kengyo

Chokling Tersar Foundation

A nonprofit foundation in the lineage of Tulku Urgyen Rinpoche, established to facilitate the preservation, practice, and study of the Tibetan Buddhist tradition known as Chokling Tersar. Lineage holders, headed by the four sons of Tulku Urgyen, are invited to the United States to give empowerment, reading transmission, and instruction. We are establishing a country retreat center to realize this aim.
ADDRESS: c/o 9 Acacia Drive, Tiburon, CA 94920
FAX: (977) 147-2529
E-MAIL: ryp@wlink.com.np
LINEAGE: Tibetan Khyentse, Kongtrul, and Chokling
SPIRITUAL HEAD: Chokyi Nyima Rinpoche
CONTACT: Erik Pema Kunsang, Director
AFFILIATION: Ka-Nying Shedrub Ling, Nepal, and Rangjung Yeshe Gomde Retreat Land, Denmark
ESTABLISHED: 1996
FACILITIES: Retreat land in the process of crystalization.
RETREATS OFFERED: Every year in late summer.
PUBLICATIONS: Rangjung Yeshe Publications (Twenty-five books, seventy booklets).

Davis Shambhala Center

The Davis Shambhala Center is a community of individuals joined in the common goal of fostering the creation of an enlightened society through the practice and study of Buddhism or the Sacred Path of Warriorship, as presented by the Vidyadhara, the Ven. Chogyam Trungpa Rinpoche. The center is the focal point of practice, education, and social interaction for the Davis Shambhala community. It is also the home of Davis Dharmadhatu, the site for local "Shambhala Training Programs," and a place where the expression of sanity and warriorship in the arts can be explored. Open to the general public.
ADDRESS: 129 E Street, Suite D-2, Davis, CA 95616
PHONES: (916) 756-3202 or (916) 758-1440
FAX: (916) 756-3202
E-MAIL: lmchenry@wheel.dcn.davis.ca.us
LINEAGE: Karma Kagyu, Nyingma, and Shambhala
SPIRITUAL HEAD: Sakyong Mipham Rinpoche
CONTACTS: Henry and Linda McHenry
AFFILIATION: Shambhala International, Halifax, Nova Scotia, Canada
FACILITIES: Urban center, bookstore, and lending library.
MEDITATION PROGRAM: Weekly scheduled meditation. Meditation instruction

available at all sittings and by appointment.

RETREATS OFFERED: Monthly Nyinthuns, "Shambhala Training"; weekly classes; occasional weekend programs.

Diamond Way Buddhist Center

Diamond Way Buddhist Center (formerly Kamtsang Choling) is a California State nonprofit organization and is part of a worldwide network of Buddhist centers in the Karma Kagyu tradition of Tibetan Buddhism. Our centers were founded and are directed by Lama Ole Nydahl and his wife, Hannah, and are under the spiritual guidance of H. E. Shamar Rinpoche, and H. H. the seventeenth Gyalwa Karmapa, Thaye Dorje. We offer the liberating and powerful meditation methods of Diamond Way Buddhism (Vajrayana) as a means of transforming our daily experience into the realization of enlightenment, which is the mind's true potential.

ADDRESS: 110 Merced Avenue, San Francisco, CA 94127
PHONE: (415) 661-6467
FAX: (415) 665-7838
E-MAIL: kclsf.aimnet.com
WWW: http://users.aimnet.com/~kclsf
LINEAGE: Karma Kagyu lineage of Tibetan Buddhism
SPIRITUAL HEAD: Seventeenth Gyalwa Karmapa, Thaye Dorje
CONTACT: Lama Ole Nydahl, Director and Teacher
AFFILIATION: Headquarters center.
ESTABLISHED: 1991
RETREATS OFFERED: Quarterly
PUBLICATIONS: Buddhism Today, international magazine.

Drikung Kagyu Center

No description available.
ADDRESS: 31000 Hasley Canyon, Castaic, CA 91384

PHONE: (805) 257-2943
LINEAGE: Tibetan Drikung Kagyu
SPIRITUAL HEAD: Ven. Khenpo Konchog Gyaltsen Rinpoche
CONTACT: John Lewis
AFFILIATION: Tibetan Meditation Center, Frederick, Maryland

Drikung Kyobpa Choling Monastery

Ven. Lama Samten teaches Buddhist philosophy, meditations, and deity yogas and leads retreats for beginners and advanced practitioners. Traditional Tibetan Buddhist chanting, music, healing, and arts are also taught. Please contact us for more information or a current monthly schedule.

ADDRESS: 1768 Sheridan Avenue, Escondido, CA 92027
PHONE: (619) 738-0089
LINEAGE: Drikung Kagyu School of Tibetan Buddhism
SPIRITUAL HEAD: His Holiness Drikung Kyabgon
CONTACT: Ven. Lama Samten
AFFILIATION: Drikung Kagyu Institute, Dehra Dun, India
ESTABLISHED: 1994
PUBLICATIONS: Periodic newsletter.

Ensenada (Mexico) Yeshe Nyingpo

For description, please see Pacific Region Yeshe Nyingpo, Ashland, Oregon.
ADDRESS: Box 431740, San Ysidro, CA 92143-1740
LINEAGE: Tibetan Nyingma
SPIRITUAL HEAD: H. H. Dudjom Rinpoche
CONTACT: Ven. Gyatrul Rinpoche, Spiritual Representative
AFFILIATION: Pacific Region Yeshe Nyingpo, Ashland, Oregon

Foundation for the Preservation of the Mahayana Tradition

Foundation for the Preservation of the Mahayana Tradition (FPMT) is an international organization of Buddhist teaching, meditation, and retreat centers; monasteries; publishing houses; hospices; healing centers; and related activities. It was founded in 1975 by Lama Thubten Zopa Rinpoche and the late Lama Thubten Yeshe and is rooted in the Tibetan Buddhist lineage of Lama Tsong Khapa. The organization is devoted to the transmission of Mahayana Buddhism worldwide through teaching, meditation, and community service.

ADDRESS: PO Box 1778, Soquel, CA 95073
PHONE: (408) 476-8435
FAX: (408) 476-4823
E-MAIL: 76734.3620@compuserve.com
LINEAGE: Tibetan Gelugpa
SPIRITUAL HEAD: Lama Thubten Zopa Rinpoche
CONTACTS: Harvey Horrocks and Petra McWilliams
AFFILIATION: FPMT
ESTABLISHED: 1974
FACILITIES: Eighty-two centers worldwide.
PUBLICATIONS: Mandala Magazine (bimonthly).

Idyllwild Dharma Center/Karma Mahasiddha Ling

The sole purpose of our organization is to provide an environment for the practice of Tibetan Buddhist meditation. Initially founded in the 1970s by the sixteenth Gyalwa Karmapa, the center began dissolving in the early eighties. In 1986 it was reformed under the guidance of the Venerable Thrangu Rinpoche, an accomplished meditation master and senior lama of the Karma Kagyu lineage.

We host an annual ten-day meditation retreat with him at Big Bear Lake, California. We also conduct weekly Chenrezig Sadhanas, celebrate Buddhist holy days, and create a support group for like-minded practitioners in our area.

ADDRESS: PO Box 1441, Idyllwild, CA 92549

PHONE: (909) 659-3401

E-MAIL: buddhafull@aol.com

LINEAGE: Tibetan Karma Kagyu

SPIRITUAL HEAD: Very Ven. Khenchen Thrangu Rinpoche

CONTACT: Lee Miracle, Center Director

AFFILIATION: Namo Buddha Seminar, Boulder, Colorado

ESTABLISHED: 1986

FACILITIES: On-site gompa.

RETREATS OFFERED: Ten-day Mahamudra retreat in the fall.

Kagyu Droden Kunchab

Lama Lodru has established study groups and gives teachings in the following cities: Sacramento, Sebastapol, San Rafael, Redwood City, and Eureka, California; and Tucson, Arizona. Please call for locations and a schedule of activities.

ADDRESS: 1892 Fell Street, San Francisco, CA 94117

PHONE: (415) 752-5454

WWW: http://www.kdk.org

LINEAGE: Tibetan

CONTACT: Lama Lodru

AFFILIATION: Founded by Kalu Rinpoche.

PUBLICATIONS: Newsletter. Call or write to be placed on our mailing list.

Khandakapala Buddhist Center

No description available.

ADDRESS: 2461 Santa Monica Boulevard, C329, Santa Monica, CA 90404

PHONE: (310) 820-3751

FAX: Same

E-MAIL: kbc@primenet.com

LINEAGE: Tibetan, New Kadampa

SPIRITUAL HEAD: Lama Geshe Kelsang Gyatso

AFFILIATION: Manjushri Mahayana Buddhist Center, Ulverston, United Kingdom

Khyung Dzong of California

We are dedicated to the dissemination and practice of Bonpo teachings as presented by the director of the Ligmincha Institute (Charlottesville, Virginia), Tenzin Wangyual Rinpoche, and the Rinpoches Lopon Tenzin Namdak and Nyima Dakpa of Menri Monastery in Dolanji, India. Bon is the indigenous religion of Tibet. Teachings and practice include the Bon Dzogchen tradition as presented in *Zhang Zhung Nyiud Gyud*, a text predating the existence of Tibet itself.

ADDRESS: Box 1607, Temple City, CA 91780-1607

PHONE: (310) 455-1200

FAX: (310) 455-3219

LINEAGE: Tibet/Bonpo

SPIRITUAL HEAD: Tenzin Wangyal Rinpoche

AFFILIATION: Ligmincha Institute

ESTABLISHED: 1989

RETREATS OFFERED: Three or four per year.

PUBLICATIONS: *Voice of Clear Light* (Ligmincha Institute).

Land of Medicine Buddha—FPMT

A member of the Foundation for the Preservation of the Mahayana Tradition (FPMT), we are a conference and retreat center located on fifty-five acres of redwood forest and meadowland, bordering the twelve-thousand-acre forest of Niscene Marks just south of Santa Cruz. The setting is peaceful and beautiful, with a pool, sauna, walking trails, and delicious vegetarian meals. Although we are a Tibetan Buddhist center, we also offer courses in transformation and healing for

Entrance to Land of Medicine Buddha in Soquel, California. (Photo courtesy of Land of Medicine Buddha.)

CALIFORNIA (*cont.*)

body, mind, and the environment from many disciplines. Double occupancy, with limited single rooms at extra charge. Private baths. No smoking or alcohol.

ADDRESS: 5800 Prescott Road, Soquel, CA 95073
PHONE: (408) 462-8383
FAX: (408) 462-8384
LINEAGE: Tibetan
SPIRITUAL HEAD: Lama Thubten Zopa Rinpoche
CONTACT: Murray Wright, Director
AFFILIATION: Foundation for the Preservation of the Mahayana Tradition (FPMT)
ESTABLISHED: 1991
FACILITIES: Twenty rooms with private baths, two meeting halls, fifty-five acres of forest and meadowland, camping.
RETREATS OFFERED: Healing courses for body, mind, and environment; Tibetan Buddhist practice; Vipassana retreats.
PUBLICATIONS: Brochure and newsletter.

Los Angeles Karma Thegsum Choling (KTC)

Los Angeles KTC was founded in 1978 by the sixteenth Gyalwa Karmapa. All are welcome to join us in our regular weekly practice and for special teaching events by visiting lamas. Lama Dudjom Dorje visits regularly from Northern California where he has lived and taught for almost ten years. Please call for detailed information regarding our regular programs and for dates and times of Chenrezig puja with ten thousand mani mantras. Interviews and meditation instruction are available by appointment. For additional information, please see listing for Karma Triyana Dharmachakra, Woodstock, New York.

ADDRESS: 3586 Tacoma Avenue, Los Angeles, CA 90065
PHONE: (213) 222-8269
E-MAIL: dechentso@aol.com
LINEAGE: Tibetan Karma Kagyu

SPIRITUAL HEAD: Ven. Khenpo Karthar Rinpoche
CONTACT: Terry Sullivan
AFFILIATION: Karma Triyana Dharmachakra, Woodstock, New York
ESTABLISHED: 1978
MEDITATION PROGRAM: Weekly practice schedule.
PUBLICATIONS: *Lion's Roar Dharma News*

Los Angeles Shambhala Center

For description, please refer to Shambhala International, Halifax, Nova Scotia, Canada.

ADDRESS: 8218 West Third Street, Los Angeles, CA 90048
PHONE: (213) 653-9342
FAX: (310) 396-8287
E-MAIL: joelwach@aol.com
LINEAGE: Tibetan Kagyu and Nyingma
SPIRITUAL HEAD: Sakyong Mipham Rinpoche
CONTACTS: Bill Roberts and Dika Ryan
AFFILIATION: Shambhala International, Halifax, Nova Scotia

Los Angeles Yeshe Nyingpo

For description, please see Pacific Region Yeshe Nyingpo, Ashland, Oregon.

ADDRESS: 627 Santa Clara Street, Apartment 4, Venice, CA 90291
PHONE: (310) 450-2559
LINEAGE: Tibetan Nyingma
SPIRITUAL HEAD: H. H. Dudjom Rinpoche
CONTACT: Ven. Gyatrul Rinpoche, Spiritual Representative
AFFILIATION: Pacific Region Yeshe Nyingpo, Ashland, Oregon

Mahakankala Buddhist Center

No description available.

ADDRESS: 32 West Anapamu Street, #297, Santa Barbara, CA 93101

PHONE: (805) 563-2771
FAX: (805) 965-3841
E-MAIL: vbc@ix.netcom.com
LINEAGE: Tibetan, New Kadampa
SPIRITUAL HEAD: Lama Geshe Kelsang Gyatso
AFFILIATION: Manjushri Mahayana Buddhist Centre, Ulverston, United Kingdom

Maitreya Institute

The Maitreya Institute is a nonprofit community-oriented organization founded by the twelfth Tai Situpa in 1985. The institute provides a forum for intercultural exchange and understanding.

ADDRESS: 3450 Sacramento Street, Suite 622, San Francisco, CA 94118
PHONE: (415) 668-5920
LINEAGE: Karma Kagyu
SPIRITUAL HEAD: Twelfth Tai Situpa Rinpoche
CONTACT: Staff
AFFILIATION: Autonomous
ESTABLISHED: 1985
FACILITIES: Rented facilities as needed.

Marin Karma Kagyu Study Group

Marin Dharma Study Group is located in the private residence of the coordinators. We host Kagyu lamas and rinpoches when they visit the Bay Area, and may sponsor events at those times. We do not provide overnight accommodations for traveling dharma students.

ADDRESS: 304 Devon Drive, San Rafael, CA 94903
PHONE: (415) 499-1778
FAX: (415) 499-3360
E-MAIL: thanka@aol.com
LINEAGE: Tibetan Karma Kagyu
SPIRITUAL HEAD: Ven. Khenpo Karthar Rinpoche

CONTACT: Tamam and Shabda Kahn
AFFILIATION: Karma Triyana Dharmachakra, Woodstock, New York
FACILITIES: Private residence.
PUBLICATIONS: *Lion's Roar Dharma News*

Ming Chi Tang

No description available.
ADDRESS: 1758 Orchard Hill Lane, Hacienda Heights, CA 91745
PHONE: (818) 912-9107
LINEAGE: Chinese Vajrayana: True Buddha School
SPIRITUAL HEAD: Grand Master Sheng-yen Lu
AFFILIATION: Autonomous

Mui Yin Tong

No description available.
ADDRESS: 131 Ladera Street, Monterey Park, CA 91754
LINEAGE: Chinese Vajrayana: True Buddha School
SPIRITUAL HEAD: Grand Master Sheng-yen Lu
AFFILIATION: Autonomous

Nyingma Institute

Fifty long-term students who work full time at one of Tarthang Tulku's centers form the core of the Nyingma Institute community. In addition, hundreds of students attend retreats, classes, workshops, or work-study programs while maintaining jobs and family responsibilities. Nyingma venues include Nyingma Institute, Dharma Publishing, and Dharma Press, as well as Odiyan Monastic Center, where long-term members undertake translation projects and extended retreats.
ADDRESS: 1815 Highland Place, Berkeley, CA 94709

PHONE: (510) 843-6812
FAX: (510) 486-1679
E-MAIL: Nyingma-institute@nyingma.org
LINEAGE: Tibetan Nyingma
SPIRITUAL HEAD: Tarthang Tulku, Founder
CONTACTS: Ralph McFall, Dean; Sylvia Gretchen
AFFILIATION: Autonomous
ESTABLISHED: 1973
FACILITIES: Residential rooms, classrooms, bookstore, meditation garden with prayer wheels and stupa.
MEDITATION PROGRAM: Evening classes.
RETREATS OFFERED: Weekend, weeklong, two- and four-month long retreats. Weekend workshops on meditation; Buddhist Studies; Kum Nye Relaxation; Human Development Training; Time, Space, and Knowledge; and Tibetan language, art, and culture.
PUBLICATIONS: *Nyingma Gateway*, quarterly.

Oakland Chapter True Buddha School

No description available.
ADDRESS: 3526 Gray Street, Oakland, CA 94601
PHONE: (510) 532-9888
FAX: (510) 261-3318
LINEAGE: Chinese Vajrayana True Buddha School
SPIRITUAL HEAD: Grand Master Sheng-yen Lu
AFFILIATION: Autonomous

Orgyen Dorje Den/Bay Area Yeshe Nyingpo

For description, please see Pacific Region Yeshe Nyingpo, Ashland, Oregon.
ADDRESS: 410 Townsend Street, Suite 406, San Francisco, CA 94107
PHONE: (415) 546-7915
LINEAGE: Tibetan Nyingma

SPIRITUAL HEAD: H. H. Dudjom Rinpoche
CONTACT: Ven. Gyatrul Rinpoche, Spiritual Representative
AFFILIATION: Pacific Region Yeshe Nyingpo, Ashland, Oregon

Orgyen Khachod Ling

Orgyen Khachod Ling was established in 1994 by His Holiness Orgyen Kusum Lingpa. The center follows the Nyingma tradition of Tibetan Buddhism, and the practices are those connected to the Longchen Nying-Thig and Pema Nying-Thig cycles of teachings. The center has Vajrakilaya as its main practice in order to tame and overcome obstacles. There is a resident lama, daily practice, and yearly visits by His Holiness. His Holiness's two sons, Tulku Hung-Kar Dorje and Tulku Dorje Trangpo, are currently living in the Berkeley/San Francisco area and have been teaching at his centers.
ADDRESS: 1042 South Keniston Avenue, Los Angeles, CA 90019
PHONE: (213) 694-1620
FAX: (213) 935-9947
LINEAGE: Tibetan Nyingma
SPIRITUAL HEAD: His Holiness Orgyen Kusum Lingpa
CONTACT: Kelley Lynch, Director
AFFILIATION: Northern Kiliya Center, Crestone, Colorado
ESTABLISHED: 1994
FACILITIES: Practice center, classroom, resident lama.
RETREATS OFFERED: Varies. Call for schedule.
PUBLICATIONS: *The Dragon*

Padmasambhava Buddhist Center

For description, please see listing for Padmasambhava Buddhist Center, New York.
ADDRESS: Box 590392, San Francisco, CA 94159

CALIFORNIA (cont.)

PHONE: (415) 221-8316
LINEAGE: Tibetan Nyingma
SPIRITUAL HEADS: Khenchen Palden Sherab Rinpoche and Khenpo Tsewang Dongyal Rinpoche
CONTACT: David Sullivan
AFFILIATION: Padmasambhava Buddhist Center, New York
RETREATS OFFERED: Summer in upstate New York; winter in West Palm Beach, Florida; others around the country.

Padma Shedrup Ling

No description available.
ADDRESS: Box 117, Fairfax, CA 94978
PHONE: (415) 485-1356
LINEAGE: Tibetan
SPIRITUAL HEAD: Lama Yonten
AFFILIATION: Autonomous
MEDITATION PROGRAM: Meditation instruction available.

Palo Alto Dharmadhatu

We are a relatively small group of strong, long-term practitioners, able to give new practitioners considerable individual attention. We offer a wide range of classes and group practice situations. For additional information, please refer to Shambhala International, Halifax, Nova Scotia, Canada.
ADDRESS: 260 Fernando, Palo Alto, CA 94306
E-MAIL: henry@netcom.com
LINEAGE: Tibetan Kagyu and Nyingma
SPIRITUAL HEAD: Sakyong Mipham Rinpoche
CONTACT: Henry Polard
AFFILIATION: Shambhala International, Halifax, Nova Scotia
ESTABLISHED: 1972
FACILITIES: Urban meditation center.

Palo Alto Karma Thegsum Choling (KTC)

Founded by the sixteenth Gyalwa Karmapa, Palo Alto KTC provides the opportunity for study and practice in the Karma Kagyu tradition of Tibetan Buddhism. All people interested in dharma are welcome, beginners and advanced students alike. For information about our weekly programs and special events, please contact the center.
ADDRESS: PO Box 60793, Palo Alto, CA 94306
PHONE: (415) 967-1145
E-MAIL: penny@jessica.stanford.edu
LINEAGE: Tibetan Karma Kagyu
SPIRITUAL HEAD: Ven. Khenpo Karthar Rinpoche
CONTACTS: Kathy Penny, Director; Lama Dudjom Dorje, Resident Teacher (based in Santa Cruz).
AFFILIATION: Karma Triyana Dharmachakra, Woodstock, New York
ESTABLISHED: 1973
PUBLICATIONS: *Lion's Roar Dharma News*

Palyul Changchub Dhargye Ling

No description available.
ADDRESS: Box 1514, Mill Valley, CA 94941
PHONE: (415) 388-4923
LINEAGE: Palyul, a subsect of the Tibetan Nyingma lineage
SPIRITUAL HEAD: H. H. Padma Norbu ("Penor")
CONTACT: Allen Schaaf
AFFILIATION: Namdroling Monastery of Byla-Kuppe, India

Purple Lotus Society

Master Samantha Chou, recognized by Grand Master Lu as the Purple Lotus Bodhisattva, started the Purple Lotus Society in a small one-room apartment in South San Francisco in 1987. She conducts weekly group cultivation and Bardo ceremonies, as well as biweekly spiritual consultations to assist individuals with their karmic difficulties. Twice-daily meditations are led by resident monks. Plans call for the establishment of a Bud-

Sangha *of the Purple Lotus Society in San Bruno, California.* (Photo courtesy of Purple Lotus Society.)

Prayer Flags from Radiant Heart

IN 1970 I JOINED A PEN PAL PROGRAM THROUGH Nyingma Institute in Berkeley, California, and began corresponding with a young Tibetan lama, Ven. Dawa Chhodak, at Sanskrit University in Varanasi. Shortly thereafter, Lama Dawa sent me a large Tibetan prayer flag inscribed with sacred symbols, prayers, and mantras. In Tibetan communities these flags are displayed outside of homes and temples, where the wind carries their beneficent vibrations across the countryside, blessing all whom the wind touches.

Fascinated by this tradition, I began redrawing traditional designs and printing my own flags, and in 1975 started a prayer flag business called "Radiant Heart." Instead of using the traditional woodblocks, I chose the more precise method of silk-screening on good-quality cotton fabric using colorfast textile paints. I sold my prints to a few stores and directly to friends by word of mouth. The profits were used to help Tibetan friends and to pay for personal meditation retreats.

Standing Avalokiteshvara. (Illustration courtesy of Timothy Clark/Radiant Heart.)

Kalachakra monogram. (Illustration courtesy of Timothy Clark/Radiant Heart.)

Now I take a stack of flags with me on every trip to Asia, where they are popular with the lamas and other Tibetans I meet. In 1990 I was exploring some caves in a remote area of northern India. An old Tibetan hermit invited me into his cave where, to my astonishment, I saw one of my flags—a colorful dharma wheel design. I have no idea how it got there. It was old and tattered so I gave him a new one.

There are still many traditional designs I would like to redraw, translate, and distribute. Over the years I've devoted more and more time to this project. Please write for a catalogue or see the prints on my Web site at http://www.asis.com/~radiant heart.

Timothy Clark

For more information, contact: Radiant Heart, Box 1272, Redway, CA 95560; e-mail: radhrt@asis.com.

CALIFORNIA *(cont.)*

dhist university in the Bay Area. A free *Purple Lotus Journal* is available upon request.

ADDRESS: 636 San Mateo Avenue, San Bruno, CA 94066

PHONE: (415) 952-9513

FAX: (415) 952-9567

WWW: http://www.dancing-bear.com/pls

LINEAGE: Chinese Vajrayana True Buddha School

SPIRITUAL HEAD: Grand Master Sheng-yen Lu

CONTACT: Vajra Master Samantha Chou, Resident Teacher

AFFILIATION: True Buddha School

ESTABLISHED: 1987

FACILITIES: Temple, limited dormitory, gift store.

RETREATS OFFERED: One-day events.

PUBLICATIONS: *Purple Lotus Journal*

Ratnashri Sangha

Ratnashri Sangha meets weekly to practice White Tara and Chenrezig meditation. Potluck dinner once a month. Welcome to all dharma friends to join in meditation and practice. Call for schedule. "May you walk in beauty, love, and peace."

ADDRESS: 2118 Hayes Street, San Francisco, CA 94117

PHONE: (415) 386-4619

LINEAGE: Tibetan Buddhist

SPIRITUAL HEAD: Khenpo Konchog Gyaltsen

CONTACT: Cindy Chang

AFFILIATION: Tibetan Meditation Center

ESTABLISHED: 1991

MEDITATION PROGRAM: Weekly meeting at 2245 Cabrillo Street, #4, San Francisco. Call for times.

Rigdzin Ling/Chagdud Gonpa Foundation

Ven. Chagdud Tulku Rinpoche teaches and initiates the meditation techniques

H. E. Chagdud Tulku Rinpoche in ceremonial regalia. (Photo ©1995 by Chagdud Gonpa/T'hondup Ling & Don Farber.)

and Buddhist philosophy represented by the Vajrayana-Dzogchen traditions of the Tibetan Nyingmapa lineage. His centers offer a daily schedule of group meditation in accordance with these traditions, interspersed with seasonally scheduled three- to five-day extended practice sessions. The meditation practices are done with the intent of taming the mind. In addition to a series of practices done by all of the students, there are the *ngondro* (foundation) practices and, ultimately, more advanced material, which is available as *ngondro* is completed.

ADDRESS: PO Box 279, Junction City, CA 96048

PHONE: (916) 623-2714

LINEAGE: Tibetan Nyingmapa

SPIRITUAL HEAD: H. E. Chagdud Tulku Rinpoche

CONTACT: Lama Padma Drimed Norbu

AFFILIATION: Headquarters of the Chagdud Gonpa Foundation.

PUBLICATIONS: Various practice texts and dharma books offered by Padma Publishing, our in-house publishing company.

Rigpa North America

Rigpa is an international network of Buddhist centers under the guidance of Sogyal Rinpoche. Born in Tibet and educated at Delhi and Cambridge Universities, Sogyal Rinpoche began teaching in the West in 1974 while continuing his studies with Dudjom Rinpoche and Dilgo Khyentse Rinpoche. He is the author of a highly acclaimed spiritual classic, *The Tibetan Book of Living and Dying*.

ADDRESS: PO Box 607, Santa Cruz, CA 95061-0607

PHONES: (408) 454-9103; Rigpa Publications: (800) 256-5262

FAX: (408) 454-0917

LINEAGE: Tibetan

SPIRITUAL HEADS: Sogyal Rinpoche and H. E. Dzogchen Rinpoche

CONTACT: Sandra Pawula, Director

AFFILIATION: Rigpa International

ESTABLISHED: 1984

FACILITIES: North American headquarters offices. Bay Area Center, 816 Bancroft Way, Berkeley, (510) 644-1858. Active centers across North America. Call for locations.

RETREATS OFFERED: The Spiritual Care for Living and Dying Program. Yearly retreats of up to three months in length. Retreats and courses in locations around North America.

PUBLICATIONS: *The Tibetan Book of Living and Dying*; Rigpa Tibetan Calendar; *View Magazine*; tapes, books, study guides.

Sakya Dechen Ling

A center established by Jetsun Kushola at the request of Bay Area residents, with an accent on, but not limited to, women practitioners. Nonsectarian, inclusive approach for committed Buddhists.

ADDRESS: 1709 Myrtle Street, Oakland, CA 94607
PHONE: (510) 465-7849
FAX: Same
LINEAGE: Tibetan Sakya
SPIRITUAL HEAD: Jetsun Kusho Chime Luding
CONTACT: Katherine Pfaff
AFFILIATION: Autonomous
ESTABLISHED: 1989
FACILITIES: City center; retreat land.
MEDITATION PROGRAM: Weekly Tara meditations, bimonthly Vajrayogini Feast practice.
RETREATS OFFERED: Individual: arrange with center.
PUBLICATIONS: Various Sadhana practice texts.

San Diego Dharma Study Group

For description, please refer to Shambhala International, Halifax, Nova Scotia, Canada.

ADDRESS: 3535 Front Street, San Diego, CA 92103
PHONE: (619) 298-4279
FAX: Same
LINEAGE: Tibetan Kagyu and Nyingma
SPIRITUAL HEAD: Sakyong Mipham Rinpoche
CONTACTS: Paul and Brenda Wagener
AFFILIATION: Shambhala International, Halifax, Nova Scotia
ESTABLISHED: 1982

San Diego Karma Thegsum Choling (KTC)

For description, see listing for Karma Triyana Dharmachakra, Woodstock, New York. Please feel free to contact us for information about meditation instruction and a current schedule of practices and events.

ADDRESS: 1236 Missouri Street, San Diego, CA 92109-2661
PHONE: (619) 483-5028
LINEAGE: Tibetan Karma Kagyu
SPIRITUAL HEAD: Ven. Khenpo Karthar Rinpoche
CONTACT: Kennon Kashima
AFFILIATION: Karma Triyana Dharmachakra, Woodstock, New York
PUBLICATIONS: *Lion's Roar Dharma News*

San Francisco Shambhala Center

San Francisco Shambhala Center is one of many practice and study centers set up under the umbrella of Shambhala International. Each center has a large amount of autonomy, but the focus of all and the base practices of each are the same. The main practice is shamatha/vipassana (tranquillity/insight) meditation. The vision of Shambhala is the creation of an enlightened society. Human wisdom and its cultural manifestations, as well as an appreciation of the world as it is, are central to the Shambhala tradition. For additional information, please see Shambhala International, Halifax, Nova Scotia, Canada.

ADDRESS: 1630 Taraval Street, San Francisco, CA 94116
PHONE: (415) 731-4426
E-MAIL: dasolman@slip.net
LINEAGE: Shambhala and Karma Kagyu
SPIRITUAL HEADS: Sakyong Mipham Rinpoche. Chogyam Trungpa Rinpoche, Founder.
CONTACTS: Bruce Del Santo and Teresa Colleton
AFFILIATION: Shambhala International
ESTABLISHED: Around 1971
FACILITIES: Center with shrine room and community room.
PUBLICATIONS: Monthly newsletter and calendar.

Santa Barbara Karma Thegsum Choling (KTC)

Please feel free to contact us for information about meditation instruction and a current schedule of practices and events. For additional information, please see Karma Triyana Dharmachakra in Woodstock, New York.

ADDRESS: 534½ Arroyo Avenue, Santa Barbara, CA 93109
PHONE: (805) 569-9440
LINEAGE: Tibetan Karma Kagyu
SPIRITUAL HEAD: Ven. Khenpo Karthar Rinpoche
CONTACT: Sherman Starr
AFFILIATION: Karma Triyana Dharmachakra, Woodstock, New York
ESTABLISHED: 1978
FACILITIES: Private home.
PUBLICATIONS: *Lion's Roar Dharma News*

Santa Cruz Karma Thegsum Choling (KTC)

Located in the foothills of the Santa Cruz Mountains, KTC was established by the sixteenth Gyalwa Karmapa in 1976 and is blessed by the activity of our resident teacher, Lama Dudjom Dorje. The center conducts frequent weekend retreats, hosts visiting lamas, and holds regular meetings for teachings and practice. Senior students offer a four-week introductory course called The Tradition of Enlightenment several times a year. Another important outreach is Dzambhala Imports, a retailer/wholesaler of dharma goods, books, and Himalayan crafts in Soquel.

ADDRESS: Box 1527, Santa Cruz, CA 95010
PHONE: (408) 462-3955 (Sandy Coca)
E-MAIL: tolmasoff@darwin.stanford.edu
LINEAGE: Tibetan Karma Kagyu
SPIRITUAL HEAD: Ven. Khenpo Karthar Rinpoche

CALIFORNIA (*cont.*)

CONTACTS: Zeinob Claire Burnham, Director. Lama Dudjom Dorje, Resident Teacher.
AFFILIATION: Karma Triyana Dharmachakra, Woodstock, New York
ESTABLISHED: 1976
FACILITIES: Traditional shrine room painted by renowned Tibetan artist Phuntsok Dorje.
MEDITATION PROGRAM: Weekly teachings by Lama Dudjom, plus either Chenrezig or Green Tara practice.
PUBLICATIONS: *Lion's Roar Dharma News*

Santa Cruz Shambhala Study Group

For description, please refer to Shambhala International, Halifax, Nova Scotia, Canada.
ADDRESS: 520 Townsend Drive, Aptos, CA 95003
FAX: (408) 685-9212 c/o Michael Rogers
LINEAGE: Tibetan Kagyu and Nyingma
SPIRITUAL HEAD: Sakyong Mipham Rinpoche
CONTACT: Michael Rogers
AFFILIATION: Shambhala International, Halifax, Nova Scotia

Saraha Buddhist Center

Saraha is a fully established Mahayana Buddhist center serving the entire Bay Area, with a variety of systematic meditation and study programs, evening drop-in classes, daily chanted meditations, and special weekend courses. Everyone is welcome to attend, regardless of previous experience or spiritual orientation. Many people find the teachings and meditations very helpful in developing a positive, stress-free attitude toward daily life.
ADDRESS: 3145 Geary Boulevard, #515, San Francisco, CA 94118-3300
PHONE: (415) 731-5973

FAX: Same
E-MAIL: saraha@netcom.com
WWW: www.webcom.com/sbc/
LINEAGE: Tibetan New Kadampa
SPIRITUAL HEAD: Lama Geshe Kelsang Gyatso
CONTACT: Gen Kelsang Togden, Resident Teacher
AFFILIATION: Manjushri Mahayana Buddhist Centre, Ulverston, United Kingdom
ESTABLISHED: 1991
MEDITATION PROGRAM: Public talks, classes, study programs.
RETREATS OFFERED: Regularly

Shingon Buddhist International Institute

Shingon is Japanese esoteric Buddhism transmitted from India to China and then to Japan in the year 804 CE by Kukai (Kobo Daishi). The central deity is Mahavairochana, represented by the Vajradhatu and Gharbakosa mandalas.
ADDRESS: Box 3757, Fresno, CA 93650
PHONE: (209) 435-0507
FAX: Same
LINEAGE: Shingon (Japanese esoteric Buddhism)
SPIRITUAL HEAD: Rev. Seicho Asahi
CONTACTS: Rev. Bill Eidson (Eijun) and Rev. Ana Harada (Shoken)
AFFILIATION: Koyasan Shingon
ESTABLISHED: 1995
FACILITIES: Ten Chiji Temple
MEDITATION PROGRAM: Ajikan, sutra reading, ritual practice, priest training.
RETREATS OFFERED: Periodic retreats and training.
PUBLICATIONS: *Esoteric Buddhist Quarterly*, *Shingon*, others.

Sonoma Valley Dharma Study Group

The Sonoma Valley Dharma Study Group is a forming Shambhala center.

Currently we offer an open house with sitting meditation twice a month. In addition we sponsor "Shambhala Training" weekends (introductory levels) and workshops in contemplative and warrior arts. Ikebana (Japanese flower arranging) is taught by Soho Sakai, a native of Japan who has been practicing ikebana since 1957. Calligraphy and Aikido master Kazuaki Tanahashi, also a native of Japan, teaches workshops in East Asian brush calligraphy. Interested parties may request to be added to our mailing list. *Mangalam!*
ADDRESS: 276 East Napa Street, Room 213, Sonoma, CA 95476
PHONE: (707) 935-3610
FAX: (415) 759-1166
E-MAIL: jjacobs@vom.com
LINEAGE: Shambhala/Tibetan Buddhism
SPIRITUAL HEAD: Sakyong Mipham Rinpoche
CONTACTS: Joseph Jacobs and Kathy Devries
AFFILIATION: Shambhala International, Halifax, Nova Scotia, Canada
ESTABLISHED: 1993
FACILITIES: Expandable facility at Sonoma Community Center
RETREATS OFFERED: Greater Bay Area Shambhala programs.
PUBLICATIONS: Members' newsletter.

Stockton Chapter True Buddha School

No description available.
ADDRESS: 6017 North El Dorado Street, Stockton, CA 95207
LINEAGE: Chinese Vajrayana: True Buddha School
SPIRITUAL HEAD: Grand Master Sheng-yen Lu
CONTACT: Rev. Chen
AFFILIATION: True Buddha School

Tibetan Aid Project

Since its founding in 1969, the Tibetan Aid Project (TAP) has been providing ongoing support for the Tibetan community in exile. Initial support involved humanitarian aid: food, medicine, clothing, and other daily necessities. As refugee communities stabilized, TAP increasingly focused on rebuilding Tibetan culture to ensure the survival of its unique tradition. Our efforts can be divided into four main categories:

Basic Survival Assistance: TAP currently offers humanitarian assistance to hundreds of monks and nuns at nineteen monasteries and nunneries inside and outside Tibet. Assistance includes money for food, clothing, and study, as well as construction and restoration of monasteries, nunneries, and schools.

Prayers for World Peace: TAP assists monks and nuns in attending peace ceremonies held annually since 1989 at four Buddhist holy sites; among them, Bodh Gaya, site of the Buddha's enlightenment.

Education: TAP offers educational materials, outreach programs, and lectures to interested groups in the United States, Europe, and South America. These programs enhance awareness of Tibetan culture, philosophy, and religion.

Preserving Tibetan Culture: TAP, the Yeshe De Project, and Dharma Publishing have together produced and shipped over sixty thousand traditional Buddhist texts, one hundred thousand art reproductions, and ten thousand handheld prayer wheels to Tibet. All are crucial in transmitting the wisdom of the Tibetan tradition.

The Tibetan Aid Project is staffed entirely by volunteers, keeping administrative costs to a minimum. These volunteers are usually work/study interns at the Nyingma institute, a retreat and meditation center in the Berkeley Hills. Interns work at the Tibetan Aid Project during the day, and take night classes at the Institute, where they are also given meals and housing. The Tibetan Aid Project provides a small stipend and a chance to put classroom lessons into practice.

Kazimieras Joseph

For more information, contact: Tibetan Aid Project, 2910 San Pablo Avenue, Berkeley, CA 94702; (800) 33-TIBET.

T'hondup Ling/Chagdud Gonpa Foundation

Chagdud Gonpa Foundation offers instruction in the traditions of Vajrayana Buddhism, especially the arts, philosophy, and meditation. Unparalleled in its swift revelation of mind's true nature, the Vajrayana incorporates all levels of Buddhist training, culminating in the pinnacle teachings of Dzogchen, the Great Perfection. His Eminence Chagdud Tulku Rinpoche established the foundation as a vehicle for bringing this rich heritage to the West. His efforts are concentrated in three areas: the development of Padma Publishing, the establishment of teaching and retreat centers, and the training of students. For additional information, see Rigdzin Ling/Chagdud Gonpa Foundation, Junction City, California.

ADDRESS: 2503 West 117th Street, Hawthorne, CA 90250
PHONE: (213) 754-0466
LINEAGE: Tibetan Vajrayana
SPIRITUAL HEAD: His Eminence Chagdud Tulku Rinpoche
CONTACT: Lama Chodrak Gyatso, Resident Teacher
AFFILIATION: Rigdzin Ling/Chagdud Gonpa Foundation, Junction City, California
ESTABLISHED: 1980
FACILITIES: Members' homes.
MEDITATION PROGRAMS: Weekly practice.
RETREATS OFFERED: One large, several small retreats per year.

Tse Chen Ling Center for Tibetan Buddhist Studies

Located in the heart of San Francisco, Tse Chen Ling offers a weekly program of guided meditation and teachings in the

Lama Chodal Gyatso, resident teacher at T'hondup Ling in Hawthorne, California. (Photo courtesy of T'hondup Ling.)

CALIFORNIA (*cont.*)

Gelugpa tradition of Tibetan Buddhism. Our resident teacher, Ven. Geshe Kelsang Wangdu, a larampa geshe from Sera Je Monastery in Karnataka, India, is shared with our sister centers, Vajrapani Institute (Boulder Creek) and Land of Medicine Buddha (Soquel). Our teaching program ranges from beginner-level classes to ongoing courses in advanced topics of Buddhist philosophy.

ADDRESS: 4 Joost Avenue, San Francisco, CA 94131
PHONE: (415) 339-8002
FAX: (415) 333-3261
E-MAIL: TCLCenter@aol.com
LINEAGE: Tibetan Gelugpa
SPIRITUAL HEAD: Ven. Lama Thubten Zopa Rinpoche
CONTACT: Carol Corradi, Director
AFFILIATION: Foundation for the Preservation of the Mahayana Tradition (FPMT)
ESTABLISHED: 1990

FACILITIES: Meditation room, bookstore/library.
MEDITATION PROGRAM: Weekly lectures, introductory teachings, initiations, programs for both beginners and advanced students.
RETREATS OFFERED: We join our sister centers for retreats.
PUBLICATIONS: *Opening the Lotus*, newsletter.

Unfettered Mind

Unfettered Mind offers individualized meditation instruction and training in Mahayana and Vajrayana methods, with a strong emphasis on their application in daily life. Consultations with Ken McLeod, a senior student of the late Kalu Rinpoche, are arranged according to interest and convenience. This format enables students to explore their own questions and to design and develop individualized approaches to spiritual training and development. Ken serves as a coach and resource. Practice/study groups and weekend retreats supplement individual consultations.

ADDRESS: 11600 Washington Place, Suite 210, Los Angeles, CA 90066
PHONE: (310) 397-1656
FAX: Same
LINEAGE: Tibetan Kagyupa
SPIRITUAL HEAD: Ken McLeod
CONTACT: Same
AFFILIATION: Autonomous
ESTABLISHED: 1990
FACILITIES: Offices in Los Angeles and Newport Beach.
RETREATS OFFERED: Four to six retreats per year on various topics.
PUBLICATIONS: Quarterly newsletter.

Vajrapani Institute

Vajrapani Institute is a Buddhist retreat center located on eighty acres of beautiful Santa Cruz mountain woodlands. Founded by the late Lama Thubten Yeshe, the center provides an opportunity to retreat from busy lives for a time of inner reflection and regeneration. Teachings and workshops offer methods for personal growth and development. The center is available for rental to outside groups. In 1989 His Holiness the Dalai Lama visited and taught at Vajrapani.

ADDRESS: PO Box 2130, Boulder Creek, CA 95006
PHONE: (408) 338-6654
FAX: (408) 338-3666
E-MAIL: 76764.2256@compuserve.com
WWW: http://www.geopages.com/Athens/2094
LINEAGE: Tibetan Gelugpa
SPIRITUAL HEAD: Lama Thubten Zopa Rinpoche
CONTACT: Amy Miller, Director
AFFILIATION: Foundation for the Preservation of the Mahayana Tradition
ESTABLISHED: 1977
FACILITIES: Retreat cabins, stupa, prostration deck, meditation hall, teacher's house, dormitory, camping.
MEDITATION PROGRAM: Daily morning meditation. Buddhist initiations given by qualified Tibetan lamas.
RETREATS OFFERED: New Year's Vajrasattva weekend; Tara, Chenrezig initiation, Palden Lhamo, and solitary retreats. Weekend courses and workshops.
PUBLICATIONS: Quarterly events schedule. Biannual newsletter.

Vajrarupini Buddhist Center

Vajrarupini Buddhist Center offers two types of meditation/study programs. The General Program consists of weekly classes that include meditation and talks on the Buddhist tradition. The Foundation Study Program allows one to deepen one's knowledge, experience, and realization of the Buddha's teachings through a

Unfettered Mind: Breaking the (Unwritten) Rules?

THE DIVERSITY OF AMERICAN SOCIETY INVITES A diversity in teaching and training formats. Since 1988, Ken McLeod has successfully pioneered an alternative teaching format. He found the center-based model largely unworkable in Los Angeles and moved to a consulting/coaching model.

Students meet with him individually on a regular or intermittent basis. They talk freely and comfortably about their practice, how it is interacting with their daily life, and where and how they lose attention during the day. Ken then offers suggestions and feedback.

This approach is for a particular kind of person: those capable of independent practice and discipline, who are self-motivated and willing to question any and all aspects of their own life and experience. Instead of following an established program of meditation and trainings, students are challenged to discover their own spiritual questions and to explore them through the teachings and methods of Buddhism. This "student-oriented" approach differs markedly from "tradition-centered" models where the emphasis is on the transmission of a teaching tradition from one generation to the next.

At Unfettered Mind, there is no center to join, no institution to serve, no set structure to follow, no belief system to adopt. Here there is room for doubt, room for questioning, room for different approaches; the functional definition of *skillful* means "whatever works."

To complement and expand the student's individual practice, Unfettered Mind offers practice/study groups and retreats that focus on specific meditation topics. The group format allows students to discuss their own experience and questions with others and to receive feedback and guidance from the teacher. The sense of shared intention is tangible, even though individual practice and interest may differ.

Ken McLeod

For more information, contact: Unfettered Mind, 11600 Washington Place, Suite 210, Los Angeles, CA 90066; (310) 397-1656.

---

structured program of dharma studies. In addition, the center conducts pujas, retreats, and introductory day-long courses.

ADDRESS: 3469 Hawk Street, San Diego, CA 92103
PHONE: (619) 692-1591
FAX: (619) 560-6454
E-MAIL: vajrarup@adnc.com
LINEAGE: Tibetan New Kadampa Tradition
SPIRITUAL HEAD: Geshe Kelsang Gyatso
AFFILIATION: Manjushri Mahayana Buddhist Centre, Ulverston, Britain
ESTABLISHED: 1995
RETREATS OFFERED: Lam Rim
PUBLICATIONS: *Full Moon*

Vajrayana Foundation/Pema Osel Ling

Our center provides daily practice, weekly teachings, and group retreats year-round. Set amid rolling hills and pristine forests and swept by ocean breezes, this 102-acre facility provides an ideal setting for group and private retreats. Amenities include heated cabins, tent sites, a swimming pool, and hiking trails. Delicious meals prepared with organically grown ingredients are served daily. Pema Osel Ling is the primary residence of Lama Tharchin Rinpoche and Tulku Thubten Rinpoche, and serves as the administrative headquarters for Vajrayana Foundation. It is situated in the Santa Cruz Mountains, seventy-five miles south of San Francisco.

ADDRESS: 2013 Eureka Canyon Road, Corralitos, CA 95076
PHONE: (408) 761-6266
FAX: (408) 761-6284
LINEAGE: Tibetan Dudjom
SPIRITUAL HEAD: Lama Tharchin Rinpoche, Resident Teacher
CONTACT: Anne Laurent
AFFILIATION: Autonomous
ESTABLISHED: 1987
FACILITIES: Lodge, cabins, campground, swimming pool, trails.
MEDITATION PROGRAM: Daily practices.
RETREATS OFFERED: Year-round group

retreats (Ngondro, Three Roots, Powa, Drupchen).

PUBLICATIONS: *Lotus Light* (membership newsletter).

Vajrayana Foundation: Los Angeles

Please see Vajrayana Foundation/Pema Osel Ling, Corralitos, California, for description.

ADDRESS: 808 4th Street, #217, Santa Monica, CA 90403-1225

PHONE: (310) 393-6996

LINEAGE: Tibetan Nyingma

SPIRITUAL HEAD: Lama Tharchin Rinpoche

CONTACT: LeRoy Griggs

AFFILIATION: Vajrayana Foundation/ Pema Osel Ling, Corralitos, California

FACILITIES: Urban meditation center in a city apartment.

MEDITATION PROGRAM: Monthly Guru Rinpoche and Yeshe Tsogyal Tsoks.

Waken Rey Tsang Temple

Master Allen Ho moved into the new Waken Rey Tsang Temple in 1996. Here he holds two fire ceremonies daily to burn away the karmic hindrances of participants. Although relatively young, he has mastered many of the intricacies of Tantric Buddhism and gives spiritual consultation to assist individuals in overcoming their life difficulties.

ADDRESS: 11657 Lower Azusa Road, El Monte, CA 91732-1353

PHONE: (818) 455-0077

WWW: http://www.ee.ucla.edu/~yang/ truebuddha.html

LINEAGE: Chinese Vajrayana: True Buddha School

SPIRITUAL HEAD: Grand Master Sheng-yen Lu

CONTACT: Master Allen Ho

AFFILIATION: Autonomous

Yeshe Khorlo

No description available.

ADDRESS: 4615 Hazelbrook Avenue, Long Beach, CA 90808

PHONE: (562) 429-1331

LINEAGE: Bhutanese/Tibetan Nyingma

SPIRITUAL HEAD: Gangteng Rinpoche

CONTACT: Charles Samuelson

AFFILIATION: Yeshe Khorlo, Inc.

COLORADO

Aspen Dharma Study Group

Our main purpose is to provide an opportunity for our members and guests to engage in regular group meditation sessions. We host Tibetan monks and lamas who come here to turn the wheel of dharma. Teachers planning a visit to the Rocky Mountain region are invited to contact us.

ADDRESS: Box 278, Woody Creek, CO 81656

PHONE: (970) 923-4090

E-MAIL: zgrubs@rof.net

LINEAGE: Tibetan Kagyu-Nyingma

SPIRITUAL HEAD: Ven. Chogyam Trungpa Rinpoche

CONTACT: Dennis Tuma

AFFILIATION: Shambhala International

ESTABLISHED: 1994

FACILITIES: All of Aspen.

MEDITATION PROGRAM: Weekly Shamatha sitting sessions.

RETREATS OFFERED: Occasional daylong Nyinthun; Shambhala training; Samadhi on Skis—The Art of Downhill Meditation.

Boulder Shambhala Center

Boulder Shambhala is the main center for Shambhala International in the United States. Our founder, the Ven. Chogyam Trungpa Rinpoche, taught three approaches, or "gates," to the spiritual life: Vajrayana Buddhism, Shambhala Training, and Nalanda Arts. (For a more de-

Boulder Shambhala Center in Boulder, Colorado. (Photo by Don Morreale.)

Parent-Child Nyinthun

CHILDREN QUIETLY BUILD FORTS OUT OF SITTING cushions while their parents practice meditation. Sound unlikely? Well, this is a common experience at the Parent-Child *Nyinthuns* (three-hour sitting sessions) held twice monthly at Boulder Shambhala Center. The children (ages two to nine) play in another part of the shrine room, looked after by a paid *sangha* teenager, while parents sit and take turns helping out in half-hour shifts.

These sessions were inspired by comments made by Ven. Khandro Rinpoche, spiritual head of the Kagyu nunnery at Rumtek in Sikkim and a respected interpreter of the teachings in the West. Rinpoche suggested that including children in their parents' practice life can be both helpful and important, and encouraged their regular participation in meditation sessions and feast practices. She advised that while children should be expected to observe a minimal amount of discipline, remain reasonably quiet, and play away from the practice area, they should also be made to feel comfortable and welcome and should want to come back. Adults, she reminds us, need to remember that "kids are still kids."

Attendance has been moderate so far, with between six and twelve parents and an equal number of children participating. Virginia Heym has brought her son Nathaniel several times and describes the sessions as "very pleasant and very powerful." Barbara Leaf says her daughters, Kate and Jenny, have a "positive feeling" about the sessions. The Family Council at Boulder Shambhala sees Parent-Child *Nyinthuns* as a step forward in their ongoing efforts to integrate children into the community, and plans to continue offering them regularly.

Mark Turnoy

For more information, contact: Boulder Shambhala Center, 1345 Spruce St., Boulder, CO 80302; (303) 444-0190.

---

tailed explanation, see the listing for Shambhala International, Halifax, Nova Scotia, Canada.) All three approaches are taught at our center. We also sponsor cooperative programs with other Buddhist groups in the area and host many of the great Tibetan Vajrayana masters when they are on teaching visits to this country.

ADDRESS: 1345 Spruce Street, Boulder, CO 80302
PHONE: (303) 444-0190
FAX: (303) 443-2975
E-MAIL: sc@indra.com
LINEAGE: Tibetan Kagyu and Nyingma
SPIRITUAL HEAD: Sakyong Mipham Rinpoche
CONTACT: Tania Leontov
AFFILIATION: Shambhala International, Halifax, Nova Scotia

ESTABLISHED: 1970
FACILITIES: Three shrine rooms, offices, classrooms.
RETREATS OFFERED: Ten-day urban retreats.
PUBLICATIONS: *The Shambhala Mirror*

Buffalo Mountain Dharma Center

We share facilities with a Rinzai Zen Group. You might say that Buffalo Mountain is the country retreat facility of Orgyen Rigjed Ling of Lafayette, Colorado. For additional information, please see Buffalo Mountain Dharma Center in the Mahayana section of this book.

ADDRESS: 8901 Hillview Road, Morrison, CO 80465

PHONE: (303) 697-0263
FAX: (303) 837-2595 c/o Lilliam Valdes-Cruz
E-MAIL: valdes-cruz.lilliam@tchden.org
LINEAGE: Tibetan Nyingma
SPIRITUAL HEAD: H. E. Chagdud Tulku Rinpoche
CONTACTS: Lilliam Valdes-Cruz and Steven Glazer
AFFILIATION: Chagdud Gonpa Foundation, Junction City, California
ESTABLISHED: 1994
FACILITIES: Yurt used as *zendo* and shrine room on mountain property; house with teacher residence; a gift store open during retreat times.
RETREATS OFFERED: In the Nyingma tradition by lamas of Chagdud Gonpa.

Rites of Passage

UPON REACHING A CERTAIN AGE, CHILDREN IN Tibet are given a herd of yaks to tend as a mark of their increasing maturity and separateness from their parents. The late Chogyam Trungpa Rinpoche felt that American eight-year-olds needed a similar rite of passage to help bring out their own sense of warriorship and compassion. So in 1983 a formal ceremony to mark the occasion was instituted at our center.

In the ritual, children enter the shrine room, followed by a group of respected elders representing different aspects of the community. The Shambhala flags are carried in, and a brief purification ceremony ensues. The preceptor then addresses the children, amplifying the themes of increased responsibility in the world and the importance of developing compassion for themselves and others.

Children and parents bow to one another in a symbolic gesture of separation. The kids offer gifts representative of their childhood and are given confirming gifts in return. Then they take a vow to be kind to themselves and to others. Four poems, one for each of the elements, are sung and danced by lively Sacred Clowns, and the ceremony concludes with the singing of the Shambhala anthem and a formal recessional.

In preparation for the ceremony, children undergo a series of classes in such "Shambhala Arts" as ikebana (flower arrangement), *kyudo* (archery), poetry, and *bugaku* (Japanese court dance). The classes further empower the children and help them to cultivate compassion in a more disciplined way. Through these rites of passage, children come to see themselves as the next generation of young warriors. Many go on to attend other programs together and to develop a sense of camaraderie and affection that will last for years to come.

Mark Turnoy

For more information, contact: Boulder Shambhala Center, 1345 Spruce St., Boulder, CO 80302; (303) 444-0190.

Rite of passage at Boulder Shambhala Center, marking the maturation of the sangha's *eight-year-olds.* (Photo courtesy of Boulder Shambhala.)

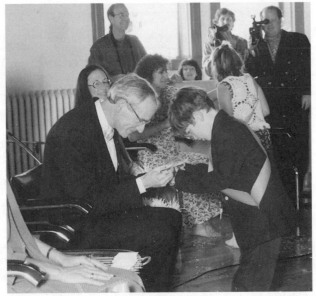

Rites of passage: the kids offer gifts representative of their childhood and are given confirming gifts in return. (Photo courtesy of Boulder Shambhala.)

Shambhala Sun Magazine

THE *SHAMBHALA SUN* IS ONE OF THE WORLD'S foremost Buddhist-inspired magazines, published in newsstand format since 1993 by students of the late Chogyam Trungpa. With its outstanding writing and striking design, the *Shambhala Sun* presents commentary on spirituality, the arts, politics, the environment, and mind-body health. Featuring such prominent figures as the Dalai Lama, Gary Snyder, Patti Smith, and Aung San Suu Kyi, the magazine strives to apply the meditative mind to all aspects of modern life. The *Shambhala Sun* is published six times per year and is available on newsstands throughout North America.

Molly De Shong

For more information, contact: *Shambhala Sun* Magazine, 1345 Spruce St., Boulder, CO 80302-4886; (902) 422-8404; http://www.shambhalasun.com.

Shambhala Sun *Magazine, published six times yearly and available on newsstands throughout North America.* (Front cover courtesy of the magazine.)

COLORADO (*cont.*)

Celtic Buddhist Society

No description available.
ADDRESS: 3435 22nd Street, Boulder, CO 80304
LINEAGE: Celtic/Tibetán
SPIRITUAL HEAD: Ven. Seonaidh
CONTACT: Same
AFFILIATION: Autonomous
ESTABLISHED: 1990
FACILITIES: Shrine rooms.
MEDITATION PROGRAM: Insight Meditation, Deity Yoga.

RETREATS OFFERED: Individual and group retreats throughout the year.

Denver Shambhala Center

Denver Shambhala Center is a branch of Shambhala International. We occupy the first floor of an office building a few blocks from downtown Denver. Meditation instruction is available but usually must be arranged. This Shambhala center is somewhat different than others since Boulder (national headquarters) and the retreat facilities of Rocky Mountain Shambhala Center and Dorje Khyung Dzong are so near to us.
ADDRESS: 718 East 18th Avenue, Denver, CO 80203
PHONE: (303) 863-8366
E-MAIL: takseng@aol.com
LINEAGE: Tibetan Karma Kagyu
SPIRITUAL HEAD: Sakyong Mipham Rinpoche
CONTACT: Gary Snyder
AFFILIATION: Shambhala International, Halifax, Nova Scotia, Canada
ESTABLISHED: 1975

Love Your Students

Since 1993 the Denver Shambhala Center has offered a series of highly successful classes through Colorado Free University, an adult continuing education program whose catalogue gets terrific distribution in this town. Through it, hundreds of people have found their way to our center. Expanding the membership, however, is not the point. The course is designed to plant seeds.

Two entry-level classes are offered, one on Hinayana (Theravada), the other on Mahayana teachings, each five weeks long. Meditation is introduced at the second session and we repeat the instructions at each succeeding class, adding five minutes of sitting each time. By the end of the course, students are able to sit for twenty-five minutes.

From hundreds of feedback sheets we've learned to accentuate the practical ("How can I use meditation in my daily life?"), to keep the jargon to near zero, and to bring a joke to start each class. We also try to articulate the many ways one can approach the dharma—intellectually, devotionally, emotionally—and to provide a sampling of these inner paths as the course unfolds.

While the importance of community has never been clearer—people crave belonging—we've discovered that without some follow-up, folks tend to disappear. So we offer a free, drop-in refresher class one evening a month, along with access to a meditation instructor and, since they're now on our mailing list, a copy of our monthly calendar of events.

The Dalai Lama expressed the guiding principle behind these classes when he said, "My religion is kindness." Love your students.

Andrew Holecek

For more information, contact: Denver Shambhala Center, 718 E. 18th Ave., Denver, CO 80203; (303) 863-8366.

COLORADO (*cont.*)

FACILITIES: Urban meditation center in an office building.

MEDITATION PROGRAM: Several practice sessions weekly.

RETREATS OFFERED: Monthly *Nyinthun* (all-day) sittings. Occasional weekend Shambhala training programs and Vajrayana feasts. Quarterly Beginners Meditation Class through Colorado Free University.

PUBLICATIONS: Monthly newsletter.

Dorje Khyung Dzong (DKD)

Located in Southern Colorado on four hundred acres of alpine meadows and woods, eighty-five hundred feet up the slopes of Mt. Greenhorn, DKD is a center for solitary retreat. There are six comfortable, well-equipped cabins. Retreatants bring their own food. For additional information, please see listing for Shambhala International, Halifax, Nova Scotia, Canada.

ADDRESS: PO Box 131, Gardner, CO 81040

PHONE: (719) 746-2264

LINEAGE: Tibetan Kagyu-Nyingma

SPIRITUAL HEAD: Sakyong Mipham Rinpoche

CONTACTS: Melissa and Bruce Robinson

AFFILIATION: Shambhala International, Halifax, Nova Scotia

FACILITIES: Six retreat cabins.

RETREATS OFFERED: DKD is open year-round for supervised solitary retreats.

Fort Collins Dharma Study Group

For a description, please see listing for Shambhala International, Halifax, Nova Scotia, Canada.

ADDRESS: 219 Sunset Street, Fort Collins, CO 80521-2147

PHONE: (970) 224-2156

LINEAGE: Tibetan Kagyu-Nyingma

SPIRITUAL HEAD: Sakyong Mipham Rinpoche

CONTACT: Fred Meyer

AFFILIATION: Shambhala International, Halifax, Nova Scotia

Karma Chang Chub Cho Tso Ling

Our *sangha* practices *Machig Logdron Chod*, the ritualistic cutting and giving up

THE PATH OF DEVOTION

of ego as symbolized by the body. We are being trained traditionally with all the accoutrements of cymbals, drums, conch shells, trumpets, and so on. Our root practices are *Sang Cho*, smoke offerings, *Chod, Chenrezig, Ngondro*, and *Dharmapalas*. Ours is a relatively small and democratic group. Those who participate can expect to have a say, as well as a share, in what is done. We embrace the ordinary magic of everyday living and challenge and enrich each other by integrating the dharma into our daily lives.

ADDRESS: 6240 West Virginia Avenue, Lakewood, CO 80226

PHONE: (303) 975-0798

FAX: Same, but wait four rings.

E-MAIL: amerbuddha@plinet.com

LINEAGE: Tibetan Nendo Kagyupa, Machig Labdrom Chod, Surmang tradition

SPIRITUAL HEADS: M. C. Nagpa Lama Kalsang Rinpoche, Vajra Master; Lama Karma Phuntshog; Choyki Wangpo, Chant Master

CONTACTS: Mike, Ralph, or Karen

AFFILIATION: Milarepa Institute Retreat Center, South India

ESTABLISHED: 1995

FACILITIES: Meet at Jefferson Unitarian Church, 14350 W. 32nd Avenue, Golden, CO 80401. Small bookstore with dharma items. Thrift store with an imports section.

Karma Thegsum Tashi Gomang (Crestone KTTG)

Karma Thegsum Tashi Gomang was founded in 1980 by the Gyalwa Karmapa, with the idea that this remote part of the country, similar in climate and natural beauty to Tibet, would be a place where the philosophy, wisdom, and culture of Tibet could be preserved and shared with others. Plans have been developed for the two hundred acres of mountain land. A stupa has been constructed. Plans also include an institute for the study and practice of traditional Tibetan medicine, retreat facilities, and a monastery. Our practice center has regular meditation sessions and is blessed by frequent lama visits.

ADDRESS: PO Box 39, Crestone, CO 81131

PHONE: (719) 256-4694

LINEAGE: Tibetan Karma Kagyu

SPIRITUAL HEAD: His Holiness the Seventeenth Gyalwa Karmapa

CONTACTS: Marianne Marstrand and Maria Pelaez

AFFILIATION: Karma Triyana Dharmachakra, Woodstock, New York

ESTABLISHED: 1980

FACILITIES: Three retreat cabins, one stupa, practice center.

Mangala Shri Bhuti

Mangala Shri Bhuti is dedicated to the study and practice of the *Longchen Nyinthig* tradition of Tibetan Buddhism. Its members are accepted on an individual basis by its spiritual head, the Ven. Dzigar Kongtrul Rinpoche, who guides them through the various practices of this lineage.

ADDRESS: PO Box 4088, Boulder, CO 80306

PHONE: (303) 494-8346

FAX: Same

LINEAGE: Tibetan Nyingma

SPIRITUAL HEAD: The Ven. Dzigar Kongtrul Rinpoche

AFFILIATION: Autonomous

ESTABLISHED: 1992

FACILITIES: Rented space in member's home.

MEDITATION PROGRAM: Weekly meditation practice.

RETREATS OFFERED: Ten-day summer seminar every other year.

PUBLICATIONS: In-house newsletter for members only.

Marpa House in Boulder, Colorado, offers communal living and a strong practice environment for dharma students. (Photo by Don Morreale.)

Marpa House

Marpa House was founded in 1973 to house students of Buddhism interested in meditation. Under the direction of the Sakyong Mipham Rinpoche, it offers long-term communal living and a strong practice environment of daily meditation and weekend programs. Four shrine rooms accommodate all levels of practitioners.

ADDRESS: 891 12th Street, Boulder, CO 80302

PHONE: (303) 444-9307

E-MAIL: marpa@shambhala.org

LINEAGE: Tibetan Karma Kagyu

SPIRITUAL HEAD: Sakyong Mipham Rinpoche

CONTACT: Jim Fladmark

AFFILIATION: Shambhala International, Halifax, Nova Scotia, Canada

ESTABLISHED: 1973

COLORADO (*cont.*)

FACILITIES: Four shrine rooms, long-term housing, communal kitchen.

MEDITATION PROGRAM: Daily meditation.

RETREATS OFFERED: Weekend programs.

Namo Buddha Seminar

Namo Buddha Seminar is engaged in promoting the activities of Thrangu Rinpoche. We offer publications, meditation retreats, and annual seminars in California, England, Nova Scotia, and Nepal.

ADDRESS: 1390 Kalmia Avenue, Boulder, CO 80304

PHONE: (303) 449-6608

FAX: (303) 440-0882

E-MAIL: CJohnson@Jeffco.k12.co.us

LINEAGE: Tibetan Kagyu

SPIRITUAL HEAD: Thrangu Rinpoche

CONTACT: Clark Johnson

AFFILIATION: Thrangu Rinpoche

ESTABLISHED: 1988

PUBLICATIONS: Namo Buddha Seminar has published more than twenty books by Thrangu Rinpoche.

Northern Kiliya Center

No description available.

ADDRESS: Box 118, Crestone, CO 81131

PHONE: (719) 256-4516

LINEAGE: Tibetan Nyingma

SPIRITUAL HEAD: H. H. Orgyen Kusum Lingpa

CONTACT: Louis Jarvis

AFFILIATION: Autonomous

FACILITIES: Country retreat facility.

MEDITATION PROGRAM: Vajrakilaya practice, Vajrapani teachings and empowerments, Pema Nying-thig (The Lotus Heart Drop of Great Perfection), Manjushri and Sarasvati teachings and empowerments.

Chagdud Tulku Rinpoche with a young sangha member at Orgyen Rigjed Ling in Lafayette, Colorado. (Photo by Steven Glazer.)

Orgyen Rigjed Ling

We offer retreats and meet biweekly for group practice, to which everyone is welcome. Our aim is to provide support for new and seasoned practitioners by furnishing a space for group practice, study, instruction, and empowerments and teachings by visiting lamas.

ADDRESS: c/o Glazer, 808 East Geneseo Street, Lafayette, CO 80026

PHONE: (303) 604-2537

LINEAGE: Tibetan Nyingma

SPIRITUAL HEAD: Chagdud Tulku Rinpoche

CONTACT: Steven Glazer

AFFILIATION: Chagdud Gonpa Foundation, Junction City, California

ESTABLISHED: 1994

FACILITIES: Members' homes; practice retreats at Buffalo Mountain Dharma Center.

RETREATS OFFERED: Weekend retreats three or four times yearly.

PUBLICATIONS: Quarterly newsletter.

Padmasambhava Buddhist Center

Khenchen Palden Sherab Rinpoche and Khenpo Tsewang Dongyal Rinpoche began giving teachings here in 1982, and in 1993 formally established their own Colorado center. The Khenpos' publishing group, Dharma Samudra, is located in Boulder. For additional information, please see listing under Padmasambhava Buddhist Center, New York, New York.

ADDRESS: 4412 Sandpiper Circle, Boulder, CO 80301

PHONE: (303) 530-5025

FAX: (303) 415-1176

LINEAGE: Tibetan Nyingma

SPIRITUAL HEADS: Khenchen Palden Sherab and Khenpo Tsewang Dongyal

CONTACT: Carl Stuendel

AFFILIATION: Padmasambhava Buddhist Center, New York

ESTABLISHED: 1993

RETREATS OFFERED: Summer retreats in upstate New York; winter retreats in West Palm Beach, Florida; plus other retreats around the country.

PUBLICATIONS: Several texts published by Dharma Samudra.

Palyul Changchub Dhargye Ling of Colorado

The Palyul lineage began in 1665 CE in eastern Tibet. It combines Ati and Mahamudra into one stream of teaching. The main practices of Palyul are the terma (treasures) of Migyur Dorje, Ratna Lingpa, and Ama Gongdu. H. H. Padma Norbu ("Penor"), Rinpoche is the eleventh throne holder of Palyul and is the supreme head of the Nyingma sect. His Holiness plans to build a retreat center and Buddhist college here in the near future.

ADDRESS: c/o Box 1514, Mill Valley, CA 94941

PHONE: (303) 543-8308

FAX: Same

LINEAGE: Palyul, a subsect of the Tibetan Nyingma lineage

SPIRITUAL HEAD: H. H. Padma Norbu ("Penor")

CONTACTS: Khenpo Tsewang Gyatso, Resident Teacher, and Michael Burroughs

AFFILIATION: Namdroling Monastery of Byla-Kuppe, India

ESTABLISHED: 1996

FACILITIES: Member's home.

RETREATS OFFERED: Bimonthly feasts based on the lunar calendar.

PUBLICATIONS: Occasional newsletter.

Rigpa Fellowship of Colorado

We meet weekly in downtown Boulder and focus on the practices of meditation and active compassion as taught by Sogyal Rinpoche, author of *The Tibetan Book of Living and Dying*. Anyone interested in the teachings of Sogyal Rinpoche is invited to attend. Please call for times and location. For additional information, see listing for Rigpa North America, Santa Cruz, California.

ADDRESS: Box 20266, Boulder, CO 80308

PHONE: (303) 702-1899

FAX: (303) 678-0403

LINEAGE: Tibetan Nyingma

SPIRITUAL HEAD: Sogyal Rinpoche

CONTACTS: Peggy Robinson and Mark Van Wagner

AFFILIATION: Rigpa North America, Santa Cruz, California

ESTABLISHED: 1994

FACILITIES: Rented facilities. Call for locations.

MEDITATION PROGRAM: Weekly meditation and study groups.

RETREATS OFFERED: We join Sogyal Rinpoche for national and international retreats, which range from a weekend to three months in duration.

(Debra Ann) Robinson's Dharma Group

No description available.

ADDRESS: 2068 Kearney Street, Denver, CO 80207

PHONE: (303) 399-6824

FAX: Same

LINEAGE: Tibetan and Indian yoga

SPIRITUAL HEAD: Ven. Thrangu Rinpoche

CONTACT: Debra Ann Robinson

AFFILIATION: Autonomous

FACILITIES: Meditation and yoga room in teacher's house; larger facilities rented for retreats.

MEDITATION PROGRAM: Weekly meditation practice, individual instruction.

RETREATS OFFERED: Weekend and weeklong retreats throughout the year.

Rocky Mountain Shambhala Center (RMSC)

RMSC is a year-round contemplative center founded by the Ven. Chogyam Trungpa Rinpoche. Situated on six hundred secluded acres of highland meadows and forests in the Colorado Rockies, RMSC provides an ideal setting for programs and retreats devoted to the study and practice of meditation in Buddhist and other contemplative traditions. We are the site for the Great Stupa of Dharmakaya. For additional information, please refer to Shambhala International, Halifax, Nova Scotia, Canada.

ADDRESS: 4921 County Road 68C, Red Feather Lakes, CO 80545

PHONE: (970) 881-2184

FAX: (970) 881-2909

E-MAIL: 75347.52@compuserve.com

LINEAGE: Tibetan Kagyu-Nyingma/ Shambhala

SPIRITUAL HEAD: Sakyong Mipham Rinpoche

CONTACT: Allyn Lyon

AFFILIATION: Shambhala International, Halifax, Nova Scotia

ESTABLISHED: 1971

FACILITIES: Summers: tents, capacity: three hundred people. Winters: dorms, capacity fifty. Individual retreat cabins.

RETREATS OFFERED: Three-month Vajradhatu Seminary; advanced Shambhala training; Vajrayana practice programs; retreats by visiting Buddhist teachers; *Dathun* (thirty-day) retreats; university-oriented contemplative studies programs.

PUBLICATIONS: *Brala*, quarterly newsletter.

Shambhala Prison Community

The Shambhala Prison Community provides meditation instruction and spiritual and pastoral counseling to the international prison community. This is done mostly on site within federal, state, and county correctional facilities in the United States and Canada and via correspondence. We also provide books, tapes, and information about Buddhism and, as much as possible, act as a clearing house for humanitarian and service-oriented work within the prison system. Although rooted in the Kagyu and Nyingma branches of Tibetan Vajrayana Buddhism, we are also an educational and nonsectarian organization that welcomes participation from all Buddhist traditions.

ADDRESS: c/o Shambhala Center, 1345 Spruce Street, Boulder, CO 80302

FAX: (303) 444-2414

LINEAGE: Tibetan Kagyu and Nyingma

CONTACT: William Karelis

AFFILIATION: Shambhala International,

Halifax, Nova Scotia, Canada (church affiliation: Vajradhatu)

ESTABLISHED: 1996

MEDITATION PROGRAM: We offer meditation instruction and spiritual counseling to the prison community, mostly within the United States prison system.

Tara Mandala

Tara Mandala supports spiritual activities in the Tibetan Buddhist tradition that are oriented toward the teachings of innate wisdom. Our principal purpose is the development of Dzogchen in the lineage of Chogyal Namkhai Norbu Rinpoche. Our spiritual director and resident teacher is Tsultrim Allione. Tara Mandala is located on five hundred acres of wild and beautiful land in the San Juan Mountains of southwestern Colorado. Throughout the year we facilitate group meditations, study groups, Vajra dance practice, teachings, and pilgrimages, as well as meditation instruction in other parts of the United States, and internationally at a number of sacred sites.

ADDRESS: PO Box 3040, 157 Hot Springs Boulevard, Pagosa Springs, CO 81147

PHONE: (970) 264-6177

FAX: (970) 264-6169

E-MAIL: 102476.3342@compuserve.com

LINEAGE: Tibetan Tantric and Dzogchen

SPIRITUAL HEADS: Tsultrim Allione and Norbu Rinpoche

CONTACT: Tsultrim Allione, Resident Director

AFFILIATION: Autonomous

ESTABLISHED: 1993, as a retreat facility

FACILITIES: Summer encampment-style retreats.

RETREATS OFFERED: Tantric, Dzogchen, Vipassana, others.

PUBLICATIONS: *Tara Mandala Newsletter*

Thubten Shadrub Ling (TSL)

Our center's Tibetan name means "Place for the learning and practice of Buddha's teachings." It was founded by Geshe Tsultim Gyeltsen of Los Angeles and has relied on the dedication, energy, and resources of a small group of friends and participating members. In 1994 a Tibetan Buddhist nun, Ani Thubten Dekyong, graciously spent fifteen months with us helping to establish TSL as the center for dharma in Colorado Springs. The Colorado College has also been very kind in providing us with a beautiful and solemn location at Shove Chapel for our weekly gatherings for teaching, prayer, and meditation.

ADDRESS: 2365 Biltmore Court, Colorado Springs, CO 80907

PHONE: (719) 635-7804

FAX: Computer on same line.

LINEAGE: Gelugpa

SPIRITUAL HEAD: Geshe Tsultim Gyeltsen

CONTACT: Roger Bosse

AFFILIATION: Thubten Dhargye Ling, Los Angeles, California

ESTABLISHED: 1981

FACILITIES: Shove Chapel on the Colorado College campus.

RETREATS OFFERED: Weekend teachings four to six times a year.

PUBLICATIONS: *TSL Newsletter*, three to four times a year.

Udiyan Maitreya Kosha

Udiyan Maitreya Kosha (UMK) was founded in 1979 by the late Lucille Schaible and her students. An American original, Ms. Schaible was a self-taught Vajra master who was recognized in her later years by the principals of the Nyingma lineage. The center is a residential community where classes in meditation, philosophy, psychology, self-healing, and related topics are offered. All UMK projects and teachings are oriented toward the understanding and practice of Tibetan Nyingma Buddhism and its appropriate presentation in the West.

ADDRESS: PO Box 300275, Denver, CO 80218

PHONE: (303) 839-9101

FAX: (303) 355-2767

LINEAGE: Tibetan Nyingma

SPIRITUAL HEAD: H. E. Shenphen Dawa Rinpoche

CONTACT: Gretchen Groth

AFFILIATION: Autonomous

ESTABLISHED: 1978 by H. H. Dudjom Rinpoche

FACILITIES: Urban meditation center with some residential apartments; bookstore and gift shop.

RETREATS OFFERED: One- to two-week retreats yearly; Vajrayana practice retreat.

Vajrayana Foundation of Colorado

For additional information, please see listing for Vajrayana Foundation, Corralitos, California.

ADDRESS: PO Box 252, Indian Hills, CO 80454

PHONE: (303) 697-1629

LINEAGE: Tibetan Nyingma-Tersar lineages of H. H. Dudjom Rinpoche

SPIRITUAL HEAD: Lama Tharchin Rinpoche

CONTACTS: Jim and Ingrid Jeffries

AFFILIATION: Vajrayana Foundation at Pema Osel Ling in Corralitos, California

ESTABLISHED: 1988

FACILITIES: Rotates among members' homes.

RETREATS OFFERED: We meet twice per month on Guru and Dakini Days (the tenth and twenty-fifth days of the lunar calendar) for "Shower of Blessings" and "Red Tara," respectively. We join our national sangha for retreats at Pema Osel Ling in Corralitos, California, for seasonal retreats with Lama Tharchin Rinpoche.

PUBLICATIONS: *Lotus Light*, newsletter from Vajrayana Foundation headquarters.

Yeshe Khorlo

The main practices of Yeshe Khorlo are the *terma* (treasures) of the fourteenth-century Bhutanese master Padma Lingpa. Gangteng Rinpoche is the ninth throne holder of the five-hundred-year-old Gangteng Gonpa Monastery and is the body emanation of Padma Lingpa. Together with the other Yeshe Khorlo centers in the United States and Canada, we have established a retreat facility in Crestone, Colorado.
ADDRESS: 1630 30th St., Box 356, Boulder, CO 80301
PHONE: (303) 543-8308
FAX: Same
LINEAGE: Bhutanese/Tibetan Nyingma
SPIRITUAL HEAD: Gangteng Rinpoche
CONTACT: Dennis Baarlaer
AFFILIATION: Yeshe Khorlo, Inc.
ESTABLISHED: 1991
FACILITIES: Members' homes.
RETREATS OFFERED: Monthly feasts on the tenth and twenty-fifth of the month (based on lunar calendar).
PUBLICATIONS: *Yeshe Khorlo*, newsletter.

CONNECTICUT

Center for Dzogchen Studies

The Center for Dzogchen Studies in New Haven, Connecticut, is a learning center that offers classes, retreats, and ongoing instruction on the teachings and practices of Dzogchen. Padma Karma Rinpoche resides and teaches at the center.
ADDRESS: 847 Whalley Avenue, New Haven, CT 06515
PHONE: (203) 387-9992
LINEAGE: Tibetan Nyingma and Kagyu
SPIRITUAL HEAD: Padma Karma Rinpoche
AFFILIATION: Santa Fe Center for Dzogchen Studies, Santa Fe, New Mexico

Padma Karma Rinpoche, Spiritual Director of the Center for Dzogchen Studies in New Haven, Connecticut. (Photo by Heidi Nevin.)

ESTABLISHED: 1994
FACILITIES: Urban meditation center.
RETREATS OFFERED: One-day retreats, monthly; three-day retreats, three times a year; individual extended retreats.
PUBLICATIONS: Monthly newsletter.

New Haven Shambhala

For a description, please refer to Shambhala International, Halifax, Nova Scotia, Canada.
ADDRESS: 319 Peck Street, New Haven, CT 06513
PHONE: (203) 776-2331
FAX: (860) 387-2913
E-MAIL: 76771.2264@compuserve.com
LINEAGE: Tibetan Kagyu-Nyingma
SPIRITUAL HEAD: Sakyong Mipham Rinpoche

CONTACT: Nealy Zimmerman
AFFILIATION: Shambhala International, Halifax, Nova Scotia
ESTABLISHED: 1978

DELAWARE

Padmasambhava Buddhist Center

For additional information, please see Padmasambhava Buddhist Center, New York, New York.
ADDRESS: 2321 Fell's Lane, Wilmington, DE 19808
PHONE: (302) 655-3364
LINEAGE: Tibetan Nyingma
SPIRITUAL HEADS: Khenchen Palden Sherab Rinpoche and Khenpo Tsewang Dongyal Rinpoche
AFFILIATION: Padmasambhava Buddhist Center, New York
RETREATS OFFERED: Summer in upstate New York; winter in West Palm Beach, Florida; others around the country.

DISTRICT OF COLUMBIA

Guhyasamaja Center

No description available.
ADDRESS: 4339 Alton Place, Washington, DC 20016
PHONE: (202) 364-8940
LINEAGE: Tibetan
CONTACT: Betty Rogers
AFFILIATION: Foundation for the Preservation of the Mahayana Tradition

Vajrayogini Buddhist Center

Vajrayogini Buddhist Center is a member of the New Kadampa Tradition (NKT) under the spiritual direction of Geshe Kelsang. All NKT centers offer one or more of Geshe Kelsang's "three study programs." The General Program provides a basic introduction to Buddhism in weekly evening classes suitable for be-

What Is Dzogchen?

DZOGCHEN IS THE DIRECT EXPERIENCE OF THE nature of mind. The word itself, a Tibetan term meaning "Great Completeness," refers to intrinsic awareness, which is the unifying quality of all experience. Recognizing this uncreated awareness means discovering our own primordial wholeness unbound by conditioned views of life.

Awareness practices introduce us directly to our own minds. By resting in relaxed presence we perceive the awakened state as existing already within us. By investigating the many facets of our ordinary experience we discover our "Great Completeness."

Rather than emphasizing theory, we bring our atten-

tion to our conceptual processes as they are, through the consistent practice of sitting meditation. This brings us into direct contact with the constant flux of our thought patterns. By simply observing the insubstantial nature of thought, the continuity of awareness within all manifestations is revealed. The Dzogchen view is thus naturally applied to every aspect of our lives. Our own experience of naked presence is a living example of how the Buddha's truths manifest within us all.

For more information, contact: Center for Dzogchen Studies, 847 Whalley Avenue, New Haven, CT 06515; (203) 387-9992.

---

ginners. The four-year Foundation Program involves the systematic study of five of Geshe Kelsang's books. Teacher Training, a seven-year program, requires the study of twelve of Geshe Kelsang's books, the keeping of commitments with regard to behavior and way of life, and the completion of several retreats.

ADDRESS: 632 D Street, Northeast, Washington, DC 20002

PHONE: (202) 544-8605

FAX: (202) 544-8605

E-MAIL: vyogini@nmaa.org

LINEAGE: Tibetan New Kadampa Tradition

SPIRITUAL HEAD: Ven. Geshe Kelsang Gyatso Rinpoche

AFFILIATION: New Kadampa Tradition Buddhist Centers (NKT)

ESTABLISHED: 1994

FACILITIES: Residential center; "beautiful meditation room."

MEDITATION PROGRAM: Daily morning

meditation on both sutra and Highest Yoga Tantra. Other *pujas* are offered regularly.

PUBLICATIONS: *Full Moon*, the magazine of NKT centers in America. Geshe Kelsang's books.

FLORIDA

Drikung Kagyu

No description available.

ADDRESS: 258 South Clearwater-Largo Road, Largo, FL 33770

PHONE: (813) 587-9534

LINEAGE: Tibetan Drikung Kagyu

SPIRITUAL HEAD: Ven. Khenpo Konchog Gyaltsen Rinpoche

CONTACT: Cynthia Verzi

AFFILIATION: Tibetan Meditation Center, Frederick, Maryland

Gainesville Karma Kagyu Study Group

We meet regularly at the Florida School of Massage, where we maintain a congenial family atmosphere and encourage people to come to whatever portion of the meetings they wish. *Sadhana* practice is for those who have taken refuge or intend to do so. It consists of alternating *Chenrezig* and *Amitabha* practice and a short Karmapa Guru Yoga practice. Our regular meetings include opening prayers, *Heart Sutra* or mantra recitation, meditation, teaching, and a short Seven Points of Mind Training practice and dedication. For additional information, please see Karma Triyana Dharmachakra, Woodstock, New York.

ADDRESS: 5785 Rudolph Avenue, St. Augustine, FL 32084

PHONE: (904) 461-8401

LINEAGE: Tibetan Karma Kagyu

SPIRITUAL HEAD: Ven. Khenpo Karthar
Rinpoche
CONTACT: Frances Norwood
AFFILIATION: Karma Triyana Dharma-
chakra, Woodstock, New York
FACILITIES: Florida School of Massage,
6421 Southwest 13th Street, Gainesville
MEDITATION PROGRAM: Weekly *sadhana*
practice and regular meeting, weekly
shamatha meditation.
PUBLICATIONS: *Lion's Roar Dharma
News*

Jacksonville Karma Kagyu Study Group (KKSG)

Jacksonville KKSG was founded in Au-
gust 1986 by the Ven. Khenpo Karthar
Rinpoche. Since that time, KKSG has
hosted lamas of the Karma Kagyu lineage
for public talks and weekend seminars
and has presented study sessions on a va-
riety of Buddhist subjects during the
group's meetings. All those interested are
welcome to call for further information.
ADDRESS: 1059 Park Street, Jacksonville,
FL 32204
PHONE: (904) 389-1317
E-MAIL: artdieties@aol.com
LINEAGE: Tibetan Karma Kagyu
SPIRITUAL HEAD: Ven. Khenpo Karthar
Rinpoche
CONTACT: Michael Turnquist
AFFILIATION: Karma Triyana Dharma-
chakra, Woodstock, New York
ESTABLISHED: 1986
FACILITIES: Urban meditation center.
PUBLICATIONS: *Lion's Roar Dharma
News*

Mitsugon-an-Tendai Buddhist Hermitage

A private *dojo* in the Florida Keys.
ADDRESS: Box 490, Key West, FL 33041
LINEAGE: Japanese Esoteric Buddhism
SPIRITUAL HEAD: Jikai Sensei Jushoku

CONTACT: Same
AFFILIATION: Autonomous
FACILITIES: *Dojo*

Padmasambhava Buddhist Center

A small, yet devoted, meditation group
practicing under the guidance of Khenpo
Palden Rinpoche and Khenpo Tsewang
Dongyal Rinpoche. The Khenpos visit
and teach us several times a year, and we
travel to receive their empowerments and
blessings. We practice and meditate
weekly for ninety minutes followed by
some time for fellowship.
ADDRESS: 655 Wildmere Avenue, Long-
wood, FL 32750
PHONE: (407) 830-4458 or 695-1297
LINEAGE: Tibetan
SPIRITUAL HEADS: Khenpo Palden Sherab
and Khenpo Tsewang Dongyal
CONTACT: Janie Floren
AFFILIATION: Padmasambhava Buddhist
Center of New York
ESTABLISHED: 1989
FACILITIES: Private meditation room in
home.
MEDITATION PROGRAM: Practice weekly.
PUBLICATIONS: *Ceaseless Echoes of the
Great Silence*

Padmasambhava Buddhist Center

The annual winter retreat with the Khen-
pos is held here in West Palm Beach. For
additional information, please see listing
under Padmasambhava Buddhist Center,
New York, New York.
ADDRESS: 1039 Churchill Circle North,
West Palm Beach, FL 33405
PHONE: (407) 586-9941
LINEAGE: Tibetan Nyingma
SPIRITUAL HEADS: Khenchen Palden
Sherab Rinpoche and Khenpo Tsewang
Dongyal Rinpoche
AFFILIATION: Padmasambhava Buddhist
Center, New York, New York

MEDITATION PROGRAM: We meet twice
weekly. Meditation instruction avail-
able. Please call for schedule.
RETREATS OFFERED: Summer in upstate
New York; winter in West Palm Beach,
Florida; others around the country.

St. Augustine Karma Kagyu Study Group

"We started this center after Nancy and I
realized we could practice more if we
didn't have to drive the forty miles to
Jacksonville to be with other Kagyu students. Khenpo Karthar visited Florida
soon after we began holding regular
Wednesday evening meetings at our
home, and we were asked if we wanted to
host him. We became an affiliate of
Karma Triyana Dharmachakra monastery in Woodstock, New York. In addi-
tion to weekly evening meditation
instruction and practice, we recite the
Chenrezig/Amitabha Sadhanas. For addi-
tional information, please see listing for
Karma Triyana Dharmachakra of Wood-
stock, New York." —*Tom Vogler*
ADDRESS: 35 San Carlos Avenue, St. Au-
gustine, FL 32084
PHONE: (904) 829-6034
FAX: (904) 829-1952
E-MAIL: tvogler@aug.com
LINEAGE: Tibetan Karma Kagyu
SPIRITUAL HEAD: Ven. Khenpo Karthar
Rinpoche
CONTACTS: Tom Vogler and Nancy Ham-
lin-Vogler
AFFILIATION: Karma Triyana Dharma-
chakra, Woodstock, New York
ESTABLISHED: 1989
FACILITIES: Shrine room.
MEDITATION PROGRAM: Weekly practice
and study, *Chenrezig/Amitabha Sad-
hana* practice.
RETREATS OFFERED: When teachers visit.
PUBLICATIONS: *Lion's Roar Dharma
News*

Sakya Kunga Dzong

No description available.
ADDRESS: 1024 Northeast 144th Street,
North Miami, FL 33161
PHONE: (305) 945-7315
LINEAGE: Tibetan Sakya
SPIRITUAL HEAD: Sakya Trizin
CONTACT: Kenneth Buscher
ESTABLISHED: 1981
FACILITIES: Shrine room.
MEDITATION PROGRAM: Weekly
RETREATS OFFERED: Occasionally

Tampa Karma Thegsum Choling (KTC)

Tampa KTC was founded in 1985 by the
Ven. Khenpo Karthar Rinpoche. Under
his guidance we are committed to providing an appropriate situation for learning and practicing the traditions of the
Karma Kagyu lineage. Meditation and
deity practices are held weekly and instruction is available by appointment. We
also host visits by distinguished Kagyu
lamas. Tampa KTC bookstore has a large
collection of titles related to the study of
Buddhism in the Kagyu tradition, as well
as many hard-to-find practice materials.
Mail-order catalogue available. For addi-
tional information, please see listing for
Karma Triyana Dharmachakra of Wood-
stock, New York.
ADDRESS: 820 South MacDill Avenue,
Tampa, FL 33609
PHONE: (813) 870-2904
E-MAIL: tdm@ix.netcom.com
LINEAGE: Tibetan Karma Kagyu
SPIRITUAL HEAD: Ven. Khenpo Karthar
Rinpoche
CONTACTS: Jill McCann and William De-
Brine
AFFILIATION: Karma Triyana Dharma-
chakra, Woodstock, New York
ESTABLISHED: 1984 by Ven. Khenpo
Karthar Rinpoche
FACILITIES: Unity Church

MEDITATION PROGRAM: Weekly meditation and deity practice.
RETREATS OFFERED: Occasional weekend
teachings of meditation and prayers by
authentic Tibetan Buddhist lamas/
teachers.
PUBLICATIONS: Books and practice materials are available.

Tub-ten Kunga Center

A "little wanna-be center" in Boca Raton,
Florida, dedicated to the bright enlight-
enment and happiness of all beings.
Weekly meditation with occasional re-
treats and notable guest speakers.
ADDRESS: 7970 Little Lane, Boca Raton,
FL 33433
PHONE: (561) 392-3318
FAX: Same
LINEAGE: Tibetan Gelugpa Lineage
SPIRITUAL HEAD: Lama Thubten Zopa
Rinpoche
CONTACT: Jacquelyn Keeley
AFFILIATION: Foundation for the Preser-
vation of the Mahayana Tradition
MEDITATION PROGRAM: Weekly medita-
tion.
RETREATS OFFERED: Occasional retreats.

United Rhyme Buddhist Society

We are a small group of students and
teachers who see ourselves more as a
community of practitioners than as a
center. Teachings are sometimes given by
our spiritual head, Lama Kunga Cheodak, a thirty-one-year-old American of
Spanish descent. We offer teachings from
all four lineages of Tibetan Buddhism,
with a special inclination towards Sakya
and Nyingmapa transmissions. Korean
Won and Chinese Zen are also taught.
Affiliated United Rhyme communities
can be found in Miami, South Carolina,
and Iquitos, Peru.
ADDRESS: PO Box 1676, Miami, FL 33233
PHONE: (305) 643-3725

FAX: (305) 649-9997
WWW: http://www.shadow.net/heruka
LINEAGE: Tibetan
SPIRITUAL HEAD: Kunga Cheodak
AFFILIATION: Autonomous
ESTABLISHED: 1996

GEORGIA

Atlanta Shambhala Center

For additional information, please refer
to Shambhala International, Halifax,
Nova Scotia, Canada.
ADDRESS: 1167 Zonolite Place, Atlanta,
GA 30306
PHONE: (404) 873-9846
E-MAIL: 73054.1730@compuserve.com
LINEAGE: Tibetan Kagyu-Nyingma
SPIRITUAL HEAD: Sakyong Mipham Rin-
poche
CONTACTS: B.J. Sharp and Kathy Tate
AFFILIATION: Shambhala International,
Halifax, Nova Scotia, Canada
FACILITIES: Urban meditation center.

Losel Shedrup Ling/Tibetan Buddhist Center of Atlanta

Losel Shedrup Ling ("Hermitage of the
Radiant Mind") was established as the
American seat of Drepung Loseling Monastery by Geshe Lobsang Tenzin, a young
monk in Atlanta completing his doctorate at Emory University. Accredited
courses at Emory University are planned.
Losel Shedrup Ling emphasizes a balanced approach to study and practice as
taught by the monastery's great lineage
masters.
ADDRESS: Woodlake Office Park, 2531
Briarcliff Road, Northeast, Suite 100,
Atlanta, GA 30329
PHONE: Twenty-four-hour activities line:
(770) 908-3358
E-MAIL: geshe@ilinks.net or
cdr@ilinks.net

www: http://www.drepung.org
LINEAGE: Gelugpa
SPIRITUAL HEAD: Geshe Lobsang Tenzin Negi, founding teacher
CONTACT: President, chosen from organizing committee.
AFFILIATION: Drepung Loseling Monastery, Karnataka, India
ESTABLISHED: 1991
FACILITIES: City center; retreat center in Mineral Bluff, Georgia.
MEDITATION PROGRAM: Weekly *shamatha*, Guru Yoga, *ngondro*, and *yamantaka*. Full moon: Mahayana Precepts and Lama Choepa. New moon: Medicine Buddha. Weekly talks by Geshe Lobsang.
RETREATS OFFERED: Teaching Retreats giving a theoretical overview of Buddhism, *ngondro*, and advanced practices. Practice Retreats: Nyung-Ney with qualified masters.
PUBLICATIONS: *The Losel Shedrup Ling Newsletter*

GUAM

Guam True Buddha School

No description available.
ADDRESS: PO Box 3146, Agana, Guam 96910
PHONE: (671) 789-1079
FAX: (671) 477-9374
LINEAGE: Chinese Vajrayana: True Buddha School
SPIRITUAL HEAD: Grand Master Sheng-yen Lu

HAWAII

Honolulu Dharma Study Group

For additional information, please refer to Shambhala International, Halifax, Nova Scotia, Canada.

ADDRESS: 1555 Pohaku Street, #A508, Honolulu, HI 96817-2836
PHONE: (808) 944-1796
FAX: (808) 944-3912
E-MAIL: bralich@hawaii.edu
LINEAGE: Tibetan Kagyu-Nyingma
SPIRITUAL HEAD: Sakyong Mipham Rinpoche
CONTACT: Philip Bralich
AFFILIATION: Shambhala International, Halifax, Nova Scotia

Kagyu Thegchen Ling

Kagyu Thegchen Ling is located in Nuuanu Valley in the city of Honolulu. Its program provides a wide variety of experiences for students of any level of interest or development. The resident lamas provide instruction in meditation techniques, give teachings and Tibetan language classes, and officiate at special events. The weekly meditation schedule includes evening silent meditation instruction and Sunday morning *Chenrezig* practice. A quarterly newsletter informs members and friends about center activities. You may call us for further information.

ADDRESS: 26 Gartley Place, Honolulu, HI 96817
PHONE: (808) 595-8989
FAX: Same
LINEAGE: Tibetan Kagyu
SPIRITUAL HEAD: H. E. Yangsi Kalu Rinpoche
CONTACT: Lama Karma Rimchen, Resident Teacher
AFFILIATION: Autonomous
ESTABLISHED: 1974
FACILITIES: Dharma center.
MEDITATION PROGRAM: Weekly and monthly meditation and puja schedule. Call for program.
PUBLICATIONS: *Empty Mirror*, quarterly.

Karma Rimay O Sal Ling/Maui Dharma Center

Maui Dharma Center was founded by the Ven. Kalu Rinpoche in 1974. Since 1983, the Ven. Lama Tenzin has been its resident teacher. Lama Tenzin conducts marriages, funerals, family and individual counseling, meditations, and blessings. The urban center can accommodate live-in students and visiting guests and offers meditation and prayer twice a day, every day. In addition to a neighborhood meditation temple, it houses a reading library, a bookstore, and a food pantry for the poor. The country retreat property is available for individual, unsupervised retreats as well as for small group retreats.

ADDRESSES: 9 Hikina Place/PO Box 1029, Paia, HI 96779
PHONE: (808) 579-8076
FAX: (808) 575-2044
E-MAIL: Krosl@maui.net
WWW: http://www.maui.net/~krosl/
LINEAGE: Karma Kagyu
SPIRITUAL HEAD: Ven. Kalu Rinpoche
CONTACT: Lama Tenzin
AFFILIATION: Connected to Kalu Rinpoche centers worldwide.
ESTABLISHED: 1974
FACILITIES: Urban meditation center; country retreat center.
MEDITATION PROGRAM: Shamatha/Vipassana, Tara, Chenrezig, Seven-Points of Mind Training, unsupervised retreats.
PUBLICATIONS: Quarterly newsletter.

Nechung Dorje Drayang Ling/Wood Valley Temple and Retreat Center

Dedicated by H. H. the Dalai Lama in October of 1980, Nechung Dorje Drayang Ling is a center for the dissemination of Buddhist teachings. It also provides facilities for other religious, secular, and community groups to hold programs in pursuit of their respective philosophies and practices. The temple hosts several programs yearly with lamas of all schools of Tibetan Buddhism. Seminars and retreats cover a wide range of subjects, from foundational philosophy to the highest yoga tantras and *Dzogchen*.

ADDRESS: PO Box 250, Pahala, HI 96777
PHONE: (808) 928-8539
FAX: (808) 928-6271
E-MAIL: nechung@aloha.net
LINEAGE: Nonsectarian
SPIRITUAL HEAD: Ven. Nechung Rinpoche, Founder
CONTACTS: Michael and Marya Schwabe
AFFILIATION: Nechung Monastery, Dharamsala, India/Lhasa, Tibet
ESTABLISHED: 1973
FACILITIES: Classic Japanese temple; meditation hall, reference library. Two-story retreat building; meditation hall, kitchen, dining room, sleeping quarters. "Towering eucalyptus, palms and bamboo . . . vivid tropical flowers."
PUBLICATIONS: *Drayang,* a biannual newsletter.

Shantideva Center

Shantideva Center sponsors teachings from qualified Tibetan lamas in the Hilo area of the Big Island of Hawaii. We have an irregular schedule, as it is dependent upon which teachers are passing through. We occasionally meet at a Japanese restaurant in Hilo to meditate and listen to dharma tapes.

ADDRESS: HCR 1, Box 4660, Keaau, HI 96749
PHONE: (808) 966-6400
FAX: Same
E-MAIL: laine@interpac.net
LINEAGE: Tibetan
SPIRITUAL HEAD: Lama Thupten Zopa Rinpoche
CONTACT: Melissa Laine

AFFILIATION: Foundation for the Preservation of the Mahayana Tradition
ESTABLISHED: 1985

Vajrayana Foundation of Hawaii/ Orgen Dechen Cho Dzong

Vajrayana Foundation of Hawaii was established in 1990 and sponsors practice and teachings throughout the Hawaiian Islands. Orgen Dechen Cho Dzong, the foundation's country retreat property, is nestled in the seclusion of a lush valley on the southernmost tip of the Big Island. With its magnificent view, rose-apple grove, and tropical fruit trees, this pure land provides sanctuary for those who seriously wish to carry out their meditation practice in a supportive setting. Under Lama Dechen Yeshe Wangmo's guidance, the center offers monthly *ngondro* intensives and hosts annual retreats with Lama Tharchin Rinpoche and others.

ADDRESS: Box 6780, Ocean View, HI 96737
PHONE: (808) 939-9889
FAX: (808) 939-8490
E-MAIL: vfh@ilhawaii.net
WWW: http://www.ilhawaii.net/~vfh/plnl.html
LINEAGE: Nyingma and Tersar Lineages of H. H. Dudjom Rinpoche
SPIRITUAL HEAD: Lama Tharchin Rinpoche
CONTACT: Lama Dechen Yeshe Wangmo, Resident Teacher
AFFILIATION: Vajrayana Foundation, Corralitos, California
ESTABLISHED: 1990
FACILITIES: Urban center and retreat sanctuary.
MEDITATION PROGRAM: Island *sanghas* meet twice monthly for *guru* and *dakini tsogs.*
PUBLICATIONS: *Pureland Hawaii,* newsletter.

ILLINOIS

Chagdud Gonpa Chicago

We follow the Tibetan Nyingmapa tradition. Weekly services, which include meditation, are held at the Quang Minh Temple and are conducted in English, Chinese, and Tibetan. Tsog (offering to the Buddha) is celebrated every fourth Sunday after group practice. Short retreats are held twice a year. Losar (Tibetan New Year) and Wesak (Buddha's birth, death, and enlightenment) are observed and empowerments are performed from time to time.

ADDRESS: 1632 South State Street, Belvidere, IL 61008
PHONE: (815) 544-6464
FAX: (815) 547-5550
E-MAIL: jchen1632@aol.com
LINEAGE: Tibetan Nyingma
SPIRITUAL HEAD: Chagdud Tulku Rinpoche
CONTACT: John Chen
AFFILIATION: Chagdud Gonpa Foundation
ESTABLISHED: 1992
FACILITIES: We use Quang Minh Temple facilities, 4429 North Damen Avenue, Chicago.
RETREATS OFFERED: Short retreats twice yearly.
PUBLICATIONS: *Windhorse,* newsletter.

Chicago Ling Shen Ching Tze

No description available.

ADDRESS: 1035 West 31st Street, Chicago, IL 60608
PHONE: (312) 927-8807
FAX: (708) 818-8988
LINEAGE: Chinese Vajrayana: True Buddha School
SPIRITUAL HEAD: Grand Master Sheng-yen Lu
AFFILIATION: True Buddha School

Chicago Ratna Shri Sangha

No description available.
ADDRESS: 3138 North Drake, Chicago,
IL 60618
PHONE: (312) 267-6224
FAX: (312) 267-1206
LINEAGE: Tibetan Drikung Kagyu
SPIRITUAL HEAD: H. H. Chetsang Rinpoche
CONTACT: Paul Larson
AFFILIATION: Tibetan Meditation Center,
Frederick, Maryland
ESTABLISHED: 1994
FACILITIES: Meet in members' homes except for large events.
RETREATS OFFERED: Periodic visits from
Ven. Khenpo Konchog Gyaltsen.
PUBLICATIONS: Irregular flyers and announcements.

Chicago Rime Center

Rime is Tibetan for "unbiased." Accordingly, Chicago Rime Center supports the development, practice, and integration of the various schools of Tibetan Buddhism. While exploring the richness unique to each, we honor the unity inherent within the vast spectrum of Tibetan Buddhist teachings. Chicago Rime Center has received the blessings of such eminent figures as H. H. Dilgo Khyentse and H. H. the Dalai Lama. Activities include weekly practice sessions, dharma talks, and bimonthly *tsog* offerings. We work to provide access to traditional teachings by notable Tibetan Buddhist masters. Call or write for current schedule. All are welcome.
ADDRESS: 4063 North Kenmore, #2,
Chicago, IL 60613
PHONE: (312) 525-1088
LINEAGE: Tibetan nonsectarian
CONTACT: Roberto Sanchez
AFFILIATION: Autonomous
MEDITATION PROGRAM: Weekly practice

sessions; dharma talks; bimonthly *tsog*
offerings.

Chicago Shambhala Center

For additional information, please refer
to Shambhala International, Halifax,
Nova Scotia, Canada.
ADDRESS: 7331 North Sheridan Road,
Chicago, IL 60626
PHONE: (773) 743-8147
FAX: (708) 256-8978 (Marita)
E-MAIL: NormChapmanMD@msn.com
LINEAGE: Tibetan Kagyu-Nyingma
SPIRITUAL HEAD: Sakyong Mipham Rinpoche
CONTACT: Robert Lehmann
AFFILIATION: Shambhala International,
Halifax, Nova Scotia
MEDITATION PROGRAM: Group practice
sessions are held twice a week. Beginning meditation instruction is available
and the public is warmly invited to attend.
RETREATS OFFERED: Chicago Shambhala
offers public lecture courses and seminars on Buddhism taught by senior students. Minimal tuition fee. Programs
and schedules are described in our
newsletter.
PUBLICATIONS: *Shambhala Newsletter*

Jewel Heart Chicago

The purpose of Jewel Heart is to perpetuate Tibetan culture and Mahayana Buddhism, with an emphasis on the tradition of Je Tsong Kapa. By offering talks, retreats, guided meditations, tapes, literature, and community service, Jewel Heart continues the practice of this living tradition. Ven. Gelek Rinpoche is Jewel Heart's spiritual director. We meet every other week at University of Chicago for meditation and discussion. Call for times and location.

ADDRESS: 2922 West Palmer, Chicago,
IL 60647
PHONES: (312) 342-8291 or (312) 702-8550
LINEAGE: Tibetan Gelugpa
SPIRITUAL HEAD: Gelek Rinpoche
CONTACT: Madonna Gauding
FACILITIES: Ida Noyes Hall, University of
Chicago
MEDITATION PROGRAM: Meditation and
discussion on first and third Sundays
monthly.
RETREATS OFFERED: Weeklong, summer,
and winter; bimonthly visits by Gelug
Rinpoche.
PUBLICATIONS: *From the Heart*, newsletter.

Karma Thegsum Choling, Chicago (KTC)

Chicago KTC was founded in the early 1980s following a visit by the Ven. Khenpo Karthar Rinpoche. We have a small but dedicated membership that practices together regularly and senior students are available to answer questions and lend support. The meditation hall is decorated with traditional pictures, statues, and offerings, and our library is stocked with hundreds of books collected by members over the years. All practice sessions are free and open to beginners. Meditation instruction is available. For additional information, please see listing for Karma Triyana Dharmachakra, Woodstock, New York.
ADDRESS: 1311 West Arthur Street,
Chicago, IL 60626
PHONE: (312) 743-5134
E-MAIL: RobertB938@aol.com
LINEAGE: Tibetan Karma Kagyu
SPIRITUAL HEAD: Ven. Khenpo Karthar
Rinpoche
CONTACT: Harold Hutton
AFFILIATION: Karma Triyana Dharmachakra, Woodstock, New York

ESTABLISHED: Around 1980

FACILITIES: Meditation hall, library, urban center.

MEDITATION PROGRAM: Weekly *Chenrezig*, *Amitabha*, Green Tara Practice (in Tibetan), and *Shamatha* meditation.

PUBLICATIONS: *Chicago KTC News*

Padmasambhava Buddhist Center

Padmasambhava Buddhist Center was established under the guidance of Khenchen Palden Sherab Rinpoche and Khenpo Tsewang Dongyal Rinpoche to promote the authentic living lineage of Tibetan Nyingma Buddhism. The Nyingma lineage stresses practice and study of the Vajrayana teachings as transmitted by Padmasambhava, Buddha Shakyamuni, and connected masters down to the present time. It is the wish of our two lamas to preserve and disseminate this ancient teaching in an effective and suitable way for American and other Western students.

ADDRESS: 2040 North Mohawk Street, Chicago, IL 60614

PHONE: (312) 951-8010

LINEAGE: Tibetan Nyingma

SPIRITUAL HEAD: Ven. Khenchen Palden Sherab Rinpoche and Ven. Khenpo Tsewang Dongyal Rinpoche

CONTACT: William Hinman

AFFILIATION: Padma Samye Ling Retreat Center in Sidney Center, New York, and other Padmasambhava Buddhist Centers

MEDITATION PROGRAM: Meditation practice and teaching is held weekly at the center. The lamas come and give teachings, empowerments, and personal guidance to practitioners regularly.

Tilopa Buddhist Center, Inc.

We offer a weekly study, practice, and meditation group. Occasionally we sponsor a visiting monk or nun who gives formal teachings. We also travel as a group to teachings in and around our area. Call for times and further information.

ADDRESS: 443 North Edward Street, Decatur, IL 62522-2211

PHONE: (217) 425-0803

FAX: (217) 423-0986

E-MAIL: tilopafpmt@aol.com

LINEAGE: Tibetan Gelugpa

SPIRITUAL HEAD: Lama Zopa Rinpoche

CONTACT: Judith Layette, Director

AFFILIATION: Foundation for the Preservation of the Mahayana Tradition (FPMT)

ESTABLISHED: 1995

FACILITIES: Second-floor suite; shrine room, living quarters.

Togmay Sangpo (formerly Wisdom Energy Center)

Originally established in 1992 as Wisdom Energy Center, Togmay Sangpo provides a continuous program of classes, seminars, and retreats in Mahayana Buddhist thought and meditation from the tradition of the Tibetan saint, Lama Je Tsong Khapa. We are associated with the Foundation for the Preservation of the Mahayana Tradition, an organization of urban meditation centers, rural retreat facilities, hospices, and a publishing company. All were founded by Lama Thupten Yeshe, a renowned teacher of Buddhism to many Western and Tibetan students.

ADDRESS: 350 West 22nd Street, Lombard, IL 60148

PHONE: (708) 629-9185

LINEAGE: Tibetan tradition of Lama Je Tsong Khapa

SPIRITUAL HEAD: Founded by Lama Thupten Yeshe.

CONTACT: Tenzin Angmo, Resident Teacher

AFFILIATION: Foundation for the Preservation of the Mahayana Tradition

ESTABLISHED: 1992

INDIANA

Ganden Dheling Buddhist Temple

In the tradition of the Tibetan tent monasteries, Ganden Dheling moved around to different members' homes during its formative years. Eventually we found a temporary home at Unity, where we meet twice a week for meditation and *Lam Rim* discussion. We've had visits from many of the great lamas of our day (Zasep Tulku Rinpoche, Kyabje Gelek Rinpoche and others) as well as from the Gyuto monks. As a result, we began having growing pains and are now fund-raising for our own temple building with a residence for our lamas. Ganden Dheling means "Joyful Isle of Bliss."

ADDRESS: PO Box 2242, Bloomington, IN 47402-2242

PHONE: (812) 337-6114

LINEAGE: Tibetan Gelugpa

SPIRITUAL HEADS: Zasep Tulku Rinpoche and Kyabje Gelek Rinpoche

CONTACT: Bruce E. Wilson

AFFILIATION: Autonomous

ESTABLISHED: 1989

FACILITIES: We meet biweekly at Unity.

MEDITATION PROGRAM: We meet once a week for meditation, and once a week for *Lam Rim* discussion.

Louisville Karma Kagyu Study Group

We offer introductory teachings and meditation instruction as well as regular *shamatha* (tranquillity meditation) and *tong len* ("sending and taking") practice. We welcome interested individuals and families to join us in creating an authentic Buddhist practice community in the Louisville area. For additional information, please see listing for Karma Triyana Dharmachakra, Woodstock, New York.

ADDRESS: 1031 Cliffwood Drive, New Albany, IN 47150

PHONE: (812) 944-5545

E-MAIL: weix1@iglou.com

LINEAGE: Tibetan Karma Kagyu

SPIRITUAL HEAD: Ven. Khenpo Karthar Rinpoche

CONTACT: Bob Weixler

AFFILIATION: Karma Triyana Dharmachakra, Woodstock, New York

PUBLICATIONS: *Lion's Roar Dharma News*

IOWA

Jalandhara Buddhist Meditation Center

Jalandhara is a Tibetan Buddhist dharma center founded by our kind teacher, the late Geshe Lobsang Namgyal (Genla). Since his death, a small group of volunteers has been bringing Tibetan lamas, monks, and nuns to Iowa City. To make these teachings available to everyone, we keep our course costs to a minimum, charging just enough to cover our expenses. Financial support from our membership allows this center to survive—and thrive—here in Iowa City. Please consider becoming a member.

ADDRESS: 627 South Governor, Iowa City, IA 52240

PHONE: (319) 338-8755

E-MAIL: dvelez@niowa.edu

LINEAGE: Tibetan Gelugpa

SPIRITUAL HEADS: Ven. Geshe Sopa Rinpoche; visiting teachers.

CONTACTS: Diana Velez and Alan Ross

AFFILIATION: Autonomous

ESTABLISHED: 1986

FACILITIES: Private home used for teachings and meditation.

MEDITATION PROGRAM: *Lam Rim* bi-weekly; weekly discussion group. Call for times.

KANSAS

Kansas City Dharmadhatu

For additional information, please refer to Shambhala International, Halifax, Nova Scotia, Canada.

ADDRESS: 2302 South Feree, Kansas City, KS 66103

PHONE: (913) 677-4835

FAX: (816) 531-2126 Attn: Network—Ann Bodnar

E-MAIL: gmmass@aol.com

LINEAGE: Tibetan Kagyu-Nyingma

SPIRITUAL HEAD: Sakyong Mipham Rinpoche

CONTACTS: Ann Bodnar and Gary Mass

AFFILIATION: Shambhala International, Halifax, Nova Scotia

YEAR ESTABLISHED: 1977

FACILITIES: Urban meditation center.

KENTUCKY

Lexington Shambhala Meditation Center

Our bid for the property was below the asking price, but the seller agreed, on two conditions: lifetime Center membership for herself, and free parking for her husband whenever games by the Kentucky Wildcats are scheduled. Our center is run by a Shambhala Council composed of six individuals using a process of cooperative deliberation. Policy decisions are by consensus. Dharma classes, Shambhala Training levels, ikebana, watercolor painting, and fund-raising concerts by local musicians are all well attended. For additional information, please see Shambhala International, Halifax, Nova Scotia, Canada.

Shambhala Meditation Center in Lexington, Kentucky. (Photo courtesy of Lexington Shambhala.)

Cafe Shambhala

SHAMBHALA MEDITATION CENTER IN LEXINGton, Kentucky, invites the public to an open house every Saturday morning from nine to noon. We call our little get-together "Cafe Shambhala." It's attended by up to a dozen guests who practice sitting meditation for the first hour, share bagels, coffee, and conversation with center members during the break, and then return to the meditation hall for a concluding period of sitting. Cafe Shambhala is offered as a friendly introduction to meditation practice. Group instruction is given at no cost and attendance does not require or imply a commitment of any kind. The Three Gateways composition of Shambhala meditation centers—Dharmadhatu, Shambhala Training, and Nalanda Contemplative Arts—provides fertile topics for discussion such as marriage, enlightened action in the work place, and art in everyday life.

Adele Prager

For more information, contact: Lexington Shambhala Meditation Center, 315 Maxwell Street, Lexington, KY 40502; (606) 225-4183.

ADDRESS: 315 Maxwell Street, Lexington, KY 40502
PHONE: (606) 225-4183
FAX: (606) 257-3909
E-MAIL: mheinz1@ukcc.uky.edu (Shelley Heinz)
LINEAGE: Tibetan Karma Kagyu
SPIRITUAL HEAD: Sakyong Mipham Rinpoche
CONTACT: Tim Struttman, Coordinator
AFFILIATION: Shambhala International, Halifax, Nova Scotia
ESTABLISHED: 1975
FACILITIES: House; Buddhist shrine room, Shambhala meditation hall, two public rooms, two kitchens, two baths.
MEDITATION PROGRAM: Meditation sessions twice a week. Dharma class. "Cafe Shambhala." Biannual *ninthun* (all-day sitting).
PUBLICATIONS: Quarterly newsletter with calendar of events.

LOUISIANA

Dhongak Tharling Dharma Center

Dhongak Tharling, a Buddhist dharma center of the Nyingma-Dzogchen lineage, opened in New Orleans on May 25, 1994. The name means "Sutra and Tantra Island of Liberation." Our teacher, the Ven. Ngawang Tsultrim Rinpoche, is a Dzogchen master of the Rigdzin Dakgyud lineage of the Nyingma School of Tibetan Buddhism. This lineage descends directly from Padmasambhava, the miraculous lotus-born master who brought the Tantric teachings to Tibet, Nepal, and Bhutan. *May all beings benefit from the establishment of this dharma center.*

ADDRESS: 4518 St. Ann, New Orleans, LA 70119
PHONE: (504) 488-4613
FAX: Same
E-MAIL: tharling@ix.netcom.com
LINEAGE: Tibetan Nyingmapa and Dzogchen
SPIRITUAL HEAD: Ven. Lama Ngawang Tsultrim
CONTACT: Ingmar K. Mounce, Secretary and Practice Leader
AFFILIATION: Tholaka Tharling Gompa, Nepal
ESTABLISHED: 1994
FACILITIES: Nonresidential

MEDITATION PROGRAM: Biweekly practice, *Guru Rinpoche Tsok* on tenth lunar day, and *Dakini Day Chod* on twenty-fifth lunar day.
PUBLICATIONS: Newsletter three times annually.

MAINE

Brunswick Dharma Study Group

Dharma Study Group of Brunswick, serving the Portland-Augusta area, is the Shambhala meditation center for southern Maine. We offer a regular schedule of group practice and weekly classes on the Kagyu Dharma. For additional information, please see Shambhala International, Halifax, Nova Scotia, Canada.

ADDRESS: 98 Elm Street, Portland, ME 04101
PHONES: (207) 967-9881 or (207) 775-6139
LINEAGE: Tibetan Kagyu-Nyingma
SPIRITUAL HEAD: Sakyong Mipham Rinpoche

The Asian Classics Input Project

THE ASIAN CLASSICS INPUT PROJECT (ACIP) was founded by scholars at Princeton University in 1987, and is engaged in locating, cataloguing, and preserving important examples of Asian classical literature in a universal digital format. It then distributes these materials without charge to users in over fifty countries, on floppy diskettes, CD-ROMs, and through the Internet.

ACIP is currently working to catalogue and input the Kangyur and Tengyur collections of classical Sanskrit Buddhist literature in Tibetan translation, written from 500 BCE to 800 CE, as well as the Sungbum collection of native Tibetan commentaries to these collections, written from 800 CE to the present time.

These three collections represent perhaps the largest body of classical philosophical literature in the world, and are estimated to contain somewhere in the area of one hundred thousand different works in fields such as epistemology, cosmology, the fine arts, psychology, logic, and medicine. These books were protected by the geographical inaccessibility of Tibet up until 1959, when political events led to the destruction of most of the libraries and books in the country.

ACIP specializes in locating the surviving copies of these texts in countries such as India, Nepal, Russia, Mongolia, and to a limited extent in Tibet itself. The texts are then input at one of approximately fifteen data entry centers located among the Tibetan refugee communities in south Asia. Here, refugees trained and equipped by the project are engaged in helping to save their own cultural heritage while simultaneously learning a vocation that will support them. In an immediate sense, input salaries earned through the project help feed over nine hundred Tibetan refugees.

For more information, contact: Asian Classics Input Project, Dr. Robert J. Taylor, 11911 Marmary Road, Gaithersburg, MD 20878; (301) 948-5569; e-mail: acip@well.com.

CONTACT: Peter Garsoe
AFFILIATION: Shambhala International, Halifax, Nova Scotia
ESTABLISHED: 1984
FACILITIES: Urban meditation center.

China Forming Dharma Study Group

For additional information, please refer to Shambhala International, Halifax, Nova Scotia, Canada.
ADDRESS: PO Box 4, Palermo, ME 04354
E-MAIL: 73123.102@compuserve.com
LINEAGE: Tibetan Kagyu-Nyingma
SPIRITUAL HEAD: Sakyong Mipham Rinpoche
CONTACT: Cindy Cochran

AFFILIATION: Shambhala International, Halifax, Nova Scotia

MARYLAND

Annapolis Mahayana Buddhist Center

All of the Buddhist centers founded by Geshe Kelsang are members of the New Kadampa Tradition (NKT). Spiritually they follow the same direction and together they constitute the NKT family, a nonprofit association of independent dharma centers united by a common spiritual path. For additional information, please see listing for Vajrayogini Buddhist Center, Washington, D.C.

ADDRESS: c/o Vajrayogini Buddhist Center, 632 D Street, Northeast, Washington, DC 20002
PHONE: (202) 544-8605
FAX: Same
E-MAIL: vyogini@nmaa.org
LINEAGE: Tibetan New Kadampa Tradition
SPIRITUAL HEAD: Ven. Geshe Kelsang Gyatso Rinpoche
CONTACT: Ven. Kadam Morten Clausen
AFFILIATION: Vajrayogini Buddhist Center, Washington, D.C. (NKT centers)
ESTABLISHED: 1996
FACILITIES: Local venues.
MEDITATION PROGRAM: Introductory evening classes and other courses offered at local venues.
PUBLICATIONS: Full Moon Magazine

Baltimore Shambhala Center

The center offers *shamatha-vipashyana* (peace-insight) meditation in a secular context and Shambhala Training to promote an enlightened society. It is also offered in the context of traditional Buddhist Hinayana, Mahayana, and Vajrayana diciplines. In addition we offer occasional contemplative art programs to complement both paths. Our center is part of an international system of Shambhala Centers founded by the Vidyadhara Chogyam Trungpa Rinpoche and directed by the Sakyong Mipham Rinpoche. For additional information, please refer to Shambhala International, Halifax, Nova Scotia, Canada.

ADDRESS: 11 East Mt. Royal Avenue, Baltimore, MD 21030
PHONE: (410) 727-2422
E-MAIL: glutryridr@aol.com
LINEAGE: Tibetan Kagyu-Nyingma
SPIRITUAL HEAD: Sakyong Mipham Rinpoche
CONTACTS: Directors: Judy Bond (Buddhist); Chris Kreeger (Shambhala Training)
AFFILIATION: Shambhala International, Halifax, Nova Scotia
ESTABLISHED: 1980
FACILITIES: Shrine rooms, classroom, kitchen, offices.
RETREATS OFFERED: Annual ten-day Working Person's Retreat, frequent weekend programs, monthly one-day retreats.
PUBLICATIONS: *Shambhala Center Newsletter*

Kunzang Palyul Choling

Kunzang Palyul Choling (KPC) is distinguished by its Spiritual Director, Jetsunma Ahkon Lhamo, the first Western woman recognized and enthroned as a *tulku*, or reincarnate lama. Programs at KPC are geared toward putting compassion and pure view into everyday prac-

Jetsunma Ahkon Lhamo, spiritual head of Kunzang Palyul Choling in Poolesville, Maryland. (Photo by John Van Beekham.)

tice. The center offers a school and other programs for children, beginner's classes, Dharma in Depth teachings, a seven-year academic curriculum, an unbroken twenty-four-hour prayer vigil for the end of suffering, short retreats, and a myriad of merit-generating projects.

ADDRESS: 18400 River Road, Poolesville, MD 20837
PHONE: (301) 428-8116
FAX: (301) 428-8245
E-MAIL: kpc@tara.org
WWW: http://www.tara.org
LINEAGE: Tibetan Nyingma
SPIRITUAL HEAD: Jetsunma Ahkon Lhamo
AFFILIATION: Namdruling Nyingmapa Monastery/Padma Norbu Rinpoche
ESTABLISHED: 1985
FACILITIES: Twenty-four-hour meditation room; fourteen stupas; library; sixty-five-acre meditation park.

RETREATS OFFERED: Annual monthlong retreat; occasional shorter ones.
PUBLICATIONS: *Vajra Voice*, quarterly.

Sakya Phuntsok Ling

Sakya Phuntsok Ling was established by Lama Kalsang Gyaltsen in order to help those interested in Buddhism come into contact with great spiritual masters and to train them in personal study and practice. A widely recognized and accomplished teacher of Buddhist philosophy and meditation, his guidance of students and direction of center activities have been praised as exemplary by the leaders of the Sakya order. He has studied both sutra and tantra extensively and spent long periods in meditative retreat. With over a decade of experience in teaching Western students, his kindness, wisdom, and practicality are warmly admired by all.

ADDRESS: 608 Ray Drive, Silver Spring, MD 20910
PHONE: (301) 589-3115
FAX: (301) 589-3111
LINEAGE: Tibetan Sakya
SPIRITUAL HEAD: His Holiness the Sakya Trizin
CONTACT: Ven. Lama Kalsang Gyaltsen, Spiritual Director
AFFILIATION: Autonomous
ESTABLISHED: 1987
RETREATS OFFERED: Periodic weekend meditation retreats in the country.

Salisbury Dharmadhatu

Salisbury Dharmadhatu is a center for the practice of Tibetan Buddhist and Shambhala meditation (*Shambhala* is a secular path of meditation open to anyone regardless of religious tradition). The center offers regular sitting practice, Shambhala Level I and beginning meditation programs. Located on the eastern shore of Maryland, thirty miles from the ocean, Dharmadhatu occupies the second floor of a Victorian building in a lively historic district. For additional information, please see Shambhala International, Halifax, Nova Scotia, Canada.

ADDRESS: 104 West Chestnut Street, Salisbury, MD 21801
PHONE: (410) 341-0941
E-MAIL: cossairt@shore.intercom.net
LINEAGE: Tibetan Kagyu-Nyingma
SPIRITUAL HEAD: Sakyong Mipham Rinpoche
CONTACTS: Betty Sue Cossairt and Etta Smith
AFFILIATION: Shambhala International, Halifax, Nova Scotia
ESTABLISHED: 1995
FACILITIES: Buddhist shrine room, Shambhala meditation hall.
RETREATS OFFERED: None
PUBLICATIONS: Newsletter

Tibetan Meditation Center

Although Tibetan Meditation Center is a small and simple group, weekends and weekday evenings are filled with classes, discussions, and meditation sessions, led by a resident lama or senior lay practitioner. The lamas are available for personal appointments and Tibetan language lessons. In addition, the spiritual director and visiting lamas conduct ceremonies or give special teachings. Our Text Project seeks to preserve the lineage's precious texts. The Achi Foundation provides support for monks and nuns. Teaching and chanting tapes and practice texts (*sadhana*) are available for purchase.

ADDRESS: 9301 Gambrill Park Road, Frederick, MD 21702
PHONE: (301) 473-5750
FAX: (301) 473-8316
LINEAGE: Tibetan Drikung Kagyu
SPIRITUAL HEAD: Khenpo Konchog Gyaltsen

CONTACT: Lama Gyursam, Resident Teacher
ESTABLISHED: 1979
FACILITIES: Small temple, residence for lamas, three and one-half acres of wooded land.
RETREATS OFFERED: Weekly study and practice sessions, occasional three- or ten-day retreats.
PUBLICATIONS: Quarterly newsletter.

Vikatadamshtri Buddhist Center of Baltimore

All the Buddhist centers founded by Geshe Kelsang are members of the New Kadampa Tradition (NKT). Spiritually they follow the same direction and together they constitute the NKT family, a nonprofit association of independent dharma centers united by a common spiritual path. For additional information, please see listing for Vajrayogini Buddhist Center, Washington, D.C.

ADDRESS: c/o Vajrayogini Buddhist Center, 632 D Street, Northeast, Washington, DC 20002
PHONE: (410) 750-6163
E-MAIL: vyogini@nmaa.org
LINEAGE: Tibetan New Kadampa Tradition (NKT)
SPIRITUAL HEAD: Ven. Geshe Kelsang Gyatso Rinpoche
CONTACT: Ven. Kadam Morten Clausen, Resident Director
AFFILIATION: Vajrayogini Buddhist Center, Washington, D.C.; other NKT centers.
ESTABLISHED: 1995
FACILITIES: Courses offered at local venues.
MEDITATION PROGRAM: Introductory evening classes, other courses.
PUBLICATIONS: *Full Moon Magazine*

Washington, DC Shambhala Center

Washington, DC Shambhala Center was founded in 1975 by the Vidyadhara, the

Ven. Chogyam Trungpa Rinpoche. Trungpa Rinpoche was a Tibetan Buddhist meditation master and a pioneer in bringing Buddhism to the West. His son, Sakyong Mipham Rinpoche, also a holder of the Kagyu and Nyingma lineages of Tibetan Buddhism and of the Shambhala teachings, now leads Shambhala International and its affiliated organizations. All programs at the center include meditation practice and vary from weekly classes to weekend programs. For additional information, please see Shambhala International, Halifax, Nova Scotia, Canada.

ADDRESS: 8719 Colesville Road, Silver Spring, MD 20910
PHONE: (301) 588-7020
FAX: (301) 270-3321 (Susan)
E-MAIL: slh27@aol.com
LINEAGE: Tibetan Kagyu-Nyingma
SPIRITUAL HEAD: Sakyong Mipham Rinpoche
CONTACT: Vivi Spicer
AFFILIATION: Shambhala International, Halifax, Nova Scotia
ESTABLISHED: 1975
FACILITIES: Office building with two shrine rooms, meditation hall, reception, kitchen, classrooms.
MEDITATION PROGRAM: Weekly sitting practice, call for times.
RETREATS OFFERED: Monthly Shambhala Training weekends.
PUBLICATIONS: *Washington, DC Shambhala Center Newsletter*

MASSACHUSETTS

American Institute for Mindfulness

The American Institute for Mindfulness was founded in 1981 during the visit of H. H. the fourteenth Dalai Lama to Harvard University. Founder Ven. Thupten Kalsang Rinpoche decided at the beginning that the institute would be nonsectarian. Since its inception, it has provided Buddhist instruction and published booklets on meditation and the mind. In

MASSACHUSETTS *(cont.)*

1986 leadership passed to Laurence O. McKinney and the institute has become a center for the emerging American Buddhist movement of practitioners independent of any Asian culture, lineage, or school. McKinney serves as Senior Columnist for *CyberSangha* magazine and is qualified to teach Tibetan meditation.

ADDRESS: Box 390309, Cambridge, MA 02139
PHONE: (617) 441-0440
FAX: Same
E-MAIL: atasyte@aol.com *or* lom@world.std.com
LINEAGE: Tibetan/Spencerian/Neuropsychological. Nonlineal lineage; we respect all of them.
CONTACT: Laurence O. McKinney, Director
AFFILIATION: Autonomous
ESTABLISHED: 1981
FACILITIES: Library, international database.
PUBLICATIONS: *Visualization Meditation*, Kalsang. *Neurotheology*, McKinney. *Important Points of the Vinaya*, Kalang. *The Last 10 Seconds of Eternity*, McKinney.

Boston Shambhala Center

Boston Shambhala is one of many centers throughout the world under the umbrella of Shambhala International. We offer sitting meditation, meditation instruction, and monthly open houses, as well as public classes and meditation intensives. We also offer a wide variety of programs designed for both beginning and advanced practitioners. For additional information, please see Shambhala International, Halifax, Nova Scotia, Canada.

ADDRESS: 646 Brookline Avenue, Brookline, MA 02146
PHONE: (617) 734-1498
E-MAIL: MSLang@aol.com

LINEAGE: Tibetan Nyingma, Karma Kagyu, and Shambhala
SPIRITUAL HEAD: Sakyong Mipham Rinpoche. Chogyam Trungpa Rinpoche, founder.
CONTACT: William Wooding, Coordinator
AFFILIATION: Shambhala International, Halifax, Nova Scotia
ESTABLISHED: circa 1970
FACILITIES: Meditation halls, kitchen, tape library
MEDITATION PROGRAM: Weekly sitting.
RETREATS OFFERED: Weekend programs.
PUBLICATIONS: Books by Chogyam Trungpa Rinpoche.

Drikung Kagyu Center

No description available.
ADDRESS: 35 Colonial Avenue, Newton, MA 02160
PHONE: (617) 332-1835
LINEAGE: Tibetan
CONTACT: Lorraine Binder

Dzogchen Community in America Inc./Tsegyalgar

Tsegyalgar is the main center for the International Dzogchen Community in America. The community practice center and administrative offices are situated in an old grammar school in the town of Conway, Massachusetts. A rural retreat center is situated in nearby Buckland County. Born in East Tibet, Namkhai Norbu Rinpoche was recognized at the age of two as the reincarnation of a great twentieth-century Dzogchen master, Adzom Drugpa. In 1960 Rinpoche moved to Italy where he became a professor of Oriental philosophy at the University of Naples. He now teaches Dzogchen practice worldwide in a nonsectarian format.

ADDRESS: PO Box 277, Conway, MA 01341
PHONE: (413) 369-4153
FAX: (413) 369-4165
E-MAIL: 74404.1141@compuserve.com
LINEAGE: Dzogchen
SPIRITUAL HEAD: Chogyal Namkhai Norbu
CONTACT: Secretary
AFFILIATION: International Dzogchen Community
ESTABLISHED: 1982
FACILITIES: Community center, retreat property.
RETREATS OFFERED: Retreat programs during the year; weekly practices.
PUBLICATIONS: *The Mirror*, newspaper of the International Dzogchen Community; *Tsegyalgar*, bimonthly newsletter.

Falmouth Dharma Study Group

For additional information, please see Shambhala International, Halifax, Nova Scotia, Canada.
ADDRESS: Box 714, Falmouth, MA 02541-0714
PHONE: (508) 457-9527
LINEAGE: Tibetan Kagyu-Nyingma
SPIRITUAL HEAD: Sakyong Mipham Rinpoche
CONTACT: Cindy Wright
AFFILIATION: Shambhala International, Halifax, Nova Scotia

Khandarohi Buddhist Center

The goal of Khandarohi Buddhist Center is to bring pure Buddhadharma to the people of our area. We have daily *pujas*, many special daylong courses and retreats, an occasional empowerment, and a weekly in-depth study of our teacher's writings. People from all denominations, faiths, and walks of life are welcome to study and visit with us.

ADDRESS: 34 Avon Street, Somerville, MA 02143

PHONE: (617) 628-2648

LINEAGE: Tibetan New Kadampa Tradition (NKT)

SPIRITUAL HEAD: Geshe Kelsang Gyatso Rinpoche

CONTACT: Gen Kelsang Lekmon

AFFILIATION: New Kadampa centers worldwide.

ESTABLISHED: 1995

FACILITIES: Residential center, beautiful *gompa* and shrine.

RETREATS OFFERED: *Lam rim* retreats offered throughout the year.

PUBLICATIONS: *Full Moon*, magazine of the NKT.

Kurukulla Center for Tibetan Buddhist Studies

Kurukulla Center offers a year-round program of classes and group practice. Our resident teacher, Geshe Tsulga of Sera Monastery, typically lives in Boston for four months during the fall and winter, where he gives classes on basic texts as well as more advanced teachings in Mahayana Buddhism. He usually grants one or two initiations per year, open to all. We also offer a yearlong introduction to Buddhism and, in Geshela's absence, hold discussion groups, do group practice, and invite visiting teachers. All are welcome to join us.

ADDRESS: PO Box 628, Astor Station, Boston, MA 02123-0628

PHONE: (617) 628-1953

E-MAIL: sr@math.bu.edu

LINEAGE: Tibetan Gelugpa

SPIRITUAL HEAD: Lama Thubten Zopa Rinpoche (head of Foundation for the Preservation of the Mahayana Tradition).

CONTACT: Geshe Tsultrim Chompel (aka Geshe Tsulga), Resident Teacher

AFFILIATION: Foundation for the Preservation of the Mahayana Tradition

ESTABLISHED: 1990

FACILITIES: Rented apartment in Jamaica Plain for Geshela and for classes.

PUBLICATIONS: *Lotus Arrow*, newsletter, available on request.

Mahasiddha Nyingmapa Center

We are a small group of students of Dodrup Chen Rinpoche, which occasionally meets for teachings and practice. Our temple and stupa are located in rural western Massachusetts. We have no residential accommodations and no regular retreat or seminar schedule. A few students who live close by meet several times each week for group practice. Our emphasis is on practice and on devotion to our teacher and tradition. Access to Rinpoche is rare and teachings are limited to the essential points necessary to practice in our current situation. Thangka prints and mandalas are available for sale. Please send for brochure.

ADDRESS: East Road, Hawley, MA 01339

PHONE: (413) 339-8339

E-MAIL: 72640.673@compuserve.com

LINEAGE: Tibetan Nyingma

SPIRITUAL HEAD: Dodrup Chen Rinpoche

AFFILIATION: Autonomous

ESTABLISHED: 1973

FACILITIES: Nonresidential temple.

MEDITATION PROGRAM: Several group practices weekly.

PUBLICATIONS: Miscellaneous prayers for use by practitioners.

Mee Yuan Buddhist Association

No description available.

ADDRESS: 360 Ward Street, Newton, MA 02159

PHONE: (617) 964-5990

LINEAGE: Chinese Vajrayana: True Buddha School

SPIRITUAL HEAD: Grand Master Sheng-yen Lu

AFFILIATION: True Buddha School

Northampton Shambhala Center

Our *sangha* consists of both families and individuals. Several of us work with Windhorse Associates, a local agency dedicated to helping people suffering from mental disturbances. Northampton Shambhala offers residents of the Pioneer Valley a place to practice and study the Buddhadharma. We have regularly scheduled introductory classes, and meditation instruction is free of charge. For additional information, please see Shambhala International, Halifax, Nova Scotia, Canada. Come sit with us!

ADDRESS: 518 Pleasant Street, #2, Northampton, MA 01060

PHONE: (413) 584-6415

LINEAGE: Tibetan Kagyu

SPIRITUAL HEAD: Sakyong Mipham Rinpoche

CONTACT: Cathy Chatwood, Coordinator

AFFILIATION: Shambhala International, Halifax, Nova Scotia

FACILITIES: Shrine room and meeting room.

MEDITATION PROGRAM: Regularly scheduled introductory classes, open houses, Shambhala Training levels, and group practice. Call for schedules.

PUBLICATIONS: *Sangha Newsletter*

Rangrig Yeshe

No description available.

ADDRESS: PO Box 1167, Stockbridge, MA 01262

PHONE: (413) 528-9932

LINEAGE: Tibetan Nyingma

SPIRITUAL HEAD: The Ven. Shyalpa Tenzin Rinpoche

AFFILIATION: Autonomous

ESTABLISHED: 1989

FACILITIES: Meditation center in Great Barrington, Massachusetts.

MEDITATION PROGRAM: Dzogchen

RETREATS OFFERED: Yearly calendar.

Sakya Institute for Buddhist Studies and Meditation/Sakya Sheidrup Ling

Sakya Sheidrup Ling was founded on the occasion of Dezhung Rinpoche's visit to Cambridge in 1980. Since that time, the center has had a continuous program of meditation and study. In 1984 we purchased land in Barre, Massachusetts, and there established a rural retreat center known as Sakya Chokhor Yangtse. We are now attempting to establish a permanent city center as well. Meanwhile, Lama Migmar Tseten teaches classes on Buddhist philosophy and meditation in rented facilities. Plans call for further development of the retreat center in Barre, where we are building a stupa, temple, and dormitories.

ADDRESS: Sakya Center, PO Box 391042, Cambridge, MA 02139

PHONE: (617) 492-2614

FAX: Same

LINEAGE: Tibetan Sakya

SPIRITUAL HEAD: H. H. Sakya Trinzin

CONTACT: Lama Migmar Tseten, Resident Teacher

AFFILIATION: Autonomous

ESTABLISHED: 1980

FACILITIES: Rented facilities and members' homes; Sakya Chokhor Yangtse retreat center in Barre, Massachusetts.

MEDITATION PROGRAM: Group meditation in members' homes.

RETREATS OFFERED: Individuals wishing to do retreats for a week, month, or year at our country property are welcome.

PUBLICATIONS: *The Sakya Satellite*

MICHIGAN

Ann Arbor Karma Thegsum Choling (KTC)

Ann Arbor KTC was founded in 1978 by the Ven. Khenpo Karthar Rinpoche. From the beginning the center has offered weekly *chenrezig* practice, as well as group sitting meditation and dharma discussion on specific texts. Our objective has been to provide information to anyone wishing to learn about and/or practice Buddhism. We host visiting lamas several times a year, facilitating contact with an unbroken transmission of meditative and religious practices that began in Tibet centuries ago. All of our programs are open to the public. For additional information, please see Karma Triyana Dharmachakra, Woodstock, New York.

ADDRESS: 614 Miner Street, Ann Arbor, MI 48103

PHONE: (313) 761-7495

E-MAIL: mannikka@umich.edu

LINEAGE: Tibetan Karma Kagyu

SPIRITUAL HEAD: Ven. Khenpo Karthar Rinpoche

CONTACT: Eleanor Mannikka

AFFILIATION: Karma Triyana Dharmachakra, Woodstock, New York

ESTABLISHED: 1978

MEDITATION PROGRAM: Weekly *shamatha*, *amitabha*, and *chenrezig* practice; dharma study. (Empowerment required for *shamatha* and *amitabha*. All practices are chanted in Tibetan.)

PUBLICATIONS: *Lion's Roar Dharma News*

Heart Center Karma Thegsum Choling (KTC)

Heart Center KTC serves the Karma Triyana Dharmachakra (KTD) community with many special projects, including the transcription and editing of Ven. Khenpo Karthar Rinpoche's teachings. We also operate *KTD Dharma Goods*, a mail-order service providing texts and practice materials from the Karma Kagyu tradition of Tibetan Buddhism. Facilities include a separate shrine building, stupa, and Heart Center House, which accommodates visiting lamas, scholars and a number of center residents. Meditation instruction is available and can be arranged by calling the center. You may also call for general information about Buddhism and Buddhist programs on our *KTD Infoline*.

ADDRESS: 315 Marion Avenue, Big Rapids, MI 49307

PHONES: (616) 796-2398; Infoline: (800) TIBETAN

E-MAIL: ktd@thenewage.com

WWW: http://thenewage.com

LINEAGE: Karma Kagyu

SPIRITUAL HEADS: H. H. Gyalwa Karmapa and Ven. Khenpo Karthar Rinpoche (his U.S. representative).

CONTACTS: Michael and Margaret Erlewine, Resident Directors

AFFILIATION: Karma Triyana Dharmachakra, Woodstock, New York

ESTABLISHED: 1985

FACILITIES: Shrine room, guest house for lamas and scholars.

MEDITATION PROGRAM: Regular visits and teachings by lamas.

Jewel Heart

Jewel Heart sponsors public talks, meditation instruction, retreat weekends, and *Lam Rim* teachings throughout the year. We also conduct a summer weeklong retreat open to new students and an intensive winter gathering for advanced Vajrayana practitioners. In support of Tibetan culture, we have sponsored a *Sacred Music, Sacred Dance* performance by the Drepung Loseling monks, raised money for the education of young monks in India, and initiated a project to create schools in Tibet. In 1994, Jewel Heart hosted a teaching and White Tara empowerment by H. H. the Dalai Lama.

ADDRESS: PO Box 7933, Ann Arbor, MI 48107-7933

PHONE: (313) 434-4411

FAX: (313) 434-0770

LINEAGE: Tibetan Gelugpa

SPIRITUAL HEAD: Kyabje Gelek Rinpoche

CONTACT: Aura Glaser

AFFILIATION: Headquarters center.

ESTABLISHED: 1989

RETREATS OFFERED: Weeklong winter and summer retreats.

PUBLICATIONS: *From the Heart*, newsletter.

Tekchen Choling

No description available.

ADDRESS: 60933 North Main Street, Jones, MI 49061-9704

PHONE: (616) 244-5474

LINEAGE: Tibetan Gelugpa

MINNESOTA

Minneapolis Karma Kagyu Study Group (KKSG)

In 1991, permission to start a Karma Kagyu Study Group in Minneapolis was requested of Khenpo Karthar Rinpoche by one of his students, Minnesota native Pamela Holtum. Happily, the request was granted. Minneapolis KKSG exists to support those who wish to study, learn, and practice the teachings of the Karma Kagyu Buddhist tradition of Tibet. Our emphasis is on daily meditation and a rapid, direct path. Beginners are very welcome to join us.

ADDRESS: 4301 Morning Side Road, Edina, MN 55416

PHONE: (612) 926-5048

LINEAGE: Tibetan Karma Kagyu

SPIRITUAL HEAD: Khenpo Karthar Rinpoche

CONTACTS: Pamela Holtum, Stu Webb, Dave Tetzlaff

AFFILIATION: Karma Triyana Dharmachakra, Woodstock, New York

ESTABLISHED: 1991

MEDITATION PROGRAM: *Shamatha, chenrezig*, Green Tara, Medicine Buddha Puja, *ngondro* practices.

Minneapolis Shambhala Center

Meditation practice is basic *Shamatha-Vipashyana*, which involves posture, attitude, and the breath. We also offer Shambhala Training, which is instruction in meditation as it relates to our life from a nonsectarian point of view. For additional information, please refer to Shambhala International, Halifax, Nova Scotia, Canada.

ADDRESS: 2425 Humbolt Avenue South, Minneapolis, MN 55405

PHONE: (612) 381-1704

FAX: (612) 724-2618 c/o Brian Spellman (call first)

LINEAGE: Tibetan Kagyu-Nyingma

SPIRITUAL HEAD: Sakyong Mipham Rinpoche

CONTACTS: Mr. M. Kassapa and Connie Brock

AFFILIATION: Shambhala International, Halifax, Nova Scotia

ESTABLISHED: 1984

Sakya Thupten Dargye Ling

His Eminence Deshung Rinpoche III (1906–1987) founded Sakya Thupten Dargye Ling in Minneapolis in 1979. The center is dedicated to providing public access on a regular basis to teachers affiliated with the Sakya order of Tibetan Buddhism.

ADDRESS: PO Box 13477, Minneapolis, MN 55414-5477

E-MAIL: mn.sakya@dierking.com

WWW: http://dierking.com/mn.sakya

LINEAGE: Sakya order of Tibetan Buddhism

SPIRITUAL HEAD: His Holiness Sakya Trizin

CONTACT: Ven. Lama Pema Wangdak, Resident Director

AFFILIATION: Sakya order of Tibetan Buddhism

ESTABLISHED: 1979

Tsechen Sakya Lhundrup Ling

We were established in August of 1994 at the request of H. H. Trinly Rinpoche, the younger brother of H. H. Dagchen Sakya, Head Lama of Sakya Monastery, North American seat of the Sakya order of Tibetan Buddhism. We follow much of the Sakya Monastery's meditation schedule. We also invite lamas from around the world to visit and give initiations and teachings. Everyone is welcome!!!

ADDRESS: Dinkytown Box 13288, Minneapolis, MN 55414

PHONE: (612) 879-9926

LINEAGE: Tibetan Sakyapa

SPIRITUAL HEADS: H. H. Trinly Rinpoche; H.H. Dagchen Sakya

CONTACT: Neil Levy

AFFILIATION: Sakya Monastery in Seattle, Washington

ESTABLISHED: 1994

FACILITIES: Various

MEDITATION PROGRAM: *Chenrezig* twice a week plus additional Green Tara special meditations. *Vajrayogini* once a month on Dakini Day. *Shiney* practice.

MISSOURI

Medical Center for Federal Prisoners (MCFP) Dharma Study Group (DSG)

MCFP DSG meets twice weekly in the prison chapel. Meditation instruction and basic Buddhist teachings are provided by the resident coordinator, him-

Clemency for Fleet Maull

IN DECEMBER 1985, FLEET MAULL BEGAN SERVING a twenty-five-year, no-parole sentence for drug-related offenses. Fleet had been a student of Chogyam Trungpa Rinpoche since 1978 and, while clearly confused about Right Livelihood, had deep devotion to Rinpoche and the teachings.

He began a solitary meditation practice in an unventilated prison mop closet. Says Fleet, "These rank-smelling closets were almost unbearably hot when you closed the door to shut out the noise, but I had to persist. So even in July and August with the temperature over 100 degrees, I would dutifully head for the closet and my daily meditation and sauna."

Fleet's practice drew the attention of other prisoners and the respect of the chaplain, and culminated in permission to create a dharma study group in the prison. That effort grew into the national Prisoners Dharma Network, through which inmates across the country receive meditation instruction, free dharma books, and contact referrals to local dharma centers and other resources.

In 1991, Fleet founded the National Prison Hospice Association, which promotes compassionate and dignified care for the dying in prisons. In addition, as a full-time instructor in the prison school, he has been teaching many of his fellow prisoners to read and write and prepare for their GED exams.

In March 1996, a clemency petition was filed with the U.S. Pardon Attorney, asking the President of the United States to commute the remainder of Fleet's sentence, based on his exceptional record of service during his incarceration. You are encouraged to write letters in support of the petition. Address them to the President and indicate clearly in the heading: "Re: Clemency Petition for Fleet Maull, #19864-044." Send a copy to the White House, another to Fleet Maull, and the original to: Office of the Pardon Attorney, U.S. Department of Justice, Washington, DC 20530.

For more information, contact: Fleet Maull, #19864-044, PO Box 4000, Springfield, MO 65801-4000.

---

self a prisoner, and by visiting Buddhist volunteers and dharma teachers. We also maintain an extensive video, audio, and print dharma library. Because this is a medical facility, the population turns over quickly, making it difficult to keep the group's momentum going. Participation ranges from five people for weekly gatherings to as many as forty for special programs. Since its start in 1986 the group has introduced hundreds of prisoners to Buddhadharma and the practice of meditation.

ADDRESS: c/o Chaplain's Office, PO Box 4000, Springfield, MO 65801-4000

LINEAGE: Tibetan Kagyu and Nyingma
SPIRITUAL HEAD: Sakyong Mipham Rinpoche
CONTACT: Fleet W. Maull, Resident Coordinator
AFFILIATION: Shambhala International, Halifax, Nova Scotia
ESTABLISHED: 1986
FACILITIES: Prison chapel.
MEDITATION PROGRAM: Twice weekly meditation, study, and discussion.
RETREATS OFFERED: Quarterly half- or full-day sitting meditation programs with visiting teachers.

MONTANA

Osel Shen Phen Ling

We're a diverse group of people with interesting backgrounds and world views. A number of us have traveled in Asia. We are committed to spiritual growth as a *sangha* and as individuals and are continuously inspired and challenged to open our minds and hearts to our Spiritual Director, Lama Zopa Rinpoche; to our other precious teachers; and to each other. All are welcome at Osel Shen Phen Ling.

ADDRESS: 7222 Siesta Drive, Missoula, MT 59802
PHONE: (406) 549-1707
LINEAGE: Tibetan Gelugpa
SPIRITUAL HEAD: Lama Zopa Rinpoche
CONTACT: Deanna Whiteside Sheriff
AFFILIATION: Foundation for the Preservation of the Mahayana Tradition
FACILITIES: We rent meeting space at University Congregational Church.
MEDITATION PROGRAM: Evening meditation and dharma readings, twice weekly. Call for times.
RETREATS OFFERED: Retreats with visiting teachers. Frequency depends upon their visits.
PUBLICATIONS: *The FPMT Mandala* and occasional newsletters.

NEBRASKA

Jewel Heart Nebraska

No description available.
ADDRESS: Box 22302, Lincoln, NE 68542
PHONE: (402) 438-5368
LINEAGE: Gelugpa
SPIRITUAL HEAD: Gelek Rinpoche
CONTACT: Kent Porter
AFFILIATION: Jewel Heart International

NEW HAMPSHIRE

Seacoast New Hampshire Dharma Study Group

For additional information, please refer to Shambhala International, Halifax, Nova Scotia, Canada.
ADDRESS: 24 Pinkham Road, Lee, NH 03824
PHONE: (603) 868-2636
LINEAGE: Tibetan Kagyu-Nyingma
SPIRITUAL HEAD: Sakyong Mipham Rinpoche
CONTACT: Phyllis Murray

AFFILIATION: Shambhala International, Halifax, Nova Scotia

NEW JERSEY

Kwan Chao True Buddha Temple

No description available.
ADDRESS: 1612 Frontage Road, Cherry Hill, NJ 08034
PHONE: (609) 795-3055
LINEAGE: Chinese Vajrayana: True Buddha School
SPIRITUAL HEAD: Grand Master Sheng-yen Lu

Mahayana Sutra and Tantra Center

The Mahayana Sutra and Tantra Center was established by Khen Rinpoche Geshe Lobsang Tharchin, who has taught for over twenty years on a wide variety of Buddhist subjects. Basic and advanced meditation classes have been offered over the years. Our lama is one of the last *geshes* to receive the Hlarampa honor (the highest scholastic achievement in monastic education) in old Tibet. Khen Rinpoche teaches in the traditional manner, giving oral commentary on various texts while translating from the Tibetan.
ADDRESS: c/o Rashi Gempil Ling Buddhist Temple, 47 East Fifth Street, Howell, NJ 07731
PHONE: (908) 364-1824
FAX: (908) 901-5940
E-MAIL: ACIP@well.com
LINEAGE: Tibetan Gelugpa
SPIRITUAL HEAD: Khen Rinpoche Geshe Lobsang Tharchin
CONTACT: Same
AFFILIATION: Autonomous
ESTABLISHED: 1975
FACILITIES: Temple, teaching room, office, monks' residence.
MEDITATION PROGRAM: Classes in *Lam*

Rim (stages on the path), debate, logic, sutra, tantra, Tibetan language.
RETREATS OFFERED: Annual retreat in August (prerequisites).
PUBLICATIONS: Newsletter, Mahayana Sutra and Tantra Press (translations). Catalogue available.

Padmasambhava Buddhist Center of Princeton

Padmasambhava Buddhist Center, under the guidance of Khenchen Palden Sherab Rinpoche and Khenpo Tsewang Dongyal Rinpoche, was established to promote Tibetan Buddhism and the ancient culture of Tibet. We endeavor to make authentic teachings available to Westerners. Emphasis is on loving-kindness and compassion combined with meditation, which are the essential practices of Buddhism. The lamas offer personal guidance and group teachings.
ADDRESS: Ani Trime, 15 Campbell Road, Kendall Park, NJ 08824
PHONE: (609) 924-6863
FAX: (609) 924-6910
LINEAGE: Tibetan Nyingma
SPIRITUAL HEADS: Khenchen Palden Sherab Rinpoche and Khenpo Tsewang Dongyal Rinpoche
CONTACT: Gelongma Karma Trime Lhamo
AFFILIATION: Padmasambhava Buddhist Center of New York
ESTABLISHED: 1994
FACILITIES: Fellowship in Prayer, 291 Witherspoon Street, Princeton, New Jersey
MEDITATION PROGRAM: Regularly scheduled practices.

Tibetan Buddhist Learning Center

No description available.
ADDRESS: 93 Angen Road, Washington, NJ 07882-9767

LINEAGE: Tibetan Gelugpa

SPIRITUAL HEAD: Founded by Geshe Wangyal

CONTACT: Joshua W. C. Cutler, Resident Director

AFFILIATION: Autonomous

ESTABLISHED: 1965

FACILITIES: Temple, teaching room, library, dorm, lama's rooms.

MEDITATION PROGRAM: Public class with prayers and meditation in the Gelugpa tradition twice a month.

RETREATS OFFERED: Occasional weekend seminars.

NEW MEXICO

Albuquerque Karma Thegsum Choling

We are a Vajrayana practice center. We receive visits from lamas in the Kagyu tradition several times per year. We offer basic meditation courses and instruction on practices done at our center. For further information, please see Karma Triyana Dharmachakra, Woodstock, New York.

ADDRESS: 139 La Plata Northwest, Albuquerque, NM 87107

PHONE: (505) 343-0692

E-MAIL: madoran@kagyu.org

LINEAGE: Tibetan Karma Kagyu

SPIRITUAL HEAD: H. H. Urguyen Trinley—seventeenth Karmapa

CONTACT: President

AFFILIATION: Karma Triyana Dharmachakra, Woodstock, New York

ESTABLISHED: 1982

FACILITIES: Shrine room in a small dedicated building.

MEDITATION PROGRAM: Meditation one night weekly; *Chenrezig/Amitabha Sadhanas,* one morning weekly; Green Tara and Medicine Buddha on Full and New Moon days. Call for times.

PUBLICATIONS: Monthly newsletter.

Albuquerque Padmasambhava Buddhist Center

For additional information, please see listing under Padmasambhava Buddhist Center, New York, New York.

ADDRESS: 479 59th Street, Northwest, Albuquerque, NM 87105

PHONE: (505) 836-9621

LINEAGE: Tibetan Nyingma

SPIRITUAL HEADS: Khenchen Palden Sherab Rinpoche and Khenpo Tsewang Dongyal Rinpoche

CONTACT: John Ojile

AFFILIATION: Padmasambhava Buddhist Center, New York, New York

RETREATS OFFERED: Summer in upstate New York; winter in West Palm Beach, Florida; others around the country.

Kagyu Shenpen Kunchab

Kagyu Shenpen Kunchab (KSK) was founded by H. E. Kalu Rinpoche to bring the profound teachings of Tibetan Buddhism to New Mexico. Rinpoche inspired his students to construct a stupa in Santa Fe under the direction of our resident teacher, Lama Dorje, and Jeremy Morrell. On his final visit to New Mexico in 1986, Kalu Rinpoche gave the center a pearl-like crystal (said to have been recovered from the cremation of Buddha Shakyamuni), which was placed at the tip of the blessing post within the spire. KSK has flourished by hosting teachers of all the major lineages of Tibetan Buddhism.

ADDRESS: 751 Airport Road, Santa Fe, NM 87505

PHONE: (505) 471-1152

FAX: (505) 471-5336

LINEAGE: Tibetan Karma Kagyu

SPIRITUAL HEAD: H. E. Kalu Rinpoche

CONTACT: Lama Karma Dorje, Resident Teacher

AFFILIATION: Kalu Rinpoche's centers

ESTABLISHED: 1983

FACILITIES: Stupa with shrine room; Noble Truth Bookstore.

RETREATS OFFERED: Varies depending on when lamas come to town.

PUBLICATIONS: KSK bimonthly newsletter.

Nibbana Foundation

We seek to (1) develop a lucid, secular, nonsectarian, and scientific presentation of Buddhadharma that is culturally comprehensible to North Americans and not necessarily incompatible with their existing religious beliefs; (2) foster and support research into the neurobiology, neurophysics, and neurophenomenology of meditation practices and altruistic states; (3) organize and sponsor courses, conferences, and retreats where Western scientists and scholars engaged in contemplative practice may gather with Buddhist scholars and clergy for purposes of dialogue, study, research, and practice; and (4) explore the practical implementation of Buddhadharma within the context of everyday life.

ADDRESS: Drawer 4367, University Station, Albuquerque, NM 87196-4367

PHONE: (505) 344-9259

FAX: (505) 342-9323

WWW: http://www.nibbana.org/samsara/

LINEAGE: Shangpa Kagyu, Rime

SPIRITUAL HEAD: Bokar Rinpoche

CONTACT: Samten Dorje, Director

AFFILIATION: Bokar Monastery, Darjeeling, West Bengal, India

ESTABLISHED: 1994

FACILITIES: Rustic facilities on rural, isolated Indian land.

RETREATS OFFERED: Three-day, eight-day, and longer.

PUBLICATIONS: *The Skandha Sheet,* quarterly journal.

Santa Fe Center for Dzogchen Studies

Santa Fe Center for Dzogchen Studies offers ongoing teachings and practice opportunities that involve an intuitive approach to the Buddha's wisdom known as the Heart Tradition. With facilitation from resident teacher Lama Pema Dzogtril, practitioners gather for regular sessions of sitting awareness practice augmented by informal discussion, dharma seminars, and workshops. In practices emphasizing direct experience of the nature of mind, habitual obscurities are allowed to display themselves and self-liberate.

ADDRESS: 329 Otero Street, Santa Fe, NM 87501

PHONE: (505) 989-4206

E-MAIL: 103624.401@compuserve.com

LINEAGE: Nyingma

CONTACT: Lama Pema Dzogtril, Resident Teacher

AFFILIATION: International Shakyamuni Heart lineage

ESTABLISHED: 1995

FACILITIES: The center offers space for sitting awareness practice, selected classes, and a library of Dzogchen, Buddhist, and related texts.

RETREATS OFFERED: Seasonal workshops and retreats.

NEW YORK

Albany Dharma Study Group

For additional information, please refer to Shambhala International, Halifax, Nova Scotia, Canada.

ADDRESS: 10 McCormick Road, Slingerlands, NY 12159

PHONE: (518) 439-7618

E-MAIL: ewrook@aol.com

LINEAGE: Tibetan Kagyu-Nyingma

SPIRITUAL HEAD: Sakyong Mipham Rinpoche

CONTACTS: Ellen and David Rook

AFFILIATION: Shambhala International, Halifax, Nova Scotia

Albany Karma Thegsum Choling (KTC)

We follow the traditional Tibetan Buddhist liturgy starting with *shinay* (calm-abiding meditation), *Lojong* (Seven Points of Mind Training), *Ngondro* (Preliminaries to Vajrayana), and the Vajrayana practices.

ADDRESS: PO Box 6545, Albany, NY 12206-0545

PHONE: (518) 437-9645

LINEAGE: Tibetan Karma Kagyu

SPIRITUAL HEAD: His Holiness the Seventeenth Gyalwa Karmapa Orgyen Dodul Trinley (Tsurphu Monastery, Tibet)

CONTACT: Laura Roth, Center Director

AFFILIATION: Karma Triyana Dharmachakra, Woodstock, New York

ESTABLISHED: 1979

FACILITIES: Meet in Laura Roth's house, shrine room.

MEDITATION PROGRAM: Scheduled practice twice weekly.

RETREATS OFFERED: Occasional all-day sittings.

PUBLICATIONS: *Drangden*, newsletter.

Aro Gar

Aro Gar is named after the place in the Himalayas where Khyungchen Aro Lingma, the source of our lineage, lived with her son Aro Yeshe in a community of her disciples. We work closely with our sister organizations in Europe in bringing the Nyingma White Tradition to the West. The White Lineages, sometimes known as the householder or nonmonastic traditions, emphasize integration of practice with everyday life. Within the yogic lineages of this tradition exists a startling variety of psychophysical methods that are brilliant in their simplicity and dynamic effectiveness.

ADDRESS: PO Box 247, Chelsea Station, New York City, NY 10113-0247

PHONES: (212) 439-4780, or in California (510) 865-1394

LINEAGE: Tibetan Nyingma Ngak-phang

SPIRITUAL HEADS: Ngakpa Chogyam Rinpoche and Khandro Dechen (a teaching couple)

AFFILIATION: Sang-ngak-cho-dzong of Great Britain

ESTABLISHED: 1983

MEDITATION PROGRAM: Weekly meditation groups in New York City and San Francisco.

RETREATS OFFERED: Open retreats and workshops available semiannually upon the visits of our lamas.

PUBLICATIONS: *Vision* and *Hidden Word*.

The Asian Classics Institute

The Asian Classics Institute is dedicated to the serious study and personal practice of the Buddha's original teachings. Under the direction of Geshe Michael Roach, the institute is part of the Mahayana Sutra and Tantra Center in Howell, New Jersey. We offer a wide range of programs, including meditation instruction, drop-in public lectures, long-term study for Buddhist teachers and Tibetan translators, Tibetan language classes, an extensive home-study correspondence course, a Buddhist monastery and nunnery for ordained Westerners, opportunities for engaged Buddhist social work, and several international Buddhist research and translation projects.

ADDRESS: PO Box 20373, New York, NY 10009

PHONE: (212) 475-7752

LINEAGE: Tibetan Gelugpa

SPIRITUAL HEAD: Geshe Michael Roach

AFFILIATION: Mahayana Sutra and Tantra Center (established by Khen Rinpoche Geshe Lobsang Tharchin)

FACILITIES: Primarily classroom for teaching.

MEDITATION PROGRAM: Meditation classes, weekly group sitting.

NEW YORK (*cont.*)

Buffalo Dharma Study Group

We're a small, informal group. When we meet, we usually sit for a while and then have readings and discussions. The director is a full-time student at State University of New York at Buffalo, so his time is limited during the semester. The summer is our best time, in terms of holding regular meetings. The leaders were among the first of Trungpa Rinpoche's students here in the United States. We uphold those traditions and practices. If any *sangha* members or truly interested non-*sangha* come through Buffalo, feel free to look us up!

ADDRESS: 1002 Charlesgate Circle, East Amherst, NY 14051
PHONE: (716) 689-8691
E-MAIL: cjackson@acsu.buffalo.edu
LINEAGE: Kagyupa/Nyingmapa
SPIRITUAL HEAD: Philip Richman
CONTACT: Clifton Jackson
AFFILIATION: Autonomous
ESTABLISHED: 1995

Chakrasambara Buddhist Center

Chakrasambara Buddhist Center was established to provide opportunities for study and practice in the context of our daily lives. Regular evening classes and occasional day courses are held in locations around New York City. In addition, we have a residential center in Brooklyn, where smaller classes are occasionally held. You are invited to visit the center, where you will find a beautiful meditation room, a book and tape library, and a warm and friendly community. For additional information, please see the listing for Vajrayogini Buddhist Center, Washington, D.C.

ADDRESS: 361 17th Street, Brooklyn, NY 11215
PHONE: (718) 788-4749
FAX: Same (contact Jo Glass)

E-MAIL: chakra@advn.com
LINEAGE: Tibetan New Kadampa Tradition
SPIRITUAL HEAD: Ven. Geshe Kelsang Gyatso Rinpoche
CONTACT: Ven. Kadam Morten Clausen, Resident Teacher
AFFILIATION: New Kadampa Tradition centers
ESTABLISHED: 1989
FACILITIES: Residential center with "meditation room available for use by all."
MEDITATION PROGRAM: Weekly General Program classes. Foundation Program (study of five of Geshe Kelsang's books).
RETREATS OFFERED: Daylong and weekend retreats.
PUBLICATIONS: *Full Moon Magazine*

Drikung Kagyu Enlightenment Institute

The Drikung Kagyu Enlightenment Institute was founded by Ven. Ayang Rinpoche, a Drikung Kagyu tulku, in 1986. His main teachers were the Karmapa and Dilgo Khentse Rinpoche. He has been coming to the United States since the early 1980s and is widely regarded as the leading *phowa* master. Our activities include a six-week introductory course on Buddhism, public talks, sponsorship of lama visits to Rochester, and a regular practice schedule. Main practices include *Mahamudra* and *Dudjom Tersar Ngondros*; Ten-level *Buddha Amitabha*; Outer, Inner, Secret *Vajrasattva*; bimonthly *Phowa*; and *Guru Rinpoche, Yeshe Tsogyel, Buddha Amitabha*, and *Milarepa Tsogs*.

ADDRESS: PO Box 25577, Rochester, NY 14625
PHONE: (716) 454-3844
E-MAIL: fhoward861@aol.com
LINEAGE: Tibetan Kagyu and Nyingma
SPIRITUAL HEAD: Ven. Ayang Rinpoche
CONTACT: Frank Howard, Director

AFFILIATION: Amitabha Foundation, Vajrayana Foundation
ESTABLISHED: 1986
FACILITIES: Dedicated city center.
RETREATS OFFERED: Various; introductory course.
PUBLICATIONS: Newsletter

Ithaca Dharma Study Group

For additional information, please refer to Shambhala International, Halifax, Nova Scotia, Canada.

ADDRESS: PO Box 4912, Ithaca, NY 14852-4912
PHONE: (607) 273-0837
LINEAGE: Tibetan Kagyu-Nyingma
SPIRITUAL HEAD: Sakyong Mipham Rinpoche
CONTACT: Andrew Cove
AFFILIATION: Shambhala International, Halifax, Nova Scotia
FACILITIES: Private home.

Kagyu Dzamling Kunchab

Kagyu Dzamling Kunchab is a Tibetan Buddhist center of the Kagyu lineage founded by meditation master Kyabje Dorje Chang Kalu Rinpoche.

ADDRESS: 35 West 19th Street #5, New York, NY 10011
PHONE: (212) 989-5989
E-MAIL: ccanon@aol.com
LINEAGE: Kagyu
SPIRITUAL HEAD: Very Ven. Kalu Rinpoche, Founder
CONTACT: Lama Norlha, Director
AFFILIATION: Autonomous
ESTABLISHED: 1976
FACILITIES: Shrine room.
MEDITATION PROGRAM: Weekly *Chenrezig* practice and dharma talk by senior students. Special events.
RETREATS OFFERED: Monthly weekend seminars by Lama Norlha. Classes in literary Tibetan.

Kagyu Thubten Choling (KTC)

KTC is Kalu Rinpoche's monastery and rural retreat center on the East Coast.

ADDRESS: 127 Sheafe Road, Wappingers Falls, NY 12590

PHONE: (914) 297-2500

LINEAGE: Tibetan Kagyu

SPIRITUAL HEAD: Very Ven. Kalu Rinpoche, Founder

CONTACT: Lama Norlha, Resident Director

AFFILIATION: Autonomous

ESTABLISHED: 1978

FACILITIES: Rural monastery and retreat center with private rooms available for short retreats.

MEDITATION PROGRAM: Daily morning and evening services are chanted in Tibetan. KTC also offers an ongoing schedule of classes in beginning and advanced literary Tibetan and in the study of dharma texts.

RETREATS OFFERED: Regular schedule of weekend seminars taught by Lama Norlha and other eminent lamas. Traditional three-year retreat program open to serious students who have lived and studied at KTC for at least one year.

Karma Triyana Dharmachakra (KTD)

KTD is a traditional Tibetan Buddhist monastery in the heart of the Catskill Mountains. It is the North American monastic seat of H. H. Gyalwa Karmapa, spiritual head of the Karma Kagyu lineage. The monastery combines traditional Tibetan design with Western architecture. The main shrine room is designed to accommodate major teachings and practices. Teachings are offered year-round and range from an introduction to Buddhism to instruction in advanced practices. Most are presented by the monastery's senior lamas or by guest teachers. Visitors are welcome; accommodations, including meals, are available. Advanced reservations required. Guided tours are conducted regularly.

ADDRESS: 352 Meads Mountain Road, Woodstock, NY 12498

PHONE: (914) 679-5906

FAX: (914) 679-4625

LINEAGE: Tibetan Karma Kagyu

SPIRITUAL HEAD: Seventeenth Gyalwa Karmapa-Ugyen Tinley Dorje

RESIDENT TEACHERS: Khenpo Karthar Rinpoche is abbot of KTD and spiritual director of all its affiliates. He was ordained in Tibet at the age of twelve and, after years of study and retreat, received the title of *Choje Lama* (Superior Dharma Master) from the sixteenth Gyalwa Karmapa. At the Karmapa's request, he came to the United States in 1976 to establish and guide the development of Karma Triyana Dharmachakra.

The Ven. Bardor Tulku Rinpoche is KTD's resident tulku (incarnate lama). Born in Tibet in 1952, he was trained under the Karmapa's direct guidance. He has lived and taught at KTD since 1978.

The Ven. Lama Dudjom Dorje holds an Acharya degree in higher Buddhist studies. He lives in California and teaches regularly at KTD and its affiliate centers.

AFFILIATION: Over the years, many at KTD have sought to create learning and practice environments in their own home communities. There are now more than two dozen meditation centers directly affiliated with the monastery. Each was established as an extension of KTD where the authentic teachings and practices of the Kagyu lineage could be made available at a local level. Affiliates are referred to as "KTCs" or "KKSGs." KTC stands for *Karma Thegsum Choling*. These are larger, longer-established groups with experienced meditation instructors. KKSGs (Karma Kagyu Study Groups) are generally newer and smaller.

ESTABLISHED: 1978

FACILITIES: Rural monastery.

RETREATS OFFERED: We offer the traditional three-year retreat; solitary retreats are also available.

PUBLICATIONS: *Densal Magazine*

Karuna Tendai Dharma Center

Karuna Tendai Dharma Center is a temple in the Japanese Tendai (Vajrayana) tradition located on a former Shaker farmstead in the Berkshire mountains. We are a community of lay and ordained, residential and nonresidential members. Activities include *Shi-kan* (Shamatha/Vipassana) meditations, teachings, counseling, contemplations, esoteric practices and spiritual retreats. Weddings, funerals, memorials, *Segaki*, blessings, and so on are provided to the *sangha* and others upon request. Bed and breakfast rooms are available.

ADDRESS: 1525 Route 295, East Chatham, NY 12060

PHONE: (518) 392-7963

FAX: Same

E-MAIL: tendai1@aol.com

LINEAGE: Japanese Tendai (Vajrayana)

SPIRITUAL HEAD: Paul Monshin Naamon; Abbot, Resident Director

AFFILIATION: Mt. Hiei/Tamon-in Temple (Japanese Tendai School of Buddhism)

ESTABLISHED: 1994

FACILITIES: Limited residence, *kodo*, *zendo*, thirty acres in Berkshire Mountains.

MEDITATION PROGRAM: Weekly meditation, lecture, meeting; daily morning practice; monthly Sunday morning meditation.

RETREATS OFFERED: Monthly weekend retreat, others by request.

PUBLICATIONS: Newsletter

NEW YORK (*cont.*)

Mother Tara Study and Meditation Group

We organize periodic teachings, primarily by Western clergy. Many are affiliated with the Foundation for the Preservation of the Mahayana Tradition. These teachers are approachable, well-trained in traditional Tibetan dharma studies, with "a foot in both worlds"—using their language skills and American cultural references to communicate their knowledge of dharma. We encourage rigorous formal study and meditation and emphasize its application to daily life in the city. We support the involvement of children. Non-Buddhists and those of all traditions are welcome.

ADDRESS: c/o Diana Abramo, 16 Montgomery Place, #1, Brooklyn, NY 11215
PHONE: (718) 789-7695
E-MAIL: dabramo@aol.com
LINEAGE: Tibetan Gelugpa
SPIRITUAL HEAD: We regard H. H. the Dalai Lama as our spiritual head.
AFFILIATION: Autonomous
ESTABLISHED: 1993
FACILITIES: Very informal. We meet at the homes of dharma students and at other local dharma centers.
MEDITATION PROGRAM: Meditation on particular Mahayana and Vajrayana teachings.
RETREATS OFFERED: Nonresidential retreat about once a year.

New York City Karma Thegsum Choling (KTC)

New York City KTC was established in 1976 by His Holiness the Gyalwa Karmapa. We provide weekend seminars, weekday classes, and practice sessions in the evenings. We sponsor a series of introductory classes and special events celebrating the Buddhist holidays. Individual meditation instruction is provided by ap-pointment. For additional information, please see listing for Karma Triyana Dharmachakra in Woodstock, New York.

ADDRESS: 412 West End Avenue #5, Intercom #19, New York, NY 10024
PHONE: (212) 580-9282
E-MAIL: slrr1@aol.com
LINEAGE: Tibetan Karma Kagyu
SPIRITUAL HEAD: Ven. Khenpo Karthar Rinpoche
CONTACT: Sandy Reese Roberts
AFFILIATION: Karma Triyana Dharmachakra, Woodstock, New York
ESTABLISHED: 1976
FACILITIES: Urban meditation center.
MEDITATION PROGRAM: *Shamatha* meditation twice weekly. *Chenrezig/Amitabha* practice for those who have taken refuge. Call for introductory class information and upcoming special events.
PUBLICATIONS: *Lion's Roar Dharma News*

New York Shambhala Center

For additional information, please refer to Shambhala International, Halifax, Nova Scotia, Canada.

ADDRESS: 118 West 22nd Street, 6th Floor, New York, NY 10011
PHONES: (212) 675-1231 (Shambhala), (212) 675-6544 (Dharmadhatu)
FAX: (212) 675-3090
E-MAIL: emirror@aol.com
LINEAGE: Tibetan Kagyu-Nyingma
SPIRITUAL HEAD: Sakyong Mipham Rinpoche
CONTACT: Dana Fulmer
AFFILIATION: Shambhala International, Halifax, Nova Scotia
ESTABLISHED: 1970
FACILITIES: Urban meditation center and country retreat facility.
RETREATS OFFERED: All types of group and individual retreats. Call for information.

Padmasambhava Buddhist Center—New York

Padmasambhava Buddhist Centers are for the most part small groups of practitioners devoted to their teachers—Khenchen Palden Sherab Rinpoche and Khenpo Tsewang Dongyal Rinpoche

Khenpo Tsewang Dongyal (left) and Khenchen Palden Sherab, spiritual heads of Padmasambhava Buddhist Center. (Photo by Ron Wagner.)

(The Khenpos). Both are sterling exemplars of the dharma. Padmasambhava centers are scattered throughout the United States, Puerto Rico, and Russia. The Khenpos have an annual summer retreat (usually in July) at Padma Samye Ling, their retreat land in upstate New York, as well as an annual winter retreat in West Palm Beach, Florida. They travel continually to their other centers during the rest of the year.

ADDRESS: Box 1533, Old Chelsea Station, NY 10011

PHONE: (212) 683-4958

LINEAGE: Tibetan Nyingma

SPIRITUAL HEADS: Khenchen Palden Sherab Rinpoche and Khenpo Tsewang Dongyal Rinpoche

AFFILIATION: Headquarters of Padmasambhava Buddhist Centers.

FACILITIES: Urban center.

RETREATS OFFERED: Summer in upstate New York; winter in West Palm Beach, Florida; others around the country.

Padma Samye Ling

This is the country retreat center for Padmasambhava. For additional information, please see listing under Padmasambhava Buddhist Center, New York, New York.

ADDRESS: Route 1, PO Box 108P, Sidney Center, NY 13839

PHONE: (607) 865-8068

LINEAGE: Tibetan Nyingma

SPIRITUAL HEAD: Khenchen Palden Sherab Rinpoche and Khenpo Tsewang Dongyal Rinpoche

AFFILIATION: Padmasambhava Buddhist Centers

FACILITIES: Country retreat property.

RETREATS OFFERED: Annual all-*sangha* summer retreat is held here.

Palden Sakya—New York City

Palden Sakya is a center for the study and practice of Tibetan Buddhism. Its supreme teacher is H. H. Sakya Trizin. The resident teacher is Ven. Lama Pema Wangdak. It offers study, contemplation, and meditation under Lama Pema's guidance. The teaching is Mahayana and Vajrayana according to the Sakyapa tradition.

ADDRESS: PO Box 1603, Cathedral Station, New York, NY 10025

PHONE: (212) 866-4339

LINEAGE: Tibetan Sakyapa

SPIRITUAL HEAD: His Holiness Sakya Trizin

CONTACT: Ven. Lama Pema Wangdak, Resident Teacher

AFFILIATION: Sakya order

ESTABLISHED: 1977

FACILITIES: Urban center on West 101st Street, New York, New York.

MEDITATION PROGRAM: *Tara, Chenrezig, Shamatha*, Buddhist study.

RETREATS OFFERED: Summer and winter retreats.

PUBLICATIONS: *Three Levels of Spiritual Perception* by Deschung Rinpoche.

Palden Sakya—Woodstock

For additional information, please refer to listing for Palden Sakya—New York City.

ADDRESS: 234 Mead Mountain Road, Woodstock, NY 12498

PHONE: (914) 679-4024

LINEAGE: Tibetan Sakyapa

SPIRITUAL HEAD: H. H. Sakya Trizin

CONTACT: Ven. Lama Pema Wangdak

AFFILIATION: Sakya order

ESTABLISHED: 1989

MEDITATION PROGRAM: *Tara, Chenrezig, Shamatha*, Buddhist study.

RETREATS OFFERED: Occasional

PUBLICATIONS: *Three Levels of Spiritual Perception* by Deschung Rinpoche.

Syracuse Dharma Study Group

For additional information, please refer to Shambhala International, Halifax, Nova Scotia, Canada.

ADDRESS: 218 Cambridge Street, Syracuse, NY 13210

PHONES: (315) 471-1527 or (315) 437-2684

FAX: (315) 437-3430 Attn: Robert Temple

LINEAGE: Tibetan Kagyu-Nyingma

SPIRITUAL HEAD: Sakyong Mipham Rinpoche

AFFILIATION: Shambhala International, Halifax, Nova Scotia

ESTABLISHED: 1977

Tibet Center

Tibet Center in downtown Manhattan follows the Gelugpa tradition of Tibetan Buddhism in its study and practice of the Buddha's teachings. This approach emphasizes the tools of logic and reasoning. Our teacher, Khyongla Rato Rinpoche, was recognized as an incarnate lama as a small child and was fully trained in Tibet. The atmosphere at our center is friendly and informal and we welcome beginners. People from over a dozen countries attend regularly. Many high lamas have taught and given initiations here. In 1991, Tibet Center sponsored the Kalachakra Initiation given by His Holiness the Dalai Lama in New York City.

ADDRESS: 359 Broadway, Fifth Floor, New York, NY 10013

PHONE: (212) 966-8504

FAX: Same

LINEAGE: Tibetan Gelugpa

SPIRITUAL HEAD: Ven. Khyongla Rato Rinpoche

AFFILIATION: Autonomous

ESTABLISHED: 1975

FACILITIES: Urban center, shrine room, library.

RETREATS OFFERED: Nonresidential private and weekend retreats.

PUBLICATIONS: Newsletter; *My Life and Lives, The Autobiography of Khyongla Rato Rinpoche.*

True Buddha Diamond Temple

No description available.

ADDRESS: 29 Forsyth Street, Third Floor, New York, NY 10002-6001
PHONE: (212) 274-1846
FAX: (718) 417-5192
LINEAGE: Chinese Vajrayana: True Buddha School
SPIRITUAL HEAD: Grand Master Sheng-yen Lu

Woodstock Karma Thegsum Choling (KTC)

Since we are so close to Karma Triyana Dharmachakra, headquarters center for the KTCs, our local group functions mostly within the sphere of the headquarters' activities. We participate in teachings, ceremonies, meditations, and social events at the monastery. We also have informal get-togethers with old and new students at individuals' homes on a regular basis. You are welcome to call if you have questions or need assistance. For additional information, please see listing for Karma Triyana Dharmachakra, Woodstock, New York.

ADDRESS: PO Box 645, Shady, NY 12409
PHONE: (914) 679-6028
E-MAIL: dmccarthy@mhv.net
LINEAGE: Tibetan Karma Kagyu
SPIRITUAL HEAD: Ven. Khenpo Karthar Rinpoche
CONTACT: Nona Howard
AFFILIATION: Karma Triyana Dharmachakra, Woodstock, New York

NORTH CAROLINA

Charlotte True Buddhist Society

No description available.

ADDRESS: 1601 East 4th Street, Charlotte, NC 28204
LINEAGE: Chinese Vajrayana: True Buddha School

SPIRITUAL HEAD: Grand Master Sheng-yen Lu

Durham Karma Thegsum Choling (KTC)

Anyone interested in Tibetan Buddhism, meditation, or other activities at our center is encouraged to call. Introductory courses are held twice a year. For additional information, please see listing for Karma Triyana Dharmachakra, Woodstock, New York.

ADDRESS: 1408 Tyler Court, Durham, NC 27701
PHONES: (919) 688-0877 or (919) 688-7509
E-MAIL: dloven@aol.com
LINEAGE: Tibetan Karma Kagyu
SPIRITUAL HEAD: Ven. Khenpo Karthar Rinpoche
CONTACT: David Loven
AFFILIATION: Karma Triyana Dharmachakra, Woodstock, New York
MEDITATION PROGRAM: Twice weekly *shamatha* meditation and dharma study. *Chenrezig* practice on Sundays.
PUBLICATIONS: *Lion's Roar Dharma News*

Durham Shambhala Center

For additional information, please refer to Shambhala International, Halifax, Nova Scotia, Canada.

ADDRESS: 353 West Main Street, Durham, NC 27701
PHONE: (919) 682-7655
FAX: (919) 962-0467 (attn. S. Gaylord)
E-MAIL: gaylords@med.unc.edu
LINEAGE: Tibetan Kagyu-Nyingma
SPIRITUAL HEAD: Sakyong Mipham Rinpoche
CONTACT: Susan Gaylord
AFFILIATION: Shambhala International, Halifax, Nova Scotia
ESTABLISHED: 1978
FACILITIES: Urban meditation center.

Greenville Karma Thegsum Choling (KTC)

Yes! There are dharma centers in rural eastern North Carolina! In addition to hosting lama visits and weekend retreats at a beautiful setting on the banks of the Pamlico Sound, the center holds two regularly scheduled meetings each week. One is a meditation/teaching session in which the principles of Mahayana Buddhism are discussed. The other is a *Chenrezig*-Medicine Buddha *puja* for those who have taken refuge and received the proper empowerments. Attendance at center activities is open to all. For additional information, please see listing for Karma Triyana Dharmachakra in Woodstock, New York.

ADDRESS: PO Box 4243, Greenville, NC 27836
PHONE: (919) 756-8315
LINEAGE: Tibetan Karma Kagyu
SPIRITUAL HEAD: Ven. Khenpo Karthar Rinpoche
CONTACT: Bonnie Snyder, Director
AFFILIATION: Karma Triyana Dharmachakra, Woodstock, New York
ESTABLISHED: 1983
FACILITIES: No "permanent" facilities.
MEDITATION PROGRAM: Meetings twice weekly for meditation, teachings, or *Chenrezig*-Medicine Buddha *puja*.
RETREATS OFFERED: Weekend retreats four or five times yearly.

Kadampa Center for the Practice of Tibetan Buddhism

Kadampa Center is a spiritual community committed to the transformation of individuals and societies through the study and practice of Tibetan Buddhism. We are part of the Foundation for the Preservation of the Mahayana Tradition, an international family of urban meditation and rural retreat centers, monasteries, publishing houses, hospices, and healing centers. We meet weekly with a full schedule of visiting teachers. Meditation retreats are held twice yearly.

ADDRESS: 7404-G Chapel Hill Road, Raleigh, NC 27607
PHONE: (919) 859-3433
FAX: (919) 460-1769
E-MAIL: 73571.701@compuserve.com
WWW: http://www.vnet.net/users/geodag/kadampa
LINEAGE: Tibetan Gelugpa
SPIRITUAL HEAD: Lama Zopa Rinpoche
CONTACT: Don Brown
AFFILIATION: Foundation for the Preservation of the Mahayana Tradition
ESTABLISHED: 1989
FACILITIES: Meditation center, 1,800 square feet.
MEDITATION PROGRAM: Regular weekly schedule.
RETREATS OFFERED: Retreats offered every six months.
PUBLICATIONS: *Prayerflag*, quarterly newsletter.

Nyingma Tantric Buddhist Group

We're a small group of Nyingma students from various lineages meeting in the Asheville area of western North Carolina.
ADDRESS: Box 100, Penrose, NC 28766
PHONE: (704) 299-4151
LINEAGE: Tibetan Nyingma
CONTACT: Susan Lindeman
AFFILIATION: Autonomous
MEDITATION PROGRAM: Weekly meditation and study. Call for schedule.

OHIO

Cincinnati Dharma Study Group

For additional information, please refer to Shambhala International, Halifax, Nova Scotia, Canada.
ADDRESS: 12 Burton Woods Lane, Cincinnati, OH 45229
PHONE: (513) 281-8606

LINEAGE: Tibetan Kagyu-Nyingma
SPIRITUAL HEAD: Sakyong Mipham Rinpoche
CONTACT: Allan Hundley
AFFILIATION: Shambhala International, Halifax, Nova Scotia

Cleveland Dharma Study Group

For additional information, please refer to Shambhala International, Halifax, Nova Scotia, Canada.
ADDRESS: 13302 Cormere Avenue #703, Cleveland, OH 44120-1569
PHONES: (216) 972-7900 (day); (216) 921-7256 (evening)
LINEAGE: Tibetan Kagyu-Nyingma
SPIRITUAL HEAD: Sakyong Mipham Rinpoche
CONTACT: Richard Dickinson
AFFILIATION: Shambhala International, Halifax, Nova Scotia

Columbus Dharma Study Group

For additional information, please refer to Shambhala International, Halifax, Nova Scotia, Canada.
ADDRESS: 2208 Arlington Avenue, #6, Columbus, OH 43221
PHONE: (614) 267-5942
FAX: (614) 752-9236 (Karen Shockey)
LINEAGE: Tibetan Kagyu-Nyingma
SPIRITUAL HEAD: Sakyong Mipham Rinpoche
CONTACT: Helen Thiry
AFFILIATION: Shambhala International, Halifax, Nova Scotia
ESTABLISHED: 1980
FACILITIES: Private home.
MEDITATION PROGRAM: Shambhala-style.

Columbus Karma Thegsum Choling (KTC)

Columbus KTC offers a regular weekly schedule of meditation practice and

classes open to the general public. Throughout the year, KTC hosts lamas and monks who give meditation instruction and Buddhist teachings, and who offer the refuge ceremony for those who wish to practice formally as Buddhists. The center features a large meditation room with a traditional Tibetan Buddhist shrine. Books, incense, and other practice materials are available for purchase. For additional information, please see listing for Karma Triyana Dharmachakra, Woodstock, New York.
ADDRESS: 231 South Grubb Street, Columbus, OH 43201
PHONE: (614) 228-6546
E-MAIL: bradleycb@aol.com
LINEAGE: Tibetan Karma Kagyu
SPIRITUAL HEAD: Ven. Khenpo Karthar Rinpoche
CONTACT: Bradley Butters, Director
AFFILIATION: Karma Triyana Dharmachakra, Woodstock, New York
ESTABLISHED: 1977
FACILITIES: Large meditation room, library, bookstore.
MEDITATION PROGRAM: Three meetings weekly for group meditation, dharma study, and/or *Chenrezig* practice. Green Tara practice on full moon days.
RETREATS OFFERED: Meditation seminars and practice weekends. Please write or call for schedule of events.
PUBLICATIONS: Bimonthly newsletter.

OREGON

Corvallis Dharma Study Group

For additional information, please refer to Shambhala International, Halifax, Nova Scotia, Canada.
ADDRESS: 1007 Northwest 31st Street, Corvallis, OR 97330-4447
PHONE: (503) 758-4649
LINEAGE: Tibetan Kagyu-Nyingma

OREGON (*cont.*)

SPIRITUAL HEAD: Sakyong Mipham Rinpoche
CONTACT: Randy Chakerian
AFFILIATION: Shambhala International, Halifax, Nova Scotia
ESTABLISHED: 1981
FACILITIES: Private home.

Dechhen Ling/Chagdud Gonpa Foundation

For description see Rigdzin Ling/Chagdud Gonpa Foundation, Junction City, California.
ADDRESS: 198 North River Road, Cottage Grove, OR 97424
PHONE: (541) 942-8619
LINEAGE: Tibetan Nyingmapa
SPIRITUAL HEAD: H. E. Chagdud Tulku Rinpoche
CONTACT: Lama Sonam Tsering
AFFILIATION: Chagdud Gonpa Foundation

Drugpa Dorje Dzin

No description available.
ADDRESS: Box 83773, Portland, OR 97283
PHONE: (206) 297-6638
LINEAGE: Tibetan
SPIRITUAL HEAD: Lama Yeshe Drugpa Thrinley Odzer
CONTACT: Gary
AFFILIATION: Autonomous
FACILITIES: Call for locations.
MEDITATION PROGRAM: Weekly *Amitabha*, Medicine Buddha, Red Tara, and *Vajrapani* practices.

Gyurme Dechen Dorje Ling (GDDL)

GDDL is a Rime (nonsectarian) center and commune promoting Tibetan Mahayana and Vajrayana Buddhism. We are associated with all four of the great Tibetan lineages (Nyingmapa, Kagyupa, Sakyapa, Gelugpa) although we adhere primarily to the Nyingmapa/Kagyupa traditions. We seek to make more accessible the teachings of Vajrayana and related psychospiritual philosophies of the Himalayas, the European alpine regions, and the Americas (Native American Medicine Wheel and related disciplines). GDDL asserts that the dissemination of these teachings is vitally important during this age. By appointment only.
ADDRESS: c/o 1517 Southwest Columbia, Portland, OR 97201
PHONE: Message: (503) 223-8223
LINEAGE: Rime: Nyingmapa, Kagyupa, Sakyapa, Gelugpa
SPIRITUAL HEADS: The Rinpoches: Dudjom, Gyalwa Karmapa, Kalu, Dilgo Khyentse, Dezhung, Sakya Dagchen, Sakya Trizin.
AFFILIATION: Autonomous, but associated with Yeshe Nyingpo/Chagdud Gonpa Foundation, and Karmapa/Kalu Rinpoche centers
ESTABLISHED: 1972
FACILITIES: Private
MEDITATION PROGRAM: *Dorje Sempa, Lamai Naljor, Phowa, Padmasambhava, Chenrezig,* Longlife to Lineages.
RETREATS OFFERED: With notice, in Wy'est (Mt. Hood) area.
PUBLICATIONS: *Padma Od'Zer (Lotus Light)*

Kagyu Changchub Chuling

A center in the Kagyu tradition of Tibetan Buddhism emphasizing calm abiding/insight meditations and Vajrayana practice. Founded by H. H. Kalu Rinpoche. Study group, meditation, group retreats, personal guidance, and instruction.
ADDRESS: 73 Northeast Monroe Street, Portland, OR 97212
PHONE: (503) 284-6697

LINEAGE: Tibetan Karma Kagyu and Shangpa
SPIRITUAL HEADS: Bokar Rinpoche; H. H. Kalu Rinpoche
CONTACT: Michael Conklin
ESTABLISHED: 1976
FACILITIES: House/dharma center.
RETREATS OFFERED: Four per year, off site.
PUBLICATIONS: Occasional newsletter.

Kagyu Yonten Gyatso

One-hundred-sixty-acre "ranch" offering luxurious camping in traditional Tibetan appliquéd tents with Central Asian interior decor. Twenty-by-thirty-foot authentically appliquéd meeting tent, optionally outfitted with authentic Vajrayana throne and equipment for ceremonies, teachings, initiations, and so on. Full kitchen offering gourmet ethnic cooking, including vegetarian and vegan. Tent and tipi accommodations for groups of up to thirty-five people (larger groups with own tents and sleeping gear). Pristine creek, swimming ponds, hiking trails through ancient fir and redwood forests, volleyball, archery, guided tours, whitewater rafting, wilderness experiences.
ADDRESS: 108 Milarepa Road, Azalea, OR 97410
PHONE: (541) 837-3636
FAX: (541) 837-3737
E-MAIL: jince@econet.org
LINEAGE: Shangpa and Karma Kagyu
SPIRITUAL HEAD: H. E. Kalu Rinpoche. No resident lama.
CONTACT: James Ince, Resident Director
AFFILIATION: H. H. the Seventeenth Gyalwa Karmapa; H. E. Kalu Rinpoche; H. E. Situ Rinpoche
ESTABLISHED: 1983
RETREATS OFFERED: Buddhist, Taoist, or selected other groups may book our center for events of their choice from three days to three months. Personal retreats considered.

Komyo Shingon Mandala, a symbol of the Shingon tradition of Japanese esoteric Buddhism depicting the full moon with the Light Mantra (Komyo Shingon) and Mantra of the Mahavairochana Tathagata (Dainichi Nyorai) in Sanskrit resting on a lotus. (Illustration © by Koyasan Shingon Shu.)

Koyasan Shingon of Portland

No description available.
ADDRESS: PO Box 1206, Portland, OR 97207-1206
PHONE: (503) 228-3154
FAX: Same
E-MAIL: ENoble@aol.com
LINEAGE: Japanese Koyasan Shingon
CONTACT: Rev. Eko Susan Noble, Resident Director
AFFILIATION: Senko-ji Temple/Koyasan Shingon Shu (1563 Shimobo, Nyukawa-mura, Ono-gun, Gifu-ken 506-21, Japan).

Newport Yeshe Nyingpo

For description please see Pacific Region Yeshe Nyingpo in Ashland, Oregon

ADDRESS: 5380 North Beaver Creek Road, Seal Rock, OR 97376
PHONE: (503) 563-5729
LINEAGE: Tibetan Nyingma
SPIRITUAL HEAD: H. H. Dudjom Rinpoche
CONTACT: Ven. Gyatrul Rinpoche, Spiritual Representative
AFFILIATION: Pacific Region Yeshe Nyingpo, Ashland, Oregon

Pacific Region Yeshe Nyingpo

Pacific Region Yeshe Nyingpo is the mother center for six Vajrayana Tibetan Buddhist centers under the direction and guidance of the Ven. Gyatrul Rinpoche, who was appointed spiritual representative by H. H. Dudjom Rinpoche. For information about practice and dharma event schedules, please contact the individual centers. See affiliate listings under: Tashi Choling (Ashland, Oregon); Portland Yeshe Nyingpo (Portland, Oregon); Newport Yeshe Nyingpo (Seal Rock, Oregon); Orgyen Dorje Den/Bay Area Yeshe Nyingpo (San Francisco, California); Los Angeles Yeshe Nyingpo (Venice, California); Ensenada (Mexico) Yeshe Nyingpo (San Ysidiro, California).
ADDRESS:Box 124, Ashland, OR 97520
PHONE: (541) 488-0477
FAX: (541) 482-0117
LINEAGE: Tibetan Nyingma
SPIRITUAL HEAD: H. H. Dudjom Rinpoche
CONTACT: Ven. Gyatrul Rinpoche, Spiritual Representative
AFFILIATION: Autonomous; headquarters center.
PUBLICATIONS: We have a complete offering of Nyingma *sadhanas* and commentaries, photos, and other dharma items available through our archives. (Write Yeshe Melong, PO Box 514, Mt. Shasta, CA 96067 or phone (916) 926-0573.)

Portland Sakya Center for Tibetan Buddhism

The Portland Sakya Center is under the spiritual direction of Jetsun Chimey Luding, sister of H. H. Sakya Trizin. She visits twice a year. The resident teacher since 1991 is (Ani) Gilda Paldron Taylor. Center members meet for two hours weekly, with a rotating program of Green Tara; Avalokiteshvara, with the transfer of merit for the dead; and Calm-Abiding Meditation. The practice time is one hour; the second hour is dedicated to teachings, study of a chosen text, or a question-and-answer period. Additional teachings and retreats are scheduled throughout the year.
ADDRESS: PO Box 14201, Portland, OR 97293-0201
PHONE: (503) 238-8097
LINEAGE: Tibetan Sakya
SPIRITUAL HEADS: H. H. Sakya Trizin, Jetsun Chimey Luding. Founded by Chogye Tri Rinpoche.
CONTACT: (Ani) Gilda Paldron Taylor
AFFILIATION: Sakya tradition worldwide.
ESTABLISHED: 1989
FACILITIES: Meets at Portland Dharma Center, 25th and Southeast Madison, Portland, Oregon.
MEDITATION PROGRAM: Two-hour weekly program of practice and study.
RETREATS OFFERED: Occasional, on flexible schedule, sometimes with visiting teachers.
PUBLICATIONS: *The Occasional Newsletter*

Portland Shambhala Center

Portland Shambhala Center was founded by the late Chogyam Trungpa Rinpoche and houses both a Dharma Study Group (DSG) and Shambhala Training. DSG offers classes in meditation and Tibetan Buddhist teachings. Shambhala Training is a nonsectarian approach to meditation that teaches us how to live with gentleness and fearlessness. We meet weekly. Meditation instruction is available. Classes are ongoing and open to the public. Open houses are held quarterly. For additional information, please refer to Shambhala International, Halifax, Nova Scotia, Canada.

ADDRESS: 1110 Southeast Alder Street, Suite 204, Portland, OR 97214

PHONE: (503) 231-4971

E-MAIL: parkerd@ohsu.edu

LINEAGE: Tibetan Kagyu-Nyingma, Shambhala

SPIRITUAL HEAD: Sakyong Mipham Rinpoche

CONTACT: Irene Lundquist

AFFILIATION: Shambhala International, Halifax, Nova Scotia

ESTABLISHED: 1976

FACILITIES: Meditation hall and reception room.

MEDITATION PROGRAM: We meet twice weekly; meditation instruction available. Call for schedule.

RETREATS OFFERED: Through Shambhala International.

Portland Yeshe Nyingpo

Nyingmapa Buddhism is a form of Tantric, Vajrayana Buddhism brought to Tibet over a thousand years ago by the great teacher Guru Rinpoche. These teachings have been passed down to us in an unbroken lineage since ancient times and with pure motivation they will bring understanding and enlightenment. Yeshe Nyingpo was established by H. H. Dudjom Rinpoche as a center for these teachings, so that both the sutras and tantras can be practiced and realized simultaneously. Our centers are guided by the Ven. Gyatrul Rinpoche, who has resided in Oregon and blessed us with his wisdom since 1976.

ADDRESS: 3200 Northwest Skyline Boulevard, Portland, OR 97229

PHONE: (503) 292-4004

FAX: Same

LINEAGE: Tibetan Nyingma

SPIRITUAL HEAD: Ven. Gyatrul Rinpoche

CONTACT: Tulku Yeshe Nyima, Resident Teacher

AFFILIATION: Pacific Region Yeshe Nyingpo; Tashi Choling Monastery in Ashland, Oregon.

ESTABLISHED: 1983

FACILITIES: Meditation center.

MEDITATION PROGRAM: Weekly meditation sessions.

RETREATS OFFERED: At Tashi Choling Monastery, Ashland, Oregon

Tashi Choling

For description please see Pacific Region Yeshe Nyingpo in Ashland, Oregon.

ADDRESS: PO Box 64, Ashland, OR 97520

PHONE: (541) 482-2399

LINEAGE: Tibetan Nyingma

SPIRITUAL HEAD: H. H. Dudjom Rinpoche

CONTACT: Ven. Gyatrul Rinpoche, Spiritual Representative

AFFILIATION: Pacific Region Yeshe Nyingpo, Ashland, Oregon

Tulo Baisi Sangha

This *sangha* was founded by Krishna Sherchan, a Thakali from northcentral Nepal who trained in Vajrayana Buddhism in Mustang (Lo Monthang). Sherchan-ji is learning English, but has two former Peace Corps volunteers who interpret for him. He prefers to keep the group small to intensify the training.

ADDRESS: 636 Northeast 30th Avenue, Portland, OR 97232

PHONE: (503) 235-0900

E-MAIL: psu11659@odin.cc.pdx.edu

LINEAGE: Nyingma-pa Vajrayana

SPIRITUAL HEAD: Krishna Sherchan

CONTACT: Same

AFFILIATION: Lupre Gompa, Nepal

ESTABLISHED: 1995

FACILITIES: Sitting group only.

MEDITATION PROGRAM: Morning sitting once a week.

RETREATS OFFERED: *Puja* once each month.

Waking Peacock Sangha

The Waking Peacock Sangha was formed in 1987 by a group of gay men who had been working together in a therapy context, and with the explicit blessings of Situ Rinpoche, a senior teacher of the Kagyu lineage. We emphasize daily meditation, contemplative study, and the liturgical practice of the Bodhisattva of Compassion as a means of realizing the Buddha's teachings on happiness, basic sanity, intelligence, and goodness—our common heritage. Commitment to daily meditation practice, regular presence at *sangha* meetings, and monthly dues are required. The *sangha* is gender and sexual-orientation *inclusive.*

ADDRESS: 3418 Northwest Thurman, Portland, OR 97210

PHONE: (503) 228-6863

LINEAGE: Tibetan Kagyu

SPIRITUAL HEAD: Situ Rinpoche

CONTACT: Eric Marcoux, Resident Teacher

AFFILIATION: Autonomous

ESTABLISHED: 1987

FACILITIES: Large shrine, meditation room in private home.

MEDITATION PROGRAM: Group meditation and study on alternate Sundays. Weekly Compassion practice.

RETREATS OFFERED: One retreat yearly, flexible.

PENNSYLVANIA

Carnegie Shambhala Study Group

For additional information, please refer to Shambhala International, Halifax, Nova Scotia, Canada.

ADDRESS: 1584 Railroad Street, #2, Carnegie, PA 15106

LINEAGE: Tibetan Kagyu-Nyingma

SPIRITUAL HEAD: Sakyong Mipham Rinpoche

AFFILIATION: Shambhala International, Halifax, Nova Scotia

Philadelphia Shambhala Center

For additional information, please refer to Shambhala International, Halifax, Nova Scotia, Canada.

ADDRESS: 2030 Sansom Street, 3rd Floor, Philadelphia, PA 19103

PHONE: (215) 568-6070

E-MAIL: phill62@ibm.net

LINEAGE: Tibetan Kagyu-Nyingma

SPIRITUAL HEAD: Sakyong Mipham Rinpoche

CONTACTS: Paul Philips, Center Coordinator (215-565-8409); Susan Wagner, Joe Stinson, Dharmadhatu Coordinators (610-325-0807)

AFFILIATION: Shambhala International, Halifax, Nova Scotia

FACILITIES: Urban meditation center.

Three Rivers Dharma Center

The Three Rivers Dharma Center began initially as a committee of the Pittsburgh Friends of Tibet. We were lucky enough to establish a relationship with Khenpo Konchog Gyaltsen Rinpoche, who agreed to direct our spiritual progress. He visits several times a year for weekend teachings. Occasionally other lamas come to teach us as well. The *sangha* gathers one evening a week at Friends Meeting House for deity meditation or other dharma-related events. Our members are working with Buddhist groups in the area to create an umbrella Buddhist Society of Pittsburgh.

ADDRESS: 100 Comrie Avenue, Braddock, PA 15104

PHONE: (412) 351-6542

LINEAGE: Drikung Kagyu

SPIRITUAL HEAD: Khenpo Konchog Gyaltsen Rinpoche

CONTACT: John Bogaard

AFFILIATION: Tibetan Meditation Center

ESTABLISHED: 1993

FACILITIES: Friends Meeting House, 4836 Ellsworth Avenue, Braddock, Pennsylvania

MEDITATION PROGRAM: Meet one evening weekly. On a rotating basis our meditations are focused on *Chenrezig, Vajrasattva, Manjushri,* and Green Tara.

RETREATS OFFERED: Occasional weekends with lama.

PUBLICATIONS: Quarterly newsletter.

Tibetan Buddhist Center of Philadelphia

No description available.

ADDRESS: 3635 Lancaster Avenue, Philadelphia, PA 19104

PHONE: (215) 222-4840

LINEAGE: Tibetan

York Mahayana Buddhist Center

All the Buddhist centers founded by Geshe Kelsang are members of the New Kadampa Tradition (NKT). Spiritually they follow the same direction and together they constitute the NKT family, a nonprofit association of independent dharma centers united by a common spiritual path. For additional information on NKT centers, please see listing for Vajrayogini Buddhist Center in Washington, D.C.

ADDRESS: York, PA

PHONE: (717) 235-4210

E-MAIL: vyogini@nmaa.org

LINEAGE: Tibetan New Kadampa Tradition

SPIRITUAL HEAD: Ven. Geshe Kelsang Gyatso Rinpoche

CONTACT: Ven. Kadam Morten Clausen

AFFILIATION: New Kadampa Tradition and Chakrasambara Buddhist Center in Brooklyn, New York.

ESTABLISHED: 1996

FACILITIES: Local venues.

MEDITATION PROGRAM: Introductory evening classes and other courses at local venues.

PUBLICATIONS: *Full Moon Magazine*

PUERTO RICO

Padmasambhava Buddhist Center—Puerto Rico

For additional information, please see listing under Padmasambhava Buddhist Center, New York, New York.

ADDRESS: 1453 San Alfonso Avenue, Altamira Rio Piedras, Puerto Rico 00912

PHONE: (809) 709-7662

LINEAGE: Tibetan Nyingma

SPIRITUAL HEADS: Khenchen Palden Sherab Rinpoche and Khenpo Tsewang Dongyal Rinpoche

AFFILIATION: Padmasambhava Buddhist Center, New York

RETREATS OFFERED: Summer in upstate New York; winter in West Palm Beach, Florida; others around the country.

SOUTH CAROLINA

Columbia Shambhala Meditation Center

Visitors are welcome at Columbia Shambhala Center whether their interest is in interfaith dialogue, a desire for study and practice, or they're just curious. Individual meditation instruction is available. Although small in number, the center's membership is diverse. There are senior Vajrayana students and instructors here with over twenty years of study and practice experience. Located one mile from

the campus of the University of South Carolina, our center is frequently visited by college students from all regions of the United States. Books are available for sale. For additional information, please refer to Shambhala International, Halifax, Nova Scotia, Canada.
ADDRESS: 2065 Blossom Street, Columbia, SC 29205
PHONE: (803) 254-9048
FAX: (803) 254-4945
LINEAGE: Tibetan Kagyu-Nyingma
SPIRITUAL HEAD: Sakyong Mipham Rinpoche
CONTACTS: Eileen Newman (803) 929-0779 and Tim Hardy (803) 732-7734
AFFILIATION: Shambhala International, Halifax, Nova Scotia
ESTABLISHED: 1975
FACILITIES: Urban center; meditation hall and classrooms.
RETREATS OFFERED: Evening and weekend programs.
PUBLICATIONS: Monthly calendar.

TENNESSEE

Clarkesville Forming Dharma Study Group

For additional information, please refer to Shambhala International, Halifax, Nova Scotia, Canada.
ADDRESS: 22 Lacy Lane, Clarkesville, TN 37043-5123
LINEAGE: Tibetan Kagyu-Nyingma
SPIRITUAL HEAD: Sakyong Mipham Rinpoche
CONTACT: Jim Hartz
AFFILIATION: Shambhala International, Halifax, Nova Scotia

Losel Shedrup Ling Tibetan Buddhist Center of Knoxville (LSLK)

LSLK is an organization of aspiring practitioners of Tibetan Buddhism in Tennes-see. We offer weekly meetings and bimonthly special events to which people of all faiths, traditions, and levels of interest are invited. Operating in close cooperation with all Drepung centers, LSLK benefits especially from the guidance of Geshe Lobsang Negi, who travels to Knoxville periodically to give retreats. He teaches with gentleness and humor and a profound understanding of the humanitarian and spiritual principles of Tibetan Buddhism.
ADDRESS: PO Box 31123, Knoxville, TN 37930-1123
PHONE: (423) 671-0472
LINEAGE: Tibetan Gelugpa
SPIRITUAL HEADS: Geshe Damdul Namgyal, Founding Spiritual Friend; Geshe Lobsang Tenzin Negi; Geshe Yeshi Lhundup
CONTACT: Bruce Seidner, President
AFFILIATION: Losel Shedrup Ling, Atlanta, Georgia; American seat of Drepung Loseling Monastery in India.
ESTABLISHED: 1993
FACILITIES: Members' homes. Rented retreat facilities.
MEDITATION PROGRAM: Two study groups and one meditation practice meeting per week.
RETREATS OFFERED: Through Drepung Loseling we bring scholars from India for long periods of residency. Guest teachers.
PUBLICATIONS: Losel Shedrup Ling of Knoxville Newsletter

Middle Tennessee Padmasambhava Buddhist Center/Padma Gochen Ling

Khenchen Palden Sherab Rinpoche and Khenpo Tsewang Dongyal Rinpoche have founded a branch of the Padmasambhava Buddhist Society in middle Tennessee. They are building a temple in an isolated rural area about halfway between Knox-ville and Nashville. A somewhat scattered sangha supports the building efforts and attends the two annual retreats. Padma Gochen Ling (The Big Door to the Land Of Enlightenment) is the only Nyingmapa retreat center between Chicago and Orlando, Florida. Once it's finished, we will intensify our retreat schedule and will make the facilities available for individual extended retreats.
ADDRESS: PO Box 3181, Cookeville, TN 38501
PHONE: (615) 678-4462
LINEAGE: Tibetan Nyingmapa
SPIRITUAL HEAD: Khenchen Palden Sherab Rinpoche and Khenpo Tsewang Dongyal Rinpoche (The Two Khenpos)
CONTACT: Susan White, Coordinator
AFFILIATION: Padmasambhava Buddhist Society
ESTABLISHED: 1987
FACILITIES: Padma Gochen Ling Retreat Center
MEDITATION PROGRAM: Evening meditation, weekly.
RETREATS OFFERED: Spring and fall weekend retreats with the Khenpos.
PUBLICATIONS: National newsletter once a year.

Padmasambhava Buddhist Center—Nashville

For additional information, please see Padmasambhava Buddhist Center, New York, New York.
ADDRESS: 4100 Nebraska Avenue, Nashville, TN 37209
PHONE: (615) 292-3752
FAX: (615) 269-6739
LINEAGE: Tibetan Nyingma
SPIRITUAL HEAD: Khenchen Palden Sherab and Khenpo Tsewang Dongyal
CONTACT: Bill French
AFFILIATION: Padmasambhava Buddhist centers
FACILITIES: Meditation room.

MEDITATION PROGRAM: Weekly evening meditation.
RETREATS OFFERED: Spring and fall at our retreat center, Padma Gochen Ling.

Turtle Hill Sangha

Established by veterans of "The Farm," the renowned 1970s commune that died of heart failure, all members initially focus on the *ngondro* and accumulation practices along with traditional Nyingma studies. We also make use of teachings by non-Buddhist masters such as Adi Da and Sri Ramakrishna. As of this writing, we are in the process of building a retreat center in rural Tennessee. Other projects include transcribing and editing Khenpo Palden Sherab's teachings and producing dharma crafts. For additional information, please see listing for Padmasambhava Center—New York.
ADDRESS: 50 Myers Road, Summertown, TN 38483
PHONE: (615) 964-2219
LINEAGE: Tibetan Nyingmapa
SPIRITUAL HEAD: Khenpo Palden Sherab Rinpoche and Khenpo Tsewang Dongyal Rinpoche (The Two Khenpos)
CONTACT: Craig Bialick
AFFILIATION: Padmasambhava Buddhist Society
ESTABLISHED: 1989
RETREATS OFFERED: Call for information.
PUBLICATIONS: *The Door to Inconceivable Wisdom and Compassion*, Sky Dancer Press.

TEXAS

Austin Shambhala Center

Austin Shambhala is a center for meditation, study, and contemplation founded by the Vidyadhara, the late Chogyam Trungpa Rinpoche. Shambhala Training—inspired by the ancient legend of an enlightened society—is presented in a progressive series of weekend study and meditation programs. Called *Heart of Warriorship*, these programs illustrate a nonsectarian path of wakefulness, gentleness, and confidence. Further expressions of a sacred world outlook can be seen in such activities as ikebana (flower arranging), *kyudo* (archery), poetics, tea ceremonies, and calligraphy. For additional information, please refer to Shambhala International, Halifax, Nova Scotia, Canada.
ADDRESS: 1702 South Fifth Street, Austin, TX 78704
PHONE: (512) 443-3263
FAX: (512) 836-1412
E-MAIL: blint@ccsi.com
LINEAGE: Tibetan Kagyu-Nyingma
SPIRITUAL HEADS: Chogyam Trungpa/Sakyong Mipham Rinpoche
CONTACTS: Darrell Reed and Jody Zemel
AFFILIATION: Shambhala International, Halifax, Nova Scotia
ESTABLISHED: 1975
FACILITIES: Meditation center with two shrine rooms.

Chenrezig Tibetan Cultural Center

The Chenrezig Tibetan Cultural Center was founded in 1990 by the Ven. Lobsang Samten, with the help of Dr. David Hall and University of Texas at El Paso (UTEP) President Diana Natalicio, in order to develop an awareness of Himalayan culture and of the Chinese occupation of Tibet. Meditation classes are conducted in Worrell Hall (Philosophy Department) and are free for all UTEP students and faculty. The center exists to foster the qualities of awareness, friendliness, compassion, understanding, and lovingkindness.
ADDRESS: University of Texas at El Paso, 127 Serrania Drive, El Paso, TX 79932-2122
PHONE: (915) 747-5451
SPIRITUAL HEAD: Ven. Lama Lobsang Samten

CONTACT: Joseph DeFlorio
AFFILIATION: Buddhist centers in Philadelphia and New York
ESTABLISHED: 1990
FACILITIES: Meditation room in Worrell Hall (Philosophy Department).

Dallas Karma Thegsum Choling (KTC)

In August 1990, KTC purchased a two-story frame house in Oak Cliff. This house was built around the turn of the century and members have done a great deal of remodeling on it. The center provides a place for the hearing, contemplation, and practice of the Buddha's teachings in the Karma Kagyu tradition. Teachers visit three or four times a year to conduct public seminars and meet personally with students. Our members humorously refer to themselves as *Dharmadillos*. For additional information, please see listing for Karma Triyana Dharmachakra, Woodstock, New York.
ADDRESS: 312 South Winnetka, Dallas, TX 75208
PHONE: (214) 948-3348
FAX: Same
E-MAIL: BillSwanson@acd.org
LINEAGE: Tibetan Karma Kagyu
SPIRITUAL HEADS: Ven. Khenpo Karthar Rinpoche; H. H. the seventeenth Karmapa, Orgyen T'rinle Dorje.
CONTACT: Bruce Roe, Resident Director
AFFILIATION: Karma Triyana Dharmachakra, Woodstock, New York
ESTABLISHED: 1984
FACILITIES: House with shrine room, capacity of about forty.
MEDITATION PROGRAM: Weekly group practice, *Shamatha* instruction, *pujas*, dharma class, Tibetan language classes.
RETREATS OFFERED: Weekend seminars when lamas visit.
PUBLICATIONS: *Dharma News* (every other month).

Dawn Mountain Tibetan Temple, Community Center, and Research Institute

We have two kinds of activities: (1) ongoing practice and instruction in Tibetan Buddhist traditions, and (2) occasional workshops in a variety of wellness-oriented techniques for enhancing mind and body. Dharma practice focuses on *Dzogchen* and on the *sutra* teachings. Wellness workshops integrate a variety of techniques helpful in alleviating stress, developing creativity, nurturing relationships, and being responsive and present in daily life.
ADDRESS: c/o Aronson, 4615 Post Oak Place, #204, Houston, TX 77027-9703
PHONE: (713) 623-0837
E-MAIL: klein-a@ricevm1.rice.edu (Anne Klein) *or* 102136.3631@ compuserve.com (Harvey Aronson)
LINEAGE: Tibetan nonsectarian (*sutra* and *Dzogchen*)
CONTACTS: Anne C. Klein and Harvey B. Aronson, Directors
ESTABLISHED: 1996
MEDITATION PROGRAM: Classes conducted by Anne and Harvey or by invited traditional or Western teachers.
RETREATS OFFERED: Occasional weekend retreats at Margaret Austin Center in Chappell Hill, Texas. Weeklong summer or winter retreats in locations to be announced.

Diamond Way Buddhist Center

Meditation center established under the direct guidance of Lama Ole Nydahl in 1992. Meditation group meets for meditation and *ngondro* practice.
ADDRESS: 804 Tall Pines, Friendswood, TX 77546
PHONE: (713) 482-2926
FAX: (713) 482-2606
LINEAGE: Karma Kagyu

SPIRITUAL HEAD: Seventeenth Karmapa Thaye Dorje

Houston Dharma Study Group

For additional information, please refer to Shambhala International, Halifax, Nova Scotia, Canada.
ADDRESS: 1902 Brimberry Street, Houston, TX 77019
PHONE: (713) 956-9269
FAX: (713) 956-9270
E-MAIL: 103337.3145@compuserve.com
LINEAGE: Tibetan Kagyu-Nyingma
SPIRITUAL HEAD: Sakyong Mipham Rinpoche
CONTACT: Celeste Budwit
AFFILIATION: Shambhala International, Halifax, Nova Scotia

Houston True Buddha Chapter

No description available.
ADDRESS: 9630 Clarewood, #A3, Houston, TX 77036
PHONE: (713) 988-8488
LINEAGE: Chinese Vajrayana: True Buddha School
SPIRITUAL HEAD: Grand Master Sheng-yen Lu

Rigpe Dorje Center

The Rigpe Dorje Center was founded in 1991 by H. E. Jamgon Kongtrul Rinpoche in the tradition of the Karma Kagyu lineage of Tibetan Buddhism. With the passing of His Eminence in 1992, the center came under the spiritual direction of Khenpo Tsultrim Gyamtso Rinpoche. Rigpe Dorje provides a place for a small group of San Antonio practitioners to meditate and study texts and tapes of Mahayana and Vajrayana teachings. We also host biannual practice and study retreats with our teachers.
ADDRESS: PO Box 690995, San Antonio, TX 78269

PHONE: (210) 525-8625
E-MAIL: rigpedorjecenter@io.com
LINEAGE: Tibetan Karma Kagyu
SPIRITUAL HEAD: Khenpo Tsultrim Gyamtso Rinpoche
CONTACT: Jan Puckett, Resident Director
AFFILIATION: Rigpe Dorje Foundation
ESTABLISHED: 1991
FACILITIES: Space is leased for programs.
RETREATS OFFERED: Biannual training programs with Khenpo Tsultrim Gyamtso Rinpoche and Dzogchen Ponlop Rinpoche.

San Antonio Shambhala Center

"What started out as a fledgling study group of three people has blossomed into a meditation center where ongoing classes and practice sessions are offered to the public. What made the difference was having a specific location for the center and a listing in the phone book. Over and over again we hear, "I had no idea anything like this was going on in San Antonio. It is heartening to connect with others who are seeking to bring some sanity to their lives through the practice of meditation." For additional information, please refer to Shambhala International, Halifax, Nova Scotia, Canada.
ADDRESS: 6233 Evers Road, Suite 100, San Antonio, TX 78238
PHONES: (210) 647-1804 or (210) 408-7227
E-MAIL: dwgordon@tenet
LINEAGE: Tibetan Kagyu-Nyingma
SPIRITUAL HEAD: Sakyong Mipham Rinpoche
CONTACT: Elisa Gonzalez
AFFILIATION: Shambhala International, Halifax, Nova Scotia
ESTABLISHED: 1995
FACILITIES: Meditation hall for ongoing practice sessions.
RETREATS OFFERED: Weekend practice intensives.
PUBLICATIONS: *Mandala*, local newsletter.

Thubten Rinchen Ling

Thubten Rinchen Ling (TRL) was founded by Geshe Tsultrim Gyeltsen in 1988. Our resident lama is Geshe Yeshe Phelgye. TRL sponsored the Texas segments of the 1990 and 1993 world tours and Sand Mandala Exhibits of the Gaden Shartse monks from India. The center also coordinated all local activities for the 1991 visit of H. H. the Dalai Lama to Houston. We sponsor five monks and several nuns in India.

ADDRESS: 10726 Carvel Lane, Houston, TX 77072
PHONE: (713) 495-6556
LINEAGE: Tibetan Gelugpa
SPIRITUAL HEAD: H. H. the Dalai Lama
CONTACT: Geshe Yeshe Phelgye, Resident Lama
AFFILIATION: Thubten Dhargye Ling of Long Beach, California.
ESTABLISHED: 1989
FACILITIES: Small center with meditation/teaching area.
MEDITATION PROGRAM: Sutra and tantra. Newcomers' meetings.
RETREATS OFFERED: Numerous

Vajradakini Buddhist Center

Vajradakini Buddhist Center was founded in 1994 by the world-renowned meditation master and scholar, Ven. Geshe Kelsang Gyatso. Buddhist teachings are presented in a form suited to the Western mind and lifestyle and can easily be integrated into our daily life. The resident teacher is Gen Kelsang Dekyi, a Buddhist nun and close disciple of Geshe Kelsang Gyatso. Gen Dekyi is a Westerner, born in England. She received oral transmissions and lineage blessings directly from Geshe Kelsang and has great depth of understanding and skill in presenting the Buddha's teachings.

ADDRESS: 4915 Junius Street, Dallas, TX 75214
PHONE: (214) 823-6385
FAX: (214) 823-6395
LINEAGE: New Kadampa Tradition
SPIRITUAL HEAD: Geshe Kelsang Gyatso
CONTACT: Gen Kelsang Dekyi, Resident Director
AFFILIATION: New Kadampa Tradition
ESTABLISHED: 1994
FACILITIES: *Gonpa* and staff residence (small house).
MEDITATION PROGRAM: Weekly general program and Sunday meditation. Classes in Austin and Denton, Texas. Please call for times and locations.
RETREATS OFFERED: Scheduled throughout the year.
PUBLICATIONS: Monthly newsletter.

UTAH

Salt Lake City Forming Dharma Study Group

For additional information, please refer to Shambhala International, Halifax, Nova Scotia, Canada.

ADDRESS: 1257 North 3100 East, Layton, UT 84040-3001
LINEAGE: Tibetan Kagyu-Nyingma
SPIRITUAL HEAD: Sakyong Mipham Rinpoche
CONTACT: Stephen Coffin
AFFILIATION: Shambhala International, Halifax, Nova Scotia
ESTABLISHED: 1976
FACILITIES: Urban meditation center.

VERMONT

Brattleboro Dharma Study Group

For additional information, please refer to Shambhala International, Halifax, Nova Scotia, Canada.

ADDRESS: 2 Flat Street, Brattleboro, VT 05301
LINEAGE: Tibetan Kagyu-Nyingma
SPIRITUAL HEAD: Sakyong Mipham Rinpoche
AFFILIATION: Shambhala International, Halifax, Nova Scotia

Burlington Shambhala Center

We are one of a large number of meditation, practice, and study centers whose parent organization is Shambhala International, founded in the early 1970s by the late Tibetan Buddhist meditation master, the Ven. Chogyam Trungpa Rinpoche. After his death in 1987, his son, the Sakyong Mipham Rinpoche, assumed leadership of the organization. Burlington Shambhala Center holds classes, meditation hours, talks, and special events, for both the general public and for our members. For additional information, please refer to Shambhala International, Halifax, Nova Scotia, Canada.

ADDRESS: 236 Riverside Avenue, Burlington, VT 05401
PHONE: (802) 658-6795
FAX: (802) 658-9516 (at Kinkos)
LINEAGE: Tibetan Kagyu-Nyingma
SPIRITUAL HEAD: Sakyong Mipham Rinpoche
CONTACT: Charlotte Brodie
AFFILIATION: Shambhala International, Halifax, Nova Scotia
ESTABLISHED: 1976
FACILITIES: Retreat center at Karmê-Chöling, Barnet, Vermont.
MEDITATION PROGRAM: Open for meditation five days a week. Meditation instruction twice monthly or by appointment. Free.

Hanover Dharma Study Group

For additional information, please refer to Shambhala International, Halifax, Nova Scotia, Canada.

ADDRESS: RR#1, Box 171, Bradford,
VT 05033
PHONES: (802) 763-7179 (home); (802)
457-2779 (work)
LINEAGE: Tibetan Kagyu-Nyingma
SPIRITUAL HEAD: Sakyong Mipham Rin-
poche
CONTACT: Donna Williams
AFFILIATION: Shambhala International,
Halifax, Nova Scotia

Karmê-Chöling Buddhist Meditation Center

Karmê-Chöling is a meditation center in
northern Vermont, founded in 1970 by
the Vidyadhara, the Ven. Chogyam Trungpa Rinpoche, author of *The Myth of
Freedom* and *Cutting Through Spiritual
Materialism*, and a pioneer in bringing
Buddhism to the West. Ours is one of
many such centers throughout North
America and Europe under the aegis
of Shambhala International. Chogyam
Trungpa's son, Sakyong Mipham Rinpoche, now leads Shambhala Interna-
tional and its affiliated organizations,
including Karmê-Chöling. The center
emphasizes the practice of meditation
based on both Buddhist and Shambhala
teachings. For additional information,
please refer to Shambhala International,
Halifax, Nova Scotia, Canada.
ADDRESS: RR1, Box 3, Barnet, VT 05821
PHONE: (802) 633-2384
FAX: (802) 633-3012
E-MAIL: karmecholing@shambhala.org
LINEAGE: Tibetan Kagyu-Nyingma
SPIRITUAL HEAD: Sakyong Mipham Rin-
poche
CONTACT: Suzann Duquette
AFFILIATION: Shambhala International,
Halifax, Nova Scotia
ESTABLISHED: 1970
FACILITIES: Architecturally, Karmê-
Chöling blends New England, Tibetan,
and Japanese design. It has six shrine
rooms, including a meditation hall that

seats two hundred. Surrounded by
meadows and woodlands, the main
building houses forty-five staff members and guests. There's also a production facility for meditation cushions, a
gift shop, vegetable garden, retreat cabins, tent sites, and a guest house in
Barnet.
MEDITATION PROGRAM: Variety of programs for beginning and advanced
practitioners. All include meditation
practice and vary in length from two
days to a month. Call for schedule.
RETREATS OFFERED: Cabin and "in-
house" retreats, programs.
PUBLICATIONS: Biannual calendar of
events.

Manchester Dharma Study Group

For additional information, please refer
to Shambhala International, Halifax,
Nova Scotia, Canada.
ADDRESS: Box 33, Manchester, VT 05254
PHONES: (802) 362-3432 (home); (802)
362-2430 (work)
LINEAGE: Tibetan Kagyu-Nyingma
SPIRITUAL HEAD: Sakyong Mipham Rin-
poche
CONTACT: Maggie Bernstein
AFFILIATION: Shambhala International,
Halifax, Nova Scotia
ESTABLISHED: 1980

Mandala Buddhist Center

Shingon is a Japanese form of esoteric
Buddhism transmitted to Japan from
India via China in the ninth century by
Kobo Daishi Kukai. Teaching that buddhahood can be achieved "in this very
body," Shingon utilizes mudra, mantra,
and visualization to uncover our inherent
awakened qualities. Set in Vermont's
beautiful Green Mountains, Mandala
Center offers an opportunity to study
and practice this rare form of Buddhism
in weekly meditations, weekend inten-

sives, and summer retreats. To both new
students and established practitioners of
any tradition, we offer a warm invitation
to visit Mandala Center and explore
Shingon.
ADDRESS: RR#1, Box 2380, Bristol,
VT 05443
PHONE: (802) 453-5038
LINEAGE: Shingon, Japanese Esoteric
Buddhism
SPIRITUAL HEAD: Rev. Jomyo Tanaka
CONTACT: James F. Kane
AFFILIATION: International Mandala As-
sociation
ESTABLISHED: 1975
FACILITIES: Farmhouse and barn on
eighty acres.
MEDITATION PROGRAM: Weekly, sched-
uled meditations and instruction, free
and open to the public.
RETREATS OFFERED: Seasonal weekend
intensives. Ten-day summer intensive
under Rev. Tanaka. Call or write for in-
formation and registration.

Milarepa Center

Located in Vermont's scenic Northeast
Kingdom, two-hundred-seventy-acre Milarepa Center is one of eighty such centers worldwide, affiliated with the
Foundation for the Preservation of the
Mahayana Tradition. We provide facili-
ties for individual and group retreats and
host qualified Buddhist meditation teach-
ers and scholars. An integrated schedule
of meditation, study, and work enables
residents to apply the Buddha's teachings
to daily life. Program attendance fees are
by donation.
ADDRESS: Barnet Mountain, Barnet,
VT 05821
PHONE: (802) 633-4136
FAX: (802) 633-3808
LINEAGE: Tibetan Gelugpa
SPIRITUAL HEAD: Lama Thubten Zopa
Rinpoche
CONTACT: Geshe Tsulga

AFFILIATION: Foundation for the Preservation of the Mahayana Tradition
ESTABLISHED: 1981
FACILITIES: Twelve-room house; facilities for individual and group retreats; garage/shop, barn, book and tape library.
PUBLICATIONS: *Repa Rag*

Rutland Dharma Study Group

For additional information, please refer to Shambhala International, Halifax, Nova Scotia, Canada.
ADDRESS: RR#1, #632, Cuttingsville, VT 05837
PHONE: (802) 773-0909
LINEAGE: Tibetan Kagyu-Nyingma
SPIRITUAL HEAD: Sakyong Mipham Rinpoche
CONTACT: Steve Butterfield
AFFILIATION: Shambhala International, Halifax, Nova Scotia

St. Johnsbury Dharma Study Group

For additional information, please refer to Shambhala International, Halifax, Nova Scotia, Canada.
ADDRESS: PO Box 58, Barnet, VT 05821
PHONE: (802) 633-4362
LINEAGE: Tibetan Kagyu-Nyingma
SPIRITUAL HEAD: Sakyong Mipham Rinpoche
CONTACT: Cathy Hinchey
AFFILIATION: Shambhala International, Halifax, Nova Scotia

Sunray Meditation Society

Sunray is an international spiritual society dedicated to planetary peace. Its purpose is to manifest the Native American ideal of Caretaker Mind, so that we may create a world of beauty upon the earth. In 1983 Sunray was designated as a Tibetan Nyingma Buddhist center by H. H. Dudjom Rinpoche. In 1986 H. H. Chet-sang Rinpoche acknowledged the meeting of Drikung Kagyu and Sunray teachings as the fulfillment of prophecy. Sunray teachings are thus a beauteous lake receiving the streams of three ancient and intact spiritual lineages, which lead us to a realization of Caretaker Mind and Bodhisattva Action.
ADDRESS: Box 269, Bristol, VT 05443
PHONE: (802) 453-4610
FAX: (802) 453-3501
E-MAIL: sunray@sover.net
LINEAGE: Cherokee Ywahoo lineage; Tibetan Nyingma and Drikung Kagyu lineages.
SPIRITUAL HEAD: Ven. Dhyani Ywahoo
AFFILIATION: Green Mountain Aniyunwiwah (Cherokee)
ESTABLISHED: 1968
FACILITIES: Sunray Peace Village Encampment (summer only) for practice, study, and retreat. Camping (tents, some RV sites) and outdoor cooking; showers and toilets available. Teachings are conducted in a large tent.
MEDITATION PROGRAM: Summertime morning and evening meditation for program participants; weekly open house.
RETREATS OFFERED: The Peacekeeper Mission—yearly foundation training—offered regionally in the United States, Canada, and Europe. Summer teachings in Native American and Buddhist studies at Sunray Peace Village. Individual retreats for practitioners.
PUBLICATIONS: *Sunray Newsletter*, quarterly.

VIRGINIA

Charlottesville Dharma Study Group

For additional information, please refer to Shambhala International, Halifax, Nova Scotia, Canada.
ADDRESS: 606 North Avenue, Charlottesville, VA 22901
PHONE: (804) 295-7593
LINEAGE: Tibetan Kagyu-Nyingma
SPIRITUAL HEAD: Sakyong Mipham Rinpoche
CONTACT: Julie Swan
AFFILIATION: Shambhala International, Halifax, Nova Scotia

Dharma Institute

Ven. Bhikshuni Tenzin Yeshe, resident director of Dharma Institute, has studied and practiced Buddhism since the 1960s and has received monastic vows from both the Dalai Lama and Thich Nhat Hanh. Her teacher, Tulku Urgyen Rinpoche, left his body in 1996, survived by four children, among whom are Chokyi Nyima Rinpoche and Tsok Nyi Rin-

Ven. Bhikshuni Tenzin Yeshe, resident director of Dharma Institute in Ruckersville, Virginia, while on a visit to Plum Village, France. (Photo by Lee Naomi.)

poche. Dharma Institute aspires to make available the works and teachings of these important dharma masters. Students of the late Tulku Urgyen are establishing a retreat center in the United States and will sponsor regular teachings based on the *Dzogchen* texts written by Tulku Urgyen and his sons.

ADDRESS: PO Box 254, Ruckersville, VA 22968
PHONE: (540) 832-5282
E-MAIL: Dharma@comet.net
LINEAGE: Tibetan Kagyu Buddhism
SPIRITUAL HEAD: Ven. Kyabje Tulku Urgyen Rinpoche
CONTACT: Ven. Bhikshuni Tenzin Yeshe (Mary Teal Coleman), Founder and Resident Director.
FACILITIES: Monastic retreat center in rural area.

Kagyu Shenpen Tharchin

We are a small, warm, and lively group of diverse individuals who have all somehow found our way to Tibetan Buddhism, Kalu Rinpoche, and Lama Norlha. We meet weekly to practice *Chenrezig, ngondro,* Green Tara, Medicine Buddha, and *shinay* meditation. Some of us participate in weekly Tibetan language classes, where we work at understanding the precise meanings of our texts. About three times a year, we are visited by Lama Norlha (Abbot of Kagyu Thubten Choling, New York), or other teachers from the Kagyu lineage.

ADDRESS: 3411 Grove Avenue, Richmond, VA 23221
PHONE: (804) 355-6657
LINEAGE: Tibetan Kagyu
SPIRITUAL HEADS: Kalu Rinpoche and Lama Norlha
CONTACTS: Bruce Frostick and Jean Hoots
AFFILIATION: Kagyu Thubten Choling, New York
ESTABLISHED: 1993

FACILITIES: Urban meditation center.
RETREATS OFFERED: Weekend seminars three times per year.

WASHINGTON

Amrita/Chagdud Gonpa Foundation

For description see Rigdzin Ling, Chagdud Gonpa Foundation in Junction City, California.

ADDRESS: 2223 Northeast 137th Street, Seattle, WA 98125
PHONE: (206) 367-7377
LINEAGE: Tibetan Nyingmapa
SPIRITUAL HEAD: H. E. Chagdud Tulku Rinpoche
CONTACT: Richard Baldwin
AFFILIATION: Chagdud Gonpa Foundation

Bellingham Dharma Study Group

For additional information, please refer to Shambhala International, Halifax, Nova Scotia, Canada.

ADDRESS: 1310 Astor, Bellingham, WA 89225
PHONE: (360) 647-5413
LINEAGE: Tibetan Kagyu-Nyingma
SPIRITUAL HEAD: Sakyong Mipham Rinpoche
CONTACTS: Jennie and Paul Warwick
AFFILIATION: Shambhala International, Halifax, Nova Scotia
ESTABLISHED: 1973
FACILITIES: Member's home.

Dharma Friendship Foundation

No description available.

ADDRESS: 3204 West Lynn Street, Seattle, WA 98199
PHONE: (206) 782-7873
LINEAGE: Tibetan

Drikung Kyobpa Choling

Tibetan Buddhist practice in the Drikung Kagyu tradition including meditations, teachings, and practices led by Ven. Lama Konchok Samten. For beginners and experienced practitioners in West Seattle.

ADDRESS: 6307 California Avenue, Southwest, 1B, Seattle, WA 98136
PHONE: (206) 937-5356
LINEAGE: Tibetan Drikung Kagyu
SPIRITUAL HEAD: Ven. Lama Konchok Samten
CONTACT: Ani Konchok Chodron
MEDITATION PROGRAM: Scheduled practice one morning and one evening per week.

Hung Kar Dudul Ling (HKDL)

After recognizing Lora Cameron Burke as a highly realized student, H. H. Kusum Lingpa asked her to open a center on Mercer Island in Seattle. *Hung Kar Dudul Ling* means "White Letter Hung Destroying Evil Influences." Kusum Lingpa is a "householder yogi" directing four monastic centers in Tibet and many new dharma centers here in the West. HKDL will have *Vajrakilaya* as its focus practice, with an emphasis on *Dzogchen* contemplation. His Holiness will make at least one extended trip to Seattle per year to teach and empower.

ADDRESS: 6630 East Mercer Way, Mercer Island, WA 98040
PHONE: (206) 232-7843
LINEAGE: Tibetan Nyingma Buddhism
SPIRITUAL HEAD: H. H. Orgyen Kusum Lingpa
CONTACTS: Lora Burgess Cameron and eight-year-old Tulku Pema Samdrup Gyatso, Resident Teachers
AFFILIATION: Vajrakilaya centers
ESTABLISHED: 1995
FACILITIES: Meditation/shrine room.
MEDITATION PROGRAM: Regular practices of *Vajrakilaya* and *Dzogchen.*
PUBLICATIONS: *HKDL Newsletter*

Kagyu Shenpen Osel Choling

Kagyu Shenpen Osel Choling is a center for the study and practice of Vajrayana Buddhism, founded through the inspiration of Kalu Rinpoche, following the tradition of the Dakgpo Kagyu. Resident Director Lama Tashi holds transmission in both the Dakgpo and Shangpa Kagyu lineages. He has practiced meditation since 1969 and has completed two three-year three-month retreats. Lama Tashi has studied with and received empowerments and transmissions from H. E. Kalu Rinpoche, Dilgo Kyentse Rinpoche, Chogyam Trungpa Rinpoche, and the seventeenth Karmapa.

ADDRESS: 4322 Burke Avenue North, Seattle, WA 98103

PHONE: (206) 632-1439

LINEAGE: Tibetan Dakgpo Kagyu

SPIRITUAL HEAD: H. E. the Very Ven. Kalu Rinpoche

CONTACT: Ven. Lama Tashi Namgyal, Resident Teacher

AFFILIATION: Kalu Rinpoche's Kagyu centers.

FACILITIES: A resident dharma center.

RETREATS OFFERED: Ongoing dharma classes with Lama Tashi and teachers such as Thrangu Rinpoche, Tai Situ Rinpoche, and Khandro Rinpoche.

PUBLICATIONS: *KSOC Newsletter*

Ling Shen Ching Tze Temple

Grand Master Lu settled in the United States in 1982 and built both Ling Shen Ching Tze Temple and a large retreat center in the Cascade Mountains. An estimated four million students have taken refuge with him and, with over three hundred chapters worldwide, his True Buddha School is recognized as a major component in Buddhism today. The Ling Shen Ching Tze Temple holds two major ceremonies each year: the New Year

Grand Master Sheng-yen Lu conducting an empowerment ceremony at Ling Shen Ching Tze Temple in Redmond, Washington. (Photo courtesy of Purple Lotus.)

Blessing (late winter) and the annual Bardo Ceremony (late summer).

ADDRESS: 17012 Northeast 40th Court, Redmond, WA 98052

PHONE: (206) 882-0916

LINEAGE: Chinese Vajrayana: True Buddha School

SPIRITUAL HEAD: Master Sheng-yen Lu

CONTACT: Rev. Lian Ning

AFFILIATION: True Buddha School

FACILITIES: Large temple.

MEDITATION PROGRAM: True Buddha Tantric Dharma.

LoJong Meditation (Nalendra Institute)

Our group is structured around a balanced program of Buddhist study (philosophy, psychology) and practice (Shamatha/Vipassana). Our primary focus is the development of special insights into the reality of phenomena and their integration into our daily life.

ADDRESS: 1826 79th Avenue, Olympia, WA 98501

PHONE: (360) 754-0963

LINEAGE: Tibetan Buddhism

SPIRITUAL HEAD: Open

CONTACT: Geshi Jamyang Tsultrim

AFFILIATION: Autonomous. Affiliated with Nalendra Institute.

ESTABLISHED: 1992

FACILITIES: Buddhist Association of Olympia

MEDITATION PROGRAM: Shamatha/Vipassana, *bodhicitta*, and Tibetan tantra practice.

RETREATS OFFERED: Annual retreat during Martin Luther King Day weekend.

Padma Ling/Chagdud Gonpa

Padma Ling Center holds daily morning and evening practice and weekly teachings by resident and visiting lamas. Our founder and spiritual head, the Ven. Chagdud Tulku Rinpoche, visits once a year. We have three prison programs and Lamas Inge and Yontan speak at area colleges. Our *sangha* extends over a large area and includes members in Washington, Oregon, Montana, Idaho, and Canada. For additional information see Rigdzin Ling/Chagdud Gonpa Foundation in Junction City, California.

ADDRESS: West 1014 Seventh Avenue, Spokane, WA 99204

PHONE: (509) 747-1559

LINEAGE: Tibetan Nyingmapa

SPIRITUAL HEAD: H. E. Chagdud Tulku Rinpoche

CONTACTS: Lama Inge Sandvoss and Lama Yontan Y. Gonpo

AFFILIATION: Chagdud Gonpa Foundation

ESTABLISHED: 1984

FACILITIES: Urban dharma center; shrine room, library, office, kitchen, living and dining rooms, nine bedrooms for residents, which include the lamas.

RETREATS OFFERED: Monthly one-day or weekend retreats, annual four-day retreat in December.

PUBLICATIONS: *Dragonsong*, quarterly newsletter.

Sakya Kachod Choling

Jetsun Kushok visits and teaches and plans to do more in the future. His Holiness Sakya Trizin gave *Lam Dre* here in 1995. The *gonpa* sits nestled on the southern slope of Mt. Dallas in the secluded west side of San Juan Island in Puget Sound. Surrounded by madrona trees and with a lovely view of Mt. Baker, it is extremely quiet, with deer and other wildlife coming up close.

ADDRESS: Box 3191/5050 B Hannah Road, Friday Harbor, WA 98250

PHONE: (360) 378-3490

FAX: Same

LINEAGE: Tibetan Vajrayana

Sakya Kachod Choling, nestled on the southern slope of Mt. Dallas on San Juan Island in Puget Sound. (Photo by Al Reid.)

Buddha Rupa at Sakya Kachod Choling. (Photo by Al Reid.)

SPIRITUAL HEADS: Jetsun Kushok Chime Luding; H. H. Sakya Trizin

CONTACT: Susan Campbell Webster

AFFILIATION: Sakya Tsechen Thubtin Ling (Jetsun Kushok's city center in Richmond, British Columbia).

ESTABLISHED: 1991

FACILITIES: *Gonpa* with two retreat rooms.

RETREATS OFFERED: Individual retreats with permission from Jetsun Kushok or H. H. Sakya Trizin.

Sakya Monastery of Tibetan Buddhism

H. H. Jigdal Dagchen Sakya and H. H. Trinly N. Sakyapa direct a wide variety of activities at Sakya Monastery, an international seat of nonsectarian Buddhist teachings and site of the Pacific Northwest branch of the Library of Tibetan

Sakya Monastery of Tibetan Buddhism in Seattle, Washington. (Photo by David Merrill.)

Works and Archives. Weekly *Chenrezig* (compassion) meditations are open to the public. Ongoing activities include refuge ceremonies, initiations, celebrations of Buddhist holy days, adult and children's classes, and observance of Tibetan New Year. An extensive program with guest lamas and visiting lecturers exposes our students to Tibetan culture and a diverse spectrum of Mahayana meditation techniques.

ADDRESS: 108 Northwest 83rd Street, Seattle, WA 98117

PHONE: (206) 789-2573

FAX: (206) 789-3994

LINEAGE: Tibetan Sakya and nonsectarian Buddhist

SPIRITUAL HEADS: H. H. Jigdal Dagchen Sakya and H. H. Trinly N. Sakyapa (Seattle); H.H. Sakya Trizin (India)

CONTACT: Adrienne Chan, Executive Administrator

AFFILIATION: Autonomous

ESTABLISHED: 1974

FACILITIES: Urban center with solitary retreat facilities.

MEDITATION PROGRAM: Weekly *Chenrezig* open to the public.

RETREATS OFFERED: "Days of Mindfulness."

PUBLICATIONS: Meditation texts.

Seattle Karma Kagyu Study Group (KKSG)

The group focus is primarily on *Shamatha, Chenrezig,* and *Ngondro* practices. We have hosted such teachers as His Eminence Tai Situ Rinpoche, Khenpo Karthar Rinpoche, Bardor Tulku Rinpoche, and Lama Dudjom Dorje. For additional information, please see listing for Karma Triyana Dharmachakra in Woodstock, New York.

ADDRESS: 2118 North 143rd Street, Seattle, WA 98133

PHONE: (206) 367-6998

E-MAIL: schiebers@msn.com

LINEAGE: Tibetan Karma Kagyu

SPIRITUAL HEAD: Ven. Khenpo Karthar Rinpoche

CONTACT: Linda Furuyama

AFFILIATION: Karma Triyana Dharmachakra, Woodstock, New York

ESTABLISHED: 1981

FACILITIES: Urban meditation center.

MEDITATION PROGRAM: One morning and one evening weekly of *Shamatha,* Green Tara Prayer, *Ngondro,* and *Amitabha* practices.

PUBLICATIONS: *Lions's Roar Dharma News*

Seattle Rigpa

We are a Tibetan Buddhist study and practice group based on Ven. Sogyal Rinpoche's work, *The Tibetan Book of Living and Dying,* and on *Dzogchen* and *Padmasambhava* practices. For additional information, please see the listing for Rigpa North America in Santa Cruz, California.

ADDRESS: 3408 South King, Seattle, WA 98122

PHONE: (206) 522-2615

LINEAGE: Tibetan Nyingma

SPIRITUAL HEAD: Sogyal Rinpoche

AFFILIATION: Rigpa North America, Santa Cruz, California

MEDITATION PROGRAM: Meditation one evening a week. Call for times and locations.

PUBLICATIONS: *The Tibetan Book of Living and Dying,* Sogyal Rinpoche.

Shambhala Center of Seattle

Shambhala Center of Seattle is one of many centers worldwide following the teachings of the Vidyadhara, the Ven. Chogyam Trungpa Rinpoche. We pursue his form of teaching and practice through the Three Gates: (1) Dharmadhatu—Kagyu/Nyingma Tibetan Buddhist practices, (2) Shambhala, or the Sacred Path of the Warrior—a secular approach to meditation, and (3) Nalanda—Sacred Arts. For additional information, please

Chenrezig

TWICE WEEKLY, STUDENTS AT SEATTLE'S SAKYA Monastery of Tibetan Buddhism practice "Chenrezig Meditation." *Chenrezig* is the Tibetan name for *Avalokiteshvara*, the Bodhisattva of Compassion. *Chenrezig* is the embodiment of compassion and lovingkindness, two aspects of enlightened mind. The Buddha taught that "lovingkindness" is the wish for all beings to be happy, and that "compassion" is the aspiration that they be free from suffering.

During *Chenrezig* meditation, the sacred six-syllable mantra *OM MANI PADME HUM*, is recited. Each sylla-ble corresponds to a particular realm of beings: the human realm, the animal realm, the hungry ghost realm, and so on. As we recite this mantra garland, we think about the beings in these realms and pray that they be free of suffering and experience great happiness.

Adrienne Chan

For more information, contact: Sakya Monastery of Tibetan Buddhism, 108 Northwest 83rd Street, Seattle, Washington 98117; (206) 789-2573.

---

refer to Shambhala International, Halifax, Nova Scotia, Canada.
ADDRESS: 919 East Pike Street, Third Floor, Seattle, WA 98122
PHONE: (206) 860-4060
E-MAILS: vincent54@aol.com *or* flipdance@speakeasy.org
LINEAGE: Tibetan Kagyu-Nyingma
SPIRITUAL HEAD: Sakyong Mipham Rinpoche
CONTACT: Bill Walters, Director
AFFILIATION: Shambhala International, Halifax, Nova Scotia
PUBLICATIONS: *Garuda*, a monthly newsletter.

Tara Mandala Practice Group

Students of Namkhai Norbu Rinpoche and Tsultrim Allione do ongoing Tibetan Buddhist practices including *Mandarava*, *Simhamulcha*, and *Chod*. This group is open only to those with transmission for Namkhai Norbu's practices.
ADDRESS: Seattle, WA
PHONE: (206) 282-1480
SPIRITUAL HEADS: Namkhai Norbu Rinpoche; Tsultrim Allione

CONTACT: Ellen Zigler
AFFILIATION: Autonomous
MEDITATION PROGRAM: One evening per week of *Mandarava, Simhamulcha,* and *Chod* practices.

Tsechen Kunkhyab Choling

H. H. Jigdal Dagchen Sakya leads Tibetan Buddhist meditation on *Chenrezig* (Avalokiteshvara), emanation of compassion. Also special observances each month according to the Tibetan lunar calendar.
ADDRESS: 4045 49th Avenue Southwest, #69, Olympia, WA 98512
PHONE: (206) 789-2573
LINEAGE: Tibetan
SPIRITUAL HEAD: H. H. Jigdal Dagchen Sakya
CONTACT: D. Farrell
AFFILIATION: "Very small branch of Sakya Monastery (Seattle)."
FACILITIES: Urban center.
MEDITATION PROGRAM: One evening and one morning per week of Tibetan Buddhist meditation on *Chenrezig*. Monthly lunar observances.

Vajralama Buddhist Center

Genkebang Jangsem teaches Kadampa Buddhism using guided meditation and relaxation techniques.
ADDRESS: c/o Genkebang Jangsem, Box 23327, Seattle, WA 98102-0627
PHONE: (206) 860-1975
LINEAGE: Tibetan Kadampa Tradition
SPIRITUAL HEAD: Genkebang Jangsem
CONTACT: Same
AFFILIATION: Autonomous
FACILITIES: University Friends Center in Seattle, Stonehouse Bookstore in Richmond.
MEDITATION PROGRAM: Introductory evening classes, guided meditation.

Vajrasamayas Trust

Ven. Kender Taylor is a licensed Vajrasattva family practitioner of tantric medicine and power practices. He gives *Padmasambhava abishekha* and practice instructions as individualized transmission. The style is outwardly informal but extremely direct, practical, and rigorous. As in ancient India, all aspects of life are integrated into the yogic prescription. Nonsectarian composite yogic practice is strongly encouraged. Emphasis is on wholeness, balance, continuity, and intensity of practice, based on appropriate technique and courage.

ADDRESS: Box 33393, Seattle, WA 98133-0393

PHONE: (206) 522-1810

FAX: Same

LINEAGE: *Arya Mata Tara, Ling Shen (Mahamudra, Padmasambhava Atiyoga), Ptesan Win Cinnunpa* (White Buffalo Calf Woman Sacred Pipe), *Kundalini Yoga, Ayurveda, Shangpa Kagyu,* and *Vimalamitra Nyingtik.*

CONTACT: Ven. Acarya Kender Taylor, Resident Director

AFFILIATION: The central Asian inner medical tantric lineages and the restoration spiritual ecology movement.

MEDITATION PROGRAM: Internal energy yogas. Wrathful Nyingma Three Roots Practice. *Atiyoga.*

WISCONSIN

Deer Park

Deer Park is the Dalai Lama's midwestern headquarters. He has been here many times and has offered at least two initiations including the first Kalachakra offered in the West.

ADDRESS: 4548 Schneider Road, Oregon, WI 53575

PHONE: (608) 835-5572

LINEAGE: Tibetan

SPIRITUAL HEAD: Geshe Lhundup Sopa

CONTACT: Jim Westbrook

AFFILIATION: Midwestern headquarters for the Dalai Lama.

FACILITIES: Temple and residence.

RETREATS OFFERED: *Lam Rim, Tara, Vajra Yogini Sadhana,* others.

Drikung Kagyu Center of Madison

We are students of the Ven. (and very joyous) Khenpo Konchog Gyaltsen Rinpoche, of the Drikung Kagyu lineage of Tibetan Buddhism. Every good teacher is a living Buddha; Khenpo Rinpoche is a very good teacher . . . therefore. . . . We are affiliated with Khenpo Rinpoche's other centers, primarily the Tibetan Meditation Center in Frederick, Maryland.

ADDRESS: 6505 Olympic Drive, Madison, WI 53705

PHONE: (608) 829-3541

LINEAGE: Tibetan, Drikung Kagyu

SPIRITUAL HEAD: Ven. Khenpo Konchog Gyaltsen Rinpoche

CONTACT: Ron Burian

AFFILIATION: Tibetan Meditation Center, Frederick, Maryland

ESTABLISHED: 1992

FACILITIES: Members' homes.

MEDITATION PROGRAM: Practice and Dharma study twice weekly.

Eau Claire Dharma Study Group

For additional information, please refer to Shambhala International, Halifax, Nova Scotia, Canada.

ADDRESS: 126 Gilbert Avenue, Eau Claire, WI 54701

PHONE: (715) 834-9612

FAX: (715) 936-2380 (Attn: Rita Gross)

LINEAGE: Tibetan Kagyu-Nyingma

SPIRITUAL HEADS: Sakyong Mipham Rinpoche; Chogyam Trungpa Rinpoche (Founder)

CONTACT: Rita Gross

AFFILIATION: Shambhala International, Halifax, Nova Scotia

ESTABLISHED: 1977

Inner Buddha Center

Paldan Lotsawa has been translating Buddhist texts for teachers and pupils of all schools of Tibetan Buddhism since 1988 and is working to revive the Jonangpa school in this way. We are Asian and American by background and are both scholars and practitioners. The following quote from Taranatha's *Buddha Guru Yoga* speaks to the reason for the center and its name:

> Eternally isolated from all
>   conceptual viewpoints,
> in me the very *dharmakaya* of the
>   conqueror dwells.
> Yet just as a flower has a dance and
>   a flower has a smell,
> there are two form bodies and so I
>   am not inconsequential.

ADDRESS: 522 State Street, Apartment C, Madison, WI 53703

PHONE: (608) 286-9154

LINEAGE: Tibetan Impartialist

SPIRITUAL HEAD: Buddha

CONTACT: Paldan Lotsawa (Jim Rutke)

AFFILIATION: Autonomous

ESTABLISHED: 1996

FACILITIES: Members' homes.

MEDITATION PROGRAM: Buddha Guru Yoga, Long-Life Tara; personal instruction in Nyingma and Sarma Tantras.

RETREATS OFFERED: Please call for scheduled retreats.

PUBLICATIONS: In preparation.

Institute of Tibetan Literary Studies

A society of translators of Tibetan literature, literary criticism, poetry, political texts, and works in the humanities and social sciences. Our magnum opus is a multivolume translation of the *Gesar of Ling Epic.* We raise grant money to support Tibetan scholars in full-time translation work. You might think of the institute as a kind of "think tank" for Tibetan translators who live, practice, study, and work together.

ADDRESS: 3487 North Cramer, Milwaukee, WI 53211

PHONE: (414) 967-0311

E-MAIL: rkornman@csd.uwm.edu

LINEAGE: Representatives of all Tibetan traditions.

CONTACT: Dr. Robin Kornman, Ph.D., Resident Director

ESTABLISHED: 1994

FACILITIES: Two residential houses, shrine room, library with computers, classrooms.

MEDITATION PROGRAM: Daily morning and evening practice for residents and visiting translators.

PUBLICATIONS: *Tibetan Institute of Literary Studies Newsletter,* biannual.

Madison Dharma Study Group

For additional information, please refer to Shambhala International, Halifax, Nova Scotia, Canada.

ADDRESS: 109 Acadia Drive, Madison, WI 53717

PHONE: (608) 833-1767

LINEAGE: Tibetan Kagyu-Nyingma

SPIRITUAL HEAD: Sakyong Mipham Rinpoche

CONTACT: Lora Wiggins

AFFILIATION: Shambhala International, Halifax, Nova Scotia

Mahayana Dharma Center

No description available.

ADDRESS: RR3, 6595 Clyde Road, Spring Green, WI 53588

PHONE: (608) 583-5311

FAX: (608) 583-4243

LINEAGE: Tibetan

SPIRITUAL HEAD: Ven. Lama Ngawang Chojar, Teacher

CONTACT: Duane Nelson, Chair

AFFILIATION: Autonomous

FACILITIES: Dharma house.

MEDITATION PROGRAM: Weekly meditation and prayer sessions, ongoing classes in Buddhist philosophy, Tibetan

language, and *Lam Rim. Lam Rim* refers to the stages of the spiritual path. It starts with the elementary aspects of the teaching and goes, stage by stage, to full enlightenment. Early stages include understanding karma and impermanence, taking refuge, and so forth.

Milwaukee Shambhala Center

For additional information, please refer to Shambhala International, Halifax, Nova Scotia, Canada.

ADDRESS: 2344 North Oakland Avenue, Milwaukee, WI 53211

PHONE: (414) 277-8020

E-MAIL: aka@csd.uwm.edu

LINEAGE: Tibetan Kagyu-Nyingma

SPIRITUAL HEAD: Sakyong Mipham Rinpoche

CONTACTS: Al Anderson, (414) 272-7191 and Richard Siebold, (414) 332-7501

AFFILIATION: Shambhala International, Halifax, Nova Scotia

ESTABLISHED: 1977

FACILITIES: Urban meditation center.

Padmasambhava Buddhist Center of Madison

No description available.

ADDRESS: 205 North Ingersoll, Madison, WI 53703

PHONE: (608) 255-4588

FAX: (608) 255-1446

E-MAIL: graphite@msn.fullfeed.com

LINEAGE: Tibetan Nyingma

SPIRITUAL HEADS: Khenchen Palden Sherab and Khenpo Tsewang Dongyal (The Two Khenpos)

CONTACT: Annalou Zeitz

AFFILIATION: Padmasambhava Buddhist Center, New York

ESTABLISHED: 1996

FACILITIES: Member's home: shrine room, lama residence room.

MEDITATION PROGRAM: One evening per

week of meditation, Guru Yoga, and Heart Sutra practice. Lunar calendar celebrations.

RETREATS OFFERED: Biannual weekend retreat and teaching with the Khenpos.

PUBLICATIONS: Yearly nationwide Padmasambhava Buddhist Centers newsletter.

CANADA
ALBERTA

Buddhist Center of Edmonton

We hold *Pho-wa* retreats, a practice that enables one to die without fear. We also hold empowerment initiations by Tschechu Rinpoche: *Chenrezig* or *Avalokiteshvara* (Loving Eyes), Green Tara, *Vajrasattva* (Diamond Mind), *Amitabha* (Buddha of Limitless Light), and Buddha of Long Life.

ADDRESS: c/o Beebe 11115 35 A Avenue, Edmonton, AB T6J 0A4

LINEAGE: Tibetan Karma Kagyu

SPIRITUAL HEADS: Lama Ole Nydahl and Shamar Rinpoche

CONTACT: Roy Beebe

AFFILIATION: Autonomous

ESTABLISHED: 1993

MEDITATION PROGRAM: Weekly, evening open meditation. We invite teachers and organize public lectures, courses, and retreats.

Chin Yin Tang Buddhist Society

No description available.

ADDRESS: 10853 98th Street, Edmonton, AB T5H 2P6

PHONE: (403) 423-0447

FAX: (403) 426-3230

LINEAGE: Chinese Vajrayana: True Buddha School

SPIRITUAL HEAD: Grand Master Sheng-yen Lu

Edmonton Shambhala Center

For additional information, please refer to Shambhala International, Halifax, Nova Scotia, Canada.

ADDRESS: 10110 124th Street #207, Edmonton, AB T5N 1P6
PHONE: (403) 482-7378
FAX: (403) 492-1186 (Attn: VDH Communications, Susan Boychuk)
E-MAIL: dveastsun@ccinet.ab.ca
LINEAGE: Tibetan Kagyu-Nyingma
SPIRITUAL HEAD: Sakyong Mipham Rinpoche
CONTACTS: Elaine Phillips and Diane Rider, Coordinators
AFFILIATION: Shambhala International, Halifax, Nova Scotia
ESTABLISHED: 1975
FACILITIES: Urban meditation center.

Gaden Samten Ling

Since its founding in 1986, Gaden Samten Ling has grown into a large *sangha* of members and friends. Its aim is to provide interested students with instruction in Tibetan Mahayana Buddhism. We meet twice weekly for regular practice, meditation, and teachings led by Geshe Kaldan. We learn the basic foundations of Buddhism and how to integrate them into our modern society. In addition, Geshe Kaldan and visiting teachers give initiations and retreats throughout the year. We hold a Tibetan Bazaar each fall and numerous other fund-raisers. Please write for more information.

ADDRESS: 9006 115th Avenue, Northwest, Edmonton, AB T5B 0L9
PHONE: (403) 468-5513
LINEAGE: Tibetan Gelugpa
SPIRITUAL HEAD: H. H. Ven. Gaden Tri Rinpoche Yeshe Dondup
CONTACT: Ven. Geshe Ngawang Kaldan, Resident Teacher
AFFILIATION: Autonomous
ESTABLISHED: 1986

FACILITIES: Meditation room, library
MEDITATION PROGRAM: *Lam Rim,* sutras, tantra. Visiting teachers offer *Vajrayogini, Heruka, Chod* teachings, *Yamantaka.*
RETREATS OFFERED: *Chenrezig*, White Tara, Green Tara, Medicine Buddha, *Vajrasattva, Zhambala.*

Karma Tashi Ling

Karma Tashi Ling is a Kagyu Tibetan Buddhist meditation society under the guidance of the Very Ven. Thrangu Rinpoche. Regular *Chenrezig* practice and meditation is held weekly (call for schedule). Guests and new members are always welcome. For those who have received the Guru Rinpoche empowerment, we perform the *Guru Rinpoche Koncho Chidu sadhana* on Sunday mornings. Private and/or group meditation instruction is available upon request.

ADDRESS: 10762 82nd Avenue, Edmonton, AB T6L 1B4
PHONE: (403) 482-6288
FAX: Same
LINEAGE: Tibetan Kagyu
SPIRITUAL HEAD: The Very Ven. Thrangu Rinpoche
CONTACT: Mike Jensen
AFFILIATION: Autonomous
ESTABLISHED: 1985
FACILITIES: Shrine room and study center.
MEDITATION PROGRAM: Twice-weekly meetings.
PUBLICATIONS: Newsletter

Marpa Gompa Changchup Ling

Marpa Gompa Changchup Ling is dedicated to the promotion, practice, and study of Tibetan Buddhism. The society is under the spiritual guidance of Vajra Acharya Lama Karma Thinley Rinpoche, living in Toronto, and his representative, resident dharma teacher Choge Susan Hutchison (Karma Khandro).

ADDRESS: 1346 Frontenac Avenue Southwest, Calgary, AB 72T 1B8
PHONE: (403) 244-2382
FAX: Same
LINEAGE: Tibetan Karma Kagyu
SPIRITUAL HEAD: Vajra Acharya Lama Karma Thinley Rinpoche
CONTACT: Choge Susan Hutchison (Karma Khandro)
AFFILIATION: Kampo Gangra Drupgyudling, Toronto, Ontario
ESTABLISHED: 1977
FACILITIES: Shrine room.
RETREATS OFFERED: Short retreats according to demand.
PUBLICATIONS: Occasional newsletter.

Pai Yuin Tang Buddhist Congregation

No description available.

ADDRESS: 1809 Centre Street North, Calgary, AB T2E 2S5
PHONE: (403) 230-7427
LINEAGE: Chinese Vajrayana: True Buddha School
SPIRITUAL HEAD: Grand Master Shengyen Lu
AFFILIATION: Ling Shen Ching Tse Temple

BRITISH COLUMBIA

Buddhist Association of Interfaith Services

Open to all interested.

ADDRESS: 5810 Wilson Ave, Duncan, BC V9L 1K4
PHONE: (250) 746-8110
LINEAGE: Tibetan Gelugpa
SPIRITUAL HEAD: H. H. the Dalai Lama
CONTACT: Jhampa Shaneman, Resident Director
AFFILIATION: Autonomous
ESTABLISHED: 1984
FACILITIES: Residential facility.

CANADA: BRITISH COLUMBIA
(*cont.*)

MEDITATION PROGRAM: Weekly meditation.

RETREATS OFFERED: Periodic weekend retreats; extensive individual retreats.

Chagdud Gonpa

For people associated with Chagdud Tulku Rinpoche.

ADDRESS: 2034 Stephens Street, Vancouver, BC V5V 3K5

PHONE: (604) 733-5583

LINEAGE: Tibetan Nyingmapa

SPIRITUAL HEAD: H. E. Chagdud Tulku Rinpoche

AFFILIATION: Autonomous. Associated with Rigdzin Ling, Chagdud Gonpa Foundation in Junction City, California.

ESTABLISHED: 1986

MEDITATION PROGRAM: Weekly meditation.

RETREATS OFFERED: Only when a teacher visits.

Dharma Group Vancouver

No description available.

ADDRESS: c/o Jolanta Pyra, #201 1230 East Eighth Avenue, Vancouver, BC V5T 1V2

PHONE: (604) 876-3875

FAX: (604) 875-9606

LINEAGE: Tibetan Kagyu

SPIRITUAL HEAD: Lama Ole Nydahl

CONTACT: Jolanta Pyra

AFFILIATION: Kamtsang Choling International Centers

Dzogchen Vancouver

No description available.

ADDRESS: #305, 11806 88th Avenue, Delta, BC V4C 3C5

PHONE: (604) 597-6990

LINEAGE: Tibetan Nyingma

SPIRITUAL HEAD: Namkhai Norbu Rinpoche

Kagyu Kunkhyab Chuling— Burnaby

We have retreat land on Saltspring Island with accommodation for private retreats and organized group seminars. Kagyu Kunkhyab Chuling offers seminars on Saltspring Island on approximately three long weekends every year—April, August, and October or November. Open to anyone interested in the Tibetan Kagyu tradition of Buddhism.

ADDRESS: 4939 Sidley Street, Burnaby, BC V5J 1T6

PHONE: (604) 434-4920

FAX: Same

E-MAIL: ldavis@eznet.ca

LINEAGE: Tibetan Kagyu

SPIRITUAL HEAD: Lama Tsengyur Rinpoche

CONTACTS: Haike Nissen and Sabina Kirst

AFFILIATION: Kalu Rinpoche/Kagyu Dharma/affiliated with other groups throughout British Columbia.

FACILITIES: Residential meditation center; rural retreat facility.

MEDITATION PROGRAM: Daily meditation and regular evening *pujas,* Tibetan language classes, Ngondro practices (summer).

RETREATS OFFERED: Three-year retreats; retreats with residential director and visiting teachers.

PUBLICATIONS: *Endless Knot,* quarterly.

Kagyu Kunkhyab Chuling— Victoria

No description available.

ADDRESS: #302, 733 Johnson Street, Victoria, BC V8W 3C7

PHONE: (604) 434-4920

LINEAGE: Tibetan Kagyu

SPIRITUAL HEAD: Kalu Rinpoche

AFFILIATION: Kagyu Kunkhyab Chuling in Burnaby, British Columbia.

ESTABLISHED: 1987

MEDITATION PROGRAM: Nightly meditation and *puja,* Shakyamuni prayer, *Chenrezig puja,* and silent and walking meditation. Call for times.

Kootenay Shambhala Centre

Kootenay Shambhala Centre began under the spiritual leadership of Chogyam Trungpa Rinpoche, when a few desperate students gathered to practice meditation in a living room. In 1979 he came to visit and a center was quickly brought into being on the third floor of a heritage building on the main street of Nelson. Still in the same location, we offer sitting meditation instruction, Shambhala Training, a variety of classes, and open houses. We meditate together in our beautiful shrine room on a regularly scheduled basis. Newcomers and explorers are welcome. For additional information, please refer to Shambhala International, Halifax, Nova Scotia.

ADDRESS: Box 136, Nelson, BC V1L 5P7

PHONE: (604) 352-1714

LINEAGE: Tibetan Kagyu-Nyingma

SPIRITUAL HEAD: Sakyong Mipham Rinpoche

CONTACT: Russel Rodgers

AFFILIATION: Shambhala International, Halifax, Nova Scotia

ESTABLISHED: 1976

FACILITIES: Urban center at 444 Baker Street; retreat cabin in the mountains.

MEDITATION PROGRAM: Thrice-weekly meditation. Call for times.

PUBLICATIONS: Bimonthly newsletter.

Kunzang Dechen Osel Ling

Kunzang Dechen Osel Ling was founded by Ven. Kalu Rinpoche in 1975 and named after his own retreat center in

Tibet. Three three-year retreats have been completed here. Both group and individual retreats of varying lengths are offered, which provide an opportunity to deepen one's practice. There are group meditations mornings and evenings daily, and silence is maintained each day until noon. Tibetan language classes and meditation instruction are available.

ADDRESS: 268 Mt. Tuam Road, Saltspring Island, BC V8K 1V5
PHONE: (604) 380-8610
LINEAGE: Tibetan
SPIRITUAL HEAD: Founded by Ven. Kalu Rinpoche
AFFILIATION: Kagyu Kunkhyab Chuling, Burnaby, British Columbia.
ESTABLISHED: 1975
FACILITIES: Residential retreat center and library.
MEDITATION PROGRAM: Two daily group meditations.
RETREATS OFFERED: Residential retreats, monthly full-day retreats, three-year retreats.

PTT Buddhist Society

No description available.

ADDRESS: 514 Keefer Street, Vancouver, BC V6A 1Y3
PHONE: (604) 255-3811
FAX: (604) 255-8894
LINEAGE: Chinese Vajrayana, True Buddha School
SPIRITUAL HEAD: Grand Master Sheng-yen Lu
AFFILIATION: Ling Shen Ching Tse Temple

Sakya Tsechen Thubten Ling

No description available.

ADDRESS: 9471 Beckwith, Richmond, BC V6X 1V8
PHONES: (604) 275-1915 and (604) 244-9550

FAX: (604) 275-1989
E-MAIL: sakya@unix.ubc.ca
LINEAGE: Tibetan Sakya
CONTACT: Jetsun Chime Luding
AFFILIATION: Shakya Monastery, India
ESTABLISHED: 1988
FACILITIES: New property in Richmond.
MEDITATION PROGRAM: *Pujas*, offerings. Jetsun is authorized for all teachings in her lineage.

Siddhartha's Intent

Dzongsar Jamyang Khyentse Rinpoche is the spiritual head of Siddhartha's Intent, a vehicle for the modern expression of traditional Buddhism through religious, educational, and social activities. A high-ranking reincarnated Tibetan lama and teacher, Rinpoche is articulate in English and well-versed in the ways of the West. Under his direction, members of Siddhartha's Intent have committed themselves to traditionally prescribed activities as a means of working toward the following goals: pacification of war, prevention of disease, and the restoration of the power of the natural elements.

ADDRESS: 486 West 26th Avenue, Vancouver, BC V5Y 2K2
PHONE: (604) 875-8552
FAX: (604) 873-8262
E-MAIL: 103430.2571@compuserve.com
LINEAGE: Rime (all four schools, mostly Nyingma-Sakya)
SPIRITUAL HEAD: H. E. Dzongsar Jamyang Khyentse Rinpoche
AFFILIATION: Siddhartha's Intent headquarters in Armdale, Nova Scotia.
ESTABLISHED: Unofficially before 1989; incorporated, 1993.
FACILITIES: Sea to Sky Retreat Centre (ssrc@cyberstore.ca)
MEDITATION PROGRAM: Group meditation during special retreat programs. Rinpoche gives teachings at least once a year. Other Rinpoches also invited to teach.

Tantric Buddhist Society/Pu T'o Tang

At Tantric Buddhist Society (TBS) the main practices are Taoist as well as Tantric and Sutric Buddhist. Weekly yoga practice sessions include mantra chanting, meditation, and buddhadharma preaching. During Buddha's Birthday celebrations we conduct ceremonies of Divine Blessing, Soul-deliverance, and *Fire` Puja*. We also perform funeral services. TBS is a retail outlet for Buddhist statues, instruments, *vajras*, bells, banners, utensils, and shrine decorations. This organization is a Canadian-government-registered nonprofit society.

ADDRESS: #100, 11800 Voyageur Way, Richmond, BC V6X 3G9
PHONE: (604) 279-0048
FAX: (604) 279-0046
E-MAIL: tichiu@skyinternet.ca
LINEAGE: Chinese Vajrayana (True Buddha School); Taoist
SPIRITUAL HEAD: Grand Master Sheng-yen Lu
CONTACT: Master Tige Chiu, Resident Director
AFFILIATION: True Buddha School
ESTABLISHED: 1994
FACILITIES: Temple
MEDITATION PROGRAM: Weekly yoga practice includes mantra, meditation, sermon.

Tashi Choling

Tashi Choling Mahayana Buddhist Meditation Society is dedicated to providing opportunities for personal, mental, creative, intellectual, and spiritual growth through traditional Tibetan Buddhist programs such as meditation, retreats, courses, philosophy, and language training.

ADDRESS: PO Box 4, Nelson, BC V1L 4P5
LINEAGE: Tibetan Gelugpa

SPIRITUAL HEAD: Venerable Zasep Tulku
Rinpoche
AFFILIATION: Autonomous
ESTABLISHED: 1980
MEDITATION PROGRAM: Weekly
RETREATS OFFERED: Occasionally
PUBLICATIONS: *Sukhasiddhi Quarterly
Newsletter*

Thubten Choling

Jhampa, a monk for fourteen years in
India, established this center in 1984.
Thubten Choling now offers a meditation
hall, one acre of land for quiet walks
around our stupa, and a small suite for
use by retreatants. Weekly teachings are
offered along with occasional weekend
retreats. The teachings are given by both
Maria and Jhampa Shaneman and offer a
pleasant adaptation of Tibetan Buddhism
to a Western cultural setting. English is
the medium for prayer and meditation.
With our proximity to the Cowichan
River and land reserve, we are truly the
western paradise.
ADDRESS: 5810 Wilson Avenue, Duncan,
BC V9L 1K4
PHONE: (604) 746-8110
FAX: (604) 746-8110, ext. 8
E-MAIL: JhampaS@duncan.island.net
WWW: http://www.mala.bc.ca/~
shanemanj/wwwhome.htm
LINEAGE: Tibetan
SPIRITUAL HEAD: H.H. the Dalai Lama
CONTACT: Jhampa Shaneman
AFFILIATION: Autonomous
ESTABLISHED: 1984
FACILITIES: Meditation hall, retreat suite,
stupa.
RETREATS OFFERED: Individual and orga-
nized groups.
PUBLICATIONS: Quarterly newsletter.

Vancouver Shambhala Center

Buddhist Open House every Monday
evening, Shambhala Open House on
Wednesday nights. Includes meditation
instruction, talk, discussion, and tea.
Bookstore offering a good selection of
books by Chogyam Trungpa Rinpoche
and other teachers. Various weekend pro-
grams; calendar and newsletter available.
For additional information, please refer
to Shambhala International, Halifax,
Nova Scotia.
ADDRESS: 3275 Heather Street,
Vancouver, BC V5Z 3K4
PHONE: (604) 874-8420
E-MAIL: mmcclen@direct.ca
LINEAGE: Tibetan Kagyu-Nyingma
SPIRITUAL HEAD: Sakyong Mipham Rin-
poche
CONTACT: Rolf Cutts, Coordinator
AFFILIATION: Shambhala International,
Halifax, Nova Scotia
FACILITIES: Meditation center.
MEDITATION PROGRAM: Weekend pro-
grams, evening classes.
PUBLICATIONS: *Vancouver Shambhala
Center Newsletter,* bimonthly.

Victoria Buddhist Dharma Society/
Sakya Thubten Kunga Choling

The Victoria Buddhist Dharma Society
was founded in 1974 by Geshe Tashi
Namgyal and reorganized by him in
1976. The center is affiliated with the
Sakya tradition of Tibetan Buddhism,
headed by H. H. Sakya Trizin, whose
headquarters are in Dehra Dun, India.
The salient feature of this center is the
presence of its resident lama.
ADDRESS: 1149 Leonard Street, Victoria,
BC V8V 2S3
PHONE: (604) 385-4828
FAX: Same
LINEAGE: Tibetan Sakya
SPIRITUAL HEAD: H. H. Sakya Trizin
CONTACTS: Geshe Tashi Namgyal, Resi-
dent Teacher; Sister Margaret, Contact
Person

AFFILIATION: Sakya Centre, Dehra Dun,
India
ESTABLISHED: 1974
FACILITIES: Daily ceremonies and medi-
tations.
RETREATS OFFERED: Several times annu-
ally.
PUBLICATIONS: Sixteen booklets and six
*sadhanas. Basics of Buddhism for Begin-
ners.*

Victoria Shambhala Center

For additional information, please refer
to Shambhala International, Halifax,
Nova Scotia.
ADDRESS: 560 Johnson Street, #304,
Market Square, Victoria, BC V8W 3C7
PHONE: (604) 383-9108
FAX: (604) 595-1919
E-MAIL: ctr@pinc.com
LINEAGE: Tibetan Kagyu-Nyingma
SPIRITUAL HEAD: Sakyong Mipham Rin-
poche
CONTACTS: Kerry Crofton, Director; Lee
and Martin White, Coordinators
AFFILIATION: Shambhala International,
Halifax, Nova Scotia

Zuru Ling Society

A Tibetan Buddhist group that sponsors
evening meditation practice. In addition,
Anita Ann McNeil conducts weekly in-
troductory classes, a weekly class on the
path of H. H. the Dalai Lama, and a Bud-
dhist Women's Support Group.
ADDRESS: #318, 336 East First Avenue,
Vancouver, BC V5T 1A7
PHONE: (604) 874-7655
E-MAIL: ezaleschuk@direct.com
LINEAGE: Tibetan Gelugpa
SPIRITUAL HEAD: Zasep Tulku Rinpoche
CONTACT: Anita Ann McNeil

AFFILIATION: Gaden Choling, Toronto, Ontario
ESTABLISHED: 1982
FACILITIES: City temple.
MEDITATION PROGRAM: Weekly beginners' instruction and study; *sadhana/ puja* practice for more advanced practitioners.
RETREATS OFFERED: When teacher visits. Also initiations.

MANITOBA

Winnipeg Dharma Study Group

For additional information, please refer to Shambhala International, Halifax, Nova Scotia.
ADDRESS: 847 Westminster Avenue, Winnipeg, MB R3G 1A7
PHONE: (204) 772-5808
LINEAGE: Tibetan Kagyu-Nyingma
SPIRITUAL HEAD: Sakyong Mipham Rinpoche
CONTACT: Dawn Rogers, Coordinator
AFFILIATION: Shambhala International, Halifax, Nova Scotia

NEW BRUNSWICK

Fredericton Shambhala Study Group

For additional information, please refer to Shambhala International, Halifax, Nova Scotia.
ADDRESS: Nortondale RR#1, Millville, NB E0H 1M0
PHONE: (506) 463-2758
LINEAGE: Tibetan Kagyu-Nyingma
SPIRITUAL HEAD: Sakyong Mipham Rinpoche
CONTACT: Vait Weber, Coordinator
AFFILIATION: Shambhala International, Halifax, Nova Scotia

NEWFOUNDLAND

St. John's Shambhala Study Group

For additional information, please refer to Shambhala International, Halifax, Nova Scotia.
ADDRESS: 21 Monchy Street, St. John's, NF A1C 5A7
PHONE: (709) 722-8056
E-MAIL: dimitri@morgan.ucs.mun.ca
LINEAGE: Tibetan Kagyu-Nyingma
SPIRITUAL HEAD: Sakyong Mipham Rinpoche
CONTACT: Mike Munro
AFFILIATION: Shambhala International, Halifax, Nova Scotia

NOVA SCOTIA

Annapolis Royal Dharma Study Group

For additional information, please refer to Shambhala International, Halifax, Nova Scotia.
ADDRESS: RR#2, Box 2047A, Granville Ferry, NS B0S 1K0
PHONE: (902) 532-7189
E-MAIL: tbell@fox.nstn.ns.ca
LINEAGE: Tibetan Kagyu-Nyingma
SPIRITUAL HEAD: Sakyong Mipham Rinpoche
CONTACT: Christine Sloan
AFFILIATION: Shambhala International, Halifax, Nova Scotia

Celtic Buddhist Society of the Crazy Heart Lineage

No description available.
ADDRESS: 6865 Quinpool Road, Halifax, NS B3L 1C5
PHONE: (902) 422-2756
LINEAGE: Celtic and Tibetan
SPIRITUAL HEAD: Ven. Seonaidh
AFFILIATION: Autonomous

ESTABLISHED: 1990
MEDITATION PROGRAM: Insight Meditation and Deity Yoga.

Dorje Denma Ling

For additional information, please refer to Shambhala International, Halifax, Nova Scotia.
ADDRESS: Willow Church Road, Tatamagouche, NS B0K 1V0
PHONE: (902) 657-9085
E-MAIL: lamabob@aol.com
LINEAGE: Tibetan Kagyu-Nyingma
SPIRITUAL HEAD: Sakyong Mipham Rinpoche
CONTACT: Bob Rader
AFFILIATION: Shambhala International, Halifax, Nova Scotia

Gampo Abbey

Gampo Abbey is a monastery of the Kagyu lineage of Tibetan Buddhism. Founded by Chogyam Trungpa Rinpoche in 1984, it is an affiliate of the Vajradhatu Buddhist Church of Canada. Located on the northeastern coast of Cape Breton Island on the beautiful Cabot Trail, the abbey is surrounded by meadows and wooded hills rising above the Gulf of St. Lawrence. The main building, completed in 1988, contains living quarters for thirty people, an excellent library, and a shrine room overlooking the ocean.
ADDRESS: Pleasant Bay, Cape Breton, NS B0E 2P0
PHONE: (902) 224-2752
FAX: (902) 224-1521
E-MAIL: gampo@shambhala.org
LINEAGE: Tibetan Kagyu-Nyingma
SPIRITUAL HEADS: Thrangu Rinpoche; Abbot. Chogyam Trungpa Rinpoche; Founder.
CONTACT: Gelongma Pema Chodron, Resident Director
AFFILIATION: Shambhala International, Halifax, Nova Scotia

A New Approach to Three-Year Retreats

WHILE STUDENTS AT SOPA CHOLING (DHARMA Place of Patience) follow the traditional Karma Kagyu cycle of practices during three-year retreats—the Six Doctrines of Naropa; Mahamudra Investigation; The Outer, Inner and Secret Practices of Vajrayogini and Chakrasamvara; and so on—there are a number of factors at this center that make the retreat both more accessible and truly unique. To begin with, all instruction, practice, and even group chanting are done in English. Instead of remaining in unbroken seclusion for the entire three years, practitioners alternate between periods of seclusion and intervals of work in the world. Participants take six years to complete the cycle of practices, spending three segments of eight to ten months inside the retreat, and an equal amount of time on the outside. This allows them to integrate practice realization into the fabric of their daily lives, and to earn money for the next segment.

In a further departure from tradition, men and women participate in the retreat together. To be sure, they live in separate wings and practice and eat independently, but they do share the facilities and join each other for bimonthly feast practices and other special occasions.

The retreat accommodates forty people in alternating groups of twenty (ten men and ten women in each group). In this way Sopa Choling is always in use as a place of advanced practice for those who wish to deepen their realization and work more skillfully and compassionately for the benefit of others.

Sopa Choling is under the guidance of the Very Venerable Thrangu Rinpoche. It is located at Gampo Abbey in Cape Breton, Nova Scotia.

Pema Chödrön

For more information, contact: Gampo Abbey/Sopa Choling, Pleasant Bay, Cape Breton, Nova Scotia, Canada B0E 2P0; (902) 224-2752.

CANADA: NOVA SCOTIA (*cont.*)
ESTABLISHED: 1983
FACILITIES: Library, shrine room, individual retreat cabins, men's and women's dormitories.
RETREATS OFFERED: Annually, two *Dathun* (monthlong sitting meditation retreats). Three-year retreats.
PUBLICATIONS: Pema Chodron's books. *Profound Path of Peace*, magazine.

Halifax Shambhala Center

For additional information, please refer to Shambhala International, Halifax, Nova Scotia.
ADDRESS: 1084 Tower Road, Halifax, NS B3H 2Y5
PHONE: (902) 420-1118

FAX: (902) 423-2750
E-MAIL: david@chem1.chem.dal.ca
LINEAGE: Tibetan Kagyu-Nyingma
SPIRITUAL HEAD: Sakyong Mipham Rinpoche
CONTACTS: Moh Hardin, Shari Vogler, and David Burkholder
AFFILIATION: Shambhala International, Halifax, Nova Scotia
ESTABLISHED: 1979
FACILITIES: Urban meditation center with some facilities for solitary retreats.

St. Margaret's Bay Shambhala Cultural Center

For additional information, please refer to Shambhala International, Halifax, Nova Scotia.

ADDRESS: 1345 Peggy's Cove Road, Tantallon, NS B0J 3J0
PHONE: (902) 826-2182
LINEAGE: Tibetan Kagyu-Nyingma
SPIRITUAL HEAD: Sakyong Mipham Rinpoche
CONTACT: Rita Armbruster
AFFILIATION: Shambhala International, Halifax, Nova Scotia

Shambhala International

Shambhala International is a network of organizations founded by meditation master Chogyam Trungpa Rinpoche and directed by his son and heir, Sakyong Mipham Rinpoche. Its activities include: (1) operation of over one hundred centers worldwide including six rural retreat

Shrine Room at Shambhala International, Halifax, Nova Scotia. (Photo by Molly Nudell.)

facilities, (2) study, practice, and preservation of Buddhist teachings, (3) presentation of a body of secular wisdom, known as the Shambhala teachings, (4) founding of the Naropa Institute, North America's only Buddhist-inspired accredited college, (5) translation of Tibetan and Sanskrit texts into English and other modern languages, (6) publication of *Shambhala Sun Magazine,* and (7) sponsorship of educational, cultural, and artistic programs.
ADDRESS: 1084 Tower Road, Halifax, NS B3H 2Y5
PHONE: (902) 425-4275
FAX: (902) 423-2750
E-MAIL: shambint@ra.isisnet.com
WWW: http://www.shambhala.org
LINEAGE: Tibetan Kagyu-Nyingma
SPIRITUAL HEAD: Sakyong Mipham Rinpoche

CONTACT: John Rockwell, Executive Director
AFFILIATION: We are Shambhala International headquarters.
ESTABLISHED: 1970
FACILITIES: Over one hundred urban and rural centers.
RETREATS OFFERED: Solitary and group practice retreats.

ONTARIO

Ajax Rigpa

This is a small study group that meets to discuss and practice the teachings of Sogyal Rinpoche, author of *The Tibetan Book of Living and Dying.*
ADDRESS: 1122-50 Exeter Road, Ajax, ON L1S 2K1

PHONE: (905) 683-7314
E-MAIL: mike.butler1@sympatico.ca
LINEAGE: Tibetan
SPIRITUAL HEAD: Sogyal Rinpoche
CONTACT: Mike Butler
AFFILIATION: Rigpa Fellowship
ESTABLISHED: 1993
FACILITIES: Members' homes.

Alliston Dharma Study Group

For additional information, please refer to Shambhala International, Halifax, Nova Scotia.
ADDRESS: 92 Wellington Street West, Alliston, ON L0M 1A0
PHONE: (705) 435-9647
E-MAIL: jimcolby@bconnex.net
LINEAGE: Tibetan Kagyu-Nyingma
SPIRITUAL HEAD: Sakyong Mipham Rinpoche
CONTACT: Myra Colby
AFFILIATION: Shambhala International, Halifax, Nova Scotia

Chandrakirti Buddhist Centre

This center focuses on "The Stages of the Path to Enlightenment," the Buddha's public teachings as practiced in Tibet. It belongs to the New Kadampa Tradition, a Western movement arising from the tradition of Je Tsong Khapa. Initiations and commentary to the tantras are available from Ven. Geshe Kelsang Gyatso Rinpoche and several of his ordained Western lineage holders.
ADDRESS: Arts Court, 2 Daly Avenue, Ottawa, ON K1N 6E2
PHONE: (613) 729-6633
FAX: (613) 729-6633
E-MAIL: dgould@aix1.uottawa.ca
LINEAGE: Tibetan New Kadampa
SPIRITUAL HEAD: Ven. Geshe Kelsang Gyatso Rinpoche
CONTACT: David Gould
AFFILIATION: New Kadampa Tradition
FACILITIES: Classes at the Arts Court.

The Gates of Shambhala

IN 1992, THE MANY ACTIVITIES OF THE ORGANIZA-tion founded by Chogyam Trungpa Rinpoche were brought under the single umbrella of Shambhala, which has three gates: Vajradhatu, Shambhala Training, and Nalanda.

At Shambhala meditation centers throughout the world, would-be students can pursue training and study in any or all of these three gates, the activities of which generally coexist within a single location. A group of meditators wishing to start a center under the auspices of Shambhala are initially called a Forming Dharma Study Group. As it grows and becomes more established it becomes a Dharma Study Group, evolving eventually into a full-fledged Shambhala center.

Vajradhatu

Vajradhatu offers a comprehensive path of Buddhist meditation and study through a network of local centers called Dharmadhatus (located within Shambhala cen-

Ven. Sakyong Mi-phan Rinpoche, Spiritual Head of Shambhala International. (Photo by Diana Church.)

ters). The Vajradhatu path provides a well-defined, graduated method of developing skillful action and wisdom through meditation practice. Shambhala centers offer a full curriculum of Buddhist classes and regular periods of sitting practice. Students participate in monthlong residential retreats (*Dathuns*), as well as Vajradhatu Seminary, an extended period of intensive practice and study conducted by Sakyong Mipham Rinpoche.

Shambhala Training

Shambhala Training is a secular path of fearless and gentle action. It is open to adherents of any spiritual tradition or of no particular tradition at all. Its path of study and practice is divided into three self-contained units. The first, "Heart of Warriorship," consists of five weekend courses or "levels." The second, "Sacred Path of Warriorship," includes six weekend levels and a two-week residential program called "Warrior Assembly." Part three, "Shambhala Training Seminary," is a three-week residential retreat. Each segment offers meditation instruction, talks, group discussion, and individual interviews.

Nalanda

Nalanda comprises a number of secular disciplines and activities that integrate art and culture with everyday life, bringing a contemplative perspective to the arts, health, education, and business. It includes such traditional disciplines as poetics, visual arts, *kyudo* (archery), ikebana (flower arranging), and tea ceremony, as well as more contemporary approaches to culture and society. Some Nalanda activities occur within structured organizations; others are pursued by practitioners on an individual basis.

For more information, contact: Shambhala International, 1084 Tower Road, Halifax, Nova Scotia, Canada B3H 2Y5; (902) 425-4275; Fax: (902) 423-2750.

Meditation for Kids

At Shambhala Middle School (grades 6–11) in Halifax, Nova Scotia, students begin and end the school day with five minutes of sitting meditation. In addition, teachers insert brief gaps of meditation into the schedule whenever major transitions occur; when moving from physical education to music class, for example. For some of the younger pupils, it's a challenge just to sit still and be quiet for those brief minutes. Older students are encouraged to watch their out breath, in traditional *shamatha* fashion, and if possible, label their thoughts and return to the breath.

Teachers and students at Shambhala Middle School in Halifax, Nova Scotia, meditate together at the end of the day. (Photo by Amanda Hester.)

Sitting to begin the day creates a gap and allows everyone to start out at the same pace. At the end of classes, it gives the kids a chance to let the day's happenings settle like dust, and provides a fresh start for the rest of their day.

Only two-thirds of our students come from meditation community families. The rest tend to look upon meditation simply as a way to relax. Their parents, however, are supportive of it and encourage the staff to include contemplative aspects in other areas of the school. Yoga, Native American chants and drumming, Oriental brush calligraphy, and the study of various religious and philosophical beliefs and movements throughout history are all part of the curriculum. New possibilities continue to arise.

From the first formal bow that begins the morning sitting to the final bow that ends the day, there is for these students a quality of remembering their own mind and being. It is hoped that this early introduction to the practice will help them to understand the value of meditation in their lives.

Jane Hester

For more information, contact: Shambhala Middle School, 5450 Russell Street, Halifax, Nova Scotia, Canada, B3K 1W9; (902) 454-6100.

CANADA: ONTARIO (*cont.*)

Chandrakirti Mahayana Buddhist Centre

Founded by Tibetan Buddhist scholar and meditation master Geshe Kelsang Gyatso, Chandrakirti Centre provides an informal and friendly atmosphere for those wishing to learn about meditation and the Buddha's teachings. We offer two study programs: the General Program introduces Buddhist teachings on subjects such as meditation, psychology, and philosophy in a series of workshops and retreats; the Foundation Program provides an opportunity to deepen our understanding of Buddhadharma through a systematic study of essential Mahayana Buddhist subjects.

ADDRESS: 1055 Yonge Street, #207, Toronto, ON M4W 2L2
PHONE: (416) 929-0734
FAX: Same
E-MAIL: chandra@pathcom.com
LINEAGE: Tibetan (Je Tsong Khapa) New Kadampa Tradition
SPIRITUAL HEAD: Ven. Geshe Kelsang Gyatso Rinpoche
CONTACT: Gen Kelsang Tharchin

New Kadampa Tradition

THE FOUNDER, LINEAGE HOLDER, AND SPIRITUAL director of the New Kadampa Tradition (NKT) is the Most Venerable Geshe Kelsang Gyatso Rinpoche, a Tibetan Buddhist Master who has lived in the United Kingdom since 1977.

Kadampa Buddhism originated with the great Indian Master, Atisha, who reintroduced Buddhism into Tibet in the eleventh century. "Ka" refers to all Buddhist Sutra and Tantra teachings, and "Dam" refers to Atisha's special way of presenting them, called the "Stages of the Path," or Lamrim.

Je Tsong Khapa (1357–1419) eventually inherited the lineage. He lived at a time when Buddhism appeared to be flourishing in Tibet, though in actual fact, confusion about the doctrine and practice was destroying its spiritual essence. Through teachings and writings of unparalleled clarity and comprehensiveness and by immaculate personal example, Je Tsong Khapa single-handedly revitalized Buddhism in Tibet, giving it a new lease on life that was to last until its introduction into the West in the present century.

Our teacher Geshe Kelsang's fifteen published texts are complete commentaries on Je Tsong Khapa's teachings and writings. Geshe-la has devised special educational programs for the systematic study of these texts. Today these programs are being offered at over two hundred NKT centers worldwide. A preeminent quality of Kadampa Buddhism is that its practitioners attain enlightenment quickly, moving from joy to joy, happily, without the difficulties advanced practitioners of other traditions have had to endure. Since the time of Je Tsong Khapa, thousands of sincere practitioners have been able to attain enlightenment, some even in as little as three years.

Gen Kelsang Tharchin

For more information, contact: Chandrakirti Mahayana Buddhist Center, 1055 Yonge Street #207, Toronto, Ontario, Canada M4W 2L2; (416) 929-0734; Fax: (416) 929-0734.

CANADA: ONTARIO (*cont.*)

AFFILIATION: Headquarters center.
ESTABLISHED: 1993
FACILITIES: Classroom, meditation room, bookshop.
RETREATS OFFERED: Weekend retreats several times a year on Buddhist psychology and philosophy.
PUBLICATIONS: Fifteen books by Geshe Kelsang Gyatso; *Full Moon*, magazine (England); *New Moon*, newsletter (Canada).

Chittamani Meditation Centre

For additional information, please refer to Gaden Choling, Toronto, Ontario.

ADDRESS: 1872 Bromley Road, Ottawa, ON K1A 1C1
PHONE: (613) 728-5416
WWW: http://wwwio.org\~gaden \aden.html
LINEAGE: Tibetan Gelugpa
SPIRITUAL HEAD: Ven. Zasep Tulku Rinpoche
CONTACT: Bob Kapitany
AFFILIATION: Gaden Choling, Toronto, Ontario

Downsview Dharma Study Group

For additional information, please refer to Shambhala International, Halifax, Nova Scotia.

ADDRESS: 25 Fourwinds Drive #402, Toronto, ON M3J 1K8
PHONE: (416) 736-0854
E-MAIL: stanleyf@yorku.ca
LINEAGE: Tibetan Kagyu-Nyingma
SPIRITUAL HEAD: Sakyong Mipham Rinpoche
CONTACT: Stanley Fefferman, Coordinator
AFFILIATION: Shambhala International, Halifax, Nova Scotia
FACILITIES: Private home.

Gaden Choling

Gaden Choling is an urban *gompa* for teachings in the Tibetan Gelugpa tradi-

Gaden Relief Projects

GADEN CHOLING MEANS "JOYOUS PLACE OF Dharma." Because of our center's Mahayana emphasis, the cultivation of love and compassion is central to our activities. Mindful of H. H. the Dalai Lama's desire to express this in social action, and moved by sympathy for the sufferings of Tibetans throughout Asia, students of Zasep Tulku Rinpoche coordinate Gaden Relief Projects as the center's volunteer-run "foreign aid" wing. Gaden Relief has become famous, despite its modest size, for its efforts in channeling medicine, books, and funds to the Tibetan refugee community in exile.

Our center raises money to supply a doctor and medicine to Sera Je Monastery in South India, and to provide uninterrupted treatment for sufferers of tuberculosis, the incidence of which is more than twice as high among Tibetan refugees as it is in the general Indian population. We're helping to rebuild Zuru monastery in the Kham province of Tibet, and we collect and send books to the science library at the Institute of Buddhist Dialectics in Dharamsala, India. We are especially active in searching for sponsors for Tibetan children, monks, and nuns in need of financial support, as we are continually receiving requests for help.

Gaden Relief Projects is a Canadian registered charity authorized to issue Canadian tax receipts for most donations.

For more information, contact: Gaden Choling, 637 Christie Street, Toronto, Ontario Canada M6G 3E6; (416) 651-3849.

---

tion. Our guru, Ven. Zasep Tulku Rinpoche, travels among his affiliated centers. Gaden Choling wishes to serve as many people as possible. We are here to create an oasis of serenity amid the busy confusion of big-city life and to offer refuge, resources, and the teachings of the Gelugpa tradition. We also sponsor aid to Tibetan refugees in India through Gaden Relief Projects.

ADDRESS: 637 Christie Street, Toronto, ON M6G 3E6
PHONE: (416) 651-3849
E-MAIL: gaden@io.org
WWW: http://wwwio.org\~gaden \gaden.html
LINEAGE: Tibetan Gelugpa
SPIRITUAL HEAD: Ven. Zasep Tulku Rinpoche
CONTACT: President
AFFILIATION: Autonomous
ESTABLISHED: 1980
FACILITIES: Urban *gompa*.

MEDITATION PROGRAM: Guest teachers, *sadhana* practice, weekly evening introductory program. Phone for information.
RETREATS OFFERED: Weekend retreats, biannual pilgrimage.
PUBLICATIONS: *Gaden Choling Newsletter* and *Gaden Notes*.

Jing Sim Branch True Buddha School

No description available.
ADDRESS: 370 Hillcrest Avenue, North York, ON M2N 3P8
PHONE: (416) 298-1069
FAX: (416) 590-1938
LINEAGE: Chinese Vajrayana, True Buddha School
SPIRITUAL HEAD: Grand Master Sheng-yen Lu

Kadam Changchub Ling

Kadam Changchub Ling, founded by Lama Karma Thinley Rinpoche, is a group of dharma practitioners and friends who meet (ir)regularly for group meditation, discussion, and sharing of understanding. We are ordinary people—householders, parents, students, professionals—committed to living the dharma in our everyday world. At present we have no "official" status, structure, or membership fees. We welcome anyone who wishes to join us in our group practice. Individual meditation instruction is available.

ADDRESS: 1290 Dorchester Avenue, Ottawa, ON K1Z 8E7
PHONE: (613) 729-9493
LINEAGE: Tibetan Kagyu
SPIRITUAL HEAD: Lama Karma Thinley Rinpoche
CONTACT: Elizabeth

AFFILIATION: Autonomous

ESTABLISHED: 1977

MEDITATION PROGRAM: Weekly group *Chenrezig* and *Vipassana* meditation; meditation instruction and counseling available.

Kampo Gangra Drubgyudling

Kampo Gangra Drubgyudling is a Vajrayana meditation center of the Karma Kagyu lineage, located in the beaches area of Toronto. Founded by Lama Karma Thinley Rinpoche, it is a charitable, nonprofit corporation. Lama Karma Thinley resides here and teaches from time to time. Shamatha meditation is offered on Sunday mornings, and the shrine rooms are available for private use at other times. Attendance at *puja* requires initiation and having taken refuge.

ADDRESS: 200 Balsam Avenue, Toronto, ON M4E 3C3

PHONE: (416) 699-5718

LINEAGE: Tibetan Karma Kagyu

SPIRITUAL HEAD: Lama Karma Thinley Rinpoche

CONTACT: Board of directors who run the center.

AFFILIATION: Autonomous

ESTABLISHED: 1973

FACILITIES: Two shrine rooms, library.

MEDITATION PROGRAM: *Shamatha* meditation on Sunday mornings.

RETREATS OFFERED: *Puja*

Karma Kagyu Centre of Toronto

Karma Kagyu Centre of Toronto is the Gyalwa Karmapa Ugyen Trinley Dorje's main facility in Canada. Most of its members are Canadian Buddhist practitioners in the Tibetan tradition. During a 1980 visit to Toronto, the Karmapa installed Choje Lama Namse Rinpoche as the cen-

Bardor Tulku Rinpoche leads puja *during a visit to the Karma Kargyu Buddhist Meditation Center of Niagara, Ontario.* (Photo by Keith I. Dixon.)

ter's resident teacher and appointed him to be his personal representative in Canada. Both beginners and advanced students are welcome.

ADDRESS: 39 Triller Avenue, Toronto, ON M6K 3B7

PHONE: (416) 778-4514

LINEAGE: Tibetan Karma Kagyu

SPIRITUAL HEAD: Choje Lama Namse Rinpoche

CONTACTS: Shelley Shakespeare and Paul Fanning

AFFILIATION: We are the Canadian seat of H. H. Gyalwa Karmapa.

ESTABLISHED: 1976

MEDITATION PROGRAM: For information about programs and retreats, please contact the center.

PUBLICATIONS: *Lion's Roar Dharma News*

Karma Kargyu Buddhist Meditation Center of Niagara

Despite the fact that our name is larger than our membership, we do have a dedicated group of practitioners and a regular program of activities. We meet one night a week for *Chenrezig puja*. Sometimes *puja* is followed by basic teachings by senior students on meditation and "the three vehicles." Approximately once a month Lama Namse Rinpoche visits our center to lead *puja* or give advanced teachings, or on occasion to lead *Nyung Nye* (a three-day fasting and meditation retreat).

ADDRESS: 4 Clayburn Avenue, St. Catharines, ON L2P 2S2

PHONE: (905) 685-9132

E-MAIL: kdixon@niagara.com

LINEAGE: Tibetan Kagyu

SPIRITUAL HEAD: Cho Je Lama Namse Rinpoche

Nyung Nye

NYUNG NYE IS A THREE-DAY FASTING RETREAT devoted to *One-thousand-armed Chenrezig* (Sanskrit: Avalokiteshvara, Bodhisattva of Compassion). Although many people find the fasting difficult and the lack of liquids on the last day even more so, for me the difficulty lay in having to sit still for the two six-to-eight-hour sessions each day. It was excruciating. Collapsed in a heap at the end of the second day, I read the translation of the *puja* and found to my relief an extensive series of prayers dealing with all of the negativity that comes up during this practice. In my case, this meant praying that the anger and frustration I was feeling be dedicated to preventing others from being reborn in the "hell realms."

There were similar prayers dealing with exhaustion, hunger, thirst, and dullness. As each hindrance arose, I was supposed to pray that my experience of it would prevent rebirth in the lower realms. In so doing, I was able to overcome these obstacles. *Nyung Nye* left me with a sense of great clarity and a feeling that I could solve whatever problems came my way.

Fred Humphrey

For more information, contact: Karma Kargyu Buddhist Meditation Center of Niagara, 4 Clayburn Avenue, St. Catharines, Ontario Canada L2P 2S2; (905) 685-9132.

CONTACT: Keith Dixon
ESTABLISHED: 1983 in Niagara
FACILITIES: Shrine room and small library of books and tapes.
RETREATS OFFERED: Occasional *Nyung Nye* retreat.

Orgyan Osal Cho Dzong

Orgyan Osal Cho Dzong is a Vajrayana temple, monastery, and retreat center in the Nyingma tradition. Situated on two hundred acres of secluded forest on the slopes of Mt. Moriah, the land has abundant wildlife. The facilities were officially inaugurated and blessed by H. H. Penor Rinpoche, Supreme Head of the Nyingma, in 1988. At that time he also bestowed the long *Chen Nying Thig* and *Zab Mo Yang Thig* cycles of teaching, which are the core practices here. Rabjam Rinpoche is the center's founder and resident lama, much loved by all for his boundless wisdom and compassion.
ADDRESS: RR3 Box 68, 1755 Lingham Lake Rd, Madoc, ON K0K 2K0

PHONE: (613) 967-7432
LINEAGE: Tibetan Nyingma
SPIRITUAL HEAD: H. H. Padma Norbu Rinpoche
CONTACT: Vajracharya Ven. Lama Jampa Rabjam Rinpoche
AFFILIATION: Palyul Namdroling Monastery, Bylakuppe, Karnataka State, India
ESTABLISHED: 1984
FACILITIES: Twenty-four-hundred-square-foot temple, fifteen individual retreat rooms, shared kitchen and bath, camping.
RETREATS OFFERED: Weekend to one-month retreats on *Shamatha, Tong Len, Deity Yoga, Dzog Chen*.
PUBLICATIONS: *Orgyan Dzong News*

Ottawa Shambhala Centre

The Ottawa Shambhala Centre provides instruction and guidance in meditative and contemplative disciplines. It is part of Shambhala International, following the vision and teachings of Tibetan meditation master Chogyam Trungpa Rinpoche and dedicated to the establishment of an enlightened society. The meditation practices and studies taught at our center are from the Kagyu/Nyingma schools, as well as from the secular Shambhala tradition of Tibet. For additional information, please refer to Shambhala International, Halifax, Nova Scotia.
ADDRESS: 982 Wellington Street, Ottawa, ON K1Y 2X8
PHONE: (613) 725-9321
FAX: (613) 725-2035
E-MAIL: 73042.1466@compuserve. com
WWW: http://infoweb.magicom/ ~Dharma/shambhala.html
LINEAGE: Tibetan Kagyu-Nyingma
SPIRITUAL HEAD: Sakyong Mipham Rinpoche
CONTACT: Bozica Costigliola
AFFILIATION: Shambhala International, Halifax, Nova Scotia
ESTABLISHED: 1978
FACILITIES: Small meditation center.

Potala Meditation Centre

Our group has weekly meditation practice with readings and discussions. In addition we do group deity practices from time to time. Throughout the year, there are longer retreats and workshops featuring teachers from the Tibetan, Theravadan, and Zen traditions. We are an open group and invite anyone interested in learning about meditation and Buddhism.

ADDRESS: 118 McComber Crescent, Thunder Bay, ON P7A 7E8
PHONE: (807) 767-7889
LINEAGE: Tibetan
SPIRITUAL HEAD: Zasep Tulku Rinpoche
ESTABLISHED: 1981
MEDITATION PROGRAM: Weekly meditation practice.
RETREATS OFFERED: Retreats and workshops with teachers from all traditions.

Pure Moon Buddhist Association

No description available.
ADDRESS: 2517 Danforth Avenue, Toronto, ON M4C 1L1
PHONE: (416) 690-7803
FAX: (416) 733-7780
LINEAGE: Chinese Vajrayana; True Buddha School
SPIRITUAL HEAD: Grand Master Sheng-yen Lu

Riwoche Society/Pemavajra Temple

Open to all who are interested in Buddhist meditation.
ADDRESS: 566 Anette Street, Toronto, ON M6S 2C2
PHONE: (416) 760-8739
LINEAGE: Tibetan Vajrayana
SPIRITUAL HEAD: Ven. Khenpo Sonam Tobgyal Rinpoche
AFFILIATION: Headquarters temple affiliated with informal branches in Ontario, United States, and Asia.
ESTABLISHED: 1990
FACILITIES: Traditional temple, meditation hall, small store.
MEDITATION PROGRAM: Weekly meditation, practice instruction, lectures by visiting teachers.
RETREATS OFFERED: Occasionally

Tengye Ling Tibetan Buddhist Centre

Ven. Bhikkshuni Tenzin Kalsang (Cho-la) is founder and Spiritual Director of Tengye Ling Tibetan Buddhist Centre. She received ordination from H. H. the Dalai Lama, as well as from Master Hsing Yun. Weekly at Tengye Ling, there are *Lam-Rim* teachings and a Dharma-In-Action Workshop. Occasionally, fully qualified tantric practitioners are invited to bestow tantric initiations. Cho-la is also a psychotherapist in the Western tradition. She teaches Buddhism in public schools and universities in the Toronto area and is available to lead workshops elsewhere. Programs are open to the general public.

ADDRESS: 11 Madison Avenue, Toronto, ON M5R 2S2
PHONE: (416) 966-4656
FAX: (416) 366-9874
E-MAIL: sangha@tengyel.ca
LINEAGE: Tibetan Gelugpa
SPIRITUAL HEAD: H. H. the Dalai Lama
CONTACT: Ven. Bhikkshuni Tenzin Kalsang (Canadian)
AFFILIATION: Autonomous in Canada and affiliated with Thukche Choling Monastery/Nunnery in Kathmandu, Nepal.
ESTABLISHED: 1990
FACILITIES: Urban meditation center.
MEDITATION PROGRAM: Diverse private and public instruction.
RETREATS OFFERED: Weekends occasionally: tantric, silent Mahayana Fast-Day Vows, or Workshop.

Canadian Bhikkshuni Tenzin Kalsang of Tengye Ling in Toronto, Ontario. (Photo courtesy of Tengye Ling.)

Toronto Shambhala Centre

Established as "Toronto Dharmadhatu Buddhist Meditation Centre" in 1973 and renamed "Toronto Shambhala Centre" in 1994, this group supports the study and practice of the Karma Kagyu and Nyingma lineages of Tibetan Buddhism as taught by the Vidyadhara the Ven. Chogyam Trungpa Rinpoche, and his son, the Sawang Osel Rangdrol Mukpo (Sakyong Mipham Rinpoche). The center also presents Shambhala Training (undergraduate, graduate, and postgraduate programs) and features Nalanda Arts and Education programs with emphasis on the Miksang School of Contemplative Photography. For additional information, please see Shambhala International, Halifax, Nova Scotia.

ADDRESS: 670 Bloor Street West, Suite 300, Toronto, ON M6G 1L2

PHONES: (416) 588-6465 or (416) 534-1278 (Daniel Vokey)

E-MAIL: bs884@freenet.toronto.on.ca *or* Daniel Vokey: dvokey@oise.on.ca

LINEAGE: Tibetan Kagyu-Nyingma

SPIRITUAL HEAD: Sakyong Mipham Rinpoche

CONTACT: Daniel Vokey, Council Secretary

AFFILIATION: Shambhala International, Halifax, Nova Scotia

MEDITATION PROGRAM: Meditation two evenings per week and all day on Sundays. Call for times.

QUEBEC

Centre Bouddhiste Kankala

Centre Bouddhiste Kankala is located in the heart of Montreal and is 95% French and 5% English. Our resident teacher is Quebec native Christine Arisferry, a close disciple of Geshe Kelsang Gyatso. She teaches the dharma "Quebecois-style," with heartfelt feeling and lots of fun! Some mornings we practice Tranquil Abiding meditation, in which students will select a picture card of a Buddha and mount it on a skewer that rises up to eye level . . . it may look a little strange having a Buddha staring you in the face, but it is a lot of fun!

ADDRESS: 2120 St. Andre #3, Montreal, QC H2C 4J9

PHONE: (514) 521-2529

LINEAGE: Tibetan Je Tsong Khapa

SPIRITUAL HEADS: Ven. Geshe Kelsang Gyatso Rinpoche; Christine Arisferry, Resident Teacher

CONTACT: Scott Ferry

AFFILIATION: New Kadampa Tradition

ESTABLISHED: 1996

MEDITATION PROGRAM: Weekly, three evening classes in French, one in English; and three morning classes in French, one in English.

Chan Hai Lei Zang

No description available.

ADDRESS: 125 Rue Charlotte, Montreal, QC H2X 1MZ

PHONE: (514) 875-9578

FAX: (514) 733-3352

LINEAGE: Chinese Vajrayana, True Buddha School

SPIRITUAL HEAD: Grand Master Shengyen Lu

Kamtsang Choling—Montreal

No description available.

ADDRESS: PO Box 385, Hudson Heights, QC J0P 1J0

PHONE: (514) 458-4640

FAX: (514) 458-0978

E-MAIL: dmarc@ego.psych.mogill.ca

LINEAGE: Tibetan Karma Kagyu

SPIRITUAL HEAD: Lama Ole Nydahl

CONTACT: Lara Braitstein, Resident Director

AFFILIATION: Kamtsang Choling International Centers

ESTABLISHED: 1993

Montreal Shambhala Centre

Montreal Shambhala Centre serves a bilingual (francophone and anglophone) community. Hence, translators are used during talks, and classes are conducted in both languages. The group is comprised of roughly one-third *Shamatha* students, one-third *Tantrikas*, and one-third *Sadhakas*. We also have a good division of *kasungs* (guards). For additional information, please refer to Shambhala International, Halifax, Nova Scotia.

Le Centre Shambhala a été fondé dans les années 70 par le Vénérable Chögyam Trungpa Rinpoche, maître Bouddhiste Tibétain décédé en 1987. Les activités du centre sont basées sur la pratique de la méditation shamatha qui vise à eveiller notre esprit et à cultiver notre bonté fondamentale. C'est un endroit où sont accessibles des enseignements spirituels qui nous permettent de nous connaître et de développer des habilités à travailler avec les autres pour créer une societé éveillée. Trois portes d'entrée sont offertes au public: Dharmadhatu, la voie bouddhique; Apprentissage Shambhala, la voie sacrée du guerrier et de la guerrière; et Nalanda, la voie des arts contemplatifs et de l'éducation. Le centre offre des sessions de méditation, des classes publiques, des causeries, et des évènements spéciaux.

ADDRESS: CP 357, LaSalle, QC H8R 3V4

PHONE: (514) 279-9115 (with answering machine)

FAX: (514) 948-3003 Attn: Natalie Boisseau

E-MAIL: cguest@aei.ca

LINEAGE: Tibetan Kagyu-Nyingma

SPIRITUAL HEAD: Sakyong Mipham Rinpoche. Chogyam Trungpa Rinpoche, founder.

AFFILIATION: Shambhala International, Halifax, Nova Scotia

ESTABLISHED: 1975

FACILITIES: Urban meditation center, dharma bookstore.

MEDITATION PROGRAM: Free meditation instruction; regularly scheduled sitting meditation; monthly open houses; public classes on Buddhist topics; *Three Yanas* classes for *Shamatha* students, *Tantrikas*, and *Sadhakas*.

RETREATS OFFERED: Biannual four- or five-day intensive sitting retreats at Christmas and Easter. Call for details.

PUBLICATIONS: Biannual program schedules.

Rigpe Dorje Centre

Rigpe Dorje offers a weekly schedule of meditation practice and classes, and sponsors seminars and practice weekends. Meditation instruction is open to all. Books, incense, and other practice materials are available. For additional information, please see Karma Triyana Dharmachakra, Woodstock, New York.

Des sessions de méditation hebdomadaires ont lieu régulièrement au Centre Rigpé Dorje, de même que des cours sur le Bouddhisme. Nous organisons aussi des séminaires et des fins de semaine de pratique intensive. Des instructions sur la méditation sont toujours disponibles pour tous. On peut trouver aussi des livres, de l'encens, et d'autres objets utiles à la pratique.

ADDRESS: 5413 St. Laurent, Suite 203, Montreal, QC H2T 1S5
PHONE: (514) 278-9793
E-MAIL: rigpemtl@citenet.net
LINEAGE: Tibetan Karma Kagyu
SPIRITUAL HEAD: Ven. Khenpo Karthar Rinpoche
CONTACTS: Judy Cutler, contact; Rosalinde Bertin, Catherine Kissel, and Stephanie Colvey, Coordinators
AFFILIATION: Karma Triyana Dharmachakra, Woodstock, New York
MEDITATION PROGRAM: *Shinay* meditation, one morning per week; *Chenrezig* meditation, one evening per week. Call for times.
PUBLICATIONS: *Lion's Roar Dharma News*

Temple Bouddhiste Tibetain

Temple Bouddhiste Tibetain represents the Gelugpa lineage. Many great lamas, including H. H. the Dalai Lama, have visited and will again visit the temple, giving teachings and initiations. Practices, meditations, ceremonies, and celebrations regularly take place. Courses are offered on a regular basis. All this was begun years ago under the compassionate guidance of the late Geshe Khenrab Gajam.

ADDRESS: 1870 Avenue de l'Église, Montreal, QC H4E 1G8
PHONE: (514) 765-3515
FAX: (514) 485-5453
E-MAIL: bdcsec6@srcing.login.qc.ca
LINEAGE: Gelugpa
SPIRITUAL HEAD: The late Geshe Khenrab Gajam
CONTACT: Gary Young
AFFILIATION: Autonomous
ESTABLISHED: 1976
FACILITIES: City center with plans for rural retreat center.
MEDITATION PROGRAM: Weekly schedule conducted in French (one evening) and English (one evening), with other activities happening according to the lunar calendar.
RETREATS OFFERED: Monthly Mahayana weekend retreats; visiting teachers three to four times per year.
PUBLICATIONS: *TBT Newsletter* (two or three times yearly).

SASKATCHEWAN

Dharma Group

We generally include some or all of the following: (1) *Anapanasati* for development of concentration, (2) *Vipassana* (Insight) Meditation to know the truth of how the universe arises and passes away, (3) chanting, (4) contemplation, (5) meditation on the body, on death, and on loving-kindness, (6) study of the Six *Paramitas* and (7) basic knowledge and information about Buddhist doctrine and exploration of its deeper meaning. Sessions in Hatha Yoga and teaching of Pranayana are also offered.

ADDRESS: #202, 2212C St. Charles Avenue, Saskatoon, SK S7M 5A7

PHONE: (306) 244-1394
LINEAGE: Tibetan Kagyu and Burmese Mahasi Sayadaw
SPIRITUAL HEAD: Gelongma Wangchuk
CONTACT: Same
AFFILIATION: Dharma Centre of Canada in Kinmount, Ontario
ESTABLISHED: 1989
FACILITIES: Shrine room in private apartment; retreats at St. Peter's Abbey in Muenster.
MEDITATION PROGRAM: Meditation, one night per week; Hatha Yoga, two nights per week.
RETREATS OFFERED: Monthly weekend retreat—sometimes Vipassana, sometimes Tibetan work.

YUKON TERRITORY

Vajra North

The purpose of Vajra North is to make authentic Mahayana teachings available by maintaining weekly practice, inviting lamas to give teachings and empowerments, and sponsoring a resident lama when supportable. May all beings benefit.

ADDRESS: 379 Valleyview Crescent, Whitehorse, YT Y1A 3C9
PHONE: (403) 667-2340
LINEAGE: Nyingma
SPIRITUAL HEAD: H. E. Chagdud Tulku Rinpoche
CONTACT: Roger Horner
AFFILIATION: Chagdud Gonpa Foundation
ESTABLISHED: 1984
FACILITIES: Private home.
MEDITATION PROGRAM: Red Tara and *Ngondro* practice in two separate sessions weekly. Call for times.
RETREATS OFFERED: Chagdud Gonpa lamas invited to give retreats, teachings, and empowerments.

PART FOUR

"Buddhayana"

*Nonsectarian Buddhism
and Mixed Traditions*

Aryaloka

MANJUVAJRA

❋

AT ARYALOKA THE RISING BELL RINGS AT SIX o'clock, calling the retreatants from their sleep. In the silence they rise. Some take a walk outside, circumambulating the twin geodesic domes that form the main building of our center. Some stroll through the trees to the riverbank and watch the insects scoot across the surface of the water. Others, like myself, take a cup of tea in the large circular sitting room.

A second bell rings and we gather in the shrine room. In silence we take our seats, sitting in lines perpendicular to the shrine, facing into the room. Some sit thoughtfully or gaze around the room at the other meditators, others watch the rising incense smoke or listen to the sound of rain on the roof. The leader enters and together we chant the Three Refuges, Five Precepts, and Threefold Salutation: "*Namo Buddaya, Namo Dharmakaya, Namo Sanghaya, Namo Nama, Om, Ah, Hum.*" Then everyone settles in for morning meditation.

The Buddhist tradition has a wide range of meditation practices. The Friends of the Western Buddhist Order (FWBO) makes use of a number of them. Everyone is taught Mindfulness of Breathing, *Metta Bhavana* (meditation on lovingkindness), and "just sitting." Those who have been ordained into the Western Buddhist Order are given additional Theravada meditations and visualizations to work on. Over the years the community of Vajraloka, a FWBO meditation center in Wales, has developed a systematic program of instruction in meditation. This approach is being adopted by most FWBO Centers throughout the world and even meditators with twenty years' experience claim that it has revolutionized their practice.

The bell rings for the beginning of a session of Mindfulness of Breathing. First I run through PIPER: Posture, Introspection, Purpose, Energy/Enthusiasm, Resolve.

Posture: First the legs and height of my seat; then the angle of my pelvis; straightened back, well balanced; the hands at the right height, without strain on the arms, supported by the lap or a small cushion; check chest, neck, shoulders, and the angle of the head.

Introspection: How am I feeling at this moment? What is on my mind? What are likely to be the distractions and hindrances to my meditation?

Purpose: What is the *purpose* of the practice? To be mindful of the breath and to develop concentration.

Enthusiasm is raised for this purpose by considering the value of mindfulness and awareness, or by remembering the experiences of meditation in the past.

Resolve: Finally, after resolving to stick with the practice and to keep trying even though it may become difficult, I set out on the practice itself.

For the first ten minutes I count my breaths at the end of each exhalation, for the second ten I count at the beginning of each inhalation, for the third I simply follow my breath, and finally I focus my awareness on the sensation of the breath as it passes through my nostrils. Every now and again I may run through PIPER, or work consciously on one of the five hindrances, or try to balance the factors of *dhyana* (meditation) as they appear in "access" concentration. Meditation is work, and I use the tools of the trade. I work without will, without forcing, as an artist will work on a poem or a carving in wood. By taking the raw material—the contents of my ordinary mind—and by shaping and directing it, I see the creative mind emerging; steadied, perfectly purified, translucent, free from blemish, purged of taint, supple and pliable, fit for wielding, established and immovable.

There have been times in my practice when I've experienced deep tranquillity, ripples of delight, torrents of ecstasy. At other times it seemed as if I would never gain even a little mindfulness. But even when there are no powerful meditation experiences, I still sense the gradual development of a more positive state, one that is clearer, brighter, friendlier, and more energetic than my normal, everyday consciousness.

The bell rings and slowly we leave our seats, form a circle, and walk around the circular shrine room, maintaining awareness of the body and the input of the senses: the perfume of the incense, the sound of creaking floorboards and swishing clothing, the taste of tea still lingering, the brush of air against the skin, the sight of knots in the pine floor, the back of the person in front of me, the shrine as I pass by. In this way, the awareness developed in sitting meditation is carried into an activity that is closer to everyday life. After about fifteen minutes the bell rings again and we take our seats for a second period of meditation.

Once again I run through PIPER, and then enter *Metta Bhavana* practice, the development of Universal Lovingkindness. *Metta* strengthens feelings of warmth and friendliness toward myself, toward a near and dear friend, a neutral person, and an enemy. Eventually that lovingkindness is directed outward ever further until all beings in the universe are included in its sphere. As the retreat progresses these feelings of friendliness toward the other retreatants increase noticeably. I even start to feel a genuine affection for their foibles.

After meditation we eat breakfast at a long, broad table beneath the spacious dome, and although the period of silence is now officially over, many choose to remain quiet, while at another table, people have begun to talk. Normally at Aryaloka silence is observed from the close of the evening *puja* to the beginning of breakfast. Often there are longer periods. When retreats begin, the silence is sometimes awkward, but gradually, as the practice takes hold, people happily slip into a quieter mode of communication.

Ben and I decide to take a walk before study group. Though we've only just met, we feel as if we have known each other for a long time. We talk of the usual things; relationships, jobs, plans, and our difficulties. We talk about how to conduct our lives in the world as we are learning to live them on retreat. What changes can we make that would enable us to live in this brighter, simpler, more loving state?

Retreats organized by the FWBO are of many types. Some are entirely devoted to meditation, others emphasize study (though meditation is always part of the program). On this retreat there is an equal amount of meditation and study.

The Buddhist tradition is often described as a treasure chest of jewels. One of the characteristics of a jewel is that it is attractive to look at. As one looks more deeply into the play of color and light it becomes ever more delightful. Study means to pick up one aspect of Buddhism and look at it, to explore all its facets and gaze deep into its heart. Only in this way do the teachings on ethics, psychology, and philosophy reveal their delightful nature. Without exception, all aspects of the Buddhist tradition are practical. Study serves to strengthen the basis on which we practice, but it also opens the mind to a wider vision and deeper understanding. It challenges our preconceived notions. It clarifies our thoughts and the way in which they influence our lives. It provides an opportunity to communicate with other people on a higher level than usual.

On retreat we study in three ways. First, people make use of the library to investigate for themselves the richness of the Buddhist literary tradition. Second, talks are given "live," by a member of the Western Buddhist Order, or from a tape by the Ven. Sangharakshita. His talks, given to Western students (in England) over the past twenty years, are informative, erudite, and inspiring. Third, we investigate traditional texts in detail in our study groups. Over the past fifteen years Sangharakshita has led study groups on over fifty texts or sections of texts from all the major Buddhist traditions; from the *Dhammapada* to the *Life and Liberation of Padmasambhava,* from the *Abhidharma* to the *Songs of Milarepa.* His method of study and commentaries are passed on by his students. Study groups are always led by qualified members of the Western Buddhist Order.

In the atmosphere of a retreat it is delightful to sit with others, to clear aside misunderstandings, and to open oneself to the vision that the text is attempting to communicate. To glimpse, however imperfectly, the purified mind of the Buddha is a powerful force of inspiration that clears away confusion. The study session lasts two hours, with ten of us sitting in a circle and going through the text, paragraph by paragraph.

I'm surprised to discover how the Buddha's words to a disciple in the forests of northern India over two thousand years ago are still relevant today. I also find that I am building a strong connection with the monks in the ancient texts, many of whom had characteristics that are instantly recognizable. In fact there are people exactly like them in this very study group, and it is here, in the study group, that the dharma—the Buddha's teaching—comes alive. His presence is felt as the material sinks deeper and fires the imagination.

After a light lunch I take a walk with a man who had visited many different Buddhist groups. He is concerned about which particular Buddhist tradition the FWBO belongs to. There are meditation practices, chanting, and study of the Pali texts—activities associated with the Theravada. Yet, there is also *puja* in which the *bodhisattvas* are mentioned and *The Heart Sutra* (a text central to the Mahayana tradition) is recited. The study and lectures are frequently based on one of the great Mahayana scriptures, or on what is clearly a Mahayana doctrine. Yet again, we meet Milarepa, Padamsambhava, *dakinis* (feminine deities), gurus, and the four foundation practices of the Vajrayana. Chinese meditation texts, Japanese poems, a modified tea ceremony, and Zen stories all may appear during the course of a retreat. As we discuss the

matter, however, it soon becomes clear that this is not simply a ragbag of Buddhist practices, but a developing Western tradition that owes its allegiance to the Three Jewels, and not to any particular school of Buddhism. It is not therefore Theravada, Mahayana, or Vajrayana, but simply *Buddhayana.*

Western cultural conditioning has presented particular problems for Western Buddhists. It has been necessary to search the whole of the Buddhist tradition to find those practices and texts that really are of practical use. Once something is found to be useful, it is incorporated into the program at FWBO's centers. Without trying to be different from, or the same as, any Eastern school, the FWBO devotes itself to discovering the best way to practice Buddhism in a modern industrialized world.

At three o'clock we are once again in the shrine room for more meditation. By this time in the afternoon I tend to get sleepy. Following the instructions for sloth and torpor, I open my eyes and look at a bright spot on the floor. Still I doze. I continually run through PIPER. I try to think of the times I have been clear and bright in meditation, but still the world swims into confusion. I try to imagine the Buddha sitting in the room, but still I cannot keep my eyes open.

Then the Buddha leaps from the shrine, transformed into a wild red *dakini,* dancing and swirling about the room, her black hair flying in all directions, her naked red body radiating energy. I sit bolt upright as a jet of energy shoots through my body, followed by another, and yet another. Then silence descends and I feel tranquil but perfectly alert. My drowsiness has vanished completely and I spend the rest of the afternoon in delightful concentration, keenly aware of my breathing and of radiating warmth to all those around me.

After dinner, which like all meals is vegetarian, we listen to a lecture by Ven. Sangharakshita—one of a series on aspects of the *bodhisattva*—which outlines the major doctrinal basis of this sublime spiritual ideal. As with the earlier study group, it provides many practical insights, as well as inspiration for working toward that ideal.

At nine o'clock we gather once again in the shrine room for the final meditation and *puja.* A *puja* is a devotional practice in seven parts, consisting of recitation, chanting, and readings from Buddhist texts, usually of the more poetic and inspirational type. Each part of the *puja* is associated with one of the seven emotional states necessary for the experience of *bodhichitta*—committing oneself to the attainment of Enlightenment for the sake of all sentient beings. The recitation and chanting with other people stimulates and gives expression to these emotional states and thus opens the door of the heart to a vision of Enlightened Mind. Enlightenment, or any level of Insight (*vipassana*), is not simply a cold intellectual understanding, but an emotionally charged realization that affects the whole being. Too easily we understand sublime spiritual truths with our intellects and assume that to be the end of the matter. While rational understanding is important, it must be allowed to penetrate the whole of our being; the emotions must also be engaged and transformed by understanding, so that insight may arise. The *puja* works directly on the emotions. With recitation, chanting, and mantras we open the heart and feel the emotions respond to the Buddha, the dharma (his teaching, the Way), the *sangha* (community of practitioners), and the *bodhisattvas*. As the final bell reverberates around the room and we sit in silence before the shrine, I watch the soft candlelight illuminating the gentle face of the Buddha figure, and the smoke of the incense rising in wisps and clouds.

For more than a hundred generations, followers of the *buddhadharma* have had this same experience. In the tropical heat of India and the cold vastness of Tibet, in the mountain temples of China and the stark *zendos* of Japan, millions of people have experienced this same tranquillity and deep sense of satisfaction. What a marvel, what a delight! Tears of joy swell into my eyes and roll slowly over my cheek.

Just sitting. Silence. Perfection

• • •

An Englishman, Manjuvajra became interested in Buddhism after reading Jack Kerouac's The Dharma Bums. *He encountered Ven. Sangharakshita in 1970 and was ordained by the Friends of the Western Buddhist Order three years later. After a ten-thousand-mile motorcycle tour of American dharma centers in 1984, he established Aryaloka, a spiritual community and retreat center in New Hampshire. He currently lives and teaches at Padmaloka Retreat Center in the United Kingdom where he is involved in the preparation of men for ordination into the Western Buddhist Order.*

Mystic Journey

BETH LOVEIN

✳

THE REVEREND JOHN W. GROFF, JR. IS AN OR-
dained Episcopal priest, poet, author, and former
monk. At least that's the standard answer. Those who
have practiced with him refer to him fondly as a "bap-
tized, Anglicized, Byzantine Buddhist." Yet that isn't
quite it either. Like all worthy teachers, he transcends la-
bels and dogma. Father John is simply a wise and loving
spiritual being. He knows that teachings of truth, no matter what persuasion, are merely fingers pointing to the
same place. And the depth and diversity of his experiences enable him to meet each student wherever he or
she happens to be. Infinitely patient, Father John is a gentle guide who constantly reminds us that what we long
for is within us, and available to all.

Father John first encountered silent Buddhist meditation on the island of Okinawa in 1959. There he studied
for six years under a venerable Zen master of the Soto
lineage. In 1965 he found his way to Pakistan and spent
the next two years with a Sufi teacher of the Golden (or
Silent) lineage. Returning to the United States he earned
an advanced degree in theology and became an ordained
Episcopal priest. Ultimately settling in Guntersville, Alabama, Father John now devotes most of his time to conducting individual private retreats at the Mystic Journey
Retreat Center.

The center is well designed for meditation—open and
airy, yet quiet and comfortable. The furnishings are taste-
ful, the single bed cozy. Retreatants prepare their own
meals and the small, fully equipped kitchen is generously
stocked with staples. Situated behind the main house, the
retreat cottage's modest, partially wooded grounds are
private and landscaped with care. It is a perfect environment for those seeking a quiet space to do serious work.

At the center, Father John offers individual retreats
with suggested stays ranging from five days to two weeks.
While on retreat you are encouraged to eat when hungry,
rest when tired, and sit. And sit. And sit. The time is
spent mostly alone in silence. Father John meets with you
informally twice a day, once in the morning and once in
the late afternoon, to listen and to discuss salient issues.

For a respite you can take the short, pleasant walk to
scenic Lake Guntersville. Or relax on the retreat house's
patio and enjoy the view. Once or twice during the week
you will be taken to a nearby park to spend time in walking meditation. Or you can just sit. And sit. And sit. You
are not required to "do" anything. But you will want to
use your time wisely.

While summer is typically retreat season at the center,
I took my initial retreat there in January. After sharing
the first evening's meal with Father John and his wonderful wife, Boots, I began my time of silence.

From the moment I arrived, I was in my "Zen bullet"
mode—very focused, very open. On the first night I woke
up a couple of times in what must have been the middle
of the night (I had no watch and couldn't be sure). At-
tributing it to excitement, I fell back to sleep. The next

morning I mentioned what happened and Father John advised that, should it occur again, I might want to get up and spend some time on the meditation cushion. It did, so I did. And every night thereafter, once or twice in the darkest dark of night, I would awake to sit.

Sometimes I sat for what seemed like only a few minutes. Other times I sat for what seemed like forever. In the beginning it was quite intriguing. After all, in addition to spending time in silence during the day, I was waking from deep and peaceful slumber to meditate more. But the novelty wore off quickly. I went through a period of irritation with the whole nocturnal scene and tried to ignore the pull. Of course that was impossible. So I just mumbled a few expletives, rolled out of bed and stumbled to the cushion. The moment I landed on the zafu my first thought was usually, *"Okay, whaaaaat?"*

After being with the excitement and the irritation, not to mention the occasional fear, I came to a place of "Who knows? Who cares?" Whatever was happening was simply happening. No more and no less. All I had to do was show up. And be open.

Throughout my time in silence I "was" many levels of awareness, and worked on and through things beyond words. Continually shifting and changing, I felt like part of some mysterious ever-beginning and never-ending symphony played by the universe. I was being. Just being. Letting come, letting go. Letting come, letting go. This is what came home.

. . .

Beth Lovein lives in the mountains of North Carolina and works as a secretary.

Mirror of Buddha: The Contemplative Practice of Naikan

GREGG KRECH AND RON GREEN

✵

> That the self advances and realizes the ten
> thousand things is delusion. That the ten
> thousand things advance and realize the self
> is enlightenment.
>
> *Dogen Zenji*

ONE OF THE REMARKABLE QUALITIES OF BUD-dhism is the understanding it gives us of the interdependence of all life. This understanding is not only the foundation of our spiritual life, but of our personal relationships to friends, colleagues, and family as well. However, for the understanding of interdependence to come alive in us, we must know it beyond our intellect. It must be woven into the fabric of our attitude and our way of being in the world. To make the Buddha's words our life, we must find some way to experience these elegant concepts on the most personal and intimate of levels. The question then is how do we go from ink spots on a page to understanding in our heart?

In Japan there is a method of self-reflection called *Naikan* (*Nai* = inner, *Kan* = observation), sometimes translated as "seeing oneself with the mind's eye." It is based on the ancient Buddhist practice of *mishirabe*. *Mishirabe* involved going into a cave and reflecting on one's life without food or sleep for days and days. The practice pushed one's body and mind to the doorstep of religious experience, but it was also dangerous. As a result of his own personal awakening during *mishirabe*, a devout Buddhist by the name of Yoshimoto Ishin vowed to develop a method that would be more accessible to people who wished to sincerely examine their lives. The method he devised was called *Naikan*.

Naikan is a method of meditative self-reflection in which we look clearly at our relationship with the world around us. As an example, let's consider something as simple as a piece of bread. When we are given bread to eat, what we are actually receiving are the gifts of a vast number of people and objects. Someone, a farmer, grew some wheat. This required rain, sunlight, minerals. Someone had to teach the farmer how to grow it and yet another person bought the crop. Someone drove the truck from the field to the mill on roads built and paid for by still others. People, specific people like you and me, ran machines to process the wheat and turn it into flour. Then it was combined with water and yeast and baked in ovens manufactured by workers using electricity—which has its own family of karmic relationships.

More people were needed to transport the finished product to the store in vehicles built by whole companies of workers. At the store you purchased it with money someone gave to you. It's your money, of course, but where did it come from? Your job? Someone hired you and others trained you. Someone gave you an education so you could find that job, use your skills, and get paid for your work. Teachers taught you how to read and write and think, how to drive a car, and to do all the countless tasks of daily living, even the task of cutting and eating the bread itself. All these people had parents who nourished and cared for them as children. Their parents had parents too.

When we take time to reflect on our lives, we see the countless efforts that have made it possible for us to have something as simple as a piece of bread. In the practice of *Naikan*, we review our entire life in this way, considering all that we have received from our parents, friends, teachers, coworkers—even those toward whom we harbor resentment such as ex-wives and ex-husbands. In so examining our lives, it's almost as if we have become that loaf of bread, shaped and formed in countless ways by others. Once we have seen this in our own personal history, we can truly say that our life depends entirely upon the support and care of others, or to put it another way, upon the grace and infinite compassion of Buddha.

But this only encompasses the first element of *Naikan* reflection. The second element involves reflection on what we have given to others. Mahayana Buddhism sets forth the *bodhisattva* ideal, but to what extent do our own lives reflect it? What in fact have we given to others? What have we done for our parents, friends, colleagues, teachers, and siblings? This question cannot be answered in the abstract: "I gave love, support, care, comfort." Rather, it must be grounded in the everyday reality of our lives: "I massaged my wife's shoulders, I washed my mother's laundry, I gave an apple to a homeless woman."

By reflecting on the giving/receiving quality of our existence, we spiritually reconcile our life's account balance. Does the world owe us, or are we in debt to the world?

We often live our lives as if the world owes us. "Why didn't I get that raise?" "Why is the pizza so late?" "How come I don't get more recognition for my work?" We expect the world to conform to our own ego-centered desires and concerns. But when I discover that I am the one who is in debt to the world, a natural desire is kindled to give, to serve others, and to travel life's path with a greater sense of gratitude, humility, and faith.

The third element of *Naikan* involves reflection on the troubles and difficulties we have caused others. As the Buddha said,

Look not at the faults of others,
at what they have done or left undone;
Rather, look at what you yourself
have done or left undone.

(*Dhammapada, verse 50*)

To be honest, mostly we tend to concentrate on how other people have caused us inconvenience and difficulty. Perhaps somebody cuts us off in traffic, or maybe the person in front of us at the post office has a lot of packages and we are kept waiting. It's easy to notice such incidents. But when we are the source of the trouble or inconvenience, we often don't notice it at all. Or if we do, we consider it an accident or unintentional, or we dismiss it as not such a big deal.

If we are willing to examine ourselves sincerely, we cannot help but see how we have been a source of difficulty and trouble to others. We become aware of how we have violated the precepts (killing, lying, stealing, and so on) and how our lives are so often driven by our self-centered desires. This is an important step in understanding ourselves and cultivating an awareness of the suffering of others. We may begin to sense the unfathomable compassion of the Buddha in our everyday lives, for true compassion is not earned, but something given us in spite of (or because of) our weaknesses and limitations.

At a *Naikan* retreat we begin by reflecting on our mother, usually from the time of our birth through age six. Then we continue to reflect in three-year increments (ages six to eight, ages nine to eleven, and so on). In this manner, our entire life in relation to our mother is examined on a period-by-period basis. We then examine our relationship to our father, siblings, spouse, children, teachers, friends, and coworkers. At the end of a period of reflection, usually ninety to one hundred and twenty minutes, the *mensetsusha* (teacher) meets with the *naikansha* (participant) to listen to his or her *Naikan* reflection. The role of the *mensetsusha* is to listen attentively and suggest the subject for the next period of reflection. Little dialogue takes place in these interviews since *Naikan* is self-reflection and what there is to be learned, is learned by searching and examining one's own direct experience.

The daily schedule at a *Naikan* retreat usually incorporates a work period (twenty minutes). There is also time for a shower and three meals. Otherwise, the entire day, from 5:30 AM to 9:30 PM is spent in quiet reflection. Though *Naikan* is rooted in Buddhist practice, retreats are open to all those with a sincere interest in examining their life. In Japan, and now Western Europe, *Naikan* is considered both a spiritual practice and a psychotherapeutic technique. Its success has established the fact that one's mental health and daily life need not be considered separate from one's religious devotion and practice. To sit quietly for a week reflecting on your existence, to rigorously examine yourself in every situation, to come face to face with your life—Who am I? How have I lived?—this is a remarkable gift. Each memory is a memory of grace.

Gregg Krech

A *Naikan* Retreat

As I kept bringing my mind back to actual events in my childhood and reflected on what I had received from my mother and father, I felt an overwhelming sadness, the sadness of seeing through the lie I had created and lived all these years. My parents were not the simple good/bad, right/wrong, nice/mean people I had made them out to be. Something melted in me. I cried for hours as memory after memory came back and I saw how much I had received from them and how little I had appreciated their efforts. I realized how self-centered I had been all my life.

After the retreat I shared the experience with my mom and told her how I'd counted up all the clothing she had washed for me in my life. I came up with forty thousand pieces of laundry!

"I'm sure you included the football uniforms," she said. "It was so hard getting the grass stains out of those jerseys."

Oops! Even after seven days of trying to remember these things, another whole area of trouble I had caused had just been opened up, and I thought I would never be done remembering it all. Even so, the practice of *Naikan* is not about guilt, though I felt plenty guilty at times during the retreat. As the days went by I found it was enough to acknowledge what I had received and the trouble I had caused. Nothing more was needed. Now, the desire to minimize the trouble I cause people is just there, and I find myself thanking people, my car, my computer, where in the past I would not have given them a second thought.

The most beautiful flower of *Naikan* for me, however, is that the illusion of isolation stemming from the sexual abuse I suffered as a child has been dispelled. Nowadays, when I notice a dark place coming, I take a deep breath and reflect on the gifts I am receiving at this very moment. How does the electricity get here to make the microwave oven work? How did I get this warm soothing water to shower in? Who should I thank for the comfortable clothes I'm wearing? There is no dark place to descend to anymore. Reality supports me at every moment. I still hurt, but the hurting doesn't make me want to hide inside, and that is worth anything.

Ron Green

· · ·

Gregg Krech has practiced Zen and Jodo Shinshu Buddhism for the past twenty years. He is the author of Naikan: The Practice of Attention and Reflection. *He currently serves as director of the ToDo Institute in Middlebury, Vermont.*

Ron Green is a senior student of Roshi John Daido Loori and is in residence at Zen Mountain Monastery in Mount Tremper, New York. He is certified in Constructive Living Counseling.

A New Year

NITA SWEENEY

✳

MY GOAL FOR NEW YEAR'S WEEKEND WAS SIM-ple: not to run screaming from the room. I had begrudgingly agreed to attend a weekend meditation retreat with my husband, Ed, a veteran meditator. Six months earlier, I had begun sitting for five minutes at a time and had recently graduated to the semiweekly, fifty-minute sits at the local *Vipassana* group. Notwithstanding my progress, two days of silence divided into forty-five-minute intervals of walking and sitting, interviews with a former Buddhist nun, and a strict vegetarian diet all sounded like pure torture to me. I spent the two-hour drive from Columbus to Loveland, Ohio regretting my decision—out loud.

"I just don't understand why you do this," I groaned. Ed, who had cut his teeth on a ten-day Rinzai retreat at Zen Mountain Monastery, allowed me to rant without interruption. "It just seems so strange and fruitless," I went on. "I have better things to do with my time."

"You might be surprised at what you learn if you give this a chance," he interjected. We had taken my Volvo station wagon, my plan being to exit quietly, check into a nearby hotel, and pick Ed up on Sunday afternoon. I noticed that he was careful to avoid even the slightest criticism of this idea. While he must have thought it absurd, I myself considered it a reasonable and necessary precaution.

"You know," Ed informed me during a lull in my tirade, "we might not get to stay in the same room."

"What?" I screeched. "Why didn't you tell me before?" My fear skyrocketed at the prospect of spending two days separated from my only connection with the outside world.

"I didn't think it was important," Ed tried to explain. "It's standard procedure at Zen retreats for men and women to room separately."

Before, I was just afraid. Now, I was furious. He had "dragged" me two hours from home to a strange environment, to sit with a bunch of people I didn't even know, to sleep in a room with a total stranger—a meditating total stranger at that.

"I will never go to another one of these [expletive deleted] meditation retreats again!"

We rode the remaining half hour in vivid silence.

Just on the other side of Loveland, we rounded a bend and I noticed a large Victorian mansion perched at the crest of a knoll. Ed touched my arm and pointed.

"The entrance is right there," he said.

I looked at him, eyes wide, and took in a long, slow breath, letting the air whistle as it entered. I had expected primitive accommodations. Instead, the elegant main house, modern adjoining cafeteria, and peaceful gardens of Grailville greeted me like a team of friendly hostesses. Ed just smiled and leaned into the silence. I pulled onto the gravel drive and followed the painted signs to "Registration."

My relief showed when the spry, graying woman registering us informed Ed and me that we would be staying (together!) in the main house. She gave Ed a knowing glance and turned her attention to the next person. We put our belongings in the room and I looked out the window at the grounds. The accommodations pleased me, so I decided not to gripe about the twin beds. We headed for the cafeteria to join the others.

Ed chose a narrow wooden table at the end of the dining hall and I placed my tray next to his. A tall, slim man who looked more like a farmhand than my idea of a meditator sat beside us. I had imagined shaved heads and flowing robes, not faded blue jeans and well-worn T-shirts. I was surprised to learn that this guy had been meditating for five years. A gentle trickle of folks continued to enter the dining room under my critical gaze. A pair of women in tie-dyed skirts and one man with dreadlocks stood out. Everyone else looked pretty much like Ed and me.

When a petite brunette entered, something about her struck me immediately, but I couldn't quite put it into words.

"Who's that?" I asked Ed.

"Jacqueline Mandell, the teacher."

"How do you know? Have you met her before?"

"No . . . just watch the way she moves."

The fluidity of her gait enchanted me. Fully present in each catlike step, she steadily, precisely, glided across the floor. Her eyes lit up as she smiled gently to each retreatant, yet her attention never wandered from the bowl of soup she carried. I was enthralled, but puzzled by this tiny woman who looked like a typical Midwesterner, yet whose determined gestures created an unintended ballet.

"How does she do that?" I asked.

"Twenty-four years of meditation," Ed replied.

I was beginning to understand and, although I wouldn't yet admit it, I had a faint suspicion that I would probably stay. After I'd finished the lentil and rice casserole, chopped salad (from the Grailville gardens), and a bar cookie for dessert, we drove across the road to the meditation hall—The Oratory—a restored hillside barn, sitting in an open field apart from the other buildings. I imagined spending long, boring hours during the next two days in this huge, looming structure. Despite the frigid temperatures, I began to sweat as we pulled into the gravel parking area. Ed hugged me. We gathered our paraphernalia and made our way inside.

The pale wooden floors of the meditation room glowed in the dim light. As my eyes adjusted, I made out long narrow benches lining the stark white, twenty-foot-high stucco walls. A teak Buddha rested on a plain oak altar. A huge wooden box, which hid a square skylight, hung from the peaked roof above the altar. A few feet in front of the altar sat an ornate meditation cushion atop a small, burgundy Oriental carpet. Two cymbal-shaped discs connected by a piece of ribbon had been placed precisely on the front edge of the rug. A microphone and attached speaker stood at attention before the cushion, which I guessed to be Jacqueline's.

Most of the others had already claimed their places. Small piles of meditation items quilted the floor: round sitting cushions in navy and black, square maroon mats, rectangular wooden benches, and an array of blankets and colorful chairs faced Jacqueline's cushion. Ed and I settled into chairs at the back of the room.

As Jacqueline entered, some people stood and bowed. Others remained seated. I looked at Ed and he shrugged, not sure of the expected protocol. Jacqueline acknowledged neither approach, but walked purposefully and peacefully to the ornate cushion and sat down with her legs crossed, her knees touching the floor in front of her.

"Good evening," she poured into the microphone, her voice as fluid as her gait. She spoke slowly in simple, short sentences, randomly broken by beams of smile. She briefly explained her Cincinnati roots and years of study in Burma, India, and Sri Lanka. "When I left Ohio to travel the world, there was no Buddhism here," she said. "Now I'm teaching Buddhism in Ohio. It's unbelievable."

Her meditation instructions were simple. Focus on the breath at either the tip of the nose or the abdomen, whichever was more pronounced. This would serve as an anchor during our practice.

"We use the breath simply because it's something we all have in common. Everybody breathes." She smiled as laughter gurgled from the audience. "When your attention wanders, which it invariably will," she chuckled, "simply bring it back to the breath. If a bodily sensation other than the breath draws your attention, observe it with full awareness and 'allowingness.' Do not push or pull on it. Let it be as it is. When the sensation passes, gently bring your awareness back to the breath. Sit as still as you can with your spine erect. Think of yourself as a marionette suspended from the ceiling by a string running up through your spine and coming out of the middle of your head."

Then she cocked her head to one side and said, "Let's begin." We sat for about forty-five minutes. The usual distractions plagued me and my mind raced. *What's Ed thinking? I hate this. What time is it? Will they notice if I look at my watch? I don't want the teacher to see me move. I wonder if Ed's horny. Can we have sex at a retreat? I wish I'd brought a good book. I'd rather be home with my friends. Why did I come here? My back hurts. . . .*

My mind wandered like a puppy learning to heel on a leash. I imagined myself gently coaxing it back to the right place. My legs ached and eventually fell asleep. I drew an audible sigh of relief when Jacqueline rang the cymbal-shaped discs together to end the session.

"Now we will move into walking meditation," she instructed. "We all walk during the day. It's a great time to bring our minds back to the present moment where we ultimately want to reside. Walking meditation helps us learn to stay in the present moment while we're moving.

"Some people prefer to walk slowly, feeling the leg move, the foot touch the floor, and the knee bend. To keep your mind on the present moment, you may choose to make a soft mental note of 'lifting, shifting, placing' as you walk.

"Others prefer to walk quickly and feel their legs moving through space. Either is fine so long as you stay present, keeping your awareness on the movement in the present moment. The phone's not for you. The mail's not for you. No one is here to see you. There's no radio to listen to and no TV to watch. There's just you and the present moment. There's no place to go, nowhere to get to, no goal to reach. Just walk. And we continue."

We formed two circles, the inner one for slow walking, the outer one for those who preferred a faster pace. We walked around and around and around the endless circle

between the massive posts that held the pitched roof above us. I felt the ridges of uneven floorboards with my bare toes and heels. Some boards squeaked as my weight shifted across them. Though I kept returning my attention to the sensations in my feet, my mind wandered and soon I was daydreaming again.

I bet the folks at work think I'm nuts. My neck is throbbing. I wonder if Ed will rub my back tonight. Sometimes that leads to something else. Oh! I shouldn't think those thoughts on retreat. Why not? Leftover guilt. Speaking of leftovers, dinner was good. I wish I hadn't eaten so much. More guilt. The man ahead of me looks angry. I bet they all know I'm new at this. I hope they're not laughing at me. How could I tell?

The thoughts jumped from one topic to another without interruption. "This must be why they call it monkey mind," I decided.

After she rang the bell, Jacqueline said we would resume in ten minutes. I did some stretching exercises and looked over at Ed, who was walking toward me. I wanted to speak to him, but he just smiled and walked past me toward the basement stairway.

During the next session, I felt as though bugs were crawling on my nose. I knew these were just itches and for a few seconds I let the sensations move across my nose and face rather than scratch and be embarrassed at having to move. As an overachiever, I feared the others would think I was a failure.

I could only stay focused for a few minutes of each period, and felt guilty about all the daydreaming and fantasizing. A couple of times I felt faint, which I later learned was from forcing the breath in and out rather than allowing it to flow in its natural rhythm.

Despite these distractions, the ease with which I fell into the pattern of alternating walking and sitting amazed me. My back ached, I nodded off at times, and my mind continued to meander, but deep within I knew I was doing something important for myself just by staying. And for several seconds that night I was "in the moment," pure and simple. Time stood still. Nothing existed but the breath and I wanted to shout, "Hey! Something incredible just happened." After that I stopped having thoughts about leaving.

At 10:00 PM on that New Year's Eve, Jacqueline rang the bell to end the last scheduled period of sitting.

"If you want to go to bed, you may leave now," she said. "If you'd like to join me in 'sitting in' the New Year, I invite you to do so. It's become something of a ritual for me."

I decided to stay and sit, to remain in that quiet place within myself for a few hours more. I knew then for certain that I would not leave the retreat and that I had found my path. I looked at Ed and he nodded. He was staying up too.

And so I continued to sit, still drifting off, thoughts scurrying, body yearning to move, wanting to scratch, to stretch—anything! At midnight, we met the distant sound of ringing church bells, local fireworks, and cheering crowds with silence—sweet, blissful silence. Jacqueline rang the bell and said simply, "Happy New Year. Rest well." Wearily, I gathered myself, put on my boots, and began the long walk back to our sleeping quarters. A peaceful smile snuck across my lips as I trudged through the dark. For me, not only a new year but a new life had begun.

. . .

Freelance writer Nita Sweeney lives in Columbus, Ohio, with her husband, Ed. She and Ed co-coordinate Mindfulness Meditation of Columbus and enjoy Ohio's growing sangha.

The "Buddhayana" Centers of North America

✳

ALABAMA

Mystic Journey Retreat Center

The center offers a small, self-contained cottage set in a quiet wooded area of pristine beauty. It provides the physical space and external silence necessary for experienced meditators or serious beginners desiring to do intensive, solitary sitting practice. Only one person is accepted into retreat at a time. While the spiritual guide's primary training is in the Japanese schools of Soto and Shingon Zen, the center is completely nonsectarian and eclectic and accepts applications from yogis of all traditions. A free comprehensive brochure is available on request.

ADDRESS: PO Box 1021, Guntersville, AL 35976
PHONE: (205) 582-5745
LINEAGE: Japanese Soto and Shingon Zen
SPIRITUAL HEAD: John Groff, Resident Teacher
AFFILIATION: Autonomous
ESTABLISHED: 1989
FACILITIES: Retreat house/*zendo.*
RETREATS OFFERED: Private intensive five- to thirty-day meditation retreats.

ARIZONA

Arizona Community of Buddhists

Our focus is on community volunteer service work.

ADDRESS: PO Box 6035, Chandler, AZ 85246-6035
PHONE: (602) 821-5939
E-MAIL: rev.terry@MCI2000.com
LINEAGE: Buddhists and non-Buddhists
CONTACT: Rev. Terry Kennard, Resident Director
AFFILIATION: Rosemead Buddhist Monastery; Center for Buddhist Development; Phoenix Vietnamese Zen Temple; Buddhist Association of Arizona State University; Phoenix Buddhist Association.
ESTABLISHED: 1995

Arizona Teachings

Arizona Teachings is a nonprofit, educational, and religious organization and dharma home to Lopon Claude d'Estree, Ken Bacher, Bonnie Cheney, Richard Laue (for Zen Desert Sangha), and the Inter-Buddhist Dialogue Group of the Network for Western Buddhist Teachers (NWBT). Messages can also be left for the Buddhist Fellowship at the University of Arizona (Claude), and Tacheria (a multifaith center for spirituality, reconciliation, and the sacred arts), and the New School for Spiritual Directors (Claude).

ADDRESS: 4725 East Sunrise Drive, #137, Tucson, AZ 85718
PHONE: (520) 882-8831
FAX: Same
E-MAIL: ati@indirect.com
CONTACT: Lopon Claude d'Estree
AFFILIATION: Autonomous

Center for Buddhist Development

We are organized for dharma study, meditation, mindfulness retreats, and lectures.

ADDRESS: PO Box 6035, Chandler, AZ 85246-6035
PHONE: (602) 821-5939
E-MAIL: rev.terry@MCI2000.com
LINEAGE: Mixed
SPIRITUAL HEAD: Bhante Chao Chu
CONTACT: Rev. Terry Kennard
AFFILIATION: Rosemead Buddhist Monastery; Arizona Community of Buddhists; Phoenix Vietnamese Zen Temple; Buddhist Association of Arizona State University; Phoenix Buddhist Association.
ESTABLISHED: 1995
FACILITIES: Meet in private home.
MEDITATION PROGRAM: Group meditation; doctrine study; *Applying Buddhist Practice in Daily Life* (discussion groups).
RETREATS OFFERED: Mindfulness retreats.
PUBLICATIONS: *Common Sense* (subscription: 7833 Emerson Place, Rosemead, CA 91770).

The Unitarian Universalist Buddhist Fellowship

ONE OF THE MORE INTERESTING ASPECTS OF Buddhism's coming west has been its encounter with Unitarian Universalism. A small denomination of around two hundred thousand members, Unitarian Universalism has had an influence in American life well beyond what its numbers might suggest.

Unitarians have been interested in Buddhism since the transcendentalist movement. In fact, the first Buddhist text translated into English was a chapter of the *Saddharmapundarika-sutra*, rendered from the French by nineteenth-century Unitarian writer and editor Elizabeth Palmer Peabody. Since that time there has been an ever increasing interest in Buddhism among Unitarians and now Unitarian Universalists.

Officially two percent of UUs currently call themselves Buddhists. In all likelihood, the percentage is larger, and growing. Unitarian Universalists have shown a keen intellectual interest in the dharma. Increasingly, they are embracing Buddhist practice as well.

Dozens of congregations encourage or sponsor Buddhist, or Buddhist-inspired, study and practice groups Every year there are more. In the 1980s a number of UU clergy and laity organized the Unitarian Universalist Buddhist Fellowship. It has remained a loosely knit organization, primarily serving as a network for UUs interested in the dharma, publishing a newsletter, maintaining a Web home page, and seeing that there are Buddhist-related activities at the annual General Assembly.

The Unitarian Universalist Buddhist Fellowship is open to anyone interested in the meeting of Buddhism

Rev. James Ishmael Ford of the Unitarian Universalist Buddhist Fellowship. (Photo courtesy of James Ishmael Ford.)

and Unitarian Universalism. It provides a bridge between these two great traditions, offering a fresh perspective on practice, social justice, and morality. The fellowship particularly encourages the involvement of parents seeking ways to raise their children within a liberal and Buddhist-friendly spiritual atmosphere.

Rev. James Ishmael Ford

For more information, contact: Unitarian Universalist Buddhist Fellowship, c/o Dr. Robert Senghas, 54 Rivermount Terrace, Burlington, VT 05401; (802) 658-6466; http://www.wp.com/uubf.

Center for Radical Aliveness

Lou has a twenty-year practice in Zen meditation under the guidance of Charlotte Joko Beck of the San Diego Zen Center. Our mission is to stop unnecessary stress and depression, allowing each individual to become fully and radically alive in body, mind, and spirit. We do this by integrating the creative arts with the principles of Zen philosophy and gestalt therapy. We offer classes and workshops in Zen meditation, Iyengar Yoga, spirit drumming, inner dance, painting, and sculpture. Write for a brochure.

ADDRESS: 7501 East Oak Street, #101, Scottsdale, AZ 85257

PHONE: (602) 954-3331

LINEAGE: Zen
SPIRITUAL HEAD: Lou Bellamak, Resident Director
AFFILIATION: Autonomous
ESTABLISHED: 1990
FACILITIES: Center

Phoenix Buddhist Network

Phoenix Buddhist Network is an organization of affiliated Buddhist groups in the greater Phoenix area. It provides a mechanism for people interested in Buddhist practice in the metropolitan area to locate a group and practice that suits them. It also provides for an informal social network of Buddhists in Arizona that crosses sectarian lines. Periodic social events are scheduled and a newsletter is published three times a year.

ADDRESS: 4701 North 35th Way, Phoenix, AZ 85018
PHONE: (602) 957-7007
LINEAGE: Nonsectarian
CONTACT: Dr. Terry Kennard, Resident Director
PUBLICATIONS: *Phoenix Buddhist Network Newsletter*

Sacred Passage

Sacred Passage offers a unique program of outdoor wilderness solo retreats. After two days of group training and preparation, individuals depart for a remote site, remaining alone for seven days. Wild nature becomes one's teacher and guide. This is followed by an integration period for sharing, grounding insights, and preparing for changes in one's life. The Sacred Passage process helps to quiet the mind, develop pristine awareness, and bring union of inner and outer nature. John Milton draws on the essential teachings of many Buddhist traditions including Dzogchen, Tantra, Zen, and Vipassana as well as Taoist and Shamanic practices.

ADDRESS: Drawer CZ, Bisbee, AZ 85603
PHONE: (520) 432-7353
FAX: (520) 432-3065
E-MAIL: sacredpa@primenet.com
SPIRITUAL HEAD: John P. Milton, Resident Director
AFFILIATION: Autonomous
ESTABLISHED: 1980
FACILITIES: Centers on preserved land in Colorado, Arizona, West Virginia, Hawaii, and Mexico.
RETREATS OFFERED: Weekend workshops. Retreats lasting from ten to 108 days in such beautiful, remote areas as Nepal, Ladakh, Cambodia, Thailand, Bali, and Australia.

Unitarian Universalist Buddhist Fellowship

Since the introduction of the first Buddhist texts to America in the mid-nineteenth century, Buddhism has been an extremely influential force among Unitarians and, since the mid-1960s, Unitarian Universalists. In recent years, we have increasingly been drawn to explore Buddhist religious practices, especially seated meditation, in order to ground the "free and responsible search for truth and meaning" that is one of the guiding principles of the Unitarian Universalist tradition. Meditation invites a direct and immediate experience of reality and provides a balance to purely intellectual inquiry.

ADDRESS: c/o Valley Unitarian Universalist Church, 1700 West Warner Road, Chandler, AZ 85224
PHONE: (602) 899-4249
E-MAIL: UUBF@uua.org
WWW: http://ns.gamewood.net:80/~casebolt/uubf.htm
CONTACT: Rev. James Ishmael Ford, Resident Director
AFFILIATION: Unitarian Universalist Association

ESTABLISHED: Informally since about 1986
FACILITIES: Church
PUBLICATIONS: *UU Sangha*

ARKANSAS

Devachan Temple

Eureka Springs, Arkansas, has always been a special place of healing. Long before throngs of people began coming in the 1800s for an assortment of mineral water cures, Native Americans were here performing spiritual ceremonies. Devachan Temple is a place of refuge where Buddhist students can come for retreats of any duration. The five precepts are observed and vegetarianism is practiced. Bhikkhuni Miao Kwang Sudharma has practiced Buddhism in Asia and the United States since 1960. Her goal is to make Buddhist teachings available through private counseling and discus-

Bhikkhuni Miao Kwang Sudharma, Director of Davachan Temple in Eureka Springs, Arkansas. (Photo courtesy of Devachan.)

sion sessions. There is no charge. All traditions are welcome.

ADDRESS: 5 Dickey Street, Eureka Springs, AR 72632

PHONE: (501) 253-7028

LINEAGE: Japanese Soto Zen, Sri Lankan Theravada, Chinese Ch'an and Pure Land

SPIRITUAL HEAD: Bhikkhuni Miao Kwang Sudharma, Director

CONTACT: Same

AFFILIATION: Autonomous

ESTABLISHED: 1980

FACILITIES: Meditation center with private rooms for solitary retreats.

MEDITATION PROGRAM: All traditions of meditation, nature walks, dharma readings, work sessions.

Ecumenical Buddhist Society

The center offers several workshops and retreats each year. Retreat leaders have come from Theravada, Mahayana, and Vajrayana traditions. Meditation sessions are open to all and are conducted at the Buddhist Center.

ADDRESS: 1010 West 3rd Street, Little Rock, AR 72201

PHONE: (501) 376-7056

FAX: (501) 664-1170

E-MAIL: ebs@aristotle.net

LINEAGE: Ecumenical, all lineages

SPIRITUAL HEADS: Lama Tharchin, Rinpoche; Lama Yeshe Wangmo; Fukushima-Roshi; and others.

AFFILIATION: Autonomous

ESTABLISHED: 1991

FACILITIES: Meditation hall with apartment for meetings and visiting teachers. Separate second location with meditation hall and one-person residence.

MEDITATION PROGRAM: Silent Zen and Vipassana sitting and walking meditation; Ngondro practice. Call for schedule.

RETREATS OFFERED: Visiting teachers

from Theravada, Mahayana, and Vajrayana traditions come regularly to offer teachings and retreats.

PUBLICATIONS: *The Ecumenical Buddhist Newsletter*

CALIFORNIA

Arya Marga Foundation

Arya Marga Foundation (AMF) was founded for the purpose of extending the scope of Buddhist education beyond the walls of the temple and meditation hall. Its activities combine traditional religious practices with ethical, environmental, and spiritual concerns. At present AMF sponsors one-day, two-day, and week-long contemplative treks in the form of pilgrimages and the circumambulation of sacred sites. By promoting both self-understanding and ecological sensitivity, AMF aims to spread Buddha Dharma as it contributes to the movement toward a nonviolent, sustainable, and socially just way of life.

ADDRESS: 2130 Fillmore Street, #124, San Francisco, CA 94115

PHONE: (415) 346-9672

FAX: Same

E-MAIL: aryamarga@igc.APC.org

LINEAGE: Japanese Pure Land, Vietnamese Mahayana Zen

SPIRITUAL HEAD: Dharma Aloka

AFFILIATION: Autonomous (work with many different centers).

ESTABLISHED: 1993

MEDITATION PROGRAM: Walking meditation. Pilgrimages; circumambulations of mountains and/or holy places.

RETREATS OFFERED: Extended walking pilgrimages; camping.

Buddhist AIDS Project

The Buddhist AIDS Project (BAP) provides free information on Buddhist re-

sources, events, and alternative services to any person living with HIV, including family, friends, caregivers, and people who are HIV negative. BAP is a grass-roots, all-volunteer, and nonsectarian organization. Among its resources are more than sixty volunteers—from physicians to body workers, psychologists to meditation instructors. BAP provides video- and audiotapes on Buddhist practice, deep relaxation, and healing.

ADDRESS: 555 John Muir Drive, #803, San Francisco, CA 94132

PHONE: (415) 522-7473

CONTACT: Administrative Committee.

AFFILIATION: Autonomous. Buddhist Peace Fellowship

ESTABLISHED: 1993

FACILITIES: Home office; meditation site.

MEDITATION PROGRAM: We support the Living Peace Meditation Community in San Francisco led by Karen Van Done, student of Thich Nhat Hanh, Stephen Levine, and Jack Kornfield.

RETREATS OFFERED: Yes

PUBLICATIONS: *BAP Flyer*, monthly. *On Meditation and AIDS: Buddhist Practice and Living with HIV* (Parallax Press).

Buddhist Alliance for Social Engagement (BASE)

BASE, founded by the Buddhist Peace Fellowship, provides a community-based structure for service and social action within the context of Buddhist training, retreat, and mentorship. In the San Francisco Bay Area, the program places volunteers at such locations as Zen Hospice, Healthcare for the Homeless, Women's Cancer Center, and at an urban community garden. Volunteers meditate, study, reflect, and act together in a community-based exploration of what it means to be a Buddhist activist.

ADDRESS: PO Box 4650, Berkeley, CA 94704

Pilgrimage with Dharma-Aloka

DURING THE LAST TWO DECADES, BUDDHISM IN the West has matured and stabilized sufficiently for us to begin establishing local pilgrimage routes in North America. There are clusters of rural dharma centers, not far from major cities, in several regions of the United States and Canada. One such mandala occurs in central California, where I began to practice long-distance walking meditation in 1991. It took three years of tramping about on the trails and back roads of the Santa Cruz Mountains to create a network of footpaths that connects nine centers and runs nearly the length of the range.

A pilgrimage from Spirit Rock to Green Gulch Farm in Marin County, California, led by Dharma-Aloka. (Photo by Libby Ingalls.)

There is also a spectacularly beautiful pilgrim's path between Spirit Rock Meditation Center and Green Gulch Farm in Marin County, and a longer course that currently extends to Mendocino and will some day reach Mount Shasta.

It's not too early for us to begin developing our own methods of walking meditation and contemplative wilderness training. Most of the necessary elements exist: monasteries and shrines, yogis, Buddhist teachers, sympathetic observers, and a public deeply concerned about the nature of our relationship to the nonhuman world. The most important elements have long been present: our sacred forests, mountains, plains, and rivers. They've always supported us. We can show our gratitude and respect by dwelling with them in holy silence and allowing them to help us realize our interdependence. In this we follow the example of the Buddha, who spent most of his ministry out of doors.

Through these activities I hope to preserve the East Asian Buddhist tradition of mountain asceticism known as the Way of Natural Wisdom. Its guidelines for living on the land, based upon walking and intentional simplicity, are a path to spiritual and ecological awakening.

Dharma-Aloka

For more information, contact: Arya Marga Foundation, 2130 Fillmore Street #124, San Francisco, CA 94115; (415) 346-9672.

CALIFORNIA *(cont.)*

PHONE: (510) 525-8596
FAX: (510) 525-7973
LINEAGE: Ecumenical
CONTACT: Diana Winston
AFFILIATION: Buddhist Peace Fellowship
ESTABLISHED: 1994
MEDITATION PROGRAM: Volunteers meditate together twice weekly.

RETREATS OFFERED: Monthly practice days. Extended five- to ten-day group retreat.

Buddhist Peace Fellowship (BPF)

Our style of open-hearted engaged Buddhism, our expanding programs in Asia and the United States, and our lively journal—*Turning Wheel*—serve as a beacon for dharma activists committed to transforming the world and themselves. Through BPF, Buddhists of many traditions explore personal and group responses to political, social, and ecological suffering. Our wide network of members, chapters, and affiliates is our greatest

The Buddhist Alliance for Social Engagement (BASE)

THE ESSENCE OF THE BUDDHA'S TEACHING IS TO put an end to suffering. Today with the planet in crisis, many of us feel the need to create and practice a socially engaged Buddhism, taking to heart the bodhisattva vow to save all sentient beings. We have looked for ways to deepen this practice and to live a life of engagement and transformation. Until now, however, no full-time program of service, meditation, and training has been available in the United States.

The Buddhist Peace Fellowship (BPF) has responded to this challenge with a new vision: Buddhist Alliance for Social Engagement (BASE). In name and conception, BPF's BASE program echoes the "base community movement" in Latin America, Asia, and elsewhere. This movement has created flexible, spiritually based communities where religious doctrine is recast into social action.

BASE provides a structure for participants to spend six months in part- to full-time service/social action work combined with Buddhist practice. Volunteer participants spend fifteen to thirty hours a week working in hospices, homeless shelters, prisons, medical clinics, and social change organizations. Other participants have paid work in these fields. They meet weekly for meditation, study, and discussion on issues of socially engaged Buddhism. In addition they participate in monthly practice days and extended two- to five-day meditation retreats. Local Buddhist activists work with volunteers as mentors, providing ongoing spiritual guidance and support.

Since 1995 there have been six BASE programs throughout California. Additional programs have been established in Colorado and Boston. BASE continues to spread on a grassroots level to different states, taking on forms appropriate to the local communities, while maintaining the spirit and intention of BASE.

Diana Winston

For more information, contact: Buddhist Peace Fellowship, PO Box 4650, Berkeley, CA 94704; (510) 525-8596.

---

strength. With its support we seek to awaken peace where there is conflict, bring insight to institutionalized ignorance, promote communication and cooperation among *sanghas*, and, in the spirit of wisdom, compassion, and harmony, offer real help wherever possible.
ADDRESS: PO Box 4650, Berkeley, CA 94704
PHONE: (510) 525-8596
FAX: (510) 525-7973
LINEAGE: Nonaffiliated
CONTACT: Alan Senauke, National Coordinator
AFFILIATION: International network of engaged Buddhists.
ESTABLISHED: 1978
RETREATS OFFERED: Periodic retreats, training, groups on engaged Buddhism. Write or call for details on programs.
PUBLICATIONS: *Turning Wheel*, quarterly.

Center for Timeless Wisdom

The Center for Timeless Wisdom offers a contemporary expression of the *Prajnaparamita* (Perfect Wisdom) and *Shunyavada* (Openness) traditions through dialogues, courses, and retreats. Our work integrates the liberating wisdom of traditions such as Zen, Dzogchen, and *Madhyamaka* (Middle Way) into a form of Buddhism that is relevant and readily accessible in a Western context. The distinguishing features of this nonaligned approach are its immediacy and directness, and the absence of ritual and unnecessary intellectualization.
ADDRESS: 555 Bryant Street, #302, Palo Alto, CA 94301
PHONE: (415) 488-4988
FAX: (415) 488-9819
E-MAIL: 100241.3546@compuserve.com
LINEAGE: Perfect Wisdom tradition
SPIRITUAL HEAD: Dr. Peter Fenner
ESTABLISHED: 1992
MEDITATION PROGRAM: Dialogues, workshops, retreats.
PUBLICATIONS: Peter Fenner, *The Ontology of the Middle Way* (Kluwer); Peter Fenner, *Reasoning into Reality* (Wisdom); Peter and Penny Fenner, *Intrinsic Freedom* (Millennium).

CALIFORNIA (*cont.*)

DharmaNet International

DharmaNet International is a central clearinghouse for Buddhist information resources around the world, both on-line and off-line. It is organized to promote and support Buddhist organizations and practitioners in whatever ways it can and to find uses for technology that make Buddhist teachings and practice freely and widely accessible. DharmaNet is committed to putting Buddhist precepts into practice through service. Dharma-Net is a one-stop source for "anything Buddhist, anywhere," and is offered freely. "All that we are is the result of what we have thought." *The Buddha*
ADDRESS: PO Box 4951, Berkeley, CA 94704-4951
E-MAIL: dharma@dharmanet.org
WWW: http://www.dharmanet.org
LINEAGE: Nondenominational. Board of advisors consists of Buddhist monastics, lay teachers, and academic professors from all Buddhist schools and lineages. DharmaNet's purpose is to bridge differences.
CONTACT: Barry Kapke, Resident Director
AFFILIATION: Autonomous
ESTABLISHED: 1991
FACILITIES: Bulletin Board Service (BBS) network: international e-mail; topical discussion areas (news groups); Internet: e-mail, news groups (under development); extensive dharma library available for on-line viewing or downloading; WWW site includes International Meditation Retreats Calendar, Buddhist E-mail Directory, Dharma Teachers Who's Who, Dharma Center Directories, "Dana" Opportunities Bulletin Board, links to all other on-line Buddhist Web sites.
MEDITATION PROGRAM: DharmaNet International offers opportunities for individuals to help type, proof, and format dharma books for electronic distribution.
PUBLICATIONS: *Gassho*, periodic electronic journal; electronic editions of books for free distribution in cooperation with dharma publishers and authors (currently over fifty titles).

Don't Worry Zendo

Informal, friendly, and nondenominational. Sitting held several nights a week in a private home in West Hollywood. One all-day sitting per month. An optional class, discussion, or sharing precedes sittings. Group leader is Michael Attie, who has been a student of Zen, Vipassana, Tibetan, and Hindu traditions for over thirty years. In good weather, sitting in the yard or on the roof, with lots of walking meditation in a pleasant neighborhood.
ADDRESS: 444 North Flores Street, Los Angeles, CA 90048
PHONE: (213) 655-8659
LINEAGE: Homegrown
SPIRITUAL HEAD: 108,000 manifestations
CONTACT: Michael Attie, Resident Director
AFFILIATION: Autonomous
ESTABLISHED: 1989
FACILITIES: Meditation hall in private home.
MEDITATION PROGRAM: Group meditation several nights a week.
RETREATS OFFERED: One all-day per month.

Garberville Dharma Center

Located some 220 miles north of San Francisco, just off Highway 101, Garberville Dharma Center offers space for the practice and study of Buddhism in the Theravadan, Zen, and Tibetan traditions. Most of our members have teachers in other areas but find it convenient to have a place to practice near their homes. We have group meditation of different styles several evenings a week. Call for current schedule.
ADDRESS: 434 Maple Lane, Garberville, CA 95440
PHONE: (707) 923-3891
FAX: (800) 853-2010
LINEAGE: Tibetan Vajrayana and Japanese Zen
CONTACT: Timothy Clark
ESTABLISHED: 1976
FACILITIES: Meditation hall.
MEDITATION PROGRAM: Group meditation several evenings weekly.

Gay Buddhist Fellowship

Gay Buddhist Fellowship exists to support Buddhist practice in the San Francisco gay community. Members come from all traditions. Currently we offer a limited meditation schedule, dharma talks, one-day sittings, retreats, classes, discussion groups, and workshops, dealing with such topics as relationships, engaged Buddhism, and practice and HIV. We publish a monthly newsletter. A steering committee is responsible for the organization's day-to-day operations, and functions on a consensus basis.
ADDRESS: 2261 Market Street #422, San Francisco, CA 94114
PHONE: (415) 974-9878
LINEAGE: Mixed traditions
SPIRITUAL HEAD: None—we are democratic!
CONTACT: Daishin David Sunseri
AFFILIATION: Autonomous
ESTABLISHED: 1990
FACILITIES: Rented
RETREATS OFFERED: One-day sittings, annual weekend retreat.
PUBLICATIONS: *Gay Buddhist Fellowship Newsletter*

Infinite Wisdom International

No description available.
ADDRESS: Box 446, Murphys, California 95247
PHONE: (209) 728-9467

Manzanita Village

Vipassana and the teachings of Thich Nhat Hanh. Meditation and Mindfulness in daily life. Engaged spirituality and deep ecology. Situated in an idyllic setting in the northern part of inland San Diego County. Retreats and residential programs. Organic gardening. Walking retreats in nearby Anza Borrego Desert and Pacific Crest Trail. Daily practice of meditation, work, and community.
ADDRESS: PO Box 67, Warner Springs, CA 92086
PHONE: (619) 782-9223
FAX: (619) 782-9223
LINEAGE: Vipassana and Zen
SPIRITUAL HEAD: Thich Nhat Hanh
CONTACTS: Christopher Reed and Michele Benzamin-Masuda
AFFILIATION: Ordinary Dharma in Santa Monica, California
ESTABLISHED: 1993
FACILITIES: Retreat center for residential programs.
RETREATS OFFERED: Three annual ten-day retreats. One annual two-month retreat. Frequent two-, three-, and four-day retreats.
PUBLICATIONS: *Ordinary Mind*, occasional newsletter.

Napa Mindfulness Community

Fluid, evolving "umbrella" organization of individuals and small groups practicing mindfulness. Includes Vipassana, Zen, and Vajrayana practitioners; also yoga and mindfulness-based stress reduction. Distinctively leaderless; senior students provide some teaching plus networking to more established centers/teachers. All participants are welcome to offer skills. Newsletter and lending library of tapes and books.
ADDRESS: 1420 Third Street, #14, Napa, CA 94559
PHONE: (707) 226-3273
CONTACT: J. Day
AFFILIATION: Autonomous
ESTABLISHED: 1990
MEDITATION PROGRAM: Several weekly or biweekly sitting groups; bimonthly gatherings; classes several times yearly.
RETREATS OFFERED: Weekends several times per year.
PUBLICATIONS: Bimonthly newsletter.

Occidental Sitting Group

This is primarily a local sitting group. Members meet one morning a week for two rounds each of sitting and walking meditation and a short dharma talk or discussion. Occasional guest teachers and daylong sittings. The leader is Bruce Fortin, a Zen priest ordained in 1976 at San Francisco Zen Center. The group's orientation is Zen and Vipassana. The teachings of Thich Nhat Hanh are influential. Members are encouraged to sit with other teachers and to attend longer retreats elsewhere. Meditation instruction (group and private) is available.
ADDRESS: 3535 Hillcrest Avenue, Sebastopol, CA 95472
PHONE: (707) 874-2234
FAX: Same
LINEAGE: Zen and Vipassana
CONTACT: Bruce Fortin
AFFILIATION: San Francisco Zen Center and Thich Nhat Hanh
ESTABLISHED: 1993
FACILITIES: Sit in local community hall.
MEDITATION PROGRAM: Group meditation one morning a week. Call for times.
RETREATS OFFERED: Daylong sittings

Open Door Sangha/Buddhist Meditation Community of Santa Barbara

Three of us (Fran Ryan, Yolanda Villareal, and Thea Howard) started Open Door Sangha as a small sitting group in 1978. We now have a mailing list of two hundred members. As the name implies, we are open to all Buddhist traditions. We sponsor four or five retreats per year led by such teachers as James Baraz, Thanissaro Bhikkhu, Christopher Reed, and Michele Benzamin-Masuda. Our *sangha* sits together one evening a week, and holds a "Day of Mindfulness" monthly from September through May. Please call or write for retreat schedules and additional information.
ADDRESS: 440 Whitman Street, #46, Goleta, CA 93117
PHONE: (805) 685-8787
FAX: (805) 893-2902
E-MAIL: thea@cosmic.physics.ucsb.edu
LINEAGE: All traditions welcome.
CONTACT: Thea Howard
AFFILIATION: Autonomous
ESTABLISHED: 1978
FACILITIES: Members' homes.
MEDITATION PROGRAM: Weekly evening sitting.
RETREATS OFFERED: Four or five retreats per year; monthly "Day of Mindfulness" from September through May.

Ordinary Dharma—Santa Monica

Vipassana and the teachings of Thich Nhat Hanh, from whom Christopher Reed has received Dharmacarya transmission. Meditation and Mindfulness in daily life, engaged spirituality, and deep ecology. We are also deeply informed by Joanna Macy and her work. Introductory classes, daily meditation practice, study groups, and Aikido in Santa Monica.

Cultivating Compassion in Caring for the Dying

INSPIRED BY A TWENTY-FIVE-HUNDRED-YEAR-OLD spiritual tradition, Zen Hospice Project (ZHP) is committed to bringing greater sensitivity and compassion to the care of people facing life-threatening illness. The project is a nationally innovative model of conscious care that provides a spectrum of collaborative volunteer programs, residential care, and training that aims to cultivate wisdom and compassion through service. As such, it is a fusion of spiritual insight and practical social action.

A primary goal of the project is to have a significant impact on the way dying people are cared for in this country. To that end, ZHP offers two basic and related programs:

Caregiver Volunteer Training: As the first step in a one-year program of service, the training approaches the fundamentals of hospice work within the broader context of meditative awareness. Volunteers make soup, change linens, give back rubs, and listen to stories of a lifetime lived and now ending. They attempt to bring to these everyday activities the open heart, mindfulness, and equanimity that are cultivated in meditation. This balanced response often transforms both the client's and the caregiver's experience of suffering and impermanence. ZHP volunteers are comprehensively trained, closely supervised by staff, nurtured by a personal spiritual practice, and emotionally supported by other volunteers and through bimonthly support meetings. Volunteer training

is offered each year in spring and fall. Although the predominant spiritual practice among volunteers is Buddhist, other traditions are respected and welcomed.

Public Education Program: Through its various educational programs, ZHP attempts to fundamentally influence traditional health care systems toward more conscious care by helping professionals to shift their view of death as being a failure to one where it is a transformative process through which they are also served, and by assisting family caregivers to avoid burn-out through discovery of their innate generosity and resourcefulness. Workshops encourage ways to demystify caregiving, investigate our response to suffering, and clarify our intention in service. Zen Hospice Project offers its mindful and integrated approach toward the care of those with life-threatening illness through presentations at national seminars, community workshops, and professional training programs. Workshops are also offered for individuals attempting to live more fully with their own life-threatening or chronic illnesses.

For more information, contact: Zen Hospice Project/San Francisco Zen Center, 273 Page Street, San Francisco, CA 94102; (415) 863-2910; e-mail: zenhospice@aol.com; www: http://www.zenhospice.org.

Regular retreats at Manzanita Village, our country retreat center.
ADDRESS: PO Box 67, Warner Springs, CA 92086
PHONE: (310) 394-6653
FAX: (619) 782-9223
E-MAIL: chanbao@AOL.COM
LINEAGE: Vipassana and Zen

SPIRITUAL HEAD: Thich Nhat Hanh
CONTACTS: Christopher Reed and Michele Benzamin-Masuda, Resident Teachers.
AFFILIATION: Manzanita Village
ESTABLISHED: 1982
FACILITIES: Meditation hall.
RETREATS OFFERED: Monthly one-day. Other retreats at Manzanita Village.

PUBLICATIONS: *Ordinary Mind,* occasional newsletter.

Rosemead Buddhist Monastery

No description available.
ADDRESS: 7833 Emerson Place, Rosemead, CA 91770

PHONE: (818) 280-1213

FAX: (818) 280-9077

E-MAIL: rev.terry@MCI2000.com

SPIRITUAL HEAD: Bhante Chao Chu, director

AFFILIATION: Center for Buddhist Development (Arizona), Los Angeles Buddhist Union.

ESTABLISHED: 1991

FACILITIES: Temple, library.

MEDITATION PROGRAM: Meditation, chanting.

RETREATS OFFERED: Monastic training.

PUBLICATIONS: *Commonsense*

San Francisco Buddhist Center

San Francisco Buddhist Center serves as the focus of a growing spiritual community. Located in the Mission District, we aim to serve the local community by providing a place dedicated to the development of positive human values. We offer a full program of courses, retreats, religious services, and festivals. Activities are funded principally through donations. Fees are negotiable for those on a low income. The center is part of the Friends of the Western Buddhist Order (FWBO), an international movement dedicated to establishing Buddhism in the modern world.

ADDRESS: 37 Bartlett Street, San Francisco, CA 94110

PHONE: (415) 282-2018

LINEAGE: Friends of the Western Buddhist Order

SPIRITUAL HEAD: Ven. Sangharakshita

CONTACT: Paramabodhi, Resident Teacher

AFFILIATION: Friends of the Western Buddhist Order

ESTABLISHED: 1993

FACILITIES: City center for meditation and Buddhism classes.

RETREATS OFFERED: Regular retreats—residential and nonresidential.

PUBLICATIONS: Many books through Windhorse Publications.

Zen Hospice Project

See accompanying article for description.

ADDRESS: 273 Page Street, San Francisco, CA 94102

PHONE: (415) 863-2910

FAX: (415) 863-1768

E-MAIL: zenhospice@aol.com

WWW: http://www.zenhospice.org

CONTACT: Frank Ostaseski

AFFILIATION: San Francisco Zen Center

ESTABLISHED: 1987

FACILITIES: Laguna Honda Hospital Hospice Unit; Victorian guest house.

COLORADO

The Buddhist/Christian Contemplative Group

This is an attempt to create a time and place where Buddhists and Christians committed to contemplative practice can come together to meditate on a weekly basis. There is a common liturgy and readings from both traditions, but the bulk of the service consists of thirty minutes of silent meditation with each person following their own religious tradition. Meets Sunday afternoons. Occasional lectures and potlucks.

ADDRESS: 1615 Ogden Street, Denver, CO 80218

PHONE: (303) 832-4929

LINEAGE: Christian and Buddhist

SPIRITUAL HEADS: Sr. Mary Luke-Tobin and Rev. Toni Cook

CONTACT: Professor Jose Cabezon

AFFILIATION: Autonomous

ESTABLISHED: 1995

FACILITIES: Sanctuary of St. Paul's United Methodist Church.

MEDITATION PROGRAM: Sunday meditation and religious service. Please call for times.

Englewood FCI Buddhist Meditation Group

This is a small group of dedicated inmates who sit together once a week in the prison chapel. Teaching duties are rotated among four volunteers: two from the Tibetan Karma Kagyu tradition and two from the Burmese and Sri Lankan Theravada traditions. Sitting is informal and discussions are freewheeling and fun. Referring to this group, Eido-Roshi once said, "Tell them they are already free."

ADDRESS: c/o Karelis, 1345 Spruce Street, Boulder, CO 80302

FAX: (303) 444-2414

LINEAGE: Tibetan Karma Kagyu. Burmese/Sri Lankan Theravada.

CONTACTS: Bill Karelis, Andrew Holecek, Don Morreale, Jeff Combelic, co-teachers.

AFFILIATION: Autonomous

ESTABLISHED: 1992

FACILITIES: Chapel at federal prison.

MEDITATION PROGRAM: Weekly sitting and dharma discussion.

RETREATS OFFERED: Occasional weekend programs.

Medicine Buddha Healing Institute

Medicine Buddha Healing Institute was founded in 1994 by the Ven. Dhamma Master Sensei Thompson. The institute provides space for people of all faiths to "learn how to heal one's self and others" through the practice of meditation. Many people have found the healing effects of Buddhist meditation extremely powerful—even miraculous. Through direct participation in our healing meditation programs, one is able to develop a high degree of transcendental wisdom, increase one's capacity for loving-kindness

Medicine Buddha

One who is not enlightened, is by definition ill.
Buddha

SAKYAMUNI BUDDHA WAS PROCLAIMED AS HUmanity's "Great Physician." He healed by teaching the dharma and also, it is said, by psychic or "miraculous" means. The incurably sick were given lessons on impermanence, while those who could be treated were taught to cultivate the "Seven Limbs of Enlightenment: mindfulness, investigation, striving, joy, tranquillity, concentration, and equanimity."

The prescription of "Morality, Meditation, and Wisdom" as a cure for disease indicates that illness, from the Buddhist perspective, is intimately linked to one's mental state. It follows then that if one's mental currents are clarified, the root cause of illness is removed and healing takes place. Healing, then, is the gradual elimination of the three inner poisons of greed, anger, and delusion, as well as the removal of karmic obstructions that have accumulated due to one's thoughts, words and deeds. These inner or psychic poisons correspond to three physiological poisons which, in imbalance, cause disease. Thus grasping generates excess wind; anger produces too much bile; and delusion yields a superabundance of phlegm.

Through the practice of meditation; participation in various *pujas* (offerings); recitation of mystical *daranis* (incantations); and the ingestion of special medicinal herbs, teas, and incense, disease can often be eradicated completely. During the healing process, insight arises and a natural transformation of one's thoughts, words, and deeds occurs. One is simultaneously cured of both mental and physical suffering.

Medicine Buddha Healing ultimately leads to the transformation of the self, to the direct apprehension of reality, and the conversion of one's suffering into the aspiration for Enlightenment.

Ven. Dhamma Master Sen Thompson

For more information, contact: Medicine Buddha Healing Institute, 720 Third Street, Fort Lupton, CO 80621; (303) 857-1993.

COLORADO (*cont.*)

and compassion, and attain and maintain peak mental and physical balance in one's everyday life.
ADDRESS: 720 Third Street, Fort Lupton, CO 80621
PHONE: (303) 857-1993
FAX: Same
E-MAIL: isg4usa@earthlink.net
WWW: http://www.isg.usa.com
LINEAGE: Nondenominational. Medicine Buddha Healing.
SPIRITUAL HEAD: Ven. Dhamma Master Sen Thompson, Director

AFFILIATION: Autonomous
ESTABLISHED: 1995
FACILITIES: Rented or donated space depending on group size.
RETREATS OFFERED: Quarterly symposia and retreats.
PUBLICATIONS: Audiocassettes/e-mail publications.

Naropa Institute

The Naropa Institute is a private, nonprofit liberal arts college offering undergraduate and graduate degrees in the arts, social sciences, and humanities. Founded by the late Chogyam Trungpa, Rinpoche, the institute is nonsectarian and characterized by its unique Buddhist educational heritage. Naropa is accredited by the North Central Association of Colleges and Schools. Our program provides an opportunity to develop skill in an area of study, openness to ever changing situations, confidence to enjoy life, and compassion to benefit society.
ADDRESS: 2130 Arapahoe Avenue, Boulder, CO 80302
PHONE: (303) 444-0202

Along the Bodhi Trail

Over there, in the center
of the flower-covered wilderness,
in the enchanted wilderness world,
beautiful with the dawn wind,
beautifully you lie with see-through freshness,
wilderness world.

Yaqui Deer Song

JUST AS THE BODHISATTVA ONCE WALKED IN THE forest, seeking quiet secluded places to practice, many of us in the West are taking time to leave the distractions and pressures of modern society for a week of walking in the mountains with supportive companions.

Such a trip offers an extraordinary opportunity to come into harmony with the rhythms and energy of the natural world. Our shared intention is to deepen the experience in an easy and unassuming way.

Mornings begin with sitting meditation. Before lunch we take our packs off and enjoy a period of slow, conscious stretching. Remaining silent on the trail or in camp, it's easier to be present for the sounds of birds, of the wind, of flowing water and, ultimately, for the silence surrounding and permeating all activity. A day or two of secluded solo practice is available for those who wish to undertake it.

During evening dharma discussions a "talking stick" is passed around. By tradition whoever holds it is given everyone's full attention and will not be interrupted. We've found that this promotes wonderfully clear and meaningful discourse.

Respect for each other as equals, sharing in the joys and suffering of human life, and following the five traditional Buddhist lay precepts during our time together form a reliable basis for mutual trust in our little community. We help each other on the trail as needed and volunteer to share camp chores.

For more intensive practice, we offer wilderness retreats led by recognized Dharma teachers. All contemplative outings and retreats are offered either as *dana* or at cost.

Terry Gustafson

For more information, contact: Rainbow Expeditions II, 7125 W. 27th Avenue, Wheat Ridge, CO 80215; (303) 239-9917.

FAX: (303) 444-0410
E-MAIL: admissions@naropa.edu
SPIRITUAL HEAD: Chogyam Trungpa, Rinpoche, Founder
CONTACT: Director of Admissions
AFFILIATION: Autonomous
ESTABLISHED: 1974
FACILITIES: Library, 3.7-acre campus, meditation hall.

MEDITATION PROGRAM: Optional meditation program for students.
RETREATS OFFERED: Some retreats as part of course work.
PUBLICATIONS: *Journal of Contemplative Psychology*; *Bombay Gin* (literary journal); *Hot Wheels*, a journal of student writing; *Naropa Weekly*, school newsletter.

Rocky Mountain Dharma Association

Rocky Mountain Dharma Association (RMDA) is a nonsectarian Buddhist organization created to support the dissemination and growth of Buddhist teachings within our community. Among its activities and benefits are (1) publication of the

RMDA Newsletter, (2) representation of members in civic and religious matters with our government, (3) representation of members for local, state, and federal grants, and (4) liaison between members and the interfaith community at large.

ADDRESS: 720 Third Street, Fort Lupton, CO 80621
PHONE: (303) 857-1993
FAX: Same
E-MAIL: isg4usa@earthlink.net
WWW: http://www.isg-usa.com
LINEAGE: Nondenominational
SPIRITUAL HEAD: Ven. Dhamma Master Sen Thompson, Director
AFFILIATION: Autonomous
ESTABLISHED: 1996
PUBLICATIONS: On-line newsletter.

Sierra Retreats/Sierra Contemplative Center

Sierra Retreats has been holding courses led by Shinzen Young at various locations near Boulder for several years. The proposed Sierra Contemplative Center (SCC) will provide a facility for daily practice and social activities and will enable us to expand the number of teachers we can bring to Colorado. Residential space for teachers will be provided. SCC will be located in a forested mountain area near Boulder.

ADDRESS: PO Box 19031, Boulder, CO 80308
PHONE: (303) 440-4153
LINEAGE: Theravada Vipassana
CONTACT: Jacquie Schechter
AFFILIATION: Autonomous
ESTABLISHED: 1992
FACILITIES: Meditation hall and support for up to one hundred participants is under development.
MEDITATION PROGRAM: Daily and weekly sittings.
RETREATS OFFERED: Long retreats led by a variety of teachers.

South Denver Buddhists

We are an informal meditation group using the facilities of a Methodist church where two of us work as caretakers. Our weekly meeting includes a short reading and thirty minutes of meditation, followed by discussion at a nearby coffeehouse. We encourage each other's practice, share insights from readings and talk about raising our children. In the future we hope to meet more frequently to explore Buddhist teachings in greater depth. New members, visitors, and inquiries are always welcome.

ADDRESS: 656 East Iowa Avenue, Denver, CO 80210
PHONE: (303) 733-7569
LINEAGE: Nondenominational
CONTACT: Richard Meier
AFFILIATION: Autonomous
ESTABLISHED: 1996
FACILITIES: Cameron Methodist Church and members' homes.
MEDITATION PROGRAM: Weekly group meditation, reading, and discussion.

Zane Sangha

Zane Sangha is a "Lilayana" practice. Both *Zane* and *Lilayana* indicate a westward movement of dharma: from *Dhyana* to *Ch'an* to *Zen* to *Zane*, and from Theravada to Mahayana to Vajrayana to "Lilayana." Our main intent is a Western vernacular translation of dharma on the practical and visceral level of living community. Our basic practices are about unification of internal and external mandala: individual focusing mandala (*Bodhi* practice), group/team mandala games (*sangha* practice), and the dharma practice of their primordial inseparability.

ADDRESS: 2635 Mapleton, #74, Boulder, CO 80302
PHONES: (303) 623-0441 (LeAnne) and (303) 541-9023 (Heath)

LINEAGE: Mahasandhi
SPIRITUAL HEAD: Atiyogi Lilananda Sambhoga
CONTACT: Z. J. Lila, DhT, Local Mis-director
AFFILIATION: Autonomous
ESTABLISHED: 1982
FACILITIES: Members' homes in Boulder and Denver.
MEDITATION PROGRAM: A variety of basic individual practices and an integrated range of group practices.
RETREATS OFFERED: Quarterly three-week fasting retreats; Year of the Fool Retreat; Various city *Siddhi* retreats.

CONNECTICUT

Meditation Center at St. John's on-the-Green

The purpose of our small *sangha* is to introduce all who come here to a variety of ways to create health, wholeness, and healing in their lives. The present format is *zazen* followed by a video and/or discussion. Sometimes we offer Tai Chi or yoga before the sitting, depending on availability of a teacher. Some of our *sangha* members teach meditation in schools, prisons, and hospitals. All of our programs are free and open to the public. Beginners are welcome (and we are all beginners)!

ADDRESS: 16 Church Street, Waterbury, CT 06702
PHONE: (203) 596-8137
FAX: (203) 757-8643
LINEAGE: Zen
SPIRITUAL HEAD: Brian Vaugh
CONTACTS: Brian Vaugh and Robin Kirsche
AFFILIATION: Autonomous
ESTABLISHED: 1990

Pentagon Meditation Club

FOUNDED IN 1976, THE PENTAGON MEDITATION Club (PMC) has a well-established reputation both within the Pentagon and throughout the world as a beacon of light for those who wish to meditate and have an impact on world peace.

Over the more than two decades since its inception, PMC has launched SDI (Spiritual Defense Initiative), inaugurated the Peace Shield Meditation Program, sponsored visits and dialogues with delegations from the former Soviet Union, and cosponsored the development of similar groups at the Environmental Protection Agency and the Department of Education.

We meet every Friday morning in the Chaplain's conference room at the Pentagon for a thirty-minute discussion period, followed by twenty-five minutes of Peace Shield Meditation. Initiated by our founder, Mr. Ed Winchester, the technique is derived, in part, from Christian centering prayer.

The practice involves centering the attention on the heart and repeating one's favorite name for God (Creator, Source, Universe, *OM*) in order to calm and focus the mind. Subsequently one recites the following, pausing after each sentence to close the eyes:

"Gently and with love and gratitude for the Divine Presence within me, I take a moment . . . to visualize myself happy and at peace. . . . I feel that place within me that yearns to love myself and other people more. . . . I see my family, friends, men, women and children throughout the world in harmony with each other. . . . I see world leaders turning to God for direction and guidance. . . . I see friends and adversaries joining together in fellowship to resolve their differences, forgiving each other and praying together for each other. . . ."

Our credo might be summed up in words spoken years ago by Ed Winchester: "Love," he said, "is the ultimate first-strike capability."

Bart Ives

For more information, contact: Pentagon Meditation Club, Box 46445, Washington, DC 20050; (703) 643-0262.

FACILITIES: St. John's on-the-Green

MEDITATION PROGRAM: Weekly evening program. Call for times.

RETREATS OFFERED: One-day retreats every few months.

(Beth) Roth

I have been teaching mindfulness meditation courses of eight to ten weeks' duration since 1993 at three locations in Connecticut: (1) Community Health Center in Meriden, an inner-city health facility. This class is taught in both Spanish and English and is open to the public. (2) Yale University School of Nursing: an accredited elective course on mindfulness meditation open to all Yale graduate and professional students. (3) The Yoga Studio in New Haven: an eight-week "Stress Reduction and Relaxation Program" geared especially towards health care, mental health, and social service workers. There is a fee for this course.

ADDRESS: 122 Canner Street, New Haven, CT 06511

PHONE: (203) 772-2335

CONTACT: Beth Roth, Resident Teacher

AFFILIATION: Autonomous

ESTABLISHED: 1993

FACILITIES: Classes at Meriden Community Health Center, Yale University School of Nursing, The Yoga Studio in New Haven.

RETREATS OFFERED: One daylong silent session with each eight-week program.

PUBLICATIONS: *Meditation in the Inner City. Meditation in the Curriculum.* "Mindfulness Meditation-Based Stress Reduction: Experience with a Bilingual Inner City Program," published in *The Nurse Practitioner Journal.*

DISTRICT OF COLUMBIA

Pentagon Meditation Club

The Pentagon Meditation Club is a non-denominational, nonprofit, private association of Department of Defense employees, their families, and non-Defense friends committed to the practice, exploration, and study of the effects of meditation, prayer, and positive thought. Our primary goal is to provide an opportunity for people to meditate in the Pentagon as part of a group. Secondarily, we provide a resource base from which people can learn more about meditation in its various forms and aspects.

ADDRESS: PO Box 46445, Washington, DC 20050

PHONE: (703) 643-0262

FAX: Same. Call first.

E-MAIL: bartonives@aol.com

CONTACT: Barton Ives, Resident Director

AFFILIATION: Office of the Chaplain, the Pentagon

ESTABLISHED: 1976

FACILITIES: Chaplain's conference room at the Pentagon.

MEDITATION PROGRAM: Instruction and open meditation, Friday mornings. Guest speakers.

RETREATS OFFERED: Join other groups in D.C. area for retreats.

PUBLICATIONS: Pentagon Meditation Club Newsletter

FLORIDA

Avalokiteshvara Buddhist Study Center

World-renowned Tibetan lamas and Zen masters teach participants the Buddhist doctrines and various meditative methods of Mahayana Buddhism (Sutrayana, Vajrayana, Rinzai, Pure Land, etc.). Includes Tibetan and Vietnamese Buddhist traditions.

Kwan Yin blesses the garden at Avalokiteshvara Buddhist Study Center, Miami, Florida. (Photo courtesy of Avalokiteshvara Buddhist Study Center.)

ADDRESS: 7550 Southwest 82nd Court, Miami, FL 33143-3818

PHONE: (305) 271-6361

FAX: (305) 271-9151

E-MAIL: lemaudao@ix.netcom.com

LINEAGE: Vajrayana (Tibetan); Rinzai Zen (Vietnamese)

SPIRITUAL HEADS: The Supreme Abbot Ven. Dr. Thich Man Giac (Vietnamese) and Geshe Ven. Dr. Lobsang Tenzin (Tibetan)

CONTACTS: Dr. Nguyen Thien, Yeshe Dorje, Resident Teachers

AFFILIATION: Vietnamese Buddhist United Churches (United States) and Drepung Loseling Monastery (Atlanta, Georgia, and India)

ESTABLISHED: 1984

FACILITIES: Urban meditation center in secluded private residence. Country re-treat facility dedicated to reading, dharma teaching, and intensive group and solitary retreats.

RETREATS OFFERED: Weekend sittings, four times a year under the master's guidance. Open to registered members or by invitation.

GEORGIA

Morning Star Institute for Holistic Studies

Morning Star Institute is a nonprofit educational organization offering workshops and retreats with leading teachers in psychological and spiritual growth. Located in a peaceful, rural area in the northeast Georgia mountains, we offer silent retreats in the contemplative traditions with an emphasis on Buddhist practice. The facilities are situated on four hundred acres near the edge of a national forest. The lodge comfortably houses twenty-five participants. Meals are vegetarian.

ADDRESS: PO Box 515, Sautee-Nacoochee, GA 30571

PHONES: (404) 633-9092 or (706) 878-2273

E-MAILS: mstarinst@aol.com or diamondh@mindspring.com

CONTACT: Linda L. Davis, Resident Director

AFFILIATION: Autonomous

ESTABLISHED: 1992

FACILITIES: Rented facilities in northeast Georgia.

RETREATS OFFERED: Buddhist and interfaith.

HAWAII

Back in Balance™

Meditation alone is but a tool to focus the mind. Meditation, along with working on a spiritual path such as the Eightfold Noble Path, the Twelve-Step Program, and so on, brings us and those we are interdependent with, back into balance. The universe remains as it is, and slowly our view expands to accept all of it.

ADDRESS: 1398 Hiahia Street, Wailuku, Maui, HI 96793
PHONE: (808) 244-0838
FAX: Same
LINEAGE: Asian-American Buddhist/ Hindu
CONTACT: Madhup Joshi, Resident Director
AFFILIATION: Autonomous
ESTABLISHED: 1996
FACILITIES: Sitting rooms. Space for three people to do overnight retreats.
MEDITATION PROGRAM: Daily sittings. Call for times.
RETREATS OFFERED: Overnight retreats on request for those wishing to learn meditation and for seasoned practitioners.

ILLINOIS

American Buddhist Association (ABA)

The ABA was founded in 1955 by the Rev. Gyomay Kubose to "study, publish and make known the principles of Buddhism and to encourage the understanding and application of these principles in the general American public." Although the organization has its roots in Japanese Buddhism (Jodo Shinshu and Zen), it considers itself an independent, nonsectarian religious organization of American Buddhists. Activities include publication of books, pamphlets, and audiovisual materials, and sponsorship of talks and lectures. We cooperate with other organizations such as the Buddhist Council of the Midwest and the National Conference of Christians and Jews.

ADDRESS: 1151 West Leland Avenue, Chicago, IL 60640
PHONE: (847) 677-8211
LINEAGE: Japanese Jodo Shinshu and Soto Zen
SPIRITUAL HEAD: Rev. Gyomay Kubose
CONTACT: Adrienne Kubose (8334 Harding, Skokie, IL 60076)
AFFILIATION: Buddhist Temple of Chicago
ESTABLISHED: 1955
FACILITIES: Buddhist Temple of Chicago

Buddhism Friendship Association

The Buddhism Friendship Association was established in 1995 by Asian Buddhists in the Chicago area and is connected with other Asian Buddhist organizations in the United States. Activities include daily chanting, meditation and talks. Services are open to all who are interested in Buddhist practice and doctrine.

ADDRESS: 950-52 West Carmen Avenue, Chicago, IL 60640
PHONE: (312) 275-0050
FAX: Same
LINEAGE: Many traditions, nonsectarian.
CONTACT: John K. Chung
ESTABLISHED: 1995
MEDITATION PROGRAM: Daily meditation, chanting, talks.

Buddhist Compassion Relief

Buddhist Compassion Relief is affiliated with other American centers in Champaign, Illinois, and Detroit, Michigan. Religious services are conducted in Chinese. Meditation is practiced on Sundays. Dana consists of monthly visits to the Port on the South Side of Chicago, as well as visits to nursing homes on Argyle Street in Chicago and Chicago's Chinatown. Families in need are also visited.

ADDRESS: 28 North Cass Avenue, Westmount, IL 60559
PHONE: (708) 963-6601
FAX: (708) 963-6602
LINEAGE: General Buddhist
CONTACT: Joe Lan Chang, Resident Teacher
AFFILIATION: American Tzu Chi Foundation
ESTABLISHED: 1993
FACILITIES: Offices
MEDITATION PROGRAM: Meditation included in Sunday services.
PUBLICATIONS: Tzu Chi World Journal, monthly.

Buddhist Council of the Midwest

The Buddhist Council of the Midwest encompasses a variety of denominations rooted in the rich traditions of their countries of origin and representing a kaleidoscope of philosophies, methodologies, and ideals. Each temple or organization is unique in itself, yet once a year we all gather for a Vesak celebration. Vesak commemorates the birth, enlightenment, and parinirvana of the Buddha. It is held each year as close as possible to the full moon of the fifth lunar month. We have celebrated Vesak together since 1984.

ADDRESS: 2400 Prairie, Evanston, IL 60201
PHONE: (847) 869-4975
FAX: (847) 869-0517
E-MAIL: jfred@wwa.com
LINEAGE: All traditions
CONTACT: Fred Babbin
AFFILIATION: We are an affiliation of dharma organizations in Chicago, northeastern Illinois, southern Wisconsin, northern Indiana, and southwestern Michigan.
RETREATS OFFERED: Annual Visakha Day (Vesak) celebration.
PUBLICATIONS: Annual Directory of Midwest Dharma Centers

Peoria Buddhist Study Group of New Horizons

No description available.

ADDRESS: PO Box 9652, Peoria, IL 61612
PHONE: (309) 682-1390
LINEAGE: General Buddhist
CONTACT: Gary Henderson
AFFILIATION: Autonomous
FACILITIES: Unitarian Universalist Church of Peoria, 908 Hamilton Boulevard, Peoria, Illinois.
MEDITATION PROGRAM: Weekly evening meditation followed by restaurant meetings. Call for times.
PUBLICATIONS: *Sangha News*

University of Chicago Buddhist Association

The University of Chicago Buddhist Association is affiliated with the Divinity School Student Association and fosters nondenominational Buddhist practice and academic activities, including meditation, discussions, talks, and interfaith meetings. Gatherings are held every week during the academic year at the University Divinity School.

ADDRESS: University of Chicago (DSA-UCBA), 1025 East 58th Street, Chicago, IL 60637
PHONE: (847) 864-7119
E-MAIL: mdamato@midway.uchicago.edu
LINEAGE: Nondenominational
CONTACT: Mario D'Amato
AFFILIATION: Divinity School Student Association
ESTABLISHED: 1994
FACILITIES: University Divinity School
MEDITATION PROGRAM: Meditation and discussion weekly. Please call for schedule. Open to the public.

KANSAS

Mindfulness Meditation Foundation

The Mindfulness Meditation Foundation is a nonsectarian, nonprofit Buddhist group unaffiliated with any particular lineage or school. We invite teachers of various lineages to come and teach us. Our goal is to be more *inclusive* and less *exclusive*. If a classification is necessary, we are American Buddhist. We meet at the Roeland Park Community Center weekly for sitting followed by a class.

ADDRESS: 3077 Merriam Lane, Kansas City, KS 66106
PHONE: (913) 432-7787
E-MAIL: AComic1@aol.com
LINEAGE: Nonsectarian American Buddhist
SPIRITUAL HEAD: Teachers from all lineages invited to teach.
CONTACT: Chuck Stanford, Director
AFFILIATION: Autonomous
FACILITIES: Roeland Park Community Center, 4850 Rosewood, Roeland Park, Kansas
MEDITATION PROGRAM: Group sitting and class one evening weekly.

Wichita Buddhist Meditation and Study Group

As there were no English-speaking Buddhist associations in the Wichita area, we decided to establish a sitting group of our own. With members from several traditions, our practice is nonsectarian. This is a new and active group that welcomes members to help broaden and strengthen our Buddhist experience.

ADDRESS: 1818 Clayton Street, Wichita, KS 67203
PHONE: (316) 945-5781
E-MAIL: fortythree@msn.com
CONTACT: Earl Griffith, Secretary
AFFILIATION: Autonomous

ESTABLISHED: February 1995
FACILITIES: Rented public building, the Civitan Center.
MEDITATION PROGRAM: We meet on Sunday mornings.
RETREATS OFFERED: Even-numbered months. Call for dates.

KENTUCKY

Louisville Community of Mindfulness

The Louisville Community of Mindfulness provides a supportive environment for anyone interested in practicing Buddhist meditation, regardless of religious affiliation or lack thereof. (Buddhist teaching is not opposed to or in competition with any other religious belief.) We take our teachings from both the Theravada and Mahayana traditions, and are inspired by such contemporary teachers as Thich Nhat Hanh, Jack Kornfield, and Joko Beck. Creating greater understanding, compassion, and loving-kindness is a goal to which we subscribe. We welcome you as a new friend and invite you to join us.

ADDRESS: 1544 Quadrant Avenue, Louisville, KY 40205
PHONE: (502) 451-2193
LINEAGE: No particular lineage.
SPIRITUAL HEAD: Inspiration from Thich Nhat Hanh, Jack Kornfield, Joko Beck, and others.
CONTACT: Bronson Rozier
AFFILIATION: Autonomous, informally affiliated with Community for Mindful Living/Order of Interbeing.
ESTABLISHED: 1993
FACILITIES: Use meditation space at ORBIS Center.
MEDITATION PROGRAM: Walking and sitting meditation on Sunday mornings, monthly recitation of the Five Precepts.
RETREATS OFFERED: Quarterly *Days of Mindfulness.*

MAINE

Friends of the Western Buddhist Order—Portland

A core of people who have been sitting together for a number of years. New people are welcome to join us.

ADDRESS: RR#3 Box 801, Woolwich, ME 04579
PHONES: (207) 828-1097 or (207) 442-8341
LINEAGE: Friends of the Western Buddhist Order
SPIRITUAL HEAD: Ven. Urgyen Sangharakshita
CONTACTS: Joanne Manoff or Deborah Henderson
AFFILIATION: Friends of the Western Buddhist Order
ESTABLISHED: 1990
FACILITIES: Rented room in a Portland office building.
MEDITATION PROGRAM: Weekly evening meditation. Call for times and location.

MASSACHUSETTS

Barre Center for Buddhist Studies

The Barre Center for Buddhist Studies is dedicated to bringing together teachers, students, scholars, and practitioners committed to exploring Buddhist thought and practice as a living tradition. We offer a variety of study and research opportunities: lectures, classes, seminars, workshops, conferences, retreats, independent study, and, in the future, a scholars-in-residence program. The center's vision calls for dialogue between different schools of Buddhism and discussions with other religious and scientific traditions. The emphasis is always on the interrelationship between study and practice and on exploring the relevance of classical teaching to contemporary life.

Barre Center for Buddhist Studies, in Barre, Massachusetts, which stresses the interrelationship between study and practice. (Photo courtesy of BCBS.)

ADDRESS: 149 Lockwood Road, Barre, MA 01005
PHONE: (508) 355-2347
FAX: (508) 355-2798
LINEAGE: Theravada; academic
CONTACTS: Andrew Olendzki and Mu Soeng
AFFILIATION: Insight Meditation Society
ESTABLISHED: 1990
FACILITIES: Residential
RETREATS OFFERED: One-day, weekend, and two-week retreats.
PUBLICATIONS: *Insight Newsletter,* Dhamma Dana Publications.

Buddhism, Meditation and Psychotherapy Group

This is an informal, friendly group of psychotherapists who are also experienced meditators. We meet monthly in one of our offices to meditate and to share our insights, thoughts, experiences, and feelings about the interface between Buddhism and psychotherapy. The responsibility for creating the structure and facilitating each meeting rotates among members. The format varies and may include discussion of specific topics such as "the concept of self in Buddhism and psychology," as well as discussion of relevant readings, case presentations, or the sharing of issues in our own lives.

ADDRESS: 274 North Pleasant Street #3, Amherst, MA 01002
PHONE: (413) 253-5494
E-MAIL: CarBee@aol.com
CONTACTS: Carla Brennan and Tetty Gorfine
AFFILIATION: Autonomous
MEDITATION PROGRAM: Monthly meditation and discussion.
ESTABLISHED: 1994

The Empty Bell

The Empty Bell is a sanctuary for the study and practice of Christian meditation and prayer. However, ours is a global, interfaith perspective, service-ori-

The Nalanda Program of Buddhist Studies

BASED ON THE MODEL OF NALANDA BUDDHIST University in ancient India where scholar-monks from all the different Buddhist schools lived, studied, and practiced together, the Barre Center for Buddhist Studies (BCBS) has been developing a program specifically intended to integrate the academic study of Buddhist doctrine with the intensive practice of meditation—all in a residential community setting.

For two weeks at a time, small groups of around fifteen students join together in morning, midday, and evening meditation, participate in lectures, discussions, and reading periods throughout the day, and join in evening seminars hosted by a wide range of visiting scholars and dharma teachers. There is unstructured time as well for students to follow their own research or meditation interests. A silent meditation retreat takes place on the intervening weekend.

The curriculum for the January intensive includes one week of Theravada studies and one week of Mahayana studies, giving the students a fairly comprehensive overview of the entire Buddhist tradition. In the summer, two two-week long programs, one each in Theravada and Mahayana studies, provide a much more in-depth study opportunity in each tradition.

The core faculty for these programs is Andrew Olendzki (Theravada Studies) and Mu Soeng (Mahayana Studies). Andrew Olendzki holds a Ph.D. in Buddhist Studies and has been the executive director of Insight Meditation Society (IMS) and BCBS since 1990. Mu Soeng, director of BCBS since 1992, was a Zen monk for eleven years. He is the author of *Thousand Peaks: Korean Zen Tradition and Teachers*, and *Heart Sutra: Ancient Buddhist Wisdom in the Light of Quantum Theory*.

Visiting faculty changes each year, and has included scholars from Harvard University, Drew University, Amherst College, Williams College, Boston College, Northeastern University, Harvard Medical School, and M.I.T.

Each participant is housed in a single room on our beautiful rural campus, with access to a well-stocked library, a tranquil meditation hall, miles of woodland trails, delicious vegetarian food, and an excellent faculty and staff. Program costs include room, board, and tuition.

Chris Phillips

For more information, contact: Barre Center for Buddhist Studies, 149 Lockwood Road, Barre, MA 01005; (508) 355-2347.

MASSACHUSETTS (*cont.*)

ented and friendly to the arts, and we give special attention to the Christian-Buddhist dialogue. All events are led by Robert A. Jonas, a psychotherapist and a Christian in the Carmelite tradition who has also received spiritual formation from the Buddhist traditions. Currently a student of *Sui-Zen*, using the Japanese bamboo flute (*shakuhachi*), he is an active member of the Society for Buddhist-Christian Studies.

ADDRESS: 105 Garfield Street, Watertown, MA 02172
PHONE: (617) 924-3497
FAX: (617) 924-1934
E-MAIL: RbtJonas@aol.com
LINEAGE: Japanese *Sui-Zen* (Blowing Zen) and Christian
SPIRITUAL HEADS: Many
CONTACTS: Robert A. Jonas, MTS, Ed.D., Resident Teacher
AFFILIATION: Autonomous
ESTABLISHED: 1992
FACILITIES: Urban Christ-*zendo*.

RETREATS OFFERED: Fall and spring Buddhist/Christian dialogue retreats. Individual, private retreats.

Friends of the Western Buddhist Order—Cambridge

FWBO—Cambridge holds regular introductory meetings in Harvard Square. Meditation classes and discussion groups meet weekly. Whatever your interest, please feel free to make use of our center to support your spiritual growth.

ADDRESS: PO Box 381171, Cambridge, MA 02238-1171
PHONE: (617) 576-7345
E-MAIL: Vajramati@aol.com
WWW: http://web.mit.edu/benbr/www/FWBOhome.htm
SPIRITUAL HEAD: Urgyen Sangharakshita (London, England)
CONTACT: Vajramati, Resident Teacher
AFFILIATION: Friends of the Western Buddhist Order
MEDITATION PROGRAM: Weekly meditation class and discussion group. Introductory meetings. Call for schedule.
PUBLICATIONS: Contact Windhorse Books, (800) 303-5728.

Harvard Buddhist Community

The Harvard Buddhist Community (HBC) was founded in 1993 to increase the interaction between persons from all Buddhist lineages in a nonsectarian spirit and to create a sense of Buddhist community at Harvard. HBC is open primarily to the university's Buddhist students, although non-Buddhist students are also welcome. Activities include interactions between ordained and nonordained members, sponsorship of educational events on Buddhist teachings and practices, organization of nonsectarian Buddhist worship services, and participation in efforts to address social and environmental issues as Buddhists.

ADDRESS: c/o Williams, 42 Francis Avenue, Cambridge, MA 02138
PHONE: (617) 493-4082
FAX: Same
LINEAGE: Nonsectarian
SPIRITUAL HEAD: Duncan Ryuken Williams (Harvard-Radcliffe Buddhist Chaplain)
AFFILIATION: Autonomous
ESTABLISHED: 1993

Mindfulness-Based Stress Management of Pioneer Valley

Each spring and fall, Carla Brennan, a transpersonal psychotherapist and Buddhist practitioner, offers a ten-week course in Mindfulness-based Stress Management called "The Art of Self-Care and Conscious Living." Advanced classes for program graduates as well as one-day retreats are scheduled periodically. The heart of the program is the practice of mindfulness—both formally in sitting, walking, and standing meditations and informally in all activities of daily life. Trained in Vipassana and Zen, Carla offers basic dharma teachings in layperson's terms.

ADDRESS: 274 North Pleasant Street, #3, Amherst, MA 01002
PHONE: (413) 253-5494
E-MAIL: CarBee@aol.com
CONTACT: Carla Brennan
AFFILIATION: Autonomous
ESTABLISHED: 1993
MEDITATION PROGRAM: Twice yearly ten-week courses. Advanced classes for graduates of the program.
RETREATS OFFERED: Periodic one-day retreats.

Mindfulness Meditation Group of Amherst

We started this group because many friends, colleagues, and clients wanted a local place to sit with others. Usually three to seven people show up for our weekly evening meeting. We sit for the first forty-five minutes (on a chair or the floor—bring your own cushion) and follow with a fifteen-minute reading from a meditation-related source. The hour ends with a brief period of silence. There is no instruction and no fee.

ADDRESS: 274 North Pleasant Street, #3, Amherst, MA 01002
PHONE: (413) 253-5494

E-MAIL: CarBee@aol.com
AFFILIATION: Autonomous
ESTABLISHED: 1995
MEDITATION PROGRAM: Weekly hour of meditation and reading.

Prison Dharma Network

Prison Dharma Network (PDN) is a nonsectarian Buddhist support network for inmates and prison volunteers. PDN regularly mails donated dharma books free of charge to interested prisoners. We also respond to requests for information and try to connect inmates with dharma center resources in their area. PDN actively networks with other prison dharma organizations, individual volunteers, and prison meditation groups in an effort to facilitate and support their work and practice. We are limited in what we can accomplish by our complete dependence on unpaid volunteer staff and by limited financial resources. Please be patient in your efforts to contact us.

ADDRESS: PO Box 912, Astor Station, Boston, MA 02123-0912
LINEAGE: Nonsectarian
SPIRITUAL HEADS: Board of Spiritual Advisors: Robert Aitken-Roshi; Bhikshuni Pema Chodron; Bernard Tetsugen Glassman-Roshi; Stephen Levine; John Daido Loori-Roshi; Sakyong Mipham-Rinpoche; Very Ven. Thrangu-Rinpoche.
CONTACT: Fleet W. Maull, Project Director
AFFILIATION: Autonomous
ESTABLISHED: 1989
FACILITIES: Borrowed office space at Shambhala Publications.
PUBLICATIONS: *The Bodhi Seed*, newsletter.

SunRay Meditation Society

No description available.

ADDRESS: 263 North Avenue, Weston, MA 02193

Buddhist Bell Chant at Wellesley College

A T THE END OF MY FIRST YEAR AS ADVISOR TO Buddhist students at Wellesley College, a group of seniors requested that I offer the traditional Korean evening bell chant as a call to worship for baccalaureate services. How exciting to be able to share this practice with college students! Even to be asked is already an indication of how far Buddhism and religious pluralism have come in this country.

To help my school, I resolved to practice thoroughly before the service. Chanting each phrase, my attention became more focused:

Mung Jong Song, *hearing the sound of the bell,*
Bon-ne Dan, *all thinking is cut off.*
Ji he jang, *wisdom grows, cognition appears.*
Bo ri sang ni ji ok, *hell is left behind.*

Walking into the crowded chapel, I was reminded of my own commencement here five years ago, and I became nervous. Trusting the practice, I sat down, watched the breath rise and fall, touched the bell, and began. Giv-ing myself to the chant wholeheartedly, anxiety dropped away. In a moment, it was finished. Our rabbi began intoning from the Book of Genesis; the service continued.

Afterward, the response was very positive. One father took me by both arms and said, "That was beautiful." Another family told me that their son had just begun monastic training in Korea. The chant, they said, had given them a point of entry into his practice and his new life.

As for me, the chanting was a renewal of my practice vow, to let go of "small self" and become "true self."

Perceiving sound,
we attain true nature
and find our way.

Ji Hyang Sunim

For more information, contact: Ji Hyang Sunim, Advisor to Buddhist Students, Office of Religious Life, Wellesley College, Wellesley, MA 02181; (617) 283-2685.

PHONE: (617) 893-3830
LINEAGE: Mixed
CONTACT: Leila Joseph
AFFILIATION: Autonomous

Wellesley Buddhist Community

Wellesley Buddhist Community was founded by alumnae of Wellesley College out of deep appreciation of the Buddha's teaching. Two of us practice with Cambridge Zen Center, which has generously donated supplies and its teachers' time. We work to support the practice of all Buddhist students and staff on the Wellesley campus. Together we develop clarity and energy and (just like the Wellesley motto) find our direction in service. The Buddhist Community has been welcomed by the college as a member of its religious life team. Practice is held three times weekly during the academic year.

ADDRESS: Office of Religious Life, Wellesley College, Wellesley, MA 02181
PHONE: (617) 283-2685
E-MAIL: jhyang@wellesley.edu
LINEAGE: All traditions.
CONTACT: Ji Hyang Sunim
AFFILIATION: Loosely affiliated with Cambridge Zen Center.

ESTABLISHED: 1995
FACILITIES: Meditation room at Houghton Chapel, Wellesley.
MEDITATION PROGRAM: Three times weekly. Call for schedule.

Wisdom Publications

Please see accompanying article.
ADDRESS: 199 Elm Street, Somerville, MA 02144
PHONE: (617) 536-3358
FAX: (617) 536-1897
E-MAIL: info@wisdompubs.org
CONTACT: Timothy McNeill, Publisher and Resident Director

Wisdom Publications

WISDOM PUBLICATIONS, A NOT-FOR-PROFIT publisher of books on Buddhism, Tibet, and related East-West themes, is dedicated to making available authentic Buddhist works for the benefit of all. We publish translations of the *Sutras* and *Tantras*, teachings of past and contemporary Buddhist masters, and original works by the world's leading Buddhist scholars. Our titles are published with an appreciation for Buddhism as a living philosophy and with the special commitment to preserve and transmit important works from all the major Buddhist traditions. Our titles are distributed worldwide and have been translated into a dozen foreign languages. Wisdom is also the exclusive North American distributor of books published by the Pali Text Society of London.

We started publishing in the late 1970s and were based in London until 1989 when we moved to an office building in Boston's historic Back Bay. Now located in Somerville, our new facility houses offices, a bookstore, and a presentation area for author talks and teaching and meditation programs. Catalogues are mailed free of charge at least twice a year.

Timothy McNeill, Publisher

For more information, contact: Wisdom Publications, 199 Elm Street, Somerville, MA 02144; (617) 536-3358.

AFFILIATION: Autonomous
ESTABLISHED: Late 1970s
FACILITIES: Space in office building.

Worcester Sitting Group

The Worcester Sitting Group began as a way for people in the Worcester area to meditate together. We have continued to sit, do walking meditation, and share tea, cookies, and conversation every Sunday evening at the home of David Rynick and Melissa Blacker. David and Melissa are students of Zen Buddhism; other group members bring the richness of their own study of Theravada, Vajrayana, Christian, and Jewish meditation to the mix. We have recently begun a second sitting evening at the First Unitarian Church, where guided meditation and interviews are offered but, alas, no cookies.
ADDRESS: 23 Berwick Street, Worcester, MA 01602-1405
PHONE: (508) 792-5189

LINEAGE: Japanese and Korean Zen
CONTACTS: Melissa Blacker and David Rynick
AFFILIATION: Autonomous
ESTABLISHED: 1993
FACILITIES: Members' homes and First Unitarian Church.
RETREATS OFFERED: Occasional one-day sittings.

MICHIGAN

Deep Spring Center for Meditation and Spiritual Inquiry

Deep Spring Center teaches and supports the deepening of nondual awareness through the practices of meditation and *spiritual inquiry*. The foundation practice is Insight Meditation. We balance Insight practice with a deepening awareness of our true nature, which is eternal and present now. Spiritual inquiry takes a broader look. Who are we? Why are we incarnate? How do we live our lives with as much wisdom and love as possible?
ADDRESS: 3455 Charing Cross Road, Ann Arbor, MI 48108
PHONE: (313) 971-3455
E-MAILS: bjbrodsky@aol.com *or* DpSpringC@aol.com
LINEAGE: Buddhist (Vipassana and Dzogchen); Quaker
SPIRITUAL HEADS: Barbara Brodsky and Aaron, a spirit whom Barbara channels. He has been a Buddhist monk, scholar, and Theravada Vipassana meditation master.
CONTACT: David Brown, Director
AFFILIATION: Autonomous
ESTABLISHED: 1990
FACILITIES: Rented facilities.
MEDITATION PROGRAM: Weekly classes, sittings; teacher-training class. There is no channeling in any meditation class.
RETREATS OFFERED: Two annual weekend retreats; ten-day retreat; three one-

Barbara Brodsky (foreground) leads Dzogchen meditation at Emrich Conference Center near Brighton, Michigan. (Photo by Celeste Zygmont.)

or two-day retreats for ongoing students.

PUBLICATIONS: Four books of Buddhist teachings from Aaron.

MINNESOTA

Common Ground Meditation Center

Common Ground is a community meditation center that provides practice opportunities for people interested in mindfulness meditation in all its forms. Programs are offered free of charge, although participants are welcome to support the center in whatever way feels appropriate given their circumstances and interest. For the most part, all work and teaching is done on a volunteer basis.

ADDRESS: 3400 East 26th Street, Minneapolis, MN 55406

PHONE: (612) 722-8260

CONTACTS: Mark Nunberg and Wynn Fricke

AFFILIATION: Autonomous

ESTABLISHED: 1993

FACILITIES: Building with studio space for meditation.

MEDITATION PROGRAM: Daily open meditations; weekly guided meditation sessions; hatha yoga; guided yogic breathing practice; six-week introduction to mindfulness meditation.

RETREATS OFFERED: Nonresidential year-end retreat.

MISSOURI

American Buddhist Center at Unity Temple on the Plaza

The American Buddhist Center is a community of meditators that provides training in meditation, as well as lecturers and workshops on Buddhist philosophy, history, and practice. We encourage understanding between Christians and Buddhists and provide opportunities for participation in Buddhist worship services and ceremonies. We also maintain a library of Buddhist materials and serve as a clearinghouse for information about other dharma organizations and activities. Our goal is to provide a place to find liberation from suffering and to awaken to our true nature.

ADDRESS: 707 West 47th Street, Kansas City, MO 64112

PHONE: (816) 561-4466

FAX: (816) 753-2221

CONTACT: Ben Worth, Resident Director

AFFILIATION: Autonomous but affiliated with Unity Temple

ESTABLISHED: 1996

FACILITIES: Meeting space, auditorium.

MEDITATION PROGRAM: Three sittings per week, weekly topic group, monthly book study, regular speaker presentations.

RETREATS OFFERED: Monthly daylong retreat.

MISSISSIPPI

Jackson Insight Meditation Group

For additional information, please see our Home page. This Web site lists titles in our lending library and provides data on upcoming events.

ADDRESS: 781 Broadmoor Drive, Jackson, MS 39206

PHONE: (601) 981-6925

FAX: (601) 982-4471

E-MAIL: luke@teclink.net

WWW: http://home.teclink.net/~luke/

CONTACTS: Luke Lundemo and Charlotte McKay, Coordinators

AFFILIATION: Autonomous

ESTABLISHED: 1990

FACILITIES: Rented space at Mississippi Yoga Center. Free lending library.

MEDITATION PROGRAM: One-hour meditation on Sundays; Classes in spring and fall.

RETREATS OFFERED: Occasional one-day, weekend, and nine-day retreats.

PUBLICATIONS: Unnamed newsletter.

MONTANA

Rocky Mountain Friends of the Western Buddhist Order

Rocky Mountain FWBO is one of several United States centers affiliated with the Friends of the Western Buddhist Order, an international Buddhist movement founded in 1967 with activities in more than two dozen countries. In Missoula we have two residential communities and a dharma center offering a variety of opportunities for meditation and devotional practice, classes, a Buddhist bookstore, and an annual calendar of local and regional retreats.

ADDRESS: 540 South Second West, Missoula, MT 59801
PHONE: (406) 543-1158
WWW: http://www.fwbo.org
LINEAGE: Friends of the Western Buddhist Order
SPIRITUAL HEAD: Sangharakshita
CONTACTS: Anandajyoti; Buddhapalita; Saramati, and Varashuri, Resident Teachers
AFFILIATION: Friends of the Western Buddhist Order
ESTABLISHED: 1991
FACILITIES: Two residential communities, dharma center, bookstore.

NEW HAMPSHIRE

Friends of the Western Buddhist Order—Aryaloka

We are pleasantly situated in wooded, rural New Hampshire. At the end of a dirt driveway bordered by pines, you will see an unusual building in the form of twin "silver"-painted geodesic domes. It may look space-age, but the FWBO is neither Space Age nor New Age. Rather, it is firmly based in traditional Buddhist teachings and practices such as meditation and ethical observance. We offer a

Study group in session at Aryaloka Community in Newmarket, New Hampshire. (Photo courtesy of Aryaloka.)

View of the east dome of Aryaloka. (Photo courtesy of Aryaloka.)

A Network of Spiritual Friends

THE FRIENDS OF THE WESTERN BUDDHIST Order (FWBO), founded by Ven. Urgyen Sangharakshita, is an international network of well over one hundred financially and legally independent organizations, including Buddhist centers, residential communities, team-based right-livelihood businesses, educational and health programs, retreat facilities, and arts centers. They are unified only by the strong bonds of spiritual friendship between the individuals involved.

In the FWBO we recognize that a sincere and effective "Going for Refuge" to the Three Jewels is the primary act of the Buddhist life. At the core of the FWBO is the Western Buddhist Order (WBO), a spiritual community of men and women who are effectively "Going for Refuge." Although the celibate spiritual life is highly valued, we do not support the traditional view that monastics are the only genuine Buddhists; members of the WBO live neither specifically "lay" nor "monastic" lifestyles. Men and women in the order have equal status. A body of "preceptors" is responsible for the ordination and training of order members.

The roles of teacher and student are less clearly defined than in many Western Buddhist groups. Instead, while affirming the hierarchy of spiritual development, we promote the development of a network of horizontal and vertical spiritual friendships. Our teaching places an equal emphasis on meditation, study, devotional practices, ethics, and the development of spiritual friendship.

Most of our businesses, residential communities, and retreat centers are single-sex because we have found that such environments provide the best conditions for spiritual development.

In the field of social action we have founded an organization that raises funds in the West for various social programs among the ex-untouchable Buddhists of India. These programs are run by Indian members of the WBO.

Manjuvajra

For more information, contact: Friends of the Western Buddhist Order, 14 Heartwood Circle, Newmarket, NH 03857; (603) 659-5456.

---

variety of retreats throughout the year from beginner level to advanced, lasting a day, weekend, week, and longer. Inside the building you will experience its spaciousness and will delight in its tranquillity.

ADDRESS: Aryaloka, 14 Heartwood Circle, Newmarket, NH 03857
PHONE: (603) 659-5456
SPIRITUAL HEAD: Urgyen Sangharakshita
CONTACTS: Silaratna or Paramashanti
AFFILIATION: Autonomous. Affiliated centers in Massachusetts, Montana, Washington, and California.
ESTABLISHED: 1985
FACILITIES: Accommodation for eighteen

to twenty people. Solitary cabin. Yoga/tai chi room.
RETREATS OFFERED: Beginners, intermediate, and advanced. Day, weekend, week, or longer.
PUBLICATIONS: *Aryaloka Mandala*, newsletter. Windhorse Publications (book publishing).

NEW JERSEY

Buddhist Sangha of South Jersey

Our group is working to adapt Buddhism to modern life in America. We have in-

corporated teachings from both Theravada and Mahayana and our members have experience in both traditions. We emphasize lay practice but we respect monasticism and support all forms of Buddhism.

ADDRESS: 164 Cheyenne Trail, Medford Lakes, NJ 08055
PHONE: (609) 953-9215
E-MAIL: wslyons@voicenet.com
LINEAGE: Nondenominational
CONTACT: Walt Lyons
AFFILIATION: Autonomous
ESTABLISHED: 1995
FACILITIES: 302 North Washington Street, #102, Moorestown, New Jersey.

MEDITATION PROGRAM: Weekly meditation, chanting, and recitation of Buddhist texts. Monthly meetings to listen to and discuss audiotapes of Buddhist teachers such as Thich Nhat Hanh. All at Moorestown address. Call for times.

RETREATS OFFERED: Occasional one-day sitting retreats.

Buddhist Study Association of Greater New York, Inc.

We function as a source of information about various Buddhist traditions and centers and provide free books on Buddhism to all who are interested. We direct institutions to Buddhist clergy, teachers, and volunteers who can serve as chaplains at hospitals, schools, colleges, police and fire departments, prisons, jails, and rehabilitation centers, and who are available for commencement exercises and other appropriate public functions. As a spiritual center, we conduct regular meetings for the study of Buddhist texts, the practice of meditation, and the enjoyment of spiritual friendship.

ADDRESS: 16 Stanford Avenue, West Orange, NJ 07052

PHONE: (201) 736-8957

FAX: (201) 736-8957 (press *51)

SPIRITUAL HEAD: Anthony Bucci, Founder

AFFILIATION: Autonomous

FACILITIES: Urban spiritual center.

MEDITATION PROGRAM: Regular meetings for meditation and the study of Buddhist texts. Please call for times.

NEW MEXICO

Lama Foundation

Established in 1968 as a "center for the awakening of consciousness," Lama Foundation is unusual in that there is no particular tradition or teacher repre-

Lama Foundation in San Cristobal, New Mexico, survived a devastating forest fire in 1996. (Photo courtesy of Lama Foundation.)

sented here. Instead, practices from all the world's great religions are taught and can be integrated into one's own path. We think of ourselves as a school of practical spirituality in which everything we do becomes an opportunity to awaken. We live closely with the land and other people, yet away from many of the stresses inherent in our culture. Whatever we go on to do in the world will have been nourished by our Lama experience.

ADDRESS: PO Box 240, San Cristobal, NM 87564

PHONE: (505) 586-1269

E-MAIL: 76375.2726@compuserve.com

CONTACT: Leslie Maclean

AFFILIATION: Ecumenical

ESTABLISHED: 1968

FACILITIES: Large community dome for dances and gatherings, a small kiva-type prayer room, a larger prayer dome, two solitary retreat huts, a library, and music room.

RETREATS OFFERED: Lama is an ecumenical center welcoming teachers from all

contemplative traditions. Buddhist retreats led by Tsultrim Allione, Sharon Salzberg, Sylvia Boorstein, Michael Freeman, Amy Schmidt, and others are regularly held here.

Ocamora Foundation

Ocamora Foundation is dedicated to serving individuals and groups wishing to pursue the path of retreat as a means of coming into peace. It is located two hours northeast of Santa Fe, New Mexico, on a 150-year-old ranch. The setting is both vast and intimate, offering a unique experience of nature unspoiled and powerful. In addition to a program of residential retreats held during the summer, Ocamora is available throughout most of the year for individuals wishing to experience a period of solitude and inner reflection.

ADDRESS: PO Box 43, Ocate, NM 87734

PHONE: (505) 666-2389

AFFILIATION: Autonomous

ESTABLISHED: 1981

The Project on Being with Dying

AS A SOCIETY, WE FACE CHALLENGING QUESTIONS about the efficacy of our health care system and the care of the dying. Death in America still exemplifies a firm denial of the transient nature of life and an aversion to pain and decay. An aging population, the widespread occurrence of cancer and AIDS, a society that is fearful of death, families that are generally unfamiliar with the care of their seriously ill members, technological developments that bring into question the ethics of life extension and termination, and a medical system challenged by questions of cost-effectiveness, all make our educational work a social imperative.

In response to a perceived need among medical professionals, social workers, clergy, and community members for a contemplative approach to working with dying people, Upaya established the "Project on Being with Dying" in 1994. The project is committed to providing innovative educational programs in the area of spiritual care for the terminally ill and for their families. It seeks to inspire a gentle revolution in our relationship to dying and living, and to serve as a means for people to explore the meaning of death in their own lives. The project encourages an approach to death that is kind, open, and dignified.

In being with dying, it is possible for us to see death and know life in terms of compassion and awakening. Indeed, exploring ways to make dying more compassionate will have far-reaching consequences for how we live our lives. In gently caring for the dying, we can more peacefully and wisely care for the living and for life itself.

Joan Halifax and Lee Moore

For more information, contact: Upaya, 1404 Cerro Gordo Road, Santa Fe, NM 87501; (505) 986-8518.

FACILITIES: Retreat center with rooms, tipi, yurt, camping.

RETREATS OFFERED: Annually one to three Vipassana meditation retreats (one of them with Bhante Gunaratana).

Santa Fe Zen Center

Santa Fe Zen Center shares Cerro Gordo Temple with Upaya (led by Joan Halifax), a Tibetan group, and other kinds of Buddhists. We sit every weekday morning (*zazen*, service, *soji*, breakfast) and one weekday evening (*zazen*, service). There are three tiny rooms at the temple available as living space for dharma students.

ADDRESS: 1404 Cerro Gordo Road, Santa Fe, NM 87501

PHONE: (505) 982-1332

CONTACT: Tom Ireland

AFFILIATION: Autonomous. Some members are affiliated with Crestone Mountain Zen Center in Crestone, Colorado.

ESTABLISHED: 1985

FACILITIES: *Zendo*, library, residential rooms.

MEDITATION PROGRAM: Daily *zazen* and services.

RETREATS OFFERED: Unaffiliated teachers lead weekend sittings at the temple.

Southwest Center for Spiritual Living

Our regular weekly meetings begin and end with thirty minutes of meditation. All events are at the Sperry Drive address. We welcome your participation.

ADDRESS: 715 Sperry Drive, Las Vegas, NM 87701

PHONE: (505) 454-1671

LINEAGE: Theravada Buddhism and Advaita Vedanta

SPIRITUAL HEAD: Dixie L. Ray

CONTACT: Same

AFFILIATION: Autonomous

ESTABLISHED: January 1993

FACILITIES: "Our house."

MEDITATION PROGRAM: Meditation weekly. Call for times.

RETREATS OFFERED: Occasional one-day retreats.

PUBLICATIONS: Newsletter every two months.

Upaya

Upaya is Sanskrit for "skillful means." *Upaya* is a way for us to practice compassion in the world. To realize compassion, we are mindful in our daily lives. We also take time to renew ourselves and to educate and train ourselves in ways to contribute to the health of the world. Upaya is a Buddhist organization that is dedicated to education and practices that foster effective action and right livelihood.

ADDRESS: 1404 Cerro Gordo Road, Santa Fe, NM 87501

PHONE: (505) 986-8518

FAX: (505) 986-8528

E-MAIL: upaya@rt66.com

LINEAGE: Vietnamese

SPIRITUAL HEAD: Thich Nhat Hanh

CONTACT: Joan Halifax, Resident Teacher

AFFILIATION: Order of Interbeing—Tiep Hien Order

ESTABLISHED: 1990

FACILITIES: Retreat house, *zendo*, office, dining building.

MEDITATION PROGRAM: Group meditation Monday through Friday.

RETREATS OFFERED: Mindfulness retreats, wilderness retreats, and programs on being with the dying.

NEW YORK

Brooklyn Buddhist Association

The Brooklyn Buddhist Association endeavors to make the Buddha's teaching available to all people, regardless of race, sex, or ethnic origin, and to share the Buddhist ideal of love and compassion for all beings. We offer a living practice of these teachings through the martial arts and related programs.

ADDRESS: 211 Smith Street, Brooklyn, NY 11201

PHONE: (718) 488-9511

FAX: (718) 797-1073

E-MAIL: sjosephj@aol.com

LINEAGE: Japanese

SPIRITUAL HEAD: Rev. Gyoko Saito

CONTACT: Rev. Shaku Joseph Jarman

AFFILIATION: Higashi Hongonji; International Zen Dojo (Chozen-ji).

ESTABLISHED: 1984

Shaku Joseph Jarman, Dharma teacher at Brooklyn Buddhist Association. (Photo by Terrance Carney/Studio L'Image.)

FACILITIES: Storefront rental used for meditation and Aikido.

MEDITATION PROGRAM: Tuesday, Wednesday, and Friday evenings. Sunday mornings. Call for times.

RETREATS OFFERED: One-week nonresidential intensive at center; one-week intensive at rented camp in Portland, Connecticut.

PUBLICATIONS: *Dojo News—Jikishinkan*

Cayuga Sangha

We are a small, informal sitting group that meets weekly for meditation and group discussion. Most participants practice Vipassana, but all silent meditators are welcome. Members have a wide range of experience.

ADDRESS: 427 North Cayuga Street, Ithaca, NY 14850

PHONE: (607) 273-0377

LINEAGE: Nondenominational

AFFILIATION: Autonomous

ESTABLISHED: 1993

FACILITIES: Sitting room.

MEDITATION PROGRAM: Weekly two-hour meditation and dharma discussion group.

RETREATS OFFERED: The group itself sponsors no retreats, but several members lead silent weekend retreats several times a year, occasionally with guest teachers.

Community of Mindfulness— New York Metro

Although the Community of Mindfulness—New York Metro is comprised primarily of people inspired by the teachings of Thich Nhat Hanh, many who sit with us are rooted in Vipassana, Zen, and Tibetan practice. Monthly "Days of Mindfulness" include precepts recitation, vegetarian potluck lunch, sitting and walking meditation, and dharma dialogue. Study groups focus on Thich Nhat Hanh's books *Blooming of a Lotus; Transformation and Healing—Sutra on the Four Establishments of Mindfulness; Old Path, White Clouds; Present Moment, Wonderful Moment;* and *Touching Peace.* Resident Director Lyn Fine was ordained as a *dharmacharya* in the Order of Interbeing in 1994.

ADDRESS: 530 West End Avenue, #5, New York, NY 10024

PHONE: (212) 501-2652 (info line)

E-MAIL: Leonoref@aol.com

LINEAGE: Vietnamese Zen, Vipassana, Tibetan Vajrayana

SPIRITUAL HEAD: Thich Nhat Hanh

CONTACT: Lyn Fine, Director

AFFILIATION: Order of Interbeing

FACILITIES: Members' homes in Manhattan, Long Island, Brooklyn, New Jersey, upstate New York. Call for locations.

RETREATS OFFERED: Monthly Day of Mindfulness; study groups.

PUBLICATIONS: Small quarterly newsletter.

Bodhiline

Up-to-the-minute information on the New York dharma scene is as close as your Touch-Tone phone with a computerized messaging system called Bodhiline, courtesy of the Buddhist Information Service of New York (BIS).

In addition to its frequently updated list of metro-area Buddhist meditation centers, bookshops, and dharma supply stores, Bodhiline provides current information on special events, as well as five-minute excerpts of recorded dharma talks. The service has been on-line since 1993 and receives anywhere from fifty to one hundred calls per week. Many Buddhist centers use it to keep members and other interested callers informed about retreats, the daily meditation schedule, Buddhist holidays, and so on. (New York centers are invited to join.) Callers may request that documents such as center schedules and our "New York Dharma Resource Guide," which lists centers and shops, and includes a list of taped dharma talks, be faxed or mailed to them.

The Buddhist Information Service is now on the Internet. Our World Wide Web site provides all of the dharma resources available on Bodhiline and more. Access detailed teachings on karma and reincarnation, or listen to excerpts of dharma talks transmitted by means of a free-streaming audio system. BIS is willing to advise others interested in setting up similar systems.

Michael Wick

For more information, contact: Buddhist Information Service of New York, 141 East Third Street #7G, New York, NY 10009; (212) 677-9394; www: http://www.infinite.org/bodhiline.

NEW YORK (*cont.*)

Dharma Group

No description available.

ADDRESS: 2 Symphony Circle, Buffalo, NY 14201

PHONE: (716) 871-1591

Friends of the Western Buddhist Order—New York City

We meet quarterly for weekends of sitting and spiritual friendship, with Vajramati visiting from Cambridge. We hope to expand to more frequent meetings as interest grows. We meet in private homes (apartments). Our founder and teacher is Urgyen Sangharakshita, who lives in London, England.

ADDRESS: Box 131, Ansonia Station, New York, New York 10023

PHONE: (212) 595-1669

LINEAGE: Nonsectarian

SPIRITUAL HEAD: Urgyen Sangharakshita (London, England)

CONTACT: Mark Aelred Sullivan

AFFILIATION: Friends of the Western Buddhist Order

FACILITIES: Members' apartments.

RETREATS OFFERED: Quarterly weekend retreats.

Mettavihara Community/Golden Dawn Center

We do a lot of community outreach work and serve as an information center for Eastern religions. Also interreligious work; unity, diversity, interfaith.

ADDRESS: 406 East 120th Street GFL, New York, NY 10035-3613

PHONE: (212) 289-8405

FAX: (212) 927-0742

LINEAGE: Triyana Vietnamese

SPIRITUAL HEAD: Bhante Suhita Dharma, Resident Director

AFFILIATION: American Buddhist Congregation

ESTABLISHED: 1984

MEDITATION PROGRAM: Daily meditation, evenings (call for times). Community service for the homeless and mentally ill.

RETREATS OFFERED: Monthly one-day retreats.

PUBLICATIONS: *Golden Dawn Sangha News*

New York Unitarian Universalist Buddhist Fellowship

A study group for both practicing Buddhists and people who simply want to learn more but are not engaged in any specific practice. Growing out of Unitarian Universalist non-creedal religious inquiry, the fellowship offers a forum for discussion of such topics as meditation techniques, ethics, and environmental issues from a Buddhist perspective. We also provide dharma books and articles from a wide variety of sources. We invite guest speakers from Buddhist temples and centers and from academia, and sponsor group visits to museums to view and discuss Buddhist art. Open to all with an interest in Buddhism.

ADDRESS: c/o Groseil, 1654 Third Avenue #2, New York, NY 10128
PHONE: (212) 427-1696
E-MAIL: dorjay@aol.com
LINEAGE: American Unitarian Universalist
CONTACT: Yvonne Groseil
AFFILIATION: Unitarian Universalist Buddhist Fellowship
ESTABLISHED: 1987
FACILITIES: Meet in homes or church halls.
PUBLICATIONS: *The Wheel*

Saddharma Cakra Buddhist Association

The Saddharma Cakra Buddhist Association was established in 1986 in Flushing, New York, by Kulapati Huang. He saw how new immigrants lacked spiritual life and would just drink and waste their time in unproductive activities, incurring the three poisons and unnecessary karma. He vowed to help them by providing a facility where they can learn methods to solve their own problems and acknowledge real, happy life. Activities include lectures on Buddhism; meditation classes and retreats; chorus; animal liberation; classes on Chinese acupuncture, calligraphy, and music; a book distribution committee; and English classes.

ADDRESS: 42-20 Kissena Boulevard #E5, Flushing, NY 11355
PHONE: (718) 886-0082
FAX: (718) 358-6058
LINEAGE: Chinese
SPIRITUAL HEAD: Rong Fang Huang
CONTACT: Simon Lin, Resident Director
AFFILIATION: Autonomous
ESTABLISHED: 1986
FACILITIES: Urban center.
MEDITATION PROGRAM: Every Friday evening.
RETREATS OFFERED: Seven-day retreat and one-month retreats in the summer (July) and winter (December/January).
PUBLICATIONS: *Association News*

Springwater Center for Meditative Inquiry and Retreats

Located on over two hundred acres of country land, Springwater Center holds silent retreats throughout the year. Except for a daily work period, all retreat activities are optional. There are no rituals or ceremonies and participants are welcome to spend time outdoors in nature. The teacher, Toni Packer, left traditional Zen practice so she could work in a more open, egalitarian way. Her approach is open listening without method or goal, discovering the workings of the conditioned mind and the silence of awareness. People who come here are free to work in whatever way they wish.

ADDRESS: 7179 Mill Street, Springwater, NY 14560
PHONE: (716) 669-2141
FAX: (716) 669-9573
LINEAGE: Nontraditional Zen
SPIRITUAL HEAD: Toni Packer, Resident Teacher
AFFILIATION: Autonomous
ESTABLISHED: 1981
FACILITIES: Country property; large retreat house; cabin.
RETREATS OFFERED: Silent retreats; most seven days, some longer, some shorter.
PUBLICATIONS: Quarterly newsletter.

Suffolk Institute for Eastern Studies

The Suffolk Institute for Eastern Studies is a not-for-profit corporation whose primary purpose is to bridge Western and Eastern approaches to life through the

Teachers of Aikido at Suffolk Institute in St. James, New York. (Photo by Rhys O'Brien.)

Change Your Mind Day

EVERY JUNE, *TRICYCLE: THE BUDDHIST REVIEW* sponsors a day of meditation in New York City's Central Park. It's called Change Your Mind Day.

As in the time of the historical Buddha, introductory meditation techniques are taught out-of-doors, free of charge and in a public space. Over the years, teachers from various Buddhist traditions, including John Daido Loori, Robert Thurman, Sharon Salzberg, His Holiness Penor-Rinpoche, Samu Sunim, Pat Enkyo O'Hara, Judith Lief, Joseph Goldstein, Ven. Kurunegoda Piyatissa, and Master Sheng-yen have introduced participants to the aims and methods of meditation. Between teachings, musicians and artists including Philip Glass and the late Allen Ginsberg have entertained the audience.

In 1995, one thousand people attended; that number doubled the following year. Because of the growing general interest in Buddhism, the numerous thriving Shao-

Ven. Samu Sunim addresses the crowd at Change Your Mind-Day. (Photo courtesy of *Tricycle* Magazine.)

The Khenpo Brothers greet Master Sheng-yen at Change Your Mind Day in Central Park, New York City. (Photo courtesy of *Tricycle* Magazine.)

lin-inspired dojos in Harlem and Chinatown, and the rapidly expanding Asian Buddhist population in New York, *Tricycle* addresses widespread interest among the city's diverse multicultural population.

Change Your Mind Day was founded on the belief that it's necessary to demystify meditation, take it out of the privileged *zendo-sangha* context, and make it accessible in a familiar and nonthreatening populist format. Change Your Mind Day is the most direct expression of *Tricycle*'s conviction that the transformation of self and society begins with a clear look at the nature of mind.

Melissa Hook

For more information, contact: *Tricycle: The Buddhist Review*, 92 Vandam Street, New York, NY 10013; (800) 950-7008; Fax: (212) 645-1493; e-mail: tricycle@echonyc.com.

study and practice of various Eastern meditative disciplines, benefiting from the wisdom gradually acquired and refined over many centuries. Classes are offered in Aikido, tai chi, and *zazen* under the supervision of Howard Pashenz, Ph.D.

ADDRESS: 330 Moriches Road, St. James, NY 11780
PHONE: (516) 584-6085
LINEAGE: Japanese/Aikido
SPIRITUAL HEAD: Howard Pashenz, Ph.D., Chief Instructor
AFFILIATION: United States Aikido Federation
ESTABLISHED: 1986
FACILITIES: Dojo
PUBLICATIONS: Informational brochure.

Tricycle: The Buddhist Review

The largest and only independent Buddhist publication in America, *Tricycle: The Buddhist Review* is dedicated to the ongoing discussion of Buddhism in the West. Articles on social issues have ranged from abortion to euthanasia to the environment. Reaching out to the culture at large, *Tricycle* has featured articles by and interviews with Spalding Gray, Oliver Stone, Richard Gere, and others. Unaffiliated with any one Buddhist school or sect, *Tricycle* is a wide-open forum for exploring contemporary and historic Buddhist activity and its impact on mainstream culture. It has been consistently recognized as a leading journal of fresh ideas.

ADDRESS: 92 Vandam Street, New York, NY 10013
PHONE: (800) 950-7008
FAX: (212) 645-1493
E-MAIL: tricycle@well.com
AFFILIATION: Autonomous
ESTABLISHED: 1991
RETREATS OFFERED: Annual day of meditation in Central Park.
PUBLICATIONS: *Tricycle: The Buddhist Review*

Zen Meditation Group of Huntington

The Zen Meditation Group of Huntington meets one evening per week for *zazen*, *kinhin*, chanting, tea, and mutual support.

ADDRESS: Unitarian Universalist Fellowship, 109 Brown's Road, Huntington, NY 11743
PHONE: (516) 423-4258
CONTACT: Robert J. Young
AFFILIATION: Unitarian Universalist Fellowship of Huntington
ESTABLISHED: 1986
FACILITIES: Large meditation room.
MEDITATION PROGRAM: Group meditation one evening per week. Please call for times.

NORTH CAROLINA

Durham Sitting Group

We've been meeting on Wednesday nights since 1984. Usually four to ten people attend. Meetings consist of thirty minutes of sitting, thirty minutes of readings or discussion, followed by another thirty minutes of sitting. Some members like to come fifteen minutes early to chant. Members practice Zen and/or Vipassana, attending retreats with a range of teachers. Visitors are welcome.

ADDRESS: 903 West Markham Avenue, Durham, NC 27701
PHONE: (919) 683-2156
FAX: Same. Call first.
LINEAGE: Mixed: Soto Zen and Vipassana
CONTACT: Sally Mason
ESTABLISHED: 1984
FACILITIES: Members' homes.
MEDITATION PROGRAM: We meet every Wednesday evening for sitting, reading, and dharma discussion.
RETREATS OFFERED: Monthly all-day sittings.

Southern Dharma Retreat Center

Southern Dharma Retreat Center provides a comfortable gathering place removed from the distractions of everyday life and fosters an atmosphere of quiet reflection where one can nurture a sense of peace and uncover the truths within the heart. It is our intention to sponsor teachers from a variety of traditions, to maintain a supportive environment for meditation, and to keep costs low. The center is located in a remote mountainous area of western North Carolina, an hour from Asheville. Facilities include a meditation hall, a dormitory for up to twenty-four people, and primitive creekside campsites with a nearby shower.

ADDRESS: Route 1 Box 34-H, Hot Springs, NC 28743
PHONE: (704) 622-7112
FAX: Same
LINEAGE: Nonprofit, nondenominational, eclectic.
CONTACTS: Susan or Eric Larsen
AFFILIATION: Autonomous
ESTABLISHED: 1978
FACILITIES: Meditation hall, dormitory, hermitages; remote mountain environment—trails, creek. Capacity: thirty.
RETREATS OFFERED: Eighteen to twenty annually, three to nine days long.
PUBLICATIONS: Biannual brochure.

Wesak Celebration of Asheville

Each year, members of various Buddhist traditions in the Asheville area join together in celebration of Buddha's birth, enlightenment, and passing. The celebration is held on the first full moon night after the spring equinox, usually in May. We feel the coincidence with spring is appropriate. We make an altar with whatever items people bring and put together a ceremony that includes something from each tradition—Theravada, Zen, and Tibetan. This has included lighting candles

Carolina Morning Designs

IN 1985 WHEN LINSI DEYO STARTED MAKING MEDItation cushions at her Carolina mountain home, the Buddhist community of North America could hardly support her fledgling cottage industry. A firm believer in "Do what you love, and the money will follow," it took Linsi a while to realize that she was barely supplying her basic living expenses. "The 'Right' part was there," says husband and business partner Patrick Clark, "but the 'Livelihood' part was questionable."

As Linsi and Patrick saw it, the mission of Carolina Morning Designs was to promote the practice of meditation, and consequently to sell cushions. But is it right to commercialize something as sacred as meditation? "This is where the rubber meets the road," says Patrick. "This is where spiritual practice hits practical mundane reality. We often reflect on this koan as we spin big plans for expanding Carolina Morning Designs."

The partners have tried to strike a balance between the demands of turning a profit on the one hand, and the inner imperative to behave ethically on the other. "If the Buddha were alive today," asks Linsi, "how would he run a business? How would he incorporate the ideals of compassion, right action, and right speech?"

After a decade of plugging away at it, the business has begun showing a modest profit. This has enabled the couple to hire employees and to be self-sufficient in rural North Carolina on "land that we love." And, they say, they've come to realize the importance of finding meaning and joy in the present moment—whatever that moment might have to offer—even if it isn't a lot of money. Please call or write for a free brochure.

Patrick Clark and Don Morreale

For more information, contact: Carolina Morning Designs, Route 67 Box 61, Cullowhee, NC 28723; (704) 293-5906.

---

and incense, various chants, circumambulation, "bathing the baby Buddha," blessing and offering food, and telling stories and folktales about the Buddha from different countries.
ADDRESS: 92 Mt. Clare Avenue, Asheville, NC 28801
PHONE: (704) 254-2092
CONTACT: Robert Wootton, Event Coordinator

OHIO

Buddhist Dharma Center of Cincinnati

The Buddhist Dharma Center of Cincinnati hosts several meditation services each week for practitioners of Vipassana, Zen, and Meditative Inquiry, and offers meditation instruction in a variety of formats. Visiting teachers lead days of meditation and weekend retreats several times yearly. Our *sangha* is modest in size, ranging from about a dozen on any Sunday morning, to five times that number for special occasions. We welcome both newcomers and seasoned sitters to our meditation hall.
ADDRESS: PO Box 23307, Cincinnati, OH 45223-0307
PHONES: (513) 281-6453, (513) 541-1650, (513) 271-0834
E-MAIL: Michael.Atkinson@UC.Edu
LINEAGE: Mixed
CONTACTS: Michael Atkinson, Bonnie Beverage, Fran Turner
AFFILIATION: Autonomous
ESTABLISHED: 1985

FACILITIES: Urban meditation hall, non-residential.
RETREATS OFFERED: One-day and weekend retreats.
PUBLICATIONS: Infrequent newsletters.

Yellow Springs Dharma Center

Yellow Springs Dharma Center is a place for the practice of meditation and the study of Buddhist teachings. It exists to promote an awareness of the effects of one's thoughts, words, and actions on the world, and seeks to create an environment that supports the growth of all beings toward happiness and peace. The center facilitates daily practice, seminars, workshops, retreats, study groups, and Buddhist poetry readings, and hosts a basic orientation to the practice of mindfulness meditation. The center also operates a lending library of dharma books, magazines, and audiotapes. We encourage you to join us.

ADDRESS: 502 Livermore Street, Yellow Springs, OH 45387
PHONE: (513) 767-9919
AFFILIATION: Autonomous
ESTABLISHED: 1993
FACILITIES: Meditation hall, library, three residential rooms.
MEDITATION PROGRAM: Daily practice; workshops; study groups.
RETREATS OFFERED: Monthly full day of sitting; annual weeklong retreat (June).

OREGON

Pure Heart

Pure Heart blends awareness, meditation, and wise compassion with leadership. Enlightened Buddhist Leadership training and retreats reflect on such topics as Responsibility as Generosity, Foundations for Empathy, Interdependence, Beneficial Speech, and Precepts and Integrity. These programs are appropriate for everyday leaders. Jacqueline Mandell has traveled extensively in Asia and has trained with the great meditation masters of three Buddhist traditions. She was authorized to teach by Ven. Mahasi Sayadaw and further encouraged in her teaching by Ven. Taungpulu Sayadaw. She continues her meditation practices in the Vajrayana tradition.

ADDRESS: Box 2085, Portland, OR 97208-2085
PHONE: (503) 790-1064
FAX: Same
LINEAGE: Buddhism
SPIRITUAL HEAD: Jacqueline Mandell, Resident Director
AFFILIATION: Autonomous
ESTABLISHED: 1996
MEDITATION PROGRAM: Meditation class

Jacqueline Mandell, resident director of Pure Heart in Portland, Oregon. (Photo courtesy of Jacqueline Mandell.)

one evening weekly. Call for times and locations.
RETREATS OFFERED: Buddhist Enlightened Leadership retreat.

PENNSYLVANIA

Buddhist Society of Pittsburgh

The Buddhist Society of Pittsburgh was established to disseminate information about—and promote the growth and cooperation of—its member groups. It also serves to meet the needs of individual Buddhist practitioners in the Pittsburgh area. Organizational meetings are held regularly. For information about the society and a listing of area Buddhist groups, please send a SASE.

ADDRESS: c/o Earth and Heaven Books, 214 South Craig Street, Pittsburgh, PA 15213
E-MAIL: dickmap@chplink.chp.edu
WWW: http://www.nauticom.net/www/dukkha

LINEAGE: All traditions.
CONTACT: Paul Dickman

Philadelphia Buddhist Association

At Philadelphia Buddhist Association, Buddhist teachings from all traditions are offered and dharma students of all levels meet in an atmosphere of openness and commitment to practice. We maintain a space for regular group sitting meditation and host teacher-led retreats and workshops throughout the year. We are always available to assist people in finding a path, in discovering the basics of Buddhism, or in enriching their current practice.

ADDRESS: 6 Old Lancaster Road, Merion, PA 19066
PHONE: (610) 660-9269
E-MAIL: buddhist@libertynet.org
WWW: http://www.libertynet.org/~buddhist
LINEAGE: Multidenominational Buddhist
CONTACT: The president. The association is guided by an elected board of directors; open board meetings.
AFFILIATION: All local Buddhist groups. Many members continue active association with their "root" dharma traditions while using PBA as a local practice center.
ESTABLISHED: 1986
FACILITIES: Meditation hall.
MEDITATION PROGRAM: Group meditation twice weekly.
RETREATS OFFERED: Monthly weekend retreats (all traditions) and all-day sittings.
PUBLICATIONS: *Philadelphia Buddhist Association Newsletter*

Won Buddhist Temple of Philadelphia

Won Buddhism grew out of the Enlightenment of its founder, the Ven. Sotaesan.

Observing the contemporary crisis in human society with his enlightened mind, Sotaesan realized that the rapid growth of material civilization was bringing about dehumanization and the overturning of traditional moral values. He proclaimed the principle "As material civilization develops, cultivate spiritual civilization accordingly." Thus, Won Buddhism is a community of religious faith and spiritual cultivation whose goal is to recover human spiritual power.

ADDRESS: 423 Abington Avenue, Glenside, PA 19038

PHONE: (215) 884-8443

FAX: (215) 886-8443

LINEAGE: Won Buddhism in Korea

SPIRITUAL HEADS: Ven. Sotaesan, Pak Chungbin

CONTACT: Bokin Kim, Resident Teacher

AFFILIATION: Autonomous

ESTABLISHED: 1987

FACILITIES: Two floors. First floor, social functions; second floor, meditation.

MEDITATION PROGRAM: Saturday afternoon class in sitting meditation and Buddhist studies. Call Dr. Kim for information.

PUBLICATIONS: *Won Buddhist Newsletter*, quarterly.

TENNESSEE

Delta Insight Group

"Memphis is a hotbed of religious intolerance, so we felt it best to establish a low-profile Buddhist presence here. Since we are in the Mississippi Delta, a word that describes both our region and the threefold nature of our practice, we called it *Delta Insight Group*. (Can you *DIG* it?) Sometimes when there are two of us sitting here, we wonder what we are about; when eight or ten people show up, we feel marvelously affirmed. The beauty of the group lies in its deep commitment to

keep it going for ourselves and the others that pass this way." —*Clark Buchner*

ADDRESS: 975 North Graham, Memphis, TN 38122

PHONES: (901) 371-0477 (work), (901) 327-2545 (home)

FAX: (901) 327-2545 (press *51)

CONTACT: Clark A. Buchner

AFFILIATION: Autonomous

ESTABLISHED: 1993

FACILITIES: Moves around to various people's homes.

MEDITATION PROGRAM: Weekly group meditation sittings. Please call for schedule and location.

Fellowship of the Lotus-Trinity

"During the 1950s, while serving in Japan with the United States Army, I fell in love with the Japanese people and began studying Buddhism to learn what makes them tick! I was drawn toward the Pure Land sect, which teaches salvation by faith in the grace of Amitabha's infinite

Vairochana, official Buddha image of the Fellowship of the Lotus Trinity in Franklin, Tennessee. (Photo courtesy of Fellowship of the Lotus Trinity.)

merit. After returning to the States, I continued my studies, first with Dr. Win Myint at Nashville Buddhist Temple, and then at San Francisco Zen Center. Now I've returned to Tennessee and my first love, the Pure Land, and have established a secular fellowship to put religious quality back into modern life."—*Malcolm Nichols*

ADDRESS: 300 Fourth Avenue South #9, Franklin, TN 37064-2657

PHONE: (615) 794-3537

LINEAGE: Japanese-Chinese True Pure Land

SPIRITUAL HEAD: The Trikaya (Vairochana-Amitabha-Shakyamuni)

CONTACT: Malcolm (Shaku In-Ken) Nichols, Director

AFFILIATION: Autonomous

ESTABLISHED: 1995

FACILITIES: Shrine

MEDITATION PROGRAM: Counseling; dharma instruction.

PUBLICATIONS: Articles about practice.

TEXAS

First Jefferson Unitarian-Universalist Meditation Group

Informal Sunday evening silent meditation.

ADDRESS: 1959 Sandy Lane, Fort Worth, TX 76112-5412

PHONE: (817) 451-1505

FAX: (817) 451-0963

E-MAIL: ccr@worldnet.att.net

ESTABLISHED: 1996

FACILITIES: Church

MEDITATION PROGRAM: Sunday evening meditation.

Kagura Kochu

We are a small, select group of dedicated people who strive to connect with life through tantric ritualization of everyday actions. Our main focus is on under-

The Margaret Austin Center

DURING THE LAST TWELVE YEARS OF HER LIFE, Margaret Austin (1918–1992) created a unique, informal retreat center on her farm near Chappell Hill, Texas. She opened her home, invited retreatants to camp on her land, and charged no fees—leaving a legacy that is a model of giving in support of the inner life.

In 1993, the Houston Zen Community joined with Insight Meditation Houston to preserve this beautiful facility as a quiet and inexpensive setting for retreats and meetings. By January 1996, hundreds of donations and in-kind contributions had made it possible to incorporate the Margaret Austin Center as a public charity, to purchase the land and buildings, and to remodel the main house and an outlying dormitory structure.

Throughout the critical fund-raising period, the center had no paid staff. The success of the project has been due almost entirely to volunteers who committed themselves over many months to legal work and architectural planning; to photography and graphic design; to coordinating events, writing proposals, and keeping books; to ham-mering, plastering, painting, installing air conditioning, and rehanging lights and fans. Volunteers also mowed, cleared brush, laid brick walkways, and raised the canopies of the great pecan trees that shade the heart of the property.

Margaret Austin embodied the joy of living. Both Steven Levine and Ram Dass became her good friends and each led several retreats at the farm. Once, when Ram Dass was expected, Margaret pitched a circus tent and more than four hundred people attended.

The center can accommodate up to fifty people overnight in bunk beds and is available for weekend and longer retreats to any appropriate group whose members need time and space in which to withdraw and renew themselves.

Jane Elioseff

For more information, contact: The Margaret Austin Center, PO Box 130124, Houston, TX 77219-0124; (713) 880-2214.

Margaret Austin Retreat Center in Houston, Texas, can accommodate up to fifty people overnight. (Photo by Paul Hester and Lisa Carol Hardaway.)

Dining hall at Margaret Austin Retreat Center. (Photo by Paul Hester and Lisa Carol Hardaway.)

standing and utilizing *intent* as it relates to the way the universe manifests itself in its various interactions. This is learned and practiced through sitting and moving meditation, lectures on "right action through right intent," martial arts, and Japanese sword and spear classes that use objects as channels of intent. We accept new members only rarely. To be admitted, one must be sponsored and go through a probationary period.

ADDRESS: PO Box 774, Caddo Mills, Texas 75135
PHONE: (214) 384-9746
FAX: (214) 490-9855
LINEAGE: Tantric
SPIRITUAL HEAD: Fumon Ayers, Resident Director
AFFILIATION: Autonomous
ESTABLISHED: 1984
FACILITIES: Meditation rooms; mat rooms for martial arts.
MEDITATION PROGRAM: Sitting and moving meditation, lecture series, martial arts meditation programs (such as Tai Chi and weapon's forms).
RETREATS OFFERED: Annual retreats for members only.

Texas Buddhist Council

Texas Buddhist Council is a clearinghouse for Buddhist concerns and information in the Lone Star State. Individual and corporate members come from a variety of ethnic backgrounds and represent the three main schools of Buddhism as well as various subsects within those schools. The council seeks to preserve and nurture the dharma in Texas, to unify practitioners through communication and interaction, and to bring Buddhism to the mainstream of American life through education and service. Council meetings and activities rotate among temples in the major metropolitan areas of the state, but center mainly in Dallas and Houston.

ADDRESS: 8727 Radio Road, Houston, TX 77075
PHONE: (800) 691-9373 (voice mail)
LINEAGE: Nine Oriental languages represented.
CONTACT: John RB Whittlesey
AFFILIATION: Autonomous
ESTABLISHED: 1992
FACILITIES: Provided, as needed, by member temples.
RETREATS OFFERED: One per year and many at affiliated temples.
PUBLICATIONS: *Texas Buddhist Directory*

VERMONT

Silent Sitting Meditation Group at Friends Meeting House

We sit together regularly on Sunday evenings. Occasionally we have a guest teacher, often from Insight Meditation Society in Barre, Massachusetts. Members of the group hold study meetings for discussion of readings and to listen to dharma tapes.

ADDRESS: c/o Fredericks, Box 39, Putney, VT 05346
PHONE: (802) 387-4395
LINEAGE: Mixed
AFFILIATION: Autonomous
ESTABLISHED: Around 1992
FACILITIES: Rented meditation room at Friends Meeting House, RT 5, Putney.
MEDITATION PROGRAM: Sunday evening group sitting; study meetings. Please call for times.

ToDo Institute

Many Buddhists find Western psychotherapy incompatible with their meditation practice. ToDo Institute is an educational center for therapies rooted in Buddhist principles. Morita Therapy focuses on action and is rooted in Zen. *Naikan* is a method of self-reflection and is

rooted in Pure Land Buddhism. Both have been adapted for Westerners by David Reynolds under the umbrella of Constructive Living. The ToDo Institute offers retreats, residential training, individual instruction, and resource materials in a woodland setting on the edge of the Green Mountains.

ADDRESS: PO Box 874, Middlebury, VT 05753
PHONE: (802) 352-9018
LINEAGE: Japanese Zen and Pure Land
CONTACT: Gregg Krech, Resident Teacher
AFFILIATION: Autonomous
ESTABLISHED: 1989
FACILITIES: Residential facility on fifty forested acres.
RETREATS OFFERED: *Naikan, Jujukinkai* (one week).
PUBLICATIONS: *Constructive Living Quarterly*

VIRGINIA

Ekoji Buddhist Sangha

Ekoji Buddhist Sangha was founded by Rev. Kenryu Tsuji, a *sensei* (teacher) for more than fifty years in the Buddhist Churches of America. At his request, the Numata Foundation purchased a building in Richmond, Virginia, and invited local Buddhist practice groups to use it. Eventually we grew and evolved into an extended dharma community. Each group holds its own practice sessions, but we all meet together on a number of special occasions during the year. We also work together to maintain and improve the temple building. The *sangha* runs a lending library and publishes a newsletter.

ADDRESS: 3411 Grove Avenue, Richmond, VA 23221
PHONE: (804) 355-6657
LINEAGE: Multidenominational service organization.

CONTACTS: Bruce Frostick and Richard Mercer

ESTABLISHED: 1986

FACILITIES: Meeting space for Buddhist groups; library.

PUBLICATIONS: *The Dharma Wheel*, quarterly newsletter.

Mountain Light Zen Center

Mountain Light Zen Center has regular *zazen* meetings and a *sesshin* schedule. However, the facility is also available for other types of workshops and seminars; groups coming for music, dance, yoga, team building, and various therapies have found that the peace, beauty, and privacy make a unique contribution to their work. The sound of falling water, a lily pond, goldfish, and flowers contribute their gentle peace. A one-hundred-year-old church with plain oak floors and a stained glass window serves as our meditation hall.

ADDRESS: 6656 Mountain Light Place, Crozet, VA 22932

PHONE: (804) 978-7770

SPIRITUAL HEAD: Donna Aiho Frantzen, Teacher/Director

AFFILIATION: Autonomous

ESTABLISHED: 1996

FACILITIES: Thirty-four acres in the Blue Ridge Mountains; meditation hall (*zendo*), dormitory space for forty.

MEDITATION PROGRAM: Regular daily sittings open to the public. Prerequisite introductory lecture.

RETREATS OFFERED: Two- to five-day retreats scheduled on request. Seven-day retreat at New Year's.

WASHINGTON

Awareness Meditation

A weaving of Vipassana, Stephen Levine's work, and the joy of wonder. Beginning with meditation, the group explores the journey of awakening into a life of curiosity, kindness, trust, and reverence.

ADDRESS: 13703 90th Avenue Northeast, Kirkland, WA 98034

PHONE: (206) 823-4203

LINEAGE: Vipassana

SPIRITUAL HEAD: Mary O'Malley, Resident Director

AFFILIATION: Autonomous

MEDITATION PROGRAM: Vipassana meditation one evening a week each in Kirkland and Puyallup and one morning a week in Bellevue. Please call for schedule and locations.

Cloud Mountain Retreat Center

Cloud Mountain is a rural Buddhist retreat center in southwest Washington, approximately two hours south of Seattle and one hour north of Portland, just off Interstate 5. It was built to provide Buddhist groups and individuals with an environment conducive to meditation and quiet contemplation or study. Cloud Mountain offers its support and facilities to all Buddhist organizations and practitioners regardless of tradition or sect. All registration is done through Northwest Dharma Association's Seattle office.

ADDRESS: 373 Agren Road, Castle Rock, WA 98611

PHONES: (360) 274-4859. Seattle office, (206) 789-5456

FAX: (360) 274-9119

E-MAIL: cloudmtn@tclcport.com

CONTACT: Karin Miles, Executive Director

AFFILIATION: Northwest Dharma Association, Seattle, Washington.

ESTABLISHED: 1984

FACILITIES: Accommodates thirty-five retreatants; two meditation halls; two dormitory buildings (private rooms available); main lodge; library; staff and teacher cottages.

RETREATS OFFERED: Regularly scheduled retreats, classes, and workshops led by monks and lay teachers representing Tibetan, Zen, and Theravada traditions.

PUBLICATIONS: *Northwest Dharma News*

Friends of the Western Buddhist Order—Richland

No description available.

ADDRESS: 2455 George Washington Way, Richland, WA 99352

PHONE: (509) 967-2331

LINEAGE: Friends of the Western Buddhist Order

SPIRITUAL HEAD: Ven. Urgyen Sangharakshita

AFFILIATION: Friends of the Western Buddhist Order

Laughing Frog Sangha

Vipassana and Zen students welcome anyone who wants to practice mindfulness. Group meets for sitting and walking practice, followed by tea. New students welcome.

ADDRESS: 22116 Urdahl Road Northwest, Poulsbo, WA 98370

PHONE: (360) 598-4247

LINEAGE: Vipassana and Zen

MEDITATION PROGRAM: Evening *zazen* and Vipassana meditation, several times each month. Call for times.

Mindfulness Community of Puget Sound

Formerly known as Peach Tea Sangha, Mindfulness Community of Puget Sound welcomes all who are interested in the teachings of Thich Nhat Hanh. Our guiding teacher is Eileen Kiera. This community was established to support our practice and teacher and to focus the work of the *sangha*. Activities include weekly sittings, monthly Days of Mindfulness, retreats, sutra classes, and a study group.

ADDRESS: 2320 East Denny Way #C, Seattle, WA 98122

PHONE: (206) 325-2839

LINEAGE: Vietnamese

SPIRITUAL HEAD: Thich Nhat Hanh. Eileen Kiera, Teacher

CONTACT: Kate Wehr

AFFILIATION: Plum Village, France (Thich Nhat Hanh's center)

ESTABLISHED: 1992

FACILITIES: We use the dojo of the Three Treasures Sangha.

MEDITATION PROGRAM: Weekly sitting sessions.

RETREATS OFFERED: Monthly Days of Mindfulness; two to three extended retreats per year. Call for details.

PUBLICATIONS: *Peach Tea Leaves*, quarterly newsletter.

Northwest Dharma Association

Northwest Dharma Association (NWDA) is a nonsectarian, nonprofit Buddhist organization created to support the dissemination and growth of Buddhist teachings in the Northwest. Among its activities is the publication of Northwest Dharma News, a bimonthly newsletter that publicizes events and activities of Buddhist groups in Washington, Oregon, and British Columbia. NWDA also sponsors activities of its own, including retreats at Cloud Mountain Retreat Center in Castle Rock, Washington.

ADDRESS: 4020 Leary Way Northwest, #300, Seattle, WA 98107

PHONE: (206) 789-5456

FAX: (206) 789-5758

E-MAIL: nwdharma@accessone.com

CONTACT: Karin Miles, Executive Director

AFFILIATION: Autonomous. Headquarters.

ESTABLISHED: 1989

RETREATS OFFERED: We sponsor retreats from all traditions at Cloud Mountain Retreat Center in Castle Rock, Washington.

PUBLICATIONS: *Northwest Dharma News*

Olympia Meditators

We are a group of Buddhists in a small community who sit together one evening a week. Meditation is followed by an hour of dharma study and discussion prompted by our readings and by video- and audiotapes. We are not aligned with any particular path; guest teachers from all Buddhist traditions are invited to give talks and offer guidance to our "leaderless" group. We spend a lot of time trying to help each other apply the teachings to everyday life.

ADDRESS: 5226 Puget Road Northeast, Olympia, WA 98516-9542

PHONE: (360) 456-1826

LINEAGE: All traditions.

AFFILIATION: Autonomous

MEDITATION PROGRAM: Weekly evening meditation, study, and discussion. Call for times.

RETREATS OFFERED: Some half-day and all-day sittings.

Open Circle

Open Circle is an eclectic Buddhist group that gathers for silent meditation practice once a week.

ADDRESS: 12801 Marble Road, Yakima, WA 98908

PHONE: (509) 965-0843

LINEAGE: Eclectic

CONTACT: Deborah Beadle

AFFILIATION: Autonomous

MEDITATION PROGRAM: We gather for meditation one evening per week. Please call for times and locations.

Seattle Buddhist Center/Friends of the Western Buddhist Order

We have two resident *dharmachari* (meditation teachers), Aryadaka and Shantinayaka, conducting activities in Seattle. We offer a regular program of meditation instruction, dharma courses, meditation, and *puja*.

ADDRESS: 2765 South Washington Street, Seattle, WA 98112

PHONE: (206) 726-0051

E-MAIL: aryadaka@aol.com

LINEAGE: Friends of the Western Buddhist Order

SPIRITUAL HEAD: Ven. Urgyen Sangharakshita

CONTACT: Dharmachari Aryadaka, Resident Director

AFFILIATION: Friends of the Western Buddhist Order

ESTABLISHED: 1985

FACILITIES: Study room; shrine room; library; bookshop.

MEDITATION PROGRAM: Open meditation, three days weekly. Please call for schedule.

RETREATS OFFERED: Frequent one-day and weekend retreats; one-week summer wilderness retreat.

PUBLICATIONS: *Dharma Friends*, newsletter.

Spokane Buddhist Fellowship

We felt Spokane needed a gateway where people who wanted to learn about Buddhism could get basic instruction and guidance. We also wanted a way to coalesce a community out of a number of individuals who had been practicing on their own. Our intention is to introduce Spokane to the many faces of Buddhism while deepening our individual practices and encouraging interdenominational *sangha*. We sponsor a small chapter of the Buddhist Peace Fellowship.

ADDRESS: 7526 North Espe Road, Spokane, WA 99207

PHONE: (509) 468-9361

LINEAGE: Friends of the Western Buddhist Order; Vipassana; Zen

CONTACT: Sarah Conover

AFFILIATION: Autonomous

ESTABLISHED: 1992

FACILITIES: Unitarian Universalist Church of Spokane

MEDITATION PROGRAM: Weekly sitting group. Call for times.

RETREATS OFFERED: Weekend retreats twice yearly; monthly miniretreats; *pujas*; workshops; potlucks.

WEST VIRGINIA

Spencer Buddhist Meditation Group

We are a small group located in a little town called Harmony in the hills of West Virginia. We meet once a month at a local church where we watch films (mostly Buddhist), listen to tapes, have discussions, and do sitting meditation. We attend retreats offered by other groups in neighboring states.

ADDRESS: Route 2 Box 99, Harmony, WV 25243

PHONE: (304) 927-1505

FAX: (304) 927-5171

E-MAIL: bel@access.mountain.net

CONTACT: Ken Lewis, "Sort-of Director"

AFFILIATION: Autonomous

ESTABLISHED: 1992

MEDITATION PROGRAM: Sitting meditation once a month.

WISCONSIN

Christine Center for Unitive Spirituality

Nestled amid three hundred acres of tranquil forest, our center has been dedicated to personal and global transformation since 1980. With a unique blend of Eastern and Western philosophies, we embrace the diversity and underlying unity of all spiritual traditions. Just beginning? Come join us in our daily practice and participate in seminars ranging from Christian Meditation to Buddhist Vipassana to Creating Conscious Relationships. Well on your way to enlightenment? Try our two-week intensive, Basic Life Transformation—a prerequisite for entrance into our school of spiritual development. Unlock your full potential!

ADDRESS: W8291 Mann Road, Willard, WI 54493

PHONE: (715) 267-7507

FAX: (715) 267-7512

CONTACT: Marylu Miller

AFFILIATION: Autonomous

ESTABLISHED: 1980

FACILITIES: Meditation hall; conference hall; twenty hermitages; hot tub; sauna; hiking; canoeing.

RETREATS OFFERED: Seminars; retreats (long and short); spiritual school; small residential community.

PUBLICATIONS: Quarterly newsletter/brochure.

CANADA

ALBERTA

International Buddhist Friends Association

The International Buddhist Friends Association (IBFA) was established in 1982 to promote the teachings of the Buddha and to encourage harmonious relations within the *sangha*. It is an umbrella organization that encourages cooperation and communication among various Alberta Buddhist groups. Its members are dedicated to working for the betterment of society as a whole. The IBFA is also committed to promoting the teachings of *buddhadharma* through various religious, educational, and cultural activities. Each May the IBFA, in conjunction with one of the local Buddhist temples, sponsors *Wesak*, a celebration of the birth, death, and enlightenment of the Buddha.

ADDRESS: 9904 106th Street, Edmonton, AB T5K 1C4

PHONE: (403) 426-2760

FAX: (403) 426-5650

E-MAIL: Steven@Hippocrates.Family. MED.ualberta.ca

SPIRITUAL HEAD: Dr. Steven Kyaw Htut Aung, Resident Director

AFFILIATION: Fifteen different Buddhist temples under IBFA.

ESTABLISHED: 1982

FACILITIES: Member temples and meditation centers.

MEDITATION PROGRAM: Annual functions, celebrations, and the like.

RETREATS OFFERED: Annual group retreat in Alberta.

PUBLICATION: *Buddhism into Year 2000* (Bangkok, Thailand).

Novayana

No description available.

ADDRESS: 13603 81st Avenue, Edmonton, AB T5R 3N7

CONTACT: Audrey Watson

BRITISH COLUMBIA

Ambedkar Memorial Association

Open to supporters of the social and religious ideology of Dr. Ambedkar.

ADDRESS: 6341 Sophia Street, Vancouver, BC V5W 2W7

LINEAGE: Indian Buddhist/Hindu

CONTACT: Mohan Bangai, Resident Director

AFFILIATION: Ambedkar Mission in Toronto, Ontario

ESTABLISHED: 1982
FACILITIES: Private home.
MEDITATION PROGRAM: Three or four
   meetings per year; guest speakers.

Denman Island Sangha

Ani Kelsang Zangmo, disciple of Geshe
Kelsang Gyatso, leads a group that meets
for regular sitting practice. A mixture of
schools and influences, but basically Bud-
dhist.
ADDRESS: 3553 Northwest Road,
   Denman Island, BC V0R 1T0
PHONE: (604) 335-0265
LINEAGE: Mixed schools and influences
SPIRITUAL HEAD: Ani Kelsang Zangmo
CONTACT: Sudasi
AFFILIATION: Autonomous
MEDITATION PROGRAM: Weekly evening
   meditation. Call for times.

Karuna Meditation Society

A nonsectarian organization offering
programs and meditation in the Soto Zen
and Mahayana Vipassana traditions.
ADDRESS: 12 West 10th Avenue #25,
   Vancouver, BC V5Y 1R6
PHONE: (604) 874-4093
LINEAGE: Soto Zen and Mahayana Vipas-
   sana
CONTACTS: Michelle Mills and Kristin
   Penn, Resident Directors
AFFILIATION: Autonomous
ESTABLISHED: 1984
MEDITATION PROGRAM: Weekly Zen
   meditation; weekly Vipassana medita-
   tion for people with life-threatening ill-
   nesses.
RETREATS OFFERED: Monthly one-day
   and periodic weekend retreats
PUBLICATION: Karuna Newsletter

Vancouver Buddhist Centre/Friends of the Western Buddhist Order

Vancouver Buddhist Centre provides a
creative atmosphere in which to practice

meditation and study Buddhism, and of-
fers an opportunity to realize dharma
within a spiritual community that recog-
nizes the realities of the modern world.
Through the fostering of spiritual friend-
ship and the development of projects
such as right-livelihood businesses and
residential communities, Vancouver
Buddhist Centre and the Friends of the
Western Buddhist Order are creating a
living Buddhist movement for the West.
ADDRESS: 456 West King Edward Avenue,
   Vancouver, BC V5Y 2J4
PHONE: (604) 877-0269
LINEAGE: Nonsectarian
SPIRITUAL HEAD: Urgyen Sangharakshita
CONTACT: Dharmachari Ariobodhi, Resi-
   dent Director
AFFILIATION: Friends of the Western
   Buddhist Order
ESTABLISHED: 1993
FACILITIES: Residential city house and
   center.
MEDITATION PROGRAM: Daily meditation
   and study; celebration of Buddhist festi-
   vals.
RETREATS OFFERED: Monthly one- or
   two-day retreats.

ONTARIO

Ambedkar Mission

Open to all who share the ideology and
social reform of Dr. Ambedkar.
ADDRESS: 49 Templeton Court,
   Scarborough, ON M1E 2C3
PHONE: (416) 284-5474
LINEAGE: Indian Buddhist
CONTACT: Darshan Chandhary,
   Chairman
AFFILIATION: Autonomous. This is the
   head office.
ESTABLISHED: 1979
FACILITIES: Meetings in a private home.
MEDITATION PROGRAM: Lectures by visit-

ing monks from India once or twice a
year.

Buddhist Association of Canada

Our library is the best one in Toronto
and is open to the public. There are seven
different kinds of Tripitaka and more
than ten thousand books on Buddhism.
We also hold a Buddhist philosophy essay
competition every year, as well as a Bud-
dhist art competition.
ADDRESS: 1330 Bloor Street West,
   Toronto, ON M6H 1P2
PHONE: (416) 537-1342
FAX: Same
SPIRITUAL HEAD: Dr. Clement Wong
CONTACT: Miss Luisianna
ESTABLISHED: 1970
PUBLICATIONS: Prajna Magazine, and
   newsletter.

Buddhist Women's Network of Toronto

Long-term and short-term projects, such
as a Directory of the Buddhist Community
of Canada, and the preparation and dis-
tribution of a Buddhist manual with a vi-
sual supplement to schools in the greater
Toronto area. Women and ideas from all
Buddhist traditions are welcome.
ADDRESS: 34 Compton Drive, Scarbor-
   ough, ON M1R 4A7
PHONE: (416) 757-6354
FAX: Same
WWW: http://www.io.org/~klima/
CONTACT: Chris Ng, Director
AFFILIATION: Autonomous
ESTABLISHED: 1993
PUBLICATION: Directory of the Buddhist
   Community of Canada

Crystal Staff

Crystal Staff is part of a network of
groups around the world established by a

native Torontonian, Namgyal Rinpoche, who has blended traditional Tibetan and Burmese Buddhism with Western esoteric teachings.

ADDRESS: PO Box 20039, Ottawa, ON K1N 9N5

PHONE: (613) 238-6511

LINEAGE: Tibetan; Burmese; Western Esoteric

SPIRITUAL HEAD: Namgyal Rinpoche

MEDITATION PROGRAM: Occasional classes.

Dharma Centre of Canada

Dharma Centre of Canada is dedicated to the awakening of all beings. Our object is to carry on the instruction and practice of meditation in order for individuals to develop compassion, wisdom, and an awareness of the nature of mind and matter. We also offer an opportunity for you to deepen your knowledge of universal laws by studying comparative religion, philosophy, and the arts and sciences. Both Western and Eastern spiritual traditions are taught. The Dharma Centre was founded by the Ven. Namgyal-Rinpoche in 1966.

ADDRESS: RR#1 Galway Road, Kinmount, ON K0M 2A0

PHONE: (705) 488-2704

FAX: (705) 488-2215

E-MAIL: dharma@ptbo.igs.net

WWW: http://www.terraport.net/ Dharma-Centre-Canada/

LINEAGE: Universalist

SPIRITUAL HEAD: Ven. Namgyal-Rinpoche

CONTACT: Mark Arneson, Resident Director

ESTABLISHED: 1966

FACILITIES: Retreat facilities on four hundred wooded acres.

RETREATS OFFERED: Formal programs and individual retreats.

PUBLICATIONS: *Dharmanews*, newsletter. Bodhi Publishing.

University of Toronto Buddhist Student Association

Our activities take place at the University of Toronto and are open to all. Our goal is to act as a liaison for Buddhist students and other interested parties and to learn dharma together. Since 1994 we have had regular meditation sessions taught by both a Theravadan monk and a Rinzai Zen teacher. We have access to dharma teachers (ordained and lay) and professors of Buddhism in Toronto and elsewhere who advise us on our activities. Many have presented lectures to the group and/or written articles for our publication.

ADDRESS: 34 Compton Drive, Scarborough, ON M1R 4A7

PHONE: (416) 757-6354

FAX: Same

E-MAIL: wisdom@ilap.com

WWW: http://www.ilap.com/wisdom

LINEAGE: Nonsectarian

SPIRITUAL HEADS: Various (see description).

CONTACT: Shan Tong

ESTABLISHED: 1984

FACILITIES: Use facilities at University of Toronto.

PUBLICATION: *Wisdom*, published three or four times a year; circulation: 2,000 copies.

SASKATCHEWAN

Saskatoon Buddhist Studies Group

Saskatoon Buddhist Studies Group grew out of a visit by a Tibetan Buddhist lama in 1990. Except during the summer months, we meet weekly in the home of one of our members. This has brought an informal and welcoming atmosphere to the group. In lieu of a teacher, we use books, audio and video teaching tapes, and each other as resources. We focus mainly on Insight and, to some extent, Tibetan meditation. Meetings consist of meditation, teaching, discussion, and social time. We are an eclectic lot; some are "Buddhists," some are not, and some are in between!

ADDRESS: 432 10th Street East, Saskatoon, SK S7N 0C9

PHONES: (306) 653-3750 or (306) 343-9727

LINEAGE: Tibetan Vajrayana/Burmese Theravada

CONTACTS: Donald Campbell and Mick Graham, Directors

AFFILIATION: Autonomous

ESTABLISHED: 1990

FACILITIES: Meet in member's home. Call for location.

MEDITATION PROGRAM: Weekly meditation and discussion.

RETREATS OFFERED: Occasional half-day, full-day, and weekend retreats.

Appendix
Dharma Centers Listed by Location

Note: The letters T, M, V, and B at the end of each entry represent the center's Yana, or Tradition: Theravada, Mahayana, Vajrayana, and "Buddhayana."

ALABAMA

Guntersville
Mystic Journey Retreat Center, B

Huntsville
Green Mountain Zen Center, M
Zen Center Of Huntsville, M

ALASKA

Anchor Point
Khawachen Dharma Center, V

Anchorage
Alaska Buddhist Society, V
Anchorage Zen Center, M
Anchorage Zen Community, M
Wat Dhamma Bhavana, T

Fairbanks
Mahakaruna Tibetan Buddhist Study Center, V

Juneau
Juneau Forming Dharma Study Group, V

ALBERTA—CANADA

Calgary
Avatamsaka Monastery, M
Calgary Theravada Meditation Society, T
Marpa Gompa Changchup Ling, V
Pai Yuin Tang Buddhist Congregation, V
Stretch Awareness, Inc., T
Vipassana Meditation Center, T

Canmore
Bow Valley Sangha, T

Edmonton
Buddhist Center of Edmonton, V
Buddhist Vihara Association of Alberta, T
Chin Yin Tang Buddhist Society, V
Edmonton Shambhala Center, V
Edmonton Shin Buddhist Dojo, M
Gaden Samten Ling, V
International Buddhist Friends Association, B
Karma Tashi Ling, V
Light of Dharma, T
Novayana, B

ARIZONA

Bisbee
Sacred Passage, B

Chandler
Arizona Community of Buddhists, B
Center for Buddhist Development, B
Unitarian Universalist Buddhist Fellowship, B
Valley Unitarian Universalist Zen Group/Desert Lotus Sangha, M

Flagstaff
Lhundrub Ling, V

Gilbert
Jodo Shu Dharma Center, M

Phoenix
Arizona Buddhist Temple, M
Desert Cactus Sangha, M
Peace House, M
Phoenix Buddhist Network, B
Vici Arizona, V

Prescott
Satisfied Mind Sangha, M

Scottsdale
Center for Radical Aliveness, B
Padma Bodhi Ling, V

Tempe
Haku-un-ji Tempe Zen Center, M
Phoenix Karma Thegsum Choling, V

Tucson
Arizona Teachings, B
Bodhisattva Institute, V
Tucson Community Meditation Center, T
Zen Desert Sangha, M

Waddell
Wat Promkunaram/Buddhist Temple of Arizona, T

ARKANSAS

Eureka Springs
Devachan Temple, B
Eureka Springs Sangha, M

Hot Springs National Park
Zen Center of Hot Springs, M

Little Rock
Ecumenical Buddhist Society, B

BRITISH COLUMBIA—CANADA

Burnaby
Kagyu Kunkhyab Chuling—Burnaby, V

Currie
Birken Forest Monastery, T

Delta
Dzogchen Vancouver, V

Denman Island
Denman Island Sangha, B

Duncan
Buddhist Association of Inter-
faith Services, V
Thubten Choling, V

Nelson
Kootenay Shambhala Centre, V
Tashi Choling, V

Powell River
Zen Fellowship, M

Richmond
International Buddhist
Society, M
Sakya Tsechen Thubten Ling, V
Tantric Buddhist Society/Pu
T'o Tang, V

Saltspring Island
Kunzang Dechen Osel Ling, V
Saltspring Island Meditation
Group, M

Vancouver
Ambedkar Memorial Associa-
tion, B
Chagdud Gonpa, V
Dharma Group Vancouver, V
Gold Buddha Sagely Monas-
tery, M
Karuna Meditation Society, B
Lions Gate Buddhist Priory, M
PTT Buddhist Society, V
Siddhartha's Intent, V
Vancouver Buddhist Centre/
Friends of the Western Bud-
dhist Order, B
Vancouver Shambhala
Center, V
Vipassana Foundation, T
Westcoast Dharma Society, T

Zen Centre of Vancouver, M
Zuru Ling, V

Victoria
Kagyu Kunkhyab Chuling—
Victoria, V
Mill Hill Mindfulness
Society, M
Victoria Buddhist Dharma So-
ciety/Sakya Thubten Kunga
Choling, V
Victoria Shambhala Center, V
Victoria Zen Centre, M
Vipassana Foundation, T

CALIFORNIA

Alameda
Aro Ter, V

Albany
Berkeley Buddhist Priory, M

Aptos
Santa Cruz Shambhala Study
Group, V
Vipassana Santa Cruz, T

Bayside
Arcata Sangha, M

Benicia
Dharma Gate Sangha, M

Berkeley
Berkeley Buddhist Monastery/
Institute of World Reli-
gions, M
Berkeley Sangha, M
Berkeley Shambhala Center, V
Berkeley Thursday Night Vi-
passana Group, T
Berkeley Zen Center, M
Buddhist Alliance for Social
Engagement (BASE), B
Buddhist Peace Fellowship
(BPF), B
California Buddhist Vihara, T
Community of Mindful
Living, M

Dhammachakka Meditation
Center, T
DharmaNet International, B
Empty Gate Zen Center, M
Inquiring Mind, T
Institute of Buddhist
Studies, M
Nyingma Institute, V
Sanghapala/East Bay Sitting
Group, T
Sixth Patriarch Zen Center, M
Tibetan Aid Project, V
Vipassana Meditation with Wes
Nisker, T

Boulder Creek
Taungpulu Kaba-Aye Monas-
tery, T
Vajrapani Institute, V

Burlingame
International Translation Insti-
tute/Dharma Realm Buddhist
Association, M

Campbell
Dharmapala Institute for Buddhist Meditation and Re-
search, Inc., T

Castaic
Drikung Kagyu Center, V

Corralitos
Vajrayana Foundation/Pema
Osel Ling, V

Costa Mesa
Newport Mesa Zen Center, M

Cuppertino
Udumbara
Sangha—Cuppertino, M

Davis
Davis Shambhala Center, V
Davis Unitarian Buddhist Med-
itation Group, T

El Monte
Waken Rey Tsang Temple, V

Encinitas
San Diego Meditation Com-
munity, T

Escondido
Drikung Kyobpa Choling
Monastery, V

Fairfax
Padma Shedrup Ling, V

Fort Bragg
Fort Bragg Sangha, M

Fremont
Wat Buddhanusorn (Thai
Temple), T

Fresno
Shingon Buddhist Interna-
tional Institute, V

Garberville
Garberville Dharma Center, B

Gardena
Rinzai Zen Temple of California, M

Glendale
Metta Meditation Center, T

Goleta
Open Door Sangha/Buddhist
Meditation Community of
Santa Barbara, B

Hacienda Heights
Hsi-Lai Temple, M
Ming Chi Tang, V

Hawthorn
T'hondup Ling/Chagdud
Gonpa Foundation, V

Hayward
Hayward Buddhist Center, M

Idyllwild
Idyllwild Dharma Center/
Karma Mahasiddha Ling, V

Joshua Tree
Dhamma Dena Dessert Vipassana Center, T

Junction City
Rigdzin Ling/Chagdud Gonpa
  Foundation, V

La Mirada
Metropolitan Vipassana, T

Laguna Beach
Laguna Beach Sangha, M

Long Beach
Blessings, Prosperity and Lon-
  gevity Monastery, M
Long Beach Buddhist
  Temple, M
Long Beach Monastery, M
Yeshe Khorlo, V

Los Altos
Palo Alto Friends Mindfulness
  Sangha, M

Los Angeles
California Buddhist
  University, M
Chua Viet Nam, M
Dharma Zen Center, M
Dharma Vijaya Buddhist Vi-
  hara, T
Don't Worry Zendo, B
Gay Zen Group, M
Gold Wheel Monastery, M
International Buddhist Medita-
  tion Center, M
International Zen Institute of
  America, M
Kanzeonji Non-Sectarian Bud-
  dhist Temple, M
Kewanee Mountain Zen Cen-
  ter, M
Lesbian Buddhist Group, M
Los Angeles Buddhist Vihara, T
Los Angeles Karma Thegsum
  Choling, V
Los Angeles Shambhala
  Center, V
Orgyen Khachod Ling, V
Rinzai-Ji Zen Center, M
Shaolin Buddhist Meditation
  Center, M

Skillful Meditation Project, T
Unfettered Mind, V
Vipassana Support Institute, T
Zen Center of Los Angeles, M
Zenshuji Soto Mission, M

Los Gatos
Jikoji, M
Los Gatos Zen Group, M

Lucerne Valley
Desert Zen Center/Monjuji, M

Maywood
Dhammakaya International
  Society of California, T

Mill Valley
Palyul Changchub Dhargye
  Ling, V

Monterey Park
Mui Yin Tong, V

Morro Bay
White Heron Sangha, M

Mount Baldy
Mount Baldy Zen Center, M

Mount Shasta
Shasta Abbey/Order of Buddhist Contemplatives, M

Mountain Center
Zen Mountain Center, M

Mountain View
Kannon Do, M

Murphys
Infinite Wisdom Interna-
  tional, B

Napa
Napa Mindfulness Commu-
  nity, B

Nevada City
Mountain Stream Meditation
  Center, T

North Fork
California Vipassana Center/
  Dhamma Mahavana, T

North Hollywood
Taoist Institute, M
Wat Thai, T

Novato
Bell Springs Hermitage, T

Oakland
Bay Zen Center, M
California Diamond Sangha/
  Oakland Dojo, M
Chabolyn Terrace Sangha, M
Fruitvale Zendo, M
Oakland Chapter True Buddha
  School, V
Oakland Sangha, M
Saddhamma Foundation, T
Sakya Dechen Ling, V

Oakville
Ati Ling/Chagdud Gonpa
  Foundation, V

Palo Alto
Center for Timeless Wisdom, B
Palo Alto Dharmadhatu, V
Palo Alto Karma Thegsum
  Choling, V

Redway
Radiant Heart, V

Redwood Valley
Abhayagiri Buddhist Monastery, T

Rosemead
Rosemead Buddhist Monas-
  tery, B

Sacramento
City of the Dharma Realm, M

San Bruno
Purple Lotus Society, V

San Diego
San Diego Dharma Study
  Group, V

San Diego Karma Thegsum
  Choling, V
San Diego Meditation
  Society, T
San Diego Vipassana Medita-
  tion Society, T
Vajrarupini Buddhist Center, V
Zen Center of San Diego, M

San Francisco
Arya Marga Foundation, B
Buddha Dendo, V
Buddhist AIDS Project, B
Diamond Way Buddhist Cen-
  ter, V
Dolores Street Dharma, T
Gay Buddhist Fellowship, B
Gold Mountain Monastery, M
Harbor Sangha, M
Hartford Street Zen Center, M
International Meditation Cen-
  ter, T
Kagyu Droden Kunchab, V
Maitreya Institute, V
Maitri: Residential Care for
  People Living with AIDS, M
Nama Rupa Foundation, T
Orgyen Dorje Den/Bay Area
  Yeshe Nyingpo, V
Padmasambhava Buddhist
  Center, V
Ratnashri Sangha, V
San Francisco Buddhist
  Center, B
San Francisco Dhamma, T
San Francisco Shambhala Cen-
  ter, V
San Francisco Mindfulness
  Community, M
San Francisco Zen Center, M
Saraha Buddhist Center, V
Tassajara Zen Mountain Cen-
  ter, M
Taungpulu Kaba-Aye Medita-
  tion Center, T
Taungpulu Kaba-Aye Monas-
  tery, T

Tse Chen Ling Center for Tibetan Buddhist Studies, V
Zen Hospice Project, B

San Jose
Gold Sage Monastery, M

San Juan
Ring of Bone Zendo, M

San Rafael
Dharma Eye Zen Center, M
Marin Karma Kagyu Study Group, V

San Ysidro
Ensenada (Mexico) Yeshe Nyingpo, V

Santa Barbara
Mahakankala Buddhist Center, V
Santa Barbara Buddhist Priory, M
Santa Barbara Karma Thegsum Choling, V

Santa Cruz
Rigpa North America, V
Santa Cruz Karma Thegsum Choling, V
Santa Cruz Sangha, M
Santa Cruz Zen Center, M

Santa Monica
Khandakapala Buddhist Center, V
Ordinary Dharma—Santa Monica, B
Santa Monica Sangha, M
Vajrayana Foundation: Los Angeles, V

Santa Rosa
California Diamond Sangha, M
Sonoma Mountain Zen Center, M
Zen Wind, M

Sausalito
Green Gulch Farm/Zen Center, M

Sebastopol
Occidental Sitting Group, B
Sebastopol Sangha, M
Stone Creek Zendo, M

Signal Hill
Signal Hill Zen Center, M

Sonoma
Moon Valley Sangha, M
Sonoma Valley Dharma Study Group, V

Soquel
Foundation for the Preservation of the Mahayana Tradition, V
Hearth Sangha, M
Land of Medicine Buddha—FPMT, V

Stanton
Ocean Eyes Zen Center, M

Stockton
Middlebar Monastery, M
Stockton Chapter True Buddha School, V

Talmage
City of Ten Thousand Buddhas/Talmage Dharma Realm Buddhist Assoc., M

Tehachapi
Mountain Spirit Center, M

Temple City
Khyung Dzong of California, V

Tiburon
Chokling Tersar Foundation, V

Turlock
Almond Blossom Sangha, M

Ukiah
Ukiah Sangha, M
Valley Center
Metta Forest Monastery, T

Venice
Los Angeles Yeshe Nyingpo, V

Vista
Three Treasures Zen Community, M

Warner Springs
Manzanita Village, B

Whittier
Dharma Kai Zen Center/Aikido Ai Dojo, M

Willits
Zen Center of Willits, M

Woodacre
Kalyana Mitta Network, T
Spirit Rock Meditation Center, T

Woodside
Mid-Peninsula Insight Meditation Center, T

COLORADO

Boulder
Boulder Shambhala Center, V
Boulder Zen Center, M
Celtic Buddhist Society, V
Great Mountain Zen Center, M
Insight Meditation Community, T
Mangala Shri Bhuti, V
Marpa House, V
Namo Buddha Seminar, V
Naropa Institute, B
Naropa Zen Group, M
Padmasambhava Buddhist Center, V
Palyul Changchub Dhargye Ling of Colorado, V
Rigpa Fellowship of Colorado, V
Shambhala Prison Community, V
Shambhala Sun Magazine, V
Sierra Retreats/Sierra Contemplative Center, B
Sugarloaf Mountain Zendo, M
University Zen Center, M

Yeshe Khorlo, V
Zane Sangha, B
Zazen Group, M

Cedaredge
Rocky Mountain Vipassana Association, T

Colorado Springs
Rocky Mountain Insight, T
Thubten Shadrub Ling, V
Treelight Productions, T

Crestone
Crestone Mountain Zen Center/Dharmasangha USA, M
Karma Thegsum Tashi Gomang (Crestone KTTG), V
Northern Kiliya Center, V

Denver
Buddhist/Christian Contemplative Group, B
Denver Shambhala Center, V
Englewood FCI Buddhist Meditation Group, B
International Buddhist Progress Society, Denver, M
(Debra Ann) Robinson's Dharma Group, V
South Denver Buddhists, B
Tuesday Night Sitting Group, T
Udiyan Maitreya Kosha, V
Vipassana Dhura Meditation Society, T
Vipassana Towers, T
Zen Center of Denver/Lotus in the Flame Temple, M

Durango
Durango Sangha, T

Fort Collins
Fort Collins Dharma Study Group, V

Fort Garland
New Traditions Retreat, T

Fort Lupton
Medicine Buddha Healing Institute, B

Rocky Mountain Dharma Association, B

Gardner
Dorje Khyung Dzong, V

Indian Hills
Vajrayana Foundation of Colorado, V

Lafayette
Lafayette Sangha, M
Orgyen Rigjed Ling, V

Lakewood
Buddhist Association of Colorado, M
Chan Nhu Buddhist Pagoda, M
Karma Chang Chub Cho Tso Ling, V

Littleton
Kwan Um Zen Community of Colorado, M

Morrison
Buffalo Mountain Dharma Center, M-V

Ouray
Colorado Mountain Zen Centers, M

Pagosa Springs
Tara Mandala, V
Red Feather Lakes
Rocky Mountain Shambhala Center, V

Wheat Ridge
Rainbow Expeditions II, B

Woody Creek
Aspen Dharma Study Group, V

CONNECTICUT

Bolton
Living Dharma Center, M

Manchester
Manchester Sangha, M

New Haven
Center for Dzogchen Studies, V
New Haven Shambhala, V
New Haven Zen Center, M
(Beth) Roth, B

Waterbury
Meditation Center at St. John's on-the-Green, B

DELAWARE

Wilmington
Padmasambhava Buddhist Center, V

DISTRICT OF
COLUMBIA
Bright Pearl Zen Group of Washington, M
Guhyasamaja Center, V
Mintwood Zendo, M
Pentagon Meditation Club, B
Vajrayogini Buddhist Center, V
Washington Buddhist Vihara, T
Zen Buddhist Center of Washington, DC/Ka Shin Zendo Genzo-Ji, M

FLORIDA

Atlantic Beach
Atlantic Beach Sangha, M

Boca Raton
Morikami Zen Group, M
Tub-ten Kunga Center, V

Gainesville
Gainesville Zen Circle, M

Hollywood
Zen Meditation Center, M

Jacksonville
Jacksonville Karma Kagyu Study Group, V
Jasksonville Zen Sangha, M

Key West
Mitsugon-an-Tendai Buddhist Hermitage, V

Largo
Bodhitree Dhamma Center, T
Circle of Vipassana, T
Drikung Kagyu, V

Longwood
Padmasambhava Buddhist Center, V

Miami
Avalokiteshvara Buddhist Study Center, B
International Zen Institute of Florida, M
Sakya Kunga Dzong, V
United Rhyme Buddhist Society, V
Wat Buddharangasi, T

Milton
Insight Meditation Group, T

Naples
Naples Community of Mindfulness, M

Port Charlotte
Charlotte County Meditation Society, T

Saint Augustine
Gainesville Karma Kagyu Study Group, V
St. Augustine Karma Kagyu Study Group, V

Seminole
Zen Meditation Group of Pinellas, M

Tallahassee
Cypress Tree Zen Center, M

Tampa
Tampa Karma Thegsum Choling, V

West Palm Beach
Padmasambhava Buddhist Center, V

Williams Island
Pure Light Sangha, M

GEORGIA

Atlanta
Atlanta Shambhala Center, V
Atlanta Soto Zen Center, M
Atlanta Zen Group, M
Losel Shedrup Ling/Tibetan Buddhist Center of Atlanta, V
Morning Star Institute for Holistic Studies, B

GUAM

Agana
Guam True Buddha School, V

HAWAII

Honaunau
Karuna Foundation/Erik Knud-Hansen, T

Honolulu
Buddhist Study Center, M
Diamond Sangha/Koko An Zendo, M
Diamond Sangha/Palolo Zen Center, M
Honolulu Dharma Study Group, V
Kagyu Thegchen Ling, V
Soto Mission, M
Vipassana Hawaii, T

Kamuela
Zen Center of Hawaii, M

Keaau
Shantideva Center, V

Lahaina
Diamond Sangha/Maui Zendo, M

Ocean View
Vajrayana Foundation of Hawaii/Orgen Dechen Cho Dzong, V

Pahala
Nechung Dorje Drayang Ling/ Wood Valley Temple and Retreat Center, V

Paia
Karma Rimay O Sal Ling/Maui Dharma Center, V

Wailuku
Back in Balance, B
Vipassana Metta Foundation, T

IDAHO

Boise
Beginner's Mind Sangha, M

Moscow
Mindfulness Sangha, M

ILLINOIS

Belvidere
Chagdud Gonpa Chicago, V

Bloomington
Bloomington-Normal Zen Group, M

Champaign
Prairie Zen Center, M

Chicago
American Buddhist Association, B
Bong Boolsa Korean Buddhist Temple, M
Buddhism Friendship Association, B
Buddhist Temple of Chicago, M
Bultasa Korean Buddhist Temple, M
Cambodian Buddhist Association/Wat Khemararan, T
Chicago Ling Shen Ching Tze, V
Chicago Ratna Shri Sangha, V
Chicago Rime Center, V
Chicago Shambhala Center, V
Harmony Zen Center, M
International Zen Dojo Sogen-kai, M
Jewel Heart Chicago, V
Kampuchean Buddhist Society, Inc./Wat Khmer Metta Temple, T
Karma Thegsum Choling, Chicago, V
Maitreya Buddhist Seminary, M
Midwest Buddhist Temple, M
Padmasambhava Buddhist Center, V
Quan Am Tu Buddhist Temple, M
Quang Minh Temple, M
Rissho Kosei-kai of Chicago, M
Suma Ching Hai International Association, M
University of Chicago Buddhist Association, B
Wat Dhammaram/Vipassana Meditation Center, T
Won Buddhism of America, M
Zen Buddhist Temple, M

Decatur
Tilopa Buddhist Center, Inc., V

Dekalb
Prairie Buddha Sangha, M

Des Plaines
Dhammaka Meditation Center of Chicago, T
Northwest Chicago Zen Group, M

Dixon
Rock River Meditation Community, T

Elmhurst
Burmese Buddhist Association, T

Evanston
Buddhist Council of the Midwest, B
Chicago Zen Center, M
Lakeside Buddha Sangha, M
Udumbara Zen Center, M

Hinsdale
Buddhadharma Meditation Center, T

Lombard
Togmay Sangpo, V

Naperville
Lotus Sangha, M

Northbrook
Zen Buddhist Temple of Chicago, M

Oak Park
Oak Park Meditation Group, T

Peoria
Peoria Buddhist Study Group of New Horizons, B

Rockford
Wat Phothikaram Lao Buddhist Temple, T

Skokie
Han-Ma-Um Zen Center, M
Kubose Dharma Legacy, M

Springfield
Buddhist Association of Central Illinois, M

Urbana
Zen Group of Champaign-Urbana, M

Westmount
Buddhist Compassion Relief, B

INDIANA

Bloomington
Ganden Dheling Buddhist Temple, V

Floyd Knobs
Red Hawk Zendo, M

Hobart
Kwan Um Zen Community of Chicago, M

Indianapolis
Indianapolis Zen Group, M

New Albany
Louisville Karma Kagyu Study Group, V

West Lafayette
West Lafayette Zazen Group, M

IOWA

Des Moines
Des Moines Sitting Group, T

Iowa City
Iowa City Zen Center, M
Jalandhara Buddhist Meditation Center, V

KANSAS

Kansas City
Kansas City Dharmadhatu, V
Mindfulness Meditation Foundation, B

Lawrence
Kansas Zen Center, M

Lenexa
Lenexa Sitting Group, T

Manhattan
Manhattan Zen Group, M

Prairie Village
Prairie Village Sitting Group, T

Wichita
Wichita Buddhist Meditation and Study Group, B

KENTUCKY

Clay City
Furnace Mountain, M

Lexington
Lexington Shambhala Meditation Center, V
Lexington Zen Center, M

Louisville
Louisville Community of Mindfulness, B

LOUISIANNA

Breaux Bridge
Udumbara Sangha—Breaux Bridge, M

Lafayette
Udumbara Sangha—Lafayette, M

New Orleans
Blue Iris Sangha, M
Dhongak Tharling Dharma Center, V
New Orleans Zen Temple, M

MAINE

Brunswick
Brunswick Sangha, M

Freeport
Center for the Awareness of Pattern, M

Lincolnville
True Heart/Mid-Coast Sangha, M

Palermo
China Forming Dharma Study Group, V

Portland
Brunswick Dharma Study Group, V

Surry
Morgan Bay Zendo, M

Waterville
Waterville Zazenkai, M

Woolwich
Friends of the Western Buddhist Order—Portland, B

MANITOBA—CANADA

Winnipeg
Winnipeg Dharma Study Group, V

MARYLAND

Annapolis
Annapolis Mahayana Buddhist Center, V

Baltimore
Baltimore Shambhala Center, V
Baltimore Zendo/Shorin-ji, M
Vikatadamshtri Buddhist Center of Baltimore, V

Bethesda
Bethesda Sangha, M

Frederick
Tibetan Meditation Center, V

Gaithersburg
Asian Classics Input Project, V

Germantown
American Zen College, M

Poolesville
Kunzang Palyul Choling, V

Potomac
Avatamsaka Hermitage, M

Salisbury
Salisbury Dharmadhatu, V

Silver Spring
Bubjusa Buddhist Temple, M
Sakya Phuntsok Ling, V
Washington, DC Shambhala Center, V
Wat Thai, T

Westminster
International Meditation Center/IMC-USA, T

MASSACHUSETTS

Amherst
Buddhism, Meditation and Psychotherapy Group, B
Living Dharma Center, M
Mindfulness-Based Stress Management of Pioneer Valley, B
Mindfulness Meditation Group of Amherst, B

Arlington
Stella Blue Sangha, M

Barre
Barre Center for Buddhist Studies, B
Insight Meditation Society, T

Boston
Kurukulla Center for Tibetan Buddhist Studies, V
Prison Dharma Network, B

Brighton
American Buddhist Shim Gum Do Association, M

Brookline
Boston Shambhala Center, V
Clear Light Society, M

Cambridge
American Institute for Mindfulness, V
Cambridge Buddhist Association, Inc., M
Cambridge Insight Meditation Center, T
Cambridge Sangha, M
Cambridge Zen Center, M
Friends of the Western Buddhist Order—Cambridge, B
Harvard Buddhist Community, B

Sakya Institute for Buddhist Studies and Meditation/Sakya Sheidrup Ling, V
Single Flower Sangha, M

Charlemont
Valley Zendo, M

Concord
Concord Sangha, M
Golden Wind Temple and White Swan Translation Center, M

Conway
Dzogchen Community in America Inc./Tsegyalgar, V

Falmouth
Falmouth Dharma Study Group, V

Framingham
Framingham Sitting Group, M

Greenfield
Keili Meditation Center, M

Harvard
Zenki, M

Hawley
Mahasiddha Nyingmapa Center, V

Maynard
Community of Interbeing, M

Newbury
Newbury Insight Meditation Center, T

Newton
Drikung Kagyu Center, V
Mee Yuan Buddhist Association, V

North Truro
Pond Village Zendo, M

Northampton
Interbeing Sangha, M

Northampton Shambhala Center, V
Northampton Zendo, M

Shelburne Falls
Vipassana Meditation Center/ Dhamma Dhara, T
West County Sangha, M

Somerville
Khandarohi Buddhist Center, V
Wisdom Publications, B

Stockbridge
Rangrig Yeshe, V

Stow
Stow Sangha, M

Sunderland
Hopping Tree Sangha, M

Watertown
Empty Bell, B

Wellesley
Boston West Sitting Group, T
Wellesley Buddhist Community, B

Wendell Depot
Dharma Seed Tape Library, T

Weston
SunRay Meditation Society, B

Worcester
Worcester Sitting Group, B

MICHIGAN

Ann Arbor
Ann Arbor Karma Thegsum Choling, V
Deep Spring Center for Meditation and Spiritual Inquiry, B
Jewel Heart, V
Maitreya Buddhist Seminary, M
Zen Buddhist Temple, M

Big Rapids
Heart Center Karma Thegsum Choling, V

Bloomfield
Traipitra's Vipassana Sitting Group, T

Dimondale
Clear Water Sangha, M

Elk Rapids
Dancing Rabbit Sangha, M

Jones
Tekchen Choling, V

Kalamazoo
Clear Mind Temple, M

Oxford
Upland Hills Ecological Awareness Center, T

MINNESOTA

Edina
Minneapolis Karma Kagyu Study Group, V

Mankato
Resources for Ecumenical Spirituality, T

Minneapolis
Clouds in Water Zen Center, M
Common Ground Meditation Center, B
Minneapolis Shambhala Center, V
Minnesota Zen Meditation Center/Ganshoji Temple, M
Minnesota Zen Meditation Center/Hokyoji, M
Sakya Thupten Dargye Ling, V
Tsechen Sakya Lhundrup Ling, V
Twin Cities Vipassana Cooperative, T

MISSISSIPPI

Jackson
Jackson Zen Group, M
Jackson Insight Meditation Group, B

Starkville
Starkville Zen Dojo, M

MISSOURI

Carthage
Heartland Insight Meditation, T

Columbia
Show Me Dharma, T

Dunnegan
Resources for Ecumenical Spirituality, T

Florissant
Wat Phrasriratanaram/Buddhist Temple of St. Louis, T

Kansas City
American Buddhist Center at Unity Temple on the Plaza, B
Mid America Dharma Group, T

Manchester
Manchester Sangha, M

Saint Louis
Missouri Zen Center, M
Saint Louis Sangha, M

Springfield
Medical Center for Federal Prisoners Dharma Study Group, V
Western Pure Land Buddhist Sangha, M

University City
Saint Louis Vipassana Meditation Group, T

MONTANA

Helena
Helena Sangha, M

Missoula
Open Way Sangha, M
Osel Shen Phen Ling, V
Rocky Mountain Friends of the Western Buddhist Order, B

Thompson Falls
Intermountain Dharma Community, T

NEBRASKA

Kearney
Kearney Zendo, M

Lincoln
Jewel Heart Nebraska, V

Omaha
Nebraska Zen Center/Shinko-kuji, M

NEVADA

Boulder City
Mojave Desert Zen Center, M

Carson City
Dharma Zephyr, T

Las Vegas
Nan Hua Zen Buddhist Society/Zen Center of Las Vegas, M
Quan Am Buddhist Temple, M
Wat Buddhapavana Las Vegas, T

NEW BRUNSWICK—CANADA

Millville
Fredericton Shambhala Study Group, V

NEW HAMPSHIRE

Barrington
Barrington Zen Center, M

Hopkinton
Bear Tree Zendo, M

Lee
Seacoast New Hampshire
Dharma Study Group, V

Newmarket
Friends of the Western Buddhist Order—Aryaloka, B

Peterborough
Peterborough Sangha, M

NEW JERSEY

Cherry Hill
Kwan Chao True Buddha Temple, V

Cinnaminson
The Zen Society/Jizo-An Monastery, M

Convent Station
Juniper Ridge Community, M

Cresskill
Zen Temple of Cresskill, M

Howell
Mahayana Sutra and Tantra
Center, V

Medford Lakes
Buddhist Sangha of South Jersey, B

Morristown
Morristown Sangha, M

Princeton
Central New Jersey Sangha, M
Padmasambhava Buddhist
Center of Princeton, V
Princeton Zen Society, M

Ramsey
Engaged Zen Foundation, M

Washington
Tibetan Buddhist Learning
Center, V

West Orange
Buddhist Study Association of
Greater New York, Inc., B

NEW MEXICO

Albuquerque
Albuquerque Karma Thegsum
Choling, V
Albuquerque Padmasambhava
Buddhist Center, V
Albuquerque Vipassana Com-
munity, T
Albuquerque Zen Center, M
Hidden Mountain Zen
Center, M
Nibbana Foundation, V
Wat Buddharam/Buddhist
Center of New Mexico, T

Arroyo Seco
Hokoji, M

El Prado
Taos Vipassana Sangha, T

Jemez Springs
Bodhi Manda Zen Center, M

Las Vegas
Southwest Center for Spiritual
Living, B

Ocate
Ocamora Foundation, B

San Cristobal
Lama Foundation, B

San Lorenzo
Southwest Sangha, T

Santa Fe
Kagyu Shenpen Kunchab, V

Mountain Cloud Zen
Center, M
One Zendo, M
Open Way Sangha, M
Santa Fe Center for Dzogchen
Studies, V
Santa Fe Vipassana Sangha, T
Santa Fe Zen Center, B
Upaya, B

Taos
Open Heart Sangha, M

NEW YORK

Albany
Albany Affiliate/Kinpu-an, M
Albany Karma Thegsum Cho-
ling, V
Albany Vipassana Sangha, T

Buffalo
Dharma Group, B
Zen Dharma Community, M

Chappaqua
Chappaqua Sangha, M

East Amherst
Buffalo Dharma Study
Group, V

East Chatham
Karuna Tendai Dharma Cen-
ter, V

East Hampton
Peaceful Dwelling Project, M

Gardiner
Plain Water Practice, M

Hempstead
Clear Mountain Zen Center, M

Huntington
Long Island Sangha, M
Zen Meditation Group of Hun-
tington, B

Ithaca
Cayuga Sangha, B
Ithaca Dharma Study Group, V

Livingston Manor
Zen Studies Society/Dai Bosatsu Zendo Kongo-ji, M

Maryknoll
Westchester, Rockland, and
Fairfield Counties Mindful-
ness Group, M

Mount Tremper
Dharma Communications, M
Lotus Peak Zendo, M
National Buddhist Prison San-
gha, M
Zen Mountain Monastery, M

New York City/Brooklyn
American Burma Buddhist As-
sociation, Inc., T
Brooklyn Buddhist Associa-
tion, B
Brooklyn Sangha, M
Brooklyn Zen Urban Temple/
Dai Gedatsu An, M
Chakrasambara Buddhist Cen-
ter, V
Mother Tara Study and Medi-
tation Group, V

*New York City/Elmhurst-
Queens*
Ch'an Meditation Center/
Dharma Drum Mountain, M

New York City/Flushing
Bo Kwang Zen Center, M
Saddharma Cakra Buddhist
Association, B

*New York City/Kew
Gardens*
American Sri Lanka Buddhist
Association, Inc./New York
Buddhist Vihara, T

New York City/Manhattan
Aro Gar, V
Asian Classics Institute, V
Buddhist Information Service
of New York, B

Chogye International Zen Center of New York, M
Community of Mindfulness—New York Metro, B
First Zen Institute of America, M
Friends of the Western Buddhist Order—New York City, B
Kagyu Dzamling Kunchab, V
Manhattan Won Buddhism, M
Mettavihara Community/Golden Dawn Center, B
New York Buddhist Church, M
New York City Karma Thegsum Choling, V
New York Shambhala Center, V
New York Unitarian Universalist Buddhist Fellowship, B
Palden Sakya—New York City, V
Reed Street Sangha, M
Soho Zendo, M
Tibet Center, V
Tricycle: The Buddhist Review, B
True Buddha Diamond Temple, V
Village Zendo, M
West 86th Street Sangha, M
West 97th Street Sangha, M
Zen Center of New York City, M
Zen Studies Society/New York Zendo Shobo-ji, M

New York City/Old Chelsea Station
Padmasambhava Buddhist Center—New York, V

New York City/Yonkers
Zen Community of New York, M

Newburgh
Budding Flower Sangha, M

Orchard Park
Buffalo Zen Group, M

Rhinebeck
Rhinebeck Sitting Group, T

Rochester
Drikung Kagyu Enlightenment Institute, V
Rochester Zen Center, M

Rye
Empty Hand Zendo, M

Sagaponack
Sagaponack Zendo, M

Saint James
Suffolk Institute for Eastern Studies, B

Saratoga Springs
Saratoga Center for Meditation and Mindful Living, M

Setauket
Long Island Zen Center, M

Shady
Woodstock Karma Thegsum Choling, V

Sidney Center
Padma Samye Ling, V

Slingerlands
Albany Dharma Study Group, V

Spencer
Ithaca Zen Center, M

Springwater
Springwater Center for Meditative Inquiry and Retreats, B

Stormville
Lotus Flower Zendo/Greenhaven Correctional Facility, M

Syosset
Buddhist Community of Bangladesh, T

Syracuse
Syracuse Dharma Study Group, V
Zen Center of Syracuse, M

Wappingers Falls
Kagyu Thubten Choling, V

Water Mill
Konzeon Zendo, M

Woodstock
Karma Triyana Dharmachakra, V
Palden Sakya—Woodstock, V
Woodstock Karma Thegsum Choling, V

NEWFOUNDLAND—CANADA

Saint John's
St. John's Shambhala Study Group, V

NORTH CAROLINA

Asheville
Asheville Vipassana Group, T
Mountain Zen Group, M
Wesak Celebration of Asheville, B
Zen Center of Asheville/Magnanimous Mind Temple, M

Burnsville
Celo Community Sangha, M

Chapel Hill
Chapel Hill Zen Group, M

Charlotte
Charlotte Community of Mindfulness, M
Charlotte True Buddhist Society, V
Charlotte Zen Meditation Society, M

Cullowhee
Carolina Morning Designs, B
Cullowhee Zen Group, M

Durham
Durham Karma Thegsum Choling, V
Durham Meditation Center, T
Durham Shambhala Center, V
Durham Sitting Group, B
Durham Unitarian Universalist Buddhist Meditation Group, M

Greenville
Greenville Karma Thegsum Choling, V

Hot Springs
Southern Dharma Retreat Center, B

Penrose
Nyingma Tantric Buddhist Group, V

Pittsboro
Squirrel Mountain Zendo/North Carolina Zen Center, M

Raleigh
Piedmont Zen Group, M
Kadampa Center for the Practice of Tibetan Buddhism, V

NOVA SCOTIA—CANADA

Cape Breton
Gampo Abbey, V

Granville Ferry
Annapolis Royal Dharma Study Group, V

Halifax
Celtic Buddhist Society of the Crazy Heart Lineage, V
Halifax Shambhala Center, V
Shambhala International, V
Shambhala Middle School, V

Tantallon
St. Margaret's Bay Shambhala Cultural Center, V

Tatamagouche
Dorje Denma Ling, V

Wolfville
White Wind Zen Community/
Wolfville Zazenkai, M

OHIO

Cincinnati
Buddhist Dharma Center of
Cincinnati, B
Cincinnati Dharma Study
Group, V
Cincinnati Sangha, M

Cleveland
Cleveland Dharma Study
Group, V
Udumbara
Sangha—Cleveland, M
Zen Shin Sangha, M

Cleveland Heights
Cleveland Heights Sangha, M

Columbus
Columbus Dharma Study
Group, V
Columbus Karma Thegsum
Choling, V
Columbus Zen Corner, M
Mindfulness Meditation of Co-
lumbus, T

Fairview Park
Cloudwater Zendo, M

Toledo
Toledo Sangha, M

Yellow Springs
Yellow Springs Dharma
Center, B

OKLAHOMA

Oklahoma City
Oklahoma City Zen Group, M

Tulsa
Chau Tam Bao Temple, M

ONTARIO—CANADA

Ajax
Ajax Rigpa, V

Alliston
Alliston Dharma Study
Group, V

Gloucester
Tu-An Pagoda, M

Kinmount
Dharma Centre Of Canada, B

Kitchener
The Ha Nguyen, M

Lindsay
Insight Retreats, T

Madoc
Orgyan Osal Cho Dzong, V

Mississauga
Westend Buddhist Centre, T

North York
Jing Sim Branch True Buddha
School, V

Ottawa
Chandrakirti Buddhist
Centre, V
Chittamani Meditation
Centre, V
Crystal Staff, B
Kadam Changchub Ling, V
Ottawa Shambhala Centre, V
Warm Snow Sangha, M
White Wind Zen
Community, M
White Wind Zen Community/
Zen Centre of Ottawa, M

Saint Catharines
Karma Kagyu Buddhist Meditation Center of Niagara, V

Sault Ste. Marie
Vipassana Meditation
Group, T

Scarborough
Ambedkar Mission, B
Ananta Kuan Yin Zen Buddhist
Institute, M
Buddhist Meditation Hermit-
age, T
Buddhist Women's Network of
Toronto, B
University of Toronto Buddhist
Student Association, B

Severn Bridge
Buddha Sasana Yeiktha of Ontario, T

Thunder Bay
Arrow River Community Cen-
ter, T
Potala Meditation Centre, V

Toronto
Buddhist Association of Can-
ada, B
Bul Kwang Sa Temple, M
Burmese Buddhist Association
of Toronto/Maha Dhammika
Temple, T
Chandrakirti Mahayana Bud-
dhist Centre, V
Downsview Dharma Study
Group, V
Gaden Choling, V
HanMaUm SeonWon of To-
ronto, M
Kampo Gangra Drub-
gyudling, V
Karma Kagyu Centre Of To-
ronto, V
Maitreya Buddhist Semi-
nary, M
Mountain Moon Sangha, M
Nine Mountains Zen Gate So-
ciety, M
Ontario Zen Center, M
Pure Moon Buddhist Associa-
tion, V
Riwoche Society/Pemavajra
Temple, V
Smiling Flower Sangha, M

Tengye Ling Tibetan Buddhist
Centre, V
Toronto Insight Meditation
Center, T
Toronto Shambhala Centre, V
Toronto Zen Centre, M
Vietnamese Zen Meditation
Group, M
Zen Buddhist Temple/
Toronto, M

OREGON

Ashland
Pacific Region Yeshe
Nyingpo, V
Siskiyou Sansui Sangha, M
Tashi Choling, V

Azalea
Kagyu Yonten Gyatso, V

Corbett
Zen Community of Oregon/
Larch Mountain Zen
Center, M

Corvallis
Corvallis Dharma Study
Group, V
Corvallis Zen Circle, M

Cottage Grove
Dechhen Ling/Chagdud Gonpa
Foundation, V

Eugene
Eugene Buddhist Priory, M
Eugene Sangha, M
Eugene Vipassana Group, T
Eugene Women's Vipassana
Group, T
Eugene Zendo, M

Independence
Independence Sangha, M

Portland
Columbia Sangha, T
Dharma Rain Zen Center, M
Drugpa Dorje Dzin, V

Gyurme Dechen Dorje Ling, V
Heartsong Sangha, T
Kagyu Changchub Chuling, V
Koyasan Shingon of Port-
   land, V
Metta Foundation, T
Portland Buddhist Priory, M
Portland Buddhist Temple, M
Portland Community of Mind-
   ful Living, M
Portland Sakya Center for Ti-
   betan Buddhism, V
Portland Shambhala Center, V
Portland Vipassana Sangha, T
Portland Yeshe Nyingpo, V
Pure Heart, B
Tulo Baisi Sangha, V
Waking Peacock Sangha, V

Redmond
Interfaith Meditation
   Group, M

Salem
Salem Meditation Circle, T
Salem Zen Sitting Group, M

Seal Rock
Newport Yeshe Nyingpo, V

PENNSYLVANIA

Ambler
Ambler Sangha, M

Braddock
Three Rivers Dharma
   Center, V

Carnegie
Carnegie Shambhala Study
   Group, V

Glenside
Won Buddhist Temple of Philadelphia, B

Library
Pittsburgh Vipassana Group, T

Merion
Philadelphia Buddhist Association, B

Muncy
Mount Equity Zendo, M

New Hope
Old Path Zendo, M

Philadelphia
Lilac Breeze Sangha, M
Philadelphia Shambhala Cen-
   ter, V
Plum Tree Zendo, M
Tibetan Buddhist Center of
   Philadelphia, V

Pittsburgh
Buddhist Society of Pitts-
   burgh, B
Laughing Rivers Sangha, M
Stillpoint, M
Zen Group of Pittsburgh, M

Reading
Zen Group of Reading, M

York
York Mahayana Buddhist Center, V

PUERTO RICO

Rio Piedras
Padmasambhava Buddhist
   Center—Puerto Rico, V

QUEBEC—CANADA

Beauport
Bo de Pagoda, M

Hudson Heights
Kamtsang Choling—Mon-
   treal, V

Lasalle
Montreal Shambhala Centre, V

Montreal
Association Zen de
   Montreal, M
Centre Bouddhiste Kankala, V
Centre Zen de la Main, M
Chan Hai Lei Zang, V
Fondation Vipassana/Eastern
   Canada Vipassana Founda-
   tion, T
International Buddhist Medita-
   tion Center of Canada, T
Montreal Zen Centre, M
Rigpe Dorje Centre, V
Temple Bouddhiste Tibetain, V

Village Des Erables
Maple Village, M

RHODE ISLAND

Cumberland
Providence Zen Center, M

SASKATCHEWAN—
CANADA

Regina
Insight Meditation Group, T

Saskatoon
Dharma Group, V
Saskatoon Buddhist Studies
   Group, B

SOUTH CAROLINA

Columbia
Columbia Shambhala Meditation Center, V

SOUTH DAKOTA

Rapid City
Laughing Teabowl Zendo, M

TENNESSEE

Clarkesville
Clarksville Forming Dharma
   Study Group, V

Cookeville
Middle Tennessee Padmasamb-
   hava Buddhist Center/Padma
   Gochen Ling, V

Franklin
Fellowship of the Lotus-
   Trinity, B

Knoxville
Losel Shedrup Ling Tibetan
   Buddhist Center Of Knox-
   ville, V

Memphis
Delta Insight Group, B

Nashville
Nashville Theravada Medita-
   tion Group/Lao Buddhpathip
   Temple, T
Nashville Zen Center, M
Padmasambhava Buddhist
   Center–Nashville, V

Summertown
Turtle Hill Sangha, V

TEXAS

Amarillo
Empty Sky/DeFalco Retreat
   Center, M

Austin
Austin Shambhala Center, V
Plum Blossom Sangha, M

Caddo Mills
Kagura Kochu, B

Dallas
Dallas Community of Mindful
   Living, M
Dallas Karma Thegsum Cho-
   ling, V
Insight Meditation Dallas, T
Maria Kannon Zen Center, M
Southwest Vipassana Medita-
   tion Center/Dhamma Siri, T
Vajradakini Buddhist Center, V

El Paso
Chenrezig Tibetan Cultural Center, V

Elgin
Zen Community of Austin, M

Fort Worth
First Jefferson Unitarian-Universalist Meditation Group, B

Friendswood
Diamond Way Buddhist Center, V

Harlingen
Sangha of the Rio Grande Valley, M

Houston
Dawn Mountain Tibetan Temple, Community Center, and Research Institute, V
Houston Buddhist Vihara, T
Houston Dharma Study Group, V
Houston True Buddha Chapter, V
Houston Zen Community, M
Insight Meditation Houston, T
Linh Son Temple, M
Margaret Austin Center, B
Phap Luan Buddhist Culture Center, T
So Lim Korean Buddhist Temple, M
Southwestern Son Academy, M
Texas Buddhist Association, M
Texas Buddhist Council, B
Thubten Rinchen Ling, V
Wat Buddhavas Thai Temple, T

Irving
Lien Hoa Monastery, T

Port Arthur
Buu Mon Buddhist Temple, T

San Antonio
Rigpe Dorje Center, V

San Antonio Shambhala Center, V
Sangha Del Corazon, M

Sugarland
Vietnam Buddhist Center, M

UTAH

Cedar City
Last Resort, T

Layton
Salt Lake City Forming Dharma Study Group, V

Salt Lake City
Kanzeon Zen Center—Utah, M
Salt Lake Sangha, M
Shaolin Chi Mantis, M

VERMONT

Barnet
Karmê-Chöling Buddhist Meditation Center, V
Milarepa Center, V
St. Johnsbury Dharma Study Group, V

Bradford
Hanover Dharma Study Group, V

Brattleboro
Brattleboro Dharma Study Group, V

Bristol
Mandala Buddhist Center, V
Sunray Meditation Society, V

Burlington
Burlington Shambhala Center, V
Zen Affiliate Of Vermont, M

Cuttingsville
Rutland Dharma Study Group, V

East Middlebury
Dharmanet, T
Green Mountain Sangha, T

Manchester
Manchester Dharma Study Group, V

Middlebury
ToDo Institute, B

Montpelier
Summer Vine Community Sangha, M

Putney
Silent Sitting Meditation Group at Friends Meeting House, B
Southern Vermont Sangha, M

Shelburne
Vermont Zen Center, M

Williston
Pot Lid Sangha, M

Woodbury
Fire on the Mountain, M

VIRGINIA

Alexandria
Washington Mindfulness, M

Charlottesville
Charlottesville Dharma Study Group, V

Crozet
Mountain Light Zen Center, B

Delaplane
Sai Sho An Zen Group, M

Earlysville
Blue Ridge Zen Group, M

Fairfax
Lotus Meditation Group, T

Leesburg
Loudin County Sangha, M

Louisa
South Anna River Sangha/Twin Oaks Community, M

Massie's Mill
Charlottesville Sangha, M

Norfolk
Mindfulness Community of Hampton Roads, M

Radford
New River Zen Community, M

Richmond
Ekoji Buddhist Sangha, B
Ekoji Buddhist Sangha Vipassana Sitting Group, T
Ekoji Jodo Shin and Chinese Pure Land Group, M
Ekoji Zen Group, M
Kagyu Shenpen Tharchin, V

Roanoke
Stone Mountain Zendo, M

Ruckersville
Dharma Institute, V

Vienna
Tuesday Mindfulness Meditation Group, M

Virginia Beach
Zen America, M

WASHINGTON

Auburn
Washington Buddhavanaram, T

Bainbridge Island
Nipponzan Myohoji, M

Bellingham
Bellingham Dharma Study Group, V
Bellingham Vipassana Meditation Group, T
Bellingham Zen Practice Group, M

Mountain Lamp Community, M

Castle Rock
Cloud Mountain Retreat Center, B

Ethel
Northwest Vipassana Center, T

Everett
Everett Meditation Society, T

Friday Harbor
Sakya Kachod Choling, V

Kirkland
Awareness Meditation, B

McKenna
North Cascades Buddhist Priory, M

Mercer Island
Hung Kar Dudul Ling, V

Olympia
Lojong Meditation (Nalendra Institute), V
Olympia Meditators, B
Tsechen Kunkhyab Choling, V

Poulsbo
Laughing Frog Sangha, B

Redmond
Ling Shen Ching Tze Temple, V

Richland
Friends of the Western Buddhist Order—Richland, B

Seattle
Amrita/Chagdud Gonpa Foundation, V

Dai Bai Zan Cho Bo Zen Temple, M
Dharma Friendship Foundation, V
Dharma Sound Zen Center, M
Dohn-O Zen and Sun-do Center, M
Drikung Kyobpa Choling, V
Gold Summit Monastery, M
HumanKind Sangha, M
Kagyu Shenpen Osel Choling, V
Mindfulness Community of Puget Sound, B
Northwest Dharma Association, B
One Drop Zendo, M
One Pine Hall Zazen Group, M
Sakya Monastery of Tibetan Buddhism, V
Seattle Buddhist Center/ Friends of the Western Buddhist Order, B
Seattle Karma Kagyu Study Group, V
Seattle Rigpa, V
Shambhala Center of Seattle, V
Tara Mandala Practice Group, V
Three Treasures Sangha Of The Pacific Northwest, M
Vajralama Buddhist Center, V
Vajrasamayas Trust, V
Vipassana Group, T

Spokane
Padma Ling—Chagdud Gonpa, V
Spokane Buddhist Fellowship, B

Whidbey Island
Whidbey Island Retreat Center of One Drop Zendo, M

Yakima
Open Circle, B

WEST VIRGINIA

Harmony
Spencer Buddhist Meditation Group, B

High View
Bhavana Society, T

WISCONSIN

Eau Claire
Eau Claire Dharma Study Group, V

Kenosha
Lake Land Zen Center, M

Madison
Drikung Kagyu Center Of Madison, V
East Side Sangha, M
Inner Buddha Center, V
Madison Dharma Study Group, V
Madison Zen Center, M
Padmasambhava Buddhist Center of Madison, V
Sacred Lakes Buddha Sangha, M

Mequon
Unitarian Church North Zen Group/Udumbara Sangha, M

Milwaukee
Crow's Caw/Udumbara Sangha, M
Institute of Tibetan Literary Studies, V
Milwaukee Shambhala Center, V
Milwaukee Zen Center, M
Mindfulness Community of Milwaukee, M

Mount Horeb
Snowflower Buddhist Sangha, M

Oregon
Deer Park, V

Port Wing
Sun Farm Sangha, M

Racine
Original Root Zen, M

Rhinelander
Dragon Flower Ch'an Temple, M

Schofield
Wausau Zen Group, M

Spring Green
Mahayana Dharma Center, V

Willard
Christine Center for Unitive Spirituality, B

YUKON TERRITORY— CANADA

Whitehorse
Vajra North, V
Yukon Dharma Society, M

Index of Dharma Center Listings

294.3
0973
Comple-
te

The Complete guide
to Buddhist Amer-
ica

DUE DATE
